PRINCIPLES OF
MICRO-
ECONOMICS

PRINCIPLES OF MICRO-ECONOMICS

ROBERT H. FRANK
Cornell University

BEN S. BERNANKE
Princeton University

McGraw-Hill
Irwin

Boston   Burr Ridge, IL   Dubuque, IA   Madison, WI   New York   San Francisco   St. Louis
Bangkok   Bogotá   Caracas   Lisbon   London   Madrid
Mexico City   Milan   New Delhi   Seoul   Singapore   Sydney   Taipei   Toronto

McGraw-Hill Higher Education

*A Division of The **McGraw-Hill** Companies*

PRINCIPLES OF MICROECONOMICS

Published by McGraw-Hill/Irwin, an imprint of The McGraw-Hill Companies, Inc., 1221 Avenue of the Americas, New York, NY, 10020. Copyright © 2001, by The McGraw-Hill Companies, Inc. All rights reserved. No part of this publication may be reproduced or distributed in any form or by any means, or stored in a data base or retrieval system, without the prior written consent of The McGraw-Hill Companies, Inc., including, but not limited to, in any network or other electronic storage or transmission, or broadcast for distance learning. Some ancillaries, including electronic and print components, may not be available to customers outside the United States.
This book is printed on acid-free paper.

2 3 4 5 6 7 8 9 0 QPD/QPD 0 9 8 7 6 5 4 3 2 1

ISBN   0-07-021991-5

Cover: Leaded glass window designed by Frank Lloyd Wright for the Avery Coonley Playhouse, Riverside, Illinois, circa 1912, 61 cm x 97.5 cm

Photo: Christie's Images, New York

Design of book: The images in the design of this book are based on elements of the architecture of Frank Lloyd Wright (1867–1959), specifically from the leaded glass windows seen in many of his houses. Wright's design was rooted in nature and based on simplicity and harmony. His windows use elemental geometry to abstract natural forms, complementing and framing the natural world outside. This concept of seeing the world through an elegantly structured framework ties in nicely to the idea of framing one's view of the world through the window of economics.

The typeface used for some of the elements was taken from the Arts and Crafts movement. The typeface, as well as the color palette, bring in the feeling of that movement in a way that complements the geometric elements of Wright's windows. The Economic Naturalist icon is visually set apart from the more geometric elements but is a representation of the inspirational force behind all of Wright's work.

Publisher: *Gary Burke*
Executive editor: *Paul Shensa*
Development editor: *Tom Thompson*
Marketing manager: *Martin Quinn*
Senior project manager: *Jean Lou Hess*
Senior production supervisor: *Michael McCormick*
Designer: *Jill Kongabel/Matthew Baldwin*
Art editor: *Nora Agbayani*
Supplement coordinator: *Becky Szura*
New media: *Ann Rogula*
Illustrators: *Mick Stevens, Elliott Banfield, Brian Barneclo, and Gini Curl*
Compositor: *GTS Graphics, Inc.*
Typeface: *10/12 Sabon Roman*
Printer: *Quebecor Printing Dubuque*

Library of Congress Cataloging-in-Publication Data

Frank, Robert H.
    Principles of microeconomics / Robert H. Frank, Ben S. Bernanke.
        p. cm.
    Includes index.
    ISBN 0-07-021991-5 (alk. paper)
    1. Microeconomics. I. Bernanke, Ben. II. Title.

HB172 .F72 2001
338.5--dc21

                                                        00-061613

DEDICATION

For Ellen

R. H. F.

For Anna

B. S. B.

ROBERT H. FRANK

Professor Frank received his B.S. from Georgia Tech in 1966, then taught math and science for two years as a Peace Corps volunteer in rural Nepal. He received his M.A. in statistics in 1971 and his Ph.D. in economics in 1972 from the University of California at Berkeley. He is the Goldwin Smith Professor of Economics at Cornell University, where he has taught since 1972, and where he currently holds a joint appointment in the Department of Economics and the Johnson Graduate School of Management. During a leave of absence from Cornell he served as chief economist for the Civil Aeronautics Board (1978–1980), a Fellow at the Center for Advanced Study in the Behavioral Sciences (1992–1993), and Professor of American Civilization at l'École des Hautes Études en Sciences Sociales in Paris (2000–2001).

Professor Frank is the author of a best-selling intermediate economics textbook—*Microeconomics and Behavior,* Fourth Edition (McGraw-Hill/Irwin, 2000). He has published on a variety of subjects, including price and wage discrimination, public utility pricing, the measurement of unemployment spell lengths, and the distributional consequences of direct foreign investment. His research has focused on rivalry and cooperation in economic and social behavior. His books on these themes include *Choosing the Right Pond: Human Behavior and the Quest for Status* (Oxford University Press, 1985) and *Passions Within Reason: The Strategic Role of the Emotions* (W.W. Norton, 1988). He and Philip Cook are coauthors of *The Winner-Take-All Society* (The Free Press, 1995), which received a Critic's Choice Award and appeared on both the *New York Times* Notable Books list and *Business Week* Ten Best list for 1995. His most recent general interest publication, *Luxury Fever* (The Free Press, 1999), was named to the *Knight-Ridder* Best Books list for 1999. He has been awarded an Andrew W. Mellon Professorship (1987–1990), a Kenan Enterprise Award (1993), and a Merrill Scholars Program Outstanding Educator Citation (1991). Professor Frank's introductory microeconomics course has graduated more than 5,000 enthusiastic economic naturalists over the years.

BEN S. BERNANKE

Professor Bernanke received his B.A. in economics from Harvard University in 1975 and his Ph.D. in economics from MIT in 1979. He taught at the Stanford Graduate School of Business from 1979 to 1985 and moved to Princeton University in 1985, where he is the Howard Harrison and Gabrielle Snyder Beck Professor of Economics and Public Affairs, and where he is currently Chairman of the Economics Department. He has consulted for the Board of Governors of the Federal Reserve, the European Central Bank, and other central banks, and he serves on a U.S. State Department committee that advises the Israeli government on economic policy. He is a Fellow of the Econometric Society, a Guggenheim Fellow, and a Research Associate of the National Bureau of Economic Research. He has been a visiting scholar at the Federal Reserve System in Boston, Philadelphia, and New York, and he is currently an advisor to the Federal Reserve Bank of New York.

Professor Bernanke's intermediate textbook, with Andrew Abel, *Macroeconomics,* Fourth Edition (Addison-Wesley, 2001), is a best seller in its field. He has authored more than 50 scholarly publications in macroeconomics, macroeconomic history, and finance. He has done significant research on the causes of the Great Depression, the role of financial markets and institutions in the business cycle, and measuring the effects of monetary policy on the economy. His two most recent books, both published by Princeton University Press, include *Inflation Targeting: Lessons from the International Experience* (with coauthors) and *Essays on the Great Depression.* He is a coeditor of the *NBER Macroeconomics Annual* and the *Journal of Business,* and he serves as associate editor for the *Journal of Financial Intermediation;* the *Journal of Money, Credit, and Banking;* and the *Review of Economics and Statistics.* He is also a member of the Editorial Board of the *Journal of Macroeconomics.* Professor Bernanke has taught principles of economics at both Stanford and Princeton.

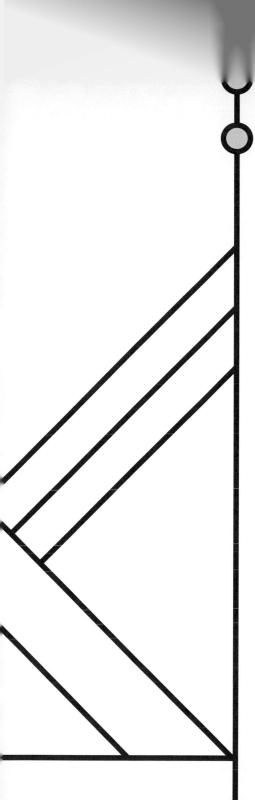

ozens of principles of economics textbooks are available, and new entries into the market appear regularly. But with many copycats and few innovators, instructors' real choices are more limited than these numbers would suggest. We wrote this book from the conviction, born of long experience in the classroom, that there is a different, and better, way to introduce beginning students to economics. In bare bones, the philosophy of this text rests on two pillars: (1) the development and repeated application of a set of core economic principles, without the usual clutter, and (2) an active, student-centered approach to learning.

A SIMPLE AGENDA

The best way to teach introductory economics—or virtually any subject, for that matter—is to expose students to repeated applications of a short list of the core ideas of the discipline. But whose short list? If we asked a thousand economists to provide their own versions, we'd get a thousand different lists. Yet to dwell on their differences would be to miss their essential similarities. Indeed, we suspect that almost all the lists would contain variants of propositions like these:

The Scarcity Principle: Having more of one good thing usually means having less of another.

The Cost-Benefit Principle: Take no action unless its marginal benefit is at least as great as its marginal cost.

The Principle of Unequal Costs: Some costs (e.g., opportunity and marginal) matter in making decisions; other costs (e.g., sunk, average) don't.

The Principle of Comparative Advantage: Everyone does best when each concentrates on the activity for which he or she is relatively most productive.

The Principle of Increasing Opportunity Cost: Use the resources with the lowest opportunity cost before turning to those with higher opportunity costs.

The Equilibrium Principle: A market in equilibrium leaves no unexploited opportunities for individuals, but may not exploit all gains achievable through collective action.

The Efficiency Principle: Efficiency is an important social goal, because when the economic pie grows larger, everyone can have a larger slice.

Our point is not that this is the best short list, but that the introductory course will be taught most effectively if it begins with a well-articulated short list of some sort, and then doggedly hammers away at it, illustrating and applying each principle in context after context. It may be hackneyed to say, but it is nonetheless true that economics is a way of thinking, not a fixed body of facts to be memorized. Beginning students often find the economic way of thinking alien and difficult to master. Repetition and focus on a few core principles are the key to developing economic thinking skills, in the same way that they are the key to learning to play the saxophone or to hit an overhead smash in tennis.

LESS IS MORE

Of course, many introductory economics textbooks pay lip service to the concepts of core ideas and thinking like an economist. And to be sure, versions of the core principles are found in many books—but often so is virtually every other economic principle that has surfaced over the past 200 years! The mind-boggling detail of these books—many of them thousand-plus-page encyclopedic reference tomes—could not have been purposely designed to camouflage more effectively the handful of principles that really matter.

All too often, students leave the introductory course never having fully grasped the essence of economic fundamentals. For example, the concept of opportunity cost—so utterly central to our understanding of what it means to think like an economist—is but one among hundreds of other concepts that go by in a blur. Opportunity cost is more important than, say, the idea that the short-run average cost curve is tangent to the long-run average cost curve at the optimal output level. But students would never realize that from the relative emphasis these topics receive in most of our introductory textbooks.

We consciously decided to write a textbook, not an encyclopedia. Our coverage includes what we believe to be the essential economic ideas and issues of the day. We have pruned much of the accumulated undergrowth, confident that students' shortest path to clear thinking about economic issues lies in becoming fluent in the basic tools of economic analysis—not in being inundated with more ideas, facts, and opinions than they can reasonably assimilate.

Repetition, however, consumes time and space. So notwithstanding our firm belief in the less-is-more approach, our book does not enter the market with the shortest page count. Instructors with Ph.D.s in economics may wonder whether so much repetition is really necessary, fearing that they will bore their students by exposing them to yet another application of the opportunity cost concept. To many, it will seem that the same time would be better spent discussing why the average fixed cost curve is asymptotic to the quantity axis.

At some point, it surely *is* better to move on to the technical properties of the average fixed cost curve. But in our view that point does not come during the principles course. For decades, each of us has had the privilege of teaching some of the best undergraduates in the world. This experience has persuaded us that when we attempt to teach less, we end up teaching more.

ECONOMIC NATURALISM

In our efforts to train students to think like economists, we aim not just for them to be *able* to apply core economic principles, but also to have an *inclination* to do so. The most effective strategy we have discovered for achieving that goal is to encourage students to become "economic naturalists." Studying biology enables people to observe and marvel at many details of the natural environment that would otherwise have escaped notice. For the naturalist, a walk in a quiet wood becomes an adventure. In much the same way, studying economics can enable students to see the everyday details of ordinary existence in a bright new light. Throughout the text, *Economic Naturalist* examples show students the relevance of economics to their world.

To illustrate, an economic naturalist is someone like Bill Tjoa, a recent student who asked, "Why do the keypad buttons on drive-up automatic teller machines have Braille dots?" A plausible answer, he reasoned, is that once the keypad molds have been manufactured, the cost of producing buttons with Braille dots is no higher than the cost of producing smooth ones. Making both types would require separate sets of molds and separate batches of inventory. If the patrons of drive-up machines found buttons with Braille dots harder to use, these extra costs might be worth incurring. But since the dots pose no difficulty for sighted users, the best and cheapest solution is to produce only keypads with dots.

In response to our challenge to employ economic principles to cast light on their own experiences, our students have tackled a host of other fascinating questions. Some recent examples from our classes:

- Why do brides spend so much money on wedding dresses, while grooms often rent cheap tuxedos, even though grooms could potentially wear their tuxedos on many other occasions and brides will never wear their dresses again? (Jennifer Dulski)

- Why, despite the proliferation of electrical appliances in the last century, do electrical outlets in newly built houses still have only two receptacles? (Beth Wollberg)

- Why do top female models earn so much more than top male models? (Fran Adams)

- Why are child safety seats required in cars but not in airplanes?" (Greg Balet)

Once students realize that they can pose and answer such questions on their own, they're hooked. A lifetime trajectory begins in which their mastery of economic principles not only doesn't decay with each year after completion of the course, but actually soars higher.

ACTIVE LEARNING

Our second guiding principle has been that active involvement by students—"student-centered" learning, in the jargon—is an essential part of an effective learning process. Merely understanding a concept—in the sense of being able to answer a test question about it the next day—is different from really *knowing* it. Even the brightest students never fully internalize a concept unless they use it repeatedly. So throughout the book, we use a number of devices to foster active learning.

- **Worked Examples.** New ideas and concepts are not simply asserted, as in most books. Instead, they are introduced by means of simple examples, usually numerical, which are worked through step-by-step in the text. These examples display the reasoning process used to reach the economic conclusion or insight, and they provide a model for the student to apply when working exercises and problems.

- **Exercises.** Following many examples, and indeed throughout each chapter, we pose in-text exercises that challenge the student to test and extend his or her understanding of the ideas being discussed. Worked-out answers to in-text exercises are provided at the end of the chapter, allowing immediate feedback.

- **Anecdotes and Illustrations.** Active learning is more likely to happen when students are engaged and motivated. We agree with Mary Poppins that a spoonful of sugar helps the medicine go down (even if the medicine is not so unpleasant). In that spirit, we have tried to make reading this text an enjoyable experience. We begin every chapter with an anecdote that motivates the discussion, and we illustrate the ideas with memorable cartoons, photographs, and original line drawings. Most important, we have striven to minimize jargon and keep the writing direct and student friendly.

- **Recap Boxes and Summaries.** To keep students focused on the forest as well as the trees, at strategic points in each chapter we have provided "recap boxes." Recaps put into a nutshell the main ideas of the previous section. The recap boxes are themselves recapitulated by bulleted end-of-chapter summaries, which are also designed to review the most important concepts presented in the chapter.

- **Core Principles Icons.** Throughout the book, whenever one of the core principles is discussed, a small icon will appear in the margin, thereby reinforcing the importance of those principles.

- **Review Questions and Problems.** Questions for review at the end of each chapter encourage the student to self-test understanding of the main ideas of the chapter. End-of-chapter problems are carefully crafted to help students internalize and extend core concepts.

THOROUGHLY MODERN MICRO

Although we believe pedagogy is extremely important, ours is not solely a book about pedagogy. Indeed, the decision about what to teach was at least as important to us as the decision of how to teach it. For example, because we believe that the most central concern of economics is efficiency, we have devoted extensive space to the concept of *economic surplus*. Introduced in Chapter 1 and applied repeatedly in Chapters 2–6, this concept is developed more fully in Chapter 7 than in any leading introductory text. Throughout the book, it underlies our ongoing argument in support of economic efficiency as an important social goal. Rather than speaking of tradeoffs between efficiency and other goals, we stress that maximizing economic surplus aids the achievement of all goals, both public and private.

A particularly distinctive feature of our book is its focus on the *normative implications of economic theory for decision making*. Basic economic reasoning tells us that rational individuals should ignore sunk costs when making choices, for example, yet many people are in fact strongly influenced by them. (Someone who has purchased a ticket for an NBA playoff game for $100 is, in practice, much more likely to drive through a snowstorm to get to the game than is an equally avid fan who won a ticket in a raffle.) Chapter 2 is devoted entirely to three pitfalls that are both widespread and important: the tendency to ignore opportunity costs, the tendency *not* to ignore sunk costs, and the tendency to confuse average and marginal costs and benefits. Throughout the book, we call students' attention to situations in which they themselves are likely to face similarly problematic choices.

Our goal of training economic naturalists has also helped dictate which topics to cover and which to leave out. Other things being equal, the more a topic enables us to make sense of our observations and experience, the stronger the case for including it. Thus, we are troubled that many people receive college degrees without ever having been exposed to ideas like the prisoner's dilemma or the tragedy of the commons. These and other *simple applications of game theory* are not only ideal vehicles for illustrating several of the core ideas of economics, but they also have enormous power to explain events in the world. In Chapter 10, we introduce students to the principles of games and strategic behavior in a highly intuitive way that does not rely on formal mathematics. We develop a limited number of simple principles that have proved entirely accessible to freshmen. In our experience, students are delighted to learn that these few principles can explain, among other things, why urban freeways are too crowded, why whales have been hunted to near extinction, why North Atlantic fisheries are near collapse, why the ozone layer is in danger, why many people fail to vote, and why the National Hockey League has a helmet rule.

ORGANIZATION

The sixteen chapters of the microeconomics split are divided into four parts of four chapters each. Part 1, which is also included in the macroeconomics split, introduces students to the most basic ideas of economics, including all the core principles that will be used throughout the book. Chapter 1 focuses on the ideas of scarcity, tradeoffs, costs, and benefits, including the fundamental notion that the desirability of any action depends on its marginal costs and benefits. Following Chapter 1 is a brief appendix that reviews the basic mathematical tools—working with equations, graphs, and tables—that students will need for the course. As mentioned earlier, Chapter 2 extends the discussion of Chapter 1 by examining some common pitfalls for decision makers, such as the sunk cost fallacy. Chapter 3 introduces the ideas of specialization and gains from trade. Finally, Chapter 4 provides an introductory overview of the tools of supply-and-demand analysis.

Part 2 explores in greater detail the concepts of demand, supply, economic surplus, and efficiency in the context of pure competition. Building on the introduction to supply and demand in Chapter 4, Chapter 5 shows how demand curves are generated by the fact that people spend their limited income in rational ways. This chapter also discusses the concept of price elasticity and its uses. Chapter 6 turns to the sellers' side of the market, showing how upward-sloping supply curves follow from profit-maximizing decisions by producers. Chapter 7 develops the concept of economic surplus and explains Adam Smith's crucial insight—that when demand and supply curves fully reflect social benefits and costs, competitive markets maximize economic surplus. Finally, Chapter 8 examines the idea of economic profit and clarifies how the quest for profit drives competitive firms to provide a socially efficient allocation of resources.

In Part 3 we study deviations from the ideal of pure competition, emphasizing that outcomes in such situations need no longer be socially efficient. Chapter 9 examines one important type of deviation from competition, the existence of monopolistic and oligopolistic firms. When only a few producers exist in a market—and in many other noncompetitive situations—behavior often takes on a strategic component. Building on this observation, Chapter 10 introduces some elementary tools of game theory, demonstrating their applicability to a variety of economic situations. Chapter 11 considers the effects of externalities—situations in which supply and demand curves do not capture the full social costs and benefits of people's choices. We show that elementary game theory—including the ideas of the prisoner's dilemma, the arms race, and the tragedy of the commons—are quite useful for analyzing many situations with externalities. Chapter 12 examines yet another deviation from the competitive ideal, the case of incomplete or asymmetric information. Among many other examples, Chapter 12 includes a discussion of the "lemons" problem in the used-car market and an explanation of why clients prefer lawyers who wear expensive suits.

Finally, Part 4 uses the tools that have been developed to approach some issues of applied economics and economic policy. Chapter 13 tackles the question of why some people earn so much more than others, with attention to factors ranging from human capital investment to discrimination to "winner-take-all" markets. Chapter 14 shows how economic principles can be used to design economic policies that mitigate the effects of market imperfections, including anti-trust policies and policies about health care, the environment, and crime. Chapter 15 discusses public goods and taxation, as well as broader issues concerning the government's role in the economy. Completing the micro split, Chapter 16 extends the analysis of Chapter 15 by considering the benefits and pitfalls of government policies to redistribute income and reduce poverty.

THE CHALLENGE

The world is a more competitive place now than it was when we started teaching in the 1970s. In arena after arena, business as usual is no longer good enough. Baseball players used to drink beer and go fishing during the off-season, but they now lift weights and ride exercise bicycles. Assistant professors used to work on their houses on weekends, but the current crop can now be found most weekends at the office. The competition for student attention has grown similarly more intense. There are many tempting courses in the typical college curriculum, and even more tempting diversions outside the classroom. Students are freer than ever to pick and choose.

Yet many of us seem to operate under the illusion that most freshmen arrive with a burning desire to become economics majors. And many of us seem not yet to have recognized that students' cognitive abilities and powers of concentration are scarce resources. To hold our ground we must become not only more selective in what we teach, but also more effective as advocates for our discipline. We must persuade students that we offer something of value.

A well-conceived and well-executed introductory course in economics can teach our students more about society and human behavior in a single term than virtually any other course in the university. This course can and should be an intellectual adventure of the first order. Not all students who take the kind of course we envisioned when writing this book will go on to become economics majors, of course. But many will, and even those who do not will leave with a sense of admiration for the power of economic ideas.

A salesperson knows that he or she often gets only one chance to make a good first impression on a potential customer. Analogously, the principles course is often our only shot at helping students appreciate the value of economics. By trying to teach them everything we know—rather than teaching them the most important things we know—we too often squander this opportunity.

SUPPLEMENTS

We believe that an ancillary package is most useful if each element in it is part of a well-considered whole. In order to ensure that our package was as integrated as possible, two solid economists and excellent teachers—Jack Mogab and Bruce McClung at Southwest Texas State University—were charged with overseeing the program. They suggested candidates, gave us advice, and provided feedback for virtually all of the components. Additionally, Jack and Bruce wrote the Study Guide and Bruce wrote the micro test bank.

FOR THE INSTRUCTOR

- **Instructor's Manual.** Prepared by Margaret Ray at Mary Washington College, this manual will be extremely useful for all teachers, but especially for those new to the job. It offers suggestions for using the Study Guide, the test bank, the Economic Naturalists, and cartoons and music for teaching; it supplies sample syllabi with assignments, sample exams, and supplemental material; and it provides for each chapter an overview, an outline, teaching objectives, Economic Naturalist discussion questions, answers to textbook questions and problems, a homework assignment with answers, and a sample quiz with answers.

- **Test Bank.** Prepared by Bruce McClung at Southwest Texas State University, this manual contain more than 2,500 multiple-choice questions categorized by Learning Objective (from the Study Guide); Learning Level (knowledge, comprehension, application, analysis); Type (graph, calculation, word problem); and Source (textbook, Study Guide, Web, unique).

- **Computerized Test Banks.** The print test bank is also available in the latest Diploma test-generating software, ensuring maximum flexibility in test preparation, including the reconfiguring of graphing exercises. This Brownstone program is the gold standard of testing programs.

- **PowerPoints.** Prepared by Rebecca Campbell at Southwest Texas State University, these slides contain all of the illustrations in the textbook, along with a detailed, chapter-by-chapter review of the important ideas presented in the textbook.

- **Overhead Transparencies.** These more than 135, four-color acetates contain all the illustrations presented in the textbook.

- **Videos.** Produced by Paul Solman, business and economics correspondent for the Lehrer News Hour and WGBH Boston, these five 10-minute segments, available on CD or tape, cover five core concepts in economics.

- **Instructor's CD-ROM.** This remarkable Windows software program, which contains the Instructor's Manual, the Computerized Test Banks, and the PowerPoints, also allows the instructor to create presentations from any of the materials on the CD or from additional material that can be imported.

- **Web Site.** The development and design of the site was overseen by Scott Simkins at North Carolina A&T State University, and much of the content was provided either by Scott or by Jim Barbour at Elon College. Both of these experienced teachers are in the forefront of a movement to make teaching using the Web easier and more valuable. For teachers there are, among other things, an online newsletter called "Teaching Using the Web" (coordinated by Mark Maier at Glendale College); the Instructor's Manual; the PowerPoints; Economics on the Web, an annotated set of URLs/links to sites of interest to economists; along with a description of what's on the student site and some Optional Material from the book.

FOR THE STUDENT

- **Study Guide.** Written by Jack Mogab and Bruce McClung at Southwest Texas State University, these three books—for Economics, Microeconomics, and Macroeconomics—provide the following elements for each chapter: a Key Point Review; a Learning Objective Grid; and Self-Tests (Key Term Matching, Multiple Choice, Problems) with answers.

- **DiscoverEcon.** This menu-driven software was developed by Gerald Nelson at the University of Illinois. It provides students with a book-specific tutorial for either microeconomics or macroeconomics. Each chapter offers two essay questions and a multiple-choice test, and when appropriate, interactive graphing problems let students observe how the economic picture is altered as data is changed. There are also links to the textbook glossary.

- **Web Site.** Based on the idea that the single most important feature of any web site is quizzing and feedback, each chapter begins with an Electronic Learning Session (eLS). Each eLS opens with a brief recap of the chapter and is followed by a pretest with answers and analysis; the test is then followed by a set of study sessions based on Economic Naturalist Exercises, Graphing Exercises, PowerPoints, and Key Terms; and the study session is finally followed by a posttest, with answers and analysis. The site also contains such useful and exciting features as Interpreting the News—articles and summaries of relevant articles with analysis and discussion questions; Videos—10-minute segments on key concepts produced by Paul Solman of WGBH in Boston; e-mail Updates—periodic sending of information/study tips; the Glossary from the textbook; and Economics on the Web—annotated URLs useful for economics students.

ACKNOWLEDGMENTS

Our thanks first and foremost go to our publisher, Gary Burke, for his unwavering faith in our project over the past several years. In an industry known for sticking with proven formulas, he has been willing from the outset to gamble that the market will embrace our somewhat unorthodox vision. Without his support and encouragement, we never could have produced this book. Tom Thompson, our development editor, was enormously helpful as he guided us with intelligence, patience, and tact through three major revisions of the original manuscript. We also thank Paul Shensa, the sponsoring editor, whose considerable experience, insightful suggestions, and extensive knowledge of the marketplace were of great help. We are especially grateful to Betty Morgan, our superb manuscript editor. And we are also grateful to the production team, whose professionalism was outstanding: Jean Lou Hess, Senior Project Manager; Michael McCormick, Senior Production Supervisor; Jill Kongabel and Matthew Baldwin, Designers; Nora Agbayani, Art Editor; Becky Szura, Supplements Coordinator, and Ann Rogula, New Media Producer.

Finally, our sincere thanks to the following teachers and colleagues, whose thorough reviews and thoughtful suggestions led to innumerable substantive improvements:

Ercument Aksoy
Los Angeles Valley College

Richard Anderson
Texas A&M University

Daniel Berkowitz
University of Pittsburgh

Guatam Bhattacharya
University of Kansas

Scott Bierman
Carleton College

Kelly Blanchard
Purdue Universtiy

Bruce Blonigen
University of Oregon

Beth Bogan
Princeton University

George Borts
Brown University

Nancy Brooks
University of Vermont

Douglas Brown
Georgetown University

Marie Bussings-Burk
Southern Indiana University

David Carr
University of Colorado

Jack Chambless
Valencia Community College

James Cover
University of Alabama

Carl Davidson
Michigan State University

Paul DePippo
Glendale Community College

Lynn Pierson Doti
Chapman College

Donald Dutkowsky
Syracuse University

Nancy Fox
Saint Joseph's College

Geoffrey Gee
California State
University–Fullerton

Jonah Gelbach
University of Maryland

Linda Ghent
East Carolina University

Kirk Gifford
Ricks College

Robert Gillette
University of Kentucky

Stephen Gohman
University of Louisville

Refet Gurkaynak
Princeton University

Mary Jean Horney
Furman University

Nancy Jianakoplos
Colorado State University

Robert Johnson
University of San Diego

William Kerby
California State
University–Sacramento

Herbert Kiesling
Indiana University

Bruce Kingma
State University of New
York–Albany

Hannes Kvaran
Glendale Community College

Leonard Lardaro
University of Rhode Island

Anthony Lima
California State
University–Hayward

Tom Love
North Central University

Steven McCafferty
The Ohio State University

Edward McNertney
Texas Christian University

William Merrill
Iowa State University

Paul Nelson
Northeast Louisiana State
University

Neil Niman
University of New Hampshire

Norman Obst
Michigan State University

Charles Okeke
Community College of Southern
Nevada

Duane Oyen
University of Wisconsin–Eau Claire

Theodore Palivos
Louisiana State University

Michael Potepan
San Francisco State University

Steve Robinson
University of North
Carolina–Wilmington

Christina Romer
University of California–Berkeley

David Romer
University of California–Berkeley

Greg Rose
Sacramento City College

Robert Rossana
Wayne State University

Richard Salvucci
Trinity University

Edward Scahill
University of Scranton

Pamela Schmitt
Indiana University

Dennis Starleaf
Iowa State University

Esther-Mirjam Sent
University of Notre Dame

John Solow
University of Iowa

Preface   ix

PART 1   **Introduction**
1   Thinking Like an Economist   3
2   Some Common Pitfalls for Decision Makers   31
3   Comparative Advantage: The Basis for Exchange   49
4   Supply and Demand: An Introduction   73

PART 2   **Competition and the Invisible Hand**
5   Demand: The Benefit Side of the Market   103
6   Perfectly Competitive Supply: The Cost Side of the Market   135
7   Efficiency and Exchange   165
8   The Quest for Profit and the Invisible Hand   195

PART 3   **Market Imperfections**
9   Monopoly and Other Forms of Imperfect Competition   221
10   Thinking Strategically   247
11   Externalities and Property Rights   273
12   The Economics of Information   297

PART 4   **Labor Markets and the Public Sector**
13   Labor Markets   321
14   The Economics of Public Policy   349
15   Public Goods and Taxation   377
16   Income Redistribution   401

Glossary   G-1

Index   I-1

PART I   **Introduction**

Chapter I   **Thinking Like an Economist**   3

Economics: Studying Choice in a World of Scarcity   4

Applying the Cost-Benefit Principle   5

    Reservation Prices   6

    Economic Surplus   6

    Opportunity Cost   7

    The Role of Economic Models   8

    To What Extent Should an Activity Be Pursued?   8

    Rationality and Imperfect Decision Makers   9

    Weighing Benefits and Costs Graphically   11

Economics: Micro and Macro   13

The Philosophy of This Text   14

Economic Naturalism   14

ECONOMIC NATURALIST I.I: Why do today's computers have so much more memory than those of a few years ago?   15

ECONOMIC NATURALIST I.2: Why is so much expensive software included with the sale of computers?   16

ECONOMIC NATURALIST I.3: Why don't auto manufacturers make cars without heaters?   17

ECONOMIC NATURALIST I.4: Why do keypads on drive-up teller machines have Braille dots?   17

Summary   18

Core Principles   18

Key Terms   18

Review Questions   18

Problems   19

Answers to In-Chapter Exercises   20

Appendix: Working with Equations, Graphs, and Tables   21

Chapter 2   **Some Common Pitfalls for Decision Makers**   31

Pitfall 1: Ignoring Opportunity Costs   32

    Recognizing the Relevant Alternative   32

    The Time Value of Money   33

ECONOMIC NATURALIST 2.I: Is it "unfair" to charge interest on a loan to a friend or family member?   35

Pitfall 2: Failure to Ignore Sunk Costs   36

Pitfall 3: Failure to Understand the Average-Marginal Distinction   39

    The Relevant Costs and Benefits Are Always Marginal   39

    Fixed and Variable Costs   42

Summary 44

Core Principles 45

Key Terms 45

Review Questions 45

Problems 45

Answers to In-Chapter Exercises 47

Chapter 3   Comparative Advantage: The Basis for Exchange   49

Exchange and Opportunity Cost   50

The Principle of Comparative Advantage   51

ECONOMIC NATURALIST 3.1: Where have all the .400 hitters gone?   53

Sources of Comparative Advantage   54

ECONOMIC NATURALIST 3.2: Why did the United States fail to retain its lead in the production of televisions and VCRs?   54

Comparative Advantage and Production Possibilities   55

Production Possibilities in a One-Person Economy   55

Factors That Influence the Production Possibilities Curve   58

Production Possibilities in a Two-Person Economy   59

How Much Does Specialization Matter?   61

A Production Possibilities Curve for a Many-Person Economy   64

Comparative Advantage and International Trade   65

Does Everyone Benefit from Trade?   68

Summary   68

Core Principles   69

Key Terms   69

Review Questions   69

Problems   69

Answers to In-Chapter Exercises   71

Chapter 4   Supply and Demand: An Introduction   73

What, How, and for Whom? Central Planning versus the Market   75

Markets and Prices   76

The Supply Curve   77

The Demand Curve   78

Market Equilibrium   79

Rent Controls Reconsidered   81

Hamburger Price Controls   84

Markets and Social Welfare   86

Cash on the Table   86

Smart for One, Dumb for All   87

Predicting and Explaining Changes in Prices and Quantities   88

Shifts in the Supply Curve   89

ECONOMIC NATURALIST 4.1: Why do book and Ph.D. dissertation manuscripts go through more revisions today than in the 1970s?   91

Shifts in Demand   92

ECONOMIC NATURALIST 4.2: Why do rents for well-located apartments in Washington go up after a government pay raise?   93

Four Simple Rules   95

ECONOMIC NATURALIST 4.3: Why do prices of some goods rise during times of heaviest consumption while others go down?   97

Summary 97

Core Principles 98

Key Terms 98

Review Questions 99

Problems 99

Answers to In-Chapter Exercises 100

PART 2 **Competition and the Invisible Hand**

Chapter 5 **Demand: The Benefit Side of the Market** 103

Needs, Wants, and the Law of Demand 104

Translating Wants into Demand 106

Measuring Wants: The Concept of Utility 106

Allocating a Fixed Income between Two Goods 108

The Rational Spending Rule 110

How Income and the Prices of Substitutes Affect Demand 112

Applying the Rational Spending Rule 113

Substitution at Work 113

ECONOMIC NATURALIST 5.1: Why do the wealthy live in smaller houses in Manhattan than in Seattle? 113

ECONOMIC NATURALIST 5.2: Why did people buy smaller cars in the 1970s but shift back to larger cars in the 1990s? 114

ECONOMIC NATURALIST 5.3: Why are automobile engines smaller in England than in the United States? 115

ECONOMIC NATURALIST 5.4: Why are waiting lines longer in poorer neighborhoods? 115

How the Distribution of Income Affects Demand 115

ECONOMIC NATURALIST 5.5: Why does a room with a view cost more in Berkeley than in Hanover? 115

Individual and Market Demand Curves 116

Horizontal Addition 117

The Straight-Line Demand Curve 117

Total Expenditure 119

Price Elasticity of Demand 122

Elasticity and Total Expenditure 123

Determinants of Price Elasticity of Demand 124

ECONOMIC NATURALIST 5.6: Will a higher tax on cigarettes curb teenage smoking? 125

Calculating Price Elasticity 125

Price Elasticity Changes along a Straight-Line Demand Curve 127

Income Elasticity and Cross-Price Elasticity of Demand 127

Two Special Cases 128

Where Do Wants Come From? 129

Summary 130

Key Terms 130

Review Questions 130

Problems 131

Answers to In-Chapter Exercises 132

Chapter 6   **Perfectly Competitive Supply: The Cost Side of the Market**   135
Thinking about Supply   136
Profit-Maximizing Firms and Perfectly Competitive Markets   139
   Profit Maximization   139
   The Demand Curve Facing a Perfectly Competitive Firm   140
   Production in the Short Run   141
   Choosing Output to Maximize Profit   142
   Price Equals Marginal Cost: The Seller's Supply Rule   144
   A Note on the Firm's Shutdown Condition   144
   Graphing Marginal Cost   145
   The "Law" of Supply   146
Determinants of Supply Revisited   147
   Technology   148
   Input Prices   148
   The Number of Suppliers   148
   Expectations   148
   Changes in Prices of Other Products   148
Applying the Theory of Supply   149
ECONOMIC NATURALIST 6.1: Why do private market forces recycle more aluminum than glass containers?   149
The Price Elasticity of Supply   151
   Defining and Calculating Elasticity of Supply   151
   Determinants of Supply Elasticity   154
   Unique and Essential Inputs: The Ultimate Supply Bottleneck   156
Using the Production Possibilities Curve to Generate Supply Curves   157
Summary   159
Key Terms   160
Review Questions   160
Problems   160
Answers to In-Chapter Exercises   162

Chapter 7   **Efficiency and Exchange**   165
Market Equilibrium and Efficiency   166
Economic Surplus   169
   Calculating Economic Surplus   169
   Efficiency Is Not the Only Goal   172
   Why Efficiency Should Be the First Goal   173
The Cost of Preventing Price Adjustments   174
   Price Ceilings   174
   Price Floors   178
   First-Come–First-Served Policies   179
ECONOMIC NATURALIST 7.1: Why does no one complain anymore about being bumped from an overbooked flight?   180
Taxes and Efficiency   183
   Who Pays a Tax Imposed on Sellers of a Good?   183
ECONOMIC NATURALIST 7.2: How will a tax on cars affect automobile prices in the long run?   184
   How a Tax Collected from a Seller Affects Economic Surplus   185
   Taxes, Elasticity, and Efficiency   187
   Taxes, External Costs, and Efficiency   188

Summary 189
Key Terms 190
Review Questions 190
Problems 190
Answers to In-Chapter Exercises 192

Chapter 8 **The Quest for Profit and the Invisible Hand** 195
The Central Role of Economic Profit 196
Three Types of Profit 196
The Effect of Market Forces on Economic Profit 201
ECONOMIC NATURALIST 8.1: Why do supermarket checkout lines all tend to be roughly the same length? 202
The Invisible Hand Theory 203
Two Functions of Price 203
The Importance of Free Entry and Exit 204
Economic Rent versus Economic Profit 205
The Effect of Cost-Saving Innovations 206
The Invisible Hand in Action 207
The Invisible Hand in Regulated Markets 207
ECONOMIC NATURALIST 8.2: Why do New York City medallions sell for more than $250,000? 208
ECONOMIC NATURALIST 8.3: Why did major commercial airlines install piano bars on the upper decks of 747s in the 1970s? 208
The Invisible Hand in Antipoverty Programs 209
The Invisible Hand in the Stock Market 210
ECONOMIC NATURALIST 8.4: Why isn't a stock portfolio consisting of America's "best-managed companies" a good investment? 212
The Distinction between an Equilibrium and a Social Optimum 213
No Cash on the Table 213
Smart for One, Dumb for All 214
ECONOMIC NATURALIST 8.5: Are there "too many" smart people working as corporate earnings forecasters? 214
Summary 215
Key Terms 216
Review Questions 216
Problems 216
Answers to In-Chapter Exercises 218

PART 3 **Market Imperfections**

Chapter 9 **Monopoly and Other Forms of Imperfect Competition** 221
Imperfect Competition 222
Different Forms of Imperfect Competition 222
The Essential Difference between Perfectly and Imperfectly Competitive Firms 222
Four Sources of Market Power 223
Exclusive Control over Important Inputs 223
Economies of Scale (Natural Monopolies) 223
Patents 224

Government Licenses or Franchises   224

Economies of Scale and the Importance of Fixed Costs   224

ECONOMIC NATURALIST 9.1: Why does Intel sell the overwhelming majority of all microprocessors used in personal computers?   227

Profit Maximization for the Monopolist   228

The Perfectly Competitive Firm's Decision Rule: A Review   228

Marginal Revenue for the Monopolist   229

The Monopolist's Profit-Maximizing Decision Rule   231

Why the Invisible Hand Breaks Down under Monopoly   233

Using Discounts to Expand the Market   235

Price Discrimination Defined   235

ECONOMIC NATURALIST 9.2: Why do many movie theaters offer discount tickets to students?   235

How Price Discrimination Affects Output   236

The Hurdle Method of Price Discrimination   238

Is the Hurdle Method Efficient?   240

Examples of the Hurdle Method   241

ECONOMIC NATURALIST 9.3: Why might an appliance retailer dent the sides of its stoves and refrigerators?   242

Summary   243

Key Terms   243

Review Questions   243

Problems   244

Answers to In-Chapter Exercises   245

Chapter 10   **Thinking Strategically**   247

The Theory of Games   248

The Three Elements of a Game   248

Nash Equilibrium   249

The Prisoner's Dilemma   251

The Original Prisoner's Dilemma   251

Prisoner's Dilemmas Confronting Imperfectly Competitive Firms   252

ECONOMIC NATURALIST 10.1: Why are cartel agreements notoriously unstable?   252

ECONOMIC NATURALIST 10.2: How did Congress unwittingly solve the television advertising dilemma for cigarette producers?   254

Prisoner's Dilemmas in Everyday Life   255

ECONOMIC NATURALIST 10.3: Why do people stand at concerts although they can see as well when everyone sits?   255

ECONOMIC NATURALIST 10.4: Why do people shout at parties?   256

Games In Which Timing Matters   256

The Ultimatum Bargaining Game   257

Credible Threats and Promises   259

Commitment Problems   262

The Strategic Role of Preferences   263

Are People Fundamentally Selfish?   264

Preferences as Solutions to Commitment Problems   265

Summary   266

Key Terms   266

Review Questions   267

Problems   267

Answers to In-Chapter Exercises   270

Chapter 11   Externalities and Property Rights   273

External Costs and Benefits   273
How Externalities Affect Resource Allocation   274
The Graphical Portrayal of Externalities   275
The Coase Theorem   275
Legal Remedies for Externalities   279
ECONOMIC NATURALIST 11.1: What is the purpose of speed limits and other traffic laws?   280
ECONOMIC NATURALIST 11.2: Why do most communities have zoning laws?   280
ECONOMIC NATURALIST 11.3: Why do many governments enact laws that limit the discharge of environmental pollutants?   280
ECONOMIC NATURALIST 11.4: What is the purpose of free speech laws?   280
ECONOMIC NATURALIST 11.5: Why does government subsidize activities that generate positive externalities?   281
The Optimal Amount of Negative Externalities Is Not Zero   281
Property Rights and the Tragedy of the Commons   282
The Problem of Unpriced Resources   282
The Effect of Private Ownership   284
When Private Ownership Is Impractical   285
ECONOMIC NATURALIST 11.6: Why do blackberries in public parks get picked too soon?   285
ECONOMIC NATURALIST 11.7: Why are shared milkshakes consumed too quickly?   285
Positional Externalities   286
Payoffs That Depend on Relative Performance   286
ECONOMIC NATURALIST 11.8: Why do football players take anabolic steroids?   287
Positional Arms Races   288
ECONOMIC NATURALIST 11.9: Why do so many grocery stores stay open all night, even in small towns?   288
Positional Arms Control Agreements   289
Social Norms as Positional Arms Control Agreements   290
Summary   292
Key Terms   293
Review Questions   293
Problems   293
Answers to In-Chapter Exercises   296

Chapter 12   The Economics of Information   297

How the Middleman Adds Value   298
The Optimal Amount of Information   300
The Cost-Benefit Test   300
The Free-Rider Problem   301
ECONOMIC NATURALIST 12.1: Why is finding a knowledgeable salesclerk often difficult?   301
ECONOMIC NATURALIST 12.2: Why did Rivergate Books, the last bookstore in its town, go out of business?   301
Two Guidelines for Rational Search   302
The Gamble Inherent in Search   303
The Commitment Problem When Search Is Costly   304
Asymmetric Information   305
The Lemons Model   306

The Credibility Problem in Trading   307

The Costly-to-Fake Principle   308

ECONOMIC NATURALIST 12.3: Why do firms use the phrase "As advertised on TV" in their print ads?   308

ECONOMIC NATURALIST 12.4: Why do companies care so much about elite educational credentials?   309

Conspicuous Consumption as a Signal of Ability   309

ECONOMIC NATURALIST 12.5: Why do many clients seem to prefer lawyers who wear expensive suits?   310

Statistical Discrimination   310

ECONOMIC NATURALIST 12.6: Why do males under 25 pay more than other drivers for auto insurance?   310

Adverse Selection   312

Disappearing Political Discourse   313

ECONOMIC NATURALIST 12.7: Why do opponents of the death penalty often remain silent?   313

ECONOMIC NATURALIST 12.8: Why do proponents of legalized drugs remain silent?   314

Summary   315

Key Terms   315

Review Questions   315

Problems   316

Answers to In-Chapter Exercises   317

PART 4   Labor Markets and the Public Sector

Chapter 13   Labor Markets   321

Wage and Salary Determination in Competitive Labor Markets   322

Monopsony: The Lone Employer in a Labor Market   325

Equilibrium in the Labor Market   328

Explaining Differences in Earnings   330

Human Capital Theory   330

Labor Unions   331

ECONOMIC NATURALIST 13.1: How do unionized firms survive competition from their nonunion counterparts?   333

Winner-Take-All Markets   333

ECONOMIC NATURALIST 13.2: Why does Kathleen Battle earn millions more than singers of slightly lesser ability?   333

ECONOMIC NATURALIST 13.3: Why did baseball salaries remain stagnant until 1975 despite large television revenues?   334

ECONOMIC NATURALIST 13.4: Why have the salaries of corporate executives been rising so rapidly?   335

Compensating Wage Differentials   336

ECONOMIC NATURALIST 13.5: Why do garbage collectors earn more than lifeguards?   336

ECONOMIC NATURALIST 13.6: Why do some advertising copywriters earn more than others?   337

ECONOMIC NATURALIST 13.7: Why did a telecommunications manufacturer offer "free" BMWs to its employees?   338

Discrimination in the Labor Market   339

Discrimination by Employers   340

Discrimination by Others   340

Other Sources of the Wage Gap   340
Comparable Worth Policies: A Costly Remedy?   342
Summary   344
Key Terms   344
Review Questions   345
Problems   345
Answers to In-Chapter Exercises   347

Chapter 14 The Economics of Public Policy   349

Public Policy toward Natural Monopoly   350
State Ownership and Management   350
State Regulation of Private Monopolies   351
Exclusive Contracting for Natural Monopoly   351
Vigorous Enforcement of Antitrust Laws   352
Marginal Cost Pricing of Public Services   353
Health Care Delivery   356
Applying the Cost-Benefit Criterion   356
Designing a Solution   358
The HMO Revolution   359
ECONOMIC NATURALIST 14.1: Why is a patient more likely to have an MRI if he has regular health insurance than if he belongs to an HMO?   360
Paying for Health Insurance   360
ECONOMIC NATURALIST 14.2: In the richest country, during an economic boom, why are the numbers of uninsured increasing?   361
Environmental Regulation   362
Taxing Pollution   362
Auctioning Pollution Permits   364
Workplace Safety Regulation   365
ECONOMIC NATURALIST 14.3: Why does the government require safety seats for infants in cars but not in airplanes?   369
Crime Control   370
ECONOMIC NATURALIST 14.4: Why do more Secret Service agents guard the President than the Vice President, and none guard professors?   370
Legalized Gambling   371
Summary   372
Key Terms   373
Review Questions   373
Problems   373
Answers to In-Chapter Exercises   375

Chapter 15 Public Goods and Taxation   377

Government Provision of Public Goods   378
Public Goods versus Private Goods   378
Paying for Public Goods   380
ECONOMIC NATURALIST 15.1: Why don't most married couples contribute equally to joint purchases?   382
The Optimal Quantity of a Public Good   383
The Demand Curve for a Public Good   383
Private Provision of Public Goods   385
ECONOMIC NATURALIST 15.2: Why do television networks favor Jerry Springer over *Masterpiece Theater?*   **386**

Additional Functions of Government 388
    Externalities and Property Rights 388
    Local, State, or Federal? 389
Sources of Ineffficiency in the Political Process 390
    Pork Barrel Legislation 390
ECONOMIC NATURALIST 15.3: Why does check-splitting make the total restaurant bill higher? 390
ECONOMIC NATURALIST 15.4: Why do legislators often support one another's pork barrel spending programs? 391
    Rent-Seeking 391
    Starve the Government 393
What Should We Tax? 394
Summary 396
Key Terms 397
Review Questions 397
Problems 397
Answers to In-Chapter Exercises 399

Chapter 16   **Income Redistribution** 401
Recent Trends in Inequality and Consumer Spending 402
Moral Concerns Raised by Income Inequality 404
    Justice as Fairness 404
    The Utilitarian Argument 405
    The Psychological Costs of Inequality 406
Practical Concerns Raised by Poverty and Income Inequality 407
    The Effect of Poverty on the Nonpoor 407
    The Effect of a Widening Income Gap on the Middle Class 408
Methods of Income Redistribution 410
    Minimum Wages 410
    The Earned-Income Tax Credit 411
    Welfare Payments and In-Kind Transfers 413
ECONOMIC NATURALIST 16.1: Why did critics charge that the AFDC program undermined family stability? 413
    The Negative Income Tax 414
    Public Employment for the Poor 416
    A Combination of Methods 416
    Benefit Levels: A State or Federal Question? 417
Paying for Income-Support Programs: Equity versus Efficiency? 418
    Adverse Effects on Incentives 418
    Tax Policy and Occupational Choice 419
ECONOMIC NATURALIST 16.2: Why are there too many singers and not enough teachers? 420
    A Progressive Consumption Tax? 424
    The Legislator's Dilemma 425
    Redistribution and Cost-Benefit Analysis 426
Summary 427
Key Terms 428
Review Questions 428
Problems 428
Answers to In-Chapter Exercises 429

Glossary G-1

Index I-1

PRINCIPLES OF
MICRO-
ECONOMICS

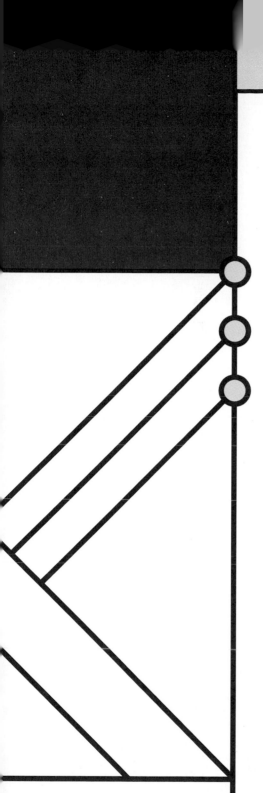

PART

1

INTRODUCTION

As you begin the study of economics, perhaps the most important thing to realize is that economics is *not* a collection of settled facts to be copied down and memorized. Mark Twain once said that nothing is older than yesterday's newspaper, and the same can be said of yesterday's economic statistics. Indeed, the only prediction about the economy that can be confidently made is that there will continue to be large, and largely unpredictable, changes.

If economics is not a set of durable facts, then what is it? Fundamentally, it is a *way of thinking* about the world. Over many years economists have developed some simple but widely applicable principles that are useful for understanding almost any economic situation, from the relatively simple economic decisions that individuals make every day to the workings of highly complex markets, such as international financial markets. The principal objective of this book, and of this course, is to help you learn these principles and how to apply them to a variety of economic questions and issues.

The four chapters of Part 1 lay out the basic economic principles that will be used throughout the book. Chapter 1 introduces the notion of scarcity—the unavoidable fact that, although our needs and wants are boundless, the resources available to satisfy them are limited. The chapter goes on to show that deciding whether to take an action by comparing the cost and benefit of the action provides a useful approach for dealing with the inevitable trade-offs that scarcity creates. Chapter 2 looks at some additional important principles for effective economic decision making, in the process identifying several pitfalls that plague many decision makers. Chapter 3 goes beyond individual decision making to consider trade among both individuals and countries. An important reason for trade is that it permits people (or countries) to specialize in the production of particular goods and services, which in turn enhances productivity and raises standards of living. Finally, Chapter 4 presents an overview of the concepts of supply and demand, perhaps the most basic and familiar tools of economists.

THINKING LIKE AN ECONOMIST

∎

How many students are in your introductory economics class? Some classes have just 20 or so. Others average 35, 100, or 200 students. At some schools, introductory economics classes may have as many as 2,000 students. What size is best?

If cost were no object, the best size for an introductory economics course—or any other course, for that matter—might be only a single student. Think about it: the whole course, all term long, with just you and your professor! Everything could be custom-tailored to your own background and ability, allowing you to cover the material at just the right pace. The tutorial format would also promote close communication and personal trust between you and your professor. And your grade would depend more heavily on what you actually learned than on the vagaries of multiple-choice exams. We may even suppose, for the sake of discussion, that studies by educational psychologists prove definitively that students learn best in the tutorial format.

Why, then, do so many universities continue to schedule introductory classes with hundreds of students? The simple reason is that costs *do* matter. They matter not just to the university administrators who must build classrooms and pay faculty salaries but also to *you*. The direct cost of providing you with your own personal introductory economics course—most notably, the professor's salary and the expense of providing a classroom in which to meet—might easily top $20,000. *Someone* has to pay these costs. In private universities, a large share of the cost would be recovered directly from higher tuition payments; in state universities, the burden would be split between higher tuition payments and higher tax payments. But in either case, the course would be unaffordable for many, if not most, students.

With a larger class size, of course, the cost per student goes down. For example, in a class of 300 students, the cost of an introductory economics

Are small classes "better" than large ones?

course might come to as little as $100 per student. Needless to say, a class that large would compromise the quality of the learning environment. But compared to the custom tutorial format, it would be dramatically more affordable.

In choosing what size introductory economics course to offer, then, university administrators confront a classic economic trade-off. In making the class larger, they lower the quality of instruction—a bad thing; but at the same time, they reduce costs and hence the tuition students must pay—a good thing.

ECONOMICS: STUDYING CHOICE IN A WORLD OF SCARCITY

Even in rich societies like the United States, *scarcity* is a fundamental fact of life. There is never enough time, money, or energy to do everything we want to do or have everything we would like to have. **Economics** is the study of how people make choices under conditions of scarcity and of the results of those choices for society.

In the class-size example just discussed, a motivated economics student might definitely prefer to be in a class of 20 rather than a class of 100, everything else being equal. But other things, of course, are not equal. Students can enjoy the benefits of having smaller classes, but only at the price of having less money for other activities. The student's choice inevitably will come down to the relative importance of competing activities.

That such trade-offs are widespread and important is one of the core principles of economics. We call it the **scarcity principle**, because the simple fact of scarcity makes trade-offs necessary. Another name for the scarcity principle is the **no-free-lunch principle** (which comes from the observation that even a lunch that is given to you takes time to eat—time you could have spent doing other useful things).

The Scarcity Principle (or the No-Free-Lunch Principle): Although we have boundless needs and wants, the resources available to us are limited. So having more of one good thing usually means having less of another.

economics the study of how people make choices under conditions of scarcity and of the results of those choices for society

Inherent in the idea of a trade-off is the fact that choice involves compromise between competing interests. Economists resolve such trade-offs by using **cost-benefit analysis,** which is based on the disarmingly simple principle that an action should be taken if, and only if, its benefits exceed its costs. We call this statement the **cost-benefit principle,** and it, too, is one of the core principles of economics:

The Cost-Benefit Principle: An individual (or a firm or a society) should take an action if, and only if, the extra benefits from taking the action are at least as great as the extra costs.

With the cost-benefit principle in mind, let's think about our class-size question again. Imagine that classrooms come in only two sizes—100-seat lecture halls and 20-seat classrooms—and that your university currently offers introductory economics courses to classes of 100 students. Question: Should administrators reduce the class size to 20 students? Answer: Reduce if, and only if, the value of the improvement in instruction outweighs its additional cost.

This rule sounds simple, but to apply it we need some way to measure the relevant costs and benefits—a task that is often difficult in practice. If we make a few simplifying assumptions, however, we can see how the analysis might work. On the cost side, suppose that the only relevant expenses are the professor's salary and the cost of a classroom big enough to hold the class. Imagine that the professor is paid $20,000 per course and that classroom space can be obtained at a cost of $30 per student per semester. Suppose further that the university charges tuition for the course equal to the direct costs of providing it. At the current class size of 100 students, the total cost is $23,000—$20,000 for the professor plus 100($30) = $3,000 for the classroom—which means that tuition is $230 per student. But if there were just 20 students in the class, the total cost would be $20,000 + 20($30) = $20,600—so tuition would be $1,030 per student.

The cost of reducing class size from 100 to 20 is simply the difference between the two tuition figures just calculated, namely, $1,030 − $230 = $800 per student. Should administrators switch to the smaller class size? If they apply the cost-benefit principle, they will realize that *the reduction in class size makes sense only if the value to students of attending the smaller class is at least $800 greater than the value of attending the larger class.*

Would you yourself (or your parents, if they are paying your tuition) be willing to part with an extra $800 for a smaller economics class? If not, and if other students feel the same way, then sticking with the larger class size makes sense. But if you and others would be willing to pay the extra tuition, then reducing the class size to 20 makes good economic sense.

Notice that the "best" class size, from an economic point of view, may not be the same as the "best" size from the point of view of an educational psychologist. The difference arises because the economic definition of "best" takes into account both the benefits *and* the costs of different class sizes. The psychologist ignores costs and looks only at the learning benefits of different class sizes.

In practice, of course, different people will feel differently about the value of smaller classes. People with high incomes, for example, tend to be willing to pay more for the advantage, which helps to explain why average class size is smaller, and tuition higher, at those private schools whose students come predominantly from high-income families.

The cost-benefit framework for thinking about the class-size problem also suggests a possible reason for the gradual increase in average class size that has been taking place in American colleges and universities. During the last 15 years, professors' salaries and the cost of classrooms have risen sharply, making smaller classes more costly. During the same period, median family income—and hence the willingness to pay for smaller classes—has remained roughly constant. When the cost of offering smaller classes goes up but willingness to pay for smaller classes does not, universities shift to larger class sizes.

Scarcity and the trade-offs that result also apply to resources other than money. Bill Gates is the richest man on earth. His wealth has been estimated at over $100 billion—more than the combined wealth of the poorest 40 percent of Americans. Gates has enough money to buy more houses, cars, vacations, and other consumer goods than he could possibly use. Yet Gates, like the rest of us, has only 24 hours each day and a limited amount of energy. So even he confronts trade-offs, in that any activity he pursues—whether it is building his business empire or planning the construction of his mansion—uses up time and energy that he could otherwise spend on other things. Indeed, someone once calculated that the value of Gates's time is so great that pausing to pick up a $100 bill from the sidewalk simply wouldn't be worth his while.

If Bill Gates saw a $100 bill lying on the sidewalk, would it be worth his time to pick it up?

APPLYING THE COST-BENEFIT PRINCIPLE

In studying choice under scarcity, we'll usually begin with the premise that people are **rational,** which means they have well-defined goals and try to fulfill them as best they can. The cost-benefit principle illustrated in the class-size example is a fundamental tool for the study of how rational people make choices.

rational person someone with well-defined goals who tries to fulfill those goals as best he or she can

As in the class-size example, often the only real difficulty in applying the cost-benefit rule is to come up with reasonable measures of the relevant benefits and costs. Only in rare instances will exact dollar measures be conveniently available. But the cost-benefit framework can lend structure to your thinking even when no relevant market data are available.

RESERVATION PRICES

To illustrate how we proceed in such cases, the following example asks you to decide whether to perform an action whose cost and benefits are described only in vague, qualitative terms.

EXAMPLE 1.1

Should you iron your shirt before going out?

You have a date for dinner in an hour, when suddenly you realize that your only clean shirt is not ironed. It doesn't look terrible, and you could certainly wear it if you had to. But you'd look and feel a little better if it were ironed, and you have the time to do it. On the other hand, you don't like to iron, and you will need 20 minutes to do the job—time that you could spend doing other things.

The cost-benefit principle says you should iron your shirt if the benefit of doing so exceeds the cost. The problem is that we don't have convenient ways to measure those benefits and costs. We can take a few simple steps, however, to generate useful estimates.

In dollar terms, the *benefit* of ironing your shirt may be defined as the largest amount of money you would be willing to pay to wear a pressed shirt to dinner rather than an unpressed shirt. How could you determine that amount? Here's a simple thought experiment that will give you an approximate estimate.

Imagine that a genie has offered to iron your shirt for a fee. If the fee were only a penny, would you accept? Assuming so, your benefit from having a pressed shirt must be at least 1 cent. If the genie's fee were $50, would you pay it? Probably not, in which case your benefit from having a pressed shirt must be less than $50. Somewhere between these two extremes lies the highest price you would be willing to pay to have your shirt ironed. To discover this price, imagine that the genie auctions off his services, starting with a price of 1 cent and raising it gradually until you refuse his last offer. For example, if you would accept the genie's offer to iron your shirt for $2.25 but would refuse the offer at $2.26, then the benefit to you of having a pressed shirt is $2.25. Another name for this benefit is your **reservation price** for having your shirt pressed—the highest price you would be willing to pay for that service.

reservation price the highest price someone is willing to pay to obtain any good or service, or the lowest payment someone would accept for giving up a good or performing a service

A similar strategy can be used to estimate the cost of ironing your shirt. This time, we want to find out the most you'd be willing to pay to avoid ironing your shirt. This is what we mean by the cost of ironing your shirt. So imagine that someone offers to hire you to iron *his* shirt for a payment of, say, $50. Would you accept? If so, we know that your cost of ironing a shirt must be less than $50. Now imagine the offer being reduced in small increments until you finally refuse the last offer. For example, if you would iron someone's shirt for $2.00 but not for $1.99, then your cost of ironing a shirt is $2.00.

In this example, the benefit of ironing your shirt (your reservation price for *having* a pressed shirt) is $2.25, and your cost for a pressed shirt (your reservation price for *ironing* the shirt) is $2.00. Because your benefit exceeds your cost, your best course of action is to iron your shirt.

ECONOMIC SURPLUS

economic surplus the economic surplus from taking any action is the benefit of taking the action minus its cost

In Example 1.1, ironing your shirt generated an **economic surplus** of $0.25, the difference between your benefit from ironing your shirt and your cost of ironing it. In general, your goal as an economic decision maker is to choose those actions that generate the largest possible economic surplus. This means taking all actions that yield a positive economic surplus, which is just another way of restating the cost-benefit principle.

OPPORTUNITY COST

Note that the fact that your best choice is to iron your shirt doesn't imply that you *enjoy* ironing it, any more than choosing a large class means that you prefer large classes to small ones. It simply means that ironing your shirt is less unpleasant than the prospect of showing up for dinner in a wrinkled shirt. Once again, you've faced a trade-off—in this case, the choice between a pressed shirt and the free time gained by going without one.

Needless to say, your mental auctions could have produced a different outcome. Suppose, for example, that the time you would need to iron your shirt is the only time you have left to study for a difficult test the next day. Or suppose you are watching one of your favorite movies on cable or that you are tired and would love a short nap. In such cases, we say that the **opportunity cost** of ironing your shirt—that is, the value of what you must sacrifice to iron your shirt—is high, and you are more likely to decide against ironing it.

In this example, if watching the last 20 minutes of the cable TV movie is the most valuable opportunity that conflicts with ironing, the opportunity cost of ironing your shirt is the dollar value you place on pursuing that opportunity—that is, the largest amount you'd be willing to pay to avoid missing the end of the movie. Note that the opportunity cost of ironing your shirt is *not* the combined value of *all* possible activities you could have pursued, but only the value of your *best* alternative—the one you would have chosen had you not ironed your shirt.

Throughout the text we will pose exercises like the one that follows. You'll find that pausing to answer them will help you to master key concepts in economics. Because doing these exercises isn't very costly (indeed, many students report that they are actually fun), the cost-benefit principle indicates that it's well worth your while to do them.

opportunity cost the opportunity cost of an activity is the value of the next-best alternative that must be forgone to undertake the activity

---

EXERCISE 1.1

If your reservation price for *having* an ironed shirt is $3 and your reservation price for *ironing* your shirt is $4, how much economic surplus would you receive from ironing your shirt? Should you iron it?

What is the opportunity cost of attending tonight's Eric Clapton concert?   **EXAMPLE 1.2**

It's rock 'n' roll hall of fame night. Eric Clapton is performing at 8 P.M. on the University of Minnesota campus, where your student ID card entitles you to free admission to all university events. Your only other alternative is to attend an 8 P.M. Bob Dylan concert at the Metrodome. Admission to the Dylan concert is $30, and you value the time and trouble involved in making the round-trip to the Metrodome at $10. If your reservation price for hearing Dylan is $50, what is your opportunity cost of attending the Clapton concert? What is your smallest reservation price for hearing Clapton that would make the Clapton concert your first choice?

By attending the Clapton concert, you give up the economic surplus you would have received by attending the Dylan concert, which is your reservation price for hearing Dylan minus the ticket price minus the cost of the trip to the Metrodome: $50 − $30 − $10 = $10. So $10 is your opportunity cost of hearing Clapton—the value of all you must sacrifice to hear him. You should attend the Clapton concert only if your reservation price for hearing Clapton is at least $10.

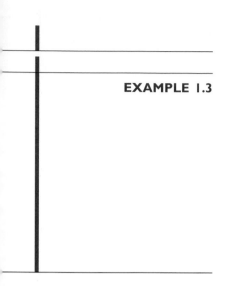

EXAMPLE 1.3

Refer to Example 1.2. Suppose your reservation price for hearing Clapton is $8? What would be your opportunity cost of hearing the Dylan concert? Which concert should you attend?

The question we must answer is "What is the value of everything you give up to attend the Dylan concert?" You give up the chance to hear Clapton, which is worth $8 to you; you give up $30 to buy the Dylan ticket; and you give up the chance to avoid the trip to the Metrodome, which is worth $10 to you. So the total value of what you give up is $8 + $30 + $10 = $48, and since this is less than your reservation price for hearing Dylan, you should attend the Dylan concert. (This is consistent with the conclusion from Example 1.2 that you should hear Dylan if your reservation price for hearing Clapton is less than $10.)

THE ROLE OF ECONOMIC MODELS

Economists use the cost-benefit principle as an abstract model of how an idealized rational individual would choose among competing alternatives. (By *abstract model* we mean a simplified description that captures the essential elements of a situation and allows us to analyze them in a logical way.) A computer model of a complex phenomenon like climate change, which must ignore many details and includes only the major forces at work, is an example of an abstract model.

Noneconomists are sometimes harshly critical of the economist's cost-benefit model on the grounds that people in the real world never conduct hypothetical mental auctions before deciding whether to iron their shirts. But this criticism betrays a fundamental misunderstanding of how abstract models can help to explain and predict human behavior. Economists know perfectly well that people don't conduct hypothetical mental auctions when they make simple decisions. All the cost-benefit principle really says is that a rational decision is one that is explicitly or implicitly based on a weighing of costs and benefits.

Most of us make sensible decisions most of the time, without being consciously aware that we are weighing costs and benefits, just as most people ride a bike without being consciously aware of what keeps them from falling. Through trial and error, we gradually learn what kinds of choices tend to work best in different contexts, just as bicycle riders internalize the relevant laws of physics, usually without being consciously aware of them.

Even so, learning the explicit principles of cost-benefit analysis can help us make better decisions, just as knowing about physics can help in learning to ride a bicycle. For instance, when a young economist was teaching his oldest son to ride a bike, he followed the time-honored tradition of running alongside the bike and holding onto his son, then giving him a push and hoping for the best. After several hours and many skinned elbows and knees, his son finally got it. A year later, someone pointed out that the trick to riding a bike is to turn slightly in whichever direction the bike is leaning. Of course! The economist passed that information along to his second son, who learned to ride almost instantly.

TO WHAT EXTENT SHOULD AN ACTIVITY BE PURSUED?

The pressed-shirt example involved the choice of whether or not to engage in an activity. But in many situations, as in the following example, the issue is not whether to pursue the activity at all but rather the *extent* to which it should be pursued.

How many pounds of compost should Heather use on her tomato patch?   **EXAMPLE 1.4**

To earn extra money over the summer, Heather grows tomatoes and sells them at the farmers' market for 20 cents per pound. By adding compost to her garden, she can increase her summer's yield, as shown in the table below. If compost costs 25 cents per pound and her goal is to make as much money as possible, how many pounds of compost should she add?

Pounds of compost	Pounds of tomatoes
0	100
1	120
2	125
3	128
4	130
5	131
6	131.5

To answer this question, note that questions of the form "Should Heather *pursue some activity*?" can be translated into the form "How many pounds of compost should Heather add?" by repeatedly posing the question "Should Heather *add an additional pound of compost*?" The answer, of course, is that Heather should add an additional pound of compost if its benefit is greater than or equal to its cost. The benefit of adding a pound of compost is the extra revenue she will get from the extra tomatoes that result; the cost of adding a pound of compost is 25 cents. If Heather starts out with no compost, she'll get 20 extra pounds of tomatoes—or 20($0.20) = $4 of extra revenue—by adding the first pound of compost. Clearly it pays to add the first pound of compost. Similar reasoning justifies adding the second, third, and fourth pounds of compost. (By adding the fourth pound of compost Heather will get 2 extra pounds of tomatoes, or 40 cents in extra revenue, which more than covers the 25-cent cost of the extra compost.) But note that if she were to add the fifth pound of compost, she'd get only one extra pound of tomatoes, whose 20-cent value is less than the cost of the compost. So Heather should add 4 pounds of compost and no more.

EXERCISE 1.2

In Example 1.4, if the cost of compost had been 50 cents/pound, not 25 cents, how many pounds of compost should Heather have added?

RATIONALITY AND IMPERFECT DECISION MAKERS

Imagine you are confronted with the question "Should I perform some action?" in which "perform some action" could mean anything from "eat another cookie" to "choose Wisconsin over Ohio State." The cost-benefit principle says that if the benefits of the action exceed its costs, then you should do it; but if the benefits fall short of the costs, then you should not do it. If its benefits and costs happen to be exactly equal, then it doesn't matter whether you perform the action or not.

Rational people will apply the cost-benefit principle most of the time, although probably in an intuitive and approximate way, rather than through explicit and precise calculation. To the extent that people are rational, their tendency to compare costs and benefits will help economists to predict their likely behavior. For example, we can predict that students from wealthy families are more likely than others to attend colleges that offer small classes.

As the next examples will make clear, however, the cost-benefit principle also proves helpful in another way. These examples demonstrate that people aren't born with an infallible instinct for weighing the relevant costs and benefits of daily decisions. Indeed, one of the rewards of teaching economics is to see how quickly it transforms students into better decision makers.

EXAMPLE I.5

Should you drive downtown to save $10 on a $20 computer game? Should you drive downtown to save $10 on a $1,050 laptop computer?

Imagine you are about to buy a $20 computer game at the nearby campus store when a friend tells you that the same game is on sale at a downtown store for only $10. Would you drive downtown, or would you buy the game at the campus store?

Now imagine that you are about to buy a $1,050 laptop computer at the nearby campus store when a friend tells you that the store downtown has the same computer for only $1,040. Would you drive downtown this time?

In the first instance, the benefit of driving downtown is the $10 you will save on the game. To estimate the cost of driving downtown, simply ask yourself this question: "What is the minimum dollar amount that someone would have to pay me before I'd be willing to drive downtown and back?" Your answer to this question is your cost of driving downtown. If you'd be willing to do it for less than $10, then you should drive downtown. Otherwise, you should buy the game from the campus store. Since the cost of driving downtown is higher for some students than for others, different people will choose differently. But although there is no uniquely correct answer to this question, most students say they would shop downtown for the game.

So far, so good. But now let's consider whether to drive downtown for the laptop computer. Again, there is no uniquely correct answer, but most students now respond that they would shop at the campus store, saying "It's not worth it to drive downtown to save $10 on a laptop costing more than $1,000." But here we have a contradiction. The benefit of driving downtown to buy the laptop is $10—exactly the same as for the computer game. And the cost of driving downtown must also be the same in both cases, since whatever inconvenience and other expense the trip entails cannot logically depend on the trip's purpose. Finally, since the respective costs and benefits of the trips are identical, someone who finds it worthwhile to drive downtown in the first case should also find it worthwhile in the second. Yet as noted, most students respond differently in the two cases.

Many feel that a $10 savings on a laptop computer is insignificant because it is such a small *proportion* of the computer's price. Yet the proportion one saves on the purchase is simply not relevant to the decision. Regardless of how big that proportion is, you should take the trip if, and only if, the dollar amount you save is enough to compensate you for the trip's cost.

EXERCISE I.3

Which is more valuable, saving $100 on a $2,000 plane ticket to Tokyo or saving $90 on a $200 plane ticket to Chicago?

EXERCISE I.4

Ask your roommates or other friends outside class to consider the questions posed in Example 1.5 and Exercise 1.3. How do you expect they will answer? Do you think those who would choose differently in the two cases will accept your explanation for why such behavior cannot be rational?

Here is another example in which many people find it difficult to apply the cost-benefit principle correctly:

Would you buy a theater ticket after losing a $10 bill? Would you buy a second ticket after losing the first?

EXAMPLE 1.6

Imagine that you've just arrived at the theater to buy your ticket when you discover that you've lost a $10 bill from your wallet. Would you buy a ticket and see the play anyway? (You have enough money left to do that.)

Now suppose that you've just arrived at the theater when you discover that you've lost the $10 ticket you purchased earlier. Would you buy another ticket and see the play anyway?

As in Example 1.5, many people say they would choose differently in these two cases. Psychologists Daniel Kahneman and Amos Tversky found that most subjects would go ahead and see the play after losing a $10 bill but would not do so after losing a ticket they had already purchased.[1] According to the cost-benefit criterion, however, choosing differently in these cases is not rational. After all, the benefit of seeing the play is the same in both cases, and the cost of seeing the play—at the moment you must decide—is exactly $10 in both.

Many people seem to feel that in the case of the lost ticket, the cost of seeing the play is not $10 but $20, the price of two tickets. In terms of the financial consequences, however, the loss of a ticket is clearly no different from the loss of a $10 bill. In each case, you must decide whether seeing the play is worth spending $10. If it is, you should see it; otherwise not. Whichever your answer, it must be the same in both cases if you are rational.

Examples 1.5 and 1.6 make the point that people sometimes choose irrationally. Not only that, the errors they make tend to be systematic: People not only make inconsistent choices, but their inconsistencies also exhibit a strong pattern.

Some economists become defensive at the mere mention of the possibility that people sometimes choose irrationally, and most textbooks don't even call attention to this possibility. We find this a curious posture, for in our view, the fact that people do not always choose rationally makes the study of economics all the more useful. And as we'll see, learning how to identify situations in which we are least apt to weigh costs and benefits correctly promises to make all of us better decision makers.

That said, we must stress that our purpose in presenting Examples 1.5 and 1.6 was not to suggest that people *generally* make irrational choices. On the contrary, most people appear to choose sensibly most of the time, especially when their decisions are important or familiar ones. The economist's focus on rational choice thus offers not only useful advice about making better decisions but also a basis for predicting and explaining human behavior. We used the cost-benefit approach in this way when discussing how rising faculty salaries and building costs have led to larger class sizes. And as we will see, similar reasoning helps to explain human behavior in virtually every other domain.

WEIGHING BENEFITS AND COSTS GRAPHICALLY

Sometimes, as in the following example, a graph proves a convenient form in which to express the costs and benefits of various levels of an activity.

How much memory should your computer have?

EXAMPLE 1.7

Suppose you can add random-access memory (RAM) to your computer at a cost of $5 per megabyte. Suppose also that the value to you of an additional megabyte of memory, measured in terms of your willingness to pay for it, is as shown by curve *MB* in Figure 1.1. How many megabytes of memory should you purchase?

[1]Amos Tversky and Daniel Kahneman, "The Framing of Decisions and the Psychology of Choice," *Science*, **211**:453–458, 1981.

FIGURE 1.1

The Marginal Cost and Benefit of Additional RAM.

Curve *MB* plots the benefit of adding an additional megabyte of memory. Curve *MC* plots the cost of an additional megabyte of memory. It is rational to continue adding memory as long as the marginal benefit of memory (curve *MB*) lies above the marginal cost of memory (curve *MC*). The optimal amount of RAM is 30 megabytes, the amount for which the marginal benefit of memory is equal to its marginal cost.

marginal benefit the marginal benefit of an activity is the increase in total benefit that results from carrying out one additional unit of the activity.

marginal cost the marginal cost of an activity is the increase in total cost that results from carrying out one additional unit of the activity.

Curve *MB* plots the value to you of an additional megabyte of memory (measured in dollars per megabyte, on the vertical axis) as a function of your computer's existing memory (measured in megabytes, on the horizontal axis). For example, the value of additional memory is $20 per megabyte if your computer has 10 megabytes of memory but only $10 if it has 20 megabytes. Curve *MB* is often called the **marginal benefit** curve, to emphasize that it shows not the *total* value of memory but the value of having *an additional unit* of memory. (*Marginal* means "extra" or "additional.")

Curve *MC* in Figure 1.1 shows the cost, in dollars, of adding an additional megabyte, assumed constant at $5. This curve is often called the **marginal cost** curve, to emphasize that it represents not the total cost of memory but the cost of adding an additional unit. The fact that curve *MC* is horizontal at $5 means that no matter how much memory your computer has, you can always add an extra megabyte at a cost of exactly $5. (Later on, we will consider examples in which the cost of adding additional units depends on the number of units you already have.)

Once we know the relevant marginal benefit and cost curves, finding the optimal quantity of memory is straightforward. Note in Figure 1.1 that if the quantity of memory your computer has is less than 30 megabytes, then the marginal benefit of adding memory (as measured by curve *MB*) is greater than its marginal cost (as measured by curve *MC*). So you should add memory if your computer currently has less than 30 megabytes.

Conversely, note that if your computer has more than 30 megabytes of memory, the marginal benefit of memory is less than its marginal cost, in which case you should have bought less memory. The optimal amount of memory is thus 30 megabytes, the amount at which the marginal benefit of memory exactly equals its marginal cost.

A common question prompted by Example 1.7 is "Why should I bother to add the thirtieth megabyte of memory if its marginal benefit is no greater than its marginal cost?" The answer is that at any amount less than 30 megabytes, the marginal benefit of memory exceeds its marginal cost. Suppose, for example, that your computer had only 29.9 megabytes of memory. The marginal benefit of additional memory would then be greater than its marginal cost (albeit by only a tiny margin), which means that you should expand. The same reasoning would apply if your computer had 29.99 megabytes, or even 29.99999. So you can always do better by expanding unless you've already got 30 megabytes.[2]

RECAP   **COST-BENEFIT ANALYSIS**

Scarcity is a basic fact of economic life. Because of it, having more of one good thing almost always means having less of another (the scarcity principle). Economics is devoted to studying how we can make intelligent choices in a world of scarcity.

The cost-benefit principle holds that an individual (or a firm or a society) should take an action if, and only if, the extra benefit from taking the action is at least as great as the extra cost. The benefit of taking any action minus the cost of taking the action is called the *economic surplus* from that action. Hence the cost-benefit principle suggests that we take only those actions with positive economic surplus.

Applying the cost-benefit principle requires measurement. The benefit of an action is your *reservation price* for having the action performed, the most you would be willing to pay someone to perform it. The cost of an action is the value of everything you must sacrifice to perform the action.

The cost-benefit principle applies not only to all-or-nothing decisions but also to decisions regarding the extent to which an activity should be pursued. The rule is to keep performing the action as long as the marginal benefit of the action exceeds its marginal cost.

ECONOMICS: MICRO AND MACRO

By convention, we use the term **microeconomics** to describe the study of individual choices and of group behavior in individual markets. **Macroeconomics**, by contrast, is the study of the performance of national economies and of the policies that governments use to try to affect that performance. Macroeconomics tries to understand the determinants of such things as the national unemployment rate, the overall price level, and the total value of national output.

Our focus in this chapter and the next is on issues that confront the individual decision maker. Further on, we'll consider economic models of groups of individuals, such as all buyers or all sellers in a specific market. Later still we will turn to broader economic issues and measures.

No matter which of these levels is our focus, however, our thinking will be shaped by the fact that although economic needs and wants are effectively unlimited, the material and human resources that can be used to satisfy them are finite. Clear thinking about economic problems must therefore always take into account the idea of trade-offs—the idea that having more of one good thing usually means having less of another. Our economy and our society are shaped to a substantial degree by the choices people have made when faced with trade-offs.

microeconomics the study of individual choice under scarcity and its implications for the behavior of prices and quantities in individual markets

macroeconomics the study of the performance of national economies and the policies that governments use to try to improve that performance.

---

[2]Note that in this example we treated your computer's memory bank as a perfectly divisible quantity. In practice, however, computer memory can be increased only by adding chunks of discrete size. A more realistic account of your decision of how much memory to buy for your computer would advise you to add the next chunk of memory if its benefit exceeds its cost. The optimal quantity of memory could then be an amount for which the benefit of the last chunk was greater than its cost. In that case, the benefit of the next discrete chunk would be less than its cost.

THE PHILOSOPHY OF THIS TEXT

Choosing the number of students to register in each class is just one of many important decisions in planning an introductory economics course. Another decision, to which the scarcity principle applies just as strongly, concerns which of many different topics to include on the course syllabus. There is a virtually inexhaustible set of topics and issues that might be covered in an introductory course, but only limited time in which to cover them. There's no free lunch. Covering some topics inevitably means omitting others.

All textbook authors are necessarily forced to pick and choose. A textbook that covered *all* the issues ever written about in economics would take up more than a whole floor of your campus library. It is our firm view that most introductory textbooks try to cover far too much. One reason each of us was drawn to the study of economics was that a relatively short list of the discipline's core ideas can explain a great deal of the behavior and events we see in the world around us. So rather than cover a large number of ideas at a superficial level, our strategy is to focus on this short list of core ideas, returning to each entry again and again, in many different contexts. This strategy will enable you to internalize these ideas remarkably well in the brief span of a single course. And the benefit of learning a small number of important ideas well will far outweigh the cost of having to ignore a host of other, less important ideas.

So far, we've already encountered two core ideas: the scarcity principle and the cost-benefit principle. As these core ideas reemerge in the course of our discussions, we'll call your attention to them. And shortly after a new core idea appears, we'll highlight it by formally restating it.

A second important element in the philosophy of this text is our belief in the importance of active learning. In the same way that you can learn Spanish only by speaking and writing it, or tennis only by playing the game, you can learn economics only by *doing* economics. Because we want you to learn how to do economics, rather than just to read or listen passively as the authors or your instructor does economics, we will make every effort to encourage you to stay actively involved.

For example, instead of just telling you about an idea, we will usually first motivate the idea by showing you how it works in the context of a specific example. Often, these examples will be followed by exercises for you to try, as well as applications that show the relevance of the idea to real life. Try working the exercises *before* looking up the answers (which are at the end of the chapter).

Think critically about the applications: Do you see how they illustrate the point being made? Do they give you new insight into the issue? Work problems at the end of the chapter, and take extra care with those relating to points that you do not fully understand. Apply economic principles to the world around you. (We'll say more about this when we discuss Economic Naturalism below.) Finally, when you come across an idea or example that you find interesting, tell a friend about it. You'll be surprised to discover how much the mere act of explaining it helps you understand and remember the underlying principles. The more actively you can become engaged in the learning process, the more effective your learning will be.

ECONOMIC NATURALISM

With the rudiments of the cost-benefit framework under your belt, you are now in a position to become an "economic naturalist," someone who uses insights from economics to help make sense of observations from everyday life. People who have studied biology are able to observe and marvel at many details of nature that would otherwise have escaped their notice. For example, while the novice may see only trees on a walk in the woods in early April, the biology student notices many different species of trees and understands why some are already into leaf while others still lie dormant. Likewise, the novice may notice that in some animal species, males are much larger than females, but the biology student knows that that pattern occurs only in species in which males take several mates. Natural selection favors larger males because their greater size helps them to prevail in the often bloody contests among males for access to females. By contrast, males tend to be roughly the same size as females in monogamous species, in which there is much less fighting for mates.

In similar fashion, learning a few simple economic principles enables us to see the mundane details of ordinary human existence in a new light. Whereas the uninitiated often fail even to notice these details, the economic naturalist not only sees them but becomes actively engaged in the attempt to understand them. Let's consider a few examples of questions economic naturalists might pose for themselves.

Why do today's computers have so much more random-access memory (RAM) than the computers of just a few years ago?

Computers sold today typically come with at least 32 megabytes of RAM, often 64. Just a few short years ago, however, personal computers rarely had more than 2 megabytes of RAM. Why this dramatic increase?

To understand this change, the economic naturalist looks for changes in the underlying costs and benefits of RAM. Having more memory is obviously a benefit, since it enables the computer to carry out more complex tasks. But memory is also costly, and this limits the amount of memory we buy. Perhaps the most important reason for the greater amount of RAM in today's computers is the dramatic drop in cost made possible by new production methods. Whereas RAM once sold for several hundred dollars per megabyte, it now costs less than $10 per megabyte. As shown in Figure 1.2, for example, a fall in the marginal cost of RAM from $10 to $5 per megabyte increases the optimal amount of memory from 20 to 30 megabytes.

Important changes have occurred on the benefit side as well. For example, graphics software uses large amounts of memory, and the drop in RAM prices has encouraged developers to make much more intensive use of graphics. The new programs are more attractive than older programs, but a computer needs a lot of extra memory to run them. The availability of these programs has thus increased the benefit of adding extra memory and in so doing has helped to fuel the move toward greater amounts of RAM.

Graphically, we represent an increase in the value of additional memory as an upward movement of the marginal benefit curve. Figure 1.3, for example, portrays an upward shift in the marginal benefit curve from curve *MB* to curve *MB'*. Such a shift means that the consumer now finds extra memory more valuable than before, no matter how much memory his or her computer has. The upward shift in the marginal benefit curve in Figure 1.3 increases the optimal amount of RAM from 30 to 40 megabytes.

FIGURE 1.2
Falling RAM Prices Increase the Optimal Amount of Memory.
When the price of memory falls from $10 per megabyte to $5 per megabyte, the optimal amount of memory increases from 20 to 30 megabytes.

FIGURE 1.3
An Increase in the Marginal Benefit of RAM Increases the Optimal Amount of Memory.
When the marginal benefit of RAM increases (when curve *MB* shifts up to become curve *MB'*), the optimal amount of memory increases from 30 to 40 megabytes.

As long as we're on the subject, let's consider one more computer-related example.

ECONOMIC NATURALIST 1.2

Why do many hardware manufacturers include more than $1,000 worth of free software with a computer selling for only slightly more than that?

The software industry is different from many others in the sense that its customers care a great deal about product compatibility. When you and your classmates are working on a project together, for example, your task will be much simpler if you all use the same word-processing program. Likewise, an executive's life will be easier at tax time if her financial software is the same as her accountant's.

The implication is that the benefit of owning and using any given software program increases with the number of other people who use that same product. This unusual relationship gives the producers of the most popular programs an enormous advantage and often makes it hard for new programs to break into the market.

Recognizing this pattern, the Intuit Corporation offered computer makers free copies of *Quicken,* its personal financial-management software. Computer makers, for their part, were only too happy to include the program, since it made their new computers more attractive to buyers. *Quicken* soon became the standard for personal financial-management programs. By giving away free copies of the program, Intuit "primed the pump," creating an enormous demand for upgrades of *Quicken* and for more advanced versions of related software. Thus *TurboTax* and *Macintax,* Intuit's personal income tax software, have become the standards for tax-preparation programs.

Inspired by this success story, other software developers have jumped onto the bandwagon. Most hardware now comes bundled with a host of free software programs. Some software developers are even rumored to *pay* computer makers to include their programs!

The free-software example illustrates a case in which the *benefit* of a product depends on the number of other people who own that product. As the next example demonstrates, the *cost* of a product may also depend on the number of others who own it.

Why don't auto manufacturers make cars without heaters?

Virtually every new car sold in the United States today has a heater. But not every car has a CD player. Why this difference?

One might be tempted to answer that although everyone *needs* a heater, people can get along without CD players. Yet heaters are of little use in places like Hawaii and southern California. What is more, cars produced as recently as the 1950s did *not* all have heaters. (The classified ad that led one young economic naturalist to his first car, a 1955 Pontiac, boasted that the vehicle had a radio, heater, and whitewall tires.)

Although heaters cost extra money to manufacture and are not useful in all parts of the country, they do not cost *much* money and are useful on at least a few days each year in most parts of the country. As time passed and people's incomes grew, manufacturers found that people were ordering fewer and fewer cars without heaters. At some point it actually became cheaper to put heaters in *all* cars, rather than bear the administrative expense of making some cars with heaters and others without. No doubt a few buyers would still order a car without a heater if they could save some money in the process. But catering to these customers is just no longer worth it.

Similar reasoning explains why certain cars today cannot be purchased without a CD player. Buyers of the 2001 BMW 740iL, for example, got a CD player whether they wanted one or not. Most buyers of this car, which sells for approximately $70,000, have high incomes, so the overwhelming majority of them would have chosen to order a CD player had it been sold as an option. Because of the savings made possible when all cars are produced with the same equipment, it would have actually cost BMW more to supply cars for the few who would want them without CD players.

The insights afforded by the preceding example suggest an answer to the following strange question:

Why do the keypad buttons on drive-up automatic teller machines have Braille dots?

Braille dots on elevator buttons and on the keypads of walk-up automatic teller machines enable blind persons to participate more fully in the normal flow of daily activity. But even though blind people can do many remarkable things, they cannot drive automobiles on public roads. Why, then, do the manufacturers of automatic teller machines install Braille dots on the machines at drive-up locations?

The answer to this riddle is that once the keypad molds have been manufactured, the cost of producing buttons with Braille dots is no higher than the cost of producing smooth buttons. Making both would require separate sets of molds and two different types of inventory. If the patrons of drive-up machines found buttons with Braille dots harder to use, there might be a reason to incur these extra costs. But since the dots pose no difficulty for sighted users, the best and cheapest solution is to produce only keypads with dots.

The preceding example was suggested by Cornell student Bill Tjoa, in response to the following assignment:

EXERCISE 1.5

In 750 words or less, use cost-benefit analysis to explain some pattern of events or behavior you have observed in your own environment.

ECONOMIC NATURALIST 1.3

ECONOMIC NATURALIST 1.4

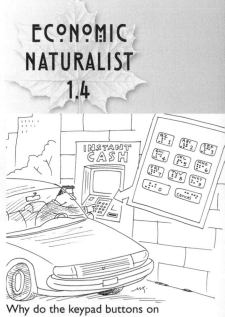

Why do the keypad buttons on drive-up automatic teller machines have Braille dots?

There is probably no more useful step you can take in your study of economics than to perform several iterations of the assignment in Exercise 1.5. Students who do so almost invariably become lifelong economic naturalists. Their mastery of economic concepts not only does not decay with the passage of time, it actually grows stronger. We urge you, in the strongest possible terms, to make this investment!

■ SUMMARY ■

• Economics is the study of how people make choices under conditions of scarcity and of the results of those choices for society. Economic analysis of human behavior begins with the assumption that people are rational—that they have well-defined goals and try to achieve them as best they can. In trying to achieve their goals, people normally face trade-offs: Because material and human resources are limited, having more of one good thing means making do with less of some other good thing.

• Our focus in this chapter was on how rational people make choices between alternative courses of action. Our basic tool for analyzing these decisions is cost-benefit analysis. The cost-benefit principle says that a person should take an action if, and only if, the benefit of that action is at least as great as its cost. The benefit of an action is measured as the largest dollar amount the person would be willing to pay to take the action. The cost of an action is measured as the dollar value of everything the person must give up to take the action.

• Often the question is not whether to pursue an activity but rather how many units of it to pursue. In these cases, the rational actor pursues additional units as long as the marginal benefit of the activity (the benefit from pursuing an additional unit of it) exceeds its marginal cost (the cost of pursuing an additional unit of it).

• In using the cost-benefit framework, we need not presume that people choose rationally all the time. Indeed, we saw examples in which people's choices departed in systematic ways from what rational decision makers would have chosen.

■ CORE PRINCIPLES ■

The Scarcity Principle (or No-Free-Lunch Principle)
Although we have boundless needs and wants, the resources available to us are limited. So having more of one good thing usually means having less of another.

The Cost-Benefit Principle
An individual (or a firm or a society) should take an action if, and only if, the extra benefits from taking the action are at least as great as the extra costs.

■ KEY TERMS ■

economic surplus (6)
economics (4)
macroeconomics (13)

marginal benefit (12)
marginal cost (12)
microeconomics (13)

opportunity cost (7)
rational person (5)
reservation price (6)

■ REVIEW QUESTIONS ■

1. A friend of yours on the tennis team says, "Private tennis lessons are definitely better than group lessons." Explain what you think your friend means by this statement. Then use the cost-benefit principle to explain why private lessons are not necessarily the best choice for everyone.

2. Assuming that both care equally about improving their tennis games, who is likely to have a higher reservation price for private tennis lessons: a McDonald's clerk or a computer programmer?

3. One of the two bicycle shops near campus is having a sale on new mountain bikes. Sam nonetheless decides to buy his new bike from the other shop, paying $30 more in the process. Describe an example of conditions under which his decision might nonetheless be considered rational.

4. True or false: Your willingness to drive downtown to save $30 on a new appliance should depend on what fraction of the total selling price $30 is. Explain.

5. Both the economics and the sociology departments have scheduled their faculty meetings on the first Wednesday of each month at 4:00 P.M. The economics department has a policy of starting its meetings at 4 o'clock sharp. The sociology department's policy is to start once 80 percent of the faculty has arrived. Discuss the relative merits of these two policies.

■ PROBLEMS ■

1. Your reservation price for having a freshly washed car when you go out to dinner is $6. The smallest amount for which you would be willing to wash someone else's car is $3.50. You are going out to dinner this evening, and your car is dirty. How much economic surplus would you receive from washing it?

2. To earn extra money in the summer, you grow tomatoes and sell them at the farmers' market for 30 cents per pound. By adding compost to your garden, you can increase your yield as shown in the following table. If compost costs 50 cents per pound and your goal is to make as much money as possible, how many pounds of compost should you add?

Pounds of compost	Pounds of tomatoes
0	100
1	120
2	125
3	128
4	130
5	131
6	131.5

3. For each long distance call anywhere in the continental United States, a new phone service will charge users 30 cents per minute for the first 2 minutes and 2 cents per minute for additional minutes in each call. Tom's current phone service charges 10 cents per minute for all calls, and his calls are never shorter than 7 minutes. If Tom's dorm switches to the new phone service, what will happen to the average length of his calls?

4. The meal plan at university A lets students eat as much as they like for a fixed fee of $500 per semester. The average student there eats 250 pounds of food per semester. University B charges $500 for a book of meal tickets that entitles the student to eat 250 pounds of food per semester. If the student eats more than 250 pounds, he or she pays extra; if the student eats less, he or she gets a refund. If students are rational, at which university will average food consumption be higher? Explain briefly.

5. Suppose random-access memory can be added to your computer at a cost of $10 per megabyte. Suppose also that the value to you of an additional megabyte of memory, measured in terms of your willingness to pay, is as shown in the following diagram. How many megabytes of memory should you purchase? Explain briefly.

6. Residents of your city are charged a fixed weekly fee of $6 for garbage collection. They are allowed to put out as many cans as they wish. The average household disposes of three cans of garbage per week under this plan. Now suppose that your city changes to a "tag" system. Each can of refuse to be collected must have a tag affixed to it. The tags cost $2 each and are not reusable. What effect do you think the introduction of the tag system will have on the total quantity of garbage collected in your city? Explain briefly.

7. Once a week, Smith purchases a six-pack of cola and puts it in his refrigerator for his two children. He invariably discovers that all six cans are gone on the first day. Jones also purchases a six-pack of cola once a week for his two children, but unlike Smith, he tells them that each may drink no more than three cans. Explain briefly why the cola lasts much longer at Jones's house than at Smith's.

8. The Wallflowers will give a free concert on the Emory University campus the same night The Traveling Wilburys will perform at a club in Buckhead. The club charges a $3 fee at the door. You choose the Wallflowers concert, but your next best choice for the evening is to hear The Wilburys. Your opportunity cost of hearing the Wallflowers is:
   a. The dollar value to you of hearing The Traveling Wilburys minus the time and money cost of driving to Buckhead and paying the door fee
   b. The time and money cost of driving to Buckhead and paying the door fee
   c. The dollar value to you of hearing The Traveling Wilburys plus the time and money cost of driving to Buckhead and paying the door fee
   d. The study time lost for Econ 101 while you listen to the Wallflowers

9. Same as Problem 8 except that this time you prefer The Traveling Wilburys and The Wallflowers would be your second choice. Your opportunity cost of going to hear The Traveling Wilburys is:
   a. The club's door fee
   b. The dollar value to you of hearing The Wallflowers minus the time and money cost of driving to Buckhead and paying the door fee
   c. The dollar value to you of hearing The Traveling Wilburys minus the time and money cost of driving to Buckhead and paying the door fee
   d. The dollar value to you of hearing The Wallflowers plus the time and money cost of driving to Buckhead plus the $3 door fee
   e. The study time lost for Econ 101 while you drive and while you listen to The Traveling Wilburys

10. As in Problem 8, The Wallflowers will give a free concert on the Emory University campus the same night The Traveling Wilburys will perform at a club in Buckhead. The club charges a $3 fee at the door. Suppose the dollar value to you of hearing The Wallflowers is $6 and the cost of your round-trip drive to Buckhead is $5. If the dollar value to you of hearing The Traveling Wilburys is $15:
   a. Which choice should you make and how much economic surplus would you receive from your evening?
   b. How would your answers be different if the dollar value of hearing The Wallflowers were $8?

■ ANSWERS TO IN-CHAPTER EXERCISES ■

1.1 The economic surplus from ironing your shirt would be $3 −$4 = −$1. Because the surplus from ironing your shirt would be negative, you should not iron it.

1.2 Adding the third pound of compost makes sense, because it increases revenue by 60 cents and costs only 50 cents. But the fourth pound of compost does not make sense, because it adds only 40 cents to revenue.

1.3 Saving $100 is $10 more valuable than saving $90, even though the percentage savings is much greater in the case of the Chicago ticket.

WORKING WITH EQUATIONS, GRAPHS, AND TABLES

■

Although many of the examples and most of the end-of-chapter problems in this book are quantitative, none require mathematical skills beyond rudimentary high school algebra and geometry. In this brief appendix we review some of the skills you'll need for dealing with these examples and problems.

One important skill is to be able to read simple verbal descriptions and translate the information they provide into the relevant equations or graphs. You'll also need to be able to translate information given in tabular form into an equation or graph, and sometimes you'll need to translate graphical information into a table or equation. The following examples illustrate all the tools you'll need.

USING A VERBAL DESCRIPTION TO CONSTRUCT AN EQUATION

We begin with an example that shows how to construct a long-distance telephone billing equation from a verbal description of the billing plan.

EXAMPLE A.1

Your long-distance telephone plan charges you $5/month plus 10 cents/minute for long-distance calls. Write an equation that describes your monthly telephone bill.

equation a mathematical expression that describes the relationship between two or more variables

variable a quantity that is free to take a range of different values

dependent variable a variable in an equation whose value is determined by the value taken by another variable in the equation

independent variable a variable in an equation whose value determines the value taken by another variable in the equation

constant (or parameter) a quantity that is fixed in value

An **equation** is a simple mathematical expression that describes the relationship between two or more **variables,** or quantities that are free to assume different values in some range. The most common type of equation we'll work with contains two types of variables: **dependent variable** and **independent variable.** In this example, the dependent variable is the dollar amount of your monthly telephone bill, and the independent variable is the variable on which your bill depends, namely, the volume of long-distance calls you make during the month. Your bill also depends on the $5 monthly fee and the 10 cents/minute charge. But in this example, those amounts are **constants,** not variables. A constant, also called a **parameter,** is a quantity in an equation that is fixed in value, not free to vary. As the terms suggest, the dependent variable describes an outcome that depends on the value taken by the independent variable.

Once you've identified the dependent variable and the independent variable, choose simple symbols to represent them. In algebra courses, X is typically used to represent the independent variable and Y the dependent variable. Many people find it easier to remember what the variables stand for, however, if they choose symbols that are linked in some straightforward way to the quantities that the variables represent. Thus, in this example, we might use B to represent your monthly *bill* in dollars and T to represent the total *time* in minutes you spent during the month on long-distance calls.

Having identified the relevant variables and chosen symbols to represent them, you are now in a position to write the equation that links them:

$$B = 5 + 0.10T, \qquad \text{(A.1)}$$

where B is your monthly long-distance bill in dollars and T is your monthly total long-distance calling time in minutes. The fixed monthly fee (5) and the charge per minute (0.10) are parameters in this equation. Note the importance of being clear about the units of measure. Because B represents the monthly bill in dollars, we must also express the fixed monthly fee and the per-minute charge in dollars, which is why the latter number appears in equation A.1 as 0.10 rather than 10. Equation A.1 follows the normal convention in which the dependent variable appears by itself on the left-hand side while the dependent variable or variables and constants appear on the right-hand side.

Once we have the equation for the monthly bill, we can use it to calculate how much you'll owe as a function of your monthly volume of long-distance calls. For example, if you make 32 minutes of calls, you can calculate your monthly bill by simply substituting 32 minutes for T in equation A.1:

$$B = 5 + 0.10(32) = 8.20. \qquad \text{(A.2)}$$

Your monthly bill when you make 32 minutes of calls is thus equal to $8.20.

EXERCISE A.1

Under the monthly billing plan described in Example A.1, how much would you owe for a month during which you made 45 minutes of long-distance calls?

GRAPHING THE EQUATION OF A STRAIGHT LINE

The next example shows how to portray the billing plan described in Example A.1 as a graph.

Construct a graph that portrays the monthly long-distance telephone billing plan described in Example A.1, putting your telephone charges, in dollars per month, on the vertical axis, and your total volume of calls, in minutes per month, on the horizontal axis.

EXAMPLE A.2

The first step in responding to this instruction is the one we just took, namely, to translate the verbal description of the billing plan into an equation. When graphing an equation, the normal convention is to use the vertical axis to represent the dependent variable and the horizontal axis to represent the independent variable. In Figure A.1, we therefore put B on the vertical axis and T on the horizontal axis. One way to construct the graph shown in the figure

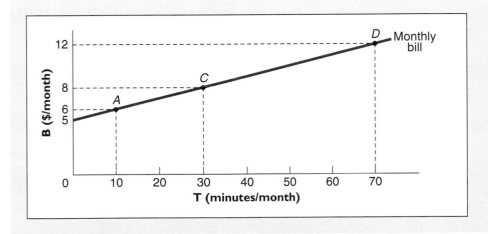

FIGURE A.1
The Monthly Telephone Bill in Example A.1.
The graph of the equation $B = 5 + 0.10T$ is the straight line shown. Its vertical intercept is 5, and its slope is 0.10.

is to begin by plotting the monthly bill values that correspond to several different total amounts of long-distance calls. For example, someone who makes 10 minutes of calls during the month would have a bill of $B = 5 + 0.10(10) = \$6$. Thus, in Figure A.1 the value of 10 minutes/month on the horizontal axis corresponds to a bill of \$6/month on the vertical axis (point A). Someone who makes 30 minutes of long-distance calls during the month will have a monthly bill of $B = 5 + 0.10(30) = \$8$, so the value of 30 minutes/month on the horizontal axis corresponds to \$8/month on the vertical axis (point C). Similarly, someone who makes 70 minutes of long-distance calls during the month will have a monthly bill of $B = 5 + 0.10(70) = \$12$, so the value of 70 minutes on the horizontal axis corresponds to \$12 on the vertical axis (point D). The line joining these points is the graph of the monthly billing equation A.1.

As shown in Figure A.1, the graph of the equation $B = 5 + 0.10T$ is a straight line. The parameter 5 is the **vertical intercept** of the line—the value of B when $T = 0$, or the point at which the line intersects the vertical axis. The parameter

vertical intercept in a straight line, the value taken by the dependent variable when the independent variable equals zero

slope in a straight line, the ratio of the vertical distance the straight line travels between any two points **(rise)** to the corresponding horizontal distance **(run)**

0.10 is the **slope** of the line, which is the ratio of the **rise** of the line to the corresponding **run**. The ratio rise/run is simply the vertical distance between any two points on the line divided by the horizontal distance between those points. For example, if we choose points A and C in Figure A.1, the rise is $8 - 6 = 2$ and the corresponding run is $30 - 10 = 20$, so rise/run $= 2/20 = 0.10$. More generally, for the graph of any equation $Y = a + bX$, the parameter a is the vertical intercept and the parameter b is the slope.

DERIVING THE EQUATION OF A STRAIGHT LINE FROM ITS GRAPH

The next example shows how to derive the equation for a straight line from a graph of the line.

EXAMPLE A.3

Figure A.2 shows the graph of the monthly billing plan for a new long-distance plan. What is the equation for this graph? How much is the fixed monthly fee under this plan? How much is the charge per minute?

FIGURE A.2

Another Monthly Long-Distance Plan.

The vertical distance between points A and C is $12 - 8 = 4$ units, and the horizontal distance between points A and C is $40 - 20 = 20$, so the slope of the line is $4/20 = 1/5 = 0.20$. The vertical intercept (the value of B when $T = 0$) is 4. So the equation for the billing plan shown is $B = 4 + 0.20T$.

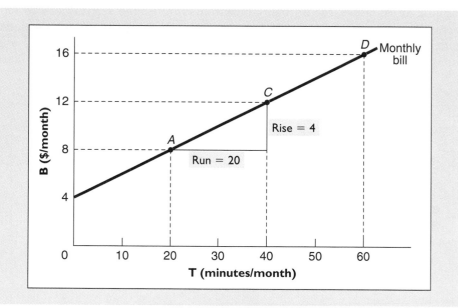

The slope of the line shown is the rise between any two points divided by the corresponding run. For points A and C, rise $= 12 - 8 = 4$, and run $= 40 - 20 = 20$, so the slope equals rise/run $= 4/20 = 1/5 = 0.20$. And since the horizontal intercept of the line is 4, its equation must be given by

$$B = 4 + 0.20T. \qquad (A.3)$$

Under this plan, the fixed monthly fee is the value of the bill when $T = 0$, which is \$4. The charge per minute is the slope of the billing line, 0.20, or 20 cents/minute.

EXERCISE A.2

Write the equation for the billing plan shown in the accompanying graph. How much is its fixed monthly fee? Its charge per minute?

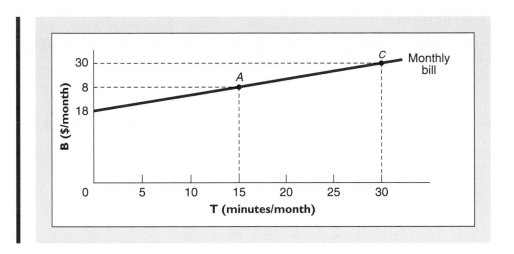

CHANGES IN THE VERTICAL INTERCEPT AND SLOPE

Examples A.4 and A.5 and Exercises A.3 and A.4 provide practice in seeing how a line shifts with a change in its vertical intercept or slope.

Show how the billing plan whose graph is in Figure A.2 would change if the monthly fixed fee were increased from $4 to $8.

An increase in the monthly fixed fee from $4 to $8 would increase the vertical intercept of the billing plan by $4 but would leave its slope unchanged. An increase in the fixed fee thus leads to a parallel upward shift in the billing plan by $4, as shown in Figure A.3. For any given number of minutes of long-distance calls, the monthly charge on the new bill will be $4 higher than on the old bill.

EXAMPLE A.4

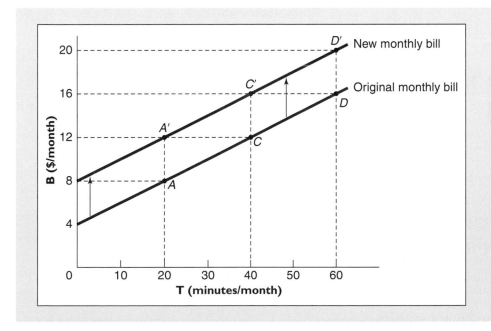

FIGURE A.3
The Effect of an Increase in the Vertical Intercept.
An increase in the vertical intercept of a straight line produces an upward parallel shift in the line.

Thus 20 minutes of calls per month costs $8 under the original plan (point *A*) but $12 under the new plan (point *A'*). And 40 minutes costs $12 under the original plan (point *C*), $16 under the new plan (point *C'*); and 60 minutes costs $16 under the original plan (point *D*), $20 under the new plan (point *D'*).

EXAMPLE A.5

Show how the billing plan whose graph is in Figure A.2 would change if the charge per minute were increased from 20 cents to 40 cents.

Because the monthly fixed fee is unchanged, the vertical intercept of the new billing plan continues to be 4. But the slope of the new plan, shown in Figure A.4, is 0.40, or twice the slope of the original plan. More generally, in the equation $Y = a + bX$, an increase in b makes the slope of the graph of the equation steeper.

FIGURE A.4

The Effect of an Increase in the Charge per Minute.

Because the fixed monthly fee continues to be $4, the vertical intercept of the new plan is the same as that of the original plan. With the new charge per minute of 40 cents, the slope of the billing plan rises from 0.20 to 0.40.

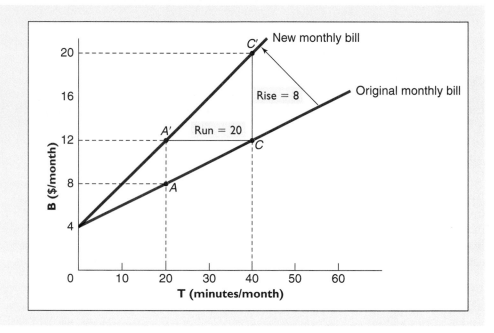

Exercise A.4 illustrates the general rule that in an equation $Y = a + bX$, a reduction in b makes the slope of the graph of the equation less steep.

CONSTRUCTING EQUATIONS AND GRAPHS FROM TABLES

Example A.6 and Exercise A.5 show how to transform tabular information into an equation or graph.

EXAMPLE A.6

Table A.1 shows four points from a monthly long-distance telephone billing equation. If all points on this billing equation lie on a straight line, find the vertical intercept of the equation and graph it. What is the monthly fixed fee? What is the charge per minute? Calculate the total bill for a month with 1 hour of long-distance calls.

TABLE A.1
Points on a Long-Distance Billing Plan

Long-distance bill ($/month)	Total long-distance calls (minutes/month)
10.50	10
11.00	20
11.50	30
12.00	40

FIGURE A.5
Plotting the Monthly Billing Equation from a Sample of Points.
Point *A* is taken from row 2, Table A.1, and point *C* from row 4. The monthly billing plan is the straight line that passes through these points.

One approach to this problem is simply to plot any two points from the table on a graph. Since we are told that the billing equation is a straight line, that line must be the one that passes through any two of its points. Thus, in Figure A.5 we use *A* to denote the point from Table A.1 for which a monthly bill of $11 corresponds to 20 minutes/month of calls (second row) and *C* to denote the point for which a monthly bill of $12 corresponds to 40 minutes/month of calls (fourth row). The straight line passing through these points is the graph of the billing equation.

Unless you have a steady hand, however, or use extremely large graph paper, the method of extending a line between two points on the billing plan is unlikely to be very accurate. An alternative approach is to calculate the equation for the billing plan directly. Since the equation is a straight line, we know that it takes the general form $B = f + sT$, where f is the fixed monthly fee and s is the slope. Our goal is to calculate the vertical intercept f and the slope s. From the same two points we plotted earlier, *A* and *C*, we can calculate the slope of the billing plan as $s = \text{rise/run} = 1/20 = 0.05$.

So all that remains is to calculate f, the fixed monthly fee. At point *C* on the billing plan, the total monthly bill is $12 for 40 minutes, so we can substitute $B = 12$, $s = 0.05$, and $T = 40$ into the general equation $B = f + sT$ to obtain

$$12 = f + 0.05(40), \tag{A.4}$$

or

$$12 = f + 2, \tag{A.5}$$

which solves for $f = 10$. So the monthly billing equation must be

$$B = 10 + 0.05T. \tag{A.6}$$

For this billing equation, the fixed fee is $10/month, the calling charge is 5 cents/minute ($0.05/minute), and the total bill for a month with 1 hour of long-distance calls is $B = 10 + 0.05(60) = \$13$, just as shown in Figure A.5.

EXERCISE A.5

The following table shows four points from a monthly long-distance telephone billing plan.

Long-distance bill ($/month)	Total long-distance calls (minutes/month)
20.00	10
30.00	20
40.00	30
50.00	40

If all points on this billing plan lie on a straight line, find the vertical intercept of the corresponding equation without graphing it. What is the monthly fixed fee? What is the charge per minute? How much would the charges be for 1 hour of long-distance calls per month?

▪ KEY TERMS ▪

constant (22)
dependent variable (22)
equation (22)
independent variable (22)

parameter (22)
rise (24)
run (24)
slope (24)

variable (22)
vertical intercept (23)

▪ ANSWERS TO IN-APPENDIX EXERCISES ▪

A.1   To calculate your monthly bill for 45 minutes of calls, substitute 45 minutes for T in equation A.1 to get $B = 5 + 0.10(45) = \$9.50$.

A.2   Calculating the slope using points A and C, we have rise $= 30 - 24 = 6$ and run $= 30 - 15 = 15$, so rise/run $= 6/15 = 2/5 = 0.40$. And since the horizontal intercept of the line is 18, its equation is $B = 18 + 0.40T$. Under this plan, the fixed monthly fee is $18, and the charge per minute is the slope of the billing line, 0.40, or 40 cents/minute.

A.3   A $2 reduction in the monthly fixed fee would produce a downward parallel shift in the billing plan by $2.

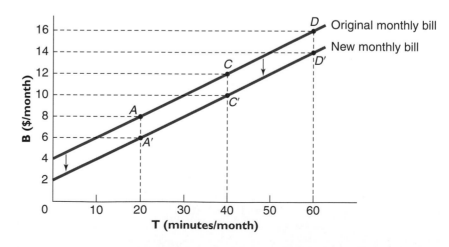

A.4 With an unchanged monthly fixed fee, the vertical intercept of the new billing plan continues to be 4. The slope of the new plan is 0.10, half the slope of the original plan.

A.5 Let the billing equation be $B = f + sT$, where f is the fixed monthly fee and s is the slope. From the first two points in the table, calculate the slope s = rise/run = 10/10 = 1.0. To calculate f, we can use the information in row 1 of the table to write the billing equation as $20 = f + 1.0(10)$ and solve for $f = 10$. So the monthly billing equation must be $B = 10 + 1.0T$. For this billing equation, the fixed fee is \$10/month, the calling charge is \$1/minute, and the total bill for a month with 1 hour of long-distance calls is $B = 10 + 1.0(60) = \$70$.

SOME COMMON PITFALLS FOR DECISION MAKERS

■

The protagonist of Roald Dahl's short story "Royal Jelly" is a bee-keeper whose infant daughter's physical development is seriously threatened by her inability to digest food. All medical interventions have failed. In desperation, the beekeeper decides to treat his daughter with massive doses of royal jelly, the substance that causes an ordinary bee to develop into a queen bee.

Only minute quantities of royal jelly are produced in any one bee colony. Because of its seemingly magical power to stimulate development, not just in bees but also in other creatures, the substance is astronomically expensive. The beekeeper's good fortune, as Dahl describes it, is that his occupation gives him access to large quantities of the precious stuff, which otherwise would have been far too expensive for a man of his modest means.

In any event, the new therapy seems to work—the baby immediately begins to gain weight when the royal jelly is mixed with her milk. Character-istically, Dahl ends his tale with a chilling twist. While changing their daughter's diaper one morning, the horrified parents notice that her torso has begun to take on the unmistakable contours of a queen bee's thorax.

Our interest in Dahl's fable lies not in its macabre ending but in its implicit claim that, to the beekeeper, royal jelly was essentially a free good. Of course, it was not a free good at all, for if the beekeeper had not fed the jelly to his daughter, he could have sold it in the marketplace. The amount for which he could have sold it was the opportunity cost of using the substance as he did. In this sense, then, the royal jelly was no less costly to the beekeeper than it would have been to an accountant or a school teacher. And he was therefore in no better position to provide it to his daughter than any other person of similar means. (Of course, in calculating how wealthy the beekeeper is, we have to take into account the value of his access to the royal jelly! Looking only at his earnings from the sale of honey would understate the total economic compensation he received from beekeeping.)

The fact that the beekeeper ignored the opportunity cost of the royal jelly when deciding whether to give it to his daughter does not mean that his decision was wrong. When a family member's health is threatened, most of us are willing to pay whatever we can afford in an effort to help. Thus, even though the opportunity cost of the royal jelly was high, its benefit might have been even higher, in which case the right decision would have been to administer it. But in that case, it would also have been the right decision for a schoolteacher or anyone else of similar means and circumstances. The important point is that using a good we already happen to own is not free.

As we noted in Chapter 1, the cost-benefit principle suggests that an introductory economics course should emphasize a short list of those principles with the greatest power to predict and explain behavior. But it also suggests that among those principles, we should focus especially on those that are most difficult to master. As we explore the cost-benefit approach in greater detail in this chapter, then, we will emphasize the errors people commonly make when trying to implement it. People often tend to ignore certain costs that they ought to take into account, for example, and sometimes they are influenced by costs that are irrelevant to the decision at hand. It is also common for people to base decisions on average costs and benefits instead of on the marginal costs and benefits called for by the cost-benefit principle.

PITFALL 1: IGNORING OPPORTUNITY COSTS

Sherlock Holmes, Arthur Conan Doyle's legendary detective, was successful because he saw details that most others overlooked. In *Silver Blaze*, Holmes is called on to investigate the theft of an expensive racehorse from its stable. A Scotland Yard inspector assigned to the case asks Holmes whether some particular aspect of the crime required further study. "Yes," Holmes replies, and describes "the curious incident of the dog in the nighttime." "The dog did nothing in the nighttime," responds the puzzled inspector. But as Holmes realized, that was precisely the problem. The watchdog's failure to bark when Silver Blaze was stolen meant that the watchdog knew the thief. This clue substantially reduced the number of suspects and eventually led to the thief's apprehension.

Opportunity costs are like dogs that fail to bark in the night.

Just as we often don't notice when a dog fails to bark, many of us tend to overlook the implicit value of activities that fail to happen. As we saw in Chapter 1, however, intelligent decisions require taking the value of forgone opportunities properly into account.

RECOGNIZING THE RELEVANT ALTERNATIVE

The opportunity cost of an activity, once again, is the value of the next-best alternative that must be forgone to engage in that activity. If ironing your shirt means not watching the last 20 minutes of a movie, then the value to you of watching the end of the movie is an opportunity cost of ironing your shirt. Many people make bad decisions because they tend to ignore the value of such forgone opportunities. To avoid overlooking opportunity costs, economists often translate questions such as "Should I iron my shirt?" into ones such as "Should I iron my shirt or watch the end of the movie?"

Should you use your frequent-flyer coupon to fly to Fort Lauderdale for spring break?

EXAMPLE 2.1

With spring break only a week away, you are still undecided about whether to go to Fort Lauderdale with a group of classmates at the University of Iowa. The round-trip airfare from Cedar Rapids is $500, but you have a frequent-flyer coupon you could use to pay for the trip. All other relevant costs for the vacation week at the beach total exactly $1,000. Your reservation price for the Fort Lauderdale vacation is $1,350. Your only alternative use for your frequent-flyer coupon is for your plane trip to Boston the weekend after spring break to attend your brother's wedding. (Your coupon expires shortly thereafter.) If the Cedar Rapids–Boston round-trip airfare is $400, should you use your frequent-flyer coupon to fly to Fort Lauderdale for spring break?

The cost-benefit criterion tells us that you should go to Fort Lauderdale if the benefits of the trip exceed its costs. If not for the complication of the frequent-flyer coupon, solving this problem would be a straightforward matter of comparing your reservation price for the week at the beach (your benefit from the trip) to the sum of all relevant costs. And since your airfare and other costs would sum to $1,500, or $150 more than your reservation price for the trip, you would not go to Fort Lauderdale.

But what about the possibility of using your frequent-flyer coupon to make the trip? Using it for that purpose might make the flight to Fort Lauderdale seem free, suggesting you would reap an economic surplus of $350 by making the trip. But doing so would also mean you would have to fork over $400 for your airfare to Boston. So the opportunity cost of using your coupon to go to Fort Lauderdale is really $400. If you use it for that purpose, the trip still ends up being a loser. In cases like these, you are much more likely to decide sensibly if you ask yourself, "Should I use my frequent-flyer coupon for this trip or save it for an upcoming trip?"

We cannot emphasize strongly enough that the key to using the concept of opportunity cost correctly lies in recognizing precisely what taking a given action prevents us from doing. To illustrate, suppose we modify Example 1.2 slightly, as follows:

Same as Example 2.1, except that now your frequent-flyer coupon expires in a week, so your only chance to use it will be for the Fort Lauderdale trip. Should you use your coupon?

EXAMPLE 2.2

Since you now have no alternative use for your coupon, the opportunity cost of using it to pay for the Fort Lauderdale trip is zero. That means your economic surplus from the trip will be $1,350 − $1,000 = $350 > 0, so you should use your coupon and go to Fort Lauderdale.

THE TIME VALUE OF MONEY

We saw that taking an action now often means being unable to take some other action in the future. To take the value of future opportunities properly into account, we need to be able to weigh future costs and benefits against those we incur or receive in the present. As the next example illustrates, having to pay someone a dollar 1 year from now is not the same as having to pay someone a dollar today.

Same as Example 2.1, except that now your best alternative use for your frequent-flyer coupon is for a flight you expect to take 1 year from now, for which the airfare is $363. If your savings account pays 10 percent interest per year, should you go to Fort Lauderdale?

EXAMPLE 2.3

Is your flight to Fort Lauderdale "free" if you travel on a frequent flyer coupon?

How does this new information alter the opportunity cost of using your coupon to travel to Fort Lauderdale? Using it now means having to pay $363 for your flight 1 year from now. The opportunity cost of using the coupon now might therefore seem to be exactly $363. But this way of thinking about the coupon misses an important aspect of opportunity cost.

The question you must ask yourself is "How much should I be willing to pay *today* to avoid making an airfare payment of $363 *one year from now?* To answer this question, you should simply ask, "How much would I have to put in my savings account today, at 10 percent annual interest, to have $363 one year from now?" The answer is $330, since that amount will earn $33 in interest (10 percent of $330) over the next year, for a total of $363.

Your economic surplus from the Fort Lauderdale trip is therefore $1,350 − $1,000 − $330 = $20, which means you should take the trip to the beach.

EXERCISE 2.1

Would your answer to Example 2.3 have been different if the annual interest rate had been 2 percent instead of 10 percent? (*Hint:* Would a deposit of $350 in your account today earn enough money to pay for your $363 air ticket 1 year from now?)

Example 2.3 and Exercise 2.1 drive home the point that the opportunity cost of a dollar spent today is not the same as the opportunity cost of a dollar spent 1 year from now. In general, the opportunity cost of resources that are expended in the future will be lower than the opportunity cost of resources that are expended in the present. The reason involves the **time value of money**—the fact that money deposited in an interest-bearing account today will grow in value over time. Indeed, the very fact that banks and other borrowers pay interest is a consequence of the opportunity cost concept.

time value of money the fact that a given dollar amount today is equivalent to a larger dollar amount in the future, because the money can be invested in an interest-bearing account in the meantime

Suppose, for example, that you owned a bank and someone deposited $1 million on January 1 without expecting to receive interest. You could then take the money and buy a productive asset, like a stock of mushrooms that would grow on an otherwise useless plot of land you own. Suppose mushrooms grow at the rate of 10 percent each year, and they sell for a constant price per pound. At the end of the year you could sell the mushrooms for $1.1 million and have $100,000 more than you started with.

But if that same option is available to the person who put his money in your bank, why should he give *you* the $100,000 he could have earned? Being a practical man, he will be willing to let you use his money only if you compensate him for the opportunity cost of not using it himself.

As the following example makes clear, paying interest on borrowed money is really no more than reimbursing the lender for the opportunity cost of not being able to use the money he has lent.

EXAMPLE 2.4 How much interest should Tom charge Dick?

Tom is a mushroom farmer. He invests all his spare cash in additional mushrooms, which require no labor and grow on otherwise useless land behind his barn. The mushrooms triple in weight during their first year, after which time they are harvested and sold at a constant price per pound. Tom's friend Dick asks Tom for a loan of $200, which he promises to repay after 1 year. How much interest must Dick pay Tom for Tom to be no worse off than if he had not made the loan?

If Tom kept the $200 and invested it in additional mushrooms, he would have 3($200) = $600 worth of mushrooms to sell after 1 year. Dick must therefore give Tom $600 − $200 = $400 in interest to prevent Tom from losing money on the loan.

Why do many people feel it is "unfair" to charge interest on a loan made to a friend or family member?

If a friend had asked you to pick up a concert ticket for her when you stopped at the Ticketmaster office, she would expect to reimburse you for the $50 you spent for it. Yet many people feel it would be unfair if you charged that same friend interest on money you loaned her. Why this difference?

Suppose you gave a friend a 1-year loan of $1,000, money that otherwise would have remained in your savings account earning interest at the annual rate of 5 percent. Had the money remained in your account, you would have earned $50 in interest. If your friend does not pay you interest on the loan, you will thus be $50 poorer at the end of the year than if you had not made her the loan. That is the opportunity cost of making her the loan. But because the $50 of forgone interest is not an explicit cost, many people tend to think of it as somehow different from other costs. To them, charging interest may seem as if you are profiting at your friend's expense. Yet it is no more unfair to ask a friend to reimburse you for interest forgone than to ask her to reimburse you for the cost of a concert ticket. If you want to make a gift of $50 to your friend—either by not accepting reimbursement for a concert ticket or by not charging interest on a loan—that is of course your privilege. But we generally do not describe people who fail to make gifts as being "unfair."

The preceding example illustrates the reciprocal relationship between costs and benefits. When taking an action results in your failing to receive a benefit that you otherwise would have received, that is a cost of taking the action. Loaning a friend money entails a cost because it results in your failure to receive the interest you would have earned had the money remained in your count. By the same token, failure to incur a cost amounts to the same thing as receiving a benefit.

As simple as the concept of opportunity cost is, it is one of the most important in economics. The art in applying the concept correctly lies in being able to recognize the most valuable alternative to a given activity.

"Just getting the hell out of here is worth the price of admission."

> **RECAP**   **THE PITFALL OF IGNORING OPPORTUNITY COSTS**
>
> When performing a cost-benefit analysis of an action, it is important to account for all relevant *opportunity costs,* defined as the values of the most highly valued alternatives that must be forgone to carry out the action. A resource (such as a frequent-flyer coupon) may have a high opportunity cost, even if you originally got it "for free," if its best alternative use has high value. The identical resource may have a low opportunity cost, however, if it has no good alternative uses.
>
> In calculating opportunity costs, it is important to take account of the time value of money. Because money can be invested in an interest-bearing account, a dollar paid or received in the future is worth less than a dollar paid or received today.

PITFALL 2: FAILURE TO IGNORE SUNK COSTS

The opportunity cost pitfall is one in which people ignore costs they ought to take into account. In another common pitfall, the reverse is true: People are influenced by costs they ought to ignore. *The only costs that should influence a decision about whether to take an action are those that we can avoid by not taking the action.* As a practical matter, however, many decision makers appear to be influenced by **sunk costs**—costs that are beyond recovery at the moment a decision is made. For example, money spent on a nontransferable, nonrefundable airline ticket is a sunk cost.

sunk cost a cost that is beyond recovery at the moment a decision must be made

Because sunk costs must be borne *whether or not an action is taken,* they are irrelevant to the decision of whether to take the action. The sunk cost pitfall (the mistake of being influenced by sunk costs) is illustrated clearly in the following examples.

EXAMPLE 2.5

Should you drive through a snowstorm to get to a basketball game?

You and your friend Joe have identical tastes. At 2 P.M. you go to the local Ticketmaster outlet and buy a $30 ticket to a basketball game to be played that night in Syracuse, 50 miles north of your home in Ithaca. Joe plans to attend the same game, but because he cannot get to the Ticketmaster outlet, he plans to buy his ticket at the game. Tickets sold at the game cost only $25, because they carry no Ticketmaster surcharge. (Many people nonetheless pay the higher price at Ticketmaster, to be sure of getting good seats.) At 4 P.M. an unexpected snowstorm begins, making the prospect of the drive to Syracuse much less attractive than before (but assuring the availability of good seats). If both you and Joe are rational, is one of you more likely to attend the game than the other?

Since you have already bought your ticket, the $30 you spent on it is a sunk cost. It is money you cannot recover, whether or not you go to the game. In deciding whether to see the game, then, you should compare the benefit of seeing the game (as measured by your reservation price, the largest dollar amount you would be willing to pay to see it) to only those *additional* costs you must incur to see the game (the opportunity cost of your time, whatever cost you assign to driving through the snowstorm, etc.). But you should not include the cost of your ticket. That is $30 you will never see again, whether you go to the game or not.

Joe, too, must weigh the opportunity cost of his time and the hassle of the drive in deciding whether to attend the game. But he must also weigh the $25 he will have to spend for his ticket. At the moment of deciding, therefore, the remaining costs Joe must incur to see the game are $25 higher than the remaining costs for you. And since you both have identical tastes—that is, since your respective benefits of attending the game are exactly the same—Joe should be less likely to make the trip. You might think the cost of seeing the game is higher for you, since your ticket cost $30, whereas Joe's will cost only $25. But at the moment of deciding whether to make the drive, the $25 is a relevant cost for Joe, whereas your $30 is a sunk cost, and hence an irrelevant one for you.

Now suppose we change the structure of Example 2.5 slightly.

Same as Example 2.5, except now a friend gives Joe a free ticket to the game at 2 P.M. Is one of you more likely to attend the game than the other?

EXAMPLE 2.6

This time neither of you faces any additional ticket expenses at the moment you must decide whether to drive through the snowstorm. Since your respective costs and benefits are the same, your decisions about whether to make the trip should also be the same.

According to the cost-benefit criterion, the decision to attend the game should not depend on whether someone bought a ticket or was given one. Yet people often seem to decide differently in the two cases. In particular, people who paid cash for a ticket often feel a need to use it, "to avoid wasting $30." People who get a free ticket seem to feel much more comfortable with the notion of staying home.

Such differences in judgment are almost surely the result of faulty reasoning. A rational decision maker weighs the benefit of seeing the game against only the *additional* costs he must incur to see it—in this example, the opportunity cost of time and the psychological cost and physical risk of driving through the snowstorm. How he came to possess a ticket in the first place has no bearing on either the relevant benefits or the relevant costs.

Here's another example in which many people seem to take sunk costs into account when they shouldn't.

How much should you eat at an all-you-can-eat restaurant?

EXAMPLE 2.7

Sangam, an Indian restaurant in Philadelphia, offers an all-you-can-eat lunch buffet for $5. Customers pay $5 at the door, and no matter how many times they refill their plates, there is no additional charge. One day, as a goodwill gesture, the owner of the restaurant tells 20 randomly selected guests that their lunch is on the house. The remaining guests pay the usual price. If all diners are rational, will there be any difference in the average quantity of food consumed by people in these two groups?

Having eaten their first helping, diners in each group confront the following question: "Should I go back for another helping?" If the benefit of so doing exceeds the cost, the answer is yes; otherwise it is no. Note that at the moment of decision about a second helping, the $5 charge for the lunch is a sunk cost. Those who paid it have no way to recover it. Thus, for both groups, the (extra) cost of another helping is exactly zero. And since the people who received the free lunch were chosen at random, there is no reason to suppose that their appetites are different from those of other diners. The benefit of another helping should be the same, on average, for people in both groups. And since their respective costs and benefits of an additional helping are the same, the two groups should eat the same number of helpings, on average.

Psychologists and economists have found experimental evidence, however, that people in such groups do not eat similar amounts.[1] In particular, those for whom the luncheon charge is waived tend to eat substantially less than those for whom the charge is not waived. People in the latter group seem somehow determined to "get their money's worth." Their implicit goal is apparently to minimize

[1]See, for example, Richard Thaler, "Toward a Positive Theory of Consumer Choice," *Journal of Economic Behavior and Organization*, 1(1), 1980.

the average cost per bite of the food they eat. Yet minimizing average cost is not a particularly sensible objective. It brings to mind the man who drove his car on the highway at night, even though he had nowhere to go, because he wanted to boost his average fuel economy. The irony is that diners who are determined to get their money's worth usually end up eating too much, as evidenced later by their regrets about having gone back for their last helpings.

The fact that the cost-benefit criterion may fail the test of prediction in examples like these does nothing to invalidate its advice about what people *should* do. If you are letting sunk costs influence your decisions, you can do better by changing your behavior.

One final sunk cost example:

EXAMPLE 2.8

Should Jennifer go to the theater or have dinner with John?

Jennifer has purchased a $50 theater ticket. On the day before the performance, John invites her to dinner the next evening. John is her chemistry lab partner, and Jennifer has been hoping he would ask her out. If she had known about John's invitation before buying the theater ticket, she would have accepted without hesitation. But it is too late to sell her theater ticket, and since John has no interest in the theater, she cannot attend both the play and the dinner. True or false: If Jennifer is rational, she will go to dinner anyway.

First a brief word about the criterion for deciding whether a statement is true or false. For a statement to be true, it must be true in *all* circumstances. If a statement can be shown to be false under *some* circumstances, it is false by definition. It need not always be untrue. So to rule on the statement posed in this example, we must ask whether it *might not* be true under some circumstances.

We'll use R^T to denote Jennifer's reservation price for going to the theater and R^D to denote her reservation price for going to dinner with John. Jennifer doesn't need to pay any money if she goes to the dinner, and since the opportunity cost of her time is the same for the two events, she can ignore that as a factor. So Jennifer's economic surplus from going to dinner with John will be R^D. Before she bought her theater ticket, the net surplus Jennifer expected to receive from going to the theater was $R^T - \$50$—the difference between her reservation price for the play and the price of a ticket.

Now, the fact that Jennifer would have chosen dinner over the theater if she had not yet bought a ticket tells us that $R^D > R^T - \$50$. *But since her theater ticket* is *already paid for, its $50 price is a sunk cost.* So Jennifer's economic surplus from going to the theater *at the moment she has to decide* will be R^T, not $R^T - \$50$. Thus she should go out to dinner with John only if $R^D > R^T$. From the information given, that may or may not be the case.

To illustrate, suppose $R^D = \$70$ and $R^T = \$80$. In that case, Jennifer would have chosen dinner over the theater before buying her ticket, because her surplus from attending the dinner ($R^D = \$70$) would have been greater than her net surplus from attending the theater ($R^T - \$50 = \$30$). But after she buys her ticket, the $50 becomes a sunk cost and thus is no longer relevant to her decision. Jennifer would gain an $80 benefit by going to the theater, and because that is more than the $70 benefit she would gain by going out to dinner with John, she would choose the theater. Because the true-false statement does not hold in this case, it is false.

EXERCISE 2.2

Refer to Example 2.8. Give examples of values of Jennifer's reservation prices for the dinner and the theater performance that are consistent with the description given in the example, but for which Jennifer's best bet *would* be to go to dinner with John.

> **RECAP** **THE PITFALL OF NOT IGNORING SUNK COSTS**
>
> When deciding whether to perform an action, it is important to ignore sunk costs—those costs that cannot be avoided even if the action is not taken. Even though a ticket to a concert may have cost you $100, if you have already bought it and cannot sell it to anyone else, the $100 is a sunk cost and should not influence your decision about whether to go to the concert.

PITFALL 3: FAILURE TO UNDERSTAND THE AVERAGE-MARGINAL DISTINCTION

As we have seen, bad decisions often result from failure to take proper account of opportunity costs and from failure to ignore sunk costs. Another common source of difficulty is confusion involving the distinction between average and marginal costs and benefits.

THE RELEVANT COSTS AND BENEFITS ARE ALWAYS MARGINAL

The cost-benefit framework emphasizes that the only relevant costs and benefits in deciding whether to pursue an activity further are *marginal* costs and benefits—those costs and benefits that correspond to the *increment* of activity under consideration. In many contexts, however, people seem more inclined to compare **average costs** and **average benefits**—total cost or benefit per unit of activity.

As Example 2.9 makes clear, increasing the level of an activity may not be justified, even though its average benefit at the current level is significantly greater than its average cost.

average cost total cost of undertaking *n* units of an activity divided by *n*

average benefit total benefit of undertaking *n* units of an activity divided by *n*

EXAMPLE 2.9

Should NASA expand the space shuttle program from four launches per year to five?

Professor Kösten Banifoot, a prominent supporter of the NASA space shuttle program, has estimated that the gains from the program are currently $24 billion per year (an average of $6 billion per launch) and that its costs are currently $20 billion per year (an average of $5 billion per launch). True or false: If these estimates are correct, NASA should definitely expand the program.

To decide whether an additional launch makes sense, we need to compare the cost of adding that launch with the benefit of adding it. The *average* benefit and *average* cost per launch for all shuttles launched thus far simply are not useful in deciding whether to expand the program. Of course, the average cost of the launches undertaken so far *might* be the same as the cost of adding another launch. But it also might be either higher or lower than the marginal cost of a launch. The same statement holds true regarding average and marginal benefits.

Suppose, for example, that the benefit of an additional launch is in fact the same as the average benefit per launch thus far, namely, $6 billion. Should NASA add another launch? Not if the cost of adding the fifth launch would be more than $6 billion. Suppose the relationship between the number of shuttles launched and the total cost of the program is as described in Table 2.1.

At the current level of four launches per year, the average cost is $20 billion/4 = $5 billion per launch. But adding a fifth launch would raise costs from $20 billion to $30 billion, so the marginal cost of the fifth launch is $10 billion. If the benefit of an additional launch is constant at $6 billion, increasing the number of launches would make no sense. Indeed, the fourth launch itself would not be justified, since it cost $8 billion and produced only $6 billion in additional

TABLE 2.1
How Total Cost Varies with the Number of Launches

Number of launches per year	Total costs per year ($billions)
1	6
2	8
3	12
4	20
5	30

benefits. On the basis of the numbers shown in the table, which are completely consistent with Professor Banifoot's data on average costs and benefits, the optimal number of launches would be only three per year.

Here's an exercise that further illustrates the importance of the average-marginal distinction.

EXERCISE 2.3

Should a basketball team's best player take all the team's shots?
   A professional basketball team has a new assistant coach. The assistant notices that one player scores on a higher percentage of his shots than other players. Based on this information, the assistant suggests to the head coach that the star player should take *all* the shots. That way, the assistant reasons, the team will score more points and win more games.
   On hearing this suggestion, the head coach fires her assistant for incompetence. What was wrong with the assistant's idea?

One of the most important practical questions we confront in life is that of how to divide our time between competing activities. As the Example 2.10 illustrates, we won't answer this question intelligently unless we're careful to distinguish between average and marginal benefits.

EXAMPLE 2.10   **How should members of a group allocate their effort in a foraging task?**

Suppose you and three friends are shipwrecked on an island. Coconut trees, which grow in clusters on both the north and south ends of the island, are your only source of food. For the past year, you and one friend have been gathering coconuts from the north end of the island, and the other two have been gathering them from the south. You and your partner have been bringing back a total of 16 coconuts each day, while your other two friends have been bringing back only 12. These harvests appear to be sustainable indefinitely. True or false: If one of the others joins the two of you on the north end of the island, your total harvest of coconuts will rise.

This statement is false for the same reason that Professor Banifoot's statement was false in Example 2.9. All we know is that the average benefit per forager is 8 coconuts on the north end of the island and 6 coconuts on the south end. We should shift someone from the south end to the north end only if the increase in coconuts gathered at the north end is more than the corresponding reduction in coconuts gathered at the south end. But suppose the relationship between the number of foragers and the total harvest at each end of the island is as shown in Table 2.2.

As the numbers in the table indicate, the current allocation of two foragers at each end of the island yields a total of 28 coconuts a day. Shifting one forager from the south end to the north will increase the number of coconuts harvested from the north end by 3 per day but will reduce the harvest from the south end

TABLE 2.2
How Coconut Harvests Depend on the Number of Foragers

		North end	South end
	1	12 coconuts/day	6 coconuts/day
Number of foragers	2	16 coconuts/day	12 coconuts/day
	3	19 coconuts/day	18 coconuts/day
	4	21 coconuts/day	24 coconuts/day

by 6, for a net reduction of 3 coconuts per day. Even though the average harvest is greater on the north end of the island, the marginal benefit of an additional forager is greater on the south end. Thus, if either you or your partner were to join the other two at the south end, the daily harvest from the north end would go down by 4 coconuts, while the harvest from the south end would go up by 6—a net gain of 2 coconuts per day.

We must emphasize again that the fact that the statements in the preceding examples were false does not mean that they could not have been true under at least some circumstances. For instance, the relationship between foragers and harvests shown in Table 2.3 is also consistent with the information given in Example 2.10. Given this relationship, sending not just one but two extra persons to the north end of the island would make sense.

TABLE 2.3
Another Example of How Coconut Harvests Depend on the Number of Foragers

		North end	South end
	1	8 coconuts/day	6 coconuts/day
Number of foragers	2	16 coconuts/day	12 coconuts/day
	3	24 coconuts/day	18 coconuts/day
	4	32 coconuts/day	24 coconuts/day

In sum, the statements in Examples 2.9 and 2.10 were false because they were based on information about average benefits or costs rather than marginal benefits or costs. To be considered true, a statement must be true in *all* circumstances; it is false if it fails to hold in even a single case.

EXERCISE 2.4

Refer to Example 2.10. If there had been not four but five of you on the island and productivity was as described in Table 2.2, how many should have foraged at each end?

Example 2.10 and Exercise 2.4, in which the problem was to allocate labor between two coconut patches, illustrate the following simple but important rule:

The criterion for allocating a resource efficiently across different activities is to allocate each unit of the resource to the production activity in which its marginal benefit is highest.

This rule applies to cases in which the resources to be allocated are not finely divisible. For instance, we cannot have 2.62 foragers on one end of the island.

In other cases, the resource to be allocated may be perfectly divisible. For example, students taking an exam have an important resource—their time—to apportion among various questions in any way they choose. For a resource that is perfectly divisible, the rule becomes:

Allocate the resource so that its marginal benefit is the same in every activity.

Applied to the task of allocating one's time on an exam, this rule suggests that the optimal allocation is one in which the number of additional points earned from the last unit of time spent on a question must be the same for all questions. Suppose a student had not allocated her time according to this rule—for example, suppose she had earned 6 points from the last unit of time spent on one question and only 2 points from the last unit of time spent on another. If her last moments spent on the first question were more productive than her last moments spent on the second, she can boost her point total score by spending more time on the first question and less time on the second.

This idea *seems* easy enough. But just as an experiment, ask several friends to consider the following example.

EXAMPLE 2.11   **How should you allocate your time on an exam?**

Suppose that in the last minute you devoted to question 1 on your physics exam you earned 4 extra points, while in the last minute you devoted to question 2 you earned 10 extra points. The total number of points you earned on these two questions were 48 and 12, respectively, and the total time you spent on each was the same. If you could take the exam again, how—if at all—would you reallocate your time between these questions?

Even though you earned four times as many points from the first question than from the second, the last minute you spent on question 2 added 6 more points to your total score than the last minute you spent on question 1. That means you should have spent more time on question 2.

How did your friends do with this problem? As obvious as the answer might seem, many people—especially those who have not had a good course in economics—often do not grasp the underlying idea. They are distracted by the fact that the average point yield per unit of time spent on question 1 is so much higher than the average yield on question 2. But that comparison, by itself, tells us nothing about how to reallocate our time.

A similar misunderstanding of the average-marginal distinction recently led a dean at a large university to complain that the university's development office had grown too large. The number of employees in this office, which raises funds for the university, had more than doubled during the past decade. To back up his claim that this growth was a bad thing, the dean cited the fact that the amount of money raised per fund-raiser was only one-third as much as it had been 10 years before. But this observation tells us nothing about whether the dean's claim is true. From the university's point of view, the number of fund-raisers should be reduced by 1 only if so doing will reduce the total funds raised by less than the cost of that employee. The fact that the average amount of money raised per employee is much smaller than it once was simply does not tell us whether that is so.

fixed cost a cost that does not vary with the level of an activity

variable cost a cost that varies with the level of activity

FIXED AND VARIABLE COSTS

Sometimes the failure to distinguish between average and marginal costs arises from a failure to distinguish between **fixed costs**—costs that do not vary with the level of an activity—and **variable costs**—costs that do vary with the level of activity.

For example, the membership fee you pay to join most health clubs is the same whether you visit the club four times a week or only once a month. This fee is a fixed cost. Once you have paid it, it is *usually* also a sunk cost—but not always. Some health clubs offer an introductory period in which a membership may be canceled with a full refund. In such cases the membership fee is a fixed cost but not a sunk cost.

Many health clubs also have tennis or racquetball courts for which they charge hourly court fees. Because these charges depend on the number of hours you play, they are variable costs. If you've already become a member and are deciding how many times a week to play racquetball, you should ignore the membership fee but take into account the hourly court fee.

How is a fixed cost different from a sunk cost? Since a sunk cost is one that is irretrievably committed, it cannot vary with the level of an activity. All sunk costs are therefore also fixed costs. But not all fixed costs are sunk costs (as in the example of a refundable membership fee).

As the next example makes clear, the ability to distinguish between fixed and variable costs is important component to sound business decisions.

Should Commercial Airlines cancel its 10:00 A.M. flight?

EXAMPLE 2.12

In an effort to improve profitability, managers of a passenger airline have considered canceling flights on the least heavily traveled routes. The typical aircraft in the airline's fleet makes 1,000 flights a year and generates the following yearly costs:

Annual interest on money borrowed to buy plane	$ 400,000
Annual interest on money borrowed to buy other equipment	400,000
Fuel	400,000
Flight crew salaries	500,000
Maintenance labor	300,000
Total	$2,000,000

Flight crew salaries and maintenance labor are constant amounts for each flight. One flight that may be dropped currently uses an aircraft that makes 1,000 flights a year, at an average cost of $2,000 per flight. An average of 30 passengers travel on this flight at a ticket price of $60 each, for total ticket revenue of $1,800 per flight. Since this flight's revenue is less than its cost, the managers cancel the flight. Is their decision a good one?

The decision is faulty because the managers have failed to distinguish between fixed and variable costs. The labor and fuel expenses they have listed are variable, but interest expenses are fixed. Because labor and fuel expenses total only $1,200 per flight—much less than the flight's $1,800 ticket revenue—the flight should not be canceled.

Needless to say, Commercial Airlines could not hope to remain in business if the ticket revenue from *each* of its flights fell short of the average cost of operating that flight. But the criterion for deciding whether any *particular* flight makes sense is to compare its ticket revenues only to those extra costs generated by that flight.

Failure to appreciate the importance of the average-marginal distinction is an important source of error, not just within the world of business but in academia, government—indeed, virtually every sphere of professional and personal life. And a little bit of knowledge can sometimes be a dangerous thing. For example, tennis star Andre Agassi appears to know what a fixed cost is but seems confused about the extent to which such costs matter in deciding how to use his $12 million jet aircraft. "There are certain fixed costs when you own a plane," he explained during a break in the action at a recent tournament, "so the more you fly it the more economic sense it makes. . . ." Exactly right! But Agassi then went on to say, "The first flight after I bought it, I took some friends to Palm Springs for lunch." Taking the plane on such trips does indeed reduce the average fixed cost per flight. But to take frivolous trips solely for the *purpose* of reducing average cost per flight makes no more sense than driving aimlessly on the highway to improve your car's average fuel economy.

RECAP **THE PITFALL OF USING AVERAGE INSTEAD OF MARGINAL COSTS AND BENEFITS**

Decision makers often have ready information about the total cost and benefit of an activity, and from these it is simple to compute the activity's average cost and benefit. A common mistake is to conclude that an activity should be increased if its average benefit exceeds its average cost. The cost-benefit principle tells us that the level of an activity should be increased if, and only if, the *marginal* benefit of doing so exceeds the *marginal* cost.

The conclusion that some costs, especially marginal costs and opportunity costs, are important, while others, like sunk costs and average costs, are irrelevant to decision making is implicit in our original statement of the cost-benefit principle (an action should be taken if, and only if, the extra benefits of taking it exceed the extra costs). Yet so important are the pitfalls of ignoring opportunity costs and taking sunk costs into account, and of confusing average with marginal costs, we enumerate these pitfalls separately as one of the core ideas for repeated emphasis.

Not All Costs Matter Equally: Some costs (e.g., opportunity costs, marginal costs) matter in making decisions; other costs (e.g., sunk costs, average costs) don't.

■ SUMMARY ■

- Our focus in this chapter was on three common pitfalls that plague decision makers in all walks of life. The first involved the failure to consider opportunity costs. The opportunity cost of an activity is the value of the next-best alternative that must be forgone to engage in that activity. Many people make bad decisions because they tend to ignore the value of forgone opportunities. We are less likely to make this mistake if we translate questions such as "Should I iron my shirt?" into ones such as "Should I iron my shirt or study for my math test?" Posing the question in this way makes relevant opportunity costs difficult to ignore. Thus, if you ask yourself "Should I use my one frequent-flyer coupon on the next flight I take?" you are more likely to decide incorrectly than if you ask "Should I use my one frequent-flyer coupon on the next flight, or should I wait and use it on another flight?"

- The second pitfall involved the tendency not to ignore sunk costs. A sunk cost is a cost that is already irretrievably committed at the moment a decision must be made. In deciding whether to drive through a snowstorm to see a concert, the amount you have already paid for your ticket simply should not matter. In deciding whether to pursue an activity, the only costs and benefits that matter are the ones that will change with your pursuit of that activity. All other costs and benefits are irrelevant.

- The third and final pitfall was the tendency to confuse average and marginal costs and benefits. In deciding whether to increase the number of space shuttle flights, comparing the average cost of current shuttle flights with their average benefit is not instructive. Instead, we must compare the cost of an additional shuttle flight with the benefit of an additional shuttle flight. Such a comparison will often yield different results from a comparison of average costs and benefits.

▪ CORE PRINCIPLES ▪

Not All Costs Matter Equally
Some costs (e.g., opportunity costs, marginal costs) matter in making decisions; other costs (e.g., sunk costs, average costs) don't.

▪ KEY TERMS ▪

average benefit (39)   fixed cost (42)   time value of money (34)
average cost (39)   sunk cost (36)   variable cost (42)

▪ REVIEW QUESTIONS ▪

1. Why might someone who is trying to decide whether to see a movie be more likely to focus on the $9 ticket price than on the $20 she would fail to earn by not babysitting?

2. Many people think of their air travel as being free when they use frequent-flyer coupons. Explain why these people are likely to make wasteful travel decisions.

3. A friend has allowed you to use her off-campus parking space while she is away for her junior year abroad. If many other students are eager to rent parking spaces off-campus, do you think your friend would be "unfair" to charge you for the use of her parking space?

4. Why is a lottery ticket that pays you $10 million now worth more than a lottery ticket that pays you $1 million each year for the next 10 years?

5. Is the nonrefundable tuition payment you made to your university this semester a sunk cost? Is it a fixed cost? How would your answers differ if your university were to offer a full tuition refund to any student who dropped out of school during the first 2 months of the semester?

▪ PROBLEMS ▪

1. Tom is a mushroom farmer. He invests all his spare cash in additional mushrooms, which grow on otherwise useless land behind his barn. The mushrooms double in weight during their first year, after which time they are harvested and sold at a constant price per pound. Tom's friend Dick asks Tom for a loan of $200, which he promises to repay after 1 year. How much interest will Dick have to pay Tom for Tom to be no worse off than if he had not made the loan? Explain briefly.

2. When John increased his computer's random-access memory by 10 megabytes, the total benefit he received from using the computer went up $55. John purchased the additional memory at a cost of $5 per megabyte, for a total cost of $50.
   a. How much economic surplus did John receive from the additional memory? Explain briefly.
   b. True or false: Because the total benefit of the additional memory was larger than its total cost, John should have added more than 10 megabytes of memory. Explain briefly.

3. A shirt company spends $1,000 per week on rent for its factory. Each shirt made at the factory requires $2 worth of cloth and $6 worth of labor and energy. If the factory produces 2,000 shirts per week:
   a. What is the average cost of a shirt?
   b. What is the marginal cost of a shirt?

   If the factory produces 3,000 shirts per week:
   c. What is the average cost of a shirt?
   d. What is the marginal cost of a shirt?

4. Fred owns four fishing boats on Seneca Lake. He knows from experience the following information about the catch per boat depending on the total number of boats he sends to either the north or south end of the lake. Based on the table below, what is the optimal allocation of Fred's boats?

Number of boats at north end	Catch per boat	Number of boats at south end	Catch per boat
1	100	1	75
2	80	2	75
3	60	3	75
4	40	4	75

5. You are shipwrecked on an island and must live only on coconuts and crabs. You divide your 8 hours of daylight between gathering coconuts and catching crabs. The following table shows how your daily crab and coconut harvests vary depending how you allocate your time.

Hours spent catching crabs	Total number of crabs caught	Hours spent gathering coconuts	Total number of gathered coconuts
1	8	1	6
2	17	2	11
3	23	3	16
4	28	4	20
5	31	5	23
6	34	6	24
7	37	7	24
8	39	8	24

If your aim is to maximize the number of crabs plus coconuts you acquire daily, how much of your time should you spend gathering coconuts? How much time should you spend catching crabs? How many coconuts and crabs will you harvest each day? (*Hint:* Efficient allocation of your time requires you to allocate each hour to the activity that yields the higher marginal benefit.)

6. You have won a prize in a state lottery. In exchange for your lottery ticket, the state government will send you a check for $424 one year from now. If bank deposits pay interest at the rate of 6 percent a year, and you already have several thousand dollars in your account, what is the lowest price at which you would be willing to sell your lottery ticket today?

7. A group has chartered a bus trip to Niagara Falls. The driver's fee is $100, the bus rental $500, and the fuel charge $75. The driver's fee is nonrefundable, but the bus rental may be canceled a week in advance at a charge of $100. At $25 a ticket, how many people must buy tickets a week before so that canceling the trip definitely will not pay?

8. Sam bought a Trek bicycle for $800 instead of a Cannondale for $1,000. Now he finds out that another bike store in town is selling the Cannondale for $800. Mike, Sam's friend, offers him $600 for his Trek. If Sam is a rational consumer, should he sell Mike his Trek and buy the Cannondale?

9. Mary planned to travel to Chicago to see Cheryl Crow in a free Lincoln Park concert, and had already purchased her $50 round-trip bus ticket (nonrefundable, nontransferable) when she found out that Adam Sandler was giving a show on the University of Illinois campus that same night for $50. Had she known about the Adam Sandler show before she bought her bus ticket, she would have chosen to go to the Sandler show. If she is a rational person and her friend Sally offers to give her one of several extra tickets she has for the Sandler show, what should she do?

10. Mandy and Tom, who live in Eugene, Oregon, have identical tastes. They both plan to attend a Paula Cole concert at the State Theater. The tickets cost $20. Mandy has bought her ticket by phone using her credit card, but Tom, who doesn't have a credit card, plans to buy his ticket at the door. On the same evening the university announces a surprise free fireworks display on campus. If Mandy had known about the fireworks display in advance, she would not have bought the theater ticket. True or false: Assuming Mandy and Tom are rational and that Mandy cannot resell her ticket, it follows that Mandy will go to the concert, while Tom will go to the fireworks display. Explain briefly.

■ ANSWERS TO IN-CHAPTER EXERCISES ■

2.1 As before, using your frequent-flyer coupon means having to pay $363 for your airfare 1 year from now. How much would you be willing to spend today to avoid having to pay $363 one year from now? Suppose you deposit $350 in your account today at 2 percent interest. By the end of one year your account would be worth $357 (the original $350 plus $7 in interest). Because that amount is not enough to pay for your $363 air ticket, the opportunity cost of using the frequent-flyer coupon now must be *more* than $350. And that means that the cost of the trip to Fort Lauderdale is greater than its $1,350 benefit, so you shouldn't go to Fort Lauderdale.

2.2 Suppose Jennifer's reservation price for attending the dinner with John is $80 and her reservation price for attending the theater is $70. With these reservation prices, she would have chosen the dinner with John had she known about it in advance. And she should also have dinner with John even if she bought a theater ticket before learning of that opportunity.

2.3 If the star player takes one more shot, some other player must take one less. The fact that the star player's *average* success rate is higher than the other player's does not mean that the probability of making his *next* shot (the marginal benefit of having him shoot once more) is higher than the probability of another player making his next shot. Indeed, if the best player took all his team's shots, the other team would focus its defensive effort entirely on him, in which case letting others shoot would definitely pay.

2.4 With 4 of you, the optimal allocation was to send 3 to the south end and 1 to the north end. Starting with that allocation, you should send the fifth person to whichever end would result in the higher marginal gain. Sending the fifth person to the south end will increase the total harvest by 6 coconuts per day, or two more than if he were sent to the north end. So the optimal allocation is 4 people on the south end and 1 on the north end.

		North end	South end
	1	12 coconuts/day	6 coconuts/day
Number of foragers	2	16 coconuts/day	12 coconuts/day
	3	19 coconuts/day	18 coconuts/day
	4	21 coconuts/day	24 coconuts/day

COMPARATIVE ADVANTAGE: THE BASIS FOR EXCHANGE

■

During a stint as a Peace Corps Volunteer in rural Nepal, a young economic naturalist employed a cook named Birkhaman, who came from a remote Himalayan village in neighboring Bhutan. Although Birkhaman had virtually no formal education, he was spectacularly resourceful. His primary duties, to prepare food and maintain the kitchen, he performed with competence and dispatch. But he also had many other skills. He could thatch a roof, butcher a goat, and repair shoes. An able tinsmith and a good carpenter, he could sew, fix a broken alarm clock, and plaster walls. On top of all that, he was a local authority on home remedies.

Birkhaman's range of skills was broad even by Nepalese standards. But even the least skilled Nepalese villager could perform a wide range of services that most Americans hire others to perform. Why this difference in skills and employment?

One might be tempted to answer that the Nepalese are simply too poor to hire others to perform these services. Nepal is indeed a poor country, whose income per person is less than one one-hundredth that of the United States. Few Nepalese have spare cash to spend on outside services. But as reasonable as this poverty explanation may seem, the reverse is actually the case. The Nepalese do not perform their own services because they are poor; rather, they are poor largely *because* they perform their own services.

The alternative to a system in which everyone is a jack-of-all-trades is one in which people *specialize* in particular goods and services, then satisfy their needs by trading among themselves. Economic systems based on specialization and the exchange of goods and services are generally far more productive than

Did this man perform most of his own services because he was poor, or was he poor because he performed most of his own services?

those with less specialization. Our task in this chapter is to investigate why this is so. In doing so we will explore why people choose to exchange goods and services in the first place, rather than having each person produce his or her own food, cars, clothing, shelter, and the like.

As this chapter will show, the reason that specialization is so productive is the existence of what economists call *comparative advantage*. Roughly, a person has a comparative advantage at producing a particular good or service, say haircuts, if that person is *relatively* more efficient at producing haircuts than at producing other goods or services. We will see that we can all have more of *every* good and service if each of us specializes in the activities at which we have a comparative advantage.

This chapter will also introduce the *production possibilities curve*, which is a graphical method of describing the combinations of goods and services that an economy can produce. The development of this tool will allow us to see much more precisely how specialization enhances the productive capacity of even the simplest economy.

EXCHANGE AND OPPORTUNITY COST

The scarcity principle (see Chapter 1) reminds us that the opportunity cost of spending more time on any one activity is having less time available to spend on others. As the following example makes clear, this principle helps explain why everyone can do better by concentrating on those activities at which he or she performs best relative to others.

EXAMPLE 3.1

Should Greg Mankiw mow his own lawn?

Professor N. Gregory Mankiw is the author of a best-selling economics textbook for which, according to press accounts, he received an advance payment from his publisher of $1.4 million. A neighborhood high school student offers to mow Professor Mankiw's lawn once each week throughout the summer for a fee of $25 per week. The student takes 2 hours to mow the lawn, a task Professor Mankiw can accomplish in only an hour. Should the professor hire the student to mow his lawn?

With his cash advance in hand, the professor can obviously *afford* to hire the student, but that isn't the question. What we want to know is whether it makes sense for him to do so. And we cannot answer that question from the information given without making a few additional assumptions.

To begin, let's assume the professor can write a book by working at it full time for a year. Let's also suppose, for the sake of simplicity, that he is equally productive during each of his 2,000 working hours per year. If he is free to take on additional writing assignments at the same rate of pay, then the time he devotes to his writing is worth ($1,400,000/year)/(2,000 hours/year) = $700/hour. And if the hour he spends mowing his lawn is time he would have been just as happy to spend writing a book, then the opportunity cost of mowing his own lawn is $700. Because the student is willing to mow the lawn for $25, we know the student's opportunity cost of mowing the lawn cannot be more than that. (If it were, he wouldn't have offered to do the job for that amount.) Given this enormous difference in opportunity costs, the professor would do far better to stick to his writing and hire the student to mow his lawn. This is so even though the professor takes only half as much time to mow the lawn as the student.

absolute advantage one person has an absolute advantage over another if he or she takes fewer hours to perform a task than the other person

comparative advantage One person has a comparative advantage over another if his or her opportunity cost of performing a task is lower than the other person's opportunity cost

In Example 3.1, economists would say the professor has an **absolute advantage** at mowing his lawn but a **comparative advantage** at writing books. He has an absolute advantage at lawn mowing because he can mow his lawn in less time than the student takes. The student has a comparative advantage at mowing lawns because his opportunity cost of mowing lawns is lower than the professor's.

The point of Example 3.1 is not that people whose time is valuable should never mow their own lawns. A pivotal assumption in that example was that the professor was equally happy to spend an hour mowing his lawn or working on his book. But suppose he was tired of working on his book and felt like getting a little exercise. Mowing his own lawn might then have made perfect sense!

THE PRINCIPLE OF COMPARATIVE ADVANTAGE

One of the most important insights of modern economics is that when two people (or two nations) have different opportunity costs of performing various tasks, they can always increase the total value of available goods and services by trading with one another. The following simple example captures the logic behind this insight.

Should Paula update her own web page?

EXAMPLE 3.2

Consider a small community in which Paula is the only bicycle mechanic and Beth is the only hyper-text markup language (HTML) programmer. Paula also happens to be an even better HTML programmer than Beth. If the amount of time each of them takes to perform these tasks is as shown in Table 3.1, and if each regards the two tasks as equally pleasant (or unpleasant), does the fact that Paula can program faster than Beth imply that Paula should update her own web page?

TABLE 3.1
Productivity Information for Paula and Beth

	Time to update a web page	Time to complete a bicycle repair
Paula	20 minutes	10 minutes
Beth	30 minutes	30 minutes

The entries in the table show that Paula has an absolute advantage over Beth in both activities. While Paula, the mechanic, needs only 20 minutes to update a web page, Beth, the programmer, needs 30 minutes. Paula's advantage over Beth is even greater when the task is fixing bikes: She can complete a repair in only 10 minutes, compared to Beth's 30 minutes.

But the fact that Paula is a better programmer than Beth does *not* imply that Paula should update her own web page. As with the professor who writes books instead of mowing lawns, the reason is that Beth has a comparative advantage over Paula at programming: She is *relatively* more productive at programming than Paula. Similarly, Paula has a comparative advantage in bicycle repair. (Remember that a person has a comparative advantage at a given task if his or her opportunity cost of performing that task is lower than another person's.)

What is Beth's opportunity cost of updating a web page? Since she takes 30 minutes to update each page—the same amount of time she takes to fix a bicycle—her opportunity cost of updating a web page is one bicycle repair. In other words, by taking the time to update a web page, Beth is effectively giving up the opportunity to do one bicycle repair. Paula, in contrast, can complete two bicycle repairs in the time she takes to update a single web page. For her, the opportunity cost of updating a web page is two bicycle repairs. Paula's opportunity cost of programming, measured in terms of bicycle repairs forgone, is twice as high as Beth's. Thus Beth has a comparative advantage at programming.

The interesting and important implication of the opportunity cost comparison summarized in Table 3.2 is that the total number of bicycle repairs and web updates accomplished if Paula and Beth both spend part of their time at each

TABLE 3.2
Opportunity Costs for Paula and Beth

	Opportunity cost of updating a web page	Opportunity cost of a bicycle repair
Paula	2 bicycle repairs	0.5 web page update
Beth	1 bicycle repair	1 web page update

activity will always be smaller than the number accomplished if each specializes in the activity in which she has a comparative advantage. Suppose, for example, that people in their community demand a total of 16 web page updates per day. If Paula spent half her time updating web pages and the other half repairing bicycles, an 8-hour workday would yield 12 web page updates and 24 bicycle repairs. To complete the remaining 4 updates, Beth would have to spend 2 hours programming, which would leave her 6 hours to repair bicycles. And since she takes 30 minutes to do each repair, she would have time to complete 12 of them. So when the two women try to be jacks-of-all-trades, they end up completing a total of 16 web page updates and 36 bicycle repairs.

Consider what would have happened had each woman specialized in her activity of comparative advantage. Beth could have updated 16 web pages on her own, and Paula could have performed 48 bicycle repairs. Specialization would have created an additional 12 bicycle repairs out of thin air.

When computing the opportunity cost of one good in terms of another, we must pay close attention to the form in which the productivity information is presented. In Example 3.2, we were told how many minutes each person needed to perform each task. Alternatively, we might be told how many units of each task each person can perform in an hour. Work through the following exercise to see how to proceed when information is presented in this alternative format.

"We're a natural, Rachel. I handle intellectual property, and you're a content-provider."

EXERCISE 3.1

Should Barb update her own web page?

   Consider a small community in which Barb is the only bicycle mechanic and Pat is the only HTML programmer. If their productivity rates at the two tasks are as shown in the table, and if each regards the two tasks as equally pleasant (or unpleasant), does the fact that Barb can program faster than Pat imply that Barb should update her own web page?

	Productivity in programming	**Productivity in bicycle repair**
Pat	2 web page updates per hour	1 repair per hour
Barb	3 web page updates per hour	3 repairs per hour

The principle illustrated by Examples 3.1 and 3.2 is so important that we state it formally as one of the core ideas of the course:

The Principle of Comparative Advantage: Everyone does best when each person (or each country) concentrates on the activities for which his or her opportunity cost is lowest.

Indeed, the gains made possible from specialization based on comparative advantage constitute the rationale for market exchange. They explain why each person does not devote 10 percent of his or her time to producing cars, 5 percent to growing food, 25 percent to building housing, 0.0001 percent to performing brain surgery, and so on. By concentrating on those tasks at which we are relatively most productive, together we can produce vastly more than if we all tried to be self-sufficient.

This insight brings us back to Birkhaman the cook. Though Birkhaman's versatility was marvelous, he was not nearly as good a doctor as someone who has been trained in medical school nor as good a repairman as someone who spends each day fixing things. If a number of people with Birkhaman's native talents had joined together, each of them specializing in one or two tasks, together they would have enjoyed more and better goods and services than each could possibly have produced on his own. Although there is much to admire in the resourcefulness of people who have learned through necessity to rely on their own skills, that path is no route to economic prosperity.

Specialization and its effects provide ample grist for the economic naturalist. Here's an example from the world of sports.

Where have all the .400 hitters gone?

In baseball, a .400 hitter is a player who averages at least four hits every 10 times he comes to bat. Though never common in professional baseball, .400 hitters used to appear reasonably frequently. Early in the twentieth century, for example, a player known as Wee Willie Keeler batted .432, meaning that he got a hit in over 43 percent of his times at bat. But since Ted Williams of the Boston Red Sox batted .406 in 1941, there has not been a single .400 hitter in the major leagues. Why not?

Some baseball buffs argue that the disappearance of the .400 hitter means today's baseball players are not as good as yesterday's. But that claim does not withstand close examination. We can document, for example, that today's players are bigger, stronger, and faster than those of Willie Keeler's day. (Wee Willie himself was just a little over 5 feet 4 inches tall and weighed only 140 pounds.)

The best analysts of baseball history, such as Bill James, argue that the .400 hitter has disappeared because the quality of play in the major leagues has *improved*, not declined. In particular, pitching and fielding standards are higher, which makes batting .400 more difficult.

ECONOMIC NATURALIST 3.1

Why has no major league baseball player batted .400 since Ted Williams did it more than half a century ago?

Why has the quality of play in baseball improved? Although there are many reasons, including better nutrition, training, and equipment, specialization has also played an important role.[1] At one time, pitchers were expected to pitch for the entire game. Now pitching staffs include pitchers who specialize in starting the game ("starters"), others who specialize in pitching two or three innings in the middle of the game ("middle relievers"), and still others who specialize in pitching only the last inning ("closers"). Each of these roles requires different skills and tactics. Pitchers may also specialize in facing left-handed or right-handed batters, in striking batters out, or in getting batters to hit balls on the ground. Similarly, few fielders today play multiple defensive positions; most specialize in only one. Some players specialize in defense (to the sacrifice of their hitting skills); these "defensive specialists" can be brought in late in the game to protect a lead. Even in managing and coaching, specialization has increased markedly. Relief pitchers now have their own coaches, and statistical specialists use computers to discover the weaknesses of opposing hitters. The net result of these increases in specialization is that even the weakest of today's teams plays highly competent defensive baseball. With no "weaklings" to pick on, hitting .400 over an entire season has become a near-impossible task.

SOURCES OF COMPARATIVE ADVANTAGE

At the individual level, comparative advantage often appears to be the result of inborn talent. For instance, some people seem to be naturally gifted at programming computers, while others seem to have a special knack for fixing bikes. But comparative advantage is more often the result of education, training, or experience. Thus we usually leave the design of kitchens to people with architectural training, the drafting of contracts to people who have studied law, and the teaching of physics to people with advanced degrees in that field.

At the national level, comparative advantage may derive from differences in natural resources or from differences in society or culture. The United States, which has a disproportionate share of the world's leading research universities, has a comparative advantage in the design of electronic computing hardware and software. Canada, which has one of the world's highest per capita endowments of farm and forest land, has a comparative advantage in the production of agricultural products. Topography and climate explain why Colorado specializes in ski resorts while Hawaii specializes in ocean resorts.

Seemingly noneconomic factors can also give rise to comparative advantage. For instance, the emergence of English as the de facto world language gives English-speaking countries a comparative advantage over non-English-speaking nations in the production of books, movies, and popular music. Even a country's institutions may affect the likelihood that it will achieve comparative advantage in a particular pursuit. For example, cultures that encourage entrepreneurship will tend to have a comparative advantage in the introduction of new products, whereas those that promote high standards of care and craftsmanship will tend to have a comparative advantage in the production of high-quality variants of established products.

ECONOMIC NATURALIST 3.2

Televisions and videocassette recorders (VCRs) were developed and first produced in the United States, but today the United States accounts for only a minuscule share of the total world production of these products. Why did the United States fail to retain its lead in these markets?

That televisions and VCRs were developed in the United States is explained in part by the country's comparative advantage in technological research, which in turn was supported by the country's outstanding system of higher education. Other contributing

---

[1]For an interesting discussion of specialization and the decline of the .400 hitter from the perspective of an evolutionary biologist, see Stephen Jay Gould, *Full House,* New York: Three Rivers Press, 1996, part three.

factors were high expenditures on the development of electronic components for the military and a culture that actively encourages entrepreneurship. As for the production of these products, America enjoyed an early advantage partly because the product designs were themselves evolving rapidly at first, which favored production facilities located in close proximity to the product designers. Early production techniques also relied intensively on skilled labor, which is abundant in the United States. In time, however, product designs stabilized, and many of the more complex manufacturing operations were automated. Both these changes gradually led to greater reliance on relatively less skilled production workers. And at that point, factories located in high-wage countries like the United States could no longer compete with those located in low-wage areas overseas.

RECAP **EXCHANGE AND OPPORTUNITY COST**

Gains from exchange are possible if trading partners have comparative advantages in producing different goods and services. You have a comparative advantage in producing, say, web pages, if your opportunity cost of producing a web page—measured in terms of other production opportunities forgone—is smaller than the corresponding opportunity costs of your trading partners. Maximum production is achieved if each person specializes in producing the good or service in which he or she has the lowest opportunity cost (the principle of comparative advantage). Comparative advantage makes specialization worthwhile even if one trading partner is more productive than others, in absolute terms, in every activity.

COMPARATIVE ADVANTAGE AND PRODUCTION POSSIBILITIES

Comparative advantage and specialization allow an economy to produce more than if each person tries to produce a little of everything. In this section we gain further insight into the advantages of specialization by first examining an imaginary economy with only one person and then noting how economic possibilities change as new people join the economy. Along the way, we will introduce a useful graph called the production possibilities curve, which can be used to describe the combinations of goods and services that a particular economy can produce.

PRODUCTION POSSIBILITIES IN A ONE-PERSON ECONOMY

We begin with a hypothetical economy consisting of a single worker who can produce two goods, coffee and Macadamia nuts. The worker lives on a small island, and "production" consists either of picking coffee beans that grow on small bushes on the island's central valley floor or picking Macadamia nuts that grow on trees on the hillsides overlooking the valley. The more time the worker spends picking coffee, the less time she has available for picking nuts. If she wants to drink more coffee than she does at present, then, she must make do with a smaller amount of nuts. Knowing how productive she is at each activity, we can easily summarize the various combinations of coffee and nuts she can pick each day if she makes full use of her available working time. This menu of possibilities is known as the **production possibilities curve.**

As the following example illustrates, constructing the production possibilities curve for a one-person economy is a straightforward matter.

production possibilities curve
a graph that describes the maximum amount of one good that can be produced for every possible level of production of the other good

EXAMPLE 3.3

What is the production possibilities curve for an economy in which Susan is the only worker?

Consider a society consisting only of Susan, who allocates her production time between coffee and nuts. Each hour per day she devotes to picking nuts yields 3 pounds of nuts, and each hour she devotes to picking coffee yields 1.5 pounds of coffee. If Susan works a total of 8 hours per day, describe her production possibilities curve—the graph that displays, for each level of nut production, the maximum amount of coffee that Susan can pick.

The vertical axis in Figure 3.1 shows Susan's daily production of coffee, and the horizontal axis shows her daily production of nuts. Let's begin by looking at two extreme allocations of her time. First, suppose she employs her entire work-

FIGURE 3.1

Susan's Production Possibilities.

For the production relationships given, the production possibilities curve is a straight line.

Production possibilities curve: All combinations of coffee and nuts that can be produced with Susan's labor

day (8 hours per day) picking coffee. In that case, since she can pick 1.5 pounds of coffee per hour, she would pick (8 hours/day)(1.5 pounds/hour) = 12 pounds per day of coffee and 0 pounds of nuts. That combination of coffee and nut production is represented by point A in Figure 3.1, the vertical intercept of Susan's production possibilities curve.

Now suppose, instead, that Susan devotes all her time to picking nuts. Since she can pick 3 pounds of nuts per hour, her total daily production would be (8 hours/day)(3 pounds/hour) = 24 pounds of nuts. That combination is represented by point B in Figure 3.1, the horizontal intercept of Susan's production possibilities curve. Because Susan's production of each good is exactly proportional to the amount of time she devotes to that good, the remaining points along her production possibilities curve will lie on the straight line that joins A and B.

For example, suppose that Susan devotes 6 hours each day to picking coffee and 2 hours to picking nuts. She will then end up with (6 hours/day)(1.5 pounds/hour) = 9 pounds of coffee per day and (2 hours/day)(3 pounds/hour) = 6 pounds of nuts. This is the point labeled C in Figure 3.1. Alternatively, if she devotes 2 hours to coffee and 6 hours to nuts, she will get (2 hours/day)(1.5 pounds/hour) = 3 pounds of coffee per day and (6 hours/day)(3 pounds/hour) = 18 pounds of nuts. This alternative combination is represented by point D in Figure 3.1.

Since Susan's production possibilities curve (PPC) is a straight line, its slope is constant. The absolute value of the slope of Susan's PPC is the ratio of its vertical intercept to its horizontal intercept: (12 pounds of coffee/day)/(24 pounds of nuts/day) = 1/2 pound of coffee/1 pound of nuts. (Be sure to keep track of the units of measure on each axis when computing this ratio.) *This ratio means that Susan's opportunity cost of an additional pound of nuts is 1/2 pound of coffee.*

Note that Susan's opportunity cost of nuts can also be expressed as the following simple formula:

$$OC_{\text{nuts}} = \frac{\text{loss in coffee}}{\text{gain in nuts}},$$

where "loss in coffee" means the amount of coffee given up and "gain in nuts" means the corresponding increase in nuts. Likewise, Susan's opportunity cost of coffee is expressed by this formula:

$$OC_{\text{coffee}} = \frac{\text{loss in nuts}}{\text{gain in coffee}}.$$

To say that Susan's opportunity cost of an additional pound of nuts is 1/2 pound of coffee is equivalent to saying that her opportunity cost of 1 pound of coffee is 2 pounds of nuts.

The production possibilities curve shown in Figure 3.1 illustrates the scarcity principle—the idea that because our resources are limited, having more of one good thing generally means having to settle for less of another (see Chapter 1). Susan can have an additional pound of coffee if she wishes, but only if she is willing to give up 2 pounds of nuts. If Susan is the only person in the economy, her opportunity cost of producing a good becomes, in effect, its price. Thus the price she has to pay for an additional pound of coffee is 2 pounds of nuts; or equivalently, the price she has to pay for an additional pound of nuts is 1/2 pound of coffee.

Any point that lies either along the production possibilities curve or within it is said to be an **attainable point,** meaning that it can be produced with currently available resources. In Figure 3.2, for example, points *A, B, C, D,* and *E* are attainable points. Points that lie outside the production possibilities curve are said to be **unattainable,** meaning that they cannot be produced using currently available resources. In Figure 3.2, *F* is an unattainable point because Susan cannot pick 9 pounds of coffee per day *and* 15 pounds of nuts. Points that lie within

attainable point any combination of goods that can be produced using currently available resources

unattainable point any combination of goods that cannot be produced using currently available resources

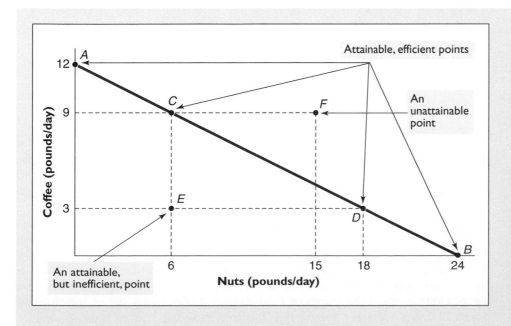

FIGURE 3.2
Attainable and Efficient Points on Susan's Production Possibilities Curve.
Points that lie either along the production possibilities curve (for example, A, C, D, and B) or within it (for example, E) are said to be attainable. Points that lie outside the production possibilities curve (for example, F) are unattainable. Points that lie along the curve are said to be efficient, while those that lie within the curve are said to be inefficient.

inefficient point any combination of goods for which currently available resources enable an increase in the production of one good without a reduction in the production of the other

efficient point any combination of goods for which currently available resources do not allow an increase in the production of one good without a reduction in the production of the other

the curve are said to be **inefficient,** in the sense that existing resources would allow for production of more of at least one good without sacrificing the production of any other good. At *E*, for example, Susan is picking only 3 pounds of coffee per day and 6 pounds of nuts, which means that she could increase her coffee harvest by 6 pounds per day without giving up any nuts (by moving from *E* to *C*). Alternatively, Susan could pick as many as 12 additional pounds of nuts each day without giving up any coffee (by moving from *E* to *D*). An **efficient point** is one that lies along the production possibilities curve. At any such point, more of one good can be produced only by producing less of the other.

FACTORS THAT INFLUENCE THE PRODUCTION POSSIBILITIES CURVE

To see how the slope and position of the production possibilities curve depend on an individual's productivity, let's compare Susan's PPC to that of a person who is less productive in both activities.

EXAMPLE 3.4   **How do changes in productivity affect the opportunity cost of nuts?**

Suppose Tom can pick 0.75 pound of nuts for each hour he devotes to picking nuts and 0.75 pound of coffee for each hour he spends picking coffee. If Tom is the only person in the economy, describe the economy's production possibilities curve.

We can construct Tom's PPC the same way we did Susan's. Note first that if Tom devotes an entire workday (8 hours/day) to coffee picking, he ends up with (8 hours/day)(0.75 pound/hour) = 6 pounds of coffee per day and 0 pounds of nuts. So the vertical intercept of Tom's PPC is *A* in Figure 3.3. If instead he devotes all his time to picking nuts, he gets (8 hours/day)(0.75 pound/hour) = 6 pounds of nuts per day and no coffee. That means the hor-

FIGURE 3.3
Tom's Production Possibilities Curve.
The less productive a person is, the closer to the origin is his PPC.

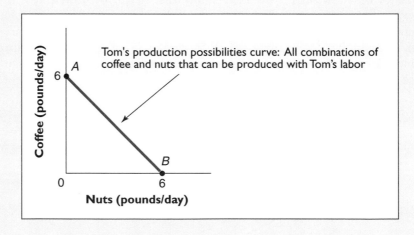

izontal intercept of his PPC is *B* in Figure 3.3. As before, because Tom's production of each good is proportional to the amount of time he devotes to it, the remaining points on his PPC will lie along the straight line that joins these two extreme points.

How does Tom's PPC compare with Susan's? Note that because Tom is less productive than Susan at both activities, the horizontal and vertical intercepts of Tom's PPC lie closer to the origin than do Susan's (see Figure 3.4). For Tom, the opportunity cost of an additional pound of nuts is 1 pound of coffee, which is twice Susan's opportunity cost of nuts. This difference in opportunity costs shows up as a difference in the slopes of their PPCs: the absolute value of the slope of Tom's PPC is 1, whereas Susan's is 1/2.

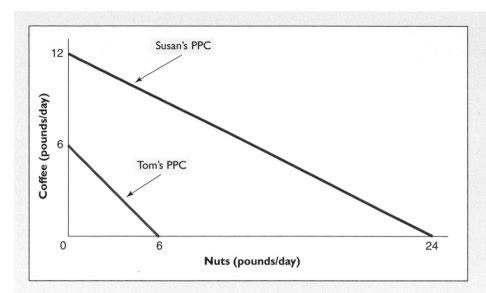

FIGURE 3.4
Individual Production Possibilities Curves Compared.
Though Tom is less productive in both activities than Susan, Tom's opportunity cost of picking coffee is only half Susan's.

But note too that while Tom is absolutely less efficient than Susan at picking coffee, his opportunity cost of coffee is actually only half Susan's. Whereas Susan must give up 2 pounds of nuts to pick an additional pound of coffee, Tom must give up only 1 pound. This difference in opportunity costs is another example of the concept of comparative advantage. Although Tom is *absolutely* less efficient than Susan at picking coffee, he is *relatively* more efficient. That is, Susan has an absolute advantage in picking both coffee and nuts, but Tom has a comparative advantage in picking coffee. Susan's comparative advantage is in picking nuts.

We cannot emphasize strongly enough that the principle of comparative advantage is a relative concept—one that makes sense only when the productivities of two or more people (or countries) are being compared. To cement this idea, work through the following exercise.

EXERCISE 3.2

Suppose Susan can pick 1.5 pounds of coffee per hour or 3 pounds of nuts per hour; Tom can pick 0.75 pound of coffee per hour and 2.25 pounds of nuts per hour. What is Susan's opportunity cost of picking a pound of nuts? What is Tom's opportunity cost of picking a pound of nuts? Where does Susan's comparative advantage now lie?

PRODUCTION POSSIBILITIES IN A TWO-PERSON ECONOMY

Why have we spent so much time defining comparative advantage? As the next examples illustrate, a comparative advantage arising from disparities in individual opportunity costs create gains for everyone.

How does the one-person economy's PPC change when a second person is added?

EXAMPLE 3.5

Suppose Susan can pick 1.5 pounds of coffee per hour or 3 pounds of nuts and Tom can pick 0.75 pound of coffee per hour or 0.75 pound of nuts. If Susan and Tom are the only two people in the economy and each works 8 hours per day, describe the production possibilities curve for the economy as a whole.

To construct the PPC for a two-person economy, we use an approach similar to the one we used for a one-person economy. To find the vertical intercept of the PPC, we ask how much coffee we would get if both Susan and Tom worked

FIGURE 3.5

The PPC for a Two-Person Economy.

Initial nut production relies on Susan, whose opportunity cost of nuts is lower than Tom's. Once Susan is fully occupied picking nuts (point *D*), additional nut production must rely on Tom.

full-time picking coffee. The answer is 18 pounds per day (12 pounds from Susan and 6 pounds from Tom), so point *A* in Figure 3.5 is the vertical intercept of the PPC. Similarly, if Susan and Tom both worked full-time picking nuts, they would make 30 pounds of nuts per day (24 pounds from Susan, and 6 from Tom). Thus point *B* in Figure 3.5 is the horizontal intercept of the PPC.

In contrast to the PPC for the one-person economy, however, the PPC for the two-person economy is not a straight line joining the two extreme points. To see why, suppose Susan and Tom were initially devoting all their time to picking coffee when they decided they would rather have some nuts. How would they launch their nut production effort? Their best bet would be to assign Susan to that task, because her opportunity cost of picking nuts is only half Tom's. Thus, if Susan spent 2 hours picking nuts while Tom continued to devote all his time to picking coffee, they would lose 3 pounds of coffee but gain 6 pounds of nuts each day. Point *C* in Figure 3.5 represents this combination.

If Susan devotes all her time to picking nuts while Tom continues to devote all his time to picking coffee, they will end up at *D* in Figure 3.5, which represents 6 pounds of coffee per day and 24 pounds of nuts. If they want to expand nut production any further, Tom will have to take some of his time away from picking coffee. But in doing so, they gain only one additional pound of nuts for each pound of coffee they lose. Notice in Figure 3.5 how the slope of the PPC changes at point *D*. To the right of point *D*, the slope of the PPC reflects Tom's opportunity cost of picking coffee rather than Susan's.

EXERCISE 3.3

To the left of point *D* in Figure 3.5, what is the slope of the production possibilities curve, and what opportunity cost does this slope represent?

The outward bow shape of the PPC for the two-person economy, then, is a consequence of individual differences in opportunity costs. As the following example shows, this distinctive shape represents expanded opportunities for both Susan and Tom.

EXAMPLE 3.6 **What is the best way to achieve a given production goal?**

Tom and Susan, a married couple, have decided to consume 12 pounds of coffee per day and 12 pounds of nuts. (They are sleepy and have 10 hungry children.)

If their productive abilities are as described in Example 3.5, how should they divide their labor?

Though Tom has a comparative advantage in picking coffee, even if he spends all his time picking coffee, he can pick only (8 hours/day)(0.75 pound/hour) = 6 pounds per day. So Susan will have to pick the additional 6 pounds of coffee to achieve their production target of 12 pounds. Since Susan is capable of picking (8 hours/day)(1.5 pounds/hour) = 12 pounds of coffee per day, she will need only 4 hours per day to pick 6 pounds. She can spend the remaining 4 hours picking nuts, which is exactly the amount of time she needs to pick their production target of 12 pounds. In terms of their two-person production possibilities curve, this allocation of labor puts Susan and Tom at point E in Figure 3.6.

FIGURE 3.6
Optimal Assignment of Production Tasks in a Two-Person Economy.
At the optimal division of labor (point E), Tom specializes completely in picking coffee, and Susan picks only as much coffee as is needed to complete their production target.

Example 3.6 illustrates the general principle that when more than one opportunity is available, we should always exploit the best opportunity first. We call this the low-hanging-fruit principle, in honor of the fruit-picker's rule of picking the most accessible fruit first:

The Principle of Increasing Opportunity Cost (or the Low-Hanging-Fruit Principle): In expanding the production of any good, first employ those resources with the lowest opportunity cost, and only afterward turn to resources with higher opportunity costs.

HOW MUCH DOES SPECIALIZATION MATTER?

In Example 3.6, Tom specialized completely in picking coffee, his area of comparative advantage (lowest opportunity cost). The reason Susan did not specialize completely in picking nuts is that had she done so, the two would have ended up with twice as many nuts (24 pounds) as they wanted to consume (12 pounds). Even so, Tom and Susan still did better through partial specialization than they could have if neither had specialized, as the following example demonstrates.

How much does specialization expand opportunity? (Part 1)

EXAMPLE 3.7

Suppose that in Example 3.6 Susan and Tom had divided their time so that each person's output consisted of half nuts and half coffee. How much worse off would they have been?

Tom can pick equal quantities of both goods by spending 4 hours each day on the production of each, which yields (4 hours/day)(0.75 pound/hour) = 3 pounds of coffee and (4 hours/day)(0.75 pound/hour) = 3 pounds of nuts. Since Susan can pick twice as many pounds of nuts in an hour as she can coffee, to get equal quantities of both goods, she must devote twice as many hours picking coffee as picking nuts. Thus she will need to spend two-thirds of a workday (16/3 hours/day) picking coffee and one-third of a workday (8/3 hours/day) picking nuts. Her output will be (16/3 hours/day)(1.5 pounds/hour) = 8 pounds of coffee per day and (8/3 hours/day)(3 pounds/hour) = 8 pounds of nuts. Their combined daily production will be only 11 pounds of coffee and 11 pounds of nuts—1 pound less of each good than when they specialized.

The relatively small gains from specialization that we saw in Example 3.7 might seem an insufficient explanation for the dramatic differences in the level of wealth across countries. While getting one extra pound of each of two goods by specializing is better than nothing, it is hardly enough to lift a society's standard of living.

This objection is a fair one. But the purpose of Example 3.7 was to demonstrate that specialization produces gains for all, even when one person enjoys an absolute advantage in both tasks, and when differences in opportunity costs are small. As the next example illustrates, the gains from specialization are considerably larger when people are both absolutely *and* relatively more efficient at their respective specialties, and when the differences in opportunity costs are more pronounced.

EXAMPLE 3.8

How much does specialization of labor expand opportunity? (Part 2)

Susan can pick 1 pound of coffee or 7 pounds of nuts in an hour. Tom can pick 7 pounds of coffee or 1 pound of nuts in an hour. Draw their combined production possibilities curve. Assuming that the two want to consume coffee and nuts in equal quantities, by how much will specialization increase their consumption?

Susan and Tom's combined PPC is shown in Figure 3.7. By working together, with Susan specializing in picking nuts and Tom specializing in picking coffee, the couple can consume (8 hours/day)(7 pounds/hour) = 56 pounds of coffee and (8 hours/day)(7 pounds/hour) = 56 pounds of nuts each day. If the two had worked separately, each would have been able to pick only 7 pounds of coffee and 7 pounds of nuts each day, for a total of 14 pounds of coffee and 14 pounds of nuts a day—only one-fourth of what they picked when they specialized.

FIGURE 3.7
An Especially Useful Division of Labor.
The gains from specialization are larger when differences in opportunity cost are larger and when individuals enjoy absolute advantage in their respective specialties.

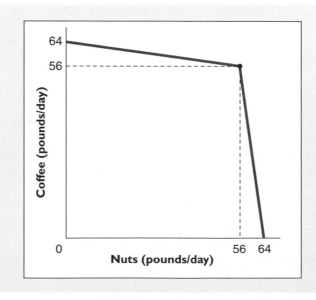

In truth, the gains from specialization will often be far more spectacular than those shown in Example 3.8. One reason is that specialization not only capitalizes on preexisting differences in individual skills but also deepens those skills through practice and experience. It also eliminates many of the switching and start-up costs people incur when they move back and forth among numerous tasks. These gains apply not only to people but also to the tools and equipment they use. Breaking a task down into simple steps, each of which can be performed by a different machine, greatly multiplies the productivity of individual workers.

Even in simple settings, these factors can combine to increase productivity hundredsfold or even thousandsfold. Consider, for instance, Adam Smith's description of work in an eighteenth-century Scottish pin factory:

> One man draws out the wire, another straightens it, a third cuts it, a fourth points it, a fifth grinds it at the top for receiving the head; to make the head requires two or three distinct operations. . . . I have seen a small manufactory of this kind where only ten men were employed . . . [who] could, when they exerted themselves, make among them about twelve pounds of pins in a day. There are in a pound upwards of four thousand pins of middling size. Those ten persons, therefore, could make among them upwards of forty-eight thousand pins in a day. Each person, therefore, making a tenth part of forty-eight thousand pins, might be considered as making four thousand eight hundred pins in a day. But if they had all wrought separately and independently, and without any of them having been educated to this peculiar business, they certainly could not each of them have made twenty, perhaps not one pin in a day. . . .[2]

The gains in productivity that result from specialization are often prodigious. They constitute the single most important explanation for why societies that don't rely heavily on specialization and exchange are rapidly becoming relics of the past.

Of course, the mere fact that specialization boosts productivity does not mean that more specialization is always better than less, for specialization also entails costs. For example, most people appear to enjoy variety in the work they do, but variety tends to be one of the first casualties as workplace tasks become ever more narrowly specialized.

[2]Adam Smith, *The Wealth of Nations,* New York: Everyman's Library, E. P. Dutton, 1910 (1776), book 1, p. 5.

Can specialization proceed too far?

Indeed, one of Karl Marx's central themes was that the fragmentation of workplace tasks often exacts a heavy psychological toll on workers. Thus, he wrote, "[A]ll means for the development of production . . . mutilate the laborer into a fragment of a man, degrade him to the level of an appendage of a machine, destroy every remnant of charm in his work and turn it into hated toil. . . ."[3]

Charlie Chaplin's 1936 film, *Modern Times*, paints a vivid portrait of the psychological costs of repetitive factory work. As an assembly worker, Chaplin's only task, all day every day, is to tighten the nuts on two bolts as they pass before him on the assembly line. Finally he snaps and walks zombielike from the factory, wrenches in hand, tightening every nutlike protuberance he encounters.

Do the extra goods made possible by specialization simply come at too high a price? We must certainly acknowledge at least the *potential* for specialization to proceed too far. Yet specialization need not entail rigidly segmented, mind-numbingly repetitive work. And it is important to recognize that *failure* to specialize entails costs as well. Those who don't specialize must accept low wages or work extremely long hours.

When all is said and done, we can expect to meet life's financial obligations in the shortest time—thereby freeing up more time to do whatever else we wish—if we concentrate at least a significant proportion of our efforts on those tasks for which we have a comparative advantage.

A PRODUCTION POSSIBILITIES CURVE FOR A MANY-PERSON ECONOMY

Most actual economies, of course, consist of millions of workers. Even so, the process of constructing a production possibilities curve for an economy of that size is really no different from the process for a one- or two-person economy. But since each worker's contribution to total output is extremely small in a large economy, production possibilities curves tend not to be kinked like the ones in preceding examples, but smoothly bowed, like the one shown in Figure 3.8.

FIGURE 3.8
Production Possibilities Curve for a Large Economy.
For an economy with millions of workers, the PPC has a gentle outward bow shape.

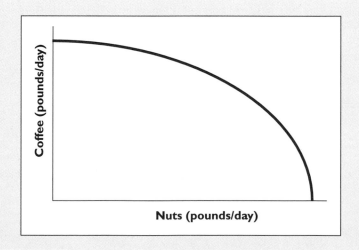

Like all production possibilities curves, the one in Figure 3.8 is downward-sloping, illustrating once again the principle of scarcity and trade-offs. If all available resources are currently engaged in the production of coffee and nuts, the only way to get more nuts is to sacrifice some coffee. Note also that the slope of the production possibilities curve in Figure 3.8 increases as the society moves toward greater production of nuts. Recall the principle of increasing opportunity

[3]Karl Marx, *Das Kapital*, New York: Modern Library, 1936 (1856), pp. 708, 709.

cost (or the low-hanging-fruit principle): In expanding nut production, people turn first to those resources that are relatively efficient at picking nuts. Only when those resources have been deployed do they turn to less efficient resources. As more and more nuts are picked, the opportunity cost of picking additional nuts rises. Note that the principle of increasing opportunity cost applies to both goods shown in Figure 3.8. Thus, as more coffee is picked, the opportunity cost of picking additional coffee rises.

> **RECAP** **COMPARATIVE ADVANTAGE AND PRODUCTION POSSIBILITIES**
>
> For an economy that produces two goods, the production possibilities curve describes the maximum amount of one good that can be produced for every possible level of production of the other good. Attainable points are those that lie on or within the curve, and efficient points are those that lie along the curve. The slope of the production possibilities curve tells us the opportunity cost of producing an additional unit of the good measured along the horizontal axis. The principle of increasing opportunity cost, or the low-hanging-fruit principle, tells us that the slope of the production possibilities curve becomes steeper as we move downward to the right. The greater the differences among individual opportunity costs, the more bow-shaped the production possibilities curve will be, and the more bow-shaped is the production possibilities curve, the greater will be the potential gains from specialization.

COMPARATIVE ADVANTAGE AND INTERNATIONAL TRADE

The same logic that leads the individuals in an economy to specialize and exchange goods with one another also leads nations to specialize and trade among themselves. As with individuals, each trading partner can benefit from exchange, even though one may be more productive than the other in absolute terms.

Can a poor nation prosper by trading with an economic superpower?

Susan and Tom are the only two workers in Islandia, a small island nation, and their production possibilities curve is as shown in Figure 3.9. The only other nation on earth has millions of workers, each of whom can produce 100 pounds

EXAMPLE 3.9

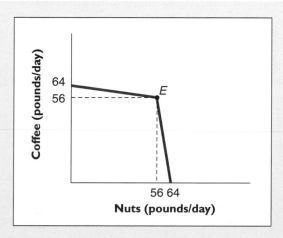

FIGURE 3.9
Production Possibilities Curve for a Small Island Nation.

of nuts or 100 pounds of coffee per hour. How does the opportunity to trade with the superpower affect consumption opportunities in Islandia?

In the economic superpower, the opportunity cost of a pound of coffee is 1 pound of nuts. The market price of 1 pound of coffee will therefore be 1 pound of nuts. (If someone tried to charge, say, 1.5 pounds of nuts for a pound of coffee, consumers could simply reduce their own nut harvest by a pound and pick an extra pound of coffee instead.) Given the superpower's size relative to the tiny nation of Islandia, in a combined market consisting of the superpower and Islandia, 1 pound of coffee will exchange for exactly 1 pound of nuts. The opportunity to trade with Islandia therefore has no perceptible impact on the citizens of the superpower.

But it has a profound impact on Susan and Tom. Suppose they were initially at point E on their PPC (Figure 3.9). Without the opportunity to trade with the superpower, they would have to give up 7 pounds of nuts to expand their coffee harvest by 1 pound. But with the opportunity to trade, they can purchase 1 pound of coffee in exchange for only 1 pound of nuts. If Islandians started at E and sold their entire 56 pounds of nuts to the superpower, they could buy an addi-

FIGURE 3.10
How Trade Expands the Menu of Possibilities.
The opportunity to trade with an economic superpower greatly expands the consumption opportunities of a smaller nation.

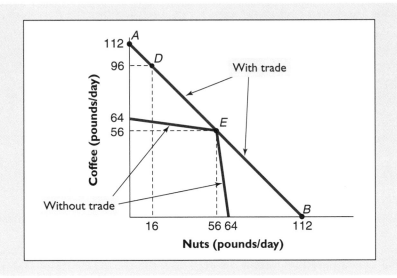

tional 56 pounds of coffee, for a total of $56 + 56 = 112$ pounds of coffee and $56 - 56 = 0$ pounds of nuts. So point A in Figure 3.10 represents their maximum possible daily coffee consumption once they can engage in trade.

Similarly, if they were initially at point E on their PPC, and lacked the opportunity to trade, they would have to sacrifice 7 pounds of coffee to obtain an additional pound of nuts. But if they could trade with the superpower, they could get an extra pound of nuts at a cost of just 1 pound of coffee. If Islandians started at D and sold their entire 56 pounds of coffee to the superpower, they could buy an additional 56 pounds of nuts, for a total of $56 + 56 = 112$ pounds of nuts and $56 - 56 = 0$ pounds of coffee. So point B in Figure 3.10 represents their maximum possible nut consumption once they can engage in trade.

A and B represent the two extreme points on Islandia's new menu of possibilities. By trading lesser quantities of coffee or nuts with the superpower, it is also possible for Islandians to achieve any point along the straight line joining A and B. For example, if Islandians started at point E and sold 40 pounds of nuts to the superpower, they could buy an additional 40 pounds of coffee, which would move them to point D, which has $56 + 40 = 96$ pounds of coffee and $56 - 40 = 16$ pounds of nuts. The opportunity to trade with the superpower thus transforms Islandia's menu of possibilities from the PPC shown in Figure 3.9 to the one labeled AB in Figure 3.10.

EXERCISE 3.4

Refer to Example 3.9. What would Islandia's new menu of possibilities look like if each citizen in the superpower could pick 100 pounds of coffee per day, as before, but only 50 pounds of nuts?

How much does trade benefit the citizens of Islandia? The answer depends on which particular combination of coffee and nuts Islandians most prefer. Suppose, for example, that they most prefer the combination at point *E* in Figure 3.11: 56 pounds of coffee per day and 56 pounds of nuts. The opportunity to trade with the superpower would then be of no benefit to them, since that combination was available to them before trade became possible (see Figure 3.9).

But suppose that in the absence of trade with the superpower, Islandians would have chosen to pick and consume only 28 pounds of coffee and 60 pounds of nuts per day (point *D* in Figure 3.11). The opportunity to trade with the superpower would then be very valuable indeed, for it would enable the Islandians

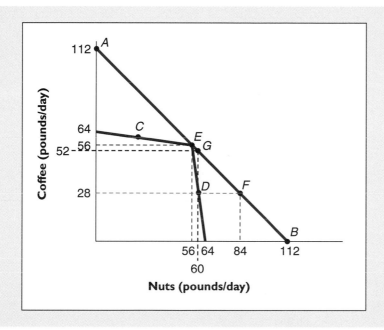

FIGURE 3.11
Gains from International Trade.
If the smaller nation was originally at *D* on its PPC, the ability to trade with the superpower enables it to increase its consumption of nuts by 24 pounds per day (by moving from *D* to *F*). Alternatively, it could increase its consumption of coffee by 24 pounds per day (by moving from *D* to *G*).

almost to double their coffee consumption without reducing their nut consumption (by moving from *D* to *G* in Figure 3.11). Or they could increase their nut consumption from 60 to 84 pounds per day without giving up any coffee (by moving from *D* to *F* in Figure 3.11). The gains from trade would also be valuable if the Islandians had initially chosen to produce at a point at which the opportunity cost of a pound of nuts was less than 1 pound of coffee—say, point *C* in Figure 3.11.

The patterns displayed in this example are at least roughly indicative of actual patterns of international trade. The volume of trade has grown substantially over time, and with some important exceptions, no single nation produces more than a small fraction of the total supply of any good or service. Thus the price at which one good exchanges for another on the world market is not much influenced by how much a good a nation itself, even an economic superpower like the United States, produces. The greater the difference between domestic opportunity costs and the world opportunity costs, the more a nation benefits from the opportunity to trade with other nations.

DOES EVERYONE BENEFIT FROM TRADE?

If trade between nations is as beneficial as our analysis seems to suggest, then why are free-trade agreements so controversial? One of the most heated issues in the 1996 presidential campaign was President Clinton's support for the North American Free Trade Agreement (NAFTA), a treaty to sharply reduce trade barriers between the United States and its immediate neighbors north and south. The treaty attracted fierce opposition from third-party candidate Ross Perot, who insisted that it would severely reduce the earnings of American workers. If exchange is beneficial, why does anyone oppose it?

The answer is that while reducing barriers to international trade increases the total value of all goods and services produced in each nation, it does not guarantee that each individual citizen will do better. One specific concern regarding NAFTA was that it would help Mexico to exploit a comparative advantage in the production of goods made by unskilled labor. Although U.S. consumers would benefit from reduced prices for such goods, many Americans feared that unskilled workers in the United States would lose their jobs to workers in Mexico.

In the end, NAFTA was enacted over the vociferous opposition of American labor unions. So far, however, studies have failed to detect significant job losses among unskilled workers in the United States.

RECAP   **COMPARATIVE ADVANTAGE AND INTERNATIONAL TRADE**

Nations, like individuals, can benefit from exchange, even though one trading partner may be more productive than the other in absolute terms. The greater the difference between domestic opportunity costs and world opportunity costs, the more a nation benefits from exchange with other nations. But expansions of exchange do not guarantee that each individual citizen will do better. In particular, unskilled workers in high-wage countries may be hurt in the short run by the reduction of barriers to trade with low-wage nations.

▪ SUMMARY ▪

- One person has an *absolute* advantage over another in the production of a good if she can produce more of that good than the other person. One person has a *comparative* advantage over another in the production of a good if she is relatively more efficient than the other person at producing that good, meaning that her opportunity cost of producing it is lower than her counterpart's. Specialization based on comparative advantage is the basis for economic exchange. When each person specializes in the task at which he or she is relatively most efficient, the economic pie is maximized, making possible the largest slice for everyone.

- At the individual level, comparative advantage may spring from differences in talent or ability or from differences in education, training, and experience. At the national level, sources of comparative advantage include these innate and learned differences, as well as differences in language, culture, institutions, climate, natural resources, and a host of other factors.

- The production possibilities curve is a simple device for summarizing the possible combinations of output that a society can produce if it employs its resources efficiently. In a simple economy that produces only coffee and nuts, the PPC shows the maximum quantity of coffee production (vertical axis) possible at each level of nut production (horizontal axis). The slope of the PPC at any point represents the opportunity cost of nuts at that point, expressed in pounds of coffee.

- All production possibilities curves slope downward because of the scarcity principle, which states that the only way a consumer can get more of one good is to settle for less of another. In economies whose workers have different opportunity costs of picking nuts, the slope of the PPC becomes steeper as consumers move downward along the curve. This change in slope illustrates the principle of increasing opportunity cost (or the low-hanging-fruit principle), which states that in expanding the production of any good, a society should first employ those resources that are relatively efficient at producing that good and only afterward turn to those that are less efficient.

- The same logic that prompts individuals to specialize in their production and exchange goods with one another also leads

nations to specialize and trade with one another. On both levels, each trading partner can benefit from an exchange, even though one may be more productive than the other, in absolute terms, for each good. For both individuals and nations, the benefits of exchange tend to be larger the larger are the differences between the trading partners' opportunity costs.

■ CORE PRINCIPLES ■

The Principle of Comparative Advantage
Everyone does best when each person (or each country) concentrates on the activities for which his or her opportunity cost is lowest.

The Principle of Increasing Opportunity Cost (or The Low-Hanging-Fruit Principle)
In expanding the production of any good, first employ those resources with the lowest opportunity cost and only afterward turn to resources with higher opportunity costs.

■ KEY TERMS ■

absolute advantage (50)
attainable point (57)
comparative advantage (50)

efficient point (58)
inefficient point (58)
production possibilities curve (55)

unattainable point (57)

■ REVIEW QUESTIONS ■

1. Explain what "having a comparative advantage" at producing a particular good or service means. What does "having an absolute advantage" at producing a good or service mean?

2. How will a reduction in the number of hours worked each day affect an economy's production possibilities curve?

3. How will technological innovations that boost labor productivity affect an economy's production possibilities curve?

4. Why does saying that people are poor because they do not specialize make more sense than saying that people perform their own services because they are poor?

5. What factors have helped the United States to become the world's leading exporter of movies, books, and popular music?

■ PROBLEMS ■

1. Consider a society whose only worker is Helen, who allocates her production time between cutting hair and baking bread. Each hour per day she devotes to cutting hair yields 4 haircuts, and each hour she devotes to baking bread yields 8 loaves of bread. If Helen works a total of 8 hours per day, graph her production possibilities curve.

2. Refer to Problem 1. Which of the points listed below is efficient? Which is attainable?
   a. 28 haircuts/day, 16 loaves/day
   b. 16 haircuts/day, 32 loaves/day
   c. 18 haircuts/day, 24 loaves/day

3. Determine whether the following statements are true or false, and briefly explain why.
   a. Toby can produce 5 gallons of apple cider or 2.5 ounces of feta cheese per hour. Kyle can produce 3 gallons of apple cider or 1.5 ounces of feta cheese per hour. Therefore, Toby and Kyle cannot benefit from specialization and trade.
   b. A doctor who can vacuum her office faster and more thoroughly than commercial cleaners should clean her office herself.

c. In an economy in which millions of workers each have different opportunity costs of producing two goods, the low-hanging-fruit principle implies that the slope of the production possibilities curve decreases in absolute value as more of the good on the horizontal axis is produced.

4. Nancy and Bill are auto mechanics. Nancy takes 4 hours to replace a clutch and 2 hours to replace a set of brakes. Bill takes 6 hours to replace a clutch and 2 hours to replace a set of brakes. If Bill and Nancy open a motor repair shop:
   a. Nancy should work only on clutches, and Bill should work only on brakes.
   b. Bill has a comparative advantage at replacing brakes.
   c. Nancy has an absolute advantage at replacing clutches.
   d. Nancy has a comparative advantage at replacing clutches.
   e. All but one of the above statements are correct.

5. Bob and Stella are a married couple. Bob takes 10 minutes to change a lightbulb and 2 minutes to fix a broken fuse. Stella takes 3 minutes to change a lightbulb and 30 seconds to fix a broken fuse. Which of the following statements is true?
   a. Stella has a comparative advantage at fixing fuses, because she can do it faster than Bob.
   b. Stella has a comparative advantage at changing lightbulbs and fixing fuses, because she can do both of them faster than Bob.
   c. Stella has an absolute advantage at changing lightbulbs and fixing fuses, because she can do both of them faster than Bob.
   d. Bob has a comparative advantage at fixing fuses, because Stella has a comparative advantage at changing lightbulbs.
   e. Stella has a comparative advantage at changing lightbulbs.

6. Larry and Harry are stranded together on a desert island. The raw materials on the island are suitable only for making beer and pizza, but their quantities are unlimited. What is scarce is labor. Harry and Larry each spend 10 hours a day making beer or pizza. The following table specifies *how much beer and pizza Harry and Larry can produce per hour.*

	Beer	**Pizza**
Harry	1 bottle per hour	0.2 pizza per hour
Larry	0.5 bottle per hour	1.5 pizzas per hour

   a. Draw the daily production possibilities curves (PPCs) for Harry and Larry.
   b. Who has an absolute advantage in making pizza? In brewing beer?
   c. Who has a comparative advantage in making pizza? In brewing beer?
   Now suppose their preferences are as follows: Harry wants 2 beers and as much pizza as he can eat each day; Larry wants 2 pizzas and as much beer as he can drink each day.
   d. If each man is self-reliant, how much beer and pizza will Harry and Larry eat and drink?
   e. Suppose the two men decide to trade with each other. Draw their joint PPC, and give an example of a trade that will make each of them better off.

7. Redo Problem 6 with the following changes:
   a. Each individual's productivity is shown in the table that follows, *which specifies the number of hours each man needs to produce a single unit of beer and pizza.*
   b. Harry wants 6 beers and as much pizza as he can eat each day, while Larry wants 2 pizzas and as much beer as he can drink each day.

	Production time for 1 beer	**Production time for 1 pizza**
Harry	5/4 hours	5/3 hours
Larry	5 hours	5/2 hours

8. Given the joint production possibilities curve in Problem 7, what would be the maximum number of pizzas available to Harry and Larry if they could buy or sell in a world market in which 1 beer could be exchanged for 1 pizza? What would be the maximum number of beers available to them?

9. Inlandia and Outlandia both can produce oranges and oil. Inlandia can produce up to 10 million tons of oranges per week or 5 million barrels of oil, or any combination of oil and oranges along a straight-line production possibilities curve linking those two points. Outlandia can produce up to 50 million tons of oranges per week or 1 million barrels of oil, or any combination along a straight-line production possibilities curve linking those points.

   a. Does the low-hanging-fruit principle apply in either of these two economies? Why or why not?

   b. Suppose Outlandia and Inlandia sign a trade agreement in which each country would specialize in the production of either oil or oranges. Which country should specialize in which commodity?

   c. If Inlandia and Outlandia are the only two economies in the world that are open to international trade, what are the maximum and minimum prices that can prevail on the world market for a ton of oranges, in terms of barrels of oil?

10. Jay, Kay, and Dee are marooned alone on the Greek island of Skorpios. They must find a way to provide themselves with food and drinking water. The following table shows how many hours each person takes to produce one unit of food or one unit of water.

	Production time for one unit of food	Production time for one unit of drinking water
Jay	1 hour	2 hours
Kay	2 hours	1 hour
Dee	4 hours	6 hours

   a. If each person can work for 12 hours a day and each person provides for him or herself, draw their individual PPCs.

   b. Suppose Jay, Kay, and Dee decide to produce food and water cooperatively, so they can gain from trade. Draw their combined production possibilities curve.

   c. If the trio wants, in aggregate, to consume 15 units of food and 12 units of water, who should specialize in food production? Who should specialize in water production? Should anyone divide his or her time between food and water production?

   d. If the trio wants, in aggregate, to consume 6 units of water and as much food as possible, who should specialize in food and who should specialize in water? Should anyone divide his or her time between food and water production? How much food will be produced?

   e. Suppose production is as in part c. Dee suggests dividing the output equally among the three of them. Assuming that the amounts of food that Jay and Kay get under this arrangement are exactly what each would have chosen if he or she had lived and worked alone, is each of them strictly better off when they share? Explain.

▪ ANSWERS TO IN-CHAPTER EXERCISES ▪

3.1

	Productivity in programming	Productivity in bicycle repair
Pat	2 web page updates per hour	1 repair per hour
Barb	3 web page updates per hour	3 repairs per hour

The entries in the table tell us that Barb has an absolute advantage over Pat in both activities. While Barb, the mechanic, can update 3 web pages per hour, Pat, the programmer, can update only 2. Barb's absolute advantage over Pat is even greater in the task of fixing bikes—3 repairs per hour versus Pat's 1.

But, as in Example 3.2, the fact that Barb is a better programmer than Pat does not imply that Barb should update her own web page. Barb's opportunity cost of updating a web page is 1 bicycle repair, whereas Pat must give up only half a bicycle repair to update a web page. Pat has a comparative advantage over Barb at programming, and Barb has a comparative advantage over Pat at bicycle repair.

3.2 Susan's opportunity cost of picking a pound of nuts is 1/2 pound of coffee. But Tom's opportunity cost of picking a pound of nuts is now only 1/3 pound of coffee. So Tom has a comparative advantage at picking nuts, and Susan has a comparative advantage at picking coffee.

3.3 The slope to the left of point D (in absolute value) is 1/2 pound of coffee per pound of nuts, which is Susan's opportunity cost of picking nuts.

3.4 In the superpower, the opportunity cost of a pound of nuts is now 2 pounds of coffee, not 1 pound. This means that Islandians can now buy or sell a pound of nuts for 2 pounds of coffee and can buy or sell a pound of coffee for 1/2 pound of nuts. So if Islandians start at point E and sell all 56 pounds of nuts they produce, they can buy an additional 112 pounds of coffee, for a total of 168 pounds of coffee. This would put them at point A in the diagram below. Alternatively, if they start at E and sell all 56 pounds of coffee they produce, they can buy an additional 28 pounds of nuts, for a total of 84 pounds of nuts, which would put them at B. The straight line AB is their new menu of opportunities.

CHAPTER 4

SUPPLY AND DEMAND: AN INTRODUCTION

■

The stock of foodstuffs on hand at any moment in New York City's grocery stores, restaurants, and private kitchens is sufficient to feed the city's 10 million residents for at most a week or so. Since most of these residents have nutritionally adequate and highly varied diets, and since almost no food is produced within the city proper, provisioning New York requires that tens of millions of pounds of food and drink be delivered to locations throughout the city each day.

No doubt many New Yorkers, buying groceries at their favorite local markets or eating at their favorite Italian restaurants, give little or no thought to the nearly miraculous coordination of people and resources that is required to feed city residents on a daily basis. But near-miraculous it is, nevertheless. Even if the supplying of New York City consisted only of transporting a fixed collection of foods to a given list of destinations each day, it would be quite an impressive operation, requiring at least a small army (and a well-managed one) to carry out.

Yet the entire process is astonishingly more complex than that. For example, the system must somehow ensure that not only *enough* food is delivered to satisfy New Yorkers' discriminating palates but also the *right kinds* of food. There mustn't be too much pheasant and not enough smoked eel, or too much bacon and not enough eggs, or too much caviar and not enough canned tuna, and so on. Similar judgments must be made *within* each category of food and drink: There must be the right amount of Swiss cheese and the right amounts of provolone, Gorgonzola, and feta.

But even this doesn't begin to describe the complexity of the decisions and actions required to provide our nation's largest city with its daily bread.

Someone has to decide where each particular type of food gets produced, and how, and by whom. Someone must decide how much of each type of food gets delivered to *each* of the tens of thousands of restaurants and grocery stores in the city. Someone must determine whether the deliveries should be made in big trucks or small ones, arrange that the trucks be in the right place at the right time, and ensure that gasoline and qualified drivers are available.

Thousands of individuals must decide what role, if any, they will play in this collective effort. Some people—just the right number—must choose to drive food delivery trucks, rather than trucks that deliver lumber. Others must become the mechanics who fix these trucks, rather than carpenters who build houses. Others must become farmers, rather than architects or bricklayers. Still others must become chefs in upscale restaurants, or flip burgers at McDonald's, instead of becoming plumbers or electricians.

Yet despite the almost incomprehensible number and complexity of the tasks involved, somehow the supplying of New York City manages to get done remarkably smoothly. Oh, a grocery store will occasionally run out of flank steak, or a diner will sometimes be told that someone else has just ordered the last serving of roast duck. But if episodes like these stick in memory, it is only because they are rare. For the most part, New York's food delivery system—like that of every other city in the country—functions so seamlessly that it attracts virtually no notice.

The situation is strikingly different in New York City's rental housing market. According to one recent estimate, the city needs between 20,000 and 40,000 new housing units each year merely to keep up with population growth and to replace existing housing that is deteriorated beyond repair. The actual rate of new construction in the city, however, is only 6,000 units per year. As a result, America's most densely populated city has been experiencing a protracted housing shortage. Yet, paradoxically, in the midst of this shortage, apartment houses are being demolished; and in the vacant lots left behind, people from the neighborhoods are planting flower gardens!

New York City is experiencing not only a growing shortage of rental housing but also chronically strained relations between landlords and tenants. In one all-too-typical case, for example, a photographer living in a loft on the Lower East Side waged an 8-year court battle with his landlord that generated literally thousands of pages of legal documents. "Once we put up a doorbell for ourselves," the photographer recalled, "and [the landlord] pulled it out, so we pulled out the wires to his doorbell."[1] The landlord, for his part, accused the photographer of obstructing his efforts to renovate the apartment. According to the landlord, the tenant preferred that the apartment remain in substandard condition, since that gave him an excuse to withhold rent payments.

Why does New York City's food distribution system work so much better than its housing market?

Same city, two strikingly different patterns. In the food industry, a huge variety of goods and services is widely available, and people (at least those with adequate income) are generally satisfied with what they receive and the choices available to them. In contrast, in the rental housing industry, there are chronic shortages and chronic dissatisfaction among both buyers and sellers. Why this difference?

The brief answer is that New York City relies on a complex system of administrative rent regulations to allocate housing units but leaves the allocation of food essentially in the hands of market forces—the forces of supply and demand. Although intuition might suggest otherwise, both theory and experience suggest that the seemingly chaotic and unplanned outcomes of market forces often can do a better job of allocating economic resources than can (for example) a government agency, even if the agency has the best of intentions.

[1]Quoted by John Tierney, "The Rentocracy: At the Intersection of Supply and Demand," *The New York Times Magazine*, May 4, 1997, p. 39.

In this chapter we'll explore how markets allocate food, housing, and other goods and services, usually with remarkable efficiency despite the complexity of the tasks. To be sure, markets are by no means perfect, and our stress on their virtues is to some extent an attempt to counteract what most economists view as an underappreciation by the general public of their remarkable strengths. But in the course of our discussion we'll see why markets function so smoothly most of the time and why bureaucratic rules and regulations rarely work as well in solving complex economic problems.

To convey an understanding of how markets work is a major goal of this course, and in this chapter we provide only a brief introduction and overview. As the course proceeds we will discuss the economic role of markets in considerably more detail, paying attention to some of the problems of markets as well as their strengths.

WHAT, HOW, AND FOR WHOM? CENTRAL PLANNING VERSUS THE MARKET

No city, state, or society—irrespective of how it is organized—can escape the need to answer certain basic economic questions. For example, how much of our limited time and other resources should we devote to building housing, how much to the production of food, and how much to providing other goods and services? What techniques should we use to produce each good? Who should be assigned to each specific task? And how should the resulting goods and services be distributed among people?

In the thousands of different societies for which records are available, issues like these have been decided in essentially one of two ways. One approach is for all economic decisions to be made centrally, by an individual or small number of individuals on behalf of a larger group. For example, in many agrarian societies throughout history, families or other small groups consumed only those goods and services that they produced for themselves, and a single clan or family leader made most important production and distribution decisions. On an immensely larger scale, the economic organization of the former Soviet Union (and other communist countries) was also largely centralized. In so-called centrally planned communist nations, a central bureaucratic committee established production targets for the country's farms and factories, developed a master plan for how to achieve the targets (including detailed instructions concerning who was to produce what), and set up guidelines for the distribution and use of the goods and services produced.

Neither form of centralized economic organization is much in evidence today. When implemented on a small scale, as in a self-sufficient family enterprise, centralized decision making is certainly feasible. For the reasons discussed in Chapter 3, however, the jack-of-all-trades approach was doomed once it became clear how dramatically people could improve their living standards by specialization—that is, by having each individual focus his or her efforts on a relatively narrow range of tasks. And with the fall of the Soviet Union and its satellite nations in the late 1980s, there are now only three communist economies left in the world: Cuba, North Korea, and China. The first two of these appear to be on their last legs, economically speaking, and China has by now largely abandoned any attempt to control production and distribution decisions from the center. The major remaining examples of centralized allocation and control now reside in the bureaucratic agencies that administer programs like New York City's rent controls—programs that are themselves becoming increasingly rare.

At the beginning of the twenty-first century we are therefore left, for the most part, with the second major form of economic system, one in which production and distribution decisions are left to individuals interacting in private markets. In the so-called capitalist, or free-market, economies, people decide for themselves which careers to pursue and which products to produce or buy. In fact, there are no *pure* free-market economies today. Modern industrial countries are more properly described as *mixed economies,* meaning that goods and services are allocated by a combination of free markets, regulation, and other forms of collective control. Still, it makes sense to refer to such systems as free-market economies, because people are for the most part free to start businesses, to shut them down, or to sell them. And within broad limits, the distribution of goods and services is determined by individual preferences backed by individual purchasing power, which in most cases comes from the income people earn in the labor market.

In country after country, markets have replaced centralized control for the simple reason that they tend to allocate goods and services so much more effectively. The popular press, and the conventional wisdom, often assert that economists disagree about important issues. (As one wag put it, "If you lay all the economists in the world end to end, they still wouldn't reach a conclusion.") The fact is, however, that there is overwhelming agreement among economists about a broad range of issues, with the great majority accepting the efficacy of markets as means for allocating society's scarce resources. For example, a recent survey found that more than 90 percent of American professional economists believe that rent regulations like the ones implemented by New York City do more harm than good. That the stated aim of these regulations—to make rental housing more affordable for middle- and low-income families—is clearly benign was not enough to prevent them from wreaking havoc on New York City's housing market. To see why, we must explore how goods and services are allocated in private markets and why nonmarket means of allocating goods and services often do not produce the expected results.

MARKETS AND PRICES

Beginning with some simple concepts and definitions, we will explore how the interactions among buyers and sellers in markets determine the prices and quantities of the various goods and services traded in those markets. We begin by defining a market: The **market** for any good consists of all the buyers and sellers of that good. So, for example, the market for hamburgers on a given day in a given place is just the set of people (or other economic actors, like firms) potentially able to buy or sell hamburgers at that time and location.

market the market for any good consists of all buyers or sellers of that good

In the market for hamburgers, sellers comprise the individuals and companies that either do sell—or might, under the right circumstances, sell—hamburgers. Similarly, buyers in this market include all individuals who buy—or might buy—hamburgers.

In most parts of the country a decent hamburger, or some other life-sustaining meal, can still be had for less than $5. Where does the market price of hamburgers come from? Looking beyond hamburgers to the vast array of other goods that are bought and sold every day, we may ask, "Why are some goods cheap and others expensive?" Aristotle had no idea. Nor did Plato, or Copernicus, or Newton. On reflection, it is astonishing that, for almost the entire span of human history, not even the most intelligent and creative minds on earth had any real inkling of how to answer that seemingly simple question. Even Adam Smith, the Scottish moral philosopher whose *Wealth of Nations* launched the discipline of economics in 1776, suffered confusion on this issue.

Smith and other early economists (including Karl Marx) thought that the market price of a good was determined by its cost of production. But although costs surely do affect prices, they cannot explain why one of Pablo Picasso's paintings sells for so much more than one of Jackson Pollock's.

Stanley Jevons and other nineteenth-century economists tried to explain price by focusing on the value people derived from consuming different goods and services. It certainly seems plausible that people will pay a lot for a good they value highly. Yet willingness to pay cannot be the whole story, either. A person deprived of water in the desert, for example, will be dead in a matter of hours, and yet water sells for less than a penny a gallon. By contrast, human beings can get along perfectly well without gold, and yet gold sells for more than $250 an ounce.

Cost of production? Value to the user? Which is it? The answer, which seems obvious to today's economists, is that both matter. Writing in the late nineteenth century, the British economist Alfred Marshall was among the first to show clearly how costs and value interact to determine both the prevailing market price for a good and the amount of it that is bought and sold. Our task in the pages ahead will be to explore Marshall's insights and gain some practice in applying them. As a first step, we introduce the two main components of Marshall's pathbreaking analysis: the supply curve and the demand curve.

Why do Pablo Picasso's paintings sell for so much more than Jackson Pollock's?

THE SUPPLY CURVE

In the market for hamburgers, the **supply curve** of hamburgers is a simple schedule, or graph, that tells us, for each possible price of hamburgers, how many hamburgers all hamburger sellers together would be willing to sell at that price.

What does the supply curve of hamburgers look like? The answer to this question is based on the logical assumption that people should be willing to sell hamburgers as long as the price they receive for them is sufficient to cover their opportunity costs of supplying them. Thus, if what people could earn by selling hamburgers is not sufficient to compensate them for what they could have earned if they had spent their time and invested their money in some other way, they will not sell hamburgers. Otherwise, they will.

In general, people differ with respect to their opportunity costs of producing and selling hamburgers: For those with limited education and work experience, the opportunity cost of selling hamburgers is relatively low (because such individuals typically do not have a lot of high-paying alternatives). For others, the opportunity cost of selling burgers is of moderate value, and for still others—like rock stars and professional athletes—it is prohibitively high. Because of these differences among people in the opportunity cost of selling hamburgers, the daily supply curve of hamburgers will be *upward-sloping* with respect to the price of hamburgers. As an illustration, see Figure 4.1, which shows a hypothetical supply curve for the hamburger market in the New York

supply curve a curve or schedule showing the total quantity of a good that sellers wish to sell at each price

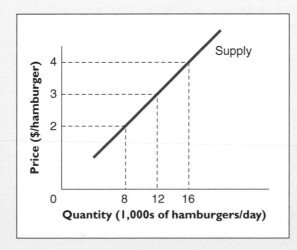

FIGURE 4.1
The Daily Supply Curve of Hamburgers in Greenwich Village.
At higher prices, sellers generally offer more units for sale.

City neighborhood of Greenwich Village on a given day. (Although economists usually refer to demand and supply "curves," we often draw them as straight lines in examples.)

Why is the supply curve for hamburgers upward-sloping? When the price of hamburgers is low—say, $2 per hamburger—only those people whose opportunity cost of selling hamburgers is less than or equal to that amount will offer hamburgers for sale. For the supply curve shown in Figure 4.1, the quantity supplied at a price of $2 will be 8,000 hamburgers per day. In that example, 8,000 hamburgers is the total quantity of hamburgers offered for sale by people whose opportunity cost of selling hamburgers is $2 per hamburger or less. If the price of hamburger were to rise above $2, however, additional sellers would find it worthwhile to offer hamburgers for sale. For example, at a price of $3, Figure 4.1 shows that the quantity of hamburgers supplied is 12,000 per day, while at a price of $4, the quantity supplied is 16,000. The higher the price, the more people find it worthwhile to supply hamburgers.

The fact that the supply curve slopes upward may be seen as a consequence of the low-hanging-fruit principle, discussed in Chapter 3. This principle tells us that as we expand the production of hamburgers, we turn first to those whose opportunity costs of producing hamburgers are lowest and only then to others with higher opportunity costs.

Stated another way, the fact that the supply curve for a good is upward-sloping reflects the fact that the marginal cost of producing the good rises as we produce more of it. If sellers are currently supplying 12,000 hamburgers a day in Figure 4.1, for example, the opportunity cost of the last hamburger produced (including the cost of meat, bun, etc., as well as the value of the supplier's time) must be $3. (If sellers could produce a 12,001st hamburger for less than that, they would have an incentive to supply it, since they can sell it for $3, which is more than it cost them to produce it. And if the cost of producing the 12,000th hamburger were greater than $3, it would not have been offered for sale at that price.) By similar reasoning, when the total quantity of hamburgers is 16,000, the opportunity cost of producing another hamburger must be $4.

THE DEMAND CURVE

demand curve a curve or schedule showing the total quantity of a good that buyers wish to buy at each price

The supply curve, by itself, does not tell us how many hamburgers will be sold in Greenwich Village on a given day, or at what price those hamburgers will sell. To find the prevailing price and quantity, we also need the demand curve for hamburgers in this market. The **demand curve** is a graph that tells us the total quantity of hamburgers that buyers wish to buy at various prices.

A fundamental property of the demand curve for a good is that it is downward-sloping with respect to price of that good. For example, the demand curve for hamburgers tells us that the higher the price of hamburgers becomes, the fewer hamburgers buyers as a whole will wish to buy. Thus the daily demand curve for hamburgers in Greenwich Village might look like the curve shown in Figure 4.2.

The demand curve in Figure 4.2 tells us that when the price of hamburgers is low—say, $2 per hamburger—buyers will want to buy 16,000 hamburgers per day, whereas they will want to buy only 12,000 at a price of $3 and only 8,000 at a price of $4. The demand curve for hamburgers—as for any other good— slopes downward for two reasons. First, as hamburgers become more expensive, some people switch to chicken sandwiches, pizza, and other foods that substitute for hamburgers. And second, people simply can't afford to buy as many hamburgers at higher prices as at lower prices.

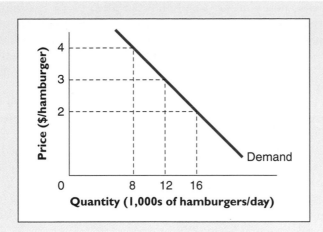

FIGURE 4.2
The Daily Demand Curve for Hamburgers in Greenwich Village.
The demand curve for any good is a downward-sloping function of its price.

MARKET EQUILIBRIUM

The concept of **equilibrium** is employed in both the physical and social sciences and is of central importance in economic analysis. In general, a system is in equilibrium when all forces at work within the system are canceled by others, resulting in a stable, balanced, or unchanging situation. In physics, for example, a ball hanging from a spring is said to be in equilibrium when the spring has stretched sufficiently that the upward force it exerts on the ball is exactly counterbalanced by the downward force of gravity. In economics, a market is said to be in equilibrium when no participant in the market has any reason to alter his or her behavior so that there is no tendency for production or prices in that market to change.

equilibrium a stable, balanced, or unchanging situation in which all forces at work within a system are canceled by others

If we want to determine the final position of a ball hanging from a spring, we need to find the point at which the forces of gravity and spring tension are balanced and the system is in equilibrium. Similarly, if we want to find the price at which a good will sell (which we will call the **equilibrium price**) and the quantity of it that will be sold (the **equilibrium quantity**), we need to find the equilibrium in the market for that good. The basic tools for finding the equilibrium in a market for some good are the supply and demand curves for that good. For reasons that we will explain, the equilibrium price and equilibrium quantity of a good are the price and quantity at which the supply and demand curves for the good intersect. For the hypothetical supply and demand curves for hamburgers in Greenwich Village, the equilibrium price will therefore be $3 per hamburger, and the equilibrium quantity of hamburgers sold will be 12,000 per day, as shown in Figure 4.3.

equilibrium price and equilibrium quantity the price and quantity of a good at the intersection of the supply and demand curves for the good

FIGURE 4.3
The Equilibrium Price and Quantity of Hamburgers in Greenwich Village.
The equilibrium quantity and price of a product are the values that correspond to the intersection of the supply and demand curves for that product.

In Figure 4.3, note that at the equilibrium price of $3 per hamburger, both sellers and buyers are "satisfied" in the following sense: Buyers are buying exactly the quantity of hamburgers they wish to buy at that price (12,000 per day), and sellers are selling exactly the quantity of hamburgers they wish to sell (also 12,000 per day). And since they are satisfied in this sense, neither buyers nor sellers face any incentives to change their behavior.

market equilibrium occurs when all buyers and sellers are satisfied with their respective quantities at the market price

Note the limited sense of the term *satisfied* in the definition of **market equilibrium.** It doesn't mean that sellers would not be pleased to receive a price higher than the equilibrium price. Rather, it means only that they're able to sell all they wish to sell at that price. Similarly, to say that buyers are satisfied at the equilibrium price doesn't mean that they would not be happy to pay less than the equilibrium price. Rather, it means only that they're able to buy exactly as many units of the good as they wish to at the equilibrium price.

Note also that if the price of hamburgers in our Greenwich Village market were anything other than $3, either buyers or sellers would not be satisfied. Suppose, for example, that the price of hamburgers were $4, as shown in Figure 4.4. At that price, buyers wish to buy only 8,000 hamburgers per day, but sellers wish

FIGURE 4.4
Excess Supply.
When price exceeds the equilibrium price, there is excess supply, or surplus, the difference between quantity supplied and quantity demanded.

to sell 16,000. And since no one can force someone to buy a hamburger against his or her wishes, this means that buyers will buy only the 8,000 hamburgers they wish to buy. So when the price exceeds the equilibrium price, it is sellers who end up being dissatisfied. At a price of $4 in this example, they are left with an **excess supply, or surplus,** of 8,000 hamburgers per day. (Note that the term *surplus* has a different meaning when used to denote excess supply than when used to denote economic surplus.)

excess supply, or surplus the difference between the quantity supplied and the quantity demanded when the price of a good exceeds the equilibrium price; sellers are dissatisfied when there is excess supply

Conversely, suppose that the price of hamburgers in our Greenwich Village market were less than the equilibrium price, say, $2 per hamburger. As shown in Figure 4.5, buyers want to buy 16,000 hamburgers per day at that price, whereas sellers want to sell only 8,000. And since sellers cannot be forced to sell hamburgers against their wishes, this time it is the buyers who end up being dissatisfied. At a price of $2 in this example, they experience an **excess demand, or shortage,** of 8,000 hamburgers per day.

excess demand, or shortage the difference between the quantity supplied and the quantity demanded when the price of a good lies below the equilibrium price; buyers are dissatisfied when there is excess demand

An extraordinary feature of private markets for goods and services is their automatic tendency to gravitate toward their respective equilibrium prices and quantities. The mechanisms by which this happens are implicit in our definitions of excess supply and excess demand. Suppose, for example, that the price of hamburgers in our hypothetical market was $4, leading to excess supply as shown in Figure 4.4. Because sellers are dissatisfied in the sense of wanting to sell more

FIGURE 4.5
Excess Demand.
When price lies below the equilibrium price, there is excess demand, the difference between quantity demanded and quantity supplied.

hamburgers than buyers wish to buy, sellers have an incentive to take whatever steps they can to increase their sales. The simplest strategy available to them is to cut their price slightly. Thus, if one seller reduced his price from $4 to, say, $3.95 per hamburger, he would attract many of the buyers who had been paying $4 for hamburgers supplied by other sellers. Those sellers, to recover their lost business, would then have an incentive to match the price cut. But notice that if all sellers lowered their prices to $3.95, there would still be considerable excess supply in the hamburger market. So sellers would face continuing incentives to cut their prices. This pressure to cut prices will not go away until the price falls all the way to $3.

Conversely, suppose that price starts out less than the equilibrium price, say, $2 per hamburger. This time it is buyers who are dissatisfied. A person who can't get all the hamburgers she wants at a price of $2 has an incentive to offer a higher price, hoping to obtain hamburgers that would otherwise have been sold to other buyers. And sellers, for their part, will be only too happy to post higher prices as long as queues of dissatisfied buyers remain.

The upshot is that price has a tendency to gravitate to its equilibrium level under conditions of either excess supply or excess demand. And when price reaches its equilibrium level, both buyers and sellers are satisfied in the technical sense of being able to buy or sell precisely the amounts they choose.

We emphasize that the mere fact that buyers and sellers are satisfied in this sense does not mean that private markets automatically result in the best of all possible worlds. For example, a poor person may be satisfied with the one hamburger he chooses to buy each day at a price of $3, but only in the sense that he *can't* buy a second hamburger without sacrificing other urgent purchases.

Social reformers often fail to understand, however, that the laws of supply and demand cannot simply be repealed by an act of the legislature. And when legislators attempt to prevent markets from reaching their equilibrium prices and quantities, they almost always do more harm than good.

RENT CONTROLS RECONSIDERED

Consider again the market for rental housing units in New York City, and suppose that the demand and supply curves for one-bedroom apartments are as shown in Figure 4.6. This market, left alone, would reach an equilibrium monthly rent of $800, at which 2 million one-bedroom apartments would be rented. Both landlords and tenants would be satisfied, in the sense that they would not wish to rent either more or fewer units at that price.

FIGURE 4.6

An Unregulated Housing Market.

For the supply and demand curves shown, the equilibrium monthly rent is $800, and 2 million apartments will be rented at that price.

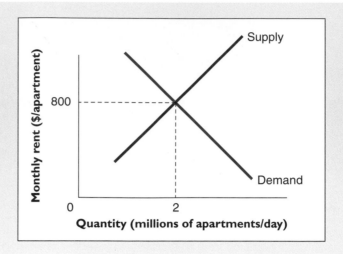

This would not necessarily mean, of course, that all is well and good. Many potential tenants, for example, might simply be unable to afford a rent of $800 per month and thus be forced to remain homeless (or to move out of the city to a cheaper location). Suppose that, acting purely out of benign motives, legislators make it unlawful for landlords to charge more than $400 per month for one-bedroom apartments. Their stated aim in enacting this law was that no person should have to remain homeless because decent housing was unaffordable.

But note in Figure 4.7 that when rents for one-bedroom apartments are prevented from rising above $400 per month, landlords are willing to supply only 1 million apartments per month, 1 million less than at the equilibrium monthly rent of $800. Note also that at the controlled rent of $400 per month, tenants want to rent 3 million one-bedroom apartments per month. (For example, many people who would have decided to live in New Jersey rather than pay $800 a month in New York will now choose to live in the city.) So when rents are prevented from rising above $400 per month, we see an excess demand for one-bedroom apartments of 2 million units each month. Put another way, the rent controls result in a housing shortage of 2 million units each month. What is more, the number of apartments actually available *declines* by 1 million units per month.

If the housing market were completely unregulated, the immediate response to such a high level of excess demand would be for rents to rise sharply. But here the law prevents them from rising above $400. Many other ways exist, however,

FIGURE 4.7

Rent Controls.

When laws prohibit rents from rising to the equilibrium level, the result is excess demand in the housing market.

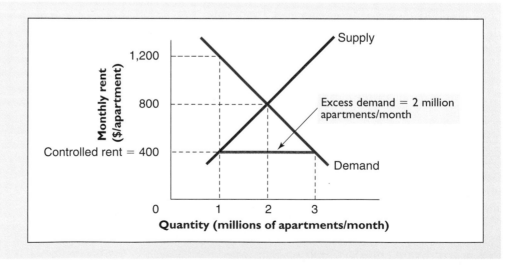

in which the pressures of excess demand can make themselves felt. For instance, owners will quickly learn that they are free to spend less on maintaining the quality of their rental units. After all, if there are scores of renters knocking at the door of each vacant apartment, a landlord has considerable room to maneuver. Leaking pipes, peeling paint, broken furnaces, and other problems are less likely to receive prompt attention—or, indeed, any attention at all—when rents are set well below market-clearing levels.

Nor are reduced availability of apartments and poorer maintenance of existing apartments the only difficulties. With an offering of only 1 million apartments per month, we see in Figure 4.7 that there are renters who would be willing to pay as much as $1,200 per month for an apartment. This pressure almost always finds ways, legal or illegal, of expressing itself. In New York City, for example, it is not uncommon to see "finder's fees" or "key deposits" as high as several thousand dollars. Owners who cannot charge a market-clearing rent for their apartments also have the option of converting them to condominiums or co-ops, which enables them to sell their assets for prices much closer to their true economic value.

Even when rent-controlled apartment owners do not hike their prices in these various ways, serious misallocations result. For instance, ill-suited roommates often remain together despite their constant bickering, because each is reluctant to reenter the housing market. Or a widow might steadfastly remain in her seven-room apartment even after her children have left home, because it is much cheaper than alternative dwellings not covered by rent control. It would be much better for all concerned if she relinquished that space to a larger family. But under rent controls, she has no economic incentive to do so.

Rent controls are not the only instance in which governments have attempted to repeal the law of supply and demand in the interest of helping the poor. During the late 1970s, for example, the federal government tried to

"If you leave me, you know, you'll never see this kind of rent again."

hold the price of gasoline below its equilibrium level out of concern that high gasoline prices imposed unacceptable hardships on low-income drivers. As with controls in the rental housing market, unintended consequences of price controls in the gasoline market made the policy an extremely costly way of trying to aid the poor. For example, gasoline shortages resulted in long lines at the pumps, a waste not only of valuable time but also of gasoline as cars sat idling for extended periods.

In their opposition to rent controls and similar measures, are economists revealing a total lack of concern for the poor? Although this claim is sometimes made by those who don't understand the issues, or who stand to benefit in some way from government regulations, there is little justification for it. *Economists simply realize that there are much more effective ways to help poor people than to give them apartments and other goods at artificially low prices.*

One straightforward approach would be to give the poor additional income and let them decide for themselves how to spend it. True, there are also practical difficulties involved in transferring additional purchasing power into the hands of the poor—most important, the difficulty of targeting cash to the genuinely needy without weakening others' incentives to fend for themselves. But there are practical ways to overcome this difficulty. For example, for far less than the waste caused by price controls, the government could afford generous subsidies to the wages of the working poor and could sponsor a generous program of public-service employment for those who are unable to find jobs in the private sector.

Regulations that peg prices below equilibrium levels have far-reaching effects on market outcomes. The following exercise asks you to consider what happens when a price control is established at a level above the equilibrium price.

EXERCISE 4.1

In the rental housing market whose demand and supply curves are shown below, what will be the effect of a law that prevents rents from rising above $1,200 per month?

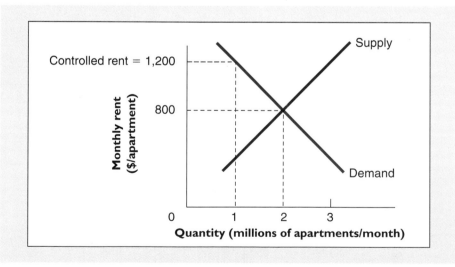

HAMBURGER PRICE CONTROLS?

The sources of the contrast between the rent-controlled housing market and the largely unregulated food markets in New York City can be seen more vividly by trying to imagine what would happen if concern for the poor led the city's leaders to implement price controls on hamburgers. Suppose, for example, that the supply and demand curves for hamburger are as shown in Figure 4.8 and that the city imposes a **price ceiling** of $2 per hamburger, making it unlawful to charge more than $2 for a hamburger. At that price, buyers want to buy 16,000 hamburgers per day, but sellers want to sell only 8,000.

price ceiling a maximum allowable price, specified by law

At a price of $2 per hamburger, every Burger King, every McDonald's, and every other fast-food restaurant in the city will have long queues of buyers trying unsuccessfully to buy hamburgers. Frustrated buyers will behave rudely to clerks, who will respond in kind. Friends of restaurant managers will begin to

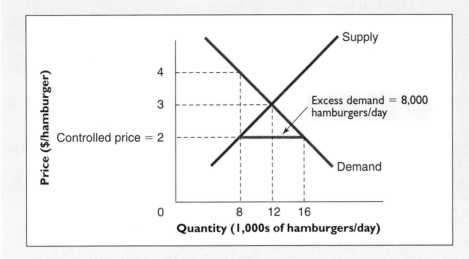

FIGURE 4.8
Price Controls in the Hamburger Market.
A price ceiling below the equilibrium price of hamburgers would result in excess demand for hamburgers.

get preferential treatment. Devious pricing strategies will begin to emerge (such as the $2 hamburger sold in combination with a $2 slice of pickle). Hamburgers will be made from poorer-quality ingredients. Rumors will begin to circulate about sources of black market hamburgers. And so on.

The very idea of not being able to buy a hamburger seems absurd, yet precisely such things happen routinely in markets in which prices are held below the equilibrium levels. For example, in communist countries (prior to their collapse) it was considered normal for people to stand in line for hours to buy basic goods, while the politically connected had first choice of those goods that were available.

RECAP **MARKETS AND PRICES**

The *market* for a good consists of the actual and potential buyers and sellers of that good. For any given price, the *supply curve* shows the total quantity that suppliers of the good would be willing to sell, and the *demand curve* shows the total quantity that demanders would be willing to buy. Suppliers are willing to sell more at higher prices (supply curves slope upward) and demanders are willing to buy less at higher prices (demand curves slope downward).

Market equilibrium, the situation in which all buyers and sellers are satisfied with their respective quantities at the market price, occurs at the intersection of the supply and demand curves. The corresponding price and quantity are called the *equilibrium price* and the *equilibrium quantity*.

Unless prevented by regulation, prices and quantities are driven toward their equilibrium values by the actions of buyers and sellers. If the price is initially too high, resulting in excess supply, dissatisfied sellers will cut their price to sell more. If the price is initially too low, resulting in excess demand, competition among buyers drives the price upward. This process continues until equilibrium is reached.

MARKETS AND SOCIAL WELFARE

Markets represent a highly effective system of allocating resources. When a market for a good is in equilibrium, the equilibrium price conveys important information to potential suppliers about the value that potential demanders place on that good. At the same time, the equilibrium price informs potential demanders about the opportunity cost of supplying the good. This rapid, two-way transmission of information is the reason that markets can coordinate an activity as complex as supplying New York City with food and drink, even though no one person or organization oversees the process.

But are the prices and quantities determined in market equilibrium socially optimal in the sense of maximizing total economic surplus? That is, does equilibrium in unregulated markets always maximize the difference between the total benefits and total costs experienced by market participants? As we see in this section, the answer is "it depends": A market that is out of equilibrium, such as the rent-controlled New York housing market, always creates opportunities for individuals to arrange transactions that will increase their individual economic surplus. However, a market for a good that is in equilibrium maximizes total, societywide economic surplus only when the supply and demand curves in the market fully reflect the costs and benefits associated with the production and consumption of that good.

CASH ON THE TABLE

When a regulation prevents the price of a good from reaching its equilibrium level, it unnecessarily reduces the total economic surplus (economic benefit less opportunity cost) available for buyers and sellers. For example, the demand curve in Figure 4.8 tells us that, with only 8,000 hamburgers being sold, there are buyers who are willing to pay $4 for additional hamburgers. The supply curve, in turn, tells us that the cost of producing additional hamburgers is only $2. The difference— $2 per hamburger—is the additional economic surplus that would result if an additional hamburger were produced and sold. One sold at a price of $3, for example, would result in an additional $1 of economic surplus for both buyer and seller.

When a market is out of equilibrium, it is always possible to identify mutually beneficial exchanges. When people have failed to take advantage of all mutually beneficial exchanges, we often say that there is "cash on the table"—the economist's metaphor for unexploited opportunities. When the price in a market is below the equilibrium price, there is cash on the table, because it will always be possible for a supplier to produce an additional unit at a cost that is lower than buyers are willing to pay for it. In the absence of a law preventing buyers from paying more than $2 per hamburger, restaurant owners would quickly raise their prices and expand their production until the equilibrium price of $3 per hamburger was reached. At that price, buyers would be able to get precisely the 12,000 hamburgers they want to buy each day. All mutually beneficial opportunities for exchange would have been exploited, leaving no more cash on the table.

Buyers and sellers in the marketplace have an uncanny ability to detect the presence of cash on the table. It is almost as if unexploited opportunities give off some exotic scent that sets off neurochemical explosions in the olfactory centers of their brains. The desire to scrape cash off the table and into their pockets is what drives sellers in each of New York City's thousands of individual food markets to work diligently to meet their customers' demands. That they succeed to a far higher degree than participants in the city's rent-controlled housing market is plainly evident. Whatever flaws it might have, the market system moves with considerably greater speed and agility than any centralized allocation mechanisms yet devised. But as we emphasize in the following section, this does not mean that markets *always* lead to the greatest good for all.

SMART FOR ONE, DUMB FOR ALL

The **efficient quantity** of any good is the quantity that maximizes the total economic surplus that results from producing and consuming the good. From the cost-benefit principle, we know that we should keep expanding production of the good as long as its marginal benefit is at least as great as its marginal cost. This means that the efficient quantity is that level for which the marginal cost and marginal benefit of the good are the same.

When the quantity of a good is less than the efficient quantity, a rearrangement boosting its production will increase total economic surplus. By the same token, when the quantity of a good exceeds the efficient quantity, reducing its production will increase total economic surplus. **Economic efficiency, or efficiency,** occurs when all goods and services in the economy are produced and consumed at levels that produce the maximum economic surplus for society.

Efficiency is an important social goal. Failure to achieve efficiency means that total economic surplus is smaller than it could have been. Movements toward efficiency make the total economic pie larger, making it possible for everyone to have a larger slice. The importance of efficiency will be a recurring theme as we move forward, and we state it here as one of the core principles:

The Efficiency Principle: Efficiency is an important social goal, because when the economic pie grows larger, everyone can have a larger slice.

Is the market equilibrium quantity of a good efficient? That is, does it maximize the total economic surplus received by participants in the market for that good? When the private market for a given good is in equilibrium, we can say that the cost *to the seller* of producing an additional unit of the good is the same as the benefit *to the buyer* of having an additional unit. If all costs of producing the good are borne directly by sellers, and if all benefits from the good accrue directly to buyers, it follows that the market equilibrium quantity of the good will equate the marginal cost and marginal benefit of the good. And this implies that the equilibrium quantity also maximizes total economic surplus.

But sometimes the production of a good entails costs that fall on people other than those who sell the good. This will be true, for instance, for goods whose production generates significant levels of environmental pollution. As extra units of these goods are produced, the extra pollution harms other people besides sellers. In the market equilibrium for such goods, the benefit *to buyers* of the last good produced is, as before, equal to the cost incurred by sellers to produce that good. But since producing that good also imposed pollution costs on others, we know that the *full* marginal cost of the last unit produced—the seller's private marginal cost plus the marginal pollution cost borne by others—must be higher than the benefit of the last unit produced. So in this case the market equilibrium quantity of the good will be higher than the socially optimal quantity. Total economic surplus would be higher if output of the good were lower. Yet neither sellers nor buyers have any incentive to alter their behavior.

Another possibility is that people other than those who buy the good may receive significant benefits from it. For instance, when a beekeeper adds an additional hive to his apiary, his neighbor's apple orchard yields a larger crop because of the higher levels of pollination caused by the bees from the extra hive. From the perspective of society as a whole, the best thing to do would be to keep adding hives until their marginal cost became equal to their marginal benefit. The marginal benefit of a hive is the value of the extra honey *plus* the value of the extra apples. Private beekeepers, however, will keep adding hives only up to the point that the cost of an extra hive is equal to the revenue from the extra honey. In this case, then, the market equilibrium quantity of beehives will be smaller than the quantity that maximizes total economic surplus. Yet individual beekeepers and individual consumers of honey have no incentive to alter their behavior.

efficient quantity the efficient quantity of a good is the quantity that results in the maximum possible economic surplus from producing and consuming the good

efficiency, or economic efficiency condition that occurs when all goods and services are produced and consumed at their respective socially optimal levels

Situations like the ones just discussed provide examples of behaviors that we may call "smart for one but dumb for all." In each case, the individual actors are behaving rationally. They are pursuing their goals as best they can, and yet there remain unexploited opportunities for gain from the point of view of the whole society. The difficulty is that these opportunities cannot be exploited by individuals acting alone. In subsequent chapters we will see how people can often organize collectively to exploit such opportunities. For now, we simply summarize this discussion in the form of the following core principle:

The Equilibrium Principle: A market in equilibrium leaves no unexploited opportunities for individuals but may not exploit all gains achievable through collective action.

For the remainder of this chapter, we will confine our attention to markets in which the supply and demand curves capture all relevant costs and benefits. Our focus will be on using supply and demand analysis to predict and explain changes in equilibrium prices and quantities.

RECAP   **MARKETS AND SOCIAL WELFARE**

When the supply and demand curves for a good reflect all significant costs and benefits associated with the production and consumption of that good, the market equilibrium will result in the largest possible economic surplus. But if people other than buyers benefit from the good, or if people other than sellers bear costs because of it, rational behavior on the part of individuals need not maximize economic surplus.

PREDICTING AND EXPLAINING CHANGES IN PRICES AND QUANTITIES

If we know how the factors that govern supply and demand curves are changing, we can make informed predictions about how prices and the corresponding quantities will change. But when describing changing circumstances in the marketplace, we must take care to recognize some important terminological distinctions. For example, we must distinguish between the meanings of the seemingly similar expressions **change in the quantity demanded** and **change in demand.** When we speak of a "change in the quantity demanded," we mean the change in quantity that people wish to buy that occurs in response to a change in price. For instance, Figure 4.9(a) depicts an increase in the quantity demanded that occurs in response to a reduction in the price of tuna. When the price falls from $5 to $4 per can, the quantity demanded rises from 2,000 to 4,000 cans per day. By contrast, when we speak of a "change in demand," we mean a *shift in the entire demand curve.* For example, Figure 4.9(b) depicts an increase in demand, meaning that at every price the quantity demanded is higher than before. In summary, a change in the quantity demanded refers to a movement *along* the demand curve, and a change in demand means a *shift* of the entire curve.

A similar terminological distinction applies on the supply side of the market. A **change in supply** means a shift in the entire supply curve, whereas **a change in the quantity supplied** refers to a movement along the supply curve.

Alfred Marshall's supply and demand model is one of the most useful tools of the economic naturalist. Once we understand the forces that govern the placements of supply and demand curves, we are suddenly in a position to make sense of a host of interesting observations in the world around us.

change in the quantity demanded a movement along the demand curve that occurs in response to a change in price

change in demand a shift of the entire demand curve

change in supply a shift of the entire supply curve

change in the quantity supplied a movement along the supply curve that occurs in response to a change in price

Δ quantity demanded
— along curve

Δ demand
— shift curve

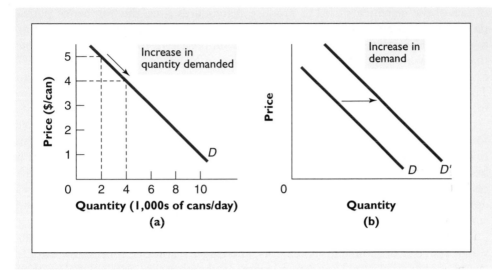

FIGURE 4.9
An Increase in the Quantity Demanded versus an Increase in Demand.
(a) An increase in quantity demanded describes a downward movement along the demand curve as price falls. (b) An increase in demand describes an outward shift of the demand curve.

SHIFTS IN THE SUPPLY CURVE

To get a better feel for how the supply and demand model enables us to predict and explain price and quantity movements, it is helpful to begin with a few simple examples. Because the supply curve is based on costs of production, anything that changes production costs will shift the supply curve and hence will result in a new equilibrium quantity and price.

What will happen to the equilibrium price and quantity of skateboards if the price of fiberglass, an ingredient for making skateboards, rises?

EXAMPLE 4.1

Suppose the initial supply and demand curves for skateboards are as shown by the curves S and D in Figure 4.10, resulting in an equilibrium price and quantity of $60 per skateboard and 1,000 skateboards per month, respectively. Since fiberglass is one of the ingredients used to produce skateboards, the effect of an increase in the price of fiberglass is to raise the cost of producing skateboards. How will this affect the supply curve of skateboards? Recall that the supply curve is upward-sloping because when the price of skateboards is low, only those potential sellers whose opportunity cost of making skateboards is low can sell boards profitably, whereas at higher prices, those with higher opportunity costs can also enter the market profitably (again, the low-hanging-fruit principle). So if the cost

FIGURE 4.10
The Effect on the Skateboard Market of an Increase in the Price of Fiberglass.
When input prices rise, supply shifts left, causing equilibrium price to rise and equilibrium quantity to fall.

of one of the ingredients used to produce skateboards rises, the number of potential sellers who can profitably sell skateboards at any given price will fall. And this, in turn, implies a leftward shift in the supply curve for skateboards. (Note that a "leftward shift" in a supply curve can also be viewed as an "upward shift" in the same curve. We will use these expressions to mean exactly the same thing.) The new supply curve (after the price of fiberglass rises) is the curve labeled S' in Figure 4.10.

Does an increase in the cost of fiberglass have any effect on the demand curve for skateboards? The demand curve tells us how many skateboards buyers wish to purchase at each price. Any given buyer is willing to purchase a skateboard if his or her reservation price for it exceeds its market price. And since each buyer's reservation price, which is based on the benefits of owning a skateboard, does not depend on the price of fiberglass, there should be no shift in the demand curve for skateboards.

In Figure 4.10, we can see what happens when the supply curve shifts leftward and the demand curve remains unchanged. For the illustrative supply curve shown, the new equilibrium price of skateboards, $80, is higher than the original price, and the new equilibrium quantity, 800 per month, is lower than the original quantity. (These new equilibrium values are merely illustrative. There is insufficient information provided in the example to determine their exact values.)

The effects on equilibrium price and quantity run in the opposite direction whenever marginal costs of production decline, as illustrated in the next example.

EXAMPLE 4.2

What will happen to the equilibrium price and quantity of new houses if the wage rate of carpenters falls?

Suppose the initial supply and demand curves for new houses are as shown by the curves S and D in Figure 4.11, resulting in an equilibrium price of $120,000 per house and an equilibrium quantity of 40 houses per month. A decline in the wage rate of carpenters reduces the marginal cost of making new houses, and this means that, for any given price of houses, more builders can profitably serve the market than before. Diagrammatically, this means a rightward shift in the supply curve of houses, from S to S'. (A "rightward shift" in the supply curve can also be described as a "downward shift.")

Does a decrease in the wage rate of carpenters have any effect on the demand curve for houses? The demand curve tells us how many houses buyers wish to purchase at each price. Because carpenters are now earning less than before,

FIGURE 4.11

The Effect on the Market for New Houses of a Decline in Carpenters' Wage Rates.
When input prices fall, supply shifts right, causing equilibrium price to fall and equilibrium quantity to rise.

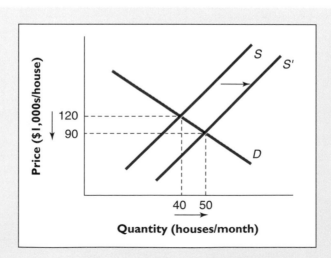

the maximum amount that they are willing to pay for houses may fall, which would imply a leftward shift in the demand curve for houses. But because carpenters make up only a tiny fraction of all potential home buyers, we may assume that this shift is insignificant. Thus, a reduction in carpenters' wages produces a significant rightward shift in the supply curve of houses, but only a negligible shift in the demand curve. We see from Figure 4.11 that the new equilibrium price, $90,000 per house, is lower than the original price, and the new equilibrium quantity, 50 houses per month, is higher than the original quantity.

Both Examples 4.1 and 4.2 involved changes in the cost of an ingredient, or input, in the production of the good in question—fiberglass in the production of skateboards and carpenters' labor in the production of houses. As the following example illustrates, supply curves also shift when technology changes.

Why do Ph.D. dissertations and book manuscripts go through so many more revisions today than in the 1970s?

Graduate students in the dark days before word processors were in widespread use could not make even minor revisions to their Ph.D. dissertations without having to retype their entire manuscripts from scratch. The availability of word-processing technology has, of course, radically changed the picture. Instead of having to retype the entire draft, now only the changes need be entered.

In Figure 4.12, the curves labeled *S* and *D* depict the supply and demand curves for revisions in the days before word processing, and the curve *S'* depicts the supply curve for revisions today. As the diagram shows, the result is not only a sharp decline in the price per revision but also a corresponding increase in the equilibrium number of revisions.

ECONOMIC NATURALIST 4.1

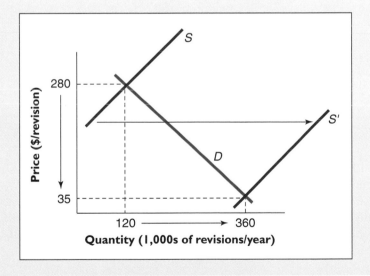

FIGURE 4.12
The Effect of Technical Change on the Market for Manuscript Revisions.
When a new technology reduces the cost of production, supply shifts right, causing equilibrium price to fall and equilibrium quantity to rise.

Changes in input prices and technology are two of the most important factors that give rise to shifts in supply curves. In the case of agricultural commodities, weather may be another important factor, with favorable conditions shifting the supply curves of such products to the right and unfavorable conditions shifting them to the left. (Weather may also affect the supply curves of nonagricultural products through its effects on the national transportation system.) Expectations of future changes in these factors may also shift current supply curves, as when the expectation of poor crops from a current drought causes suppliers to withhold supplies from existing stocks in the hope of selling at higher prices in the future.

SHIFTS IN DEMAND

The preceding examples involved changes that gave rise to shifts in supply curves. Next, we'll look at what happens when demand curves shift. In the following example, the shift in demand results from events outside the particular market itself.

EXAMPLE 4.3

What will happen to the equilibrium price and quantity of tennis balls if court rental fees decline?

Let the initial supply and demand curves for tennis balls be as shown by the curves S and D in Figure 4.13, where the resulting equilibrium price and quantity are $1 per ball and 40 million balls per month, respectively. Tennis courts and tennis balls are what economists call **complements**, goods that are more valuable when used in combination than when used alone. Tennis balls, for example, would be of little value if there were no tennis courts on which to play. (Tennis balls would still have *some* value even without courts—for example, to the parents who pitch them to their children for batting practice.) As tennis courts become cheaper to use, people will respond by playing more tennis, and this will increase their demand for tennis balls. A decline in court rental fees will thus shift

complements two goods are complements in consumption if an increase in the price of one causes a leftward shift in the demand curve for the other

FIGURE 4.13
The Effect on the Market for Tennis Balls of a Decline in Court Rental Fees.
When the price of a complement falls, demand shifts right, causing equilibrium price and quantity to rise.

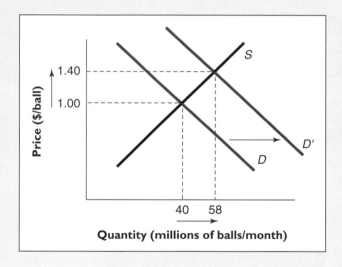

the demand curve for tennis balls rightward to D'. (A "rightward shift" of a demand curve can also be described as an "upward shift.")

Note in Figure 4.13 that for the illustrative demand shift shown, the new equilibrium price of tennis balls, $1.40, is higher than the original price, and the new equilibrium quantity, 58 million balls per month, is higher than the original quantity.

EXAMPLE 4.4

What will happen to the equilibrium price and quantity of overnight letter delivery service as more people gain access to the Internet?

Suppose that the initial supply and demand curves for overnight letter deliveries are as shown by the curves S and D in Figure 4.14 and that the resulting equilibrium price and quantity are denoted P and Q. E-mail messages and overnight letters are examples of what economists call **substitutes**, meaning that, in many applications at least, the two serve similar functions for people. (Many noneconomists would call them substitutes, too. Economists don't *always* choose obscure terms for important concepts!) When two goods or services are substitutes, a decrease in the effective price of one will cause a leftward shift in the demand curve for the other. (A "leftward shift" in a demand curve can also be described

substitutes two goods are substitutes in consumption if an increase in the price of one causes a rightward shift in the demand curve for the other as a "downward shift.") An increase in Internet access is, in effect, a decline in the price of a substitute for overnight delivery for affected users. Diagrammatically, this means a leftward shift in the demand curve for overnight delivery service to D' in Figure 4.14.

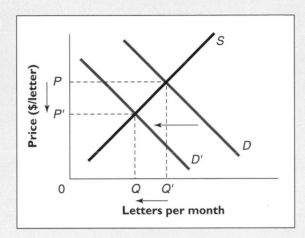

FIGURE 4.14
The Effect on the Market for Overnight Letter Delivery of a Decline in the Price of Internet Access.
When the price of a substitute falls, demand shifts left, causing equilibrium price and quantity to fall.

As the figure shows, both the new equilibrium price P' and the new equilibrium quantity Q' are lower than the initial values P and Q. More widespread Internet access probably won't put Federal Express and UPS out of business, but it will definitely cost them many customers.

To summarize, economists define goods as substitutes if an increase in the price of one causes a rightward shift in the demand curve for the other. By contrast, goods are complements if an increase in the price of one causes a leftward shift in the demand curve for the other.

The concepts of substitutes and complements enable you to answer questions like the one posed in the following exercise.

EXERCISE 4.2

How will a decline in airfares affect bus fares and the price of hotel rooms in resort communities?

Demand curves are shifted not just by changes in the prices of substitutes and complements but also by other factors that change the amounts that people are willing to pay for a given good or service. One of the most important such factors is income.

When the federal government implements a large pay increase for government employees, why do rents for apartments located near Washington Metro Stations go up relative to rents for apartments located far away from Metro Stations?

For the citizens of Washington, D.C., a substantial proportion of whom are government employees, it is more convenient to live in an apartment located 1 block from the nearest subway station than to live in one that is 10 blocks away. These conveniently located apartments thus command relatively high rents. Suppose the initial demand and supply curves for such apartments are as shown in Figure 4.15. Following a federal pay raise, some government employees who live in less convenient apartments will be willing and able to use part of their extra income to bid for more conveniently located apartments, and those who already live in such apartments will be willing and able to pay more to keep them. The effect of the pay raise

ECONOMIC NATURALIST 4.2

FIGURE 4.15

The Effect of a Federal Pay Raise on the Rent for Conveniently Located Apartments in Washington, D.C.

An increase in income shifts demand for a normal good to the right, causing equilibrium price and quantity to rise.

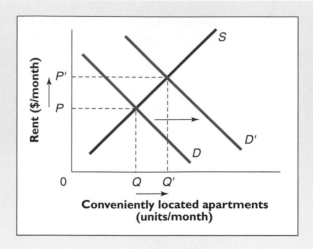

is thus to shift the demand curve for conveniently located apartments to the right, as indicated by the demand curve labeled D' in Figure 4.15. As a result, both the equilibrium price and quantity of such apartments, P' and Q', will be higher than before.

It might seem natural to ask how there could be an increase in the number of conveniently located apartments, which might appear to be fixed by the constraints of geography. But one must never underestimate the ingenuity of sellers when they confront an opportunity to make money by supplying more of something that people want. For example, if rents rose sufficiently, some landlords might respond by converting warehouse space to residential use. Or perhaps people with cars and no pressing need to live near a subway station might sell their apartments to landlords, thereby freeing them up for people eager to rent them.

When incomes increase, the demand curves for most goods will behave like the demand curve for conveniently located apartments, and in recognition of that fact, economists have chosen to call such goods **normal goods.**

Nor all goods are normal goods, however. In fact, the demand curves for some goods actually shift leftward when income goes up, and such goods are called **inferior goods.**

When would having more money tend to make you want to buy less of something? In general, this will happen in the case of goods for which there exist attractive substitutes that sell for only slightly higher prices. Apartments in an unsafe, inconveniently located neighborhood are an example. Most residents would choose to move out of such neighborhoods as soon as they could afford to, which means that an increase in income would cause the demand for such apartments to shift leftward.

Ground beef with high fat content is another example of an inferior good. For health reasons, most people prefer grades of meat with low fat content, and when they do buy high-fat meats it is usually a sign of budgetary pressure. When people in this situation receive higher incomes, they usually switch quickly to leaner grades of meat.

normal good a good whose demand curve shifts rightward when the incomes of buyers increase

inferior good a good whose demand curve shifts leftward when the incomes of buyers increase

EXERCISE 4.3

Normal and inferior goods were defined in terms of how their demand curves were affected by an increase in income. How will a *decrease* in income affect the demand for a normal good? An inferior good?

Preferences, or tastes, are another important factor that determines whether a given good will meet the cost-benefit test. Steven Spielberg's films *Jurassic Park* and *The Lost World* appeared to kindle a powerful, if previously latent, preference among children for toy dinosaurs. In the wake of these films, the demand for such toys shifted sharply to the right. And the same children who couldn't find enough dinosaur toys suddenly seemed to lose interest in toy designs involving horses and other present-day animals, whose respective demand curves shifted sharply to the left.

FOUR SIMPLE RULES

For supply and demand curves that have the conventional slopes (upward-sloping for supply curves, downward-sloping for demand curves), the preceding examples illustrate the four basic rules that govern how shifts in supply and demand affect equilibrium prices and quantities. These rules are summarized in Figure 4.16.

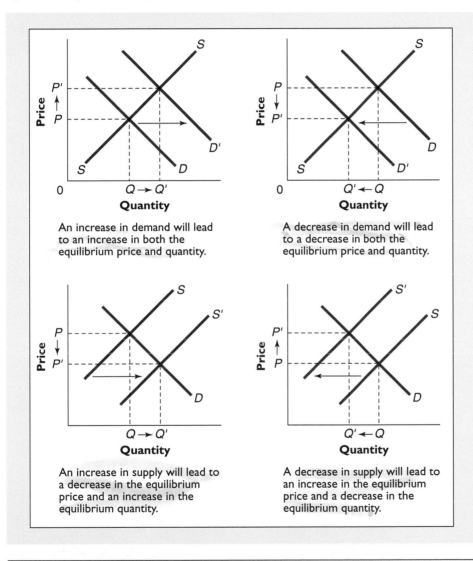

FIGURE 4.16
Four Rules Governing the Effects of Supply and Demand Shifts.

RECAP   **FACTORS CAUSING AN INCREASE IN SUPPLY (SUPPLY CURVE SHIFTS RIGHT)**

1. A decrease in the cost of materials, labor, or other inputs used in the production of the good or service
2. An improvement in technology that reduces the cost of producing the good or service

When these factors move in the opposite direction, supply will shift left.

> **RECAP**   **FACTORS CAUSING AN INCREASE IN DEMAND (DEMAND CURVE SHIFTS RIGHT)**
>
> 1. A decrease in the price of complements to the good or service
> 2. An increase in the price of substitutes for the good or service
> 3. An increase in income (for a normal good)
> 4. An increased preference by demanders for the good or service
> 5. An increase in the population of potential buyers
>
> When these factors move in the opposite direction, demand will shift left.

The qualitative rules summarized in Figure 4.16 hold for supply or demand shifts of any magnitude, provided the curves have their conventional slopes. But as the next example demonstrates, when both supply and demand curves shift at the same time, the direction in which equilibrium price or quantity changes will depend on the relative magnitudes of the shifts.

EXAMPLE 4.5

How do shifts in *both* demand and supply affect equilibrium quantities and prices?

What will happen to the equilibrium price and quantity in the corn tortilla chip market if both the following events occur: (1) researchers discover that the oils in which tortilla chips are fried are harmful to human health, and (2) the price of corn harvesting equipment falls?

The discovery regarding the health effects of the oils will shift the demand for tortilla chips to the left, because many people who once bought chips in the belief that they were healthful will now switch to other foods. The decline in the price of harvesting equipment will shift the supply of chips to the right, because additional farmers will now find it profitable to enter the corn market. In Figure 4.17(a) and (b), the original supply and demand curves are denoted by *S* and *D*, while the new curves are denoted by *S'* and *D'*. Note that in both parts, the shifts lead to a decline in the equilibrium price of chips.

But note also that the effect of the shifts on equilibrium quantity cannot be determined without knowing their relative magnitudes. Taken separately, the demand shift causes a decline in equilibrium quantity, whereas the supply shift causes an increase in equilibrium quantity. The net effect of the two shifts thus depends on which of the individual effects is larger. In Figure 4.17(a), the demand shift dominates, so equilibrium quantity declines. In Figure 4.17(b), the supply shift dominates, so equilibrium quantity goes up.

FIGURE 4.17
The Effects of Simultaneous Shifts in Supply and Demand.
When demand shifts left and supply shifts right, equilibrium price falls, but equilibrium quantity may either rise [part (b)] or fall [part (a)].

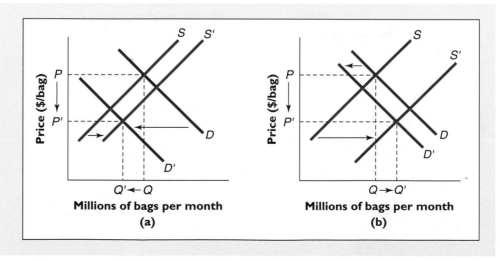

Millions of bags per month
(a)

Millions of bags per month
(b)

The following exercise asks you to consider a simple variation on the problem posed in Example 4.5.

EXERCISE 4.4

What will happen to the equilibrium price and quantity in the corn tortilla chip market if both the following events occur: (1) researchers discover that a vitamin found in corn helps protect against cancer and heart disease; and (2) a swarm of locusts destroys part of the corn crop?

Why do the prices of some goods, like airline tickets to Europe, go up during the months of heaviest consumption, while others, like sweet corn, go down?

Seasonal price movements for airline tickets are primarily the result of seasonal variations in demand. Thus, ticket prices to Europe are highest during the summer months because the demand for tickets is highest during those months, as shown in Figure 4.18(a) (where the w and s subscripts denote winter and summer values, respectively).

By contrast, seasonal price movements for sweet corn are primarily the result of seasonal variations in supply. The price of sweet corn is lowest in the summer months because its supply is highest during those months [Figure 4.18(b)].

ECONOMIC NATURALIST 4.3

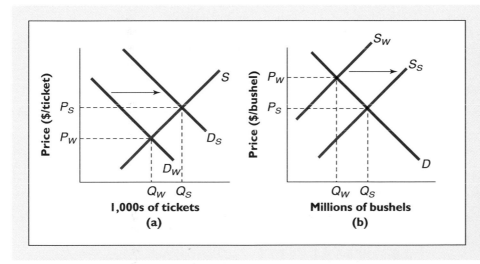

1,000s of tickets
(a)

Millions of bushels
(b)

FIGURE 4.18
Seasonal Variation in the Air Travel and Corn Markets.
(a) Prices are highest during the period of heaviest consumption when heavy consumption is the result of high demand. (b) Prices are lowest during the period of heaviest consumption when heavy consumption is the result of high supply.

■ SUMMARY ■

- Eighteenth-century economists tried to explain differences in the prices of goods by focusing on differences in their cost of production. But this approach cannot explain why a conveniently located house sells for more than one that is less conveniently located. Early nineteenth-century economists tried to explain price differences by focusing on differences in what buyers were willing to pay. But this approach cannot explain why the price of a lifesaving appendectomy is less than that of a surgical facelift.

- Alfred Marshall's model of supply and demand explains why neither cost of production nor value to the purchaser (as measured by willingness to pay) is, by itself, sufficient to

explain why some goods are cheap and others are expensive. To explain variations in price, we must examine the interaction of cost and willingness to pay. As we saw in this chapter, goods differ in price because of differences in their respective supply and demand curves.

- The supply curve is an upward-sloping line that tells what quantity sellers will offer at any given price. The demand curve is a downward-sloping line that tells what quantity buyers will demand at any given price. Market equilibrium occurs when the quantity buyers demand at the market price is exactly the same as the quantity that sellers offer. The equilibrium price-quantity pair is the one at which the demand and supply curves intersect. In equilibrium, market price measures both the value of the last unit sold to buyers and the cost of the resources required to produce it.

• When the price of a good lies above its equilibrium value, there is an excess supply, or surplus, of that good. Excess supply motivates sellers to cut their prices, and price continues to fall until the equilibrium price is reached. When price lies below its equilibrium value, there is excess demand, or shortage. With excess demand, dissatisfied buyers are motivated to offer higher prices, and the upward pressure on prices persists until equilibrium is reached. A remarkable feature of the market system is that, relying only on the tendency of people to respond in self-interested ways to market price signals, it somehow manages to coordinate the actions of literally billions of buyers and sellers worldwide. When shortages and surpluses do occur, they tend to be small and brief, except in markets where regulations prevent full adjustment of prices.

• When the supply and demand curves for a good reflect all significant costs and benefits associated with the production and consumption of that good, the market equilibrium price will guide people to produce and consume the quantity of the good that results in the largest possible economic surplus. This conclusion does not apply if others, beside buyers, benefit from the good (as when orchard owners benefit from beehives), or if others besides sellers bear costs because of the good (as when its production generates pollution). In such cases, rational behavior on the part of individuals does not result in the greatest gain for all.

• The efficiency of markets in allocating resources does not eliminate social concerns about how goods and services are distributed among different people. For example, we often lament the fact many buyers enter the market with too little income to buy even the most basic goods and services. Concern for the well-being of the poor has motivated many governments to intervene in a variety of ways to alter the outcomes of market forces. Sometimes these interventions take the form of laws that peg prices below their equilibrium levels. Such laws almost invariably generate harmful, if unintended, consequences. Programs like rent-control laws, for example, lead to severe housing shortages, black marketeering, and a rapid deterioration of the relationship between landlords and tenants.

• If the difficulty is that the poor have too little money, the best solution is to discover ways of boosting their incomes directly. The law of supply and demand cannot be repealed by a legislature. But legislatures do have the capacity to alter the underlying forces that govern the shape and position of supply and demand schedules.

• The basic supply and demand model is a primary tool of the economic naturalist. Changes in the equilibrium price of a good, and in the amount of it traded in the marketplace, can be predicted on the basis of shifts in its supply or demand curves. The following four rules hold for any good with a downward-sloping demand curve and an upward-sloping supply curve:

1. An increase in demand will lead to an increase in equilibrium price and quantity.

2. A reduction in demand will lead to a reduction in equilibrium price and quantity.

3. An increase in supply will lead to a reduction in equilibrium price and an increase in equilibrium quantity.

4. A decrease in supply will lead to an increase in equilibrium price and a reduction in equilibrium quantity.

• Incomes, tastes, population, and the prices of substitutes and complements are among the factors that shift demand schedules. Supply schedules, in turn, are primarily governed by such factors as technology, input prices, and, for agricultural products, the weather.

■ CORE PRINCIPLES ■

The Efficiency Principle
Efficiency is an important social goal, because when the economic pie grows larger, everyone can have a larger slice.

The Equilibrium Principle
A market in equilibrium leaves no unexploited opportunities for individuals but may not exploit all gains achievable through collective action.

■ KEY TERMS ■

change in demand (88)   demand curve (78)   equilibrium price (79)
change in quantity demanded (88) economic efficiency (87)   equilibrium quantity (79)
change in quantity supplied (88) efficiency (87)   excess demand (80)
change in supply (88)   efficient quantity (87)   excess supply (80)
complements (92)   equilibrium (79)   inferior good (94)

market (76)   price ceiling (85)   supply curve (77)
market equilibrium (80)   shortage (80)   surplus (80)
normal good (94)   substitutes (92)

■ REVIEW QUESTIONS ■

1. Why isn't knowing how much it costs to produce a good sufficient to predict its market price?

2. Distinguish between the meaning of the expressions "change in demand" and "change in the quantity demanded."

3. Last year a government official proposed that gasoline price controls be imposed to protect the poor from rising gasoline prices. What evidence could you consult to discover whether this proposal was enacted?

4. Explain why, in unregulated markets, the equilibrium principle suggests that excess demand and excess supply tend to be fleeting.

5. Give an example of behavior you have observed that could be described as "smart for one but dumb for all."

■ PROBLEMS ■

1. State whether the following pairs of goods are complements or substitutes. (If you think a pair is ambiguous in this respect, explain why.)
   a. Tennis courts and squash courts
   b. Squash racquets and squash balls
   c. Ice cream and chocolate
   d. Cloth diapers and paper diapers

2. How would each of the following affect the U.S. market supply curve for corn?
   a. A new and improved crop rotation technique is discovered.
   b. The price of fertilizer falls.
   c. The government offers new tax breaks to farmers.
   d. A tornado sweeps through Iowa.

3. Indicate how you think each of the following would affect demand in the indicated market:
   a. An increase in family income on the demand for Adirondack vacations
   b. A study linking beef consumption to heart disease on the demand for hamburgers
   c. A relaxation of immigration laws on the demand for elementary school places
   d. An increase in the price of audiocassettes on the demand for CDs
   e. An increase in the price of CDs on the demand for CDs

4. An Arizona student claims to have spotted a UFO over the desert outside of Tucson. How will his claim affect the supply of binoculars in Tucson stores?

5. What will happen to the equilibrium price and quantity of oranges if the wages paid to farm workers rise?

6. How will an increase in the birthrate affect the equilibrium price of land?

7. What will happen to the equilibrium price and quantity of fish if it is discovered that fish oils help prevent heart disease?

8. What will happen to the equilibrium price and quantity of beef if the price of chicken feed increases?

9. Use supply and demand analysis to explain why hotel room rental rates near your campus during parents' weekend and graduation weekend might differ from the rates charged during the rest of the year.

10. How will a new law mandating an increase in required levels of automobile insurance affect the equilibrium price and quantity in the market for new automobiles?

11. Suppose the current issue of *The New York Times* reports an outbreak of mad cow disease in Nebraska, as well as the discovery of a new breed of chickens that gains more weight than existing breeds from the same amount of food. How will these developments affect the equilibrium price and quantity of chicken sold in the United States?

12. What will happen to the equilibrium quantity and price of potatoes if population increases and a new, higher yielding variety of potato plant is developed?

13. What will happen to the equilibrium price and quantity of apples if apples are discovered to help prevent colds and a fungus kills 10 percent of existing apple trees?

14. What will happen to the equilibrium quantity and price of corn if the price of butter increases and the price of fertilizer decreases?

15. Tofu was available 25 years ago only from small businesses operating in Chinese quarters of large cities. Today tofu has become popular as a high-protein health food and is widely available in supermarkets throughout the United States. At the same time, production has evolved to become factory-based using modern food-processing technologies. Draw a diagram with demand and supply curves depicting the market for tofu 25 years ago and the market for tofu today. Given the information above, what does the demand-supply model predict about changes in the volume of tofu sold in the United States between then and now? What does it predict about changes in the price of tofu?

▪ ANSWERS TO IN-CHAPTER EXERCISES ▪

4.1 Since landlords are permitted to charge less than the maximum rent established by rent-control laws, a law that sets the maximum rent at $1,200 will have no effect on the rents actually charged in this market, which will settle at the equilibrium value of $800 per month.

4.2 Travel by air and travel by bus are substitutes, so a decline in airfares will shift the demand for bus travel to the left, resulting in lower bus fares and fewer bus trips taken. Travel by air and the use of resort hotels are complements, so a decline in airfares will shift the demand for resort hotel rooms to the right, resulting in higher hotel rates and an increase in the number of rooms rented.

4.3 A decrease in income will shift the demand curve for a normal good to the left and will shift the demand curve for an inferior good to the right.

4.4 The vitamin discovery shifts the demand for chips to the right, and the crop losses shift the supply of chips to the left. Both shifts result in an increase in the equilibrium price of chips. But depending on the relative magnitude of the shifts, the equilibrium quantity of chips may either rise [part (a) of figure] or fall [part (b) of figure].

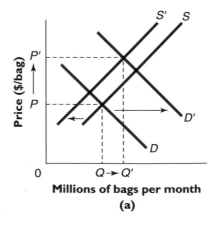

Millions of bags per month
(a)

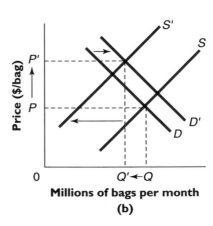

Millions of bags per month
(b)

PART

2

COMPETITION AND THE INVISIBLE HAND

■

Having grasped the basic core principles of economics, you are now in a position to sharpen your understanding of how consumers and firms behave. In Part 2 our focus will be on how things work in an idealized perfectly competitive economy in which consumers are perfectly informed and no firm has market power.

In our review of supply and demand in Part 1, we asked you simply to assume the law of demand, which says that demand curves are downward-sloping. In Chapter 5 we will see that this law is a simple consequence of the fact that people spend their limited incomes in rational ways. We will also explore the concept of price elasticity, which describes the sensitivity of purchase decisions to variations in price. In Chapter 6 our focus will shift to the seller's side of the market, where our task will be to see why upward-sloping supply curves are a consequence of production decisions taken by firms whose goal is to maximize profit.

Our agenda in Chapter 7 is to develop more carefully and fully the concept of economic surplus introduced in Part 1 and to investigate the conditions under which unregulated markets generate the largest possible economic surplus. We will also explore why attempts to interfere with market outcomes often lead to unintended and undesired consequences.

Finally, in Chapter 8 we will investigate the economic forces by which the invisible hand of the marketplace guides profit-seeking firms and satisfaction-seeking consumers in ways that, to a surprising degree, serve society's ends. These forces encourage aggressive cost cutting by firms, even though the resulting gains will eventually take the form of lower prices rather than higher profits. We will also see why misunderstanding of competitive forces often results in costly errors, both in everyday decision making and in government policy.

DEMAND: THE BENEFIT SIDE OF THE MARKET

Many illicit drug users commit crimes to finance their addiction. The connection between drugs and crime has led to calls for more vigorous efforts to stop the smuggling of illicit drugs. But can such efforts reduce the likelihood that your laptop computer will be stolen in the next month?

If attempts to reduce the supply of illicit drugs are successful, their effect will be to increase the market price of drugs. (From our basic supply and demand analysis, we can see that this increase in price is caused by a leftward shift in the supply curve for drugs.) The law of demand tells us that drug users will respond by consuming a smaller quantity of drugs. But the amount of crime drug users commit depends not on the *quantity* of drugs they consume but rather on their *total expenditure* on drugs. Depending on the specific characteristics of the demand curve for illicit drugs, a price increase might reduce total expenditure on drugs, but it could also raise total expenditure.

Suppose, for example, that extra border patrols shift the supply curve in the market for illicit drugs to the left, as shown in Figure 5.1. As a result, the equilibrium quantity of drugs would fall from 50,000 to 40,000 ounces per day, and the price of drugs would rise from $50 to $80 per ounce. The total amount spent on drugs, which was $2,500,000 per day (50,000 ounces/day times $50/ounce), would rise to $3,200,000 per day (40,000 ounces/day times $80/ounce). In this case, then, efforts to stem the supply of drugs would actually increase the likelihood of your laptop being stolen.

Other benefits from stemming the flow of illicit drugs might still outweigh the resulting increase in crime. But knowing that the policy might increase drug-related crime would clearly be useful to law enforcement authorities.

FIGURE 5.1
The Effect of Extra Border Patrols on the Market for Illicit Drugs.
Extra patrols shift supply leftward and reduce the quantity demanded but may actually increase the total amount spent on drugs.

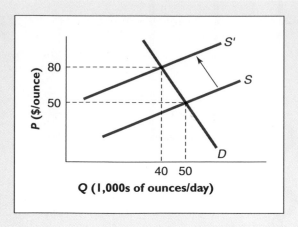

Our task in this chapter will be to explore the demand side of the market in greater depth than was possible in Chapter 4. There we merely asked you to accept as an intuitively plausible claim that the quantity demanded of a good or service declines as its price rises. This relationship is known as the law of demand, and we will see how it emerges as a simple consequence of the assumption that people spend their limited incomes in rational ways. In the process, we will see more clearly the dual roles of income and substitution as factors that account for the law of demand.

We will also explore the relationship between the price for which a good sells and the total amount that consumers spend on it. In the illicit drug example just considered, the increase in price led to an increase in total spending. In many other cases, an increase in price will lead to a reduction in total spending. Why this difference? The underlying phenomenon that explains this pattern, we will see, is elasticity of demand, a measure of the extent to which quantity demanded responds to variations in price.

Could reducing the supply of illegal drugs cause an increase in drug-related burglaries?

NEEDS, WANTS, AND THE LAW OF DEMAND

On the northern border of a large university in the East, a creek widens to form a picturesque lake, fondly remembered by generations of alumni as a popular recreation spot. Over the years, the lake gradually silted in, and by the late 1980s it had become impossible even to paddle a canoe across it. A generous alumnus then sponsored an effort to restore the lake. Heavy dredging equipment hauled out load after load of mud, and months later the lake was finally silt-free.

To mark the occasion, the university held a ceremony. Bands played, the president spoke, a chorus sang, and distinguished visitors applauded the donor's generosity. Hundreds of faculty and students turned out for the festivities. Spotting a good opportunity to promote their product, the proprietors of a local ice cream store set up a temporary stand at the water's edge, with a large sign announcing "Free Ice Cream."

Word spread. Soon scores of people were lined up waiting to try out Vanilla Almond Delight, Hazelnut Cream, and Fudge Faire. The ice cream was plentiful, and because it was free, everyone could obviously afford it. Or so it seemed. In fact, many people who wanted ice cream that day never got any. The reason, of course, was that they found waiting in a long line too steep a price.

When a good or service is scarce, it must somehow be rationed among competing users. In most markets, monetary prices perform that task. But in the case of a stand offering free ice cream, waiting time becomes the effective rationing device. Having to stand in line is a cost, no less so than having to part with some money.

This example drives home the point that although the demand curve is usually described as a relationship between the quantity demanded of a good and its monetary price, the relationship is really much more general. At bottom, the demand curve is a relationship between the quantity demanded and *all* costs—monetary and nonmonetary—associated with acquiring a good. We can thus restate the **law of demand** as follows:

The Law of Demand: **People do less of what they want to do as the cost of doing it rises.**

By stating the law of demand this way, we can see it as a direct consequence of the cost-benefit principle, which says that an activity should be pursued if (and only if) its benefits are at least as great as its costs. Recall that we measure the benefit of an activity by the highest price we'd be willing to pay to pursue it—namely, our reservation price for the activity. When the cost of an activity rises, it is more likely to exceed our reservation price, and we are therefore less likely to pursue that activity.

The law of demand applies to BMWs, cheap key rings, and "free" ice cream, not to mention compact discs, manicures, medical care, and acid-free rain. It stresses that a "cost" is the sum of *all* the sacrifices—monetary and nonmonetary, implicit and explicit—we must make to engage in an activity.

How much are you willing to pay for the latest Alanis Morisette CD? The answer will clearly depend on how you feel about her music. To Morisette's die-hard fans, buying the new release might seem absolutely essential; they'd pay a steep price indeed. But those who don't like Morisette's music may not be willing to buy it at any price.

In everyday language, we distinguish between goods and services people need and ones they merely want. For example, we might say that someone wants a ski vacation in Utah, but what he really needs is a few days off from his daily routine; or that someone wants a house with a view, but what she really needs is shelter from the elements. Likewise, since people need protein to survive, we might say a severely malnourished person needs more protein. But it would strike us as odd to say that anyone—even a malnourished person—needs more prime filet of beef, since health can be restored by consuming far less expensive sources of protein.

Economists like to emphasize that once we have achieved bare subsistence levels of consumption—the amount of food, shelter, and clothing required to maintain our health—we can abandon all reference to needs and speak only in terms of wants. This linguistic distinction helps us think more clearly about the true nature of our choices.

For instance, someone who says "Californians don't have nearly as much water as they need" will tend to think differently about water shortages than someone who says "Californians don't have nearly as much water as they want when the price of water is low." The first person is likely to focus on regulations to prevent people from watering their lawns or on projects to capture additional runoff from the Sierra Nevada mountains. The second person is more likely to focus on the low price of water in California. Whereas remedies of the first sort are often costly and extremely difficult to implement, raising the price of water is both simple and effective.

Why does California experience chronic water shortages? Some might respond that the state must serve the needs of a large population with a relatively low average annual rainfall. Yet other states, like New Mexico, have even less rainfall per person and do not experience water shortages nearly as often as California.

California's problem exists because local governments sell water at extremely low prices, which encourages Californians to use water in ways that make no sense for a state with low rainfall. For instance, rice, which is well suited for conditions in high-rainfall states like South Carolina, requires extensive irrigation in California. But because California farmers can obtain water so cheaply, they plant and flood hundreds of thousands of acres of rice paddies each spring in the Central Valley. It takes 2,000 tons of water to produce 1 ton of rice, but many other grains can be produced with only half that amount. If the price of California water were higher, farmers would simply switch to other grains.

Likewise, cheap water encourages homeowners in Los Angeles and San Diego to plant water-intensive lawns and shrubs, like the ones common in the East and Midwest. By contrast, residents of cities like Santa Fe, New Mexico, where water prices are high, choose native plantings that require little or no watering.

TRANSLATING WANTS INTO DEMAND

The scarcity principle reminds us that although our resources are finite, our appetites for good things are boundless. Even if we had unlimited bank accounts, we'd quickly run out of the time and energy needed to do all the things we wanted to do. Our challenge is to use our limited resources to fulfill our desires to the greatest possible degree. And that leaves us with this practical question: How should we allocate our incomes among the various goods and services that are available? To answer that question, it helps to begin by recognizing that the goods and services we buy are not ends in themselves but rather means for satisfying our desires.

MEASURING WANTS: THE CONCEPT OF UTILITY

Economists use the concept of *utility* to represent the satisfaction people derive from their consumption activities. The assumption is that people try to allocate their incomes so as to maximize their satisfaction, a goal referred to as *utility maximization.*

We begin by imagining that the utility associated with different activities can be measured. The nineteenth-century British economist Jeremy Bentham wrote of a "utilometer," a device that could be used to measure the amount of utility provided by different consumption activities. Such a device doesn't exist, but if it did, we could use it to assign a numerical utility value to every activity—watching a movie, eating a cheeseburger, and so on. The utilometer measures utility in utils, much as a thermometer measures temperature in degrees Fahrenheit or Celsius.

Finally, we make the following plausible assumption: The consumer's goal is to maximize the total number of utils obtained from the goods consumed. The trick is to find that maximum—the combination of goods that provides the most "bang for the buck."

Let's begin with an unusually simple problem, the one facing a consumer who reaches the front of the line at a free ice cream stand. How many cones of ice cream should this person, whom we'll call Lamar, ask for? Table 5.1 shows the relationship between the total number of ice cream cones Lamar eats per hour and the total utility, measured in utils per hour, he derives from them.

Note that the measurements in the table are stated in terms of cones per hour and utils per hour. Why "per hour"? Because without an explicit time dimension, we would have no idea whether a given quantity was a lot or a little. Five ice cream cones in a lifetime isn't much, but five in an hour would be more than most of us would care to eat.

As the entries in Table 5.1 show, Lamar's total utility increases with each cone he eats, up to the fourth cone. Eating 4 cones per hour makes him happier than eating 3, which makes him happier than eating 2, and so on. But beyond 4 cones per hour, consuming more ice cream actually makes Lamar less happy. The fifth cone reduces his total utility from 187 utils per hour to 184 utils per hour.

TABLE 5.1
Lamar's Total Utility from Ice Cream Consumption

Cone quantity (cones/hour)	Total utility (utils/hour)
0	0
1	100
2	150
3	175
4	187
5	184

We can display the utility information in Table 5.1 graphically, as in Figure 5.2. Note in the graph that the more cones per hour Lamar eats, the more utils he gets—but again only up to the fourth cone. Once he moves beyond 4 cones, his total utility begins to decline. Lamar's happiness reaches a maximum of 187 utils when he eats 4 cones per hour. At that point he has no incentive to eat the fifth cone, even though it's absolutely free. Eating the fifth cone actually makes him worse off.

Table 5.1 and Figure 5.2 illustrate another important aspect of the relationship between utility and consumption—namely, that the additional utility from

FIGURE 5.2
Lamar's Total Utility from Ice Cream Consumption.
For most goods, utility rises at a diminishing rate with additional consumption.

additional units of consumption declines as total consumption increases. Thus, while 1 cone per hour is a *lot* better—by 100 utils—than zero, 4 cones per hour is just a *little* better than 3 (just 12 utils worth).

The term **marginal utility** denotes the amount by which total utility changes when consumption changes by one unit. In Table 5.2, the third column shows the marginal utility values that correspond to changes in Lamar's level of ice cream consumption. For example, the second entry in column 3 represents the increase in total utility (measured in utils per cone) when Lamar's consumption rises from 1 cone per hour to 2. Note that the marginal utility entries in column 3 are placed midway between the rows of the preceding columns, to indicate that marginal utility corresponds to the movement from one consumption quantity to the next. Thus we would say that the marginal utility of moving from 1 to 2 cones per hour is 20 utils per cone.

marginal utility the additional utility gained from consuming an additional unit of a good

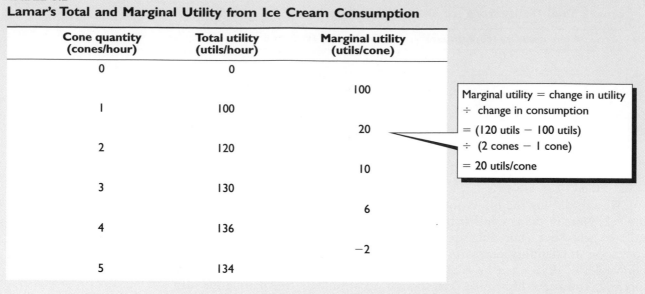

TABLE 5.2
Lamar's Total and Marginal Utility from Ice Cream Consumption

Cone quantity (cones/hour)	Total utility (utils/hour)	Marginal utility (utils/cone)
0	0	
		100
1	100	
		20
2	120	
		10
3	130	
		6
4	136	
		−2
5	134	

Marginal utility = change in utility ÷ change in consumption
= (120 utils − 100 utils) ÷ (2 cones − 1 cone)
= 20 utils/cone

Law of Diminishing Marginal Utility: As consumption of a good increases beyond some point, the additional utility gained from an additional unit of the good tends to decline.

This pattern of diminishing marginal utility holds true not just for Lamar but also for most consumers of most goods. If we have one brownie or one Ferrari, we're happier than we are with none; if we have two, we'll be even happier—but not twice as happy, and so on. Although this pattern is called a law, there are exceptions. Indeed, some consumption activities even seem to exhibit *increasing* marginal utility. For example, an unfamiliar song may seem irritating the first time you hear it, then gradually become more tolerable the next few times you hear it. Before long, you may discover that you *like* the song, and may even find yourself singing it in the shower. Notwithstanding such exceptions, the law of diminishing marginal utility is a plausible characterization of the relationship between utility and consumption for many goods. Unless otherwise stated, we'll assume that it holds for the various goods we discuss.

What will Lamar do when he gets to the front of the line? At that point, the opportunity cost of the time he spent waiting is a sunk cost and is hence irrelevant to his decision about how many cones to order. And since there is no monetary charge for the cones, the cost of ordering an additional one is zero. According to the cost-benefit criterion, Lamar should therefore continue to order cones as long as the marginal benefit (here, the marginal utility he gets from an additional cone) is greater than or equal to zero. Thus he should order 4 cones.

In this highly simplified example, Lamar's utility-maximization problem is just like the one he'd confront if he were deciding how much water to drink from a public fountain. (Solution: Keep drinking until the marginal utility of water declines to zero.)

ALLOCATING A FIXED INCOME BETWEEN TWO GOODS

Most of us confront considerably more complex purchase decisions than the one Lamar faced. For one thing, we generally must make decisions not just about a single good but about many. Another complication is that the cost of consuming additional units of each good will rarely be zero.

To see how to proceed in more complex cases, suppose Lamar must decide how to spend his fixed income on two different goods each with a positive price. Should he spend all his income on one of the goods or part of it on each? The law of diminishing marginal utility suggests that spending all one's income on a single good isn't a good strategy. Rather than devote more and more money to the purchase of a good we already consume in large quantities (and whose marginal utility is therefore relatively low), we generally do better to spend that money on other goods we don't have many of, whose marginal utility will likely be higher.

The simplest way to illustrate how economists think about the spending decisions of a utility-maximizing consumer is to work through an example like the following.

How many vanilla ice cream cones and chocolate sundaes should Lamar consume?

EXAMPLE 5.1

The free ice cream bonanza is over, and Lamar now has a fixed income of $10 per week to spend at the ice cream parlor. Also, a torn ligament has forced him to resign from the track team, so his appetite for ice cream is considerably smaller than it was. His two favorite choices are vanilla cones and chocolate sundaes. Sundaes sell for $2 and vanilla cones for $1. The number of utils Lamar derives from consuming different amounts of each are as shown in Table 5.3. If Lamar's goal is to maximize the utility he derives from his $10 weekly spending on ice cream, how much of each should he eat?

TABLE 5.3
Utility from Two Types of Ice Cream Consumption

Vanilla cones per week	Utils/week from cones	Chocolate sundaes per week	Utils/week from sundaes
0	0	0	0
1	36	1	50
2	50	2	80
3	60	3	105
4	68	4	120
5	75	5	130
6	80	6	138
7	84	7	144
8	82	8	148
9	81	9	150
10	80	10	151

Lamar wants to maximize the total number of utils he gets from eating two types of ice cream—cones and sundaes—on a $10 weekly budget. His spending limit, or *budget constraint,* is $10. One way Lamar can solve his problem is to list all the combinations of cones and sundaes that cost $10 per week and then choose the one that delivers the highest total utility. Suppose he spends the entire $10 on cones. At $1 apiece, that gives him 10 cones per week, yielding a total utility of 80 utils per week.

Now compare that to what happens if Lamar splits up his budget. Suppose, for example, that he buys only 6 cones, which leaves $4 to spend on sundaes (enough to buy 2 per week). That gives him 80 utils/week from cones + 80 utils/week from sundaes = 160 utils/week, or twice as many utils per week as he got by spending all his income on cones.

Table 5.4 shows the various cone and sundae combinations Lamar can buy without exceeding his $10 weekly budget constraint.

A glance at the table shows that Lamar's *optimal combination* of goods is 4 cones per week and 3 sundaes. His total utility from that combination is 173 utils per week—more than he'd get from any of the other affordable combinations. In other words, the **optimal combination** is the *affordable* combination that delivers *maximum total utility*.

optimal combination of goods
the affordable combination that yields the highest total utility

TABLE 5.4
Affordable Combinations of Cones and Sundaes

Cone/sundae combinations	Total utility (utils/week)
10 cones, 0 sundaes	80 + 0 = 80
8 cones, 1 sundae	82 + 50 = 132
6 cones, 2 sundaes	80 + 80 = 160
4 cones, 3 sundaes	68 + 105 = 173
2 cones, 4 sundaes	50 + 120 = 170
0 cones, 5 sundaes	0 + 130 = 130

EXERCISE 5.1

In Example 5.1, the combination consisting of 8 cones per week and 4 sundaes per week gives a total utility of 202 utils per week. Why isn't that combination Lamar's best choice?

THE RATIONAL SPENDING RULE

If Lamar is to achieve the highest possible utility from the $10 per week he spends on ice cream, he must divide his purchases between the two types so that the marginal utility of the last dollar spent on each good is as large as possible. (If it were not, he could achieve higher total utility by spending his last dollar differently.) Let's see if that condition is satisfied when Lamar buys 4 cones per week and 3 sundaes. Table 5.3A reproduces the utility information given in Example 5.1.

Note that the marginal utility of Lamar's third sundae is 25 utils (the difference between the 105 utils he gets from 3 sundaes and the 80 utils he gets from 2). And since the third sundae costs him $2, his marginal utility per dollar is 25 utils/$2, or 12.5 utils per dollar. Could he have gotten more utils per dollar had he spent $2 on cones instead? Spending $1 more on cones would move him from 4 cones per week to 5, which would increase his total utility from cones by 7 utils per week (the difference between the 75 utils he gets from 5 cones and the 68 utils he gets from 4). Buying a sixth cone would increase his total utility by only 5 utils, for a total increase of 12 utils, significantly less than the 25 utils he would get from an extra sundae. Shifting more money to cones would thus prevent Lamar from achieving the largest possible marginal utility from his last dollars spent on each type.

Note that when Lamar allocates his budget optimally (that is, when he buys 4 cones per week and 3 sundaes), he receives 12.5 utils per dollar from his last purchase of sundaes but only 8 utils per dollar from his last purchase of vanilla cones. If this discrepancy strikes you as a problem, your economic intuition has served you well. Since Lamar is getting more bang for his buck (more utils per dollar) from his last sundae purchase than from his last cone purchase, it would seem that he ought to be spending more heavily on sundaes.

TABLE 5.3A
Utility from Two Types of Ice Cream Consumption

Vanilla cones per week	Utils/week from cones	Chocolate sundaes per week	Utils/week from sundaes
0	0	0	0
1	36	1	50
2	50	2	80
3	60	3	105
4	68	4	120
5	75	5	130
6	80	6	138
7	84	7	144
8	82	8	148
9	81	9	150
10	80	10	151

The way the example is structured, however, Lamar can purchase cones and sundaes *only in whole-number amounts*. Spending more on sundaes would thus require a move from 3 sundaes a week to 4. And because buying a fourth sundae would yield only 7.5 utils per dollar—less than he would get by spending the same amount on cones—Lamar is better off if he stops at 3 sundaes.

In actual experience, the inability to divide goods and services into fractional amounts is seldom an insurmountable problem. After all, if Lamar could do better by consuming, say, 3.2 sundaes per week instead of 3, he could accomplish that by consuming 32 sundaes every 10 weeks (which works out to an average of 3.2 per week).

Whenever goods can be consumed in fractional quantities, we can use the following important rule—the **Rational Spending Rule**—to solve the consumer's allocation problem.

The Rational Spending Rule: Spending should be allocated across goods so that the marginal utility per dollar is the same for each good.

The Rational Spending Rule tells us that if Lamar can purchase ice cream in fractional amounts, he should continue shifting from cones to sundaes until the marginal utility per dollar he obtains from the two goods becomes equal.

The Rational Spending Rule can be expressed in the form of a simple formula. If we use MU_C to denote Lamar's marginal utility from cone consumption (measured in utils per cone) and P_C to denote the price of cones in dollars (measured in dollars per cone), then the ratio MU_C/P_C will represent Lamar's marginal utility per dollar spent on cones. Similarly, if we use MU_S to denote Lamar's marginal utility from sundae consumption, and P_S to denote the price of sundaes, then MU_S/P_S will represent his marginal utility per dollar spent on sundaes. The marginal utility per dollar will be exactly the same for the two types—and hence total utility will be maximized—when the following simple equation is satisfied:

The Rational Spending Rule for Two Goods:

$$\frac{MU_C}{P_C} = \frac{MU_S}{P_S}.$$

The Rational Spending Rule is easily generalized to apply to spending decisions regarding large numbers of goods. In its most general form, it says that the ratio of marginal utility to price must be the same for each good the consumer buys. If the ratio were higher for one good than for another, the consumer could always increase her total utility by buying more of the first good and less of the second.

Notice that we have not chosen to classify the Rational Spending Rule as one of the core principles of economics. We omit it from this list not because the rule is unimportant but because it follows directly from the cost-benefit principle. And as we noted earlier, there is considerable advantage in keeping the list of core principles as small as possible. (If we included 200 principles on this list, there's a good chance you wouldn't remember any of them a few years from now.)

HOW INCOME AND THE PRICES OF SUBSTITUTES AFFECT DEMAND

In Chapter 4 we made the plausible assumption that the demand for any good or service depends on factors like income and the prices of substitutes. As you apply the Rational Spending Rule to work through the following exercises, you'll see more clearly *why* demand depends on factors like these.

EXERCISE 5.2

How should Lamar from Example 5.1 allocate his spending between cones and sundaes if he has $14 per week rather than $10 per week to spend on ice cream?

From among the combinations of goods that are affordable, the utility-maximizing consumer chooses the combination that provides the highest total utility. Extra income stimulates demand by enlarging the set of affordable combinations—by making it possible to buy more of each good than before.

EXERCISE 5.3

Suppose that Lamar again has a budget of $10 per week to allocate between vanilla ice cream cones and chocolate sundaes. The utilities he derives from different quantities of each are again as given in Example 5.1, and chocolate sundaes again sell for $2 apiece. How many units of each type will Lamar buy if the price of vanilla cones is $2 rather than $1?

If you worked through Exercise 5.3 successfully, you saw that a rise in the price of cones caused Lamar to increase his consumption of sundaes. Now consider a more streamlined way of explaining why a change in the price of one good affects demands for other goods. When consumption goods can be purchased in fractional quantities, the Rational Spending Rule requires that the ratio of marginal utility to price be the same for all goods. This means that if the price of one good goes up, the ratio of its current marginal utility to its new price will be lower than for other goods. Consumers can then increase their total utility by devoting smaller proportions of their incomes to that good and larger proportions to others.

> **RECAP** **TRANSLATING WANTS INTO DEMAND**
>
> The scarcity principle challenges us to allocate our incomes among the various goods that are available so as to fulfill our desires to the greatest possible degree. The optimal combination of goods is that affordable combination that yields the highest total utility. For goods that are perfectly divisible, the Rational Spending Rule tells us that the optimal combination is one for which the marginal utility per dollar is the same for each good. If this condition were not satisfied, the consumer could increase her utility by spending less on goods for which the marginal utility per dollar was lower and more on goods for which the marginal utility per dollar was higher.

APPLYING THE RATIONAL SPENDING RULE

The real payoff from learning the law of demand and the Rational Spending Rule lies not in working through hypothetical examples but in using these abstract concepts to make sense of the world around you. To encourage you in your efforts to become an economic naturalist, we turn now to a sequence of examples.

SUBSTITUTION AT WORK

In the first of these examples, we focus on the role of substitution. When the price of a good or service goes up, rational consumers generally turn to less expensive substitutes. Can't meet the payments on a new car? Then buy a used one, or rent an apartment on a bus or subway line. French restaurants too pricey? Then go out for Chinese food, or eat at home more often. National Football League tickets too high? Watch the game on television, or read a book. Can't afford a book? Check one out of the library, or download some reading matter from the Internet. Once you begin to see substitution at work, you will be amazed by the number and richness of the examples that confront you every day.

Why do the wealthy in Manhattan live in smaller houses than the wealthy in Seattle?

Microsoft cofounder Paul Allen lives in a 70,000-square-foot house in Seattle, Washington. His house is large even by the standards of Seattle, many of whose wealthy residents live in houses with more than 10,000 square feet of floor space. By contrast, persons of similar wealth in Manhattan rarely live in houses larger than 5,000 square feet. Why this difference?

   For people trying to decide how large a house to buy, the most obvious difference between Manhattan and Seattle is the huge difference in housing prices. The cost of land alone is several times higher in Manhattan than in Seattle, and construction costs are also much higher. Although plenty of New Yorkers could *afford* to build a 70,000-square-foot mansion, Manhattan housing prices are so high that they simply choose to live in smaller houses and spend what they save in other ways—on lavish summer homes in eastern Long Island, for instance. New Yorkers also eat out and go to the theater more often than their wealthy counterparts in other U.S. cities.

ECONOMIC NATURALIST 5.1

   An especially vivid illustration of substitution occurred during the late 1970s, when fuel shortages brought on by interruptions in the supply of oil from the Middle East led to sharp increases in the price of gasoline and other fuels. In a variety of ways—some straightforward, others remarkably ingenious—consumers changed their behavior to economize on the use of energy. They formed carpools; switched to public transportation; bought four-cylinder cars; moved closer to work; took fewer trips; turned down their thermostats; installed insulation, storm windows, and solar heaters; and bought more efficient appliances. Many people even moved farther south to escape high winter heating bills.

As the next example points out, consumers not only abandon a good in favor of substitutes when it gets more expensive but also return to that good when real prices return to their original levels.

ECONOMIC NATURALIST 5.2

real price dollar price of a good relative to the average dollar price of all other goods and services

nominal price absolute price of a good in dollar terms

Why did people turn to four-cylinder cars in the 1970s, only to shift back to six- and eight-cylinder cars in the 1990s?

In 1973, the price of gasoline was 38 cents per gallon. The following year the price shot up to 52 cents per gallon in the wake of a major disruption of oil supplies. A second disruption in 1979 drove the 1980 price to $1.19 per gallon. These sharp increases in the price of gasoline led to big increases in the demand for cars with four-cylinder engines, which delivered much better fuel economy than the six- and eight-cylinder cars most people had owned. After 1980, however, fuel supplies stabilized, and prices rose only slowly, reaching $1.40 per gallon by 1999. Yet despite the continued rise in the price of gasoline, the switch to smaller engines did not continue. By the late 1980s, the proportion of cars sold with six- and eight-cylinder engines began rising again. Why this reversal?

The key to explaining these patterns is to focus on changes in the **real price** of gasoline. When someone decides how big an automobile engine to choose, what matters is not the **nominal price** of gasoline but the price of gasoline *relative* to all other goods. After all, for consumers faced with a decision of whether to spend $1.40 for a gallon of gasoline, the important question is how much utility they could get from other things they could purchase with the same money. Even though the price of gasoline has continued to rise slowly in nominal, or dollar, terms since 1981, it has declined sharply relative to the price of other goods. Indeed, in terms of real purchasing power, the 1999 price was actually slightly lower than the 1973 price. (That is, in 1999, $1.40 bought slightly more goods and services than 38 cents bought in 1973.) It is this decline in the real price of gasoline that accounts for the reversal of the trend toward smaller engines.

A sharp decline in the real price of gasoline also helps account for the explosive growth in sport utility vehicles in the 1990s. More than 4 million SUVs were sold in the United States in 1997, up from only 750,000 in 1990. Some of them—like the Ford Excursion—weigh more than 7,500 pounds (three times as much as a Honda Civic) and get less than 10 miles per gallon on city streets. Vehicles like these would have been dismal failures during the 1970s, but they're by far the hottest sellers in the current cheap-energy environment.

"We motored over to say hi!"

Here's another closely related example of the influence of price on spending decisions.

Why are automobile engines smaller in England than in the United States?

In England, the most popular model of BMW's 5-series car is the 516i, while in the United States it is the 528i. The engine on the 516i is more than 40 percent smaller than the engine on the 528i. Why this difference?

In both countries, BMWs appeal to professionals with roughly similar incomes, so the difference cannot be explained by differences in purchasing power. Rather, it is the direct result of the heavy tax the British levy on gasoline. With tax, a gallon of gasoline sells for almost $6 in England—more than four times the price in the United States. This difference in price encourages the British to choose smaller, more fuel-efficient engines.

ECONOMIC NATURALIST 5.3

THE IMPORTANCE OF INCOME DIFFERENCES

The most obvious difference between the rich and the poor is that the rich have higher incomes. To explain why the wealthy generally buy larger houses than the poor, we need not assume that the wealthy feel more strongly about housing than the poor. A much simpler explanation is that the total utility from housing, as with most other goods, increases with the amount that one consumes.

As the next example illustrates, income influences the demand for not only housing and other goods, but also quality of service.

Why are waiting lines longer in poorer neighborhoods?

As part of a recent promotional campaign, a Baskin-Robbins retailer offered free ice cream at two of its franchise stores. The first store was located in a high-income neighborhood, the second in a low-income neighborhood. Why was the queue for free ice cream longer in the low-income neighborhood?

Residents of both neighborhoods must decide whether to stand in line for free ice cream or go to some other store and avoid the line by paying the usual price. If we make the plausible assumption that people with higher incomes are more willing than others to pay to avoid standing in line, we should expect to see shorter lines in the high-income neighborhood.

ECONOMIC NATURALIST 5.4

Similar reasoning helps explain why lines are shorter in grocery stores that cater to high-income consumers. Keeping lines short at *any* grocery store means hiring more clerks, which means charging higher prices. High-income consumers are more likely than others to be willing to pay for shorter lines.

HOW THE DISTRIBUTION OF INCOME AFFECTS DEMAND

People whose incomes differ substantially spend their incomes in different ways. For example, the proportion of income a person spends on food tends to fall as income rises, whereas the proportion of income spent on foreign travel tends to rise as income rises. This observation suggests that the demand for specific goods may differ from one city to another, not just because of differences in *average* incomes but also because of differences in the way income is distributed among people.

Why does a house with a view cost more in Berkeley than in Hanover?

In many cities, such as Berkeley, California, and Hanover, New Hampshire, a small proportion of homesites are located on hillsides with commanding views. Most homeowners think that having a view is desirable. If lots with views sold for the same price as lots without views, virtually every homeowner would buy a lot with a view. Since homesites with views are in limited supply, however, they command a

ECONOMIC NATURALIST 5.5

significant price premium. But why is this premium more than 50 percent in Berkeley but less than 30 percent in Hanover?

The average income in Hanover is not much lower than in Berkeley, but incomes are much less equally distributed in Berkeley than in Hanover. Berkeley attracts executives and entrepreneurs from the entire San Francisco Bay area, people who earn significantly more than the top earners in Hanover, most of whom work for Dartmouth College. The result is that the effective demand for homesites with views is much stronger in Berkeley than in Hanover. In both cities the houses with views tend to go to the highest earners, but the premium for a view is much higher in Berkeley because its top earners make so much more money.

To illustrate, suppose the supply of homesites with views is essentially fixed in each city, as indicated by the vertical supply curves shown in Figure 5.3, and that people in both cities have identical tastes regarding views. But because the incomes of the top earners in Berkeley are much higher than the incomes of the top earners in Hanover, the demand curve for homesites with views in Berkeley lies significantly to the right of the corresponding demand curve for Hanover. And that explains the significantly higher premium for views in Berkeley.

FIGURE 5.3
The Price for a House with a View.
If the average income level is the same in two cities, then the city in which income is more unequally distributed, as in (a), will have higher demand for luxury goods such as homesites with views.

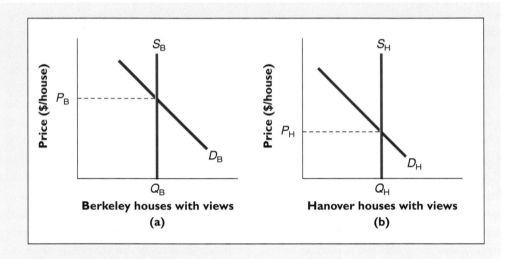

Berkeley houses with views
(a)

Hanover houses with views
(b)

RECAP   **APPLYING THE RATIONAL SPENDING RULE**

Application of the Rational Spending Rule highlights the important roles of income and substitution in explaining differences in consumption patterns—among individuals, among communities, and across time. The rule also highlights the fact that real, as opposed to nominal, prices and income are what matter. The demand for a good falls when the real price of a substitute falls or the real price of a complement rises. Patterns of demand may differ between communities of the same average real-income level if the distributions of income within those communities differ significantly.

INDIVIDUAL AND MARKET DEMAND CURVES

If we know what each individual's demand curve for a good looks like, how can we use that information to construct the market demand curve for the good? We must add together the individual demand curves, a process that is straightforward but requires care.

HORIZONTAL ADDITION

Suppose that there are only two buyers—Smith and Jones—in the market for canned tuna and that their demand curves are as shown in Figure 5.4(a) and (b). To construct the market demand curve for canned tuna, we simply announce a sequence of prices and then add the quantity demanded by each buyer at each price. For example, at a price of $4 per can, Smith demands 8 cans per week [Fig. 5.4(a)] and Jones demands 2 cans per week [Fig. 5.4(b)], for a market demand of 10 cans per week [Fig. 5.4(c)].

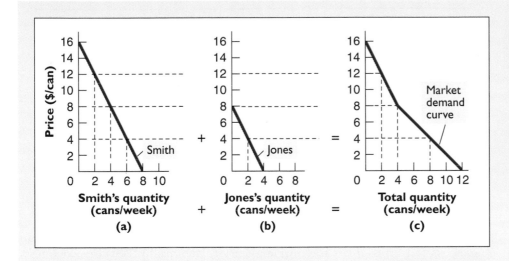

FIGURE 5.4

Individual and Market Demand Curves for Canned Tuna.

The quantity demanded at any price on the market demand curve (c) is the sum of the individual quantities (a) and (b) demanded at that price.

The process of adding individual demand curves to get the market demand curve is known as *horizontal addition,* a term used to emphasize that we are adding quantities, which are measured on the horizontal axes of individual demand curves.

Figure 5.5(a) illustrates the special case in which each of 1,000 consumers in the market has the same demand curve. To get the market demand curve in this case, we simply multiply each quantity on the representative individual demand curve by 1,000 [Fig. 5.5(b)].

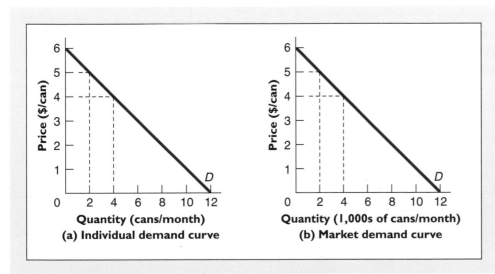

FIGURE 5.5

The Individual and Market Demand Curves When All Buyers Have Identical Demand Curves.

When individual demand curves are identical, we get the market demand curve by multiplying each quantity on the individual demand curve by the number of consumers in the market.

THE STRAIGHT-LINE DEMAND CURVE

The law of demand requires only that the demand curve for a good or service slope downward. It makes no predictions about the specific shape of the curve.

It is often convenient, however, to draw demand curves as downward-sloping straight lines, as we did in Chapter 4.

Market demand curves may be shown not only in graphical form but in two other forms as well. One is to summarize the market demand relationship in the form of a table. For example, the linear market demand curve shown in Figure 5.5(b) may be also represented as Table 5.5.

TABLE 5.5
The Market Demand for Canned Tuna in Tabular Form

Price ($/can)	Quantity (1,000s of cans/month)
0	12
1	10
2	8
3	6
4	4
5	2
6	0

A third alternative—and one especially handy for straight-line demand curves—is to express the market demand curve algebraically. Because economists have adopted the convention of plotting price on the vertical axis and quantity on the horizontal axis, we write the general formula of a straight-line demand curve as follows:

$$P = b - mQ,$$

where P denotes the price of the good, usually measured in dollars per unit; Q denotes the quantity demanded, in physical units per unit of time; b denotes the vertical intercept of the demand curve, and $-m$ represents its slope.

To illustrate, suppose we want to write the equation for the market demand curve shown in Figure 5.6 [which is the same as the one in Figure 5.5(b)].

To begin, we can see from the graph that b, the vertical intercept of the demand curve, is 6. The slope is the ratio of the vertical distance between any

FIGURE 5.6
The Market Demand Curve for Canned Tuna.

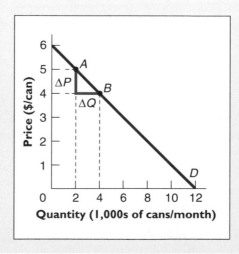

two points on the line (the "rise") to the corresponding horizontal distance (the "run"). For example, if we look at the segment of the demand curve between the points labeled A and B, the rise is $\Delta P = -1$ (since the line falls a vertical distance of 1 unit between A and B), and the corresponding run is $\Delta Q = 2{,}000$. Thus the slope of the demand curve shown is $-m = \Delta P / \Delta Q = -1/2{,}000$. Knowing both the slope and vertical intercept of the demand curve, we also know that its equation must be

$$P = 6 - \left(\frac{1}{2{,}000}\right)Q.$$

To check that this equation is indeed correct, let's see if it works for the two points we started with. Does the equation hold, for example, if we plug in $P = 5$ and $Q = 2{,}000$? Sure enough, $5 = 6 - (1/2{,}000)(2{,}000)$. Similarly, we can verify that $4 = 6 - (1/2{,}000)(4{,}000)$.

EXERCISE 5.4

Find the equation of the linear demand curve for movie tickets shown in the following diagram.

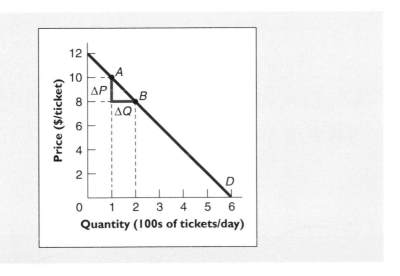

TOTAL EXPENDITURE

Given the market demand curve for a good, the total amount consumers spend on the good will depend on the price for which it is sold. And by definition, the total expenditure on a good per day is simply the number of units bought each day times the price for which it sells.

To illustrate, calculate how much moviegoers will spend on tickets each day if the demand curve is as shown in Figure 5.7 and the price is $2 per ticket. The demand curve tells us that at a price of $2 per ticket, 500 tickets per day will be sold, so total expenditure at that price will be $1,000 per day. If tickets sell not for $2 but for $4 apiece, 400 tickets will be sold each day, so total expenditure at the higher price will be $1,600 per day.

Note that the total amount consumers spend on a product each day must equal the total amount sellers of the product receive. That is, the terms **total expenditure** and **total revenue** are simply two sides of the same coin.

It might seem that an increase in the market price of a product should always result in an increase in the total revenue received by sellers. But although that happened in the case we just saw, it needn't always be so. The law of demand

Total expenditure = total revenue the dollar amount consumers spend on a product is equal to the dollar amount sellers receive

FIGURE 5.7
The Demand Curve for Movie Tickets.
An increase in price from $2 to $4 per ticket increases total expenditure on tickets.

tells us that when the price of a good rises, people will buy less of it. The two factors that govern total revenue—price and quantity—thus will always move in opposite directions. When price goes up and quantity goes down, the product of the two may go either up or down.

Note, for example, that for the demand curve shown in Figure 5.8 (which is the same as the one we just saw in Figure 5.7), a rise in price from $8 to $10 per ticket will cause total expenditure on tickets to go down. Thus people will spend $1,600 per day on tickets at a price of $8, but only $1,000 per day at a price of $10.

The general rule illustrated by these examples is that a price increase will produce an increase in total revenue whenever it is greater, in percentage terms, than the corresponding percentage reduction in quantity demanded. Although the two

FIGURE 5.8
The Demand Curve for Movie Tickets.
An increase in price from $8 to $10 per ticket results in a fall in total expenditure on tickets.

price increases (from $2 to $4 and from $8 to $10) were of the same absolute value—$2 in each case—they are much different when expressed as a percentage of the original price. An increase from $2 to $4 represents a 100 percent increase in price, whereas an increase from $8 to $10 represents only a 25 percent increase in price. And although the quantity reductions caused by the two price increases were equal in absolute terms, they too are very different when expressed as percentages of the quantities originally sold. Thus, although the decline in quantity demanded was 100 tickets per day in each case, it was just a 20 percent reduction in the first case (from 500 units to 400) but a 50 percent reduction in the second (from 200 units to 100). In the second case, the negative effect on total expenditure of the 50 percent quantity reduction outweighed the positive effect of the 25 percent price increase. The reverse happened in the first case: The 100 percent increase in price (from $2 to $4) outweighed the 20 percent reduction in quantity (from 5 units to 4 units).

Example 5.2 provides further insight into the relationship between total revenue and price.

For the demand curve shown in Figure 5.9, draw a separate graph showing how total expenditure varies with the price of movie tickets.

EXAMPLE 5.2

FIGURE 5.9
The Demand Curve for Movie Tickets.

The first step in constructing this graph is to calculate total expenditure for a sample of price points on the demand curve and record the results, as in Table 5.6.

The next step is to plot total expenditure at each of the price points on a graph, as in Figure 5.10. Finally, sketch the curve by joining these points. (If greater accuracy is required, you can use a larger sample of points than the one shown in Table 5.6.)

TABLE 5.6
Total Expenditure as a Function of Price

Price ($/ticket)	Total expenditure ($/day)
12	0
10	1,000
8	1,600
6	1,800
4	1,600
2	1,000
0	0

Note in Figure 5.10 that as the price per ticket increases from 0 to $6, total expenditure increases. But as the price rises from $6 to $12, total expenditure decreases. Total expenditure reaches a maximum of $1,800 per day at a price of $6.

The pattern observed in Example 5.2 holds true in general. For a straight-line demand curve, total expenditure is highest at the price that lies on the mid-point of the demand curve.

FIGURE 5.10

Total Expenditure as a Function of Price.
For a good whose demand curve is a straight line, total expenditure reaches a maximum at the price corresponding to the midpoint of the demand curve.

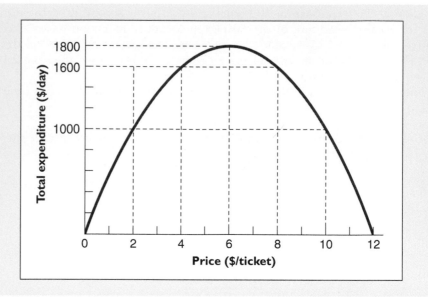

RECAP   INDIVIDUAL AND MARKET DEMAND CURVES

To generate the market demand curve for a good, we add the individual demand curves of market participants horizontally. Although demand curves for actual goods will seldom be straight lines, they often can be well approximated as straight lines, especially when our concern is with the effects of small variations in quantity or price.

Total expenditure on a good is the product of its price and the quantity bought. Total revenue received by the seller of a good is the product of its price and the quantity sold. Because the quantity bought equals the quantity sold, total revenue must equal total expenditure. For a straight-line demand curve, total expenditure reaches a maximum at the midpoint along the demand curve.

PRICE ELASTICITY OF DEMAND

When the price of a good or service rises, the quantity demanded falls. But as we have seen, to predict the effect of the price increase on total expenditure, we must also know how much quantity will fall. The quantity demanded of some goods, such as salt, is not very sensitive to changes in price. Indeed, even if the price of salt were to double, or to fall by half, most people would alter their consumption of it hardly at all. For other goods, however, the quantity demanded is extremely responsive to changes in price. As we saw earlier, for example, when energy prices rose in the 1970s, gasoline consumption fell sharply.

price elasticity of demand the percentage change in the quantity demanded of a good that results from a 1 percent change in its price

The **price elasticity of demand** for a good is a measure of the responsiveness of the quantity demanded of that good to changes in its price. Formally, the price elasticity of demand for a good is defined as the percentage change in the quantity demanded that results from a 1 percent change in its price. For example, if the price of beef falls by 1 percent and the quantity demanded rises by 2 percent, then the price elasticity of demand for beef has a value of -2.

Strictly speaking, the price elasticity of demand will always be negative (or zero) because price changes always move in the opposite direction from changes in quantity demanded. So for convenience, we can drop the negative sign and speak of price elasticities in terms of absolute value. The demand for a good is said to be **elastic** with respect to price if the absolute value of its price elasticity is greater than 1. It is said to be **inelastic** if the absolute value of its price elasticity is less than 1. Finally, demand is said to be **unit elastic** if the absolute value of its price elasticity is equal to 1. (See Figure 5.11.)

elastic the demand for a good is elastic with respect to price if its price elasticity of demand is greater than 1

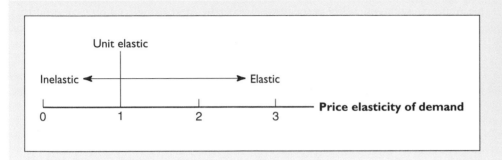

FIGURE 5.11
Elastic and Inelastic Demand.
Demand for a good is called elastic, unit elastic, or inelastic with respect to price if the price elasticity is greater than 1, equal to 1, or less than 1, respectively.

ELASTICITY AND TOTAL EXPENDITURE

Sellers of goods and services will often have a strong interest in being able to answer such questions as "Will consumers spend more on my product if I sell more units at a lower price or fewer units at a higher price?" As it turns out, the answer to this question depends critically on the elasticity of demand. Suppose, for example, that the business manager of a rock band knows that 5,000 tickets to the band's weekly summer concerts can be sold if the price is set at $20 per ticket. If the elasticity of demand for tickets is equal to 3.0, will total ticket revenue go up or down in response to a 10 percent increase in the price of tickets?

Total revenue from ticket sales is currently ($20/ticket)(5,000 tickets/week) = $100,000/week. The fact that the price elasticity of demand for tickets is 3 implies that a 10 percent increase in price will produce a 30 percent reduction in the number of tickets sold, which means that ticket sales will fall to 3,500/week. Total expenditure on tickets will therefore fall to (3,500 tickets/week)($22/ticket) = $77,000/week, which is significantly less than the current spending total.

This example illustrates the following important rule regarding the relationship between price elasticity and the effect of a price increase on total expenditure:

For a product whose price elasticity is greater than 1, an increase in price will reduce total expenditure, and a reduction in price will increase total expenditure.

Let's look at the intuition behind this rule. Total expenditure is the product of price and quantity. For an elastically demanded product, the percentage change in quantity will be larger than the corresponding percentage change in price. Thus the change in sales will more than offset the change in revenue per unit sold.

Now let's see how total spending responds to a price increase when demand is *inelastic* with respect to price. Suppose that in the case just considered, the elasticity of demand for tickets is not 3.0 but 0.5. How will total revenue respond to a 10 percent increase in ticket prices? This time the number of tickets sold will fall by only 5 percent to 4,750 tickets/week, which means that total expenditure on tickets will rise to (4,750 tickets/week)($22/ticket) = $104,500/week, or $4,500/week more than the current expenditure level.

As this example illustrates, the effect of a price change on total expenditure when demand is inelastic runs in the opposite direction from the effect when demand is elastic:

inelastic the demand for a good is inelastic with respect to price if its price elasticity of demand is less than 1

unit elastic the demand for a good is unit elastic with respect to price if its price elasticity of demand is equal to 1

For a product whose price elasticity of demand is less than 1, an increase in price will increase total expenditure, and a cut in price will reduce total expenditure.

Again, the intuition behind this rule is straightforward. For a product whose demand is inelastic with respect to price, the percentage change in quantity demanded will be smaller than the corresponding percentage change in price. Thus the change in revenue per unit sold will more than offset the change in the number of units sold.

The relationship between elasticity and the effect of a price change on total revenue are summarized in Table 5.7, where the symbol ϵ is used to denote elasticity.

TABLE 5.7
Elasticity and the Effect of a Price Change on Total Revenue

$\epsilon > 1$	Price increase causes reduction in total revenue.	Price reduction causes increase in total revenue.
$\epsilon < 1$	Price increase causes increase in total revenue.	Price reduction causes reduction in total revenue.

DETERMINANTS OF PRICE ELASTICITY OF DEMAND

What factors determine the price elasticity of demand for a good or service? To answer this question, recall that before a rational consumer buys any product, the product must first pass the cost-benefit test. For instance, consider a good (such as a dorm refrigerator) that, if you buy it at all, you buy only one unit. Suppose that, at the current price, you have decided to buy it. Now imagine that the price goes up by 10 percent. Will a price increase of this magnitude be likely to make you change your mind? The answer will depend on factors such as the following.

Substitution possibilities When the price of a product you want to buy goes up significantly, you are likely to ask yourself, "Is there some other good that can do roughly the same job but for less money?" If the answer is yes, then you can escape the effect of the price increase by simply switching to the substitute product. But if the answer is no, you are more likely to stick with your current purchase.

These observations suggest that the price elasticity of demand will tend to be higher for products for which close substitutes are readily available. Salt, for example, has no close substitutes, which is one reason that the demand for it is highly inelastic. Note, however, that while the quantity of salt people demand is highly insensitive to price, the same cannot be said of the demand for any specific brand of salt. After all, despite what salt manufacturers say about the special advantages of their own labels, consumers tend to regard one brand of salt as a virtually perfect substitute for another. Thus, if Morton were to raise the price of its salt significantly, people would simply switch to some other brand.

The vaccine against rabies is another product for which there are essentially no attractive substitutes. A person who is bitten by a rabid animal and does not take the vaccine faces a certain and painful death. So most people in that position would pay any price they could afford rather than do without the vaccine.

Budget share Suppose the price of key rings suddenly were to double. How would that affect the number of key rings you buy? If you're like most people, it would have no effect at all. Think about it—a doubling of the price of a 25 cent item that you buy only every year or two is simply nothing to worry about.

If the price of salt were to double, would you use less of it?

By contrast, if the price of the new car you were about to buy suddenly doubled, you would definitely want to check out possible substitutes, such as a used car or a smaller new model. You might also consider holding onto your current car a little longer. The larger the share of your budget an item accounts for, the greater is your incentive to look for substitutes when the price of the item rises. Big-ticket items therefore tend to have higher price elasticities of demand.

Time Home appliances come in a variety of models, some more energy-efficient than others. As a general rule, the more efficient an appliance is, the higher its price. If you were about to buy a new air conditioner and the electric rates suddenly rose sharply, it would be in your interest to buy a more efficient machine than you had originally planned. But suppose you had already bought the machine before you learned of the rate increase. In all likelihood, it would not pay you to discard the machine right away and replace it with a more efficient model. Rather, you would wait until the machine wore out, or until you moved, before making the switch.

As this example illustrates, substitution of one product or service for another takes time. Some substitutions occur in the immediate aftermath of a price increase, but many others take place years or even decades later. For this reason, the price elasticity of demand for any good or service will be higher in the long run than in the short run.

An understanding of the factors that govern price elasticity of demand is necessary not only to make sense of consumer behavior but also to design effective public policy. Consider, for example, the debate about how taxes affect teenage smoking.

Will a higher tax on cigarettes curb teenage smoking?

Consultants hired by the tobacco industry have testified in Congress against higher cigarette taxes aimed at curbing teenage smoking. The main reason teenagers smoke is that their friends smoke, these consultants testified, and they concluded that higher taxes would have little effect. Does the consultants' testimony make economic sense?

The consultants are almost certainly right that peer influence is the most important determinant of teen smoking. But that does not imply that a higher tax on cigarettes would have little impact on adolescent smoking rates. Because most teenagers have small disposable incomes (that is, most have little money to spend at their own discretion), cigarettes constitute a significant share of a teenage smoker's budget. The price elasticity of demand is thus likely to be far from negligible. For at least some teenage smokers, a higher tax would make smoking unaffordable. And among those who could afford the higher prices, at least some others would choose to spend their money on other things rather than pay the higher prices.

Given that the tax would affect at least *some* teenage smokers, the consultants' argument begins to unravel. If the tax deters even a small number of smokers directly through its effect on the price of cigarettes, it will also deter others indirectly by reducing the number of peer role models who smoke. And those who refrain because of these indirect effects will in turn no longer influence others to smoke, and so on. So even if the direct effect of higher cigarette taxes on teen smoking is small, the cumulative effects may be extremely large. The mere fact that peer pressure may be the primary determinant of teen smoking therefore does not imply that higher cigarette taxes will have no significant impact on the number of teens who smoke.

ECONOMIC NATURALIST 5.6

CALCULATING PRICE ELASTICITY

We defined price elasticity of demand as the percentage change in quantity demanded that occurs in response to a 1 percent change in price. Another way of phrasing this definition is to say that price elasticity is the proportion by which quantity demanded changes divided by the corresponding proportion by which price changes. For example, if a 5 percent change in price causes quantity demanded to fall by 10 percent, the price elasticity of demand is 10 percent/5 percent = 2.0. By defining elasticity in this way, we can construct a simple formula that enables us to calculate the price elasticity of demand for a product using only minimal information about its demand curve.

Suppose we let P represent the current price of a good and Q the quantity demanded at that price. Similarly, let ΔP represent a small change in the current price and ΔQ the resulting change in quantity demanded. (See Figure 5.12.) The expression $\Delta P/P$ will then stand for the proportion by which price changes when

FIGURE 5.12
A Graphical Interpretation of Price Elasticity of Demand.
Price elasticity of demand at any point along a straight-line demand curve is the ratio of price to quantity at that point times the reciprocal of the slope of the demand curve.

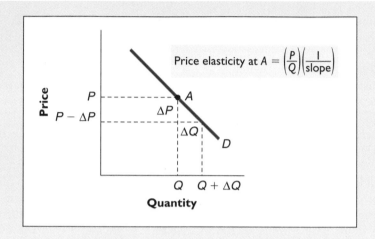

Price elasticity at $A = \left(\dfrac{P}{Q}\right)\left(\dfrac{1}{slope}\right)$

P changes by ΔP, and $\Delta Q/Q$ will stand for the corresponding proportion by which quantity changes. The formula for price elasticity may then be written as

$$\text{Price elasticity} = \epsilon = \left(\frac{\Delta Q}{Q}\right)\bigg/\left(\frac{\Delta P}{P}\right).$$

One attractive feature of this formula for elasticity is that it has a straightforward graphical interpretation. Thus, if we want to calculate the price elasticity of demand at point A on the demand curve shown in Figure 5.12, we can begin by rewriting the right-hand side of the equation as $(P/Q)(\Delta Q/\Delta P)$. And since the slope of the demand curve is equal to $\Delta P/\Delta Q$, $\Delta Q/\Delta P$ is the reciprocal of that slope: $\Delta Q/\Delta P = 1/\text{slope}$. So the price elasticity of demand at point A, denoted ϵ_A, has the following simple formula:

$$\epsilon_A = \left(\frac{P}{Q}\right)\bigg/\left(\frac{1}{slope}\right).$$

To illustrate how convenient this graphical interpretation of elasticity can be, suppose we want to find the price elasticity of demand at point A on the demand curve in Figure 5.13. The slope of this demand curve is the ratio of its vertical intercept to its horizontal intercept: $20/5 = 4$, so $1/\text{slope} = 1/4$. (Actually, the slope is -4, but we ignore the minus sign for convenience, since price elasticity always has the same sign.) The ratio P/Q at point A is $8/3$, so the price elasticity at point A is equal to $(P/Q)(1/\text{slope}) = (8/3)(1/4) = 2/3$.

EXERCISE 5.5

What is the price elasticity of demand when $P = 4$ on the demand curve in Figure 5.13?

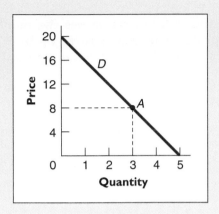

FIGURE 5.13
Calculating Price Elasticity of Demand.
The price elasticity of demand at A is given by $(P/Q)(1/\text{slope}) = (8/3)(1/4) = 2/3$.

PRICE ELASTICITY CHANGES ALONG A STRAIGHT-LINE DEMAND CURVE

As a glance at our elasticity formula makes clear, price elasticity has a different value at every point along a straight-line demand curve. The slope of a straight-line demand curve is constant, which means that 1/slope is also constant. But the price-quantity ratio, P/Q, declines as we move down the demand curve. Thus the elasticity of demand declines steadily as we move downward along a straight-line demand curve.

If we think back to the definition of elasticity as the percentage change in quantity demanded divided by the corresponding percentage change in price, this pattern makes sense. After all, a price movement of a given absolute size is small in percentage terms when it occurs near the top of the demand curve, where price is high, but large in percentage terms when it occurs near the bottom of the demand curve, where price is low. Likewise, a quantity movement of a given absolute value is large in percentage terms when it occurs near the top of the demand curve, where quantity is low, and small in percentage terms when it occurs near the bottom of the curve, where quantity is high.

INCOME ELASTICITY AND CROSS-PRICE ELASTICITY OF DEMAND

The **elasticity of demand** for a good can be defined not only with respect to its own price but also with respect to the prices of substitutes or complements, or even to income. For example, the elasticity of demand for peanuts with respect to the price of cashews—also known as the cross-price elasticity of peanuts with respect to cashew prices—is the percentage by which the quantity of peanuts demanded changes in response to a 1 percent change in the price of cashews.

Unlike the elasticity of demand for a good with respect to its own price, these other elasticities may be either positive or negative, so it is important to note their algebraic signs carefully. The income elasticity of demand for inferior goods, for example, is negative, while the income elasticity of demand for normal goods is positive. When the **cross-price elasticity of demand for two goods** is positive—as in the peanuts-cashews example—the two goods are substitutes. When it is negative, the two goods are complements. The elasticity of demand for tennis racquets with respect to court rental fees, for example, is less than zero.

income elasticity of demand the percentage by which a good's quantity demanded changes in response to a 1 percent change in income

cross-price elasticity of demand for two goods the percentage by which the quantity demanded of the first good changes in response to a 1 percent change in the price of the second

EXERCISE 5.6

If a 10 percent increase in income causes the number of students who choose to attend private universities to go up by 5 percent, what is the income elasticity of demand for private universities?

TWO SPECIAL CASES

There are two important exceptions to the general rule that elasticity declines along straight-line demand curves. Note that the horizontal demand curve Figure 5.14(a) has a slope of zero, which means that the reciprocal of its slope is infi-

FIGURE 5.14
Perfectly Elastic and Perfectly Inelastic Demand Curves.

The horizontal demand curve (a) is perfectly elastic, or infinitely elastic, at every point. Even the slightest increase in price leads consumers to desert the product in favor of substitutes. The vertical demand curve (b) is perfectly inelastic at every point. Consumers do not, or cannot, switch to substitutes even in the face of large increases in price.

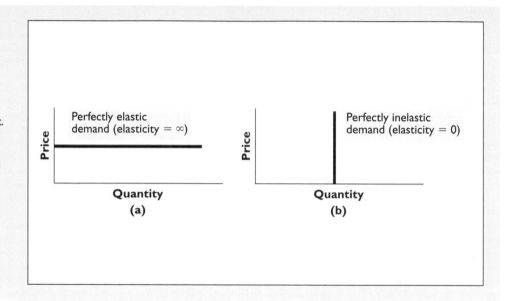

nite. Price elasticity of demand is thus infinite at every point along a horizontal demand curve. Such demand curves are said to be **perfectly elastic.**

In contrast, the demand curve in Figure 5.14(b) is vertical, which means that its slope is infinite. The reciprocal of its slope is thus equal to zero. Price elasticity of demand is thus exactly zero at every point along the curve. For this reason, vertical demand curves are said to be **perfectly inelastic.**

perfectly elastic the demand for a good is perfectly elastic with respect to price if its price elasticity of demand is infinite

perfectly inelastic the demand for a good is perfectly inelastic with respect to price if its price elasticity of demand is zero

---

RECAP   PRICE ELASTICITY OF DEMAND

The price elasticity of demand for a good is the percentage change in the quantity demanded that results from a 1 percent change in its price. Mathematically, the elasticity of demand at a point along a demand curve is equal to $(P/Q)(1/\text{slope})$, where P and Q represent price and quantity and $(1/\text{slope})$ is the reciprocal of the slope of the demand curve at that point.

For a product whose price elasticity is greater than 1, an increase in price will reduce total expenditure, and a reduction in price will increase total expenditure. For a product whose price elasticity of demand is less than 1, an increase in price will increase total expenditure, and a cut in price will reduce total expenditure.

The price elasticity of demand for a good or service tends to be larger when substitutes for the good are more readily available, when the good's share in the consumer's budget is larger, and when consumers have more time to adjust to a change in price.

When the elasticity of demand for one good with respect to the price of another good is positive, the two goods are substitutes; when this cross-price elasticity of demand is negative, the two goods are complements. A normal good has positive income elasticity of demand, and an inferior good has negative income elasticity of demand.

WHERE DO WANTS COME FROM?

Wants (also called *preferences* or *tastes*) are an important determinant of how much people are willing to pay for specific goods and services. Where do wants come from? Many tastes—such as the taste for water on a hot day or for a comfortable place to sleep at night—are largely biological in origin. But many others are heavily shaped by culture, and even basic cravings may be socially molded. For example, people raised in southern India develop a taste for hot curry dishes, while those raised in England generally prefer milder foods.

Tastes for some items may remain stable for many years, but tastes for others may be highly volatile. Although books about the *Titanic* disaster have been continuously available since the vessel sank in the spring of 1912, not until the appearance of James Cameron's blockbuster film did these books begin to sell in large quantities. In the spring of 1998, 5 of the 15 books on *The New York Times* paperback bestseller list were about the *Titanic* itself or one of the actors in the film. Yet none of these books, or any other book about the *Titanic,* made the bestseller list in 1999. Still, echoes of the film continued to reverberate in the marketplace. In the years since its release, for example, demand for ocean cruises has grown sharply, and several television networks have introduced shows set on cruise ships.

As discussed in the tobacco tax example, peer pressure is another example of how social forces often influence demand. Indeed, it is often the most important single determinant of demand. For instance, if our goal is to predict whether a young man will purchase an illegal recreational drug, knowing how much income he has is not very helpful. Nor does knowing the prices of whiskey and other legal substitutes for illicit drugs. Although these factors do influence purchase decisions, by themselves they are weak predictors. But if we know that most of the young man's best friends are heavy drug users, there is a reasonably good chance that he will use drugs as well.

Another important way in which social forces shape demand is in the relatively common desire to own products that are recognized as the best of their kind. For instance, many people want to hear Luciano Pavorotti sing, not just because of the high quality of his voice, but because he is widely regarded as the world's best—or at least the world's best known—tenor.

Consider, too, the decision of how much to spend on an interview suit. As the employment counselors never tire of reminding us, making a good first impression is extremely important when you go for a job interview. At the very least, it means showing up in a suit that looks good. But looking good is a relative concept. If everyone else shows up in a $200 suit, you'll look good if you show up in a $300 suit. But you won't look as good in that same $300 suit if everyone else shows up in suits costing $1,000. The amount you'll choose to spend on an interview suit, then, clearly depends on how much others in your circle are spending.

■ SUMMARY ■

- The rational consumer allocates income among different goods so that the marginal utility gained from the last dollar spent on each good is the same. This rational spending rule gives rise to the law of demand, which states that people do less of what they want to do as the cost of doing it rises. Here, *cost* refers to the sum of all monetary and nonmonetary sacrifices—explicit and implicit—that must be made to engage in the activity.

- The ability to substitute one good for another is an important factor behind the law of demand. Because virtually every good or service has at least some substitutes, economists prefer to speak in terms of wants rather than of needs. We face choices, and describing our demands as needs is misleading because it suggests we have no options.

- The demand curve is a schedule that shows the amounts of a good people want to buy at various prices. Demand curves can be used to summarize the price–quantity relationship for a single individual, but more commonly we employ them to summarize that relationship for an entire market. At any quantity along a demand curve, the corresponding price represents the amount by which the consumer (or consumers) would benefit from having an additional unit of the product. For this reason, the demand curve is sometimes described as a summary of the benefit side of the market.

- The price elasticity of demand is a measure of how strongly buyers respond to changes in price. It is the percentage change in quantity demanded that occurs in response to a 1 percent change in price. The demand for a good is called elastic with respect to price if its price elasticity is more than 1, inelastic if its price elasticity is less than 1, and unit elastic if its price elasticity is equal to 1.

- A cut in price will increase total spending on a good if demand is elastic, but reduce it if demand is inelastic. An increase in price will increase total spending on a good if demand is inelastic but reduce it if demand is elastic. Total expenditure on a good reaches a maximum when price elasticity of demand is equal to 1.

- Goods such as salt, which occupy only a small share of the typical consumer's budget and have few or no good substitutes, tend to have low price elasticity of demand. Goods like new cars of a particular make and model, which occupy large budget shares and have many attractive substitutes, tend to have high price elasticity of demand. Price elasticity of demand is higher in the long run than in the short run because people often need time to adjust to price changes.

- The price elasticity of demand at a point along a demand curve can also be expressed as the formula $\epsilon = (\Delta Q/Q)/(\Delta P/P)$. Here, P and Q represent price and quantity at that point, and ΔQ and ΔP represent small changes in price and quantity. For straight-line demand curves, this formula can also be expressed as $\epsilon = (P/Q)(1/\text{slope})$. These formulations tell us that price elasticity declines in absolute terms as we move down a straight-line demand curve.

■ KEY TERMS ■

cross-price elasticity of demand (127)
elastic (123)
income elasticity of demand (127)
inelastic (123)
law of demand (105)
law of diminishing marginal utility (108)

marginal utility (107)
nominal price (114)
optimal combination of goods (110)
perfectly elastic (128)
perfectly inelastic (128)
price elasticity of demand (122)

rational Spending Rule (111)
real price (114)
total expenditure (119)
total revenue (119)
unit elastic (123)

■ REVIEW QUESTIONS ■

1. Why do economists prefer to speak of demands arising out of "wants" rather than "needs"?

2. Why does the law of diminishing marginal utility encourage people to spread their spending across many different types of goods?

3. Under what conditions will an increase in the price of a product lead to a reduction in total spending for that product?

4. Why do economists pay little attention to the algebraic sign of the elasticity of demand for a good with respect to its own price, yet they pay careful attention to the algebraic sign of the elasticity of demand for a good with respect to another good's price?

5. Why does the elasticity of demand for a good with respect to its own price decline as we move down along a straight-line demand curve?

▪ PROBLEMS ▪

1. In which type of restaurant do you expect the service to be more prompt and courteous: an expensive gourmet restaurant or an inexpensive diner? Explain your answer.

2. Tom has a weekly allowance of $24, all of which he spends on pizza and movie rentals, whose prices are $6 and $3, respectively. His total utility is the sum of the utility he derives from each of these consumption activities. If these utilities vary with the amounts consumed as shown in the following table, and pizzas and movie rentals are consumable only in integer amounts, how many pizzas and how many movie rentals should Tom consume each week?

Pizzas/week	Utils/week from pizza	Movie rentals/ week	Utils/week from rentals
0	0	0	0
1	20	1	40
2	38	2	46
3	54	3	50
4	68	4	54
5	80	5	56
6	90	6	57
7	98	7	57
8	104	8	57

3. Martha's current marginal utility from consuming orange juice is 75 utils per ounce, and her marginal utility from consuming coffee is 50 utils per ounce. If orange juice costs 25 cents per ounce and coffee costs 20 cents per ounce, is Martha maximizing her total utility from the two beverages? If so, explain how you know. If not, how should she rearrange her spending?

4. The following schedule shows the number of packs of bagels bought in Davis, California, each day at a variety of prices.

Price of bagels ($/pack)	Number of packs purchased per day
6	0
5	3,000
4	6,000
3	9,000
2	12,000
1	15,000
0	18,000

   a. Graph the daily demand curve for packs of bagels in Davis.
   b. Derive an algebraic expression for the demand schedule you graphed.
   c. Calculate the price elasticity of demand at the point on the demand curve where the price of bagels is $3.
   d. If all bagel shops increased the price of bagels from $3 to $4, what would happen to total revenue?
   e. Calculate the price elasticity of demand at a point on the demand curve where the price of bagels is $2.
   f. If bagel shops increased the price of bagels from $2 to $3, what would happen to total revenue?
   g. Show on the graph in part a the inelastic and elastic regions of the demand curve.

5. Suppose, while rummaging through your uncle's closet, you found the original painting of *Dogs Playing Poker,* a valuable piece of art. You decided to set up a display in your uncle's garage. The demand curve to see this valuable piece of art is $P = 12 - 2Q$, where P is dollars per visit and Q is the number of visitors per day.
   a. Draw the demand curve for the painting.
   b. How many people would view the painting if you charged them nothing?
   c. What is the price elasticity of demand when the price is $4?

6. Is the demand for a particular brand of car, like a Chevrolet, likely to be more or less price-elastic than the demand for all cars?

7. Among the following groups—senior executives, junior executives, and students—which is likely to have the most and which is likely to have the least price-elastic demand for membership in the Association of Business Professionals?

8. At point A on the following demand curve, how will a 1 percent increase in the price of the product affect total expenditure on the product?

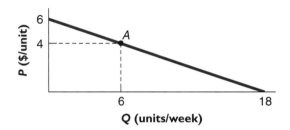

9. Andy is selling Economics Department T-shirts. The vertical axis of his demand curve measures the price of T-shirts in dollars, and the horizontal axis measures the quantity demanded in T-shirts per week. The absolute value of the slope of his demand curve is 2, and if Andy's goal is to maximize revenue from selling the T-shirts, the price he should charge, in dollars, will be:
   a. Half as large as the number of shirts he will sell at that price.
   b. Twice as large as the number of shirts he will sell at that price.
   c. Equal to the number of shirts he will sell at that price.
   d. Low enough to sell as many T-shirts as possible.
   e. There is not enough information here to answer this question.

10. In an attempt to induce citizens to conserve energy, the government enacted regulations requiring that all air conditioners be more efficient in their use of electricity. After this regulation was implemented, government officials were then surprised to discover that people used even more electricity than before. Using the concept of price elasticity, explain how this might have happened.

▪ ANSWERS TO IN-CHAPTER EXERCISES ▪

5.1 To buy 8 cones per week and 4 sundaes would cost $16, which is $2 more than Lamar has to spend.

5.2 Suppose Lamar starts with his previous optimal combination—4 cones per week and 3 sundaes—then allocates his additional $4 one step at a time—either by spending $2 on an additional sundae or by spending that same $2 on 2 more cones. If he buys a fourth sundae for $2, he'll get 15 extra utils, or 7.5 utils per dollar. For the same money, he could buy 2 additional cones, which would give him 12 extra utils, or 6 utils per dollar. Since the first option is better, Lamar should spend the first $2 of his additional $4 weekly ice cream budget on sundaes. That gives him 4 cones and 4 sundaes, with an additional $2 to spend. He can spend it either on a fifth sundae or on 2 more cones. If he buys the fifth sundae, he'll get 10 extra utils, or 5 utils per dollar. If he buys 2 more cones, he'll get 12 extra utils, or 6 utils per dollar. So cones are the better choice this time. Proceeding in this manner, Lamar ends up buying 6 cones per week and 4 sundaes, a combination that yields 200 utils per week. The increase in his income has increased his demands for both cones and more sundaes.

Vanilla cones per week	Utils/week from cones	Chocolate sundaes per week	Utils/week from sundaes
0	0	0	0
1	36	1	50
2	50	2	80
3	60	3	105
4	68	4	120
5	75	5	130
6	80	6	138
7	84	7	144
8	82	8	148
9	81	9	150
10	80	10	151

5.3. As we saw earlier, when the price of cones was $1 apiece, Lamar's best bet was to buy 4 cones per week and 3 sundaes. But with the price of cones now $2 instead of $1, he cannot afford to buy 4 cones and 3 sundaes (whose combined price is $14, or $4 more than his $10 weekly budget). So he needs to cut back, and the best place to start is with the good that delivers less marginal utility per dollar. The marginal utility per dollar delivered by the fourth cone is now only 8 utils/$2 = 4 utils per dollar, much less than the marginal utility per dollar delivered by the third sundae (which is still 12.5 utils per dollar). At 3 cones and 3 sundaes a week, he is still spending $2 too much, and the solution is to reduce consumption of cones still further (since giving up the third cone sacrifices only 5 utils per dollar, or less than he'd lose by giving up a sundae). Having cut back to 2 cones and 3 sundaes, he's spending exactly $10 per week. Now suppose he cuts his cone consumption from 2 to 1. By so doing he'll lose another 14 utils, or 7 utils per dollar saved. And if he then spends that $2 on an additional sundae, he'll gain 15 utils, or 7.5 utils per dollar. So Lamar's best bet this time is to consume 1 cone and 4 sundaes per week, which gives him a total of 156 utils per week.

5.4 The vertical intercept of this demand curve is 12, and its slope is $\Delta P/\Delta Q = -2/100 = -1/50$. So the equation for this demand curve is $P = 12 - (1/50)Q$.

5.5. At point *A* in the following diagram, $P/Q = 4/4 = 1$. The slope of this demand curve is $20/5 = 4$, so $\epsilon = 1(1/\text{slope}) = 1/4$.

5.6. Income elasticity = percentage change in quantity demanded/(percentage change in income) = 5 percent/10 percent = 0.5.

6

PERFECTLY COMPETITIVE SUPPLY: THE COST SIDE OF THE MARKET

■

Cars that took more than 50 hours to be assembled in the 1970s are now built in less than 8 hours. Similar productivity growth has occurred in many other manufacturing industries. Yet in many service industries, productivity has grown only slowly, if at all. For example, the London Philharmonic Orchestra performs Beethoven's Fifth Symphony with no fewer musicians today than it did in 1850. And it still takes a barber about half an hour to cut someone's hair, just as it always has.

Given the spectacular growth in manufacturing workers' productivity, it is no surprise that their real wages have risen more than fivefold during the last century. But how to explain why real wages for service workers have risen just as much? If barbers and musicians are no more productive than they were at the turn of the century, why are they now paid five times as much?

An answer is suggested by the observation that the opportunity cost of pursuing any given occupation is the most one could have earned in some other occupation. Most people who become barbers or musicians could instead have chosen jobs in manufacturing. If workers in service industries were not paid roughly as much as they could have earned in other occupations, many of them would not have been willing to work in service industries in the first place.

The trajectories of wages in manufacturing and service industries illustrate the intimate link between the prices at which goods and services are offered for sale in the market and the opportunity cost of the resources required to

Why are barbers paid five times as much now as in 1900, even though they can't cut hair any faster than they could then?

produce them. Whereas our focus in Chapter 5 was on the buyer's side of the market, our focus here will be on the seller's side. Earlier, we saw that the demand curve is a schedule that tells how many units buyers wish to purchase at different prices. Our task here is to gain insight into the factors that shape the supply curve, the schedule that tells how many units suppliers wish to sell at different prices.

Although the demand side and the supply side of the market differ in several ways, many of these differences are superficial. Indeed, the behavior of both buyers and sellers is in an important sense fundamentally the same. After all, the two groups confront essentially similar questions—in the buyer's case, "Should I buy another unit?" and in the seller's case, "Should I sell another unit?" What is more, buyers and sellers use the same criterion for answering these questions. Thus a rational consumer will buy another unit if its benefit exceeds its cost, and a rational seller will sell another unit if the cost of making it is less than the extra revenue that results from selling it (the familiar cost-benefit principle again).

THINKING ABOUT SUPPLY

Do you live in a state that requires refundable soft drink container deposits? If so, you've probably noticed that some people always redeem their own containers, while other people pass up this opportunity, leaving their used containers to be recycled by others. The recycling of used containers is a service, and its production obeys the same logic that applies to the production of other goods and services. As the following sequence of recycling examples makes clear, the supply curve for a good or service is rooted in the individual's choice of whether to produce it.

EXAMPLE 6.1   **How much time should Harry spend recycling soft drink containers?**

Harry is trying to decide how to divide his time between his job as a dishwasher in the dining hall, which pays $6/hour for as many hours as he chooses to work, and gathering soft drink containers to redeem for deposit, in which case his pay depends on both the deposit per container and the number of containers he finds. Earnings aside, Harry is indifferent between the two tasks, and the number of containers he will find depends, as shown in the accompanying table, on the number of hours per day he searches:

Search time (hours/day)	Total number of containers found	Additional number of containers found
0	0	
		600
1	600	
		400
2	1,000	
		300
3	1,300	
		200
4	1,500	
		100
5	1,600	

If the containers can be redeemed for 2 cents each, how many hours should Harry spend searching for containers?

For each additional hour Harry spends searching for soft drink containers, he loses the $6 he could have earned as a dishwasher. This is his hourly opportunity cost of searching for soft drink containers. His benefit from each hour spent searching for containers is the number of additional containers he finds (shown in column 3 of the table) times the deposit he collects per container. Since he can redeem each container for 2 cents, his first hour spent collecting containers will yield earnings of $600(\$0.02) = \$12$, or \$6 more than he could have earned as a dishwasher.

By the cost-benefit principle, then, Harry should spend his first hour of work each day searching for soft drink containers rather than washing dishes. A second hour searching for containers will yield 400 additional containers, for additional earnings of \$8, so it too satisfies the cost-benefit test. A third hour spent searching yields 300 additional containers, for $300(\$0.02) = \$6$ of additional earnings. Since this is exactly what Harry could have earned washing dishes, he is indifferent between spending his third hour of work each day on one task or the other. For the sake of discussion, however, we'll assume that he resolves ties in favor of searching for containers, in which case he will spend 3 hours each day searching for containers.

What is the lowest redemption price that would induce Harry to spend at least 1 hour per day recycling? Since he will find 600 containers in his first hour of search, a 1 cent deposit on each container would enable him to match his \$6/hour opportunity cost. More generally, if the redemption price is p and the next hour spent searching yields ΔQ additional containers, then Harry's additional earnings from searching the additional hour will be $p(\Delta Q)$. This means that the smallest redemption price that will lead Harry to search another hour must satisfy the equation

$$p(\Delta Q) = \$6.$$

How high would the redemption price of containers have to be to induce Harry to search for a second hour? Since he can find $\Delta Q = 400$ additional containers if he searches for a second hour, the smallest redemption price that will lead him to do so must satisfy $p(400) = \$6$, which solves for $p = 1.5$ cents.

EXERCISE 6.1

In Example 6.1, calculate the smallest container redemption prices that will lead Harry to search a third, fourth, and fifth hour.

By searching for soft drink containers, Harry becomes, in effect, a supplier of container-recycling services. In Exercise 6.1, we saw that Harry's reservation prices for his third, fourth, and fifth hours of container search are 2, 3, and 6 cents, respectively. Having calculated these reservation prices, we can now plot his supply curve of container-recycling services. This curve, which plots the redemption price per container on the vertical axis and the number of containers recycled each day on the horizontal axis, is shown in Figure 6.1. Harry's individual supply curve of container-recycling services tells us the number of containers he is willing to recycle at various redemption prices.

Like the supply curves we saw in Chapter 4, the supply curve in Figure 6.1 is upward-sloping. There are exceptions to this general rule, but sellers of most goods will offer higher quantities at higher prices than at lower prices.

The relationship between the individual and market supply curves for a product is analogous to the relationship between the individual and market demand curves. The quantity that corresponds to a given price on the market demand curve is the sum of the quantities demanded at that price by all individual buyers in the market. Likewise, the quantity that corresponds to any given price on the market supply curve is the sum of the quantities supplied at that price by all individual sellers in the market.

FIGURE 6.1

An Individual Supply Curve for Recycling Services.

When the deposit price increases, it becomes attractive to abandon alternative pursuits to spend more time searching for soft drink containers.

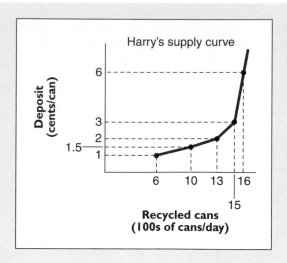

Suppose, for example, that the supply side of the recycling-services market consists only of Harry and his identical twin, Barry, whose individual supply curve is the same as Harry's. To generate the market supply curve, we first put the individual supply curves side by side, as shown in Figure 6.2(a) and (b). We then announce a price, and for that price we add the individual quantities supplied to obtain the total quantity supplied in the market. Thus, at a price of 3 cents/container, both Harry and Barry wish to recycle 1,500 cans/day, so the total market supply at that price is 3,000 cans/day. Proceeding in like manner for a sequence of prices, we generate the market supply curve for recycling services shown in Figure 6.2(c). This is the same process of horizontal summation by which we generated market demand curves from individual demand curves in Chapter 5.

FIGURE 6.2

The Market Supply Curve for Recycling Services.

To generate the market supply curve (c) from the individual supply curves (a) and (b), we add the individual supply curves horizontally.

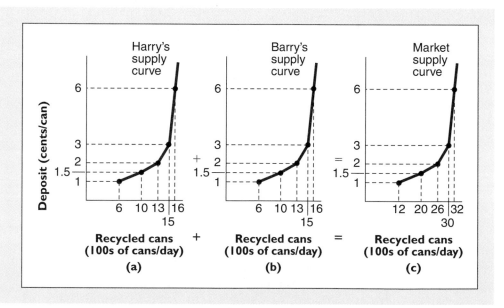

Alternatively, if there were many suppliers with individual supply curves identical to Harry's, we could generate the market supply curve by simply multiplying each quantity value on the individual supply curve by the number of suppliers. For instance, Figure 6.3 shows the supply curve for a market in which there are 1,000 suppliers with individual supply curves like Harry's.

Why do individual supply curves tend to be upward-sloping, at least in the short run? One explanation is suggested by the principle of increasing opportunity cost, or the low-hanging-fruit principle. Container recyclers should always

FIGURE 6.3
The Market Supply Curve with 1,000 Identical Sellers.
To generate the market supply curve for a market with 1,000 identical sellers, we simply multiply each quantity value on the individual supply curve by 1,000.

look first for the containers that are easiest to find, such as those in plain view in readily accessible locations. As the redemption price rises, it will pay to incur the additional cost of searching farther from the beaten path.

If all individuals have identical upward-sloping supply curves, the market supply curve will be upward-sloping as well. But there is an important additional reason for the positive slope of market supply curves—namely, that individual suppliers generally differ with respect to their opportunity costs of supplying the product. (The principle of increasing opportunity cost applies not only to each individual searcher but also *across* individuals.) Thus, whereas people facing unattractive employment opportunities in other occupations may be willing to recycle soft drink containers even when the redemption price is low, those with more attractive options will recycle only if the redemption price is relatively high.

In summary then, the upward slope of the supply schedule reflects the fact that costs tend to rise when producers expand production in the short run, partly because each individual exploits her or his most attractive opportunities first, but also because different potential sellers face different opportunity costs.

PROFIT-MAXIMIZING FIRMS AND PERFECTLY COMPETITIVE MARKETS

PROFIT MAXIMIZATION

To explore the nature of the supply curve of a product more fully, we must say more about the goals of the organizations that supply the product and the kind of economic environment in which they operate. In virtually every economy, goods and services are produced by a variety of organizations that pursue a host of different motives. The Red Cross supplies blood because its organizers and donors want to help people in need, the local government fixes potholes because the mayor was elected on a promise to do so, karaoke singers perform because they like public attention, and car wash employees are driven primarily by the hope of making enough money to pay their rent.

Notwithstanding this rich variety of motives, *most* goods and services offered for sale in a market economy are sold by private firms whose main reason for existing is to earn **profit** for their owners. A firm's profit is the difference between the total revenue it receives from the sale of its product and all costs it incurs, both explicit and implicit, in producing it.

profit the total revenue a firm receives from the sale of its product minus all costs— explicit and implicit—incurred in producing it

profit-maximizing firm a firm whose primary goal is to maximize the difference between its total revenues and total costs

A **profit-maximizing firm** is one whose primary goal is to maximize the amount of profit it earns. The supply curves that economists use in standard supply and demand theory are based on the assumption that goods are sold by profit-maximizing firms in **perfectly competitive markets,** which are markets in which individual firms have no influence over the market prices of the products they sell. Any single firm, being just one of many sellers of the product, cannot hope to charge more than its rivals and has no motive to charge less. Because of their inability to influence market price, perfectly competitive firms are often described as **price takers.**

perfectly competitive market a market in which no individual supplier has significant influence on the market price of the product

The market for operating systems for desktop computers, more than 90 percent of which are sold by Microsoft, is not perfectly competitive because Microsoft has enough presence in that market to have significant control over the prices it charges. For example, if Microsoft were to raise the price of its latest edition of its Windows operating system by, say, 20 percent, some consumers might switch to Macintosh or Linux, and others might postpone their next upgrade; but many—perhaps even most—would continue with their plans to buy.

price taker a firm that has no influence over the price at which it sells its product

By contrast, if an individual wheat farmer were to charge even just 10 cents more than the current market price for a bushel of wheat, the farmer wouldn't be able to sell any wheat at all. The wheat farmer is a stereotypical example of a perfectly competitive firm—one of a host of essentially similar firms that sell a tiny fraction of their industry's output of a highly standardized product. If any one perfectly competitive seller were to raise its price, buyers would simply switch to another seller.

THE DEMAND CURVE FACING A PERFECTLY COMPETITIVE FIRM

From the perspective of an individual firm in a perfectly competitive market, what does the demand curve for its product look like? Since the firm can sell as much or as little as it wishes at the prevailing market price, the demand curve for its product is perfectly elastic at the market price. Figure 6.4(a) shows the market demand and supply curves intersecting to determine a market price of P_0. Figure 6.4(b) shows the product demand curve D_i as seen by any individual firm in this market, a horizontal line at the market price level P_0.

FIGURE 6.4

The Demand Curve Facing a Perfectly Competitive Firm.

(a) The market demand and supply curves intersect to determine the market price of the product. (b) The individual firm's demand curve (D_i) is a horizontal line at the market price.

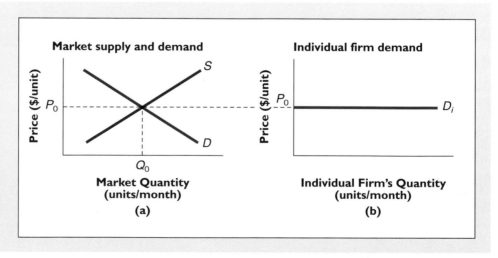

imperfectly competitive firm a firm that has at least some control over the market price of its product

Many of the conclusions of the standard supply and demand model also hold for **imperfectly competitive firms:** those firms, like Microsoft, that have at least some ability to vary their own prices. But certain other conclusions do not, as we will see when we examine the behavior of such firms more closely in Chapter 9.

Since a perfectly competitive firm has no control over the market price of its product, it needn't worry about choosing the level at which to set that price. As we've seen, the equilibrium market price in a competitive market comes from the intersection of the industry supply and demand curves. The challenge confronting the perfectly competitive firm is to choose its output level so that it makes as much profit as it can at that price. As we investigate how the competitive firm responds to this challenge, we'll see once again the pivotal role of our core principle that some costs are more important than others.

PRODUCTION IN THE SHORT RUN

To help gain a deeper understanding of the origins of the supply curve, consider a perfectly competitive firm confronting the decision of how much to produce. The firm in question is a small company that makes glass bottles. To keep things simple, suppose that the silicon required for making bottles is available free of charge from a nearby desert, and that the only costs the firm incurs are the wages it pays its employees and the lease payment on its bottle-making machine. The employees and the machine are the firm's only two **factors of production**—inputs used to produce goods and services. In more complex examples, factors of production might also include land, structures, entrepreneurship, and possibly others, but for the moment we consider only labor and capital.

factor of production an input used in the production of a good or service

When we refer to the **short run,** we mean a period of time during which at least some of the firm's factors of production cannot be varied. (For our bottle maker, the short run is that period of time during which the firm cannot alter the capacity of its bottle-making machine.) By contrast, when we speak of the **long run,** we refer to a time period of sufficient length that all the firm's factors of production are variable.

short run a period of time sufficiently short that at least some of the firm's factors of production are fixed

Table 6.1 shows how the company's bottle production depends on the number of hours its employees spend on the job each day.

long run a period of time of sufficient length that all the firm's factors of production are variable

TABLE 6.1
Employment and Output for a Glass Bottle Maker

Number of bottles/day	Number of employee-hours/day
0	0
100	1
200	2
300	4
400	7
500	11
600	16
700	22

law of diminishing returns a property of the relationship between the amount of a good or service produced and the amount of a variable factor required to produce it; the law says that when some factors of production are fixed, increased production of the good eventually requires ever larger increases in the variable factor

The output-employment relationship described in Table 6.1 exhibits a pattern common to many such relationships. Each time we move down one row in the table, output grows by 100 bottles/day, but note in column 2 that larger and larger increases in the amount of labor are necessary to achieve this increase. Economists refer to this pattern as the **law of diminishing returns,** and it always refers to situations in which at least some factors of production are held fixed. In the current example, the **fixed factor of production** is the bottle-making machine, and the **variable factor of production** is labor. In the context of this example, the law of diminishing returns says simply that

fixed factor of production an input whose quantity cannot be altered in the short run

variable factor of production an input whose quantity can be altered in the short run successive increases in bottle output require ever larger increases in labor input. The reason for this pattern often entails some form of congestion. For instance, in an office with three secretaries and only a single word processor, we would not expect to get three times as many letters typed per hour as in an office with only one secretary, because only one person can use a word processor at a time.

CHOOSING OUTPUT TO MAXIMIZE PROFIT

Suppose the lease payment for the company's bottle-making machine and the building that houses it is $40/day, and it must be paid whether or not the company makes any bottles. This payment is both a fixed cost (since it does not depend on the number of bottles per day the firm makes) and, for the duration of the lease, a sunk cost. For short, we'll refer to this cost as the company's *capital cost*. In Examples 6.2 to 6.5, we'll explore how the company's decision about how many bottles to make depends on the price of bottles, the wage rate, and the cost of capital.

EXAMPLE 6.2

If bottles sell for $35/hundred and if the employee's wage is $10/hour, how many bottles should the company described above produce each day?

The company's goal is to maximize its profit, which is the difference between the revenue it collects from the sale of bottles and the cost of its labor and capital. Table 6.2 shows how the daily number of bottles produced (denoted Q) is related to the company's revenue, employment, costs, and profit.

TABLE 6.2
Output, Revenue, Costs, and Profit

Q (bottles/ day)	Total revenue ($/day)	Total labor cost ($/day)	Total cost ($/day)	Profit ($/day)
0	0	0	40	−40
100	35	10	50	−15
200	70	20	60	10
300	105	40	80	25
400	140	70	110	30
500	175	110	150	25
600	210	160	200	10
700	245	220	260	−15

To see how the entries in Table 6.2 are constructed, examine the revenue, cost, and profit values that correspond to 200 units of output (row 3). Total revenue is $70, the company's receipts from selling 200 bottles at $35/hundred. To make 200 bottles, the firm's employee had to work 2 hours (see Table 6.1), and at a wage of $10/hour that translates into $20 of total labor cost. When the firm's fixed capital cost of $40/day is added to its total labor cost, we get the total cost entry of $60/day in column 4. The firm's daily profit, finally, is total revenue − total cost = $70 − $60 = $10, the entry in column 5.

From a glance at the final column in Table 6.2, we see that the company's maximum profit, $30/day, occurs when it produces 400 bottles/day.

EXAMPLE 6.3

Same as Example 6.2, except now bottles sell for $45/hundred.

As we see in the entries of Table 6.3, the only consequence of the change in selling price is that total revenue, and hence profit, is now higher than before at every output level. As indicated by the entries of the final column, the company now does best to produce 500 bottles/day, 100 more than when the price was only $35/hundred.

TABLE 6.3
Output, Revenue, Costs, and Profit

Q (bottles/ day)	Total revenue ($/day)	Total labor cost ($/day)	Total cost ($/day)	Profit ($/day)
0	0	0	40	−40
100	45	10	50	−5
200	90	20	60	30
300	135	40	80	55
400	175	70	110	70
500	220	110	150	75
600	270	160	200	70
700	315	220	260	55

EXAMPLE 6.4

Same as Example 6.2, except now the wage rate is $12/hour.

With a higher wage rate, labor costs are higher at every level of output, as shown in column 3, Table 6.4, and maximum profit now occurs when the firm produces 300 bottles/day, or 100 fewer than when the wage rate was $10/hour.

TABLE 6.4
Output, Revenue, Costs, and Profit

Q (bottles/ day)	Total revenue ($/day)	Total labor cost ($/day)	Total cost ($/day)	Profit ($/day)
0	0	0	40	−40
100	35	12	52	−17
200	70	24	64	6
300	105	48	88	17
400	140	84	124	16
500	175	132	172	3
600	210	192	232	−22
700	245	264	304	−59

Consider one final variation:

EXAMPLE 6.5

Same as Example 6.2, except now the capital cost is not $40/day but $70.

The entries in Table 6.5 are just like those in Table 6.2 except that each entry in the total cost column (column 4) is $30 higher than before, with the result that each entry in the profit column (column 5) is $30 lower. Note, however, that the profit-maximizing number of bottles to produce is again 400/day, precisely the same as when capital cost was only $40/day. When the company produces 400 bottles daily, its daily profit is 0, but at any other output level its profit would have been negative; that is, it would have been making a loss.

TABLE 6.5
Output, Revenue, Costs, and Profit

Q (bottles/ day)	Total revenue ($/day)	Total labor cost ($/day)	Total cost ($/day)	Profit ($/day)
0	0	0	70	−70
100	35	10	80	−45
200	70	20	90	−20
300	105	40	110	−5
400	140	70	140	0
500	175	110	180	−5
600	210	160	230	−20
700	245	220	290	−45

PRICE EQUALS MARGINAL COST: THE SELLER'S SUPPLY RULE

The observation that the profit-maximizing quantity for a firm to supply does not depend on its fixed costs is not an idiosyncrasy of this example. That it holds true in general is an immediate consequence of the cost-benefit principle, which says that a firm should increase its output if, and only if, the *extra* benefit exceeds the *extra* cost. If the firm expands production by 100 bottles/day, its benefit is the extra revenue it gets, which in this case is simply the price of 100 bottles. The cost of expanding production by 100 bottles is by definition the marginal cost of producing 100 bottles—the amount by which total cost increases when bottle production rises by 100/day. The cost-benefit principle thus tells us that the perfectly competitive firm should keep expanding production as long as the price of the product is greater than marginal cost.

When the law of diminishing returns applies (that is, when some factors of production are fixed), marginal cost goes up as the firm expands production. Under these circumstances, the firm's best option is to supply that level of output for which price and marginal cost are exactly equal.

Note in Example 6.5 that if the company's capital cost had been any more than $70/day, it would have made a loss at *every* possible level of output. As long as it still had to pay its capital cost, however, its best bet would have been to continue producing 400 bottles/day. It is better, after all, to experience a smaller loss than a larger one. If a firm in that situation expected conditions to remain the same, though, it would want to get out of the bottle business as soon as its equipment lease expired.

A NOTE ON THE FIRM'S SHUTDOWN CONDITION

It might seem that a firm that can sell as much output as it wishes at a constant market price would *always* do best in the short run by producing and selling the output level for which price equals marginal cost. But there are exceptions to this rule. Suppose, for example, that the market price of the firm's product falls so low that its revenue from sales is smaller than its variable cost when price equals marginal cost. The firm should then cease production for the time being. By shutting down, it will suffer a loss equal to its fixed costs. But by remaining open, it would suffer an even larger loss.

EXERCISE 6.2

In Example 6.2, suppose bottles sold not for $35/hundred but for only $5. Calculate the profit corresponding to each level of output, as in Example 6.2, and verify that the firm's best option is to cease operations in the short run.

GRAPHING MARGINAL COST

To plot the marginal cost curve for a specific company, we would need to know how total cost changes for every possible change in output. In Examples 6.2 to 6.5, however, we know the firm's cost for only a small sample of production values. Even with this limited information, though, we can construct a reasonable approximation of the firm's marginal cost curve. For instance, note in Example 6.2 that when the firm expands production from 100 to 200 bottles/day, its increase in cost is $10. When we graph the marginal cost curve, what output level should this $10 marginal cost correspond to? Strictly speaking, it corresponds neither to 100 nor 200 but to the movement between the two. On the graph we thus show the $10 marginal cost value corresponding to an output level midway between 100 and 200 bottles/day, namely, 150 bottles/day, as in Figure 6.5. Similarly, when the firm in Example 6.2 expands from 200 to 300 bottles/day, its costs go up by $20, so we plot a marginal cost of $20 with the output level 250 in Figure 6.5. Proceeding in this fashion, we generate the marginal cost curve shown in the diagram.

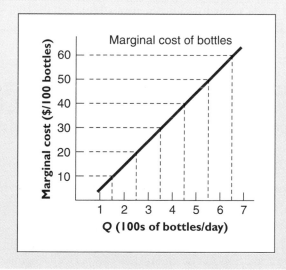

**FIGURE 6.5
The Firm's Marginal Cost of Production.**
The firm's cost goes up by $10 when it expands production from 100 to 200 bottles/day. The marginal cost of the increased output is thus $10, and by convention we plot that value at a point midway between 100 and 200 bottles/day.

Suppose the market price facing the seller whose marginal cost curve is shown in Figure 6.5 is $25/hundred. If the firm's goal is to make as much profit as possible, how many bottles should it sell? It should sell the quantity for which marginal cost is equal to $25/hundred, and as we see in Figure 6.6, that quantity is 300 bottles/week.

To gain further confidence that 300 must be the profit-maximizing quantity when the price is $25/hundred, first suppose that the firm had sold some amount less than that, say, only 200 bottles/day. Its benefit from expanding output by one bottle would then be the bottle's market price, here 25 cents (since bottles sell

FIGURE 6.6

Price = Marginal Cost: The Perfectly Competitive Firm's Profit-Maximizing Supply Rule.

If price is less than marginal cost, the firm can increase its profit by expanding production and sales. If price exceeds marginal cost, the firm can increase its profit by producing and selling less output.

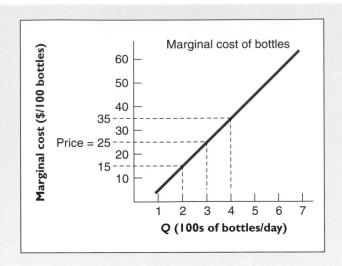

for $25/hundred, each individual bottle sells for 25 cents). The cost of expanding output by one bottle is equal (by definition) to the firm's marginal cost, which at 200 bottles/day is only $15/100 = 15 cents (see Figure 6.6). So by selling the 201st bottle for 25 cents and producing it for an extra cost of only 15 cents, the firm will increase its profit by 25 − 15 = 10 cents/day. Similarly, we can show that for *any* quantity less than the level at which price equals marginal cost, the seller can boost profit by expanding production.

Conversely, suppose the firm is currently selling more than 300 bottles/day—say, 400—at a price of $25/hundred. From Figure 6.6 we see that marginal cost at an output of 400 is $35/100 = 35 cents per bottle. If the firm then contracts its output by one bottle/day, it would cut its costs by 35 cents while losing only 25 cents in revenue. As before, its profit would grow by 10 cents/day. The same argument can be made regarding any quantity larger than 300, so if the firm is currently selling an output at which price is less than marginal cost, it can always do better by producing and selling fewer bottles.

We have thus established that if the firm were selling fewer than 300 bottles/day, it could earn more profit by expanding, and that if it were selling more than 300, it could earn more by contracting. It follows that at a market price of $25/hundred, the seller does best by selling 300 units per week, the quantity for which price and marginal cost are exactly the same.

EXERCISE 6.3

For a bottle price of $25/hundred, calculate the profit corresponding to each level of output, as in Example 6.2, and verify that the profit-maximizing output is 300 bottles/day.

As further confirmation of the claim that the perfectly competitive firm maximizes profit by setting price equal to marginal cost, note in Figure 6.6 that when marginal cost is equal to a price of $35/hundred, the corresponding quantity is 400 bottles/day. This is the same as the profit-maximizing quantity we identified for that price in Table 6.2.

THE "LAW" OF SUPPLY

The law of demand tells us that consumers buy less of a product when its price rises. If there were an analogous law of supply, it would say that producers offer more of a product for sale when its price rises. Is there such a law? We know that supply curves are essentially marginal cost curves, and that because of the law of diminishing returns, marginal cost curves are upward-sloping in the short run. And so there is indeed a law of supply that applies as stated in the short run.

In the long run, however, the law of diminishing returns does not apply. (Recall that it holds only if at least some factors of production are fixed.) Because firms can vary the amounts of *all* factors of production they use in the long run, they can often double their production by simply doubling the amount of each input they use. In such cases costs would be exactly proportional to output, and the firm's marginal cost curve in the long run would be horizontal, not upward-sloping. So for now we'll say only that the "law" of supply holds as stated in the short run but not necessarily in the long run. For both the long run and the short run, however, *the perfectly competitive firm's supply curve is its marginal cost curve.*[1]

Every quantity of output along the market supply curve represents the summation of all the quantities individual sellers offer at the corresponding price. So the correspondence between price and marginal cost exists for the market supply curve as well as for the individual supply curves that lie behind the market supply curve. That is, *for every price-quantity pair along the market supply curve, price will be equal to each seller's marginal cost of production.*

This is why we sometimes say that the supply curve represents the cost side of the market, whereas the demand curve represents the benefit side of the market. At every point along a market demand curve, price represents what buyers would be willing to pay for an additional unit of the product—and this, in turn, is how we measure the amount by which they would benefit by having an additional unit of the product. Likewise, at every point along a market supply curve, price measures what it would cost producers to expand production by one unit.

RECAP   **THE COMPETITIVE FIRM'S SUPPLY CURVE**

The perfectly competitive firm faces a horizontal demand curve for its product, meaning that it can sell any quantity it wishes at the market price. In the short run, the firm's goal is to choose the level of output that maximizes its profits. Under a broad range of conditions, it will accomplish this goal by choosing the output level for which its marginal cost is equal to the market price of its product. The perfectly competitive firm's supply curve is its marginal cost curve, which is upward-sloping in the short run because of the law of diminishing returns.

DETERMINANTS OF SUPPLY REVISITED

What factors give rise to changes in supply? (Again, remember that a *change in supply* refers to a shift in the entire supply curve, as opposed to a movement along the curve, which we call a *change in the quantity supplied*.) A seller will offer more units if the benefit of selling extra output goes up relative to the cost of producing it. And since the benefit of selling output in a perfectly competitive market is a fixed market price beyond the seller's control, our search for factors that influence supply naturally focuses on the cost side of the calculation. Examples 6.2 to 6.5 suggest why the following five factors, among others, will affect the likelihood that a product will satisfy the cost-benefit test for a given supplier.

---

[1]Again, this rule holds subject to the provision that total revenue exceeds variable production cost at the output level for which price equals marginal cost.

TECHNOLOGY

Perhaps the most important determinant of production cost is technology. Improvements in technology make it possible to produce additional units of output at lower cost. This shifts each individual supply curve downward and hence shifts the market supply curve downward as well. Over time, the introduction of more sophisticated machinery has resulted in dramatic increases in the number of goods produced per hour of effort expended. Every such development gives rise to an outward shift in the market supply curve.

But how do we know technological change will reduce the cost of producing goods and services? Might not new equipment be so expensive that producers who used it would have higher costs than those who relied on earlier designs? If so, then rational producers simply would not use the new equipment. The only technological changes rational producers will adopt are those that will reduce their cost of production.

INPUT PRICES

Whereas technological change generally (although not always) leads to gradual shifts in supply, changes in the prices of important inputs can give rise to large supply shifts literally overnight. For example, the price of crude oil, which is the most important input in the production of gasoline, rose suddenly in 1979, and the resulting leftward shift in supply caused gasoline prices to rise almost immediately.

Similarly, when wage rates rise, the marginal cost of any business that employs labor also rises, shifting supply curves to the left. When interest rates fall, the opportunity cost of capital equipment also falls, causing supply to shift to the right.

THE NUMBER OF SUPPLIERS

Just as demand curves shift to the right when population grows, supply curves also shift to the right as the number of individual suppliers grows. For example, if container recyclers die or retire at a higher rate than new recyclers enter the industry, the supply curve for recycling services will shift to the left. Conversely, if a rise in the unemployment rate leads more people to recycle soft drink containers (by reducing the opportunity cost of time spent recycling), the supply curve of recycling services will shift to the right.

EXPECTATIONS

Expectations about future price movements can affect how much sellers choose to offer in the current market. Suppose, for example, that recyclers expect the future price of aluminum to be much higher than the current price because of the growing use of aluminum components in cars. The rational recycler would then have an incentive to withhold aluminum from the market at today's lower price, thereby to have more available to sell at the higher future price. Conversely, if recyclers expected next year's price of aluminum to be lower than this year's, their incentive would be to offer more aluminum for sale in today's market.

CHANGES IN PRICES OF OTHER PRODUCTS

Apart from technological change, perhaps the most important determinant of supply is variation in the prices of other goods and services that sellers might produce. Prospectors, for example, search for those precious metals for which the surplus of benefits over costs is greatest. When the price of silver rises, many people stop looking for gold and start looking for silver. Conversely, when the price of platinum falls, many platinum prospectors shift their attention to gold.

APPLYING THE THEORY OF SUPPLY

Whether the activity is producing new soft drink containers or recycling used ones, or indeed any other production activity at all, the same logic governs all supply decisions in perfectly competitive markets (and in any other setting in which sellers can sell as much as they wish to at a constant price): Keep expanding output until marginal cost is equal to the price of the product. This logic helps us understand why recycling efforts are more intensive for some products than others.

When recycling is left to private market forces, why are many more aluminum beverage containers recycled than glass ones?

In both cases, recyclers gather containers until their marginal costs are equal to the containers' respective redemption prices. When recycling is left to market forces, the redemption price for a container is based on what companies can sell it (or the materials in it) for. Aluminum containers can be easily processed into scrap aluminum, which commands a high price, and this leads profit-seeking companies to offer a high redemption price for aluminum cans. By contrast, the glass from which glass containers are made has only limited resale value, and this leads profit-seeking companies to offer very low redemption prices for glass containers.

The high redemption prices for aluminum cans induce many people to track down these cans, whereas the low redemption prices for glass containers leads most people to ignore the containers. If recycling is left completely to market forces, then, we would expect to see aluminum soft drink containers quickly recycled, whereas glass containers would increasingly litter the landscape. This is in fact the pattern we do see in states without recycling laws. (More on how these laws work in a moment.) This pattern is a simple consequence of the fact that the supply curves of container-recycling services are upward-sloping.

The acquisition of valuable raw materials is only one of two important benefits from recycling. The second benefit is that, by removing litter, recycling makes the environment more pleasant for everyone. As the next example suggests, this second benefit might easily justify the cost of recycling substantial numbers of glass containers.

ECONOMIC NATURALIST 6.1

What is the socially optimal amount of recycling of glass containers?

Suppose that the 60,000 citizens of Burlington, Vermont, collectively would be willing to pay 6 cents for each glass container removed from their local environment.

EXAMPLE 6.6

FIGURE 6.7
The Supply Curve of Container Recycling Services for Burlington, Vermont.

Market supply curve of glass container recycling services

Redemption price (cents/container)

Number of containers recycled (1,000s of containers per day)

If the local market supply curve of glass container recycling services is as shown in Figure 6.7, what is the socially optimal level of glass container recycling?

Suppose the citizens of Burlington authorize their city government to collect tax money to finance litter removal. If the benefit of each glass container removed, as measured by what residents are collectively willing to pay, is 6 cents, the government should offer to pay 6 cents for each glass container recycled. To maximize the total economic surplus from recycling, we should recycle that number of containers for which the marginal cost of recycling is equal to the 6 cent marginal benefit. Given the market supply curve shown, the optimal quantity is 16,000 containers/day, and that is how many will be redeemed when the government offers 6 cents/container.

Although 16,000 containers/day will be removed from the environment in Example 6.6, others will remain. After all, some containers are discarded in remote locations, and a redemption price of 6 cents per container is simply not high enough to induce people to track them all down.

So why not offer an even higher price and get rid of *all* glass container litter? For Example 6.6, the reason is that the marginal cost of removing the 16,001st glass container each day is greater than the benefit of removing it. Total economic surplus is largest when we remove litter only up to the point that the marginal benefit of litter removal is equal to its marginal cost, which occurs when 16,000 containers/day are recycled. To proceed past that point is actually wasteful.

Many people become upset when they first hear economists say that the socially optimal amount of litter is greater than zero. In the minds of these people, the optimal amount of litter is *exactly* zero. But this position completely ignores the scarcity principle. Granted, there would be benefits from reducing litter further, but there would also be costs. Spending more on litter removal therefore means spending less on other useful things. No one would insist that the optimal amount of household dirt is zero. (If someone does make this claim, ask him why he doesn't stay home all day vacuuming the dust that is accumulating in his absence.) If it doesn't pay to remove all the dust from your house, it doesn't pay to remove all the bottles from the environment. Precisely the same logic applies in each case.

If 16,000 containers/day is the optimal amount of litter removal, can we expect the individual spending decisions of private citizens to result in that amount of litter removal? Unfortunately we cannot. The problem is that anyone who paid for litter removal individually would bear the full cost of those services while reaping only a tiny fraction of the benefit. In Example 6.6, the 60,000 citizens of Burlington reaped a total benefit of 6 cents per container removed, which means a benefit of only $(6/60,000) = 0.0001$ cent per person! Someone who paid 6 cents for someone else to remove a container would thus be incurring a cost 60,000 times greater than her share of the resulting benefit.

Note that the incentive problem here is similar to the one we saw in the case of the beekeeper and orchard owner discussed in Chapter 4. The orchard owner planted too few trees because even though he bore the full cost of planting each tree, part of the extra benefit from extra trees accrued to the beekeeper, whose bees were thereby able to produce extra honey. Similarly, the beekeeper kept too few hives because even though he bore the full cost of each additional hive, part of the benefit of extra hives accrued to the orchard owner, whose trees were thereby more fully pollinated.

In the case of glass container litter, in short, we have an example in which private market forces do not produce the best attainable outcome for society as a whole. Even people who carelessly toss containers on the ground rather than recycle them are often offended by the unsightly landscape to which their own actions contribute. Indeed, this is why they often support laws mandating adequate redemption prices for glass containers.

Is the socially optimal quantity of litter zero?

© Galen Rowell/Corbis

Activities that generate litter are a good illustration of the equilibrium principle described in Chapter 4. People who litter do so not because they don't care about the environment, but because their private incentives make littering misleadingly attractive. Recycling requires some effort, after all, yet no individual's recycling efforts have a noticeable effect on the quality of the environment. The soft drink-container deposit laws enacted by numerous states were a simple way to bring individual interests more closely into balance with the interests of society as a whole. The vast majority of container litter disappeared almost literally overnight in states that enacted these laws.

EXERCISE 6.4

If the supply curve of glass container recycling services is as shown in the following diagram and each of the city's 60,000 citizens would be willing to pay 0.00005 cent for each glass container removed from the landscape, at what level should the city government set the redemption price for glass containers, and how many containers will be recycled each day?

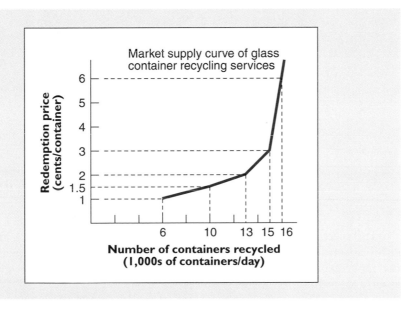

THE PRICE ELASTICITY OF SUPPLY

DEFINING AND CALCULATING ELASTICITY OF SUPPLY

On the buyer's side of the market, we use price elasticity of demand to measure the responsiveness of quantity demanded to changes in price. On the seller's side of the market, the analogous measure is **price elasticity of supply,** which is defined as the percentage change in quantity supplied that occurs in response to a 1 percent change in price. For example, if a 1 percent increase in the redemption price of glass containers leads to a 2 percent increase in the quantity supplied, the price elasticity of supply of recycled glass containers would be 2.0.

The mathematical formula for price elasticity of supply at any point is the same as the corresponding expression for price elasticity of demand:

$$\text{Price elasticity of supply} = \frac{\Delta Q/Q}{\Delta P/P}, \tag{6.1}$$

where P and Q are the price and quantity at that point, ΔP is a small change in the initial price, and ΔQ is the resulting change in quantity.

price elasticity of supply the percentage change in the quantity supplied that will occur in response to a 1 percent change in the price of a good or service

As with the corresponding expression for price elasticity of demand, Equation 6.1 can be rewritten as $(P/Q)(\Delta Q/\Delta P)$. And since $\Delta Q/\Delta P$ is the reciprocal of the slope of the supply curve, the right-hand side of Equation 6.1 is equal to $(P/Q)(1/\text{slope})$—the same expression we saw for price elasticity of demand. Price and quantity are always positive, as is the slope of the typical short-run supply curve, which implies that price elasticity of supply will be a positive number at every point.

Consider the supply curve in Figure 6.8. The slope of this supply curve is 1/3, so the reciprocal of this slope is 3. Using the formula, this means that the price elasticity of supply at A is $(4/12)(3) = 1$. The corresponding expression at B, $(5/15)(3)$, yields exactly the same value. Indeed, because the ratio P/Q is the same at every point along the supply curve shown, price elasticity of supply will be exactly 1 at every point along this curve. Note the contrast between this result and our earlier finding that price elasticity of demand declines as we move downward along any straight-line demand curve.

FIGURE 6.8

Graphically Calculating the Price Elasticity of Supply.

Price elasticity of supply is $(P/Q)(1/\text{slope})$, which at A is $(4/12)(12/4) = 1$, exactly the same as at B. The price elasticity of supply is equal to 1 at any point along a straight-line supply curve that passes through the origin.

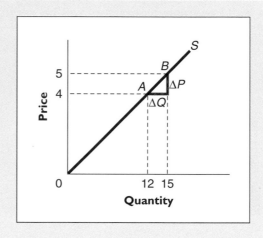

The special property that explains why price elasticity equals 1 at every point in this illustration is that the supply curve was a straight line through the origin. For movements along any such line, both price and quantity always change in exactly the same proportion.

Elasticity is not constant, however, along straight-line supply curves like the one in Figure 6.9, ones that do not pass through the origin. Although the slope of this supply curve is equal to 1 at every point, the ratio P/Q declines as we move to the right along the curve. Elasticity at A is equal to $(4/2)(1) = 2$ and declines to $(5/3)(1) = 5/3$ at B.

FIGURE 6.9

A Supply Curve for Which Price Elasticity Declines As Quantity Rises.

For the supply curve shown, 1/slope is the same at every point, but the ratio P/Q declines as Q increases. So Elasticity = $(P/Q)(1/\text{slope})$ declines as quantity increases.

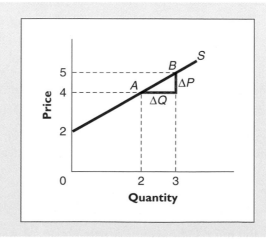

On the buyer's side of the market, two important polar cases were demand curves with infinite price elasticity and zero price elasticity. As Examples 6.7 and 6.8 illustrate, analogous polar cases exist on the seller's side of the market.

What is the elasticity of supply of land within the borough limits of Manhattan?

Land in Manhattan sells in the market for a price, just like aluminum or corn or automobiles or any other product. And the demand for land in Manhattan is a downward-sloping function of its price. For all practical purposes, however, its supply is completely fixed. No matter whether its price is high or low, the same amount of it is available in the market. The supply curve of such a good is vertical, and its price elasticity is zero at every price. Supply curves like the one in Figure 6.10 are said to be **perfectly inelastic.**

EXAMPLE 6.7

perfectly inelastic supply curve
a supply curve whose elasticity with respect to price is zero

FIGURE 6.10
A Perfectly Inelastic Supply Curve.
Price elasticity of supply is zero at every point along a vertical supply curve.

What is the elasticity of supply of lemonade?

EXAMPLE 6.8

Suppose that the ingredients required to bring a cup of lemonade to market and their respective costs are listed as follows:

Paper cup	2.0 cents
Lemon	3.8 cents
Sugar	2.0 cents
Water	0.2 cents
Ice	1.0 cents
Labor (30 seconds @ $6/hour)	5.0 cents

If these proportions remain the same no matter how many cups of lemonade are made, and the inputs can be purchased in any quantities at the stated prices, draw the supply curve of lemonade and compute its price elasticity.

Since each cup of lemonade costs exactly 14 cents to make, no matter how many cups are made, the supply curve of lemonade is a horizontal line at 14 cents/cup (Figure 6.11). The price elasticity of supply of lemonade is infinite.

Whenever additional units of a good can be produced by using the same combination of inputs, purchased at the same prices, as have been used so far, the supply curve of that good will be horizontal. Such supply curves are said to be **perfectly elastic.**

perfectly elastic supply curve
a supply curve whose elasticity with respect to price is infinite

Example 6.8 is a good illustration of how economists use the terms long run and short run. Even though the time span over which lemonade production takes place may be brief, all factors of production were assumed to be variable. By

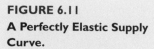

FIGURE 6.11

A Perfectly Elastic Supply Curve.

The elasticity of supply is infinite at every point along a horizontal supply curve.

definition, then, the example describes what happens when output changes in the long run, and the law of diminishing returns therefore does not apply. For the specific production process described, the marginal cost curve is constant—at 14 cents/cup—not upward-sloping.

DETERMINANTS OF SUPPLY ELASTICITY

Examples 6.7 and 6.8 suggest some of the factors that govern the elasticity of supply of a good or service. The lemonade case in Example 6.8 was one whose production process was essentially like a cooking recipe. For such cases, we can exactly double our output by doubling each ingredient. If the price of each ingredient remains fixed, the marginal cost of production for such goods will be constant, and hence their horizontal supply curves. Again, when all factors of production can be increased, the law of diminishing returns does not apply, and so the supply curve need not be upward-sloping.

Example 6.7 of land in Manhattan is a contrast in the extreme. The inputs used to produce land in Manhattan—even if we knew what they were—could not be duplicated at any price.

The key to predicting how elastic the supply of a good will be with respect to price is to know the terms on which additional units of the inputs involved in producing that good can be acquired. In general, the more easily additional units of these inputs can be acquired, the higher the price elasticity of supply will be. The following four factors (among others) govern the ease with which additional inputs can be acquired by a producer.

Flexibility of inputs To the extent that production of a good requires inputs that are also useful for the production of other goods, it is relatively easy to lure additional inputs away from their current uses, making supply of that good relatively elastic with respect to price. Thus the fact that lemonade production requires labor with only minimal skills means that a large pool of workers could shift from other activities to lemonade production if a profit opportunity arose. Brain surgery, by contrast, requires elaborately trained and specialized labor, which means that even a large price increase would not increase available supplies, except in the very long run.

Mobility of inputs If inputs can be easily transported from one site to another, an increase in the price of a product in one market will enable a producer in that market to summon inputs from other markets. For example, the supply of agricultural products is made more elastic with respect to price by the fact that thousands of farmworkers are willing to migrate northward during the growing season. The supply of entertainment is similarly made more elastic by the willingness of entertainers to hit the road. Circus performers, lounge singers, comedians, and even exotic dancers often spend a substantial fraction of their

time away from home. For instance, according to a 1996 *New York Times* arti-
cle, the top exotic dancers "basically follow the action, so the same entertainers
who worked the Indianapolis 500 now head to Atlanta for the Olympics."

For most goods, the price elasticity of supply increases each time a new canal
is dug, or when a new highway is built, or when the telecommunications network improves, or indeed when any other development makes it easier to find
and transport inputs from one place to another.

Ability to produce substitute inputs The inputs required to produce finished diamond gemstones include raw diamond crystal, skilled labor, and elaborate cutting and polishing machinery. In time, the number of people with the requisite skills can be increased, as can the amount of specialized machinery. The
number of raw diamond crystals buried in the earth is probably fixed in the same
way that Manhattan real estate is fixed, but unlike Manhattan real estate, rising
prices will encourage miners to spend the effort required to find a larger proportion of those crystals. Still, the supply of natural gemstone diamonds tends to
be relatively inelastic because of the difficulty of augmenting the number of diamond crystals.

The day is close at hand, however, when gemstone makers will be able to produce synthetic diamond crystals that are indistinguishable from real ones. Indeed,
there are already synthetic crystals that fool even highly experienced jewelers. The
introduction of a perfect synthetic substitute for natural diamond crystals would
increase the price elasticity of supply of diamonds (or, at any rate, the price elasticity of supply of gemstones that look and feel just like diamonds).

Time Because it takes time for producers to switch from one activity to
another and because it takes time to build new capital goods and train additional
skilled workers, the price elasticity of supply will be higher for most goods in the
long run than in the short run. In the short run, a manufacturer's inability to
augment existing stocks of capital equipment and skilled labor may make it
impossible to expand output beyond a certain limit. But if a shortage of managers is the bottleneck, new MBAs can be graduated in only 2 years. Or if a
shortage of legal staff is the problem, new lawyers can be trained in 3 years. In
the long run, firms can always buy new equipment, build new factories, and hire
additional skilled workers.

"In six more weeks, these M.B.A.s will be ready for market."

The conditions that gave rise to the perfectly elastic supply curve for lemonade in Example 6.8 are also satisfied for many other products in the long run. If a product can be copied (in the sense that any company can acquire the design and other technological information required to produce it) and if the inputs needed for its production are used in roughly fixed proportions and are available at fixed market prices, then the long-run supply curve for that product will be horizontal. But as we will presently see, many products do not satisfy these conditions, and their supply curves remain steeply upward-sloping, even in the very long run.

UNIQUE AND ESSENTIAL INPUTS: THE ULTIMATE SUPPLY BOTTLENECK

Fans of professional basketball are an enthusiastic bunch. Directly through their purchases of tickets and indirectly through their support of television advertisers, they spend literally billions of dollars each year on the sport. But these dollars are not distributed evenly across all teams. A disproportionate share of all revenues and product endorsement fees accrue to the people associated with consistently winning teams, and at the top of this pyramid generally stands the National Basketball Association's championship team.

Consider the task of trying to produce a championship team in the NBA. What are the inputs you would need? Talented players, a shrewd and dedicated coach and assistants, trainers, physicians, an arena, practice facilities, means for transporting players to away games, a marketing staff, and so on. And whereas some of these inputs can be acquired at reasonable prices in the marketplace, many others cannot. Indeed, the most important input of all—highly talented players—is in extremely limited supply. *This is so because the very definition of a talented player is inescapably relative: Simply put, such a player is one who is better than most others.*

Given the huge payoff that accrues to the NBA championship team, it is no surprise that the bidding for the most talented players has become so intense. If there were a long list of 7-foot 3-inch 325-pound centers, the Los Angeles Lakers wouldn't have had to pay Shaquille O'Neal $120 million over a 7-year contract. But of course the supply of such players is extremely limited. Many hungry organizations would like nothing better than to claim the NBA championship each year, yet no matter how much each is willing to spend, only one can succeed. The supply of NBA championship teams is perfectly inelastic with respect to price even in the very long run.

Sports champions are by no means the only important product whose supply elasticity is constrained by the inability to reproduce unique and essential inputs. In the movie industry, for example, although the supply of movies starring Jim Carrey is not perfectly inelastic, there are only so many films he can make each year. Because his films consistently generate huge box office revenues, scores of film producers want to sign him for their projects. But because there isn't enough of him to go around, his salary per film is more than $20 million.

In the long run, unique and essential inputs are the only truly significant supply bottlenecks. If it were not for the inability to duplicate the services of such inputs, most goods and services would have extremely high price elasticities of supply.

USING THE PRODUCTION POSSIBILITIES CURVE TO GENERATE SUPPLY CURVES

Recall Islandia, the simple economy in Chapter 3, in which Susan and Tom could produce either of two goods: coffee or Macadamia nuts. Our task in this section will be to see how the information implicit in Islandia's production possibilities curve enables us to construct supply curves for each product. To begin, the individual members' productivity information is reproduced in Table 6.6.

TABLE 6.6
Productivity for Two Workers

	Coffee productivity	Nut productivity
Susan	1.5 pounds/hour	3 pounds/hour
Tom	0.75 pound/hour	0.75 pound/hour

As we saw earlier, the opportunity cost of 1 pound of nuts is 1/2 pound of coffee for Susan and 1 pound of coffee for Tom. The production possibilities curve for this economy is reproduced in Figure 6.12.

How can we use the information in the production possibilities curve to construct Islandia's supply curves in world markets for coffee and nuts? Suppose Islandians could sell, or buy, coffee or nuts in the world market at fixed prices. If the price of 1 pound of nuts in the world market were less than 1/2 pound of coffee, the citizens of Islandia simply would not offer any nuts for sale in the world market. To see why, examine what would happen if they did. Suppose, for example, that they could get 1/4 pound of coffee by selling a pound of nuts in the world market and that they were selling 1 pound of nuts/day at that price (picked by Susan, as called for by the low-hanging-fruit principle, since her opportunity cost of picking nuts is lower than Tom's). Why should Islandia continue to make that sale? After all, it can get an extra 1/2 pound of coffee if Susan shifts full-time to picking coffee. As the supply curve in Figure 6.13 indicates, Islandians will supply 0 pounds of nuts to the world market when the price of nuts is lower than 1/2 pound of coffee.

Once the price of nuts rises to 1/2 pound of coffee, however, Susan should no longer pick coffee. At that price, Islandians will offer 24 pounds of nuts/day

FIGURE 6.12

Opportunity Cost of Food at Different Points along the Production Possibilities Curve.

At A, the opportunity cost of 1 pound of nuts is 1/2 pound of coffee. At B, the opportunity cost of 1 pound of nuts is 1 pound of coffee.

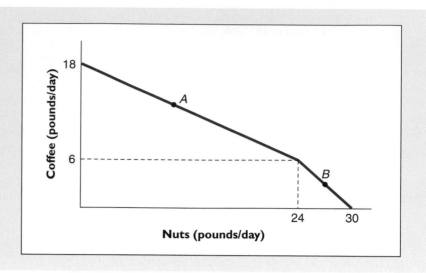

FIGURE 6.13

Islandia's Supply Curve for Nuts.

Since Susan's opportunity cost of producing nuts is only 1/2 pound of coffee, Islandia will supply no nuts when the world price of nuts is less than that. When the price of nuts is above Susan's opportunity cost but below Tom's (1 pound of coffee), Islandia will sell all the nuts Susan can pick. For nut prices larger than 1 pound of coffee, both Tom and Susan will sell all the nuts they can pick.

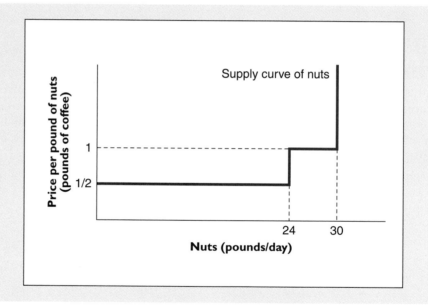

for sale in the world market (the full amount that Susan can pick each day). Similarly, once the price of 1 pound of nuts reaches 1 pound of coffee, Tom should switch from coffee to nut production, which means that Islandians will supply a total of 30 pounds of nuts/day (Susan's 24 pounds plus Tom's 6 pounds) at that price. For nut prices above 1 pound of coffee, the Islandians's supply curve of nuts is perfectly inelastic, since they are unable to supply any more than 30 pounds of nuts/day.

The procedure for constructing Islandia's supply curve for coffee involves essentially parallel reasoning. If the slope of the production possibilities curve at any point represents the opportunity cost of 1 pound of nuts, the reciprocal of that slope represents the opportunity cost of 1 pound of coffee at that point. Thus the opportunity cost of a pound of coffee is 2 pounds of nuts at A in Figure 6.12 and 1 pound at B.

When the world price of 1 pound of coffee is less than 1 pound of nuts, Islandians will supply no coffee to the world market. Once the price of coffee reaches 1 pound of nuts, Tom should supply 6 pounds of coffee. And for world coffee prices at or above 2 pounds of nuts, Susan should add her offering of 12 pounds of coffee/day, for a total of 18 pounds of coffee/day. Islandia's supply curve for coffee is thus as shown in Figure 6.14.

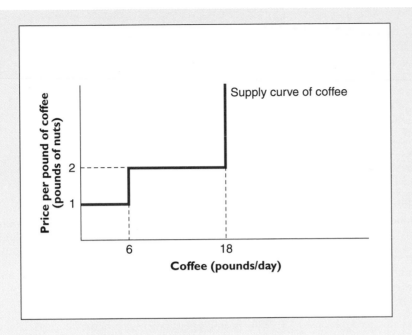

FIGURE 6.14
Islandia's Supply Curve for Coffee.
When the world price of coffee is less than Tom's opportunity cost of picking coffee (1 pound of nuts), Islandia will sell no coffee. When the price of coffee is between Tom's opportunity cost and Susan's (2 pounds of nuts), Islandia will sell all the coffee Tom can pick (6 pounds/day). When the price of coffee is above 2 pounds of nuts, Islandia will sell all the coffee Tom and Susan can pick (18 pounds/day).

▪ SUMMARY ▪

- The supply curve for a good or service is a schedule that for any price tells us the quantity sellers wish to supply at that price. The prices at which goods and services are offered for sale in the market depend, in turn, on the opportunity cost of the resources required to produce them.

- Supply curves tend to be upward-sloping, at least in the short run, partly because of the low-hanging-fruit principle. Generally, rational producers will always take advantage of their best opportunities first, moving on to more difficult or costly opportunities only after their best ones have been exhausted. Reinforcing this tendency is the law of diminishing returns, which says that when some factors of production are held fixed, the amount of additional variable factors required to produce successive increments in output grows larger.

- For perfectly competitive markets—or, more generally, for markets in which individual sellers can sell whatever quantity they wish at constant price—the seller's best option is to sell that quantity of output for which price equals marginal cost. The supply curve for the seller thus coincides with his or her marginal cost curve, the curve that measures the cost of producing additional units of output. This is why we sometimes say the supply curve represents the cost side of the market (in contrast to the demand curve, which represents the benefit side of the market).

- An important terminological distinction from the demand side of the market also applies on the supply side of the

market. *A change in supply* means a shift in the entire supply curve, whereas *a change in the quantity supplied* means a movement along the supply curve. The factors that cause supply curves to shift include technology, input prices, the number of sellers, expectations of future price changes, and the prices of other products that firms might produce.

- Price elasticity of supply is defined as the percentage change in quantity supplied that occurs in response to a 1 percent change in price. The mathematical formula for the price elasticity of supply at any point is $(\Delta Q/Q)/(\Delta P/P)$, where P and Q are the price and quantity at that point, ΔP is a small change in the initial price, and ΔQ is the resulting change in quantity. This formula can also be expressed as $(P/Q)(1/\text{slope})$, where $1/\text{slope}$ is the reciprocal of the slope of the supply curve.

- The price elasticity of supply of a good will depend on how difficult or costly it is to acquire additional units of the inputs involved in producing that good. In general, the more easily additional units of these inputs can be acquired, the higher the price elasticity of supply will be. It is easier to expand production of a product if the inputs used to produce that product are similar to inputs used to produce other products, if inputs are relatively mobile, or if an acceptable substitute for existing inputs can be developed. And like the price elasticity of demand, the price elasticity of supply is greater in the long run than in the short run. Except for the existence of unique and essential inputs, all goods and services would have highly elastic supply curves in the long run.

▪ KEY TERMS ▪

factor of production (141)
fixed factor of production (141)
imperfectly competitive firm (140)
law of diminishing returns (141)
long run (141)

perfectly competitive market (140)
perfectly elastic supply curve (153)
perfectly inelastic supply curve (153)
price elasticity of supply (151)
price taker (140)

profit (139)
profit-maximizing firm (140)
short run (141)
variable factor of production (141)

▪ REVIEW QUESTIONS ▪

1. Explain why you would expect supply curves to slope upward on the basis of the principle of increasing opportunity cost.

2. Which do you think is more likely to be a fixed factor of production for an ice cream producer during the next 2 months, its factory building or its workers who operate the machines? Explain.

3. Economists often stress that congestion helps account for the law of diminishing returns. With this in mind, explain

why it would be impossible to feed all the people on earth with food grown in a single flowerpot, even if unlimited water, labor, seed, fertilizer, sunlight, and other inputs were available.

4. True or false: The perfectly competitive firm should *always* produce the output level for which price equals marginal cost.

5. Why is supply elasticity higher in the long run than in the short run?

▪ PROBLEMS ▪

1. Zoe is trying to decide how to divide her time between her job as a wedding photographer, which pays $27/hour for as many hours as she chooses to work, and as a fossil collector, in which her pay depends both on the price of fossils and the number of fossils she finds. Earnings aside, Zoe is indifferent between the two tasks, and the number of fossils she can find depends on the number of hours a day she searches, as shown in the following table.

Hours/day	Total fossils/day
1	5
2	9
3	12
4	14
5	15

a. Derive a table with price in dollar increments from $0 to $30 in the first column and the quantity of fossils Zoe is willing to supply per day at that price in the second column.

b. Plot these points in a graph with price on the vertical axis and quantity per day on the horizontal axis. What is this curve called?

2. A price-taking firm makes air conditioners. The market price of one of their new air conditioners is $120. Its total cost information is given in the following table.

Air conditioners/day	Total cost ($/day)
1	100
2	150
3	220
4	310
5	405
6	510
7	650
8	800

How many air conditioners should the firm produce per day if its goal is to maximize its profit?

3. The Paducah Slugger Company makes baseball bats out of lumber supplied to it by Acme Sporting Goods, which pays Paducah $10 for each finished bat. Paducah's only factors of production are lathe operators and a small building with a lathe. The number of bats per day it produces depends on the number of employee-hours per day, as shown in the following table.

Number of bats/day	Number of employee-hours/day
0	0
5	1
10	2
15	4
20	7
25	11
30	16
35	22

 a. If the wage is $15/hour and Paducah's daily capital cost for the lathe and building is fixed at $60, what is the profit-maximizing quantity of bats?
 b. What would be the profit-maximizing number of bats if the capital cost were not $60/day but only $30?

4. In Problem 3, how would Paducah's profit-maximizing level of output be affected if the government imposed a tax of $10/day on the company? What would Paducah's profit-maximizing level of output be if the government imposed a tax of $2 per bat?

5. Explain how the following would affect supply in the indicated market:
 a. An increase in the world price of honey in the market for beeswax candles.
 b. An increase in the world price of cauliflower in the market for cabbage. (Assume the demand for cabbage does not shift.)
 c. An increase in the world price of ice cream in the market for ice cream.

6. How would each of the following affect the U.S. market supply curve for corn?
 a. A new high-yielding genetic strain of corn is discovered.
 b. The price of fertilizer falls.
 c. The government offers corn farmers a subsidy of $1/bushel.

7. The price elasticity of supply for Basmati rice (an aromatic strain of rice) is likely to be:
 a. Higher in the long run than the short run, because farmers cannot easily change their decisions about how much Basmati rice to plant once the current crop has been planted.
 b. High, because consumers have a lot of other kinds of rice and other staple foods to choose from.
 c. Low in both the long run and short run, because rice farming requires only unskilled labor.

d. High in both the long run and the short run because the inputs required to produce Basmati rice can easily be duplicated.

8. What are the respective price elasticities of supply at *A* and *B* on the supply curve shown in the following figure?

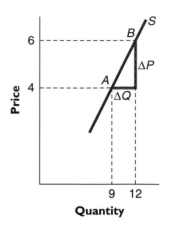

9. The supply curves for the only two firms in a competitive industry are given by $P = 2Q_1$ and $P = 2 + Q_2$, where Q_1 is the output of firm 1 and Q_2 is the output of firm 2. What is the market supply curve for this industry? (*Hint:* Graph the two curves side by side, then add their respective quantities at a sample of different prices.)

10. Jay, Kay, and Dee are marooned on an island in the Bahamas. They must find a way to provide themselves with food and drinking water. The following table shows how many hours it takes each person to produce one unit of food or one unit of water.

	Time to produce one unit of food	Time to produce one unit of water
Jay	1 hour	2 hours
Kay	2 hours	1 hour
Dee	4 hours	6 hours

a. If each person has 12 hours of daylight available to work, draw the individual production possibility curves when each person provides for himself or herself.
b. Suppose food and water are also produced on a neighboring island and a boat becomes available at no cost to allow trade between the islands. Draw the supply curve for water on the island inhabited by Jay, Kay, and Dee, where the vertical axis represents the price of water in terms of food. Then draw the supply curve for food on their island, where the vertical axis represents the price of food in terms of water.

■ ANSWERS TO IN-CHAPTER EXERCISES ■

6.1 Since Harry will find 300 containers if he searches a third hour, we find his reservation price for searching a second hour by solving $p(300) = \$6$, for $p = 2$ cents. His reservation prices for additional hours of search are calculated in an analogous way.

Fourth hour: $p(200) = \$6$, so $p = 3$ cents;
Fifth hour: $p(100) = \$6$, so $p = 6$ cents.

6.2 The profit figures corresponding to a price of $5/hundred are as shown in the last column of the following table, where we see that the profit-maximizing output (which here means the loss-minimizing output) is 0 bottles/day. Note that the company actually loses $40/day at that output level. But it would lose even more if it produced any other amount. If the company expects conditions to remain unchanged, it will want to go out of the bottle business as soon as its equipment lease expires.

Q (bottles/day)	Total revenue ($/day)	Total labor cost ($/day)	Total cost ($/day)	Profit ($/day)
0	0	0	40	−40
100	5	10	50	−45
200	10	20	60	−50
300	15	40	80	−65
400	20	70	110	−90
500	25	110	150	−125
600	30	160	200	−170
700	35	220	260	−225

6.3 The profit figures corresponding to a price of $25/hundred are as shown in the last column of the following table, where we see that the profit-maximizing output (which here means the loss-minimizing output) is 300 bottles/day. Note that the company actually loses $5/day at that output level. But as long as it remains committed to its daily lease payment of $40, it would lose even more if it produced any other amount. If the company expects conditions to remain unchanged, it will want to go out of the bottle business as soon as its equipment lease expires.

Q (bottles/day)	Total revenue ($/day)	Total labor cost ($/day)	Total cost ($/day)	Profit ($/day)
0	0	0	40	−40
100	25	10	50	−25
200	50	20	60	−10
300	75	40	80	−5
400	100	70	110	−10
500	125	110	150	−25
600	150	160	200	−50
700	175	220	260	−85

6.4 That each of the city's 60,000 residents is willing to pay 0.00005 cents for each bottle removed means that the collective benefit of each bottle removed is (60,000)(0.00005) = 3 cents. So the city should set the redemption price at 3 cents, and from the supply curve we see that 15,000 bottles/day will be recycled at that price.

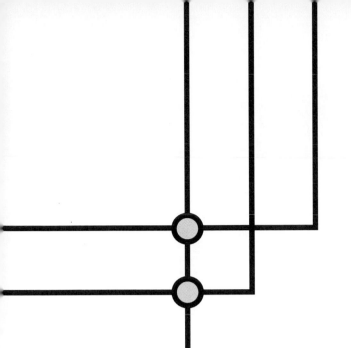

EFFICIENCY AND EXCHANGE

■

Armando Lopez sat watching the Republican National Convention on television one August night as one orator after another extolled the virtues of the free enterprise system. "The greatest engine of progress mankind has ever witnessed," one of the speakers called it. "A rising tide that will lift all boats," said another.

Lopez, however, was skeptical, for although he had worked hard and played by society's rules, his standard of living had been deteriorating rather than improving. Downsized from his draftsman's position at an aircraft plant the year before, Lopez was working as a janitor for a local office-cleaning company, the best job he had been able to find after months of search. He could not afford to repair the leaky roof and faulty plumbing at his house in East Los Angeles. Indeed, his two older children had dropped out of college because he could no longer afford their tuition bills. Although his commute to work was only 6 miles each way, freeway congestion made it a 90-minute trip most mornings. His wife's recurrent asthma attacks, triggered by local air pollution, had recently worsened. Without health insurance, the family's medical bills had been mounting rapidly. And there had been four deaths from drive-by shootings in their neighborhood in the last year.

Given the stark contrast between his own experience and the lofty claims of the orators he was listening to, Lopez's skepticism about the virtues of the free enterprise system was understandable. Yet informed students of the market system understand that it never could have been expected to prevent Lopez's problems in the first place. *In certain domains*—indeed, in very broad domains—markets are every bit as remarkable as even their strongest proponents assert. Yet there are many problems they simply cannot be expected to solve. For example, private markets cannot by themselves guarantee an income distribution that most people regard as fair. Nor can they ensure clean air, uncongested highways, or safe neighborhoods.

"I know we live in troubled times, but I don't seem to be troubled."

But markets do enable society to produce sufficient resources to meet all these goals and more. In virtually all successful societies, however, markets are supplemented by active political coordination in at least some instances. We will almost always achieve our goals more effectively if we know what tasks private markets can do well and then let them perform those tasks. Unfortunately, the discovery that markets cannot solve *every* problem seems to have led some critics to conclude that markets cannot solve *any* problems. This misperception is a dangerous one, because it has prompted attempts to prevent markets from doing even those tasks for which they are ideally suited.

Our task in this chapter will be to explore why many tasks are best left to the market. We will develop more carefully the concept of economic surplus introduced in Chapter 1, and we will explore the conditions under which unregulated markets generate the largest possible economic surplus. We will also discuss why attempts to interfere with market outcomes often lead to unintended and undesired consequences.

MARKET EQUILIBRIUM AND EFFICIENCY

As noted in Chapter 4, the mere fact that markets coordinate the production of such a large and complex list of goods and services is reason enough to marvel at them. But economists make an even stronger claim, namely, that markets not only produce these goods but also produce them as efficiently as possible.

efficient (or Pareto-efficient)
a situation is efficient if no change is possible that will help some people without harming others

The term **efficient,** as economists use it, has a narrow technical meaning. When we say that market equilibrium is efficient, we mean simply this: *If price and quantity take anything other than their equilibrium values, a transaction that will make at least some people better off without harming others can always be found.* This concept of efficiency is also known as **Pareto efficiency,** after Vilfredo Pareto, the nineteenth-century Italian economist who introduced it.

Why is market equilibrium efficient in this sense? The answer to this question involves a straightforward application of the cost-benefit principle. The following examples will illustrate the kinds of welfare-enhancing transactions that become possible whenever a market is out of equilibrium.

Why is holding the price of milk below its equilibrium level inefficient?   **EXAMPLE 7.1**

Suppose the supply and demand curves for milk are as shown in Figure 7.1 and the current price of milk is $1/gallon. Describe a transaction that will benefit both buyer and seller.

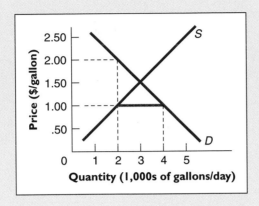

FIGURE 7.1
A Market in Which Price Is Below the Equilibrium Level.
In this market, milk is currently selling for $1/gallon, $0.50 below the equilibrium price of $1.50/gallon.

At a price of $1, sellers offer only 2,000 gallons of milk a day. At that quantity, buyers value an extra gallon of milk at $2 (the price that corresponds to 2,000 gallons a day on the demand curve, which represents what buyers are willing to pay for an additional gallon). We also know that the cost of producing an extra gallon of milk is only $1 (the price that corresponds to 2,000 gallons a day on the supply curve, which equals marginal cost).

Furthermore, a price of $1/gallon leads to excess demand of 2,000 gallons/day, which means that many dissatisfied buyers cannot buy as much milk as they want at the going price. Now suppose a supplier sells an extra gallon of milk to the most eager of these buyers for $1.25, as in Figure 7.2. Since the extra gallon cost only $1 to produce, the seller is $0.25 better off than before. And since the most eager buyer values the extra gallon at $2, that buyer is $0.75 better off than before. In sum, the transaction creates an extra $1 of economic surplus out of thin air!

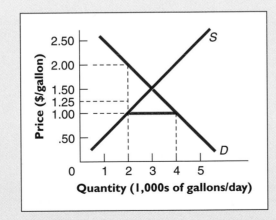

FIGURE 7.2
How Excess Demand Creates an Opportunity for a Surplus-Enhancing Transaction.
At a market price of $1/gallon, the most intensely dissatisfied buyer is willing to pay $2 for an additional gallon, which a seller can produce at a cost of only $1. If this buyer pays the seller $1.25 for the extra gallon, the buyer gains an economic surplus of $0.75 and the seller gains an economic surplus of $0.25.

Note that none of the other buyers or sellers is harmed by this transaction. Thus milk selling for only $1/gallon cannot be efficient. Indeed, if milk sells for *any* price below $1.50/gallon (the market equilibrium price), we can design a transaction in which each participant's benefit exceeds his or her cost, which means that selling milk for any price less than $1.50/gallon cannot be efficient.

EXERCISE 7.1

In Example 7.1, suppose that milk initially sells for 50 cents/gallon. Describe a transaction that will create additional economic surplus for both buyer and seller without causing harm to anyone else.

EXAMPLE 7.2

Why is holding the price of milk above its equilibrium level inefficient?

Suppose the current price of milk is $2/gallon with the same demand and supply curves as in Example 7.1. Describe a transaction that would benefit both buyer and seller.

With the price now above the equilibrium level, we have an excess supply of 2,000 gallons/day (see Figure 7.3). Suppose the most dissatisfied producer sells a gallon of milk for $1.75 to the buyer who values it most highly. This buyer, who would have been willing to pay $2, will be $0.25 better off than before. Likewise the producer, who would have been willing to sell milk for as little as $1/gallon (the marginal cost of production at 2,000 gallons/day), will be $0.75 better

FIGURE 7.3
How Excess Supply Creates an Opportunity for a Surplus-Enhancing Transaction.
At a market price of $2/gallon, dissatisfied sellers can produce an additional gallon of milk at a cost of only $1, which is $1 less than a buyer would be willing to pay for it. If the buyer pays the seller $1.75 for an extra gallon, the buyer gains an economic surplus of $0.25 and the seller gains an economic surplus of $0.75.

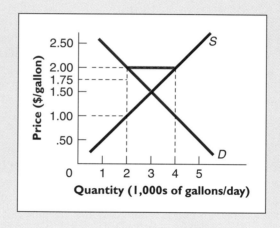

off than before. As in Example 7.1, the new transaction creates $1 of additional economic surplus without harming any other buyer or seller. Since we could design a similar surplus-enhancing transaction at any price above the equilibrium level, selling milk for more than $1.50/gallon cannot be efficient.

Indeed, the market equilibrium price is the *only* price at which buyers and sellers cannot design a surplus-enhancing transaction. In this specific, limited sense, free markets are said to allocate goods and services efficiently.

Actually, to claim that market equilibrium is always efficient even in this limited sense is an overstatement. The claim holds only if buyers and sellers are well informed, if markets are perfectly competitive, and if the demand and supply curves satisfy certain other restrictions. For example, market equilibrium will not be efficient if the individual marginal cost curves that add up to the market supply curve fail to include all relevant costs of producing the product. As we saw in Chapter 4, for example, if production generates pollution that harms others, then the true cost of expanding output will be higher than indicated by the market supply curve. The equilibrium output will be inefficiently large and the equilibrium price inefficiently low.

Likewise, market equilibrium will not be efficient if the individual demand curves that make up the market demand curve do not capture all the relevant benefits of buying additional units of the product. For instance, if a homeowner's willingness to pay for ornamental shrubs is based only on the enjoyment she gains from them, and not on any benefits that may accrue to the neighbors, the market demand curve for shrubs will understate their value to the neighborhood. The equilibrium quantity of ornamental shrubs will be inefficiently small, and the market price for shrubs will be inefficiently low.

We will take up such market imperfections in greater detail in later chapters. For now, we will confine our attention to perfectly competitive markets whose demand curves capture all relevant benefits and whose supply curves capture all relevant costs. For such goods, market equilibrium will always be efficient in the limited sense described earlier.

RECAP **EQUILIBRIUM AND EFFICIENCY**

When a market is not in equilibrium—either because price is above the equilibrium level or below it—the quantity exchanged is always less than the equilibrium level. At such a quantity, a transaction can always be made in which both buyer and seller benefit from the exchange of an additional unit of output. A market in equilibrium is said to be efficient, or Pareto-efficient, meaning that no reallocation is possible that will benefit some people without harming others.

ECONOMIC SURPLUS

In Chapter 1 we first encountered the concept of economic surplus, which in a buyer's case is the difference between the most she would have been willing to pay for a product and the amount she actually pays for it. The same concept applies to sellers of goods and services, for whom economic surplus is the difference between what they are paid for the goods they sell and the smallest amount they would have been willing to accept. In any given market, **total economic surplus** is the sum of all economic surplus attributable to participation in that market by buyers and sellers. Stated another way, it is a measure of the total amount by which buyers and sellers benefit from their participation in the market.

total economic surplus the total economic surplus in a market is the sum of all the individual economic surpluses gained by buyers and sellers who participate in the market

CALCULATING ECONOMIC SURPLUS

To see how total economic surplus is actually measured, we'll consider a hypothetical market for a good with 11 potential buyers and 11 potential sellers, each of whom can buy or sell a maximum of one unit of the good each day. The first potential seller's marginal cost is $1 per unit, the second potential seller's is $2, the third potential seller's is $3, and so on. Similarly, the first potential buyer's reservation price for the product is $11, the second buyer's reservation price is $10, the third buyer's reservation price is $9, and so on. The supply and demand curves for this market will have the staircase shapes shown in Figure 7.4. We can think of these curves as digital counterparts of the traditional analog demand and supply curves. (If the units shown on the horizontal axis were fine enough, these digital curves would be visually indistinguishable from their analog counterparts.)

The equilibrium price in the market shown in Figure 7.4 is $6/unit, and the equilibrium quantity is 6 units/day. Neither buyer nor seller will receive any surplus from the exchange of the sixth unit, since their respective reservation prices for that unit are exactly $6, the same as its market price. But the first five units yielded surplus for both buyers and sellers. The buyer of the first unit, for

FIGURE 7.4
A Market with "Digital" Supply and Demand Curves.
When a product can be sold only in whole-number amounts, its demand and supply curves have the staircase shapes shown.

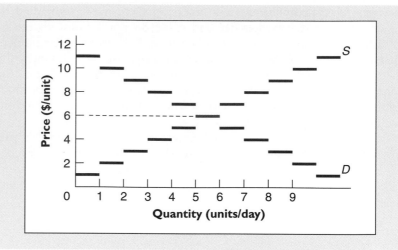

consumer surplus the economic surplus gained by the buyers of a product as measured by the cumulative difference between their respective reservation prices and the price they actually paid.

producer surplus the economic surplus gained by the sellers of a product as measured by the cumulative difference between the price received and their respective reservation prices.

example, would have been willing to pay $11 for it, but since the market price was only $6, the buyer received a surplus of exactly $5. Likewise the seller of the first unit, who would have been willing to supply it for as little as his marginal cost of $1, also received a surplus of $5. The buyer of the second unit, who would have been willing to pay as much as $10, received a surplus of $4, the same as the seller, who would have been willing to sell the unit for $2. For both buyer and seller, the surplus was $3 on the third unit, $2 on the fourth unit, and $1 on the fifth unit.

If we add all the buyers' surpluses, we get a total of $15 of buyers' surplus each day. This total is often referred to as **consumer surplus**. The sum of the corresponding surpluses for sellers is also $15/day. This total is often referred to as **producer surplus**. As we'll see in later examples, the surplus received by buyers and sellers need not always be the same. The total economic surplus for this market is the sum of consumer surplus and producer surplus, or $30/day, which corresponds to the combined blue and green areas in Figure 7.5.

FIGURE 7.5
Consumer and Producer Surplus.
Consumer surplus (blue region) is the cumulative difference between the most that buyers are willing to pay for each unit and the price they actually pay. Producer surplus (green region) is the cumulative difference between the price at which producers sell each unit and the smallest amounts they would be willing to accept.

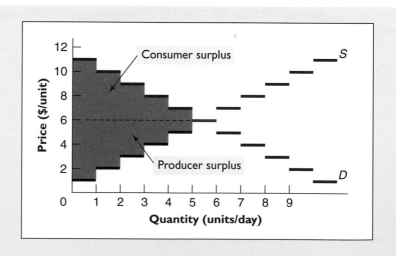

EXERCISE 7.2

Calculate producer surplus and consumer surplus for a market like the one just described, except that the buyers' reservation prices for each unit are $2 higher than before. (That is, how big would the surpluses be if the demand and supply curves were as shown in the following diagram?)

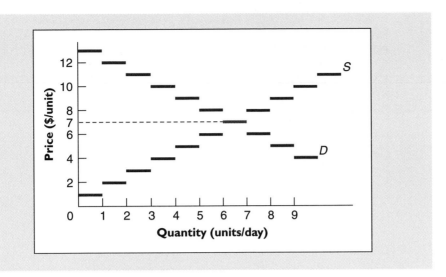

Now suppose we want to measure total economic surplus in a market with conventional straight-line supply and demand curves. As Example 7.3 illustrates, this task is a simple extension of the method used for digital supply and demand curves.

How much do buyers and sellers benefit from their participation in the market for milk?

Consider the market for milk whose demand and supply curves are shown in Figure 7.6, which has an equilibrium price of \$2/gallon and an equilibrium quantity of 4,000 gallons/day. How much total economic surplus do the participants in this market reap?

In Figure 7.6, note first that, as in Figure 7.5, the last unit exchanged each day generates no surplus at all, either for buyers or sellers. Note also that for all milk sold up to 4,000 gallons/day, buyers receive consumer surplus and

EXAMPLE 7.3

FIGURE 7.6
Supply and Demand in the Market for Milk.
For the supply and demand curves shown, the equilibrium price of milk is \$2/gallon and the equilibrium quantity is 4,000 gallons/day.

sellers receive producer surplus, just as in Figure 7.5. For sellers, the surplus is the cumulative difference between market price and marginal cost. For buyers, the surplus is the cumulative difference between the most they would be willing to pay for milk (as measured on the demand curve) and the price they actually pay.

Total consumer surplus received by buyers in the milk market is thus the blue triangle between the demand curve and the market price in Figure 7.7. Note that this area is a right triangle whose vertical arm is $h = \$1$/gallon and whose

FIGURE 7.7

Total Economic Surplus in the Market for Milk. Consumer surplus is the area of the blue triangle ($2,000/day). Producer surplus is the area of the green triangle ($4,000/day). Total economic surplus is the sum of the two, or $6,000/day.

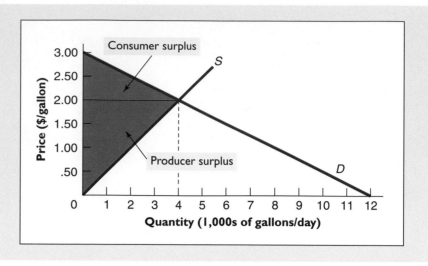

horizontal arm is b = 4,000 gallons/day. And since the area of any triangle is equal to $(1/2)bh$, consumer surplus in this market is equal to

$$(1/2)(4,000 \text{ gallons/day})(\$1/\text{gallon}) = \$2,000/\text{day}.$$

Likewise, total producer surplus is the green triangle between the supply curve and the market price. The height of this triangle is h = \$2/gallon and the base is b = 4,000 gallons/day, so producer surplus is equal to

$$(1/2)(4,000 \text{ gallons/day})(\$2/\text{gallon}) = \$4,000/\text{day}.$$

The total economic surplus from this milk market is the sum of consumer and producer surplus, or $6,000/day.

A useful way of thinking about this surplus is to ask what is the highest price consumers and producers would pay, in the aggregate, for the right to continue participating in the milk market. For buyers, the answer is $2,000/day, since that is the amount by which their combined benefits exceed their combined costs. Sellers would pay up to $4,000/day, since that is the amount by which their combined benefits exceed their combined reservation prices. All together, then, buyers and sellers would be willing to pay up to $6,000/day for the right to continue participating in this market.

That economic surplus is the amount by which buyers and sellers benefit from participating in a market sheds further light on the economist's claim that market equilibrium is efficient. At any price other than the equilibrium price, the total economic surplus produced by a market will be less than it would be at the equilibrium price. Stated another way, the equilibrium price and quantity serve to maximize the total economic surplus created by a market.

EFFICIENCY IS NOT THE ONLY GOAL

The fact that market equilibrium maximizes economic surplus is an attractive feature, to be sure. Bear in mind, however, that "efficient" does not mean the same thing as "good." For example, the market for milk may be in equilibrium at a price of $2/gallon, yet many poor families may be unable to afford milk for their children at that price. Still others may not even have a place for their children to sleep.

Efficiency is a concept based on predetermined attributes of buyers and sellers—their incomes, tastes, abilities, knowledge, and so on. Through the combined effects of individual cost-benefit decisions, these attributes give rise to the supply and demand curves for each good produced in an economy. If we are concerned about inequality in the distribution of attributes like income, we should not be surprised to discover that markets do not always yield outcomes we like.

Most of us could agree, for example, that the world would be a better one if poor families had enough income to feed their families adequately. The claim that equilibrium in the market for milk is efficient means simply that *taking people's incomes as given,* the resulting allocation of milk cannot be altered so as to help some people without at the same time harming others.

To this a critic of the market system might respond: So what? As such critics rightly point out, imposing costs on others may be justified if doing so will help those with sufficiently important unmet demands. For example, most people would prefer to fund homeless shelters with their tax dollars rather than let the homeless freeze to death. Arguing in these terms, American policymakers responded to rapid increases in the price of oil in the late 1970s by imposing price controls on home heating oil. And many of us might agree that if the alternative had been to take no action at all, price controls might have been justified in the name of social justice.

But the economist's concept of market efficiency makes clear that there *must* be a better alternative policy. Price controls on oil prevent the market from reaching equilibrium, and as we saw, that means forgoing transactions that would benefit some people without harming others.

WHY EFFICIENCY SHOULD BE THE FIRST GOAL

Efficiency is important not because it is a desirable end in itself but because it enables us to achieve all our other goals to the fullest possible extent. Whenever a market is out of equilibrium, it is always possible to generate additional economic surplus. To gain additional economic surplus is to gain more of the resources we need to do the things we want to do. Whenever any market is out of equilibrium, there is waste, and waste is always a bad thing.

RECAP ECONOMIC SURPLUS

The economic surplus generated by a market is the total dollar amount by which buyers and sellers benefit from their participation in that market. It is the sum of consumer surplus and producer surplus. Consumer surplus is the cumulative difference between what buyers would have been willing to pay for the product and the price they actually do pay. Graphically it is the area between the demand curve and the market price. Producer surplus is the cumulative difference between the market price and the reservation prices at which producers would have been willing to make their sales. Graphically it is the area between market price and the supply curve.

Total economic surplus in a market is maximized when exchange occurs at the equilibrium price. But the fact that equilibrium is "efficient" in this sense does not mean the same as "good." All markets can be in equilibrium, yet many people may lack sufficient income to buy even basic goods and services. Still, it is important to permit markets to reach equilibrium, because when economic surplus is maximized, it is possible to pursue every goal more fully.

THE COST OF PREVENTING PRICE ADJUSTMENTS

PRICE CEILINGS

price ceiling a law or regulation that prevents sellers from charging more than a specified amount

During 1979, an interruption in oil supplies from the Middle East caused the price of home heating oil to rise by more than 100 percent. Concern about the hardship this sudden price increase would impose on poor families in northern states led the government to impose a **price ceiling** in the market for home heating oil. This price ceiling prohibited sellers from charging more than a specified amount for heating oil.

Example 7.4 illustrates why imposing a price ceiling on heating oil, although well intended, was a bad idea.

EXAMPLE 7.4

How much waste does a price ceiling on heating oil cause?

Suppose the demand and supply curves for home heating oil are as shown in Figure 7.8, in which the equilibrium price is $1.40/gallon. And suppose that at that price, many poor families cannot heat their homes adequately. Out of concern for the poor, legislators pass a law setting the maximum price at $1.00/gallon. How much lost economic surplus does this policy cost society?

FIGURE 7.8

Economic Surplus in an Unregulated Market for Home Heating Oil.
For the supply and demand curves shown, the equilibrium price of home heating oil is $1.40/gallon, and the equilibrium quantity is 3,000 gallons/day. Consumer surplus is the area of the blue triangle ($900/day). Producer surplus is the area of the green triangle (also $900/day).

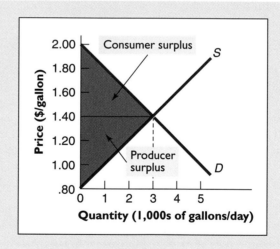

First, let's calculate the surplus without price controls. If this market is not regulated, 3,000 gallons/day will be sold at a price of $1.40/gallon. In Figure 7.8, the economic surplus received by buyers is the area of the blue triangle. Since the height of this triangle is $0.60/gallon and its base is 3,000 gallons/day, its area is equal to (1/2)(3,000 gallons/day)($0.60/gallon) = $900/day. The economic surplus received by producers is the area of the green triangle. Since this triangle also has an area of $900/day, total economic surplus in this market will be $1,800/day.

If the price of heating oil is prevented from rising above $1.00/gallon, only 1,000 gallons/day will be sold, and the total economic surplus will be reduced by the area of the lined triangle in Figure 7.9. Since the height of this triangle is $0.80/gallon, and its base is 2,000 gallons/day, its area is (1/2)(2,000 gallons/day)($0.80/gallon) = $800/day. Producer surplus falls from $900/day in the unregulated market to the area of the green triangle, or (1/2)(1,000 gallons/day)($0.20/gallon) = $100/day, which is a loss of $800/day. Thus the loss in total economic surplus is equal to the loss in producer surplus, which means

FIGURE 7.9
The Waste Caused by Price Controls.
By limiting output in the home heating oil market to 1,000 gallons/day, price controls cause a loss in economic surplus of $800/day (area of the lined triangle).

that the new consumer surplus must be the same as the original consumer surplus. To verify that, note that consumer surplus under controls is the area of the blue figure, which is again $900/day. (*Hint:* To compute this area, first split the figure into a rectangle and a triangle.) By preventing the home heating oil market from reaching equilibrium, price controls waste $800 of producer surplus per day without creating any additional surplus for consumers!

Defenders of price controls might respond that those poor families who managed to buy some heating oil at the lower price received welcome budget relief. Yes, but the same objective could have been accomplished in a much less costly way, namely, by giving the poor more income with which to buy heating oil. But can the poor, who have limited political power, really hope to receive income transfers that would enable them to heat their homes? On reflection, the answer to this question would seem to be yes, *if the alternative is to impose price controls that would be even more costly than the income transfers.* After all, the price ceiling as implemented ends up costing heating oil sellers $800/day in lost economic surplus. So they ought to be willing to pay some amount less than $800/day in additional taxes to escape the burden of controls. The additional tax revenue could finance income transfers that would be far more beneficial to the poor than price controls.

This point is so important, and so often misunderstood by voters and policymakers, that we will emphasize it by putting it another way. Think of the economic surplus from a market as a pie to be divided among the various market participants. Figure 7.10(a) represents the $1,000/day total economic surplus available to participants in the home heating oil market when the government limits the price of oil to $1/gallon. We have divided this pie into two slices labeled *R* and *P,* to denote the surpluses received by rich and poor participants. Figure 7.10(b) represents the $1,800/day total economic surplus available when the price of home heating oil is free to reach its equilibrium level. This pie is divided among rich and poor participants in the same proportion as the pie in part (a).

The important point to notice is this: *Because the pie in the part (b) is larger, both rich and poor participants in the home heating oil market can get a bigger slice of the pie than they would have had under price controls.* Price controls prevent people and firms from engaging in transactions that pass the cost-benefit test. Rather than tinker with the market price of oil, it is in everyone's interest to simply transfer additional income to the poor.

Supporters of price controls may object that income transfers to the poor might weaken people's incentive to work, and thus might prove extremely costly

FIGURE 7.10

When the Pie Is Larger, Everyone Can Have a Bigger Slice.

Any policy that reduces total economic surplus is a missed opportunity to make everyone better off.

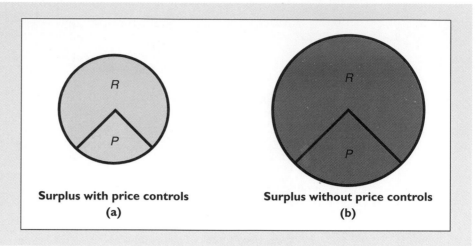

Surplus with price controls
(a)

Surplus without price controls
(b)

in the long run. Difficult issues do indeed arise in the design of programs for transferring income to the poor—issues we will consider in some detail in later chapters. But for now, suffice it to say that ways exist to transfer income without undermining work incentives significantly. One such method is the *earned-income tax credit,* a program that supplements the wages of low-income workers. Given such programs, transferring income to the poor will always be more efficient than trying to boost their living standard through price controls.

Rent controls are another example of a price ceiling. As discussed in Chapter 4, rent controls prevent landlords from charging more than a specified amount for rental housing. Tenants lucky enough to find a rent-controlled apartment often end up paying less than they would have in the absence of rent controls. But rent controls also prevent the housing market from reaching equilibrium and are thus inefficient. As Example 7.5 illustrates, alternatives to rent controls that will do even more for tenants can always be found.

EXAMPLE 7.5

By how much do rent controls reduce economic surplus in the rental housing market?

Suppose the supply and demand curves for rental housing units are as shown in Figure 7.11. By how much will a law that prevents rents from exceeding $100/month reduce the total economic surplus of participants in the rental housing market?

Without rent control the equilibrium rent in this market would be $200/month, and the equilibrium quantity would be 4,000 apartments/month. The blue triangle in Figure 7.11 represents the economic surplus for renters. The height of this triangle is $800/apartment, and its base is 4,000 apartments/month, so its area is equal to (1/2)(4,000 apartments/month)($800/apartment) = $1,600,000/month. Economic surplus for landlords is represented by the green triangle in Figure 7.11. This triangle has the same base as the blue triangle, and a height of $200/month, so its area is (1/2)(4,000 apartments/month)($200/month) = $400,000/month. Total economic surplus in this unregulated market—the sum of consumer surplus and producer surplus—is thus $2,000,000/month.

With rents capped at $100/month, however, only 2,000 apartments/month are rented. The reduction in total surplus is equal to the area of the lined triangle in Figure 7.12: (1/2)($500/month)(2,000 apartments/month) = $500,000/month. Producer surplus falls from $400,000/month in the unregulated market to the area of the green triangle: (1/2)($100/month)(2,000 apartments/month) = $100,000/month. Consumer surplus falls from $1,600,000/month in the unregulated market to the area of the blue figure, only $1,400,000. (Again, to calculate the area of the blue figure, first split the figure into a rectangle and a triangle.)

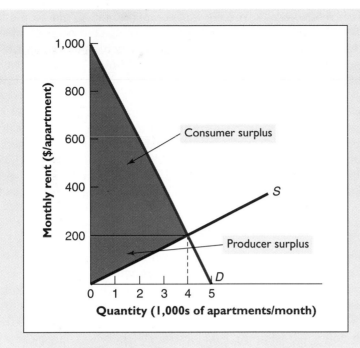

FIGURE 7.11
Economic Surplus in an Unregulated Housing Market.
For the supply and demand curves shown, consumer surplus (area of the blue triangle) is $1,600,000/month and producer surplus (area of the green triangle) is $400,000/month. Total economic surplus is $2,000,000/month.

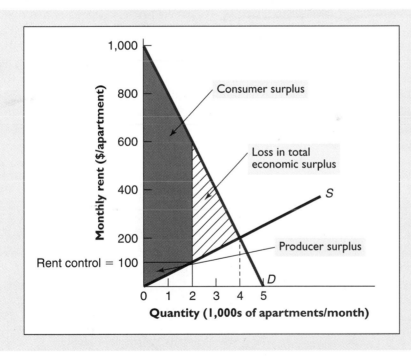

FIGURE 7.12
Lost Surplus from Rent Control.
When rent is prevented from rising above $100/month, the quantity of apartments rented falls from 4,000/month to 2,000/month. The resulting total loss of economic surplus is equal to the area of the lined triangle, $500,000/month.

These reductions in economic surplus constitute pure waste—no different, from the perspective of participants in this market, than if someone had siphoned that much cash out of their bank accounts each month and thrown it into a bonfire.

EXERCISE 7.3

How much total economic surplus would have been lost if the rent ceiling had been set at $150 instead of $100?

Compared to rent control, a much better policy would be to give low-income tenants some additional income and then let them bid for housing on the open market. Those rent control advocates who complain that no one would be willing to give low-income tenants extra money must be asked to explain why people would be willing to tolerate rent controls, which are so much *more* costly than income transfers. Logically, if people are willing to support rent controls, they should be even more eager to support income transfers to low-income tenants.

That is not to say that the poor reap no benefit at all from rent controls. Again, those who are lucky enough to find an apartment that meets their needs often end up paying substantially less than they would in an unregulated market. The point is that more can be done for the poor. Their problem is that they have too little income, so the simplest and best solution is not to regulate the prices of the goods they and others buy but to give them more money.

PRICE FLOORS

price floor *a law or regulation that guarantees that suppliers will receive at least a specified amount for their product*

Whereas a price ceiling prevents sellers from charging more than a specified amount, a **price floor** guarantees that suppliers will receive at least a specified amount for their product. But unlike a price ceiling, which attempts to hold price below its equilibrium level, a price floor attempts to peg price above its equilibrium level. And unlike the imposition of a price ceiling, in which the government's only responsibility is to impose penalties on sellers who charge too much, the imposition of a price floor requires the government to become an active participant on the buyer's side of the market. For when price is pegged above the equilibrium level, an excess supply develops, which consumers cannot be forced to buy against their wishes.

Agricultural price supports are an example of a price floor. They are another attempt by the government to prevent markets from reaching equilibrium to provide benefits for deserving citizens. But as Example 7.6 demonstrates, price ceilings and price floors do have one fundamental characteristic in common: Both stand in the way of actions that satisfy the cost-benefit test, and both therefore reduce total economic surplus.

EXAMPLE 7.6

By how much do price supports for wheat reduce total economic surplus?

Suppose the supply and demand for wheat are as shown in Figure 7.13. The government offers to buy as much wheat as necessary to clear the market at a price of $40/ton. Assuming that the government then gives the wheat it buys to the consumers who value it most, by how much will price supports reduce the total economic surplus generated in the wheat market?

FIGURE 7.13
Equilibrium in an Unregulated Wheat Market.
In the absence of a government price support, 3 million tons of wheat/day are sold at a price of $30/ton.

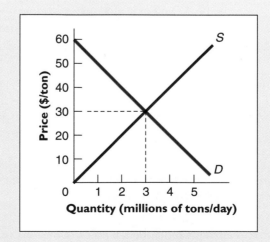

Without the price support, the equilibrium price in this market would be $30/ton. With the price support set at $40/ton, the public purchases 2 million tons/month and the government purchases the remaining 2 million tons offered by farmers at that price. If the government then gives the wheat to the consumers who value it most, the total quantity consumed is 4 million tons/month. The first million pounds that are given away effectively restore the economic surplus that would have been produced had the market been left unregulated (see Figure 7.14), since the cost of producing this wheat is the same as before and the same consumers end up getting it. But the second million pounds the government gives away cost farmers more to produce (as measured by the supply curve) than what buyers were willing to pay for it (as measured by the demand curve). The resulting reduction in economic surplus is represented by the area of the pale blue triangle in Figure 7.14, which is $10 million/month.

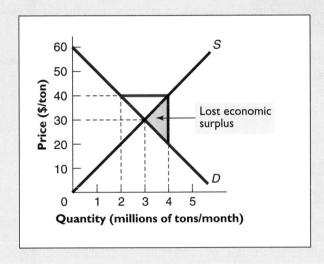

FIGURE 7.14
Lost Surplus from Price Supports for Wheat.
A price support of $40/ton results in 4,000 tons of wheat/month being produced, of which the government buys half and the public buys half. Lost economic surplus from the program is equal to $10 million/month.

Unfortunately, the actual reduction in surplus is likely to be much larger than $10 million/month, because the government is generally unable to give the wheat away to those people who value it most. Indeed, the wheat purchased by the government often spoils or is eaten by rodents before it can be sold or given away. If the government's goal were to help wheat farmers, administrators would have done better to leave the price of wheat alone and simply give farmers some extra money.

EXERCISE 7.4

In Example 7.6, by how much would total economic surplus be reduced by the price support if none of the wheat purchased by the government were given to consumers?

FIRST-COME–FIRST-SERVED POLICIES

Governments are not the only institutions that attempt to promote social goals by preventing markets from reaching equilibrium. Some universities, for example, attempt to protect access by low-income students to concerts and sporting events by selling a limited number of tickets below the market-clearing price on a first-come–first-served basis.

The commercial airline industry was an early proponent of the use of the first-come–first-served allocation method, which it used to ration seats on overbooked flights. Throughout the industry's history, most airlines have routinely accepted more reservations for their flights than there are seats on those flights. Most of the time, this practice causes no difficulty, because many reservation holders don't show up to claim their seats. Indeed, if airlines did not overbook their flights, most flights would take off with many empty seats, forcing airlines to charge higher ticket prices to cover their costs.

The only real difficulty is that every so often, more people actually do show up for a flight than there are seats on the plane. Until the late 1970s, airlines dealt with this problem by boarding passengers on a first-come–first-served basis. For example, if 120 people showed up for a flight with 110 seats, the last 10 people to arrive were "bumped," or forced to wait for the next available flight.

The bumped passengers often complained bitterly, and no wonder, since many of them ended up missing important business meetings or family events. As the following example illustrates, there was fortunately a simple solution to this problem, one that was almost blocked by a public interest group that failed to appreciate how rich and poor alike can benefit when an efficient policy replaces an inefficient one.

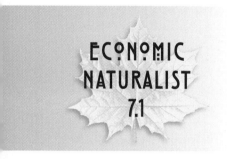

Why are passenger complaints about overbooked flights a thing of the past?

ECONOMIC NATURALIST 7.1

Why does no one complain anymore about being bumped from an overbooked flight?

In 1978, airlines abandoned their first-come–first-served policy in favor of a new procedure. Since then, their practice has been to solicit volunteers to give up their seats on oversold flights in return for a cash payment or free ticket. Now, the only people who give up their seats are those who volunteer to do so in return for compensation. And hence the complete disappearance of complaints about being bumped from overbooked flights.

Example 7.7 illustrates how we might attempt to quantify the loss in surplus that results from first-come–first-served policies.

EXAMPLE 7.7

Which of the two policies—first-come–first-served or compensation for volunteers—is more efficient?

The difficulty with the first-come–first-served policy is that it gives little weight to the interests of passengers with pressing reasons for arriving at their destination on time. Such passengers can sometimes avoid losing their seats by showing up early, but passengers coming in on connecting flights often cannot control when they arrive. And the cost of showing up early is likely to be highest for precisely those people who place the highest value on not missing a flight (such as business executives, whose opportunity cost of waiting in airports is high). How big is the efficiency loss that results from first-come–first served?

For the sake of illustration, suppose that 37 people show up for a flight with only 33 seats. One way or another, four people will have to wait for another flight. Suppose we ask each of them, "What is the most you would be willing to pay to fly now rather than wait?" Typically, different passengers will have different reservation prices for avoiding the wait. Suppose the person who is most willing to pay would pay up to $60 rather than miss the flight; that the person secondmost willing to pay would pay up to $59; that the person thirdmost willing to pay would pay up to $58; and so on. In that case, the person with the smallest reservation price for avoiding the wait would have a reservation price of $24. For the entire group of 37 passengers, the average reservation price for avoiding the wait would be ($60 + $59 + $58 + $\cdots$ + $24)/37 = $42.

Given the difficulty of controlling airport arrival times, the passengers who get bumped under the first-come–first-served policy are not likely to differ systematically from others with respect to their reservation price for not missing the flight. On average, then, the total cost imposed on the four bumped passengers would be four times the average reservation price of $42, or $168. As far as those four passengers are concerned, that total is a pure loss of consumer surplus.

How does this cost compare with the cost imposed on bumped passengers when the airline compensates volunteers? Suppose the airline solicits volunteers by conducting an informal auction, increasing its cash compensation offer by $1 increments until it has the desired number of volunteers. As the incentive to stay behind rises, more people will volunteer; those whose reservation prices are the lowest will volunteer first. In this example, offers below $24 would generate no volunteers. An offer of $24 would generate one volunteer; an offer of $25 would generate two volunteers; and so on. A compensation payment of $27 would generate the necessary four volunteers.

What is the net cost of the compensation policy? While the airline pays out (4)($27) = $108 in compensation payments, not all that amount represents lost economic surplus. Thus the passenger whose reservation price for missing the flight is $24 receives a net gain in economic surplus of $3—the difference between the $27 compensation payment and her $24 reservation price. Similarly, those whose reservation prices were $25 and $26 receive a net gain of $2 and $1, respectively. The cost of the cash compensation policy net of these gains is thus $108 − $6 = $102, or $66 less than under the first-come–first-served policy.

The compensation policy is more efficient than the first-come–first-served policy because it establishes a market for a scarce resource that would otherwise be allocated by nonmarket means. Figure 7.15 shows the supply and demand curves for seats under the compensation policy. In this market, the equilibrium price of not having to wait is $27. People who choose not to volunteer at that price incur an opportunity cost of $27 to not miss the flight. The four people who do volunteer accept $27 as ample compensation—indeed, more than ample for three of them.

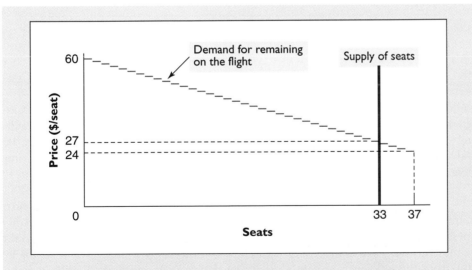

FIGURE 7.15
Equilibrium in the Market for Seats on Oversold Flights.
The demand curve for remaining on the flight is generated by plotting the reservation prices in descending order. The equilibrium compensation payment for volunteers who give up their seats is $27— the price at which four passengers volunteer to wait and the remaining 33 choose not to wait.

An interesting footnote to this example is that the airlines' policy change evoked a fierce protest from the Aviation Consumer Action Project (ACAP), a group that portrayed itself as a watchdog for the interests of airline passengers. ACAP's concern was that the shift to a system of compensation payments would mean that poor people would most often end up waiting for the next flight. This was a curious objection, for several reasons. Although the people who volunteer to wait in return for a compensation payment probably have lower incomes, on average, than those who don't volunteer, the income distributions of the two groups overlap considerably. Many financially comfortable persons with no pressing appointments will gladly volunteer to wait, while many people with lower incomes will choose not to. But more important, the previous policy of first-come–first-served was manifestly less attractive to the poor than the new policy. After all, passengers give up their seats under the volunteer policy only when they find the payment offered sufficient to compensate for the inconvenience of waiting. We may suspect that few poor persons would be grateful if ACAP had succeeded in persuading the government to block the switch to compensation payments.

EXAMPLE 7.8

How should a tennis pro handle the overbooking problem?

Anticipating a high proportion of no-shows, a tennis pro routinely books five people for each of his group lesson slots, even though he is able to teach only three people at a time. One day, all five people show up for their lessons at 10 A.M., the first lesson slot of the morning. Their respective arrival times and the maximum amounts each would be willing to pay to avoid postponing his or her lesson are as given in the following table.

Player	Arrival time	Reservation price
Ann	9:50 A.M.	$ 4
Bill	9:52 A.M.	$ 3
Carrie	9:55 A.M.	$ 6
Dana	9:56 A.M.	$ 10
Earl	9:59 A.M.	$ 3

If the tennis pro accommodates the players on a first-come–first-served basis, by how much will total economic surplus be smaller than if he had offered cash compensation to induce two volunteers to reschedule? Which system is more efficient?

The result of using a first-come–first-served policy will be that Dana and Earl, the last two to arrive, will have to postpone their lessons. Since the cost of waiting is $10 for Dana and $3 for Earl, the total cost of the first-come–first-served policy is $13.

Suppose that the pro instead had offered cash compensation payments to elicit volunteers. If he offered a payment of $3, both Bill and Earl would be willing to wait. The total cost of the cash compensation policy would therefore be only $6, or $7 less than under the first-come–first-served policy. So the cash compensation policy is more efficient.

You might feel tempted to ask why the tennis pro would bother to offer cash compensation when he has the option of saving the $6 by continuing with his current policy of first-come–first-served. Or why, for that matter, an airline would bother to offer cash compensation to elicit volunteers to wait for the next flight. But from the efficiency principle we know that it is possible for *everyone* to do better under an efficient policy than under an inefficient one. (When the pie is bigger, everyone can have a larger slice.) Exercise 7.5 asks you to design such a transaction for the tennis lesson example.

EXERCISE 7.5

Describe a set of cash transfers in Example 7.7 that would make each of the five students and the tennis pro better off than under the first-come–first-served policy.

In practice, transactions like the one called for in Exercise 7.5 would be cumbersome to administer. Typically, the seller is in a position to solve such problems more easily by offering cash payments to elicit volunteers, and then financing those cash payments by charging slightly higher prices. Buyers, for their part, are willing to pay the higher prices because they value the seller's promise not to cancel their reservations without compensation.

RECAP **THE COST OF BLOCKING PRICE ADJUSTMENTS**

In an effort to increase the economic welfare of disadvantaged consumers, governments often implement policies that attempt to prevent markets from reaching equilibrium. Price ceilings attempt to make housing and other basic goods more affordable for poor families, and price floors attempt to boost the incomes of sellers in distress, typically family farmers. Private organizations also implement policies that prevent markets from reaching equilibrium, such as allocation on a first-come–first-served basis.

Such policies always reduce total economic surplus relative to the alternative of letting prices seek their equilibrium levels. It is always possible to design alternative policies under which rich and poor alike fare better.

TAXES AND EFFICIENCY

WHO PAYS A TAX IMPOSED ON SELLERS OF A GOOD?

Politicians of all stripes seem loath to propose new taxes. But when additional public revenue must be raised, most seem to feel more comfortable proposing taxes paid by sellers than taxes paid by consumers. When pressed to explain this preference, many respond that businesses can more easily afford to pay extra taxes. Yet as Example 7.9 illustrates, the burden of a tax collected from the sellers of a good need not fall exclusively on sellers.

How will the imposition of a tax of $1/pound collected from potato farmers affect the equilibrium price and quantity of potatoes?

EXAMPLE 7.9

Suppose the demand and supply curves for potatoes have the conventional slopes as shown by D and S in Figure 7.16, resulting in an initial equilibrium price and quantity of $3/pound and 3 million pounds/month, respectively. From the farmers' perspective, the imposition of a tax of $1/pound is essentially the same as a $1 increase in the marginal cost of producing each pound of potatoes, and hence the tax results in an upward shift in the supply curve by $1/pound.

As shown in Figure 7.16, the new equilibrium price (including the tax) will be $3.50, and the new equilibrium quantity will be 2.5 million pounds/month. The net price per pound received by producers is $1 less than the price paid by the consumer, or $2.50. Even though the tax was collected entirely from potato sellers, the burden of the tax fell on both buyers and sellers—on buyers, because they pay $0.50/pound more than before the tax, and on sellers, because they receive $0.50/pound less than before the tax.

The burden of the tax need not fall equally on buyers and sellers, as in Example 7.9. Indeed, as the following example illustrates, a tax levied on sellers may end up being paid almost entirely by buyers.

FIGURE 7.16

The Effect of a Tax on the Equilibrium Quantity and Price of Potatoes.

With no tax, 3 million pounds of potatoes are sold each month at a price of $3/pound. With a tax of $1/pound collected from sellers, consumers end up paying $3.50/pound (including tax), while sellers receive only $2.50/pound (net of tax). Equilibrium quantity falls from 3 million pounds/month to 2.5 million.

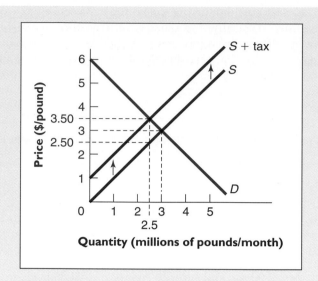

ECONOMIC NATURALIST 7.2

How will a tax on cars affect automobile prices in the long run?

Suppose that, given sufficient time, all the inputs required to produce cars can be acquired in unlimited quantities at fixed market prices. If the inputs required to produce each car cost $10,000, how will the long-run equilibrium price of automobiles be affected if a tax of $100/car is levied on manufacturers?

The fact that all the inputs needed to build cars can be acquired at constant prices suggests that the long-run marginal cost of making cars is constant, or, in other words, that the long-run supply curve of cars is horizontal at $10,000/car. A tax of $100/car effectively raises marginal cost by $100/car and thus shifts the supply curve upward by exactly $100. If the demand curve for cars is as shown by curve D in Figure 7.17, the effect is to raise the equilibrium price of cars by exactly $100, to $10,100. The equilibrium quantity falls from 2 million cars/month to 1.9 million.

Although the long-run supply curve shown in Figure 7.17 is in one sense an extreme case (since its price elasticity is infinite), it is by no means an unrepresentative one. For as we discussed in Chapter 6, the long-run supply curve will tend to be horizontal when it is possible to acquire more of all the necessary inputs at constant prices. As a first approximation, this can be accomplished for many—perhaps even most—goods and services in a typical economy.

FIGURE 7.17

The Effect of a Tax on Sellers of a Good with Infinite Price Elasticity of Supply.

When the supply curve for a good is perfectly elastic, the burden of a tax collected from sellers falls entirely on buyers.

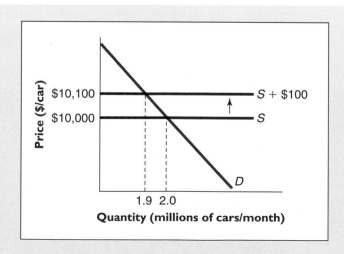

For goods with perfectly elastic supply curves, the entire burden of any tax is borne by the buyer.[1] That is, the increase in the equilibrium price is exactly equal to the tax. For this empirically relevant case, then, there is special irony in the common political practice of justifying taxes on business by saying that businesses have greater ability to pay than consumers.

HOW A TAX COLLECTED FROM A SELLER AFFECTS ECONOMIC SURPLUS

We saw earlier that perfectly competitive markets distribute goods and services efficiently if demand curves reflect all relevant benefits and supply curves reflect all relevant costs. In Example 7.10, we'll consider how the imposition of a tax on a product might affect a market's efficiency.

How does a tax on potatoes affect economic efficiency?

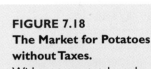

EXAMPLE 7.10

Suppose the supply and demand for potatoes are as shown by the curves S and D in Figure 7.18. How would the imposition of a tax of $1/pound, collected from potato sellers, affect total economic surplus in the potato market?

In the absence of a tax, 3 million pounds of potatoes/month would be sold at a price of $3/pound, and the resulting total economic surplus would be $9 million/month (the area of the pale blue triangle in Figure 7.18).

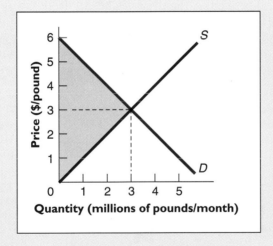

FIGURE 7.18
The Market for Potatoes without Taxes.
Without taxes, total surplus in the potato market equals the area of the pale blue triangle, $9 million/month.

With a tax of $1/pound collected from potato sellers, the new equilibrium price of potatoes would be $3.50/pound (of which sellers receive $2.50, net of tax), and only 2.5 million pounds of potatoes would be sold each month (see Figure 7.19). The total economic surplus reaped by buyers and sellers in the potato market would be the area of the pale blue triangle shown in Figure 7.19, which is $6.25 million/month, or $2.75 million less than before.

This drop in surplus may sound like an enormous loss. But it is a misleading figure, because it fails to take account of the value of the additional tax revenue collected, which is equal to $2.5 million/month ($1/pound on 2.5 million pounds of potatoes). If the government needs to collect no more than a given total amount of tax revenue to pay for the services it provides, then the potato tax revenue should enable it to reduce other taxes by $2.5 million/month. So although buyers and sellers lose $2.75 million/month in economic surplus from their participation in the potato market, they also enjoy a $2.5 million reduction

[1]In the example given, the tax was collected from sellers. If you go on to take intermediate microeconomics, you will see that the same conclusions apply when a tax is collected from buyers.

FIGURE 7.19

The Effect of a $1/pound Tax on Potatoes.

A $1/pound tax on potatoes would cause an upward shift in the supply curve by $1. Total surplus would shrink to the area of the pale blue triangle, $6.25 million/month.

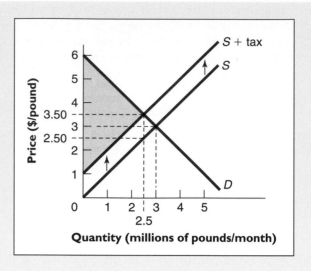

in the other taxes they pay. On balance, then, their net reduction in economic surplus is only $0.25 million.

Graphically, the loss in economic surplus caused by the imposition of the tax can be shown as the area of the small pale blue triangle in Figure 7.20. This loss in surplus is often described as the **deadweight loss** from the tax.

Still, a loss in economic surplus, however small, is something people would prefer to avoid, and taxes like the one just described undoubtedly reduce economic surplus in the markets on which they are imposed. As Federal Reserve Board Chairman Alan Greenspan has remarked, "All taxes are a drag on economic growth. It's only a question of degree."[2]

deadweight loss the deadweight loss caused by a policy is the reduction in economic surplus that results from adoption of that policy

FIGURE 7.20

The Deadweight Loss Caused by a Tax.

For the market shown, the loss in economic surplus caused by a tax of $1/pound of potatoes equals the area of the small pale blue triangle, or $250,000/month.

A tax reduces economic surplus because it distorts the basic cost-benefit criterion that would ordinarily guide efficient decisions about production and consumption. In Example 7.10, the cost-benefit test tells us that we should expand potato production up to the point at which the benefit of the last pound of potatoes consumed (as measured by what buyers are willing to pay for it) equals the cost of producing it (as measured by the producer's marginal cost). That condition was satisfied in the potato market before the tax, but it is not satisfied once

[2]*The Wall Street Journal*, March 26, 1997, p. A1.

the tax is imposed. In Figure 7.20, for example, note that when potato consumption is 2.5 million pounds/month, the value of an additional pound of potatoes to consumers is $3.50, whereas the cost to producers is only $2.50, not including the tax. (The cost to producers, including the tax, is $3.50/pound, but again we note that this tax is not a cost to society as a whole because it offsets other taxes that would otherwise have to be collected.)

Is a tax on potatoes necessarily "bad"? (When economists say that a policy, such as a tax, is "bad," they mean that it lowers total economic surplus.) To answer this question, we must first identify the best alternative to taxing potatoes. You may be tempted to say, "Don't tax anything at all!" On a moment's reflection, however, you will realize that this is surely not the best option. After all, a country that taxed nothing could not pay for even the most minimal public services, such as road maintenance, fire protection, and national defense. And a country without at least minimal defense capability could not hope to maintain its independence for long. (In Chapter 15 we will consider why we often empower government to provide public goods.) On balance, if taxing potatoes were the best way to avoid doing without highly valued public services, then a small deadweight loss in the potato market would be a small price indeed.

So the real question is whether there are other things we could tax that would be better than taxing potatoes. The problem with a tax on any activity is that if market incentives encourage people to pursue the "right" amount of the activity (that is, the surplus-maximizing amount), then a tax will encourage them to pursue too little of it. As economists have long recognized, this observation suggests that taxes will cause smaller deadweight losses if they are imposed on goods for which the equilibrium quantity is not highly sensitive to changes in production costs.

TAXES, ELASTICITY, AND EFFICIENCY

Suppose the government put a tax of 50 cents/pound on table salt. How would this affect the amount of salt you and others use? In Chapter 5 we saw that the demand for salt is highly inelastic with respect to price, because salt has few substitutes and occupies only a minuscule share in most family budgets. Because the imposition of a tax on table salt would not result in a significant reduction in the amount of it consumed, the deadweight loss from this tax on would be relatively small. More generally, the deadweight loss from a per-unit tax imposed on the seller of a good will be smaller the smaller is the price elasticity of demand for the good.

Figure 7.21 illustrates how the deadweight loss from a tax declines as the demand for a good becomes less elastic with respect to price. In both parts, the original supply and demand curves yield an equilibrium price of $2/unit and an equilibrium quantity of 24 units/day. The deadweight loss from a tax of $1/unit imposed on the good shown in part (a) is the area of the pale blue triangle in part (a), which is $2.50/day. The demand curve D_2 in part (b) is less elastic at the equilibrium price of $2 than the demand curve D_1 in part (a), which follows from the fact that P/Q is the same in both cases, while 1/slope is smaller in part (b). The deadweight loss from the same $1/unit tax imposed on the good in part (b) is the area of the pale blue triangle in part (b), which is only $1.50/day.

The reduction in equilibrium quantity that results from a tax on a good will also be smaller the smaller is the elasticity of supply of the good. In Figure 7.22, for example, the original supply and demand curves for the markets portrayed in parts (a) and (b) yield an equilibrium price of $2/unit and an equilibrium quantity of 72 units/day. The deadweight loss from a tax of $1/unit imposed on the good shown in part (a) is the area of the pale blue triangle in part (a), which is $7.50/day. The supply curve s_2 in part (b) is less elastic at the equilibrium price than the supply curve s_1 in part (a), again because P/Q is the same in both cases,

FIGURE 7.21

Elasticity of Demand and the Deadweight Loss from a Tax.

At the equilibrium price and quantity, price elasticity of demand is smaller for the good shown in (b) than for the good shown in (a). The area of the deadweight loss triangle in (b) ($1.50/day) is smaller than the area of the deadweight loss triangle in (a) ($2.50/day).

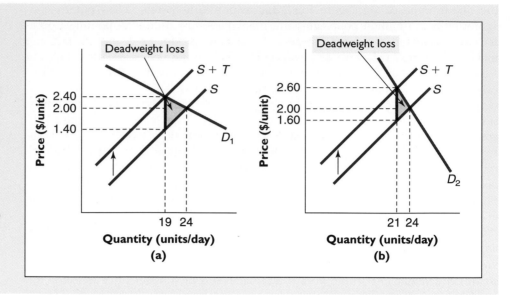

(a)   **(b)**

FIGURE 7.22

Elasticity of Supply and the Deadweight Loss from a Tax.

At the equilibrium price and quantity, price elasticity of supply is smaller for the good shown in (b) than for the good shown in (a). The area of the deadweight loss triangle in (b) ($4.50/day) is smaller than the area of the deadweight loss triangle in (a) ($7.50/day).

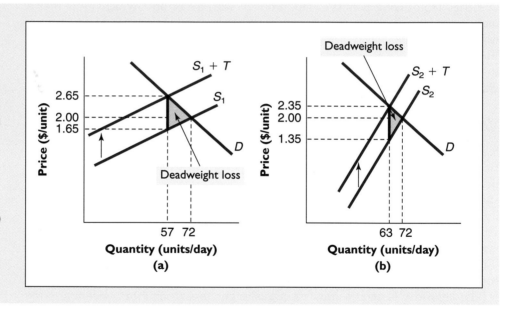

(a)   **(b)**

while 1/slope is smaller in part (b). The deadweight loss from the same $1/unit tax imposed on the good in part (b) is the area of the pale blue triangle in part (b), which is only $4.50/day.

The deadweight loss from a tax imposed on a good whose supply curve is perfectly inelastic will be zero. This explains why many economists continue to favor the tax Henry George advocated in the nineteenth century. George proposed that all taxes on labor and goods be abolished and replaced by a single tax on land. Such a tax, he argued, would cause no significant loss in economic surplus because the supply of land is almost perfectly inelastic.

TAXES, EXTERNAL COSTS, AND EFFICIENCY

Even more attractive than taxing land, from an efficiency standpoint, is taxing activities that people tend to pursue to excess. We mentioned activities that generate environmental pollution as one example; in later chapters we will discuss others. Whereas a tax on land does not reduce economic surplus, a tax on pollution can actually increase total economic surplus. Taxes on activities that cause harm to others kill two birds with one stone: They generate revenue to pay for useful public services and at the same time discourage people from pursuing the harmful activities. The notion that taxes always and everywhere constitute an obstacle to efficiency simply does not withstand careful scrutiny.

RECAP   TAXES AND EFFICIENCY

A tax levied on the seller of a product has the same effect on equilibrium quantity and price as a rise in marginal cost equal to the amount of the tax. The burden of a tax imposed on sellers will generally be shared among both buyers and sellers. In the extreme case of a good whose elasticity of supply is infinite, the entire burden of the tax is borne by buyers.

A tax imposed on a product whose supply and demand curves embody all relevant costs and benefits associated with its production and use will result in a deadweight loss—a reduction in total economic surplus in the market for the taxed good. Such taxes may nonetheless be justified if the value of the public services financed by the tax outweighs this deadweight loss. In general, the deadweight loss from a tax on a good will be smaller the smaller are the good's price elasticities of supply and demand. Taxes on activities that generate harm to others may produce a net gain in economic surplus, even apart from the value of public services they finance.

■ SUMMARY ■

- When the supply and demand curves for a product capture all the relevant costs and benefits of producing that product, then market equilibrium for that product will be efficient. In such a market, if price and quantity do not equal their equilibrium values, a transaction can be found that will make at least some people better off without harming others.

- Total economic surplus is a measure of the amount by which participants in a market benefit by participating in it. It is the sum of total consumer surplus and total producer surplus in the market. For an individual buyer, the economic surplus from a transaction is the difference between the most the buyer would have been willing to pay and the amount actually paid. For an individual seller, the economic surplus from a transaction is the difference between the revenue received and the lowest amount at which the seller would have been willing to make the sale. Total economic surplus in a market is the sum of all producer and consumer surplus in that market. One of the attractive properties of market equilibrium is that it maximizes the value of total economic surplus.

- Efficiency should not be equated with social justice. If we believe that the distribution of income among people is unjust, we will not like the results produced by the intersection of the supply and demand curves based on that income distribution, even though those results are efficient.

- Even so, we should always strive for efficiency because it enables us to achieve all our other goals to the fullest possible extent. Whenever a market is out of equilibrium, the economic pie can be made larger. And with a larger pie, everyone can have a larger slice.

- Regulations or policies that prevent markets from reaching equilibrium—such as rent controls, price supports for agricultural products, and first-come–first-served allocation schemes—are often defended on the grounds that they help the poor. But such schemes reduce economic surplus, meaning that we can find alternatives under which both rich and poor would be better off. The main difficulty of the poor is that they have too little income. Rather than try to control the prices of the goods they buy, we could do better to enact policies that raise the incomes of the poor, and then let prices seek their equilibrium levels. Those who complain that the poor lack the political power to obtain the income transfers they need must explain why the poor have the power to impose regulations that are far more costly than income transfers.

- Critics often complain that taxes make the economy less efficient. A tax will indeed reduce economic surplus if the supply and demand curves in the market for the taxed good reflect all the relevant costs and benefits of its production and consumption. But this decline in surplus may be more than offset by the increase in economic surplus made possible by public goods financed with the proceeds of the tax. The best taxes are ones imposed on activities that would otherwise be pursued to excess, such as activities that generate environmental pollution. Such taxes not only do not reduce economic surplus, they actually increase it.

■ KEY TERMS ■

consumer surplus (170)
deadweight loss (186)
efficient (or Pareto-efficient) (166)

price ceiling (174)
price floor (178)
producer surplus (170)

total economic surplus (169)

■ REVIEW QUESTIONS ■

1. Why do economists emphasize efficiency as an important goal of public policy?

2. You are a senator considering how to vote on a policy that would reduce the economic surplus of workers by $100 million/year but increase the economic surplus of retirees by $1 million/year. What additional measure might you combine with the policy to assure that the overall result is a better outcome for everyone?

3. Why does the loss in total economic surplus directly experienced by participants in the market for a good that is taxed overstate the overall loss in economic surplus that results from the tax?

4. Why is compensating volunteers to relinquish their seats on overbooked flights more efficient than a policy of first-come–first-served?

5. Why do price supports reduce economic surplus?

■ PROBLEMS ■

1. Calculate the producer and consumer surplus for the market whose demand and supply curves are shown as follows.

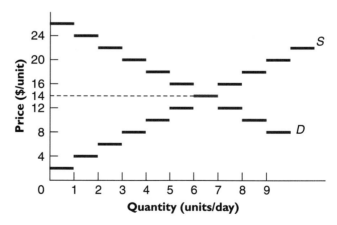

2. Suppose the weekly demand curve for wristwatches in Lincoln, Nebraska, is given by the equation $P = 12 - 0.25Q$, and the weekly supply of wristwatches is given by the equation $P = 6 + 0.75Q$, where P is the dollar price of a wristwatch. Sketch the weekly demand and supply curves in Lincoln, and calculate:
   a. The weekly consumer surplus
   b. The weekly producer surplus
   c. The maximum weekly amount that producers and consumers in Lincoln would be willing to pay to be able to buy and sell wristwatches in any given week

3. Refer to Problem 2. Suppose a coalition of students from Lincoln High School succeeds in persuading the local government to impose a price ceiling of $7.50 on wristwatches, on the grounds that local suppliers are taking advantage of teenagers by charging exorbitant prices.
   a. Calculate the weekly shortage of wristwatches that will result from this policy.
   b. Calculate the total economic surplus lost every week as a result of the price ceiling.
   c. In the face of the price ceiling, describe a transaction that would benefit both a buyer and a seller of wristwatches.

4. The Kubak crystal caves are renowned for their stalactites and stalagmites. The warden of the caves offers a tour each afternoon at 2 P.M. sharp. Only four people per day can see the caves without disturbing their fragile ecology. Occasionally, however, more than four people want to see the caves on the same day. The following table shows the list of people who wanted to see the caves on September 24, 2001, together with their respective times of arrival and reservation prices for taking the tour that day.

	Arrival time	Reservation price ($)
Herman	1:48	20
Jon	1:50	14
Kate	1:53	30
Jack	1:56	15
Penny	1:57	40
Fran	1:59	12
Faith	2:00	17

a. If the tour is "free" and the warden operates it on a first-come–first-served basis, what will the total consumer surplus be for the four people who get to go on the tour on that day?

b. Suppose the warden solicits volunteers to postpone their tour by offering increasing amounts of cash compensation until only four people still wish to see the caves that day. If he gives each volunteer the same compensation payment, how much money will he have to offer to generate the required number of volunteers? What is the total economic surplus under this policy?

c. Why is the compensation policy more efficient than the first-come-first-served policy?

d. Describe a way of financing the warden's compensation payments that will make everyone, including the warden, either better off or no worse off than under the first-come–first-served approach.

5. Suppose the weekly demand for a certain good, in thousands of units, is given by the equation $P = 8 - Q$, and the weekly supply of the good by the equation $P = 2 + Q$, where P is the price in dollars.

a. Calculate the total weekly economic surplus generated at the market equilibrium.

b. Suppose a per-unit tax of $2, to be collected from sellers, is imposed in this market. Calculate the direct loss in economic surplus experienced by participants in this market as a result of the tax.

c. How much government revenue will this tax generate each week? If the revenue is used to offset other taxes paid by participants in this market, what will be their net reduction in total economic surplus?

6. A price support for milk will lead to a loss of economic efficiency because:

a. It will raise the marginal cost of milk above the marginal benefit of milk to consumers.

b. It will cause a reduction in economic surplus.

c. It will lead consumers to buy less milk than they would otherwise have bought.

d. All of the above.

7. The government of Islandia, a small island nation, imports heating oil at a price of $2/gallon and makes it available to citizens at a price of $1/gallon. If Islandians' demand curve for heating oil is given by $P = 6 - Q$, where P is the price per gallon in dollars and Q is the quantity in millions of gallons per year, how much economic surplus is lost as a result of the government's policy?

8. Refer to Problem 7. Suppose each of the 1 million Islandian households has the same demand curve for heating oil.

a. What is the household demand curve?

b. How much consumer surplus would each household lose if it had to pay $2/gallon instead of $1/gallon for heating oil, assuming there were no other changes in the household budget?

c. With the money saved by not subsidizing oil, by how much could the Islandian government afford to cut each family's annual taxes?

d. If the government abandoned its oil subsidy and implemented the tax cut, by how much would each family be better off?

e. How does the resulting total gain for the 6 million families compare with your calculation of the lost surplus in Problem 7?

9. Phil's demand curve for visits to the Gannett walk-in medical clinic is given by $P = 48 - 8Q$, where P is the price per visit in dollars and Q is the number of visits per semester. The marginal cost of providing medical services at Gannett is $24/visit. Phil has a choice between two health policies, A and B. Both policies cover all the costs of any serious illness from which Phil might suffer. Policy A also covers the cost of visits to the walk-in clinic, while policy B does not. Thus if Phil chooses policy B, he must pay $24/visit to the walk-in clinic.

a. If the premiums the insurance company charges for policies A and B must cover their respective costs, by how much will the two premiums differ, and what will be the difference in Phil's total expenditure for medical care under the two policies?

b. Which policy will Phil choose?

c. What is the most Phil would be willing to pay for the right to continue buying that policy?

10. Is a company's producer surplus the same as its profit? (*Hint:* A company's total cost is equal to the sum of all marginal costs incurred in producing its output, plus any fixed costs.)

■ ANSWERS TO IN-CHAPTER EXERCISES ■

7.1 At a price of 50 cents/gallon, there is excess demand of 4,000 gallons/day. Suppose a seller produces an extra gallon of milk (marginal cost = 50 cents) and sells it to the buyer who would value it most (reservation price = $2.50) for $1.50. Both buyer and seller will gain an additional economic surplus of $1, and no other buyers or sellers will be hurt by the transaction.

7.2 The new equilibrium price becomes $7/unit. Consumer surplus is now $(13 - 7) + (12 - 7) + (11 - 7) + (10 - 7) + (9 - 7) + (8 - 7) = \$21$. Producer surplus is $(7 - 1) + (7 - 2) + (7 - 3) + (7 - 4) + (7 - 5) + (7 - 6) = \$21$. Total economic surplus is $42.

7.3 The new lost surplus is the area of the lined triangle in the following figure: (1/2)($250/month)(1,000 apartments/month) = $125,000/month.

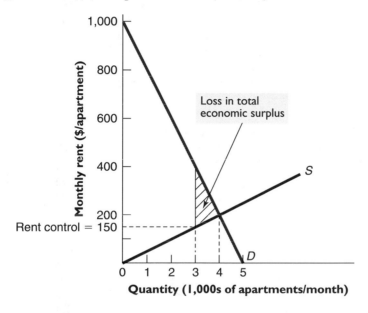

Loss in total economic surplus

Rent control = 150

7.4 With the price support set at $40/ton, the public again purchases 2 million tons/month, and the government purchases the remaining 2 million tons farmers offer at that price. If none of the wheat purchased by the government goes to consumers, it will generate no benefit. So compared to the case without price supports, the lost benefit is equal to the area under the demand curve between 2 and 3 million tons/month. The cost of producing the extra 1 million tons/month, which is the area under the supply curve between 3 and 4 million tons/month, is also lost. The total loss in economic surplus caused by the price support is thus the area of the pale blue region shown in the following diagram, which is $70 million/month.

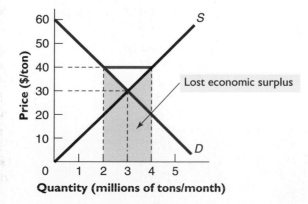

Lost economic surplus

7.5 Under first-come–first-served, Dana will have to postpone his lesson. Since Dana would be willing to pay up to $10 to avoid postponing it, he will be better off if we charge him, say, $8, and let him take Bill's place at the scheduled time. We could then give $4 to Bill, which would make him $1 better off than if he had not postponed his lesson. The remaining $4 of Dana's payment could be distributed by giving $1 each to Ann, Carrie, Earl, and the tennis pro.

Player	Arrival time	Reservation price ($)
Ann	9:50 A.M.	$ 4
Bill	9:52 A.M.	3
Carrie	9:55 A.M.	6
Dana	9:56 A.M.	10
Earl	9:59 A.M.	3

8

THE QUEST FOR PROFIT AND THE INVISIBLE HAND

■

The market for ethnic cuisine in Ithaca, New York, offered few choices in the mid-1970s: The city had one Japanese, two Greek, four Italian, and three Chinese restaurants. But now, some 25 years later and with essentially the same population, Ithaca has one Sri Lankan, two Indian, one Spanish, three Thai, two Korean, two Vietnamese, four Mexican, three Greek, seven Italian, and eight Chinese restaurants. In at least some of the city's other markets, however, the range of available choices has narrowed. For example, several companies provided telephone answering service in 1972, but only one does so today.

Rare indeed is the marketplace in which the identities of the buyers and sellers remain static for extended periods. New businesses enter, established ones leave. There are more body-piercing studios in Ithaca now and fewer watch repair shops, more marketing consultants and fewer intercity bus companies; and more appliances in stainless steel or black finishes, fewer in avocado or coppertone.

Driving these changes is the businessowner's quest for profit. Businesses migrate to industries and locations in which profit opportunities abound and desert those whose prospects appear bleak. In perhaps the most widely quoted passage from his landmark treatise, *The Wealth of Nations,* Adam Smith wrote:

> It is not from the benevolence of the butcher, the brewer, or the baker that we expect our dinner, but from their regard of their own interest. We address ourselves not to their humanity, but to

Why do most American cities now have more tattoo parlors and fewer watch repair shops than in 1972?

their self-love, and never talk to them of our necessities, but of their advantage.[1]

Smith went on to argue that although the entrepreneur "intends only his own gain," he is "led by an invisible hand to promote an end which was no part of his intention." As Smith saw it, even though self-interest is the prime mover of economic activity, the end result is an allocation of goods and services that serves society's collective interests remarkably well. If producers are offering "too much" of one product and "not enough" of another, profit opportunities immediately alert entrepreneurs to that fact and provide incentives for them to take remedial action. All the while, the system exerts relentless pressure on producers to hold the price of each good close to its cost of production, and indeed to reduce that cost in any ways possible.

Our task in this chapter is to gain deeper insight into the nature of the forces that guide the invisible hand. What exactly does "profit" mean? How is it measured, and how does the quest for it serve society's ends? And if competition holds price close to the cost of production, why do so many entrepreneurs become fabulously wealthy? We will also discuss cases in which misunderstanding of Smith's theory results in costly errors, both in everyday decision making and in the realm of government policy.

THE CENTRAL ROLE OF ECONOMIC PROFIT

The economic theory of business behavior is built on the assumption that the firm's goal is to maximize its profit. So we must be clear at the outset about what, exactly, profit means.

THREE TYPES OF PROFIT

explicit costs the actual payments a firm makes to its factors of production and other suppliers

accounting profit the difference between a firm's total revenue and its explicit costs

implicit costs all the firm's opportunity costs of the resources supplied by the firm's owners

economic profit the difference between a firm's total revenue and the sum of its explicit and implicit costs; also called excess profit

The economist's understanding of profit is different from the accountant's, and the distinction between the two is important in understanding how the invisible hand works. Accountants define the annual profit of a business as the difference between the revenue it takes in over the year and its **explicit costs** for the period, which are the actual payments the firm makes to its factors of production and other suppliers. Profit thus defined is called **accounting profit**.

$$\text{Accounting profit} = \text{Total revenue} - \text{Explicit costs}.$$

Accounting profit is the most familiar profit concept in everyday discourse. It is the one that companies use, for example, when they provide statements about their profits in press releases or annual reports.

Economists, by contrast, define profit as the difference between the firm's total revenue and not just its explicit costs but also its **implicit costs,** which are the opportunity costs of all resources supplied by the firm's owners. Profit thus defined is called **economic profit, or excess profit.**

$$\text{Economic profit} = \text{Total revenue} - \text{Explicit costs} - \text{Implicit costs}.$$

To illustrate the difference between accounting profit and economic profit, consider a firm with $400,000 in total annual revenue whose only explicit costs are workers' salaries that total $250,000/year. The owners of this firm have supplied machines and other capital equipment with a total market value of $1 million. This firm's accounting profit, then, is the difference between its total revenue of $400,000/year and its explicit costs of $250,000/year, or $150,000/year.

[1] Adam Smith, *The Wealth of Nations,* New York: Everyman's Library, E. P. Dutton, 1910 (1776), book 1.

To calculate the firm's economic profit, we must first calculate the opportunity cost of the resources supplied by the firm's owners. Suppose the current annual interest rate on savings accounts is 10 percent. Had owners not invested in capital equipment, they could have earned an additional $100,000/year interest by depositing their $1 million in a savings account. So the firm's economic profit is $400,000/year − $250,000/year − $100,000/year = $50,000/year.

Note that this economic profit is smaller than the accounting profit by exactly the amount of the firm's implicit costs—the $100,000/year opportunity cost of the resources supplied by the firm's owners. This difference between a business's accounting profit and its economic profit is called its **normal profit.** Normal profit is simply the opportunity cost of the resources supplied to a business by its owners.

Figure 8.1 illustrates the difference between accounting and economic profit. Part (a) represents a firm's total revenues, while parts (b) and (c) show how these revenues are apportioned among the various cost and profit categories.

normal profit the opportunity cost of the resources supplied by the firm's owners; Normal profit = Accounting profit − Economic profit

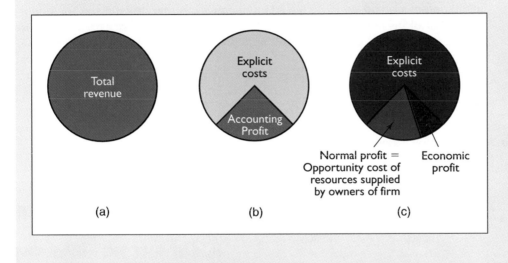

(a)   (b)   (c)

FIGURE 8.1
The Difference between Accounting Profit and Economic Profit.
(a) A firm's total revenues.
(b) Accounting profit is the difference between total revenue and explicit costs.
(c) Normal profit is the opportunity cost of all resources supplied by firm's owners. Economic profit is the difference between total revenue and all costs, explicit and implicit (also equal to the difference between accounting profit and normal profit).

"All I know, Harrison, is that I've been on the board forty years and have yet to see an excess profit."

Examples 8.1 to 8.5 illustrate why the distinction between accounting and economic profit is so important.

EXAMPLE 8.1   **Should Pudge Buffet stay in the farming business?**

Pudge Buffet is a corn farmer who lives near Lincoln, Nebraska. His payments for land and equipment rental and other supplies come to $10,000/year. The only input he supplies is his own labor, and he considers farming just as attractive as his only other employment opportunity, managing a retail store at a salary of $11,000/year. Apart from the matter of pay, Pudge is indifferent between farming and being a manager. Corn sells for a constant price per bushel in an international market too large to be affected by changes in one farmer's corn production. Pudge's revenue from corn sales is $22,000/year. What is his accounting profit? His economic profit? His normal profit? Should he remain a corn farmer?

As shown in Table 8.1, Pudge's accounting profit is $12,000/year, the difference between his $22,000 annual revenue and his $10,000 yearly payment for land, equipment, and supplies. His economic profit is that amount less the opportunity cost of his labor, which is the $11,000/year he could have earned as a store manager. Thus he is making an economic profit of $1,000/year. Finally, his normal profit is the $11,000 opportunity cost of the only resource he supplies, namely, his labor. Since Pudge likes the two jobs equally well, he will be better off by $1,000/year if he remains in farming.

TABLE 8.1
Revenue, Cost, and Profit Summary for Example 8.1

Total revenue ($/year)	Explicit costs ($/year)	Implicit costs ($/year)	Accounting profit (= Total revenue − Explicit costs) ($/year)	Economic profit (= Total revenue − Explicit costs − Implicit costs) ($/year)	Normal profit (= Implicit costs) ($/year)
22,000	10,000	11,000	12,000	1,000	11,000

EXAMPLE 8.2   **If Pudge's annual revenue falls by $2,000, should he stay in farming?**

Refer to Example 8.1. How will Pudge's economic profit change if his annual revenue from corn production is not $22,000 but $20,000? Should he continue to farm?

As shown in Table 8.2, Pudge's accounting profit is now $10,000, the difference between his $20,000 annual revenue and his $10,000/year payment for land, equipment, and supplies. His economic profit is that amount minus the opportunity cost of his labor—again, the $11,000/year he could have earned as a store manager. So Pudge is now earning a negative economic profit, −$1,000/year.

TABLE 8.2
Revenue, Cost, and Profit Summary for Example 8.2

Total revenue ($/year)	Explicit costs ($/year)	Implicit costs ($/year)	Accounting profit (= Total revenue − Explicit costs) ($/year)	Economic profit (= Total revenue − Explicit costs − Implicit costs) ($/year)	Normal profit (= Implicit costs) ($/year)
20,000	10,000	11,000	10,000	−1,000	11,000

As before, his normal profit is the $11,000/year opportunity cost of his labor. Although an accountant would say Pudge is making an annual profit of $10,000, that amount is less than a normal profit for his activity. An economist would therefore say that he is making an **economic loss** of $1,000/year. Since Pudge likes the two jobs equally well, he will be better off by $1,000/year if he leaves farming to become a manager.

economic loss an economic profit that is less than zero

EXERCISE 8.1

Refer to Example 8.1. Pudge can now be not only a farmer or a store manager, he can also choose to be a ski instructor at $8,000/year. If the store manager's salary were $13,000/year, Pudge would be indifferent between being a ski instructor and being a store manager. (At a manager's salary less than $13,000/year, he would prefer to be a ski instructor.) Should Pudge remain in farming?

You might think that if Pudge could just save enough money to buy his own land and equipment, his best option would be to remain a farmer. But as Example 8.3 makes clear, that impression is based on a failure to perceive the difference between accounting profit and economic profit.

Does owning one's own land make a difference?

EXAMPLE 8.3

Refer to Example 8.2. Suppose Pudge's Uncle Warren, who owns the farmland Pudge has been renting, dies and leaves Pudge that parcel of land. If the land could be rented to some other farmer for $6,000/year, should Pudge remain in farming?

As shown in Table 8.3, if Pudge continues to farm his own land, his accounting profit will be $16,000/year, or $6,000 more than before. But his economic profit will be the same as before——$1,000/year—because Pudge must deduct the $6,000/year opportunity cost of farming his own land. If other farmers have tastes like Pudge's and face similar outside employment opportunities, the normal profit from owning and operating a farm like his will be $17,000/year, the opportunity cost of the land and labor provided by the farmer. But since Pudge earns an accounting profit of only $16,000, he will again do better to abandon farming for the managerial job.

TABLE 8.3
Revenue, Cost, and Profit Summary for Example 8.3

Total revenue ($/year)	Explicit costs ($/year)	Implicit costs ($/year)	Accounting profit (= Total revenue − Explicit costs) ($/year)	Economic profit (= Total revenue − Explicit costs − Implicit costs) ($/year)	Normal profit (= Implicit costs) ($/year)
20,000	4,000	17,000	16,000	−1,000	17,000

Needless to say, Pudge would be wealthier as an owner than he was as a renter. But the question of whether to remain a farmer is answered the same way whether Pudge rents his farmland or owns it.

What would happen if *all* farmers in Lincoln earned less than normal profit?

EXAMPLE 8.4

Suppose the conditions confronting Pudge Buffet in Example 8.2 are essentially the same as those confronting all other farmers in Lincoln, Nebraska; that is, all earn less than a normal profit. What economic changes will result?

If all farmers in Lincoln are earning a negative economic profit, some farmers will begin switching to other activities. As they abandon farming, however, the market price for farmland—and hence its opportunity cost—will begin to fall. It will continue to fall until farmers in Lincoln can once again earn a normal profit. Specifically, the price of land will fall until the yearly rental for a farm like Pudge's is only $5,000, for at that rent the accounting profit of those who farmed their own land would be $16,000/year, exactly the same as normal profit. Their economic profit would be zero.

EXAMPLE 8.5

What will happen if all farmers earn *more* than a normal profit?

Suppose corn growers farm 80 acres of their own land, which sells for $1,000/acre. Each farm's revenue from corn sales is $20,000/year. Equipment and other supplies cost $4,000/year, and the current annual interest rate on savings accounts is 5 percent. Farmers can earn $11,000/year in alternative jobs that they like equally well as farming. What is normal economic profit for these farmers? How much accounting profit will they earn? How much economic profit? Is their economic situation stable? If not, how is it likely to change?

As shown in Table 8.4, accounting profit—the difference between the $20,000 annual revenue and the $4,000 annual expense for equipment and supplies—is $16,000/year, as in Example 8.3. Normal profit is the opportunity cost of the farmer's time and land—$11,000 for his time and $4,000 for his land (since had he sold the land for $80,000 and put the money in the bank at 5 percent interest, he would have earned $4,000/year in interest)—for a total of $15,000. Accounting profit thus exceeds normal profit by $1,000/year, which means that farmers are earning an economic profit of $1,000/year.

TABLE 8.4
Revenue, Cost, and Profit Summary for Example 8.5

Total revenue ($/year)	Explicit costs ($/year)	Implicit costs ($/year)	Accounting profit (= Total revenue − Explicit costs) ($/year)	Economic profit (= Total revenue − Explicit costs − Implicit costs) ($/year)	Normal profit (= Implicit costs) ($/year)
20,000	4,000	15,000	16,000	1,000	15,000

To see whether this situation is stable, we must ask whether people have an incentive to change their behavior. Consider the situation from the perspective of a manager who is earning $11,000/year. To switch to farming, he would need to borrow $80,000 to buy land, which would mean interest payments of $4,000/year. With $20,000/year in revenue from corn sales and $4,000/year in expenses for supplies and equipment, in addition to $4,000/year in interest payments, the manager would earn an accounting profit of $12,000/year. And since that amount is $1,000/year more than the opportunity cost of the manager's time, he will want to switch to farming. Indeed, *all* managers will want to switch to farming. At current land prices, there is cash on the table in farming.

As we know from the equilibrium principle, however, such situations are not stable. There is only so much farmland to go around, so as demand for farmland increases, its price will begin to rise. The price will keep rising until there is no longer any incentive for managers to switch to farming.

How much must the price of land rise to eliminate the incentive to switch? If 80 acres of land sold for $100,000 (that is, if land sold for $1,250/acre), the interest on the money borrowed to buy a farm would be $5,000/year, an amount that would make workers indifferent between farming or being a manager. But if land sells for anything less than $1,250/acre, there will be excess demand for farmland.

THE EFFECT OF MARKET FORCES ON ECONOMIC PROFIT

A firm's normal profit is just a cost of doing business. Thus the owner of a firm that earns no more than a normal profit has managed only to recover the opportunity cost of the resources invested in the firm. By contrast, the owner of a firm that makes a positive economic profit earns more than the opportunity cost of the invested resources; the owner earns a normal profit and then some. Naturally, everyone would be delighted to earn more than a normal profit, and no one wants to earn less. The result is that those markets in which firms are earning an economic profit tend to attract additional resources, whereas markets in which firms are experiencing economic losses tend to lose resources.

In Examples 8.1 to 8.5 discussed in the last section, we assumed that the price of corn was set in a world market too large to be influenced by the amount of corn produced in any one locality. More generally, however, we need to consider the effects of supply shifts on price.

Consider first the effect of an influx of resources in a market in which firms are currently earning an economic profit. As new firms enter the market, the supply curve will shift to the right, causing a reduction in the price of the product (see Figure 8.2).

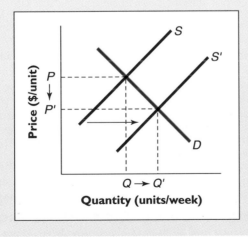

FIGURE 8.2
The Effect of Positive Economic Profit on Entry.
A market in which firms earn a positive economic profit will attract new firms from other markets. The resulting increase in supply will lead to a reduction in market price.

If firms continue to earn a positive economic profit at the new, lower price P', additional firms will enter, causing the market price to fall still further. The process will continue until economic profit is driven down to zero—that is, until price is just sufficient to cover all costs, including a normal profit.

Now consider the effect of resources moving out of a market in which businesses are currently experiencing an economic loss. As firms leave, the market supply curve shifts to the left, causing the price of the product to rise, as shown in Figure 8.3. Firms will continue to exit until the price rises to cover all resource costs—including the opportunity cost of the resources that owners have invested in their firms. The economic loss firms have been sustaining will be eliminated.

FIGURE 8.3

The Effect of Economic Losses on Market Exit.
Firms tend to leave a market when they experience an economic loss. The result is a leftward shift in the supply curve and a corresponding increase in price. Firms will continue to leave the market until the price rises enough to cover all costs, including the opportunity cost of resources supplied by a firm's owners.

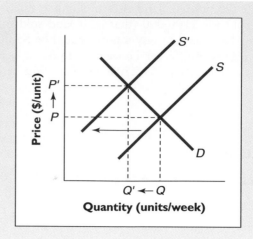

The net result of these resource movements is that in the long run all firms will tend to earn zero economic profit. Their *goal* is not to earn zero profit. Rather, the zero-profit tendency is a consequence of the dynamics of their entry into and exit from the market. As the equilibrium principle predicts, when people confront an opportunity for gain, they are almost always quick to exploit it.

Why do supermarket checkout lines all tend to be roughly the same length?

Pay careful attention the next few times you go grocery shopping, and you'll notice that the lines at all the checkout stations tend to be roughly the same length. Suppose you saw one line that was significantly shorter than the others as you wheeled your cart toward the checkout area. Which line would you choose? The shorter one, of course; and because most shoppers would do the same, the short line seldom remains shorter for long.

EXERCISE 8.2

Use the equilibrium principle to explain why all lanes on a crowded, multi-lane freeway move at about the same speed.

RECAP THE CENTRAL ROLE OF ECONOMIC PROFIT

A firm's accounting profit is the difference between its revenue and the sum of all explicit costs it incurs. Economic profit is the difference between the firm's revenue and *all* costs it incurs—both explicit and implicit. Normal profit is the opportunity cost of the resources supplied by the owners of the firm. When a firm's accounting profit is exactly equal to the opportunity cost of the inputs supplied by the firm's owners, the firm's economic profit is zero. Industries in which firms earn a positive economic profit tend to attract new firms, shifting industry supply to the right. Firms tend to leave industries in which they sustain an economic loss, shifting supply curves to the left. In each case, the supply movements continue until economic profit reaches zero.

THE INVISIBLE HAND THEORY

TWO FUNCTIONS OF PRICE

In the free enterprise system, market prices serve two important and distinct functions. The first, the **rationing function of price**, is to distribute scarce goods among potential claimants, assuring that those who get them are the ones who value them most. Thus, if three people want the only antique clock for sale at an auction, the clock goes home with the person who bids the most for it. The second function, the **allocative function of price**, is to direct productive resources to different sectors of the economy. Resources leave markets in which price cannot cover the cost of production and enter those in which price exceeds the cost of production.

Both the allocative and rationing functions of price underlie Adam Smith's celebrated **theory of the invisible hand** of the market. Recall that Smith thought the market system channels the selfish interests of individual buyers and sellers so as to promote the greatest good for society. The carrot of economic profit and the stick of economic loss, he argued, were the only forces necessary to assure not only that existing supplies in any market would be allocated efficiently, but also that resources would be allocated across markets to produce the most efficient possible mix of goods and services.

We must emphasize that Smith's invisible hand theory does not mean that market allocation of resources is optimal in every way. It simply means that markets are efficient in the limited technical sense discussed in Chapter 7. Thus, if the current allocation differs from the market equilibrium allocation, the invisible hand theory implies that we can reallocate resources in a way that makes some people better off without harming others. We can gain additional insight into Smith's theory by working through a series of simple examples.

What happens in a city with "too many" hairstylists and "not enough" aerobics instructors?

According to the invisible hand theory, the right number of haircuts and aerobics classes for a community are determined by the intersections of the respective supply and demand curves. For a specific community, suppose that means 50 haircuts/day and 20 aerobics classes/day, as shown in Figure 8.4. Why,

rationing function of price distributes scarce goods to those consumers who value them most highly

allocative function of price directs resources away from overcrowded markets and toward markets that are underserved

invisible hand theory a theory stating that the actions of independent, self-interested buyers and sellers will often result in the most efficient allocation of resources

EXAMPLE 8.6

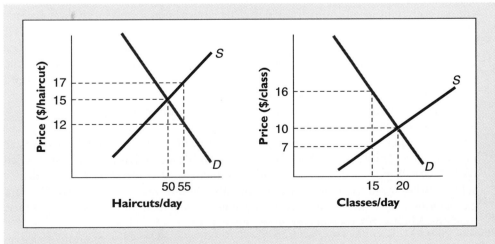

FIGURE 8.4
An Imbalance in the Markets for Haircuts and Aerobics Classes.
In a market for too many haircuts and not enough aerobics classes, hairstylists will suffer economic losses and aerobics instructors will enjoy economic profits. Eventually, stylists will leave haircutting for other occupations, and others will become aerobics instructors. The shift in resources will continue until all economic profits and losses are eliminated.

according to Adam Smith, would 55 haircuts/day and 15 aerobics classes be worse? What resource movements would occur in response to those production levels?

Note that when the market for haircuts is in equilibrium, the $15 value that buyers receive from the last haircut purchased is exactly equal to the $15 cost of producing it, which includes a salary sufficient to cover the stylist's opportunity cost. If instead stylists offer 55 haircuts/day, the last haircut will fail the cost-benefit test: Its value ($12) will be less than the stylist's marginal cost of producing it ($17). By contrast, if aerobics instructors offer five fewer aerobics classes than the market equilibrium number, the value of the last lesson ($16) will be far higher than the instructor's marginal cost of producing it ($7).

By definition, a situation in which there are "too many" hairstylists and "too few" aerobics instructors is one in which stylists earn less than the opportunity cost of their time, while aerobics instructors earn more than the opportunity cost of theirs. Stated another way, stylists earn an economic loss and aerobics instructors earn an economic profit. Over time, economic losses will induce some stylists to leave the haircutting market, and economic profits will lure new instructors to the aerobics teaching market. These resource movements will continue until there are only enough stylists to provide 50 haircuts/day and enough aerobics instructors to provide 20 classes/day—the equilibrium output levels in the two markets.

Those people who leave the haircutting market will not necessarily enter the aerobics teaching market, however. Indeed, given the sheer number of occupations a former hairstylist might choose to pursue, the likelihood of such a switch is low. Nor does the invisible hand theory imply an immediate adjustment of resources. In some markets, especially labor markets, the required movements might take months or even years. But if the supply and demand curves remain stable, the markets will eventually reach equilibrium prices and quantities.

THE IMPORTANCE OF FREE ENTRY AND EXIT

The allocative function of price cannot operate unless firms can enter new markets and leave existing ones at will. If new firms could not enter a market in which existing firms were making a large economic profit, economic profit would not tend to fall to zero over time, and price would not tend to gravitate toward the cost of production.

barrier to entry any force that prevents firms from entering a new market

Forces that inhibit firms from entering new markets are sometimes called **barriers to entry**. In the book publishing market, for example, the publisher of a book enjoys copyright protection granted by the government. Copyright law forbids other publishers from producing and selling their own editions of protected works. This barrier allows the price of a popular book to remain significantly above its cost of production for an extended period, all the while generating an economic profit for its publisher. (A copyright provides no *guarantee* of a profit, and indeed most new books actually generate an economic loss for their publishers.)

Barriers to entry may result from practical constraints as well as legal ones. Some economists, for example, have argued that the compelling advantages of product compatibility have created barriers to entry in the computer software market. Since more than 90 percent of new desktop computers come with Microsoft's Windows software already installed, rival companies have difficulty selling other operating systems, whose use would prevent most users from exchanging files with friends and colleagues. This fact, more than any other, explains Microsoft's spectacular profit history.

No less important than the freedom to enter a market is the freedom to leave. When the airline industry was regulated by the federal government, air carriers were often required to serve specific markets, even though they were losing money in them. When firms discover that a market, once entered, is difficult or impossible to leave, they become reluctant to enter these new markets. Barriers to exit thus become barriers to entry. Without reasonably free entry and exit, then, the implications of Adam Smith's invisible hand theory cannot be expected to hold.

All things considered, however, producers enjoy a high degree of freedom of entry in most U.S. markets. Because free entry is one of the defining characteristics of a perfectly competitive market, unless otherwise stated, we will assume its existence.

ECONOMIC RENT VERSUS ECONOMIC PROFIT

Microsoft chairman Bill Gates is the wealthiest man on the planet, largely because the problem of compatibility prevents rival suppliers from competing effectively in the many software markets dominated by his company. Yet numerous people have become fabulously rich even in markets with no conspicuous barriers to entry. If market forces push economic profit toward zero, how can that happen?

The answer to this question hinges on the distinction between economic profit and **economic rent.** Most people think of rent as the payment they make to a landlord or the supplier of a dorm refrigerator, but the term *economic rent* has a different meaning. Economic rent is that portion of the payment for an input that is above the supplier's reservation price for that input. Suppose, for example, that a landowner's reservation price for an acre of land is $100/year. That is, suppose he would be willing to lease it to a farmer as long as he received an annual payment of at least $100, but for less than that amount he would rather leave it fallow. If a farmer gives him an annual payment not of $100 but of $1,000, the landowner's economic rent from that payment will be $900/year.

Economic profit is like economic rent in that it, too, may be seen as the difference between what someone is paid (the businessowner's total revenue) and her reservation price for remaining in business (the sum of all her costs, explicit and implicit). But whereas competition pushes economic profit toward zero, it has no such effect on the economic rent for inputs that cannot be replicated easily. For example, although the lease payments for land may remain substantially above the landowner's reservation price, year in and year out, new land cannot come onto the market to reduce or eliminate the economic rent through competition. There is, after all, only so much land to be had.

As Example 8.7 illustrates, economic rent can accrue to people as well as land.

economic rent that part of the payment for a factor of production that exceeds the owner's reservation price, the price below which the owner would not supply the factor

How much economic rent will a talented chef get?

EXAMPLE 8.7

A community has 100 restaurants, 99 of which employ chefs of normal ability at a salary of $30,000/year, the same as the amount they could earn in other occupations that are equally attractive to them. But the 100th restaurant has an unusually talented chef. Because of her reputation, diners are willing to pay 50 percent more for the meals she cooks than for those prepared by ordinary chefs. Owners of the 99 restaurants with ordinary chefs each collect $300,000/year in revenue, which is just enough to assure that each earns exactly a normal profit. If the talented chef's opportunities outside the restaurant industry are the same as those of ordinary chefs, how much will she be paid by her employer at equilibrium? How much of her pay will be economic rent? How much economic profit will her employer earn?

Because diners are willing to pay 50 percent more for meals cooked by the talented chef, the owner who hires her will take in total receipts not of $300,000/year but of $450,000. In the long run, competition should assure that the talented chef's total pay each year will be $180,000/year, the sum of the $30,000 that ordinary chefs get and the $150,000 in extra revenues for which she is solely responsible. Since the talented chef's reservation price is the amount she could earn outside the restaurant industry—by assumption, $30,000/year, the same as for ordinary chefs—her economic rent is $150,000/year. The economic profit of the owner who hires her will be exactly zero.

Since the talented chef's opportunities outside the restaurant industry are no better than an ordinary chef's, why is it necessary to pay the talented chef so much? Suppose her employer were to pay her only $60,000, which they both would consider a generous salary, since it is twice what ordinary chefs earn. The employer would then earn an economic profit of $120,000/year, since his annual revenue would be $150,000 more than that of ordinary restaurants, but his costs would be only $30,000 more.

But this economic profit would create an opportunity for the owner of some other restaurant to bid the talented chef away. For example, if the owner of a competing restaurant were to hire the talented chef at a salary of $70,000, the chef would be $10,000/year better off, and the rival owner would earn an economic profit of $110,000/year rather than his current economic profit of zero. Furthermore, if the talented chef is the sole reason that a restaurant earns a positive economic profit, the bidding for that chef should continue as long as any economic profit remains. Some other owner will pay her $80,000, still another $90,000, and so on. Equilibrium will be reached only when the talented chef's salary has been bid up to the point that no further economic profit remains—in Example 8.7, at an annual paycheck of $180,000.

This bidding process assumes, of course, that the reason for the chef's superior performance is that she possesses some personal talent that cannot be copied. If instead it were the result of, say, training at a culinary institute in France, then her privileged position would erode over time as other chefs sought similar training.

THE EFFECT OF COST-SAVING INNOVATIONS

When economists speak of perfectly competitive firms, they have in mind businesses whose contribution to total market output is too small to have a perceptible impact on market price. As explained in Chapter 6, such firms are often called price takers: They take the market price of their product as given and then produce that quantity of output for which marginal cost equals that price.

This characterization of the competitive firm gives the impression that the firm is essentially a passive actor in the marketplace. Yet for most firms, that is anything but the case. As Example 8.8 illustrates, even those firms that cannot hope to influence the market prices of their products have very powerful incentives to develop and introduce cost-saving innovations.

EXAMPLE 8.8

How do cost-saving innovations affect economic profit in the short run? In the long run?

Forty merchant marine companies operate supertankers that carry oil from the Middle East to the United States. The cost per trip, including a normal profit, is $500,000. An engineer at one of these companies develops a more efficient propeller design that results in fuel savings of $20,000/trip. How will this innovation affect the company's accounting and economic profits? Will these changes persist in the long run?

In the short run, the reduction in a single firm's costs will have no impact on the market price of transoceanic shipping services. The firm with the more efficient propeller will thus earn an economic profit of $20,000/trip (since its total revenue will be the same as before, while its total costs are now $20,000/trip lower). As other firms learn about the new design, however, they will begin to adopt it, causing their individual supply curves to shift downward (since the marginal cost per trip at these firms will drop by $20,000). The shift in these individual supply curves will cause the market supply curve to shift, which in turn will result in a lower market price for shipping and a decline in economic profit at the firm where the innovation originated. When all firms have adopted the new efficient design, the long-run supply curve for the industry will have shifted downward by $20,000/trip, and each company will again be earning only a normal profit. At that point, any firm that did *not* adopt the new propeller design would suffer an economic loss of $20,000/trip.

The incentive to come up with cost-saving innovations to reap economic profit is one of the most powerful forces on the economic landscape. Its beauty, in terms of the invisible hand theory, is that competition among firms assures that the resulting cost savings will be passed along to consumers in the long run.

RECAP   **THE INVISIBLE HAND THEORY**

In market economies, the allocative and rationing functions of prices guide resources to their most highly valued uses. Prices influence how much of each type of good gets produced (the allocative function). Firms enter those industries in which prices are sufficiently high to sustain an economic profit and leave those in which low prices result in an economic loss. Prices also direct existing supplies of goods to the buyers who value them most (the rationing function).

Economic rent is the amount by which the payment to a factor of production exceeds the supplier's reservation price. Unlike economic profit, which is driven toward zero by competition, economic rent may persist for extended periods, especially in the case of factors with special talents that cannot easily be duplicated.

Early adopters of cost-saving innovations enjoy temporary economic profits. But as additional firms adopt the innovations, the resulting downward supply shift causes price to fall. In the long run, economic profit returns to zero, and all cost savings are passed on to consumers.

THE INVISIBLE HAND IN ACTION

To help develop your intuition about how the invisible hand works, we will examine how it helps us gain insight into patterns we observe in a variety of different contexts.

THE INVISIBLE HAND IN REGULATED MARKETS

The carrot of economic profit and the stick of economic loss guide resource movements in regulated markets no less than in unregulated ones. Consider the taxi industry, which many cities regulate by licensing cabs. These licenses are often called medallions, because they are issued in the form of a metal shield that must be affixed to the hood of the cab, where enforcement officials can easily see it. Cities that regulate cabs in this fashion typically issue fewer medallions than the equilibrium number of taxicabs in similar markets that are not regulated. Officials then allow the medallions to be bought and sold in the marketplace. As the next example demonstrates, the issuance of taxi medallions alters the equilibrium quantity of taxicabs but does not change the fundamental rule that resources flow in response to profit and loss signals.

ECONOMIC NATURALIST 8.2

Why do New York City taxicab medallions sell for more than $250,000?

Because New York City issues far fewer taxi medallions than would-be taxi owners could operate profitably, the equilibrium passenger fare is higher than the direct cost of operating a taxicab. Suppose the cost of operating a cab full-time—including car, fuel, maintenance, depreciation, and the opportunity cost of the driver's time, but excluding the purchase price of a medallion—is $40,000/year, and a cab in full-time operation will collect $60,000/year in fares. If the annual interest rate on savings accounts is 8 percent, how much will a medallion cost at equilibrium? Will the owner of a medallion earn an economic profit?

If the medallion were free and could not be sold to others, its owner would earn an economic profit of $20,000/year, the difference between $60,000 in fares and $40,000 in operating cost. But the equilibrium principle tells us that the lure of this economic profit would induce outsiders to enter the taxi industry, which could be done by purchasing an owner's medallion.

How much would the entrant be willing to pay for a medallion? If one were available for, say, $100,000, would it be a good buy? Since $100,000 in the bank would earn only $8,000/year in interest, but would bring $20,000 in earnings if used to purchase a taxi medallion, the answer must be yes. In fact, when the annual interest rate is 8 percent, a rational buyer's reservation price for a stream of economic profits of $20,000/year is the amount of money the buyer would have to put in the bank to earn that much interest each year—namely, $250,000. At any amount less than that, medallions would be underpriced.

Clearly, the owner of a $250,000 medallion has a valuable asset. The opportunity cost of using it to operate a taxi is forgone interest of $20,000/year. So the medallion owner who takes in $60,000 in fares actually covers only the cost of the resources invested in the operation. The owner's economic profit is zero. From the perspective of the medallion owner, the $20,000 difference between the owner's fares and explicit costs is an economic rent.

EXERCISE 8.3

How much would the medallion in the preceding example sell for if the annual interest rate were not 8 percent but 4 percent?

Another regulated market in which the invisible hand was very much in evidence was the regulated commercial airline industry. Until late 1978, airlines were heavily regulated by the Civil Aeronautics Board (CAB), an agency of the federal government. Carriers could not provide air service between two cities unless they were given explicit permission to do so. The CAB also prescribed what fares carriers could charge. The standard practice was to set fares well above the cost of providing service on most routes, and then require carriers to use some of the resulting economic profit to pay for service on sparsely traveled routes. But as the following example illustrates, the CAB failed to reckon with the invisible hand.

ECONOMIC NATURALIST 8.3

Why did major commercial airlines install piano bars on the upper decks of Boeing 747s in the 1970s?

At the high airfares the CAB established on the New York to Los Angeles and other large transcontinental routes in the 1970s, any air carrier that managed to fill a flight with passengers would have earned tens of thousands of dollars in economic profit on that one flight alone. The invisible hand theory tells us that resources will flow into any market in which economic profit is positive and out of any market in which economic profit is negative, eventually driving economic profit to zero. But although an influx of resources will normally cause prices to fall in an unregulated market, the CAB's rules prevented fares from falling. The rules could not prohibit carriers from competing with one another in other ways, however. Because passengers care not only about fares but also about the frequency of service, a carrier can steal business from rivals simply by adding another flight. Carriers did so, adding flights to their routes until economic profit disappeared. The CAB's goal of generating surplus revenue to pay for service on sparsely traveled routes was doomed from the start.

Adding insult to injury, the policy of setting high fares on heavily traveled routes was wasteful, insofar as it resulted in so many flights on those routes that each left with a substantial number of empty seats. Carrier executives quickly realized that they could fill many of those seats by offering service enhancements that would lure passengers away from other airlines. For instance, one carrier converted the upper deck of its 747s to a piano bar, and other airlines quickly followed suit. Others offered elaborate meals. Recognizing this difficulty, the CAB responded by trying to regulate the kinds of food carriers could serve, leading in one case to a protracted legal squabble over the definition of a sandwich.

The problem is not that the extra amenities carriers offered were of *no* value whatever to passengers. Piano bars and more frequent flights were obviously of value to many travelers. But for efficiency's sake, additional amenities should be offered only if their benefit exceeds their cost, and most passengers would not voluntarily have paid for the high level of amenities air carriers offered in the 1970s. Evidence for this claim comes from the operations of several intrastate airlines, which were exempt from federal regulation. Unregulated carriers in California provided service on the San Francisco to San Diego route for about half the fare charged by regulated carriers on the Washington to Boston route of the same distance. Though the California carriers were free to offer more frequent service and more elaborate in-flight amenities, passengers voted with their dollars to sacrifice those amenities for lower airfares.

THE INVISIBLE HAND IN ANTIPOVERTY PROGRAMS

As Example 8.9 shows, failure to understand the logic of the invisible hand can lead not only to inefficient government regulation but also to antipoverty programs that are doomed to fail.

How will an irrigation project affect the incomes of poor farmers?

EXAMPLE 8.9

Suppose unskilled workers must choose between working in a textile mill at $8,000/year and growing rice on a rented parcel of farmland. One worker can farm an 80-acre rice parcel, which rents for $5,000/year. Such farms yield $16,000/year in revenue, and the total nonlabor costs of bringing the crop to market are $3,000/year. The net incomes of rice farmers are thus $8,000/year, the same as those of textile workers. A state legislator has introduced a bill to fund an irrigation project that would double the output of rice on farms operated by tenant farmers. If the state's contribution to the total supply of rice is too small to affect the price, how will the project affect the incomes of tenant farmers over the long run?

The direct effect of the project will be to double rice yields, which means that each farmer will sell $32,000 worth of rice per year rather than $16,000. If nothing else changed, farmers' incomes would rise from $8,000/year to $24,000/year. But the equilibrium principle tells us that farmers cannot sustain this income level. From the perspective of textile workers, there is cash on the table in farming. Seeing an opportunity to triple their incomes, many will want to switch to farming. But since the supply of land is fixed, farm rents will rise as textile workers begin bidding for them. They will continue to rise as long as farmers can earn more than textile workers. The long-run effect of the project, then, will be to raise the rent on rice farms, from $5,000/year to $21,000/year (since at the higher rent the incomes of rice farmers and textile workers will again be the same). Thus the irrigation project will increase the wealth of landowners but will have no long-run effect on the incomes of tenant farmers.

THE INVISIBLE HAND IN THE STOCK MARKET

One of the most competitive markets in the world is the market for stocks and bonds on Wall Street in New York. And as we will see, public understanding of how the invisible hand works in this market is often no better than the state legislator's understanding of how the rice market works.

Calculating the Value of a Share of Stock

A share of stock in a company is a claim to a share of the current and future accounting profits of that company. Thus, if you own 1 percent of the total number of shares of a company's stock, you effectively own 1 percent of the company's annual accounting profit, both now and in the future. (We say "effectively" because companies generally do not distribute their accounting profit to shareholders each year; many reinvest their earnings in the company's operations. Such reinvestment benefits the stockholder by enlarging the company and increasing its future accounting profit.) The price of a share of stock depends not only on a company's accounting profit, however, but also on the market rate of interest, as Example 8.10 illustrates.

EXAMPLE 8.10

How much will a share of stock sell for?

Suppose we know with certainty that a company's accounting profit will be $1 million this year and every year. If the company has issued a total of 1,000 shares of stock and the annual interest rate is 5 percent, at what price will each share sell?

Because there are 1,000 shares of stock, each share entitles its owner to one one-thousandth of the company's annual accounting profit, or $1,000/year. Owning this stock is like having a bank deposit that earns $1,000/year in interest. To calculate the economic value of the stock, therefore, we need only ask how much an investor would need to deposit in the bank at 5 percent interest to generate an annual interest payment of $1,000. The answer is $20,000, and that is the price that each share will command in the stock market.

Calculating the Present Value of Future Costs and Benefits

Someone who is trying to estimate how much a business is worth must take into account that earnings received in the future are less valuable than earnings received today. Consider a company whose only accounting profit, $14,400, will occur exactly 2 years from now. At all other times its accounting profit will be exactly zero. How much is ownership of this company worth?

To answer this question, we need to employ the concept of the *time value of money*, which we first encountered in Chapter 2. Our goal is to compute what economists call the **present value** of a $14,400 payment to be received in 2 years. We can think of this present value as the amount that would have to be deposited in an interest-bearing bank account today to generate a balance 2 years from today of $14,400. Let PV denote present value, and let r be the market rate of interest, measured as a fraction. (For example, an annual interest rate of 10 percent would correspond to $r = 0.10$.) If we put PV in the bank today at the interest rate r, we will have $PV(1 + r)$ 1 year from now and $PV(1 + r)^2$ 2 years from now. So to find the present value of a $14,400 payment to be received 2 years from now we simply solve the equation $14,400 = PV(1 + r)^2$ and get $PV = \$14,400/(1 + r)^2$. If the interest rate is 20 percent, then $PV = \$14,400(1.2)^2 = \$10,000$. To verify this answer, note that $10,000 deposited at 20 percent interest today would grow to $10,000(1 + 0.2) = \$12,000$ by the end of 1 year, and that amount left on deposit for a second year would grow to $12,000(1 + 0.2) = \$14,400$.

More generally, when the interest rate is r, the present value of a payment M to be received T years from now is given by the equation $PV = M/(1 + r)^T$.

present value when the annual interest rate is r, the present value (PV) of a payment M to be received T years from now is the amount that would have to be deposited today at an annual interest rate r to generate a balance of M after T years: $PV = M/(1 + r)^T$

EXERCISE 8.4

What is the present value of a payment of $1,728 to be received 3 years from now if the annual interest rate is 20 percent?

The Efficient Markets Hypothesis

In practice, of course, no one knows with certainty what a company's future profits will be. So the current price of a share of stock will depend not on the actual amount of future profits but on investors' estimates of them. These estimates incorporate information about current profits, prospects for the company's industry, the state of the economy, demographic trends, and a host of other factors. As this information changes, investors' estimates of future profits change with it, along with the prices of a share of stock.

How fast does new information affect the price of a stock? With blazing speed, according to the **efficient markets hypothesis.** The theory says that the current price of a stock incorporates all available information relevant to the company's earnings.

The plausibility of this theory is evident if we think for a moment about what might happen if it were false. Suppose, for example, that at 9:00 A.M. on Monday, October 14, some investors acquire new information to the effect that the company in Example 8.10 will realize accounting profits not of $1 million/year but $2 million. That information implies that the new equilibrium price for each share of its stock should be $40,000. Now suppose that the price were to remain at its current level ($20,000) for 24 hours before rising gradually to $40,000 over the next 2 weeks. If so, an investor privy to this information could double her wealth in 2 weeks without working hard, taking any risk, or even being lucky. All she would have to do is invest all her wealth in the stock at today's price of $20,000/share.

We may safely assume that there is no shortage of investors who would be delighted to double their wealth without having to work hard or take risks. But in the example just described, they would have to buy shares of the stock within 24 hours of learning of the new profit projections. As eager investors rushed to buy the stock, its price would rise quickly so that those who waited until the end of the day to buy would miss much of the opportunity for gain. To get the full advantage of the new information, they would have to make their purchases earlier in the day. As more and more investors rushed to buy shares, the window of opportunity would grow narrower and narrower. In the end, the duration of the opportunity to profit from the new information may be just a few minutes long.

In practice, of course, new information often takes time to interpret, and different investors may have different beliefs about exactly what it means. Early information may signal an impending change that is far from certain. As time passes, events may confirm or contradict the implications of the earlier information. The usual pattern is for information to emerge in bits and pieces and for stock prices to adjust in small increments as each new bit of information emerges. But this does not mean that the price of a stock adjusts gradually to new information. Rather, it means that new information usually emerges gradually. And as each piece of new information emerges, the market reacts almost instantly.

For instance, when a Florida jury awarded a lung cancer patient $750,000 in damages in July of 1996, the price of tobacco stocks plummeted roughly 20 percent *within minutes*. The award broke a long series of legal precedents in which tobacco companies were not held liable for the illnesses suffered by smokers. When the verdict was announced, no one knew whether it would be reversed on appeal, or whether it would influence future verdicts in such cases. Yet investors who had been monitoring the case carefully knew instantly when the verdict was announced that the industry faced the possibility of massive new financial liabilities. To the extent that further court decisions confirm that possibility, the price of tobacco stocks will fall still further.

efficient markets hypothesis the theory that the current price of stock in a corporation reflects all relevant information about its current and future earnings prospects

Despite such persuasive evidence in favor of the efficient markets hypothesis, many investors seem to believe that information about the next sure investment bonanza is as close as their broker's latest newsletter. Securities salespersons in New York routinely call investors to offer the latest tips on how to invest their money. The difficulty is that by the time information reaches investors in this way, days, weeks, or even months will have gone by, and the information will have been already incorporated into any stock prices for which it might have been relevant.

The Wall Street Journal publishes a feature in which a group of leading investment advisors predicts which stocks will increase most in price during the coming months. The *Journal* then compares the forecasts with the performance of a randomly selected set of stocks. The usual finding is that the randomly selected portfolios perform little differently from the ones chosen by the "experts." Some of the experts do better than average, others worse. This pattern is consistent with the economist's theory that the invisible hand moves with unusual speed to eliminate profit opportunities in financial markets.

Why isn't a stock portfolio consisting of America's "best-managed companies" a good investment?

Each year *Fortune* magazine asks executives at the nation's largest companies to list those U.S. firms, excluding their own, that are managed most efficiently. Imagine that you see the results of this survey and immediately purchase 100 shares of stock in each of the top 10 companies on the list. How well might you expect those stocks to perform relative to a randomly selected portfolio?

A stock is said to "perform well" if its price rises more rapidly than the prices of other stocks. Changes in the price of a company's stock depend not on investors' current beliefs about the company's accounting profit but on changes in those beliefs. Suppose, for the sake of argument, that the "best-managed" companies had higher accounting profits than other companies at the time of the Fortune survey. Because the prices you paid for their stocks would have reflected those higher earnings, there would be no reason to expect their prices to rise more rapidly than those of other stocks.

But won't the accounting profits of a well-managed company be likely to grow more rapidly than those of other companies? Perhaps, but even so, beliefs to that effect would also be reflected in current stock prices. Indeed, the stocks of many software, biotechnology, and Internet commerce companies sell at high prices years before they ever post their first dollar of accounting profit.

An understanding of the invisible hand theory might even lead us to question whether a "well-managed" company will have higher accounting profit than other companies. After all, if an unusually competent manager were known to be the reason a company consistently posted a positive economic profit, other companies could be expected to bid for the manager's services, causing her salary to rise. And the market for the manager's services will not reach equilibrium until her salary has captured all the gains for which her talent is responsible.

We must stress that our point in the preceding examples is *not* that good management doesn't matter. Good management is obviously better than bad management, for it increases total economic surplus. The point is that the reward for good performance tends to be captured by those who provide that performance. And that is a good thing, insofar as it provides powerful incentives for everyone to perform well.

RECAP   THE INVISIBLE HAND IN ACTION

The quest for advantage guides resources not only in perfectly competitive markets but also in heavily regulated ones. Firms can almost always find ways to expand sales in markets in which the regulated price permits an economic profit or to withdraw service from markets in which the regulated price results in an economic loss.

An understanding of the invisible hand theory is also important for the design of antipoverty programs. An irrigation program that makes land more productive, for example, will raise the incomes of tenant farmers only temporarily. In the long run, the gains from such projects tend to be captured as rents to landowners.

The efficient markets hypothesis says that the price of a firm's stock at any moment reflects all available information that is relevant for predicting the firm's future earnings. This hypothesis identifies several common beliefs as false—among them that stocks in well managed companies perform better than stocks in poorly managed ones, and that ordinary investors can make large financial gains by trading stocks on the basis of information reported in the news media.

THE DISTINCTION BETWEEN AN EQUILIBRIUM AND A SOCIAL OPTIMUM

NO CASH ON THE TABLE

The examples discussed in the preceding section illustrate the equilibrium principle, which tells us that when a market reaches equilibrium, no further opportunities for gain are available to individuals. This principle implies that the market prices of resources that people own will eventually reflect their economic value. (As we will see in later chapters, the same cannot be said of resources that are not owned by anyone, such as fish in international waters.)

The equilibrium principle is sometimes misunderstood to mean that there are *never* any valuable opportunities to exploit. For example, the story is told of two economists on their way to lunch when they spot what appears to be a $100 bill lying on the sidewalk. When the younger economist stoops to pick up the bill, his older colleague restrains him, saying, "That can't be a $100 dollar bill." "Why not?" asks the younger colleague. "If it were, someone would have picked it up by now," the older economist replies.

The equilibrium principle means not that there *never* are any unexploited opportunities but that there are none when the market is *in equilibrium*. Occasionally a $100 bill does lie on the sidewalk, and the person who first spots it and picks it up gains a windfall. Likewise, when a company's earnings prospects improve, *somebody* must be the first to recognize the opportunity, and that person can make a lot of money by purchasing the stock quickly.

Still, the equilibrium principle is important. It tells us, in effect, that there are only three ways to earn a big payoff: to work especially hard, to have some unusual skill, talent, or training, or simply to be lucky. The person who finds a big bill on the sidewalk is lucky, as are many of the investors whose stocks perform better than average. Other investors whose stocks do well achieve their gains through hard work or special talent. For example, the legendary investor Warren Buffett, whose portfolio has grown in value at almost three times the stock market average for the last 40 years, spends long hours studying annual financial reports and has a remarkably keen eye for the telling detail. Thousands of others work just as hard, yet never even match the market averages.

It is important to stress, however, that a market being in equilibrium implies only that no additional opportunities are available *to individuals*. It does not imply that the resulting allocation is necessarily best from the point of view of society as a whole.

SMART FOR ONE, DUMB FOR ALL

Adam Smith's profound insight was that the individual pursuit of self-interest often promotes the broader interests of society. But unlike some of his modern disciples, Smith was under no illusion that *always* is the case. Note, for example, Smith's elaboration on his description of the entrepreneur led by the invisible hand "to promote an end which was no part of his intention":

> Nor is it *always* the worse for society that it was no part of it. By pursuing his own interest he *frequently* promotes that of society more effectively than when he really intends to promote it. [Italics supplied.][2]

As Smith was well aware, the individual pursuit of self-interest often does not coincide with society's interest. In Chapter 4 we cited activities that generate environmental pollution as an example of conflicting economic interests, noting that behavior in those circumstances may be described as smart for one, but dumb for all. As the following example suggests, extremely high levels of investment in earnings forecasts can also be smart for one, dumb for all.

ECONOMIC NATURALIST 8.5

Are there "too many" smart people working as corporate earnings forecasters?

Stock analysts use complex mathematical models to forecast corporate earnings. The more analysts invest in the development of these models, the more accurate the models become. Thus the analyst whose model produces a reliable forecast sooner than others can reap a windfall buying stocks whose prices are about to rise. Given the speed with which stock prices respond to new information, however, the results of even the second-fastest forecasting model may come too late to be of much use. Individual stock analysts thus face a powerful incentive to invest more and more money in their models in the hope of generating the fastest forecast. Does this incentive result in the socially optimal level of investment in forecast models?

Beyond some point, increased speed of forecasting is of little benefit to society as a whole, whose interests suffer little when the price of a stock moves to its proper level a few hours more slowly. If *all* stock analysts spent less money on their forecasting models, *someone's* model would still produce the winning forecast, and the resources that might otherwise be devoted to fine-tuning the models could be put to more valued uses. Yet if any one individual spends less, she can be sure the winning forecast will not be hers.

The invisible hand went awry in the situation just described because the benefit of an investment to the individual who made it was larger than the benefit of that investment to society as a whole. In later chapters we will discuss a broad class of investments with this property. In general, the efficacy of the invisible hand depends on the extent to which the individual costs and benefits of actions

---

[2]Adam Smith, *The Wealth of Nations*, New York: Everyman's Library, E. P. Dutton, 1910 (1776), book 1.

taken in the marketplace coincide with the respective costs and benefits of those actions to society. These exceptions notwithstanding, some of the most powerful forces at work in competitive markets clearly promote society's interests.

RECAP **EQUILIBRIUM VERSUS SOCIAL OPTIMUM**

A market in equilibrium is one in which no additional opportunities for gain remain available to individual buyers or sellers. The equilibrium principle describes powerful forces that help push markets toward equilibrium. But even if all markets are in equilibrium, the resulting allocation of resources need not be socially optimal. Equilibrium will not be socially optimal when the costs or benefits to individual participants in the market differ from those experienced by society as a whole.

■ SUMMARY ■

- Accounting profit is the difference between a firm's revenue and its explicit expenses. It differs from economic profit, which is the difference between revenue and the sum of the firm's explicit and implicit costs. Normal profit is the difference between accounting profit and economic profit. It is the opportunity cost of the resources supplied to a business by its owners.

- The quest for economic profit is the invisible hand that drives resource allocation in market economies. Markets in which businesses earn an economic profit tend to attract additional resources, whereas markets in which businesses experience an economic loss tend to lose resources. If new firms enter a market with economic profits, that market's supply curve shifts to the right, causing a reduction in the price of the product. Prices will continue to fall until economic profits are eliminated. By contrast, the departure of firms from markets with economic losses causes the supply curve in such markets to shift left, increasing the price of the product. Prices will continue to rise until economic losses are eliminated. In the long run, market forces drive economic profits and losses toward zero.

- When market supply and demand curves reflect the underlying costs and benefits to society of the production of a good or service, the quest for economic profit assures not only that existing supplies are allocated efficiently among individual buyers but also that resources are allocated across markets in the most efficient way possible. In any other allocation than the one generated by the market, resources could be rearranged so as to benefit some people without harming others.

- Economic rent is the portion of the payment for an input that exceeds the reservation price for that input. If a professional baseball player is willing to play for as little as $100,000/year, but is paid $15 million, he earns an economic rent of $14,900,000/year. While the invisible hand drives economic profit toward zero over the long run, economic rent can persist indefinitely, because replicating the services of players like Ken Griffey, Jr., is impossible. Talented individuals who are responsible for the superior performance of a business will tend to capture the resulting financial gains as economic rents.

- Failure to understand the logic of Adam Smith's invisible hand often compromises the design of regulatory programs. For instance, when regulation prevents firms from lowering prices to capture business from rivals, firms generally find other ways in which to compete. Thus, if airline regulators set passenger fares above cost, air carriers will try to capture additional business by offering extra amenities and more frequent service. Likewise, many antipoverty programs have been compromised by failure to consider how incentives change people's behavior.

- A share of stock in a company is a claim to a share of the current and future accounting profits of that company. The price of a share of stock depends not only on its accounting profits but on the market rate of interest, since the interest rate affects the present value of future costs and benefits. When the annual interest rate is r, the present value (PV) of a payment M to be received (or paid) T years from now is the amount that would have to be deposited in an account today at interest rate r to generate a balance of M after T years: $PV = M/(1 + r)^T$.

- According to the efficient markets hypothesis, the market price of a stock incorporates all currently available information that is relevant to that company's earnings. If this hypothesis were untrue, people could earn large sums of money without working hard, having talent, or being lucky.

- The equilibrium principle implies that if someone owns a valuable resource, the market price of that resource will fully reflect its economic value. The implication of this principle is not that lucrative opportunities never exist but rather that such opportunities cannot exist when markets are in equilibrium.

- Exceptions to the invisible hand theory arise when the benefit of an investment to an individual differs from its benefit to society as a whole. Such conflicting incentives give rise to

behavior that is smart for one but dumb for all. But despite such exceptions, the invisible hand of the market works remarkably well much of the time. One of the market system's most important contributions to social well-being is the pressure it creates to adopt cost-saving innovations. Competition among firms assures that the resulting cost savings get passed along to consumers in the long run.

▪ KEY TERMS ▪

accounting profit (196)
allocative function of price (203)
barrier to entry (204)
economic loss (199)
economic profit (196)

economic rent (205)
efficient markets hypothesis (211)
explicit costs (196)
implicit costs (196)
invisible hand theory (203)

normal profit (197)
present value (210)
rationing function of price (203)

▪ REVIEW QUESTIONS ▪

1. Why do most cities in the United States now have more radios but fewer radio repair shops than they did in 1960?

2. How can a businessowner who earns $10 million/year from his or her business credibly claim to earn zero economic profit?

3. Why do market forces drive economic profit but not economic rent toward zero?

4. Why did airlines that once were regulated by the government generally fail to earn an economic profit, even on routes with relatively high fares?

5. Why is a payment of $10,000 to be received 1 year from now more valuable than a payment of $10,000 to be received 2 years from now?

▪ PROBLEMS ▪

1. True or false: Explain why the following statements are true or false:
   a. The economic maxim "There's no cash on the table" means that there are never any unexploited economic opportunities.
   b. Firms in competitive environments make no accounting profit when the market is in long-run equilibrium.
   c. Firms that can introduce cost-saving innovations can make an economic profit in the short run.

2. Explain why new software firms that give away their software products at a short-run economic loss are nonetheless able to sell their stock at positive prices.

3. John Jones owns and manages a café in Collegetown whose annual revenue is $5,000. Annual expenses are shown in the following list:

Labor	$2,000
Food and drink	500
Electricity	100
Vehicle lease	150
Rent	500
Interest on loan for equipment	1,000

   a. Calculate John's annual accounting profit.
   b. John could earn $1,000/year as a recycler of aluminum cans. However, he prefers to run the café. In fact, he would be willing to pay up to $275/year to run the café rather than to recycle. Is the café making an economic profit? Should John stay in the café business? Explain.

c. Suppose the café's revenues and expenses remain the same, but recyclers' earnings rise to $1,100/year. Is the café still making an economic profit? Explain.

d. Suppose John had not had to get a $10,000 loan at an annual interest rate of 10 percent to buy equipment, but instead he had invested $10,000 of his own money in equipment. How would your answers to parts a and b change?

e. If John can earn $1,000/year as a recycler and he likes recycling just as well as running the café, how much additional revenue would the café have to collect each year to earn a normal profit?

4. The city of New Orleans has 200 advertising companies, 199 of which employ designers of normal ability at a salary of $100,000/year. Paying this salary, each of the 199 firms makes a normal profit on $500,000 in revenue. However, the 200th company employs Janus Jacobs, an unusually talented designer. This company collects $1,000,000 in revenues because of Jacobs's talent.

a. How much will Jacobs earn? What proportion of his annual salary will be economic rent?

b. Why won't the advertising company for which Jacobs works be able to earn an economic profit?

5. Explain carefully why, in the absence of a patent, a technical innovation invented and pioneered in one tofu factory will cause the supply curve for the entire tofu industry to shift to the right. What will finally halt the rightward shift?

6. The government of the Republic of Self-Reliance has decided to limit imports of machine tools to encourage development of locally made machine tools. To do so, the government offers to sell a small number of machine tool import licenses. To operate a machine tool import business costs $30,000, excluding the cost of the import license. An importer of machine tools can expect to earn $50,000/year. If the annual interest rate is 10 percent, for how much will the government be able to auction the import licenses? Will the owner of a license earn an economic profit?

7. Unskilled workers in a poor cotton-growing region must choose between working in a factory for $6,000/year or being a tenant cotton farmer. One farmer can work a 120-acre farm, which rents for $10,000/year. Such farms yield $20,000 worth of cotton each year. The total nonlabor cost of producing and marketing the cotton is $4,000/year. A local politician whose motto is "working people come first" has promised that if he is elected, his administration will fund a fertilizer, irrigation, and marketing scheme that will triple cotton yields on tenant farms at no charge to tenant farmers.

a. If the market price of cotton would be unaffected by this policy and no new jobs would be created in the cotton-growing industry, how would the project affect the incomes of tenant farmers in the short run? In the long run?

b. Who would reap the benefit of the scheme in the long run? How much would they gain each year?

8. You have a friend who is a potter. He holds a permanent patent on an indestructible teacup whose sale generates $30,000/year more revenue than production costs. If the annual interest rate is 20 percent, what is the market value of his patent?

9. You have an opportunity to buy an apple orchard that produces $25,000/year in total revenue. To run the orchard, you would have to give up your current job, which pays $10,000/year. If you would find both jobs equally satisfying, and the annual interest rate is 10 percent, what is the highest price you would be willing to pay for the orchard?

10. Louisa, a renowned chef, owns one of the 1,000 spaghetti restaurants in Sicily. Each restaurant serves 100 plates of spaghetti a night at $5/plate. Louisa knows she can develop a new sauce at the same cost as the current sauce, which would be so tasty that all 100,000 spaghetti eaters would buy her spaghetti at $10/plate. There are two problems: Developing the new sauce would require some experimental cost, and the other spaghetti producers could figure out the recipe after 1 day.

a. What is the highest experimental cost Louisa would be willing to incur?

b. How would your answer change if Louisa could enforce a year-long patent on her new sauce? (Assume that the interest rate is zero.)

■ ANSWERS TO IN-CHAPTER EXERCISES ■

8.1 Since Pudge is indifferent between being a ski instructor or a store manager if the store manager's salary is $13,000/year, his economic surplus as a ski instructor at $8,000/year is $2,000/year higher than as a manager at $11,000/year. Thus his economic surplus as a ski instructor is $1,000/year higher than it would be if he stayed in farming. Pudge should become a ski instructor.

8.2 If each lane did not move at about the same pace, any driver in a slower lane could reduce his or her travel time by simply switching to a faster one. People will exploit these opportunities until each lane moves at about the same pace.

8.3 If the taxi medallion were available for free, it would still command an economic profit of $20,000/year. So its value is still the answer to the question "How much would you need to put in the bank to generate interest earnings of $20,000/year?" When the interest rate is 4 percent/year, the answer is $500,000, or twice what the medallion was worth at an interest rate of 8 percent.

8.4 $PV = \$1,728/(1.2)^3 = \$1,000.$

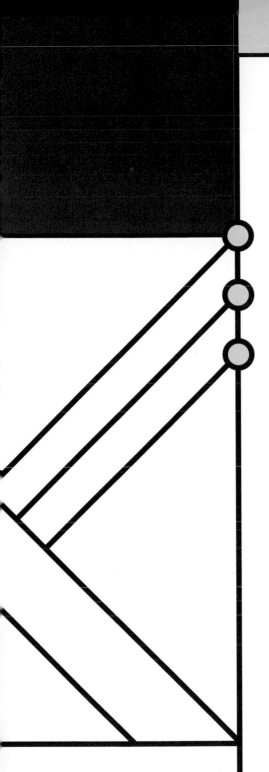

PART

3

MARKET IMPERFECTIONS

■

We now abandon Adam Smith's frictionless world to investigate what happens when people and firms interact in markets plagued by a variety of imperfections. Not surprisingly, the invisible hand that served society so well in the perfectly competitive world often goes astray in this new environment.

Our focus in Chapter 9 will be on how markets served by only one or a small number of firms differ from those served by perfectly competitive firms. We will see that although monopolies often escape the pressures that constrain the profits of their perfectly competitive counterparts, the two types of firms also have many important similarities.

In Chapter 10 we will investigate how the allocation of resources is affected when activities generate costs or benefits that accrue to people not directly involved in those activities. We will see that if parties cannot easily negotiate with one another, the self-serving actions of individuals usually will not lead to efficient outcomes.

In Chapters 1 to 10 economic decision makers confronted an environment that was essentially fixed. In Chapter 11, however, we will discuss cases in which people can expect their actions to alter the behavior of others, as when a firm's decision to advertise or launch a new product induces a rival to follow suit. Interdependencies of this sort are the rule rather than the exception, and we will explore how to take them into account using simple theories of games.

Although the invisible hand theory assumes that buyers and sellers are perfectly informed about all relevant options, this assumption is almost never satisfied in practice. In Chapter 12 we will explore how basic economic principles can help imperfectly informed individuals and firms make the best use of the limited information they possess.

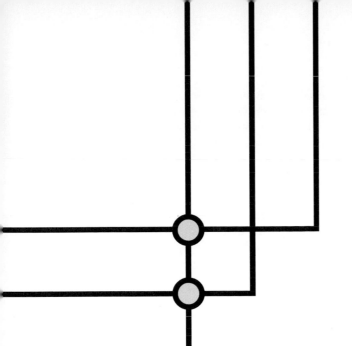

MONOPOLY AND OTHER FORMS OF IMPERFECT COMPETITION

■

Several years ago, schoolchildren around the country became obsessed with the game of Magic. To play, you need a deck of Magic Cards, available only from the creators of the game. But unlike ordinary playing cards, which can be bought in most stores for only a dollar or two, a deck of Magic Cards sells for upward of $10. And since Magic Cards cost no more to manufacture than ordinary playing cards, their producer earns an enormous economic profit.

In a normal competitive market, entrepreneurs would see this economic profit as cash on the table. It would entice them to offer Magic Cards at slightly lower prices so that eventually the cards would sell for roughly their cost of production, just as ordinary playing cards do. But Magic Cards have been on the market for several years now, and that hasn't happened. The reason is that the cards are copyrighted, which means the government has granted the creators of the game an exclusive license to sell them.

The holder of a copyright is an example of an **imperfectly competitive firm**, or **price setter**, that is, a firm with at least some latitude to set its own price. The competitive firm, by contrast, is a price taker, a firm with no influence over the price of its product.

Our focus in this chapter will be on the ways in which markets served by imperfectly competitive firms differ from those served by perfectly competitive firms. One salient difference is the imperfectly competitive firm's ability, under certain circumstances, to charge more than its cost of production. But if the producer of Magic Cards could charge any price it wished, why does it charge only $10? Why not $100, or even $1,000? We'll see that even though such a company may be the only seller of its product, its pricing freedom is far from

Why do Magic Cards sell for 10 times as much as ordinary playing cards, even though they cost no more to produce?

price setter or imperfectly competitive firm a firm with at least some latitude to set its own price

pure monopoly the only supplier of a unique product with no close substitutes

oligopolist a firm that produces a product for which only a few rival firms produce close substitutes

monopolistically competitive firm one of a large number of firms that produce slightly differentiated products that are reasonably close substitutes for one another

absolute. We'll also see how some imperfectly competitive firms manage to earn an economic profit, even in the long run, and even without government protections like copyright. And we'll explore why Adam Smith's invisible hand is less in evidence in a world served by imperfectly competitive firms.

IMPERFECT COMPETITION

The perfectly competitive market is an ideal; the actual markets we encounter in everyday life differ from the ideal in varying degrees. In a classification scheme whose arbitrariness most economists would feel hard pressed to defend, economics texts usually distinguish among three types of imperfectly competitive market structures.

DIFFERENT FORMS OF IMPERFECT COMPETITION

Farthest from the perfectly competitive ideal is the **pure monopoly**, a market in which a single firm is the lone seller of a unique product. The producer of Magic Cards is a pure monopolist, as are many providers of electric power. If the residents of Miami don't buy their electricity from the Florida Power and Light Company, they simply do without.

Somewhat closer to the perfectly competitive ideal is **oligopoly**, the market structure in which only a few firms sell a given product. Examples include the market for long-distance telephone service, in which firms like AT&T, Sprint, and MCI are the principal providers. Closer still to perfect competition is the industry structure known as **monopolistic competition**, which typically consists of a relatively large number of firms that sell the same product with slight differentiations. Examples of this structure include local gasoline stations, which differ not so much in the gas they sell as in their physical locations.

As we'll see in the next section, the essential characteristic that differentiates imperfectly competitive firms from perfectly competitive firms is the same in each of the three cases. So for convenience, we'll use the term *monopolist* to refer to any of the three types of imperfectly competitive firms.

THE ESSENTIAL DIFFERENCE BETWEEN PERFECTLY AND IMPERFECTLY COMPETITIVE FIRMS

In advanced economics courses, professors generally devote much attention to the analysis of subtle differences in the behavior of different types of imperfectly competitive firms. Far more important for our purposes, however, will be to focus on the single, common feature that differentiates all imperfectly competitive firms from their perfectly competitive counterparts—namely, that *whereas the perfectly competitive firm faces a perfectly elastic demand curve for its product, the imperfectly competitive firm faces a downward-sloping demand curve.*

In the perfectly competitive industry, the supply and demand curves intersect to determine an equilibrium market price. At that price, the perfectly competitive firm can sell as many units as it wishes. It has no incentive to charge more than the market price, because it won't sell anything if it does so. Nor does it have any incentive to charge less than the market price, because it can sell as many units as it wants to at the market price. The perfectly competitive firm's demand curve is thus a horizontal line at the market price, as we saw in Chapter 6.

By contrast, if a local gasoline retailer—an imperfect competitor—charges a few pennies more than its rivals for a gallon of gas, some of its customers may desert it. But others will remain, perhaps because they are willing to pay a little extra to continue stopping at their most convenient location. An imperfectly competitive firm thus faces a negatively sloped demand curve. Figure 9.1 summarizes this contrast between the demand curves facing perfectly competitive and imperfectly competitive firms.

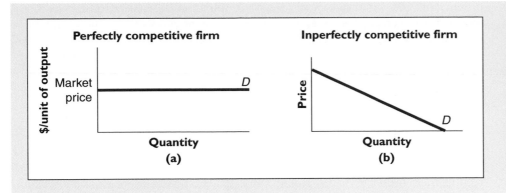

FIGURE 9.1
The Demand Curves Facing Perfectly and Imperfectly Competitive Firms.
(a) The demand curve confronting a perfectly competitive firm is perfectly elastic at the market price.
(b) The demand curve confronting an imperfectly competitive firm is downward-sloping.

RECAP **IMPERFECT COMPETITION**

Perfect competition is an ideal case, at best only approximated in actual industries. Economists study three other types of market structure that differ in varying degrees from perfect competition: monopoly, an industry with only one seller of a unique product; oligopoly, an industry with only a few sellers; and monopolistic competition, an industry in which many firms sell products that are close, but imperfect, substitutes for one another. The demand curve confronting a perfectly competitive firm is perfectly elastic at the market price, while the demand curve confronting an imperfectly competitive firm is downward-sloping.

If the Sunoco station at State and Meadow Streets raised its gasoline prices by 3 cents/gallon, would all its customers shop elsewhere?

FOUR SOURCES OF MARKET POWER

Firms that confront downward-sloping demand curves are sometimes said to enjoy **market power,** a term that refers to their ability to set the prices of their products. A common misconception is that a firm with market power can sell any quantity at any price it wishes. It cannot. All it can do is pick a price-quantity combination along its demand curve. If the firm chooses to raise its price, it must settle for reduced sales.

Why do some firms have market power while others do not? Since market power often carries with it the ability to charge a price above the cost of production, such power tends to arise from factors that limit competition. In practice, the following four factors often confer such power: exclusive control over inputs, economies of scale, patents, and government licenses or franchises.

EXCLUSIVE CONTROL OVER IMPORTANT INPUTS

If a single firm controls an input essential to the production of a given product, that firm will have market power. For example, to the extent that some tenants are willing to pay a premium for office space in the country's tallest building, the Sears Tower, the owner of that building has market power.

ECONOMIES OF SCALE (NATURAL MONOPOLIES)

When a firm doubles all its factors of production, what happens to its output? If output exactly doubles, the firm's production process is said to exhibit **constant returns to scale.** If output more than doubles, the production process is said to exhibit **increasing returns to scale,** or **economies of scale.** When production is subject to economies of scale, the average cost of production declines as the

market power a firm's ability to raise the price of a good without losing all its sales

constant returns to scale a production process is said to have constant returns to scale if, when all inputs are changed by a given proportion, output changes by the same proportion

increasing returns to scale a production process is said to have increasing returns to scale if, when all inputs are changed by a given proportion, output changes by more than that proportion; also called *economies of scale* number of units produced increases. For example, in the generation of electricity, the use of larger generators lowers the unit cost of production. The markets for such products tend to be served by a single seller, or perhaps only a few sellers, because having a large number of sellers would result in significantly higher costs. A monopoly that results from economies of scale is called a **natural monopoly**.

natural monopoly a monopoly that results from economies of scale

PATENTS

Patents give the inventors or developers of new products the exclusive right to sell those products for a specified period of time. By insulating sellers from competition for an interval, patents enable innovators to charge higher prices to recoup their product's development costs. Pharmaceutical companies, for example, spend millions of dollars on research in the hope of discovering new drug therapies for serious illnesses. The drugs they discover are insulated from competition for an interval—currently 17 years in the United States—by government patents. For the life of the patent, only the patent holder may legally sell the drug. This protection enables the patent holder to set a price above the marginal cost of production to recoup the cost of the research on the drug. In the same way, copyrights protect the authors of published works.

GOVERNMENT LICENSES OR FRANCHISES

The Yosemite Concession Services Corporation has an exclusive license from the U.S. government to run the lodging and concession operations at Yosemite National Park. One of the government's goals in granting this monopoly was to preserve the wilderness character of the area to the greatest degree possible. And indeed, the inns and cabins offered by the Yosemite Concession Services Company blend nicely with the valley's scenery. No garish neon signs mar the national park as they do in places where rivals compete for the tourist's dollars.

By far the most important and enduring of these four sources of market power is economies of scale. Lured by economic profit, firms almost always find substitutes for exclusive inputs. Thus, real estate developer Donald Trump has proposed a building taller than the Sears Tower, to be built on the west side of Manhattan. Likewise, firms can often evade patent laws by making slight changes in design of products. Patent protection is only temporary, in any case. Finally, governments grant very few franchises each year. But economies of scale are both widespread and enduring.

ECONOMIES OF SCALE AND THE IMPORTANCE OF FIXED COSTS

As we saw in Chapter 2, variable costs are those that vary with the level of output produced, while fixed costs are independent of output. Strictly speaking, there are no fixed costs in the long run, because all inputs can be varied. But as a practical matter, start-up costs often loom large for the duration of a product's useful life. Most of the costs involved in the production of computer software, for example, are fixed costs of this sort, one-time costs incurred in writing and testing the software. Once those tasks are done, additional copies of the software can be produced at a very low marginal cost. A good such as software, whose production entails large fixed costs and low variable costs, will be subject to significant economies of scale. Because by definition fixed costs don't increase as output increases, the average cost of production for such goods will decline sharply as output increases.

To illustrate, consider a production process for which total cost is given by the equation $TC = F + MQ$, where F is fixed cost, M is marginal cost (assumed constant in this illustration), and Q is the level of output produced. For the production process with this simple total cost function, variable cost is simply MQ, the product of marginal cost and quantity. The average cost per unit of output, TC/Q, is equal to $F/Q + M$. As Q increases, average cost declines steadily, because the fixed costs are spread out over more and more units of output.

Figure 9.2 shows the total production cost [part (a)] and average cost per unit [part (b)] for a firm with the total cost curve $TC = F + MQ$ and the corresponding average cost curve $AC = F/Q + M$. The average cost curve [part (b)] shows the decline in per unit cost as output grows. Though average cost is always higher than marginal cost for this firm, the difference between the two diminishes as output grows. At extremely high levels of output, average cost becomes very close to marginal cost *(M)*. Because the firm is spreading out its fixed cost over an extremely large volume of output, fixed cost per unit becomes almost insignificant.

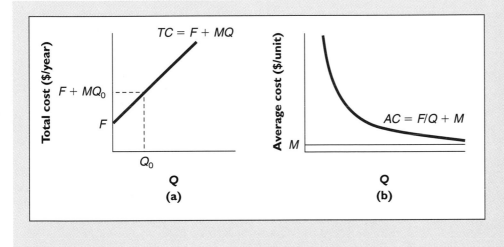

FIGURE 9.2
Total and Average Costs for a Production Process with Economies of Scale.
For a firm whose total cost curve of producing Q units of output per year is $TC = F + MQ$, total cost (a) rises at a constant rate as output grows, while average cost (b) declines. Average cost is always higher than marginal cost for this firm, but the difference becomes less significant at high output levels.

As Examples 9.1 and 9.2 illustrate, the importance of economies of scale depends on how large fixed cost is in relation to marginal cost.

Two video game producers, Nintendo and Sega, each have fixed costs of $200,000 and marginal costs of $0.80/game. If Nintendo produces 1 million units/year and Sega produces 1.2 million, how much lower will Sega's average production cost be?

EXAMPLE 9.1

Table 9.1 summarizes the relevant cost categories for the two firms. Note in the bottom row that Sega enjoys only a 3 cent average cost advantage over Nintendo. Even though Nintendo produces 20 percent fewer copies of its video game than Sega, it does not suffer a significant cost disadvantage because fixed cost is a relatively small part of total production cost.

TABLE 9.1
Costs for Two Computer Game Producers (1)

	Nintendo	Sega
Annual production	1,000,000	1,200,000
Fixed cost	$200,000	$200,000
Variable cost	$800,000	$960,000
Total cost	$1,000,000	$1,160,000
Average cost per game	$1.00	$0.97

But note how the picture changes when fixed cost looms large relative to marginal cost.

EXAMPLE 9.2

Two video game producers, Nintendo and Sega, each have fixed costs of $10,000,000 and marginal costs of $0.20/video game. If Nintendo produces 1 million units/per year and Sega produces 1.2 million, how much lower will Sega's average production cost be?

TABLE 9.2
Costs for Two Computer Game Producers (2)

	Nintendo	Sega
Annual production	1,000,000	1,200,000
Fixed cost	$10,000,000	$10,000,000
Variable cost	$200,000	$240,000
Total cost	$10,200,000	$10,240,000
Average cost per game	$10.20	$8.53

The relevant cost categories for the two firms are now summarized in Table 9.2. The bottom row shows that Sega enjoys a $1.67 average cost advantage over Nintendo, substantially larger than in Example 9.1.

If the video games the two firms produce are essentially similar, the fact that Sega can charge significantly lower prices and still cover its costs should enable it to attract customers away from Nintendo. As more and more of the market goes to Sega, its cost advantage will become self-reinforcing. Table 9.3 shows how a shift of 500,000 units from Nintendo to Sega would cause Nintendo's average cost to rise to $20.20/unit, while Sega's average cost would fall

TABLE 9.3
Costs for Two Computer Game Producers (3)

	Nintendo	Sega
Annual production	500,000	1,700,000
Fixed cost	$10,000,000	$10,000,000
Variable cost	$100,000	$340,000
Total cost	$10,100,000	$10,340,000
Average cost per game	$20.20	$6.08

to $6.08/unit. The fact that a firm could not long survive at such a severe disadvantage explains why the video game market is served now by only a small number of firms.

EXERCISE 9.1

How big will Sega's unit cost advantage be if it sells 2,000,000 units/year, while Nintendo sells only 300,000?

An important worldwide economic trend during recent decades is that an increasing share of the value embodied in the goods and services we buy stems from fixed investment in research and development. For example, in 1984 some

80 percent of the cost of a computer was in its hardware (which has relatively high marginal cost); the remaining 20 percent was in its software. But by 1990 those proportions were reversed. Fixed cost now accounts for about 85 percent of total costs in the computer software industry, whose products are included in a growing share of ordinary manufactured goods.

Why does Intel sell the overwhelming majority of all microprocessors used in personal computers?

The fixed investment required to produce a new leading-edge microprocessor such as the Intel Pentium chip currently runs upward of $2 billion. But once the chip has been designed and the manufacturing facility built, the marginal cost of producing each chip is only pennies. This cost pattern explains why Intel currently sells more than 80 percent of all microprocessors.

As fixed cost becomes more and more important, the perfectly competitive pattern of many small firms, each producing only a small share of its industry's total output, becomes less common. For this reason, we must develop a clear sense of how the behavior of firms with market power differs from that of the perfectly competitive firm.

RECAP   **FOUR SOURCES OF MARKET POWER**

A firm's power to raise its price without losing its entire market stems from its exclusive control of important inputs, patents, government licenses, or economies of scale. By far the most important and enduring of these is economies of scale. For a firm that enjoys economies of scale, the average cost per unit of output declines as output grows. This cost advantage explains why many industries are dominated by either a single firm or a small number of firms.

PROFIT MAXIMIZATION FOR THE MONOPOLIST

Regardless of whether a firm is a price taker or a price setter, economists assume that its basic goal is to maximize its profit. Another commonality is that the operational decision confronting both types of firm is to select the output level that results in the greatest possible difference between total revenue and total cost. But there are some important differences in how the two types of firm carry out this decision. To help focus attention on these differences, we begin with a brief review of how the perfectly competitive firm chooses the profit-maximizing level of output.

THE PERFECTLY COMPETITIVE FIRM'S DECISION RULE: A REVIEW

Recall from Chapter 6 that a perfectly competitive firm is typically one among many firms that produce products that are essentially perfect substitutes for one another. As the following example reminds us, the competitive firm maximizes profit by selling that quantity of output at which marginal cost equals the market price.

EXAMPLE 9.3

How many watermelons should a farmer produce?

Consider a perfectly competitive watermelon farmer whose marginal cost is shown in Figure 9.3. If this grower can sell as many tons of melons as he chooses at a price of $200/ton, how many tons should he sell to maximize his profit?

FIGURE 9.3
The Profit-Maximizing Output Level for a Perfectly Competitive Watermelon Farmer.
At a market price of $200/ton, the perfectly competitive farmer maximizes profit by selling 18 tons of watermelon a year, the quantity for which price equals marginal cost.

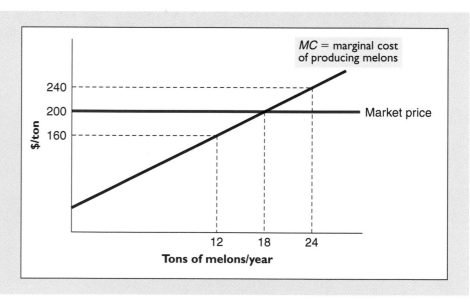

A competitive firm, or a monopolist for that matter, should expand its production if and only if the benefit of doing so exceeds the cost. If the farmer in this example were producing only 12 tons/year, his marginal cost would be $160/ton, while his benefit from expanding production would be the market price for which he can sell the melons, $200/ton. So this farmer should expand his production of melons until he reaches 18 tons/year, the quantity at which marginal cost exactly equals the market price.

For both the perfectly competitive firm and the monopolist, the marginal benefit of expanding output is the additional revenue the firm will receive if it sells one additional unit of output. In both cases, this marginal benefit is called the firm's **marginal revenue.** For the perfectly competitive firm, marginal revenue is exactly equal to the market price of the product.

marginal revenue the change in a firm's total revenue that results from a one-unit change in output

MARGINAL REVENUE FOR THE MONOPOLIST

The logic of profit maximization is precisely the same for the monopolist as for the perfectly competitive firm. In both cases, the firm keeps expanding output as long as the benefit of doing so exceeds the cost. The calculation of marginal cost is also precisely the same for the monopolist as for the perfectly competitive firm. *The only significant difference between the two cases concerns the calculation of marginal revenue.*

As we have seen, marginal revenue for a competitive firm is simply the market price. If that price is $6, then the marginal benefit of selling an extra unit is exactly $6. *To a monopolist, in contrast, the marginal benefit of selling an additional unit is strictly less than the market price.* As Examples 9.4 to 9.6 make clear, the reason is that while the perfectly competitive firm can sell as many units as it wishes at the market price, the monopolist can sell an additional unit only if it cuts the price—and it must do so not just for the additional unit but for the units it is currently selling.

How much extra revenue would a monopolist get by expanding output?

EXAMPLE 9.4

A monopolist with the demand curve shown in Figure 9.4 is currently selling 2 units of output at a price of $6/unit. What would be its marginal benefit from selling an additional unit?

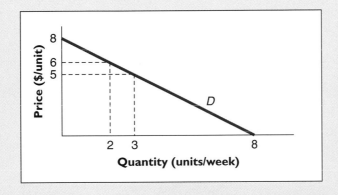

**FIGURE 9.4
The Monopolist's Benefit from Selling an Additional Unit.**
The monopolist shown receives $12/week in total revenue by selling 2 units/week at a price of $6 each. This monopolist could earn $15/week by selling 3 units/week at a price of $5 each. In that case, the benefit from selling the third unit would be $15 − $12 = $3, less than its selling price of $5.

This monopolist's total revenue from the sale of 2 units/week is ($6/unit)(2 units/week) = $12/week. Its total revenue from the sale of 3 units/week would be $15/week. The difference—$3/week—is the marginal revenue from the sale of the third unit each week. Note that this amount is not only smaller than the original price ($6) but smaller than the new price ($5) as well.

EXERCISE 9.2

Calculate marginal revenue for the monopolist in Example 9.4 as it expands output from 3 to 4 units/week, and then from 4 to 5 units/week.

Consider again the monopolist whose demand curve is shown in Figure 9.4. In Example 9.4 and Exercise 9.1, we saw that a sequence of increases in output—from 2 to 3, from 3 to 4, and from 4 to 5—could yield marginal revenue of $3, $1, and −$1, respectively. We can display these results in tabular form, as in Table 9.4.

TABLE 9.4
Marginal Revenue for a Monopolist ($/unit)

Quantity	Marginal revenue
2	
	3
3	
	1
4	
	−1
5	

Note in the table that the marginal revenue values are displayed in between the two quantity figures to which they correspond. For example, when the firm expanded its output from 2 units/week to 3, its marginal revenue was $3/unit. Strictly speaking, this marginal revenue corresponds to neither quantity but to the movement between those quantities, hence its placement in the table. Likewise, in moving from 3 to 4 units/week, the firm earned marginal revenue of $1/unit so that figure is placed midway between the quantities of 3 and 4, and so on.

To graph marginal revenue as a function of quantity, we would plot the marginal revenue for the movement from 2 to 3 units of output per week ($3) at a quantity value of 2.5, because 2.5 lies midway between 2 and 3. Similarly, we would plot the marginal revenue for the movement from 3 to 4 units/week ($1) at a quantity of 3.5 units/week, and the marginal revenue for the movement from 4 to 5 units/week (−$1) at a quantity of 4.5. The resulting marginal revenue curve *MR*, is shown in Figure 9.5.

FIGURE 9.5
Marginal Revenue in Graphical Form.
Because a monopolist must cut price to sell an extra unit, not only for the extra unit sold but also for all existing units, marginal revenue from the sale of the extra unit is less than its selling price.

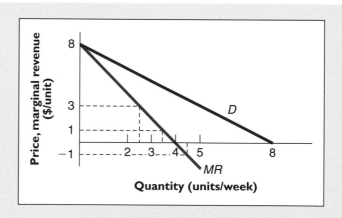

More generally, consider a monopolist with a straight-line demand curve whose vertical intercept is *a* and whose horizontal intercept is Q_0, as shown in Figure 9.6. This monopolist's marginal revenue curve will also have a vertical intercept of *a*, and it will be twice as steep as the demand curve. Thus its horizontal intercept will be not Q_0, but $Q_0/2$, as shown in Figure 9.6.

Marginal revenue curves can also be expressed algebraically. If the formula for the monopolist's demand curve is $P = a - bQ$, then the formula for its marginal revenue curve will be $MR = a - 2bQ$. If you have had calculus, this relationship is easy to derive,[1] but even without calculus you can verify it by working through a few numerical examples. First, translate the formula for the

[1] For those who have had an introductory course in calculus, marginal revenue can be expressed as the derivative of total revenue with respect to output. If $P = a - bQ$, then total revenue will be given by $TR = PQ = aQ - bQ^2$, which means that $MR = dTR/dQ = a - 2bQ$.

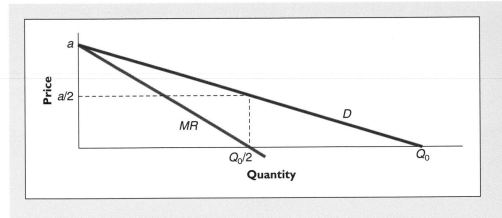

FIGURE 9.6
The Marginal Revenue Curve for a Monopolist with a Straight-Line Demand Curve.
For a monopolist with the demand curve shown, the corresponding marginal revenue curve has the same vertical intercept as the demand curve, and a horizontal intercept only half as large as that of the demand curve.

demand curve into a diagram, and then construct the corresponding marginal revenue curve graphically. Reading from the graph, write the formula for that marginal revenue curve.

What is the marginal revenue curve that corresponds to a specific demand curve?

EXAMPLE 9.5

Find the formula for the marginal revenue curve for the monopolist whose demand curve is given by $P = 10 - (1/2)Q$.

Figure 9.7(a) shows the demand curve for this monopolist. In Figure 9.7(b), we use the fact that the marginal revenue curve has the same vertical intercept as the demand curve and a horizontal intercept half as large as the demand curve's horizontal intercept. Since the demand curve has a slope of $-1/2$ and since the marginal revenue curve is twice as steep as the demand curve, the slope of the marginal revenue curve must be -1. And since the marginal revenue curve has the same vertical intercept as the demand curve, its formula must be $MR = 10 - Q$, as shown in Figure 9.7(b).

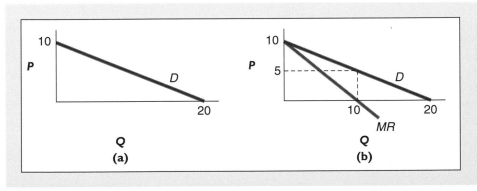

FIGURE 9.7
The Marginal Revenue Curve for a Specific Demand Curve.
If the formula for the monopolist's demand curve is $P = a - bQ$, the formula for the corresponding marginal revenue curve is $MR = a - 2bQ$.

THE MONOPOLIST'S PROFIT-MAXIMIZING DECISION RULE

Having derived the monopolist's marginal revenue curve, we are now in a position to describe how the monopolist chooses the output level that maximizes profit. As in the case of the perfectly competitive firm, the cost-benefit principle says that the monopolist should continue to expand output as long as the gain from doing so exceeds the cost. At the current level of output, the benefit from expanding output is the marginal revenue value that corresponds to that output level. The cost of expanding output is the marginal cost at that level of output. Whenever marginal revenue exceeds marginal cost, the firm should expand.

Conversely, whenever marginal revenue falls short of marginal cost, the firm should reduce its output. *Profit is maximized at the level of output for which marginal revenue precisely equals marginal cost.*

When the monopolist's profit-maximizing rule is stated in this way, we can see that the perfectly competitive firm's rule is actually a special case of the monopolist's rule. When the perfectly competitive firm expands output by one unit, its marginal revenue exactly equals the product's market price (because the perfectly competitive firm can expand sales by a unit without having to cut the price of existing units). So when the perfectly competitive firm equates price with marginal cost, it is also equating marginal revenue with marginal cost.

EXAMPLE 9.6 **What is the monopolist's profit-maximizing output level?**

Consider a monopolist with the demand and marginal cost curves shown in Figure 9.8. If this firm is currently producing 12 units/week, should it expand or contract production? What is the profit-maximizing level of output?

FIGURE 9.8
The Demand and Marginal Cost Curves for a Monopolist.
At the current output level of 12 units/week, price equals marginal cost. Since the monopolist's price is always greater than marginal revenue, marginal revenue must be less than marginal cost, which means this monopolist should produce less.

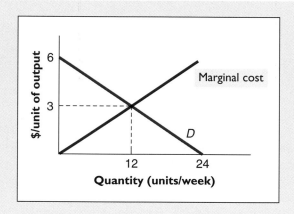

In Figure 9.9, we begin by constructing the marginal revenue curve that corresponds to the monopolist's demand curve. It has the same vertical intercept as the demand curve, and its horizontal intercept is half as large. Note that the monopolist's marginal revenue at 12 units/week is zero, which is clearly less than its marginal cost of $3/unit. This monopolist will therefore earn a higher profit by contracting production until marginal revenue equals marginal cost, which occurs at an output level of 8 units/week. At this profit-maximizing output level, and the firm will charge $4/unit, the price that corresponds to 8 units/week on the demand curve.

FIGURE 9.9
The Monopolist's Profit-Maximizing Output Level.
This monopolist maximizes profit by selling 8 units/week, the output level at which marginal revenue equals marginal cost. The profit-maximizing price is $4/unit, the price that corresponds to the profit-maximizing quantity on the demand curve.

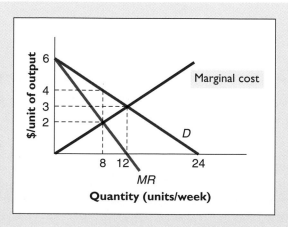

EXERCISE 9.3

Find the profit-maximizing price and level of output for a monopolist with the demand curve $P = 12 - Q$ and the marginal cost curve $MC = 2Q$, where P is the price of the product in dollars per unit and Q is output in units per week.

RECAP **PROFIT MAXIMIZATION FOR THE MONOPOLIST**

Both the perfectly competitive firm and the monopolist maximize profit by choosing the output level at which marginal revenue equals marginal cost. But whereas marginal revenue equals market price for the perfectly competitive firm, it is always less than market price for the monopolist.

WHY THE INVISIBLE HAND BREAKS DOWN UNDER MONOPOLY

In our discussion of equilibrium in perfectly competitive markets in Chapter 7, we saw conditions under which the self-serving pursuits of consumers and firms were consistent with the broader interests of society as a whole. Let's explore whether the same conclusion holds true for the case of imperfectly competitive firms.

Consider the monopolist in Example 9.6. Is this firm's profit-maximizing output level efficient from society's point of view? For any given level of output, the corresponding price on the demand curve indicates the amount buyers would be willing to pay for an additional unit of output. When the monopolist is producing 8 units/week, the marginal benefit to society of an additional unit of output is thus $4 (see Figure 9.9.) And since the marginal cost of an additional unit at that output level is only $2 (again, see Figure 9.9), society would gain a net benefit of $2/unit if the monopolist were to expand production by one unit above the profit-maximizing level. Because this economic surplus is not realized, the profit-maximizing monopolist is socially inefficient.

Recall that the existence of inefficiency means that the economic pie is smaller than it might be. If that is so, why doesn't the monopolist simply expand production? The answer is that the monopolist would gladly do so, if only there were some way to maintain the price of existing units and cut the price of only the extra units. As a practical matter, however, that is not always possible.

Consider again the monopolist in Example 9.6, whose demand and marginal cost curves are reproduced in Figure 9.10. For the market served by this monopolist, what is the socially efficient level of output?

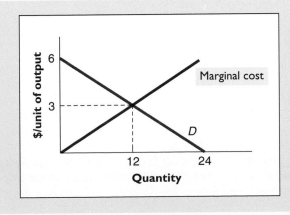

FIGURE 9.10
The Demand and Marginal Cost Curves for a Monopolist.
The socially optimal output level is 12 units/week, the quantity for which the marginal benefit *to the public* is exactly the same as marginal cost.

At any output level, the cost to society of an additional unit of output is the same as the cost to the monopolist, namely, the amount shown on the monopolist's marginal cost curve. The marginal benefit *to society* (not to the monopolist) of an extra unit of output is simply the amount people are willing to pay for it, which is the amount shown on the monopolist's demand curve. To achieve social efficiency, the monopolist should expand production until the marginal benefit to society equals the marginal cost, which in this case occurs at a level of 12 units/week. Social efficiency is thus achieved at the output level at which the market demand curve intersects the monopolist's marginal cost curve.

The fact that marginal revenue is less than price for the monopolist results in a deadweight loss. For the monopolist just discussed, the size of this deadweight loss is equal to the area of the pale blue triangle in Figure 9.11, which is (1/2)($2/unit)(4 units/week) = $4/week. That is the amount by which total economic surplus is reduced because the monopolist produces too little.

FIGURE 9.11
The Deadweight Loss from Monopoly.
A loss in economic surplus results because the profit-maximizing level of output (8 units/week) is less than the socially optimal level of output (12 units/week). This deadweight loss is the area of the pale blue triangle, $4/week.

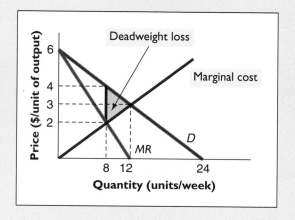

For a monopolist, profit maximization occurs when marginal cost equals marginal revenue. Since the monopolist's marginal revenue is always less than price, the monopolist's profit-maximizing output level is always below the socially efficient level. Under perfect competition, by contrast, profit maximization occurs when marginal cost equals the market price—the same criterion that must be satisfied for social efficiency. This difference explains why the invisible hand of the market is less evident in monopoly markets than in perfectly competitive markets.

If perfect competition is socially efficient and monopoly is not, why isn't monopoly against the law? The nation's legislators have in fact tried to limit the extent of monopoly through the antitrust laws. But even the most enthusiastic proponents of those laws recognize the limited utility of the legislative approach, since the alternatives to monopoly often entail problems of their own.

Suppose, for example, that a monopoly results from a patent that prevents all but one firm from manufacturing some highly valued product. Would society be better off without patents? Probably not, because eliminating such protection would discourage innovation. Virtually all successful industrial nations grant some form of patent protection, which gives firms a chance to recover the research and development costs without which new products would seldom reach the market.

Or suppose that the market in question is a natural monopoly—one that, because of economies of scale, is most cheaply served by a single firm. Would society do better to require this market to be served by many small firms, each with significantly higher average costs of production? Such a requirement would merely replace one form of inefficiency with another.

In short, we live in an imperfect world. Monopoly is socially inefficient, and that, needless to say, is bad. But the alternatives to monopoly aren't perfect, either.

> **RECAP** **WHY THE MONOPOLIST PRODUCES "TOO LITTLE" OUTPUT**
>
> The monopolist maximizes profit at the output level for which marginal revenue equals marginal cost. Because its profit-maximizing price exceeds marginal revenue, and hence also marginal cost, the benefit to society of the last unit produced (the market price) must be less than the cost of the last unit produced (the marginal cost). So the output level for an industry served by a profit-maximizing monopolist is smaller than the socially optimal level of output.

USING DISCOUNTS TO EXPAND THE MARKET

The source of inefficiency in monopoly markets is the fact that the benefit to the monopolist of expanding output is less than the corresponding benefit to society. From the monopolist's point of view, the price reduction the firm must grant existing buyers to expand output is a loss. But from the point of view of those buyers, each dollar of price reduction is a gain—one dollar more in their pockets.

Note the tension in this situation, which is similar to the tension that exists in all other situations in which the economic pie is smaller than it might otherwise be. As the efficiency principle reminds us, when the economic pie grows larger, everyone can have a larger slice. To say that monopoly is inefficient means that steps could be taken to make some people better off without harming others. If people have a healthy regard for their own self-interest, why doesn't someone take those steps? Why, for example, doesn't the monopolist from the earlier examples sell 8 units of output at a price of $4, and then once those buyers are out the door, cut the price for more price-sensitive buyers?

PRICE DISCRIMINATION DEFINED

Sometimes the monopolist does precisely that. Charging different buyers different prices for the same good or service is a practice known as **price discrimination.** Examples of price discrimination include senior citizens' and children's discounts on movie tickets, supersaver discounts on air travel, and rebate coupons on retail merchandise.

Attempts at price discrimination seem to work effectively in some markets, but not in others. Buyers are not stupid, after all; if the monopolist periodically offered a 50 percent discount on the $8 list price, those who were paying $8 might anticipate the next price cut and postpone their purchases to take advantage of it. In some markets, however, buyers may not know, or simply may not take the trouble to find out, how the price they pay compares to the prices paid by other buyers. Alternatively, the monopolist may be in a position to prevent some groups from buying at the discount prices made available to others. In such cases, the monopolist can price-discriminate effectively.

price discrimination the practice of charging different buyers different prices for essentially the same good or service

Why do many movie theaters offer discount tickets to students?

Whenever a firm offers a discount, the goal is to target that discount to buyers who would not purchase the product without it. People with low incomes generally have lower reservation prices for movie tickets than people with high incomes. Because students generally have lower disposable incomes than working adults, theater owners can expand their audiences by charging lower prices to students than to adults. Student discounts are one practical way of doing so. Offering student discounts also entails no risk of some people buying the product at a low price and then reselling it to others at a higher price.

ECONOMIC NATURALIST 9.2

HOW PRICE DISCRIMINATION AFFECTS OUTPUT

In Examples 9.7 to 9.9 we will see how the ability to price-discriminate affects the monopolist's profit-maximizing level of output. First we will consider a baseline case in which the monopolist must charge the same price to every buyer.

EXAMPLE 9.7   **How many manuscripts should Carla edit?**

Carla supplements her income as a teaching assistant by editing term papers for undergraduates. There are eight students/week for whom she might edit, each with a reservation price as given in the following table.

Student	Reservation price
A	$40
B	38
C	36
D	34
E	32
F	30
G	28
H	26

Carla is a profit maximizer. If the opportunity cost of her time to edit each paper is $29 and she must charge the same price to each student, how many papers should she edit? How much economic profit will she make? How much accounting profit?

Table 9.5 summarizes Carla's total and marginal revenue at various output levels. To generate the amounts in the total revenue column, we simply multiplied the corresponding reservation price by the number of students whose reservation prices were at least that high. For example, to edit 4 papers/week (for

TABLE 9.5
Total and Marginal Revenue from Editing

Student	Reservation price ($/paper)	Total revenue ($/week)	Marginal revenue ($/paper)
A	40	40	40
B	38	76	36
C	36	108	32
D	34	136	28
E	32	160	24
F	30	180	20
G	28	196	16
H	26	208	12

students *A, B, C,* and *D*), Carla must charge a price no higher than *D*'s reservation price ($34). So her total revenue when she edits 4 papers/week is (4)($34) = $136/week. Carla should keep expanding the number of students she serves as long as her marginal revenue exceeds the opportunity cost of her time. Marginal revenue, or the difference in total revenue that results from adding another student, is shown in the last column of Table 9.5.

Note that if Carla were editing 2 papers/week, her marginal revenue from editing a third paper would be $32. Since that amount exceeds her $29 opportunity cost, she should take on the third paper. But since the marginal revenue of taking on a fourth paper would be only $28, Carla should stop at 3 papers/week. The total opportunity cost of the time required to edit the 3 papers is (3)($29) = $87, so Carla's economic profit is $108 − $87 = $21/week. Since Carla incurs no explicit costs, her accounting profit will be $108/week.

What is the socially efficient number of papers for Carla to edit?

EXAMPLE 9.8

Again, suppose that Carla's opportunity cost of editing is $29/paper and that she could edit as many as 8 papers/week for students whose reservation prices are again as listed in the following table.

Student	Reservation price
A	$40
B	38
C	36
D	34
E	32
F	30
G	28
H	26

What is the socially efficient number of papers for Carla to edit? If she must charge the same price to each student, what will her economic and accounting profits be if she edits the socially efficient number of papers?

Students *A* to *F* are willing to pay more than Carla's opportunity cost, so serving these students is socially efficient. But students *G* and *H* are unwilling to pay at least $29 for Carla's services. The socially efficient outcome, therefore, is for Carla to edit 6 papers/week. To attract that number, she must charge a price no higher than $30/paper. Her total revenue will be (6)($30) = $180/week, slightly more than her total opportunity cost of (6)($29) = $174/week. Her economic profit will thus be only $6/week. Again, because Carla incurs no explicit costs, her accounting profit will be the same as her total revenue, $180/week.

If Carla can price-discriminate, how many papers should she edit?

EXAMPLE 9.9

Suppose Carla is a shrewd judge of human nature. After a moment's conversation with a student, she can discern that student's reservation price. The reservation prices of her potential customers are again as given in the following table. If Carla confronts the same market as before, but can charge students their respective reservation prices, how many papers should she edit, and how much economic and accounting profit will she make?

Student	Reservation price
A	$40
B	38
C	36
D	34
E	32
F	30
G	28
H	26

Carla will edit papers for students A to F and charge each exactly his or her reservation price. Because students G and H have reservation prices below $29, Carla will not edit their papers. Carla's total revenue will be $40 + $38 + $36 + $34 + $32 + $30 = $210/week, which is also her accounting profit. Her total opportunity cost of editing 6 papers is (6)($29) = $174/week, so her economic profit will be $210 − $174 = $36/week, $30/week more than when she was constrained to charge each customer the same price.

perfectly discriminating monopolist a firm that charges each buyer exactly his or her reservation price

A monopolist who can charge each buyer exactly his or her reservation price is called a **perfectly discriminating monopolist.** Notice that when Carla was discriminating among customers in this way, her profit-maximizing level of output was exactly the same as the socially efficient level of output: 6 papers/week. With a perfectly discriminating monopoly, there is no loss of efficiency. All buyers who are willing to pay a price high enough to cover marginal cost will be served.

Note that although total economic surplus is maximized by a perfectly discriminating monopolist, consumers would have little reason to celebrate if they found themselves dealing with such a firm. After all, consumer surplus is exactly zero for the perfectly discriminating monopolist. In this instance, total economic surplus and producer surplus are one and the same.

In practice, of course, perfect price discrimination can never occur, because no seller knows each and every buyer's precise reservation price. But even if some sellers did know, practical difficulties would stand in the way of their charging a separate price to each buyer. For example, in many markets the seller could not prevent buyers who bought at low prices from reselling to other buyers at higher prices, capturing some of the seller's business in the process. Despite these difficulties, price discrimination is widespread. But it is generally *imperfect price discrimination,* that is, price discrimination in which at least some buyers are charged less than their reservation prices.

THE HURDLE METHOD OF PRICE DISCRIMINATION

The profit-maximizing seller's goal is to charge each buyer the highest price that buyer is willing to pay. Two primary obstacles prevent sellers from achieving this goal. First, sellers don't know exactly how much each buyer is willing to pay. And second, they need some means of excluding those who are willing to pay a high price from buying at a low price. These are formidable problems, which no seller can hope to solve completely.

hurdle method of price discrimination the practice by which a seller offers a discount to all buyers who overcome some obstacle

One common method by which sellers achieve a crude solution to both problems is to require buyers to overcome some obstacle to be eligible for a discount price. This method is called the **hurdle method of price discrimination.** For example, the seller might sell a product at a standard list price and offer a rebate to any buyer who takes the trouble to mail in a rebate coupon.

The hurdle method solves both the seller's problems, provided that buyers with low reservation prices are more willing than others to jump the hurdle. Because the decision to jump the hurdle is subject to the cost-benefit test, such a link seems to exist. As noted earlier, buyers with low incomes are more likely than others to have low reservation prices (at least in the case of normal goods). Because of the low opportunity cost of their time, they are more likely than others to take the trouble to send in rebate coupons. Rebate coupons thus target a discount toward those buyers whose reservation prices are low and who therefore might not buy the product otherwise.

A **perfect hurdle** is one that separates buyers precisely according to their reservation prices, and in the process imposes no cost on those who jump the hurdle. With a perfect hurdle, the highest reservation price among buyers who jump the hurdle will be lower than the lowest reservation price among buyers who choose not to jump the hurdle. In practice, perfect hurdles do not exist. Some buyers will always jump the hurdle, even though their reservation prices are high. And hurdles will always exclude at least some buyers with low reservation prices. Even so, many commonly used hurdles do a remarkably good job of targeting discounts to buyers with low reservation prices. In the examples that follow, we will assume for convenience that the seller is using a perfect hurdle.

perfect hurdle one that completely segregates buyers whose reservation prices lie above some threshold from others whose reservation prices lie below it, imposing no cost on those who jump the hurdle

How much should Carla charge for editing if she uses a perfect hurdle?

EXAMPLE 9.10

Suppose Carla again has the opportunity to edit as many as 8 papers/week for the students whose reservation prices are as given in the following table. This time she can offer a rebate coupon that gives a discount to any student who takes the trouble to mail it back to her. Suppose further that students whose reservation prices are at least $36 never mail in the rebate coupons, while those whose reservation prices are below $36 always do so.

Student	Reservation price
A	$40
B	38
C	36
D	34
E	32
F	30
G	28
H	26

If Carla's opportunity cost of editing each paper is again $29, what should her list price be, and what amount should she offer as a rebate? Will her economic profit be larger or smaller than when she lacked the discount option (Example 9.7)?

The rebate coupon allows Carla to divide her original market into two submarkets in which she can charge two different prices. The first submarket consists of students *A, B,* and *C,* whose reservation prices are at least $36, and who therefore will not bother to mail in a rebate coupon. The second submarket consists of students *D* to *H,* whose lower reservation prices indicate a willingness to use rebate coupons.

In each submarket, Carla must charge the same price to every buyer, just like an ordinary monopolist. She should therefore keep expanding output in each submarket as long as marginal revenue in that market exceeds her marginal cost. The relevant data for the two submarkets are displayed in Table 9.6.

On the basis of the entries in the marginal revenue column for the list price submarket, we see that Carla should serve all three students *(A, B,* and *C)*, since marginal revenue for each exceeds $29. Her profit-maximizing price in the list price submarket is $36, the highest price she can charge in that market and still sell her services to students *A, B,* and *C.* For the discount price submarket, marginal revenue exceeds $29 only for the first two students *(D* and *E)*. So the profit-maximizing price in this submarket is $32, the highest price Carla can charge and still sell her services to *D* and *E.* (A discount price of $32 means that students who mail in the coupon will receive a rebate of $4 on the $36 list price.)

Note that the rebate offer enables Carla to serve a total of five students/week, compared to only three without the offer (see Example 9.7). Carla's combined total revenue for the two markets is (3)($36) + 2($32) = $172/week. Since her opportunity cost is $29/paper, or a total of (5)($29) = $145/week, her economic profit is $172/week − $145/week = $27/week, $6 more than when she did not offer the rebate.

TABLE 9.6
Price Discrimination with a Perfect Hurdle

Student	List Price Submarket Reservation price ($/paper)	Total revenue ($/week)	Marginal revenue ($/paper)
			40
A	40	40	
			36
B	38	76	
			32
C	36	108	
Discount Price Submarket			
			34
D	34	34	
			30
E	32	64	
			26
F	30	90	
			22
G	28	112	
			18
H	26	130	

EXERCISE 9.4

Refer to Example 9.10. How much should Carla charge in each submarket if she knows that only those students whose reservation prices are below $34 will use rebate coupons?

IS THE HURDLE METHOD EFFICIENT?

We are so conditioned to think of discrimination as bad that we may be tempted to conclude that price discrimination must run counter to the public interest. In Example 9.10, however, both consumer and producer surplus were actually enhanced by the monopolist's use of the hurdle method of price discrimination. To show this, we compare consumer and producer surplus when Carla employs the hurdle method (Example 9.10) to the corresponding values when she charges the same price to all buyers (Example 9.7).

When Carla had to charge the same price to every customer, she edited only the papers of students A, B, and C, each of whom paid a price of $36. We can tell at a glance that the total surplus must be larger under the hurdle method, because not only are students A, B, and C served at the same price ($36), but also students E and F are now served at a price of $32.

To confirm this intuition, we can calculate the exact amount of the surplus. For any student who hires Carla to edit her paper, consumer surplus is the difference between her reservation price and the price actually paid. In both the single price and discount price examples, student A's consumer surplus is thus $40 − $36 = $4; student B's consumer surplus is $38 − $36 = $2; and student C's consumer surplus is $36 − $36 = 0. Total consumer surplus in the list price submarket is thus $4 + $2 = $6/week, which is the same as total consumer surplus in Example 9.7. But now the discount price submarket generates additional consumer surplus. Specifically, student D receives $2/week of consumer surplus, since this student's reservation price of $34 is $2 more than the discount price of $32. So total consumer surplus is now $6 + $2 = $8/week, or $2/week more than before.

Carla's producer surplus also increases under the hurdle method. For each paper she edits, her producer surplus is the price she charges minus her reservation price ($29). In the single price case, Carla's surplus was (3)($36 − $29) = $21/week. When she offers a rebate coupon, she earns the same producer surplus as before from students A, B, and C, and an additional (2)($32 − $29) = $6/week from students D and E. Total producer surplus with the discount is thus $21 + $6 = $27/week. Adding that amount to the total consumer surplus of $8/week, we get a total economic surplus of $35/week with the rebate coupons, $8/week more than without the rebate.

Note, however, that even with the rebate, the final outcome is not socially efficient, because Carla does not serve student F, even though this student's reservation price of $30 exceeds her opportunity cost of $29. But though the hurdle method is not perfectly efficient, it is still more efficient than charging a single price to all buyers.

EXAMPLES OF THE HURDLE METHOD

Once you grasp the principle behind the hurdle method of price discrimination, you will begin to see examples of it all around you. Next time you visit a grocery, hardware, or appliance store, for instance, notice how many different product promotions include cash rebates. Temporary sales are another illustration of the hurdle method. Most of the time, stores sell most of their merchandise at the "regular" price but periodically offer special sales at a significant discount. The hurdle in this instance is taking the trouble to find out when and where the sales occur and then going to the store during that period. This technique works because buyers who care most about price (mainly, those with low reservation prices) are more likely to monitor advertisements carefully and buy only during sale periods.

To give another example, book publishers typically launch a new book in hardcover form at a price from $20 to $30, and a year later they bring out a paperback edition priced between $5 and $15. In this instance, the hurdle involves having to wait the extra year and accepting a slight reduction in the quality of the finished product. People who are strongly concerned about price end up waiting for the paperback edition, while those with high reservation prices usually spring for the hardback.

Or take the example of automobile producers, who typically offer several different models with different trim and accessories. Although GM's actual cost of producing a Cadillac may be only $2,000 more than its cost of producing a Chevrolet, the Cadillac's selling price may be $10,000 to $15,000 higher than the Chevrolet's. Buyers with low reservation prices purchase the Chevrolet, while those with high reservation prices are more likely to choose the Cadillac.

Commercial air carriers have perfected the hurdle method to an extent matched by almost no other seller. Their supersaver fares are often less than half their regular coach fares. To be eligible for these discounts, travelers must purchase their tickets 7 to 21 days in advance, and their journey must include a Saturday night stayover. Vacation travelers can more easily satisfy these restrictions than business travelers, whose schedules often change at the last moment and whose trips seldom involve Saturday stayovers. And—no surprise—the business traveler's reservation price tends to be much higher than the vacation traveler's.

Many sellers employ not just one hurdle but several by offering deeper discounts to buyers who jump successively more difficult hurdles. For example, movie producers release their major films to first-run theaters at premium prices, then several months later to neighborhood theaters at a few dollars less. Still later they make the films available on pay-per-view cable channels, then release them on video, and finally permit them to be shown on network television. Each successive hurdle involves waiting a little longer, and in the case of the televised versions, accepting lower quality. These hurdles are remarkably effective in segregating moviegoers according to their reservation prices.

Recall that the efficiency loss from single-price monopoly occurs because to the monopolist the benefit of expanding output is smaller than the benefit to society as a whole. The hurdle method of price discrimination reduces this loss by giving the monopolist a practical means of cutting prices for price-sensitive buyers only. In general, the more finely the monopolist can partition a market using the hurdle method, the smaller the efficiency loss. Hurdles are not perfect, however, and some degree of efficiency will inevitably be lost.

ECONOMIC NATURALIST 9.3

Why might an appliance retailer instruct its clerks to hammer dents into the sides of its stoves and refrigerators?

The Sears "Scratch 'n' Dent Sale" is another example of how retailers use quality differentials to segregate buyers according to their reservation prices. Many Sears stores hold an annual sale in which they display appliances with minor scratches and blemishes in the parking lot at deep discounts. People who don't care much about price are unlikely to turn out for these events, but those with very low reservation prices often get up early to be first in line. Indeed, these sales have proven so popular that it might even be in a retailer's interest to put dents in some of its sale items deliberately.

Would a profit-maximizing appliance retailer ever deliberately damage its own merchandise?

> ### RECAP   USING DISCOUNTS TO EXPAND THE MARKET
>
> A price-discriminating monopolist is one who charges different prices to different buyers for essentially the same good or service. A common method of price discrimination is the hurdle method, which involves granting a discount to buyers who jump over a hurdle, such as mailing in a rebate coupon. An effective hurdle is one that is more easily cleared by buyers with low reservation prices than by buyers with high reservation prices. Such a hurdle enables the monopolist to expand output and thereby reduce the deadweight loss from monopoly pricing.

■ SUMMARY ■

- Our concern in this chapter was the conduct and performance of the imperfectly competitive firm, a firm that has at least some latitude to set its own price. Economists often distinguish among three different types of imperfectly competitive firms: the pure monopolist, the lone seller of a product in a given market; the oligopolist, one of only a few sellers of a given product; and the monopolistic competitor, one of a relatively large number of firms that sell similar though slightly differentiated products.

- Although advanced courses in economics devote much attention to differences in the behavior among these three types of firms, our focus was on the common feature that differentiates them from perfectly competitive firms. Whereas the perfectly competitive firm faces an infinitely elastic demand curve for its product, the imperfectly competitive firm faces a downward-sloping demand curve. For convenience, we use the term *monopolist* to refer to any of the three types of imperfectly competitive firms.

- Monopolists are sometimes said to enjoy market power, a term that refers to their power to set the price of their product. Market power stems from exclusive control over important inputs, from economies of scale, and from patents and government licenses or franchises. The most important and enduring of these four sources of market power is economies of scale.

- Unlike the perfectly competitive firm, for which marginal revenue exactly equals market price, the monopolist realizes a marginal revenue that is always less than its price. This shortfall reflects the fact that to sell more output, the monopolist must cut the price not only to additional buyers but to existing buyers as well. For the monopolist with a straight-line demand curve, the marginal revenue curve has the same vertical intercept and a horizontal intercept that is half as large as the intercept for the demand curve.

- Whereas the perfectly competitive firm maximizes profit by producing at the level at which marginal cost equals the market price, the monopolist maximizes profit by equating marginal cost with marginal revenue, which is significantly lower than the market price. The result is an output level that is best for the monopolist but smaller than the level that would be best for society as a whole. At the profit-maximizing level of output, the benefit of an extra unit of output (the market price) is greater than its cost (the marginal cost). At the socially efficient level of output, where the monopolist's marginal cost curve intersects the demand curve, the benefit and cost of an extra unit are the same.

- Both the monopolist and its potential customers can do better if the monopolist can grant discounts to price-sensitive buyers. The extreme example is the perfectly discriminating monopolist, who charges each buyer exactly his or her reservation price. Such producers are socially efficient, because they sell to every buyer whose reservation price is at least as high as the marginal cost.

- One common method of targeting discounts toward price-sensitive buyers is the hurdle method of price discrimination, in which the buyer becomes eligible for a discount only after overcoming some obstacle, such as mailing in a rebate coupon. This technique works well because those buyers who care most about price are more likely than others to jump the hurdle. While the hurdle method reduces the efficiency loss associated with single-price monopoly, it does not completely eliminate it.

■ KEY TERMS ■

constant returns to scale (223)	marginal revenue (228)	perfect hurdle (239)
economies of scale (223)	market power (223)	perfectly discriminating monopolist (238)
hurdle method of price discrimination (238)	monopolistically competitive firm (222)	price discrimination (235)
imperfectly competitive firm (221)	natural monopoly (224)	price setter (221)
increasing returns to scale (223)	oligopolist (222)	pure monopoly (222)

■ REVIEW QUESTIONS ■

1. What important characteristic do all three types of imperfectly competitive firm share?

2. True or false: A firm with market power can sell whatever quantity it wishes at whatever price it chooses.

3. Why do most successful industrial societies offer patents and copyright protection, even though these protections enable sellers to charge higher prices?

4. Why is marginal revenue always less than price for a monopolist but equal to price for a perfectly competitive firm?

5. True or false: Because a natural monopolist charges a price greater than marginal cost, it necessarily earns a positive economic profit.

▪ PROBLEMS ▪

1. Two car manufacturers, Saab and Volvo, have fixed costs of $1 billion and marginal costs of $10,000/car. If Saab produces 50,000 cars/year and Volvo produces 200,000, calculate the average production cost for each company. On the basis of these costs, which company's market share do you think will grow in relative terms?

2. State whether the following statements are true or false, and explain why.
   a. In a perfectly competitive industry the industry demand curve is horizontal, whereas for a monopoly it is downward-sloping.
   b. Perfectly competitive firms have no control over the price they charge for their product.
   c. For a natural monopoly, average cost declines as the number of units produced increases over the relevant output range.

3. A single-price profit-maximizing monopolist:
   a. Causes excess demand, or shortages, by selling too few units of a good or service.
   b. Chooses the output level at which marginal revenue begins to increase.
   c. Always charges a price above the marginal cost of production.
   d. Also maximizes marginal revenue.
   e. None of the above statements is true.

4. If a monopolist could perfectly price-discriminate:
   a. The marginal revenue curve and the demand curve would coincide.
   b. The marginal revenue curve and the marginal cost curve would coincide.
   c. Every consumer would pay a different price.
   d. Marginal revenue would become negative at some output level.
   e. The resulting pattern of exchange would still be socially inefficient.

5. Explain why price discrimination and the existence of slightly different variants of the same product tend to go hand in hand. Give an example from your own experience.

6. What is the socially desirable price for a natural monopoly to charge? Why will a natural monopoly that attempts to charge the socially desirable price invariably suffer an economic loss?

7. TotsPoses, Inc., a profit-maximizing business, is the only photography business in town that specializes in portraits of small children. George, who owns and runs TotsPoses, expects to encounter an average of eight customers per day, each with a reservation price shown in the following table.

Customer	Reservation price ($/photo)
A	50
B	46
C	42
D	38
E	34
F	30
G	26
H	22

   a. If the total cost of each photoportrait is $12, how much should George charge if he must charge a single price to all customers? At this price, how many portraits will George produce each day? What will be his economic profit?
   b. How much consumer surplus is generated each day at this price?
   c. What is the socially efficient number of portraits?
   d. George is very experienced in the business and knows the reservation price of each of his customers. If he is allowed to charge any price he likes to any consumer, how many portraits will he produce each day, and what will his economic profit be?

e. In this case, how much consumer surplus is generated each day?

f. Suppose George is permitted to charge two prices. He knows that customers with a reservation price above $30 never bother with coupons, whereas those with a reservation price of $30 or less always use them. At what level should George set the list price of a portrait? At what level should he set the discount price? How many photoportraits will he sell at each price?

g. In this case, what is George's economic profit, and how much consumer surplus is generated each day?

8. Suppose that the University of Michigan Cinema is a local monopoly whose demand curve for adult tickets on Saturday night is $P = 12 - 2Q$, where P is the price of a ticket in dollars and Q is the number of tickets sold in hundreds. The demand for children's tickets on Sunday afternoon is $P = 8 - 3Q$, and for adult tickets on Sunday afternoon, $P = 10 - 4Q$. On both Saturday night and Sunday afternoon, the marginal cost of an additional patron, child or adult, is $2.

a. What is the marginal revenue curve in each of the three submarkets?

b. What price should the cinema charge in each of the three markets if its goal is to maximize profit?

9. Suppose you are a monopolist in the market for a specific video game. Your demand curve is given by $P = 80 - Q/2$, and your marginal cost curve is $MC = Q$. Your fixed costs equal $400.

a. Graph the demand and marginal cost curve.

b. Derive and graph the marginal revenue curve.

c. Calculate and indicate on the graph the equilibrium price and quantity.

d. What is your profit?

e. What is the level of consumer surplus?

10. Beth is a second-grader who sells lemonade on a street corner in your neighborhood. Each cup of lemonade costs Beth 20 cents to produce; she has no fixed costs. The reservation prices for the 10 people who walk by Beth's lemonade stand each day are listed in the following table.

Person	A	B	C	D	E	F	G	H	I	J
Reservation Price	$1.00	$0.90	$0.80	$0.70	$0.60	$0.50	$0.40	$0.30	$0.20	$0.10

Beth knows the distribution of reservation prices (that is, she knows that one person is willing to pay $1, another $0.90, and so on), but she does not know any specific individual's reservation price.

a. Calculate the marginal revenue of selling an additional cup of lemonade. (Start by figuring out the price Beth would charge if she produced only one cup of lemonade, and calculate the total revenue; then find the price Beth would charge if she sold two cups of lemonade; and so on.)

b. What is Beth's profit-maximizing price?

c. At that price, what are Beth's economic profit and total consumer surplus?

d. What price should Beth charge if she wants to maximize total economic surplus?

e. Now suppose Beth can tell the reservation price of each person. What price would she charge each person if she wanted to maximize profit? Compare her profit to the total surplus calculated in part d.

▪ ANSWERS TO IN-CHAPTER EXERCISES ▪

9.1 The relevant cost figures are as shown in the following table, which shows that the Sega's unit-cost advantage is now $50.20 - $5.20 = $45.00.

	Nintendo	Sega
Annual production	200,000	2,000,000
Fixed cost	$10,000,000	$10,000,000
Variable cost	$40,000	$400,000
Total cost	$10,040,000	$10,400,000
Average cost per game	$50.20	$5.20

9.2   When the monopolist expands from 3 to 4 units/week, total revenue rises from $15 to $16/week, which means that the marginal revenue from the sale of the fourth unit is only $1/week. When the monopolist expands from 4 to 5 units/week, total revenue drops from $16 to 15/week, which means that the marginal revenue from the sale of the fifth unit is actually negative, or −$1/week.

9.3   For the demand curve $P = 12 - Q$, the corresponding marginal revenue curve is $MR = 12 - 2Q$. Equating MR and MC, we solve the equation $12 - 2Q = 2Q$ for $Q = 3$. Substituting $Q = 3$ into the demand equation, we solve for the profit-maximizing price, $P = 12 - 3 = 9$.

9.4   As the marginal revenue column in the following table shows, Carla should again serve students A, B, and C in the list price submarket (at a price of $36), and only student E in the discount submarket (at a price of $32).

Student	Reservation price ($/paper)	Total revenue ($/week)	Marginal revenue ($/paper)
List Price Submarket			
			40
A	40	40	
			36
B	38	76	
			32
C	36	108	
			28
D	34	136	
Discount Price Submarket			
			32
E	32	32	
			28
F	30	60	
			24
G	28	84	
			20
H	26	104	

THINKING
STRATEGICALLY

At a Christmas Eve dinner party in 1997, actor Robert DeNiro pulled singer Tony Bennett aside for a moment. "Hey Tony—there's a film I want you in," DeNiro said. He was referring to the project that became the 1999 Warner Brothers hit comedy *Analyze This,* in which the troubled head of a crime family, played by DeNiro, seeks the counsel of a psychotherapist, played by Billy Crystal. In the script, both the mob boss and his therapist are big fans of Bennett's music.

Bennett heard nothing further about the project for almost a year. Then his son and financial manager, Danny Bennett, got a phone call from Warner Brothers, in which the studio offered Tony $15,000 to sing "Got the World on a String" in the movie's final scene. As Danny described the conversation, ". . . they made a fatal mistake. They told me they had already shot the film. So I'm like: 'Hey, they shot the whole film around Tony being the end gag and they're offering me $15,000?'"[1]

Warner Brothers wound up paying $200,000 for Bennett's performance.

In business negotiations, as in life, timing can be everything. If executives at Warner Brothers had thought the problem through carefully, they would have negotiated with Bennett *before* shooting the movie. At that point Bennett would have realized that the script could be rewritten if he asked too high a fee. By waiting, studio executives left themselves with no other option than to pay Bennett's price.

---

[1]As quoted by Geraldine Fabrikant, "Talking Money with Tony Bennett," *The New York Times,* May 2, 1999, Money & Business, p. 1.

The payoff to many actions depends not only on the actions themselves but also on when they are taken and how they relate to actions taken by others. In previous chapters, economic decision makers confronted an environment that was essentially fixed. This chapter will focus on cases in which people must consider the effect of their behavior on others. For example, an imperfectly competitive firm will want to weigh the likely responses of rivals when deciding whether to cut prices or to increase the advertising budget. Interdependencies of this sort are the rule rather than the exception in economic and social life. To make sense of the world we live in, then, we must take these interdependencies into account.

THE THEORY OF GAMES

In chess, tennis, or any other game, the payoff to a given move depends on what your opponent does in response. In choosing your move, therefore, you must anticipate your opponent's responses, how you might respond, and what further moves your own response might elicit. To analyze such situations, in which the payoffs to different actors depend on the actions their opponents take, economists and other behavioral scientists have devised the mathematical theory of games.

THE THREE ELEMENTS OF A GAME

basic elements of a game the players, the strategies available to each player, and the payoffs each player receives for each possible combination of strategies

Any game has three **basic elements:** the players, the list of possible actions (or strategies) each player can choose from, and the payoffs the players receive for each combination of strategies. How these elements combine to form the basis of a theory of behavior will become clear in the context of the following illustrative examples.

EXAMPLE 10.1

Should United Airlines spend more money on advertising?

Suppose that United Airlines and TWA are the only air carriers that serve the Chicago–St. Louis market. Each currently earns an economic profit of $6,000/flight on this route. If United increases its advertising spending in this market by $1,000/flight and TWA spends no more on advertising than it does now, United's profit will rise to $8,000/flight and TWA's will fall to $2,000. If both spend $1,000 more on advertising, each will earn an economic profit of $5,500/flight. These payoffs are symmetric, so if United stands pat while TWA increases its spending by $1,000, United's economic profit will fall to $2,000/flight and TWA's will rise to $8,000. If each must decide independently whether to increase spending on advertising, what should United do?

Think of this situation as a game. What are its three elements? The players are the two airlines, each of which must choose one of two strategies: to raise spending by $1,000 or to leave it the same. The payoffs are the economic profits that correspond to the four possible scenarios resulting from their choices. One way to summarize the relevant information about this game is to display the players, strategies, and payoffs in the form of a simple table called a **payoff matrix** (see Table 10.1).

payoff matrix a table that describes the payoffs in a game for each possible combination of strategies

Confronted with the payoff matrix in Table 10.1, what should United Airlines do? The essence of strategic thinking is to begin by looking at the situation from the other party's point of view. Suppose TWA assumes that United will raise its spending on advertising (the top row in Table 10.1). In that case, TWA's best bet would be to follow suit (the left column in Table 10.1). Why is the left column TWA's best response when United chooses the top row? TWA's economic profits, given in the upper left cell of Table 10.1, will be $5,500 as compared to only $2,000 if it keeps spending level (see the upper right cell).

TABLE 10.1
The Payoff Matrix for an Advertising Game

		TWA	
		Raise ad spending	Leave ad spending the same
United	Raise ad spending	$5,500 for United $5,500 for TWA	$8,000 for United $2,000 for TWA
	Leave ad spending the same	$2,000 for United $8,000 for TWA	$6,000 for United $6,000 for TWA

Alternatively, suppose TWA assumes that United will keep its ad spending level (that is, United will choose the bottom row in Table 10.1). In that case, TWA would still do better to increase spending, because it would earn $8,000 (the lower left cell) as compared to only $6,000 if it keeps spending level (lower right cell). In this particular game, no matter which strategy United chooses, TWA will earn a higher economic profit by increasing its spending on advertising. And since this game is perfectly symmetric, a similar conclusion holds for United: No matter which strategy TWA chooses, United will do better by increasing its spending on ads.

When one player has a strategy that yields a higher payoff no matter which choice the other player makes, that player is said to have a **dominant strategy.** Not all games involve dominant strategies, but both players in this game have one, and that is to increase spending on ads. For both players, to leave ad spending the same is a **dominated strategy**—one that leads to a lower payoff than an alternative choice, regardless of the other player's choice.

Notice, however, that when each player chooses the dominant strategy, the resulting payoffs are smaller than if each had left spending unchanged. When United and TWA increase their spending on ads, each earns only $5,500 in economic profits as compared to the $6,000 each would have earned without the increase. (We'll say more below about this apparent paradox.)

dominant strategy one that yields a higher payoff no matter what the other players in a game choose

dominated strategy any other strategy available to a player who has a dominant strategy

NASH EQUILIBRIUM

A game is said to be in equilibrium if each player's strategy is the best he or she can choose, given the other players' strategies. This definition of equilibrium is sometimes called a **Nash equilibrium,** after the Nobel laureate John Nash, who developed the concept in the early 1950s. When a game is in equilibrium, no player has any incentive to deviate from his or her current strategy.

If each player in a game has a dominant strategy, as in Example 10.1, equilibrium occurs when each player follows that strategy. But even in games in which not every player has a dominant strategy, we can often identify an equilibrium outcome. Consider, for instance, the following variation on the advertising game in Example 10.1.

Nash equilibrium any combination of strategies in which each player's strategy is his or her best choice, given the other players' strategies

Should TWA spend more money on advertising?

Suppose United Airlines and TWA are the only carriers that serve the Chicago–St. Louis market. Their payoff matrix for advertising decisions is shown in Table 10.2. Does United have a dominant strategy? Does TWA? If each firm does the best it can, given the incentives facing the other, what will be the outcome of this game?

EXAMPLE 10.2

TABLE 10.2
Equilibrium When One Player Lacks a Dominant Strategy

		TWA	
		Raise ad spending	Leave ad spending the same
United	Raise ad spending	$3,000 for United $8,000 for TWA	$8,000 for United $4,000 for TWA
	Leave ad spending the same	$4,000 for United $5,000 for TWA	$5,000 for United $2,000 for TWA

In this game, no matter what United does, TWA will do better to raise its ad spending, so raising the advertising budget is a dominant strategy for TWA. United, however, does not have a dominant strategy. If TWA raises its spending, United will do better to stand pat; if TWA stands pat, however, United will do better to spend more. But even though United does not have a dominant strategy, we can still predict what is likely to happen in this game. After all, United's managers know what the payoff matrix is, so they can predict that TWA will spend more on ads (since that is TWA's dominant strategy). Thus the best strategy for United, given the prediction that TWA will spend more on ads, is to keep its own spending level. If both players do the best they can, taking account of the incentives each faces, this game will end in the lower left cell of the payoff matrix: TWA will raise its spending on ads and United will not. (Note that when both players are positioned in the lower left cell, neither has any incentive to change its strategy.)

EXERCISE 10.1

What should United and TWA do if their payoff matrix is modified as follows?

		TWA	
		Raise ad spending	Leave ad spending the same
United	Raise ad spending	$3,000 for United $8,000 for TWA	$4,000 for United $5,000 for TWA
	Leave ad spending the same	$8,000 for United $4,000 for TWA	$5,000 for United $2,000 for TWA

RECAP   THE THEORY OF GAMES

The three elements of any game are the players, the list of strategies from which they can choose, and the payoffs to each combination of strategies. Players in some games have a dominant strategy, one that yields a higher payoff regardless of the strategies chosen by other players.

Equilibrium in a game occurs when each player's strategy choice yields the highest payoff available, given the strategies chosen by other players. Such a combination of strategies is called a Nash equilibrium.

THE PRISONER'S DILEMMA

The game in Example 10.1 belongs to an important class of games called the **prisoner's dilemma.** In the prisoner's dilemma, when each player chooses his dominant strategy, the result is unattractive to the group of players as a whole.

prisoner's dilemma a game in which each player has a dominant strategy, and when each plays it, the resulting payoffs are smaller than if each had played a dominated strategy

THE ORIGINAL PRISONER'S DILEMMA

Example 10.3 recounts the original scenario from which the prisoner's dilemma drew its name.

Should the prisoners confess?

Two prisoners, Horace and Jasper, are being held in separate cells for a serious crime that they did in fact commit. The prosecutor, however, has only enough hard evidence to convict them of a minor offense, for which the penalty is a year in jail. Each prisoner is told that if one confesses while the other remains silent, the confessor will go scot-free and the other will spend 20 years in prison. If both confess, they will get an intermediate sentence of years. (These payoffs are summarized in Table 10.3.) The two prisoners are not allowed to communicate with one another. Do they have a dominant strategy? If so, what is it?

EXAMPLE 10.3

TABLE 10.3
The Payoff Matrix for a Prisoner's Dilemma

		Jasper	
		Confess	Remain silent
Horace	Confess	5 years for each	0 years for Horace / 20 years for Jasper
	Remain silent	20 years for Horace / 0 years for Jasper	1 year for each

In this game, the dominant strategy for each prisoner is to confess. No matter what Jasper does, Horace will get a lighter sentence by speaking out. If Jasper confesses, Horace will get 5 years (upper left cell) instead of 20 (lower left cell). If Jasper remains silent, Horace will go free (upper right cell) instead of spending a year in jail (lower right cell). Because the payoffs are perfectly symmetric, Jasper will also do better to confess, no matter what Horace does. The difficulty is that when each follows his dominant strategy and confesses, both will do worse than if each had shown restraint. When both confess, they each get 5 years (upper left cell) instead of the 1 year they would have gotten by remaining silent (lower right cell). Hence the name of this game, the prisoner's dilemma.

EXERCISE 10.2

GM and Chrysler must both decide whether to invest in a new process. Games 1 and 2 below show how their profits depend on the decisions they might make. Which of these games is a prisoner's dilemma?

	Game 1 Chrysler	
	Don't invest	Invest
Don't invest	10 for each	4 for GM / 12 for Chrysler
Invest	12 for GM / 4 for Chrysler	5 for each

	Game 2 Chrysler	
	Don't invest	Invest
Don't invest	4 for GM / 12 for Chrysler	5 for each
Invest	10 for each	12 for GM / 4 for Chrysler

The prisoner's dilemma is one of the most powerful metaphors in all of human behavioral science. Countless social and economic interactions have pay-off structures analogous to the one confronted by the two prisoners. Some of those interactions occur between only two players, as in the examples just discussed; many others involve larger groups. But regardless of the number of players involved, the common thread is one of conflict between the narrow self-interest of individuals and the broader interests of larger communities.

PRISONER'S DILEMMAS CONFRONTING IMPERFECTLY COMPETITIVE FIRMS

cartel a coalition of firms that agrees to restrict output for the purpose of earning an economic profit

A **cartel** is any coalition of firms that conspires to restrict production for the purpose of earning an economic profit. As we will see in the next example, the problem confronting oligopolists who are trying to form a cartel is a classic illustration of the prisoner's dilemma.

Why are cartel agreements notoriously unstable?

Consider a market for bottled water served by only two firms, Aquapure and Mountain Spring. Each firm can draw water free of charge from a mineral spring located on its own land. Customers supply their own bottles. Rather than compete with one another, the two firms decide to collude by selling water at the price a profit-maximizing pure monopolist would charge. Under their agreement (which constitutes a cartel), each firm would produce and sell half the quantity of water demanded by the market at the monopoly price (see Figure 10.1). The agreement is not legally enforceable, however, which means that each firm has the option of charging less than the agreed price. If one firm sells water for less than the other firm, it will capture the entire quantity demanded by the market at the lower price.

FIGURE 10.1
The Market Demand for Mineral Water.
Faced with the demand curve shown, a monopolist with zero marginal cost would produce 1,000 bottles/day (the quantity at which marginal revenue equals zero) and sell them at a price of $1.00/bottle.

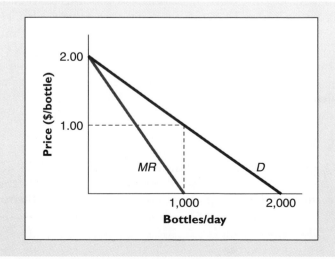

Why is this agreement likely to collapse?

Since the marginal cost of mineral water is zero, the profit-maximizing quantity for a monopolist with the demand curve shown in Figure 10.1 is 1,000 bottles/day, the quantity for which marginal revenue equals marginal cost. At that quantity, the monopoly price is $1/bottle. If the firms abide by their agreement, each will sell half the market total, or 500 bottles/day at a price of $1/bottle, for an economic profit of $500/day.

But suppose Aquapure reduced its price to $0.90/bottle. By underselling Mineral Spring, it would capture the entire quantity demanded by the market, which as shown in Figure 10.2 is 1,100 bottles/day. Aquapure's economic profit would rise from $500/day to ($0.90/bottle)(1,100 bottles/day) = $990/day, almost twice as much as before. In the process, Mountain Spring's economic profit would fall from $500/day to zero. Rather than see its economic profit disappear, Mountain Spring would match Aquapure's price cut, recapturing its original 50 percent share of the market. But when each firm charges $0.90/bottle and sells 550 bottles/day, each earns an economic profit of ($0.90/bottle)(550 bottles/day) = $495/day, or $5/day less than before.

Suppose we view the cartel agreement as an economic game in which the two available strategies are to sell for $1/bottle or to sell for $0.90/bottle. The payoffs are the economic profits that result from these strategies. Table 10.4 shows the payoff matrix for this game. Each firm's dominant strategy is to sell at the lower price, yet in following that strategy, each earns a lower profit than if each had sold at the higher price.

The game does not end with both firms charging $0.90/bottle. Each firm knows that if it cuts the price a little further, it can recapture the entire market, and in the process earn a substantially higher economic profit. At every step the rival firm will match any price cut, until the price falls all the way to the marginal cost—in this example, zero.

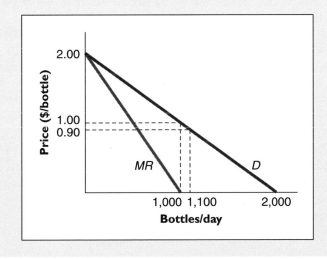

FIGURE 10.2
The Temptation to Violate a Cartel Agreement.
By cutting its price from $1/bottle to $0.90/bottle, Aquapure can sell the entire market quantity demanded at that price, 1,100 bottles/day, rather than half the monopoly quantity of 1,000 bottles/day.

TABLE 10.4
The Payoff Matrix for a Cartel Agreement

		Mountain Spring	
		Charge $1/bottle	Charge $0.90/bottle
Aquapure	Charge $1/bottle	$500/day for each	0 for Aquapure $990/day for Mt. Spring
	Charge $0.90/bottle	$990/day for Aquapure 0 for Mt. Spring	$495/day for each

Cartel agreements confront participants with the economic incentives inherent in the prisoner's dilemma, which explains why such agreements have historically been so unstable. Usually a cartel involves not just two firms, but several, an arrangement that can make retaliation against price cutters extremely difficult. In many cases, discovering which parties have broken the agreement is difficult. For example, the Organization of Petroleum Exporting Countries (OPEC), a cartel of oil producers formed in the 1970s to restrict oil production, has no practical way to prevent member countries from secretly pumping oil offshore in the dead of night.

ECONOMIC NATURALIST 10.2

How did Congress unwittingly solve the television advertising dilemma confronting cigarette producers?

In 1970, Congress enacted a law making cigarette advertising on television illegal after January 1, 1971. As evidenced by the steadily declining proportion of Americans who smoke, this law seems to have achieved its stated purpose of protecting citizens against a proven health hazard. But the law also had an unintended effect, which was to increase the economic profit of cigarette makers, at least in the short run. In the year before the law's passage, manufacturers spent more than $300 million on advertising, about $60 million more than they spent during the year after the law was enacted. Much of the saving in advertising expenditures in 1971 was reflected in higher cigarette profits at year-end. But if eliminating television advertising made companies more profitable, why didn't the manufacturers eliminate the ads on their own?

When an imperfectly competitive firm advertises its product, its demand curve shifts rightward, for two reasons. First, people who have never used that type of product learn about it, and some buy it. Second, people who consume a different brand of the product may switch brands. The first effect boosts sales industrywide; the second merely redistributes existing sales.

Although advertising produces both effects in the cigarette industry, its primary effect is brand switching. Thus the decision of whether to advertise confronts the individual firm with a prisoner's dilemma. Table 10.5 shows the payoffs facing a pair of cigarette producers trying to decide whether to advertise. If both firms advertise on TV (upper left cell), each earns a profit of only $10 million/year as compared to a profit of $20 million/year for each if neither advertises (lower right cell). Clearly, both will benefit if neither advertises.

Yet note the powerful incentive that confronts each firm. RJR sees that if Philip Morris doesn't advertise, RJR can earn higher profits by advertising ($35 million/year)

TABLE 10.5
Cigarette Advertising as a Prisoner's Dilemma

		Philip Morris	
		Advertise on TV	Don't advertise on TV
RJR	Advertise on TV	$10 million/year for each	$35 million/year for RJR $5 million/year for Philip Morris
	Don't advertise on TV	$5 million/year for RJR $35 million/year for Philip Morris	$20 million/year for each

than by not advertising ($20 million/year). RJR also sees that if Philip Morris does advertise, RJR will again earn more by advertising ($10 million/year) than by not advertising ($5 million/year). Thus RJR's dominant strategy is to advertise. And because the payoffs are symmetric, Philip Morris's dominant strategy is also to advertise. So when each firm behaves rationally from its own point of view, the two together do worse than if they had both shown restraint. The Congressional ad ban forced cigarette manufacturers to do what they could not have accomplished on their own.

PRISONER'S DILEMMAS IN EVERYDAY LIFE

As the following examples make clear, the prisoner's dilemma helps the economic naturalist to make sense of human behavior not only in the world of business, but in other domains of life as well.

Why do people often stand at concerts, even though they can see just as well when everyone sits?

A few years ago, an economic naturalist went with friends to hear Diana Ross sing. They bought good seats, some 20 rows from the stage. But before Ross had finished her first song, several people in front of them rose to their feet, presumably to get a better view. In doing so, they blocked the line of sight for others behind them, forcing those people to stand to see better. Before long, the entire crowd was standing. Then a few people in the front rows climbed atop their seats, blocking the views of those behind them and forcing them to stand on their seats too. The seats had fold-up bottoms, so from time to time someone who stood too close to the pivot point would tumble as the seat popped into its vertical position. All things considered, the outcome was far less satisfactory than if everyone had remained seated. Why this pattern of self-defeating behavior?

To understand what happened at the concert, note that standing is self-defeating only when viewed from the group's perspective. From the individual's perspective, however, standing passes the cost-benefit test. No matter what others do, an individual sees better by standing than by sitting. Suppose for the sake of discussion that you and other members of the audience would be willing to pay $2 to avoid standing and $3 to get a better view (or avoid having a worse one). In this multiperson prisoner's dilemma, you are one player and the rest of the audience is the other. The two strategies are to stand or to sit. Suppose everyone is seated to begin with. The payoffs you and others face will depend on the combination of strategies that you and others choose, as shown Table 10.6.

The payoff of 0 in the lower right cell of the payoff matrix reflects the fact that when everyone remains seated, everyone is just as well off as before. Your payoff of −$3 in the lower left cell reflects the fact that if you sit while others stand, you will have a worse view. Your payoff of −$2 in the upper left cell reflects the fact that when

Since standing is tiring and the view is no better when everyone stands than when everyone sits, why do people often stand at concerts?

TABLE 10.6
Standing Versus Sitting at a Concert as a Prisoner's Dilemma

		Others	
		Stand	Sit
You	Stand	−$2 for each	$1 for you −$3 for others
	Sit	−$3 for you $1 for others	0 for each

you and others stand, you must endure the $2 cost of standing, even though you don't get a better view. Finally, your $1 payoff in the upper right cell represents the difference between your $3 benefit and your $2 cost of standing when you stand while others sit.

These payoffs mean that your dominant strategy is to stand. If others stand, you will get −$2 by standing, which is better than the −$3 you will get by sitting. If others sit, you will get $1 by standing, which is better than the $0 you will get by sitting. Since this game is symmetric, the dominant strategy for others is also to stand. Yet when everyone stands, everyone gets a payoff of −$2, which is $2 worse than if everyone had remained seated. As in all prisoner's dilemmas, the choice that is more attractive from the perspective of the individual turns out to be less attractive from the perspective of the group.

ECONOMIC NATURALIST 10.4

Why do people shout at parties?

Whenever large numbers of people gather for conversation in a closed space, the ambient noise level rises sharply. After attending such gatherings, people often complain of sore throats and hoarse voices. If everyone spoke at a normal volume at parties, the overall noise level would be lower, and people would hear just as well. So why do people shout?

Again the problem involves the difference between individual incentives and group incentives. Suppose everyone starts by speaking at a normal level. But because of the crowded conditions, conversation partners have difficulty hearing one another, even when no one is shouting. The natural solution, from the point of view of the individual, is to simply raise one's voice a bit. But that is also the natural solution for everyone else. And when everyone speaks more loudly, the ambient noise level rises, so no one hears any better than before.

No matter what others do, the individual will do better by speaking more loudly. Doing so is a dominant strategy for everyone, in fact. Yet when everyone follows the dominant strategy, the result is worse (no one can hear well) than if everyone had continued to speak normally. While shouting is wasteful, individuals acting alone have no better option. If anyone were to speak softly while others shout, that person wouldn't be heard. No one wants to go home with raw vocal cords, but people apparently prefer that cost to the alternative of not being heard at all.

RECAP   **THE PRISONER'S DILEMMA**

The prisoner's dilemma is a game in which each player has a dominant strategy, and in which the payoff to each player when each chooses that strategy is smaller than if each had chosen a dominated strategy. Incentives analogous to those found in the prisoner's dilemmas help to explain a broad range of behavior in business and everyday life—among them, excessive spending on advertising, cartel instability, standing at concerts, and shouting at parties.

GAMES IN WHICH TIMING MATTERS

In the games discussed so far, players were assumed to choose their strategies simultaneously, and which player moved first didn't particularly matter. For example, in the prisoner's dilemma, players would follow their dominant strategies even if they knew in advance what strategies their opponents had chosen. But in other situations, such as the negotiations between Warner Brothers and Tony Bennett described at the beginning of this chapter, timing is of the essence.

THE ULTIMATUM BARGAINING GAME

Another such game is illustrated in Example 10.4.

Should Michael accept Tom's offer?

EXAMPLE 10.4

Tom and Michael are subjects in an experiment. The experimenter begins by giv-ing $100 to Tom, who must then propose how to divide the money between him-self and Michael. Tom can propose any division he chooses, provided the pro-posed amounts are whole dollars and he offers Michael at least $1. Suppose Tom proposes X for himself and $(100 − X)$ for Michael, where X is a whole num-ber no larger than 99. Michael must then say whether he accepts the proposal. If he does, each will get the proposed amount. But if Michael rejects the pro-posal, each player will get zero, and the $100 will revert to the experimenter. If Tom and Michael know they will play this game only once, and each wants to make as much money for himself as possible, what should Tom propose?

A payoff matrix is not a useful way to summarize the information in this game, because it says nothing about the timing of each player's move. For games in which timing matters, a **decision tree**, or **game tree**, is more useful. This type of diagram describes the possible moves in the sequence in which they may occur and lists the final payoffs for each possible combination of moves.

The decision tree for the game in Example 10.4 is shown in Figure 10.3. At A, Tom begins the game by making his proposal. At B, Michael responds to Tom's proposal. If he accepts (the top branch of the tree), Tom will get X and Michael will get $(100 − X)$. If he refuses (the bottom branch of the tree), both will get nothing.

decision tree (or game tree) a diagram that describes the possible moves in a game in sequence and lists the payoffs that correspond to each possible combination of moves

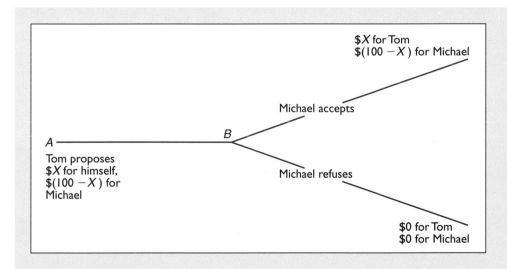

FIGURE 10.3
Decision Tree for Example 10.4.
This decision tree shows the possible moves and payoffs for the game in Example 10.4 in the sequence in which they may occur.

In thinking strategically about this game, the key for Tom is to put himself in Michael's shoes and imagine how he might react to various proposals. Because he knows Michael's goal is to make as much money as possible, he knows that Michael will accept his offer no matter how small, because the alternative is to reject it and get nothing. For instance, suppose Tom proposes $99 for himself and only $1 for Michael (see Figure 10.4). At B, Michael's best option is to accept the offer. This is a Nash equilibrium, because neither player has any incentive to deviate from the strategy he chose.

This type of game has been called the **ultimatum bargaining game,** because of the power of the first player to confront the second player with a take-it-or-leave-it offer. Michael could refuse a one-sided offer from Tom, but doing so would make him worse off than if he accepted it.

ultimatum bargaining game one in which the first player has the power to confront the second player with a take-it-or-leave-it offer

FIGURE 10.4

Tom's Best Strategy in an Ultimatum Bargaining Game.

Because Tom can predict that Michael will accept any positive offer, Tom's income-maximizing strategy at *A* is to offer Michael the smallest positive amount possible, $1.

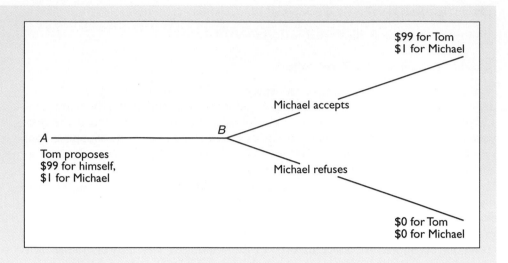

Example 10.5 illustrates the importance of the timing of moves in determining the outcome of the ultimatum bargaining game.

EXAMPLE 10.5

What should Michael's acceptance threshold be?

Suppose we change the rules of the ultimatum bargaining game slightly so that Michael has the right to specify *in advance* the smallest offer he will accept. Once Michael announces this number, he is bound by it. If Tom's task is again to propose a division of the $100, what amount should Michael specify?

This seemingly minor change in the rules completely alters the game. Once Michael announces that $Y is the smallest offer he will accept, his active role in the game is over. If Y is $60 and Tom proposes $X for himself and $(100 − X) for Michael, his offer will be rejected automatically if X exceeds 40. The decision tree for this game is shown in Figure 10.5.

When Michael announces that $Y is the smallest offer he will accept, the best Tom can do is to propose $(100 − Y) for himself and $Y for Michael. If he proposes any amount less than $Y for Michael, both will get nothing at all. Since this reasoning holds for any value of Y less than 100, Michael's best bet is to announce an acceptance threshold of $99—the largest whole number that is less

FIGURE 10.5

The Ultimatum Bargaining Game with an Acceptance Threshold.

If Michael can commit himself to a minimum acceptable offer threshold at *A*, he will fare dramatically better than in the standard ultimatum bargaining game.

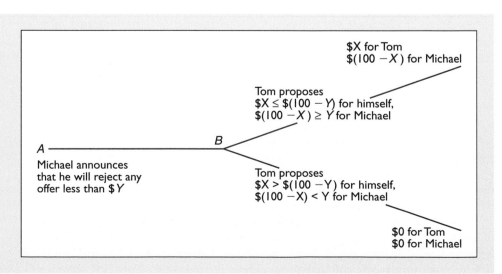

than $100. The equilibrium outcome of the game will then be $99 for Michael and only $1 for Tom, exactly the opposite of the outcome when Tom had the first move.

CREDIBLE THREATS AND PROMISES

Why couldn't Michael have threatened to refuse a one-sided offer in the original version of the game? While nothing prevented him from doing so, such a threat would not have been credible. In the language of game theory, a **credible threat** is one that is in the threatener's interest to carry out when the time comes to act. The problem in the original version of the game is that Michael would have no reason to carry out his threat to reject a one-sided offer in the event he actually received one. Once Tom announced such an offer, refusing it would not pass the cost-benefit test.

The concept of a credible threat figured prominently in the negotiations between Warner Brothers managers and Tony Bennett over the matter of Mr. Bennett's fee for performing in *Analyze This*. Once most of the film had been shot, managers knew they couldn't threaten credibly to refuse Mr. Bennett's salary demand, because at that point adapting the film to another singer would have been prohibitively costly. In contrast, a similar threat made before production of the movie had begun would have been credible.

credible threat a threat to take an action that is in the threatener's interest to carry out

"Listen to me, John. Tell them this is our final offer. Let 'em know we'll take an option at twenty-five million over five years—not a penny more, not a minute longer! If they balk, stall them for time and get back to me."

Here is another example in which one person suffers as a result of the inability to make a credible threat.

Is it safe to steal Veronica's briefcase?

EXAMPLE 10.6

When Veronica travels out of town on business, she usually brings along an expensive briefcase. A stranger takes a liking to her briefcase and assumes that because Veronica is an economist, she must be a self-interested, rational person. If the cost to Veronica of pressing charges in the event her briefcase is stolen exceeds the value of the briefcase, can the stranger safely steal it?

Provided the thief's assumptions about Veronica are correct, he can get away with his crime. To press charges once her briefcase has been stolen, Veronica must call the police, and will probably miss her flight home. Months later, she will have to return to testify at the thief's trial, and she may have to endure hostile cross-examination by the thief's attorney. Since these costs clearly exceed the value of the briefcase, a rational, self-interested person would simply write off the briefcase. But if Veronica could somehow have made a credible threat to press charges in the event her briefcase was stolen, she could have deterred the thief. The problem is that the thief knows the cost of retaliation will exceed the benefit, so the threat is not credible.

credible promise a promise to take an action that is in the promiser's interest to keep

Just as in some games credible threats are impossible to make, in others **credible promises** are impossible. A credible promise is one that is in the interests of the promiser to keep when the time comes to act. In Example 10.7, both players suffer because of their inability to make a credible promise.

EXAMPLE 10.7

Will the kidnapper release his victim?

A kidnapper who has seized a hostage for ransom suddenly changes his mind. He wants to set his victim free but is afraid that the victim will go to the police. Although the victim promises not to do so, both realize that he will have no incentive to keep his promise once he is free. The victim also realizes that the kidnapper would still pose a threat to him, out of fear that the victim may change his mind and go to the police. So if only to protect himself from the possibility of further harm, the victim has a powerful incentive to go to the police once he is free. Finally, if the victim goes to the police, the kidnapper will be caught and executed. The kidnapper desperately wants to set his victim free, but he prefers survival to execution. What will the kidnapper do?

The decision tree for the situation in Example 10.7 is shown in Figure 10.6. At *A*, the victim promises not to go to the police. He knows his life depends on the credibility of his promise, and at the moment he makes it, he sincerely means to keep it.

At *B* the kidnapper must decide what to do. If he sets his victim free (top branch at *B*), they reach *C*, where the victim must decide whether to go to the police. If the victim keeps his promise to remain silent (bottom branch at *C*), the kidnapper survives as a continuing threat to the victim. But if the victim goes to the police (top branch at *C*), the kidnapper will be caught and executed, and the victim will be safe. Since the victim prefers the second outcome, he will go to the police if freed. *And since the kidnapper can anticipate what will happen if the*

FIGURE 10.6
Decision Tree for the Kidnapper Game.
Both the kidnapper and the victim want to see the victim freed, but because the victim's promise to remain silent is not credible, the kidnapper kills him.

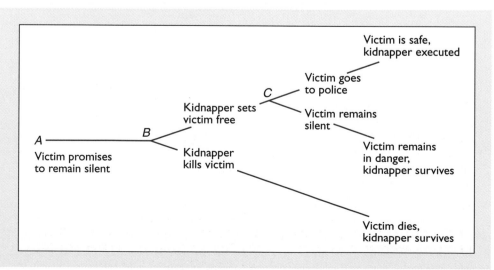

game reaches C, he cannot let the game reach that point. His only hope of survival is to choose the bottom branch at *B*. The irony is that both he and the victim strongly prefer the alternative in which he sets the victim free and the victim remains silent.

Here is another instance in which both parties suffer because of the inability to make a credible promise.

Should the businessowner open a remote office?

EXAMPLE 10.8

The owner of a thriving business wants to start up an office in a distant city. If she hires someone to manage the new office, she can afford to pay a weekly salary of $1,000—a premium of $500 over what the manager would otherwise be able to earn—and still earn a weekly economic profit of $1,000 for herself. The owner's concern is that she will not be able to monitor the manager's behavior. The owner knows that by managing the remote office dishonestly, the manager can boost his take-home pay to $1,500 while causing the owner an economic loss of $500/week. If the owner believes that all managers are selfish income maximizers, will she open the new office?

The decision tree for the remote office game is shown in Figure 10.7. At *A*, the managerial candidate promises to manage honestly, which brings the owner to *B*, where she must decide whether to open the new office. If she opens it, they reach *C*, where the manager must decide whether to manage honestly. If the manager's only goal is to make as much money as he can, he will manage dishonestly (bottom branch at *C*), since that way he will earn $500 more than by managing honestly (top branch at *C*).

FIGURE 10.7
Decision Tree for the Remote Office Game.
The best outcome is for the manager to open the office at *B* and for the manager to manage the office honestly at *C*. But if the manager is purely self-interested and the owner knows it, this path will not be an equilibrium outcome.

So if the owner opens the new office, she will end up with an economic loss of $500. If she had not opened the office (bottom branch at *B*), she would have realized an economic profit of zero. Since zero is better than −$500, the owner will choose not to open the remote office. In the end, the opportunity cost of the manager's inability to make a credible promise is $1,500: the manager's forgone $500 salary premium and the owner's forgone $1,000 return.

EXERCISE 10.3

mith and Jones are playing a game in which Smith has the first move at in the following decision tree. Once Smith has chosen either the top or ottom branch at *A*, Jones, who can see what Smith has chosen, must choose the top or bottom branch at *B* or *C*. If the payoffs at the end of each branch are as shown, what is the equilibrium outcome of this game? If before Smith chose, Jones could make a credible commitment to choose either the top or bottom branch when his turn came, what would he do?

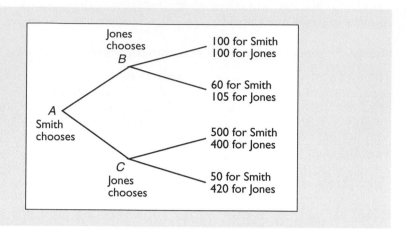

COMMITMENT PROBLEMS

commitment problem a situation in which people cannot achieve their goals because of an inability to make credible threats or promises

Games like the one in Exercise 10.3, as well as the prisoner's dilemma, the cartel game, the ultimatum bargaining game, the kidnapper game, and the remote office game, confront players with a **commitment problem**, a situation in which they have difficulty achieving the desired outcome because they cannot make credible threats or promises. If both players in the prisoner's dilemma (Example 10.3) could make a binding promise to remain silent, both would be assured of a shorter sentence. Hence the logic of the underworld code of *omerta,* under which the family of anyone who provides evidence against a fellow mob member is killed. A similar logic explains the adoption of military arms control agreements, in which opponents sign an enforceable pledge to curtail weapons spending.

The commitment problem in the kidnapper game (Example 10.7) could be solved if the victim could find some way of committing himself to remain silent once released. The economist Thomas Schelling suggests the following way out of the dilemma: "If the victim has committed an act whose disclosure could lead to blackmail, he may confess it; if not, he might commit one in the presence of his captor, to create a bond that will ensure his silence."[2] (Perhaps the victim could allow the kidnapper to photograph him in the process of some unspeakable act.) The blackmailable act serves as a **commitment device**, something that provides the victim with an incentive to keep his promise. Doing so will be unpleasant for him once he is freed, but clearly less so than not being able to make a credible promise.

commitment device a way of changing incentives so as to make otherwise empty threats or promises credible

Businessowners seem well aware of commitment problems in the workplace and have adopted a variety of commitment devices to solve them. Consider, for example, the problem confronting the owner of a restaurant. She wants her table staff to provide good service so that customers will enjoy their meals and come back in the future. And since good service is valuable to her, she would be willing to pay waiters extra for it. For their part, waiters would be willing to provide good service in return for the extra pay. The problem is that the owner cannot always monitor whether the waiters do provide good service. Her concern is that, having been paid extra for it, the waiters may slack off when she isn't looking. Unless the owner can find some way to solve this problem, she will not pay

---

[2]Thomas Schelling, *The Strategy of Conflict,* Cambridge, Mass.: Harvard University Press, 1960, pp. 43, 44.

extra, the waiters will not provide good service, and she, they, and the diners will suffer. A better outcome for all concerned would be for the waiters to find some way to commit themselves to good service.

Restaurateurs in many countries have tried to solve this commitment problem by encouraging diners to leave tips at the end of their meals. The attraction of this solution is that the diner is *always* in a good position to monitor service quality. The diner should be happy to reward good service with a generous tip, since doing so will help to ensure good service in the future. And the waiter has a strong incentive to provide good service, because he knows that the size of his tip may depend on it.

The various commitment devices just discussed—the underworld code of *omerta*, military arms control agreements, the tip for the waiter—all work because they change the material incentives facing the decision makers. But as Example 10.9 illustrates, changing incentives in precisely the desired way is not always practical.

Will leaving a tip at an out-of-town restaurant affect the quality of service you receive?

EXAMPLE 10.9

Will Sylvester leave a tip when dining on the road?

Sylvester has just finished a $100 steak dinner at a restaurant on Interstate 81, some 500 miles from home. The waiter provided good service. If Sylvester cares only about himself, will he leave a tip?

Once the waiter has provided good service, there is no way for him to take it back if the diner fails to leave a tip. In restaurants patronized by local diners, failure to tip is not a problem, because the waiter can simply provide poor service the next time a nontipper comes in. But the waiter lacks that leverage with out-of-town diners. Having already received good service, Sylvester must choose between paying $100 or $115 for his meal. If he is an essentially selfish person, the former choice may be a compelling one.

> **RECAP** **GAMES IN WHICH TIMING MATTERS**
>
> The outcomes in many games depend on the timing of each player's move. For such games, the payoffs are best summarized by a decision tree rather than a payoff matrix.
>
> The inability to make credible threats and promises often prevents people from achieving desired outcomes in many games. Games with this property are said to confront players with commitment problems. Such problems can sometimes be solved by employing commitment devices—ways of changing incentives to facilitate making credible threats or promises.

THE STRATEGIC ROLE OF PREFERENCES

In all the games we have discussed so far, players were assumed to care only about obtaining the best possible outcome for themselves. Thus each player's goal was to get the highest monetary payoff, the shortest jail sentence, the best chance of survival, and so on. The irony, in most of these games, is that players do not attain the best outcomes. Better outcomes can sometimes be achieved by altering the material incentives selfish players face, but not always.

If altering the relevant material incentives is not possible, commitment problems can sometimes be solved by altering people's psychological incentives. As Example 10.10 illustrates, in a society in which people are strongly conditioned to develop moral sentiments—feelings of guilt when they harm others, feelings of sympathy for their trading partners, feelings of outrage when they are treated unjustly—commitment problems arise less often than in more narrowly self-interested societies.

EXAMPLE 10.10   **In a moral society, will the businessowner open a remote office?**

Consider again the owner of the thriving business who is trying to decide whether to open an office in a distant city (Example 10.8). Suppose the society in which she lives is one in which all citizens have been strongly conditioned to behave honestly. Will she open the remote office?

Suppose, for instance, that the managerial candidate would suffer guilt pangs if he embezzled money from the owner. Most people would be reluctant to assign a monetary value to guilty feelings. But for the sake of discussion, let's suppose that those feelings are so unpleasant that the manager would be willing to pay at least \$10,000 to avoid them. On this assumption, the manager's payoff if he manages dishonestly will not be \$1,500 but \$1,500 − \$10,000 = −\$8,500. The new decision tree is shown in Figure 10.8.

FIGURE 10.8
The Remote Office Game with an Honest Manager.
If the owner can identify a managerial candidate who would choose to manage honestly at *C*, she will hire that candidate at *B* and open the remote office.

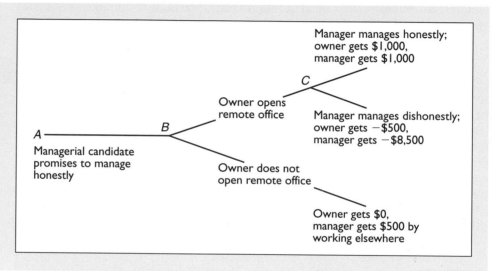

In this case, the best choice for the owner at *B* will be to open the remote office, because she knows that at *C* the manager's best choice will be to manage honestly. The irony, of course, is that the honest manager in this example ends up richer than the selfish manager in Example 10.8, who earned only a normal salary.

ARE PEOPLE FUNDAMENTALLY SELFISH?

As Example 10.10 suggests, the assumption that people are self-interested in the narrow sense of the term does not always capture the full range of motives that govern choice in strategic settings. Think, for example, about the last time you had a meal at an out-of-town restaurant. Did you leave a tip? If so, your behavior was quite normal. Researchers have found that tipping rates in restaurants patronized mostly by out-of-town diners are essentially the same as in restaurants patronized mostly by local diners.

Reflect also on how you would behave in some of the other games we have discussed. In the ultimatum game, what would you do if your partner proposed \$99 for himself and only \$1 for you? Would you reject the offer? If so, you are not alone. Two findings of extensive laboratory studies of the ultimatum bargaining game challenge the assumption that most players are narrowly self-interested. First, the most common proposal by the first player in this game is not a 99-1 split, but a 50-50 split. And second, on the few occasions when the first player does propose a highly one-sided split, the second player almost always rejects it. Subjects who reject the offer often mention the satisfaction they experienced at having penalized the first player for an "unfair" offer.

Indeed, there are many exceptions to the outcomes predicted on the basis of the assumption that people are self-interested in the most narrow sense of the term. People who have been treated unjustly often seek revenge even at ruinous cost to themselves. Every day people walk away from profitable transactions whose terms they believe to be "unfair." And the British spent vast sums to defend the desolate Falkland Islands, even though they had little empire left against which to deter future aggression. (The Argentine writer Jorge Luis Borges likened the Falklands war to two bald men fighting over a comb.) In these and countless other ways, people do not seem to be pursuing self-interest narrowly defined. And if motives beyond narrow self-interest are significant, we must take them into account in attempting to predict and explain human behavior.

PREFERENCES AS SOLUTIONS TO COMMITMENT PROBLEMS

Economists tend to view preferences as ends in themselves. Taking them as given, they calculate what actions will best serve those preferences. This approach to the study of behavior is widely used by other social scientists and by game theorists, military strategists, philosophers, and others. In its standard form, it assumes purely self-interested preferences for present and future consumption goods of various sorts, leisure pursuits, and so on. Concerns about fairness, guilt, honor, sympathy, and the like typically play no role.

Preferences clearly affect the choices people make in strategic interactions. Sympathy for one's trading partner can make a businessperson trustworthy even when material incentives favor cheating. A sense of justice can prompt a person to incur the costs of retaliation, even when incurring those costs will not undo the original injury. It can also induce people to reject one-sided offers, even when their wealth would be increased by accepting them.

Note, however, that although preferences can clearly shape behavior in these ways, that alone does not solve commitment problems. The solution to such problems requires not only that a person *have* certain preferences, but also that others have some way of *discerning* them. Unless the businessowner can identify the trustworthy employee, that employee cannot land a job whose pay is predicated on trust. Unless the predator can identify a potential victim whose character will motivate retaliation, that person is likely to become a victim. And unless a person's potential trading partners can identify him as someone predisposed to reject one-sided offers, he will not be able to deter such offers.

From among those whom we might engage in ventures requiring trust, can we identify reliable partners? If people could make *perfectly* accurate character judgments, they could always steer clear of dishonest persons. That people continue to be victimized at least occasionally by dishonest persons suggests that perfectly reliable character judgments are either impossible to make or prohibitively expensive.

Vigilance in the choice of trading partners is an essential element in solving (or avoiding) commitment problems, for if there is an advantage in being honest and being perceived as such, there is an even greater advantage in only *appearing* to be honest. After all, a liar who appears trustworthy will have better opportunities than one who glances about furtively, sweats profusely, and has difficulty making eye contact. Indeed, the liar will have the same opportunities as an honest person but will get higher payoffs because the liar will exploit them to the fullest.

In the end, the question of whether people can make reasonably accurate character judgments is an empirical one. Experimental studies have shown that even on the basis of brief encounters involving strangers, subjects are adept at predicting who will cooperate and who will defect in prisoner's dilemma games. For example, in one experiment in which only 26 percent of subjects defected, the accuracy rate of predicted defections was more than 56 percent. One might expect that predictions regarding those we know well would be even more accurate.

Do you know someone who would return an envelope containing $1,000 in cash to you if you lost it at a crowded concert? If so, then you accept the claim that personal character helps people to solve commitment problems. As long as honest individuals can identify at least some others who are honest, and can interact selectively with them, honest individuals can prosper in a competitive environment.

RECAP **THE STRATEGIC ROLE OF PREFERENCES**

Most applications of the theory of games assume that players are self-interested in the narrow sense of the term. In practice, however, many choices, such as leaving tips in out-of-town restaurants, appear inconsistent with this assumption.

The fact that people seem driven by a more complex range of motives makes behavior more difficult to predict but also creates new ways of solving commitment problems. Psychological incentives can often serve as commitment devices when changing players' material incentives is impractical. For example, people who are able to identify honest trading partners and interact selectively with them are able to solve commitment problems that arise from lack of trust.

▪ SUMMARY ▪

- Economists use the mathematical theory of games to analyze situations in which the payoffs of one's actions depend on the actions taken by others. Games have three basic elements: the players; the list of possible actions, or strategies, from which each player can choose; and the payoffs the players receive for those strategies. The payoff matrix is the most useful way to summarize this information in games in which the timing of the players' moves is not decisive. In games in which the timing of moves does matter, a decision tree provides a much more useful summary of the information.

- A dominant strategy is one that yields a higher payoff regardless of the strategy chosen by the other player. In some games, such as the prisoner's dilemma, each player has a dominant strategy. The equilibrium occurs in such games when each player chooses his or her dominant strategy. In other games, not all players have a dominant strategy.

- Although the equilibrium outcome of any game is any combination of choices in which each player does the best he can, given the choices made by others, the result is often unattractive from the perspective of players as group. The prisoner's dilemma has this feature. The incentive structure of this game helps explain such disparate social dilemmas as excessive advertising, military arms races, and failure to reap the potential benefits of interactions requiring trust.

- Individuals can often resolve these dilemmas if they can make binding commitments to behave in certain ways. Some commitments, such as those involved in military arms control agreements, are achieved by altering the material incentives confronting the players. Other commitments can be achieved by relying on psychological incentives to counteract material payoffs. Moral sentiments like guilt, sympathy, and a sense of justice often foster better outcomes than can be achieved by narrowly self-interested players. For this type of commitment to work, the relevant moral sentiments must be discernible by one's potential trading partners.

▪ KEY TERMS ▪

basic elements of a game (248)
cartel (266)
commitment device (262)
commitment problem (262)
credible promise (260)

credible threat (259)
decision tree (257)
dominant strategy (249)
dominated strategy (249)
game tree (257)

Nash equilibrium (249)
payoff matrix (248)
prisoner's dilemma (251)
ultimatum bargaining game (257)

▪ REVIEW QUESTIONS ▪

1. Explain why a military arms race is an example of a prisoner's dilemma.

2. Why did Warner Brothers make a mistake by waiting until the filming of *Analyze This* was almost finished before negotiating with Tony Bennett to perform in the final scene?

3. Suppose General Motors is trying to hire a small firm to manufacture the door handles for Pontiac sedans. The task requires an investment in expensive capital equipment that cannot be used for any other purpose. Why might the president of the small firm refuse to undertake this venture without a long-term contract fixing the price of the door handles?

4. Would you be irrational to refuse a one-sided offer in an ultimatum bargaining game if you knew that you would be playing that game many times with the same partner?

5. Describe the commitment problem that narrowly self-interested diners and waiters would confront at restaurants located on interstate highways. Given that in such restaurants tipping does seem to assure reasonably good service, do you think people are always selfish in the narrowest sense?

▪ PROBLEMS ▪

1. In studying for his economics final, Sam is concerned about only two things: his grade and the amount of time he spends studying. A good grade will give him a benefit of 20; an average grade, a benefit of 5; and a poor grade, a benefit of 0. By studying a lot, Sam will incur a cost of 10; by studying a little, a cost of 6. Moreover, if Sam studies a lot and all other students study a little, he will get a good grade and they will get poor ones. But if they study a lot and he studies a little, they will get good grades and he will get a poor one. Finally, if he and all other students study the same amount of time, everyone will get average grades. Other students share Sam's preferences regarding grades and study time.
   a. Model this situation as a two-person prisoner's dilemma in which the strategies are to study a little and to study a lot, and the players are Sam and all other students. Include the payoffs in the matrix.
   b. What is the equilibrium outcome in this game? From the students' perspective, is it the best outcome?

2. Consider the following "dating game," which has two players, A and B, and two strategies, to buy a movie ticket or a baseball ticket. The payoffs, given in points, are as shown in the following matrix. Note that the highest payoffs occur when both A and B attend the same event.

		B	
		Buy movie ticket	Buy baseball ticket
A	Buy movie ticket	2 for A 3 for B	0 for A 0 for B
	Buy baseball ticket	1 for A 1 for B	3 for A 2 for B

Assume that players A and B buy their tickets separately and simultaneously. Each must decide what to do knowing the available choices and payoffs but not what the other has actually chosen. Each player believes the other to be rational and self-interested.
   a. Does either player have a dominant strategy?
   b. How many potential equilibriums are there? (*Hint:* To see whether a given combination of strategies is an equilibrium, ask whether either player could get a higher payoff by changing his or her strategy.)
   c. Is this game a prisoner's dilemma? Explain.

d. Suppose player *A* gets to buy his or her ticket first. Player *B* does not observe *A*'s choice but knows that *A* chose first. Player *A* knows that player *B* knows he or she chose first. What is the equilibrium outcome?

e. Suppose the situation is similar to part d, except that player *B* chooses first. What is the equilibrium outcome?

3. Blackadder and Baldrick are rational, self-interested criminals imprisoned in separate cells in a dark medieval dungeon. They face the prisoner's dilemma displayed in the following matrix.

		Blackadder	
		Confess	Deny
Baldrick	Confess	5 years for each	0 years for Baldrick 20 years for Blackadder
	Deny	0 years for Blackadder 20 years for Baldrick	1 year for each

Assume that Blackadder is willing to pay $1,000 for each year by which he can reduce his sentence below 20 years. A corrupt jailer tells Blackadder that before he decides whether to confess or deny the crime, she can tell him Baldrick's decision. How much is this information worth to Blackadder?

4. The owner of a thriving business wants to open a new office in a distant city. If he can hire someone who will manage the new office honestly, he can afford to pay that person a weekly salary of $2,000 ($1,000 more than the manager would be able to earn elsewhere) and still earn an economic profit of $800. The owner's concern is that he will not be able to monitor the manager's behavior and that the manager would therefore be in a position to embezzle money from the business. The owner knows that if the remote office is managed dishonestly, the manager can earn $3,100 while causing the owner an economic loss of $600/week.

a. If the owner believes that all managers are narrowly self-interested income maximizers, will he open the new office?

b. Suppose the owner knows that a managerial candidate is a devoutly religious person who condemns dishonest behavior and who would be willing to pay up to $15,000 to avoid the guilt she would feel if she were dishonest. Will the owner open the remote office?

5. Imagine yourself sitting in your car in a campus parking lot that is currently full, waiting for someone to pull out so that you can park your car. Somebody pulls out, but at the same moment a driver who has just arrived overtakes you in an obvious attempt to park in the vacated spot before you can. Suppose this driver would be willing to pay up to $10 to park in that spot and up to $30 to avoid getting into an argument with you. (That is, the benefit of parking is $10, and the cost of an argument is $30.) At the same time the other driver guesses, accurately, that you too would be willing to pay up to $30 to avoid a confrontation and up to $10 to park in the vacant spot.

a. Model this situation as a two-stage decision tree in which the other driver's bid to take the space is the opening move and your strategies are (1) to protest and (2) not to protest. If you protest (initiate an argument), the rules of the game specify that the other driver has to let you take the space. Show the payoffs at the end of each branch of the tree.

b. What is the equilibrium outcome?

c. What would be the advantage of being able to be able to communicate credibly to the other driver that your failure to protest would be a significant psychological cost to you?

6. Newfoundland's fishing industry has recently declined sharply due to overfishing, even though fishing companies were supposedly bound by a quota agreement. If all fishing companies had abided by the agreement, yields could have been maintained at high levels.

a. Model this situation as a prisoner's dilemma in which the players are Company *A* and Company *B* and the strategies are to keep the quota and break the quota. Include appropriate payoffs in the matrix. Explain why overfishing is inevitable in the absence of effective enforcement of the quota agreement.

b. Provide another environmental example of a prisoner's dilemma.

c. In many potential prisoner's dilemmas, a way out of the dilemma for a would-be cooperator is to make reliable character judgments about the trustworthiness of potential partners. Explain why this solution is not available in many situations involving degradation of the environment.

7. Consider the following game, called matching pennies, which you are playing with a friend. Each of you has a penny hidden in your hand, facing either heads up or tails up (you know which way the one in your hand is facing). On the count of "three" you simultaneously show your pennies to each other. If the face-up side of your coin matches the face-up side of your friend's coin, you get to keep the two pennies. If the faces do not match, your friend gets to keep the pennies.

a. Who are the players in this game? What are each player's strategies? Construct a payoff matrix for the game.

b. Is there a dominant strategy? If so, what?

c. Is there an equilibrium? If so, what?

8. Consider the following game. Harry has four quarters. He can offer Sally from one to four of them. If she accepts his offer, she keeps the quarters Harry offered her and Harry keeps the others. If Sally declines Harry's offer, they both get nothing ($0). They play the game only once, and each cares only about the amount of money he or she ends up with.

a. Who are the players? What are each player's strategies? Construct a decision tree for this ultimatum bargaining game.

b. Given their goal, what is the optimal choice for each player?

9. Two airplane manufacturers are considering the production of a new product, a 150-passenger jet. Both are deciding whether to enter the market and produce the new plane. The payoff matrix is as shown (payoff values are in millions of dollars).

| | | **Airbus** | |
		Produce	Don't produce
Boeing	Produce	−5 for each	100 for Boeing 0 for Airbus
	Don't produce	0 for Boeing 100 for Airbus	0 for each

The implication of these payoffs is that the market demand is large enough to support only one manufacturer. If both firms enter, both will sustain a loss.

a. Identify two possible equilibrium outcomes in this game.

b. Consider the effect of a subsidy. Suppose the European Union decides to subsidize the European producer, Airbus, with a check for $25 million if it enters the market. Revise the payoff matrix to account for this subsidy. What is the new equilibrium outcome?

c. Compare the two outcomes (pre- and post-subsidy). What qualitative effect does the subsidy have?

10. Jill and Jack both have two pails that can be used to carry water down from a hill. Each makes only one trip down the hill, and each pail of water can be sold for $5. Carrying the pails of water down requires considerable effort. Both Jill and Jack would be willing to pay $2 each to avoid carrying one bucket down the hill and an additional $3 to avoid carrying a second bucket down the hill.

a. Given market prices, how many pails of water will each child fetch from the top of the hill?

b. Jill and Jack's parents are worried that the two children don't cooperate enough with one another. Suppose they make Jill and Jack share their revenues from selling the water equally. Given that both are self-interested, construct the payoff matrix for the decisions Jill and Jack face regarding the number of pails of water each should carry. What is the equilibrium outcome?

■ ANSWERS TO IN-CHAPTER EXERCISES ■

10.1 In game 1, no matter what Chrysler does, GM will do better to invest, and no matter what GM does, Chrysler will do better to invest. Each has a dominant strategy, but in following it, each does worse that if it had not invested. So game 1 is a prisoner's dilemma. In game 2, no matter what Chrysler does, GM again will do better to invest; but no matter what GM does, Chrysler will do better *not* to invest. Each has a dominant strategy, and in following it, each gets a payoff of 10—5 more than if each had played its dominated strategy. So game 2 is not a prisoner's dilemma.

Game 1

		Chrysler	
		Don't invest	Invest
GM	Don't invest	10 for each	4 for GM 12 for Chrysler
	Invest	12 for GM 4 for Chrysler	5 for each

Game 2

		Chrysler	
		Don't invest	Invest
GM	Don't invest	4 for GM 12 for Chrysler	5 for each
	Invest	10 for each	12 for GM 4 for Chrysler

10.2 No matter what TWA does, United will do better to leave ad spending the same. No matter what United does, TWA will do better to raise ad spending. So each player will play its dominant strategy: TWA will raise its ad spending, and United will leave its ad spending the same.

		TWA	
		Raise ad spending	Leave ad spending the same
United	Raise ad spending	$3,000 for United $8,000 for TWA	$4,000 for United $5,000 for TWA
	Leave ad spending the same	$8,000 for United $4,000 for TWA	$5,000 for United $2,000 for TWA

10.3 Smith assumes that Jones will choose the branch that maximizes his payoff, which is the bottom branch at either *B* or *C*. So Jones will choose the bottom branch when his turn comes, no matter what Smith chooses. Since Smith will do better (60) on the bottom branch at *B* than on the bottom branch at *C* (50), Smith will choose the top branch at *A*. So the equilibrium in this game is for Smith to choose the top branch at *A* and Jones to choose the bottom branch at *B*. Smith gets 60, and Jones gets 105. If Jones could make a credible commitment to choose the top branch no matter what, both would do better. Smith would choose the bottom branch at *A* and Jones would choose the top branch at *C*, giving Smith 500 and Jones 400.

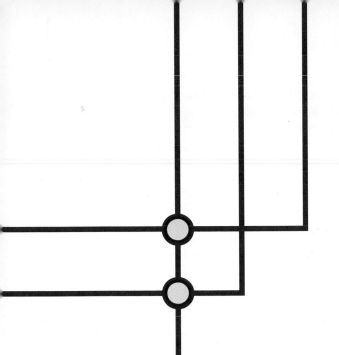

EXTERNALITIES AND PROPERTY RIGHTS

■

A droll television ad for a British brand of pipe tobacco opens with a distinguished looking gentleman sitting quietly on a park bench, smoking his pipe and reading a book of poetry. Before him lies a pond, unrippled except for a mother duck swimming peacefully with her ducklings. Suddenly a raucous group of teenage boys bursts onto the scene with a remote-controlled toy warship. Yelling and chortling, they launch their boat and maneuver it in aggressive pursuit of the terrified ducks.

Interrupted from his reverie, the gentleman looks up from his book and draws calmly on his pipe as he surveys the scene before him. He then reaches into his bag, pulls out a remote control of his own, and begins manipulating the joystick. The scene shifts underwater, where a miniature submarine rises from the depths of the pond. Once the boys' boat is in the sub's sights, the gentleman pushes a button on his remote control. Seconds later, the boat is blown to smithereens by a torpedo. The scene fades to a close-up of the tobacco company's label.

EXTERNAL COSTS AND BENEFITS

Many activities generate costs or benefits that accrue to people not directly involved in those activities. These effects are generally unintended. They are called **external costs** and **benefits**—**externalities,** for short. From the pipe smoker's point of view, the noise generated by the marauding boys was an external cost. And had others been disturbed by the boys' rowdiness, they may well have regarded the pipe smoker's retaliatory gesture as an external benefit.

***external cost (or negative
externality)*** a cost of an
activity that falls on people
other than those who pursue
the activity

***external benefit (or positive
externality)*** a benefit of an
activity received by people other
than those who pursue the
activity

externality an external cost or
benefit of an activity

This chapter focuses on how externalities affect the allocation of resources. Adam Smith's theory of the invisible hand applies to an ideal marketplace in which externalities do not exist. In such situations, Smith argued, the self-interested actions of individuals would lead to socially efficient outcomes. We will see that when the parties affected by externalities can easily negotiate with one another, the invisible hand will still produce an efficient outcome.

But in many cases, such as the scene depicted in the tobacco ad, negotiation is impractical. In those cases, the self-serving actions of individuals simply will not lead to efficient outcomes. Because externalities are widespread, the attempt to forge solutions to the problems they cause is one of the most important rationales, not only for the existence of government but for a variety of other forms of collective action as well.

HOW EXTERNALITIES AFFECT RESOURCE ALLOCATION

The way in which externalities distort the allocation of resources can be seen clearly in the next several examples.

EXAMPLE 11.1

Does the honeybee keeper face the right incentives? (Part 1)

Phoebe earns her living as a keeper of honeybees. Her neighbors on all sides grow apples. Because bees pollinate apple trees as they forage for nectar, the more hives Phoebe keeps, the larger the harvests will be in the surrounding orchards. If Phoebe takes only her own costs and benefits into account in deciding how many hives to keep, will she keep the socially optimal number of hives?

For the orchard owners, Phoebe's hives constitute an external benefit, or a positive externality. If she takes only her own personal costs and benefits into account, she will add hives only until the added revenue she gets from the last hive just equals the cost of adding it. But since the orchard owners also benefit from additional hives, the total benefit of adding another hive at that point will be greater than its cost. Phoebe, then, will keep too few hives.

EXAMPLE 11.2

Does the honeybee keeper face the right incentives? (Part 2)

As in Example 11.1, Phoebe earns her living as a keeper of honeybees. But now her neighbors are not apple growers but an elementary school and a nursing home. The more hives Phoebe keeps, the more students and nursing home residents will be stung by bees. If Phoebe takes only her own costs and benefits into account in deciding how many hives to keep, will she keep the socially optimal number of hives?

For the students and nursing home residents, Phoebe's hives constitute an external cost, or a negative externality. If she considers only her own costs and benefits in deciding how many hives to keep, she will continue to add hives until the added revenue from the last hive is just enough to cover its cost. But since Phoebe's neighbors also incur costs when she adds a hive, the benefit of the last hive at that point will be smaller than its cost. Phoebe, in other words, will keep too many hives.

Every activity involves costs and benefits. When all the relevant costs and benefits of an activity accrue directly to the person who carries it out—that is, when the activity generates no externalities—the level of the activity that is best for the individual will be best for society as a whole. But when an activity generates externalities, be they positive or negative, individual self-interest does not produce the best allocation of resources. Individuals who consider only their own costs and benefits will tend to engage too much in activities that generate negative externalities and too little in activities that generate positive externalities. When an activity generates both positive and negative externalities, private and social interests will coincide only in the unlikely event that the opposing effects offset one another exactly.

THE GRAPHICAL PORTRAYAL OF EXTERNALITIES

The effects of externalities on resource allocation can be portrayed graphically, as in Figure 11.1. In part (a), Private MC (for marginal cost) is the supply curve of a product whose production is accompanied by an external cost of XC per unit. The market equilibrium level of output is Q_{pvt}, the output level at which the demand curve D intersects Private MC. Note that Q_{pvt} is larger than the socially optimal level of output, Q_{soc}, the output level at which the demand curve intersects Social MC. Social MC, the socially optimal supply curve of the product, is the result of adding the external cost XC to every value along Private MC.

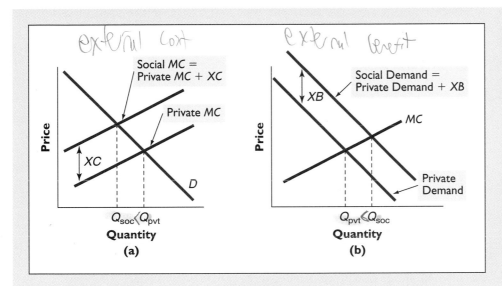

FIGURE 11.1

How External Costs and Benefits Affect Resource Allocation.

The market equilibrium level of output (Q_{pvt}) is larger than the socially optimal level (Q_{soc}) for products accompanied by external costs [part (a)] but smaller than the socially optimal level for products accompanied by external benefits [part (b)].

In Figure 11.1(b), Private Demand is the demand curve for a product whose production generates an external benefit of XB per unit. The market equilibrium quantity of this good, Q_{pvt}, is the output level at which Private Demand intersects the supply curve of the product *(MC)*. This time Q_{pvt} is smaller than the socially optimal level of output, Q_{soc}. Q_{soc} is the output level at which MC intersects the socially optimal demand curve (Social Demand), which is the result of adding the external benefit XB to every value along Private Demand.

Externalities thus distort the allocation of resources in an otherwise efficient market. When externalities are present, the individual pursuit of self-interest will not result in the largest possible economic surplus. And when it does not, the outcome is by definition inefficient.

THE COASE THEOREM

To say that a situation is inefficient means that it can be rearranged in a way that would make at least some people better off without harming others. Such situations, we have seen, are a source of creative tension. The existence of inefficiency, after all, means that there is cash on the table, which usually triggers a race to see who can capture it. For example, we saw that because monopoly pricing results in an inefficiently low output level, the potential for gain gave monopolists an incentive to make discounts available to price-sensitive buyers. As the next examples illustrate, the inefficiencies that result from externalities create similar incentives for remedial action.

EXAMPLE 11.3

Will Abercrombie dump toxins in the river? (Part 1)

Abercrombie's factory produces a toxic waste by-product. If Abercrombie dumps it in the river, he causes damage to Fitch, a fisherman located downstream. The toxins are short-lived and cause no damage to anyone other than Fitch. At a cost, Abercrombie can filter out the toxins, in which case Fitch will suffer no damage at all. The relevant gains and losses for the two individuals are listed in Table 11.1.

TABLE 11.1
Costs and Benefits of Eliminating Toxic Waste (Part 1)

	With filter	Without filter
Gains to Abercrombie	$100/day	$130/day
Gains to Fitch	$100/day	$50/day

If the law does not penalize Abercrombie for dumping toxins in the river, and if Abercrombie and Fitch cannot communicate with one another, will Abercrombie operate with or without a filter? Is that choice socially efficient?

Since Abercrombie earns $30/day more without a filter than with one, his natural incentive is to operate without one. But the outcome when he does so is socially inefficient. Thus, when Abercrombie operates without a filter, the total daily gain to both parties is only $130 + $50 = $180, compared to $100 + $100 = $200 if Abercrombie had operated with a filter. The daily cost of the filter to Abercrombie is only $130 − $100 = $30, which is smaller than its daily benefit to Fitch of $100 − $50 = $50. The fact that Abercrombie does not install the filter implies a squandered daily surplus of $20.

EXAMPLE 11.4

Will Abercrombie dump toxins in the river? (Part 2)

Suppose the costs and benefits of using the filter are as in Example 11.3 except that Abercrombie and Fitch can now communicate with one another at no cost. Even though the law does not require him to do so, will Abercrombie use a filter?

This time, Abercrombie will use a filter. Recall from Chapter 7 the observation that when the economic pie grows larger, everyone can have a larger slice. Because use of a filter would result in the largest possible economic surplus, it would enable both Abercrombie and Fitch to have a larger net gain than before. Fitch thus has an incentive to *pay* Abercrombie to use a filter. For example, suppose Fitch offers Abercrombie $40/day to compensate him for operating with a filter. Both Abercrombie and Fitch will then be exactly $10/day better off than before, for a total daily net gain of $20.

EXERCISE 11.1

In Example 11.4, what is the largest whole-dollar amount by which Fitch could compensate Abercrombie for operating with a filter and still be better off than before?

Ronald Coase, a professor at the University of Chicago Law School, was the first to see clearly that if people can negotiate with one another at no cost over the right to perform activities that cause externalities, they will always arrive at an efficient solution. This insight, which is often called the **Coase theorem,** is a profoundly important idea, for which Coase (rhymes with "dose") was awarded the 1991 Nobel Prize in Economics.

Why, you might ask, should Fitch pay Abercrombie to filter out toxins that would not be there in the first place if not for Abercrombie's factory? The rhetorical force of this question is undeniable. Yet Coase points out that externalities are reciprocal in nature. The toxins do harm Fitch, to be sure, but preventing Abercrombie from emitting them would penalize Abercrombie, by exactly $30/day. Why should Fitch necessarily have the right to harm Abercrombie? Indeed, as Example 11.5 illustrates, even if Fitch had that right, he would exercise it only if filtering the toxins proved the most efficient outcome.

Coase theorem *if at no cost people can negotiate the purchase and sale of the right to perform activities that cause externalities, they can always arrive at efficient solutions to the problems caused by externalities*

Will Abercrombie dump toxins in the river? (Part 3)

EXAMPLE 11.5

Suppose the law says that Abercrombie may *not* dump toxins in the river unless he has Fitch's permission. If the relevant costs and benefits of filtering the toxins are as shown in Table 11.2, and if Abercrombie and Fitch can negotiate with one another at no cost, will Abercrombie filter the toxins?

TABLE 11.2
Costs and Benefits of Eliminating Toxic Waste (Part 3)

	With filter	Without filter
Gains to Abercrombie	$100/day	$150/day
Gains to Fitch	$100/day	$70/day

Note that this time the most efficient outcome is for Abercrombie to operate without a filter, for the total daily surplus in that case will be $220 as compared to only $200 with a filter. Under the law, however, Fitch has the right to insist that Abercrombie use a filter. We might expect him to exercise that right, since his own gain would rise from $70 to $100/day if he did so. But because this outcome would be socially inefficient, we know that each party can do better.

Suppose, for example, that Abercrombie gives Fitch $40/day in return for Fitch's permission to operate without a filter. Each would then have a net daily gain of $110, which is $10 better for each of them than if Fitch had insisted that Abercrombie use a filter. Abercrombie's pollution harms Fitch, sure enough. But failure to allow the pollution would have caused even greater harm to Abercrombie.

These examples drive home the point that when externalities are a source of inefficiency, the affected parties will search for the outcome with the highest total economic surplus. And that is precisely what will happen, provided they can negotiate with one another at no cost.

Externalities are hardly rare and isolated occurrences. On the contrary, finding examples of actions that are altogether free of them is difficult. And because externalities can distort the allocation of resources, recognizing them and dealing intelligently with them are important. Consider the following example of an externality that arises because of shared living arrangements.

Will Ann and Betty share an apartment?

EXAMPLE 11.6

Ann and Betty can live together in a two-bedroom apartment for $600/month, or separately in 2 one-bedroom apartments, each for $400/month. If the rent paid were the same for both alternatives, the two women would be indifferent between living together or separately, except for one problem: Ann talks constantly on the telephone. Ann would pay up to $250/month for this privilege. Betty, for her part, would pay up to $150/month to have better access to the phone. If the two cannot install a second phone line, should they live together or separately?

Ann and Betty should live together only if the benefit of doing so exceeds the cost. The benefit of living together is the reduction in their rent. Since 2 one-bedroom apartments would cost a total of $800/month, compared to $600 for a two-bedroom unit, their benefit from living together is $200/month. Their cost of living together is the least costly accommodation they can make to Ann's objectionable telephone habits. Since Ann would be willing to pay up to $250/month to avoid changing her behavior, the $200 rent saving is too small to persuade her to change. But Betty is willing to put up with Ann's behavior for a compensation payment of only $150/month. Since that amount is smaller than the total saving in rent, the least costly solution to the problem is for Betty to live with Ann and simply put up with her behavior.

 Table 11.3 summarizes the relevant costs and benefits of this shared living arrangement. The cost-benefit principle tells us that Ann and Betty should live together if and only if the benefit of living together exceeds the cost. The cost of the shared living arrangement is not the sum of all possible costs but the least costly accommodation to the problem (or problems) of shared living. Since the $200/month saving in rent exceeds the least costly accommodation to the phone problem, Ann and Betty can reap a total gain in economic surplus of $50/month by sharing their living quarters.

TABLE 11.3
The Gain in Surplus from Shared Living Arrangements

Benefits of Shared Living		
Total cost of separate apartments	**Total cost of shared apartment**	**Rent savings from sharing**
(2)($400/month) = $800/month	$600/month	$200/month

Costs of Shared Living			
Problem	**Ann's cost of solving problem**	**Betty's cost of solving problem**	**Least costly solution to the problem**
Ann's phone usage	Curtailed phone usage: $250/month	Tolerate phone usage: $150/month	Betty tolerates Ann's phone usage: $150/month

Gain in Surplus from Shared Living		
Rent savings ($200/month) −	Least costly accommodation to shared living problems ($150/month) =	Gain in surplus: $50/month

Some people might conclude that Ann and Betty should not live together, because if the two share the rent equally, Betty will end up paying $300/month—which when added to the $150 cost of putting up with Ann's phone behavior comes to $50 more than the cost of living alone. As persuasive as that argument may sound, however, it is mistaken. The source of the error, as Example 11.7 makes clear, is the assumption that the two must share the rent equally.

What is the highest rent Betty would be willing to pay for the two-bedroom apartment?

EXAMPLE 11.7

In Example 11.6, what is the highest rent Betty would be willing to pay to share an apartment with Ann?

Betty's alternative is to live alone, which would mean paying $400/month, her reservation price for a living arrangement with no phone problem. Since the most she would be willing to pay to avoid the phone problem is $150/month, the highest monthly rent she would be willing to pay for the shared apartment is $400 − $150 = $250. If she pays that amount, Ann will have to pay the difference, namely, $350/month, which is clearly a better alternative for Ann than paying $400 to live alone.

How much should Ann and Betty pay if they agree to split their economic surplus equally?

EXAMPLE 11.8

If Ann and Betty agree to live together and split the resulting gain in economic surplus equally, how much rent will each of them pay?

As we saw in Table 11.3, the total rent saving from the shared apartment is $200, and since the least costly solution to the phone problem is $150, the monthly gain in economic surplus is $50. We know that Ann's reservation price for living together is $400/month and Betty's is $250 (see Example 11.7). So if the two women want to split the $50 monthly surplus equally, each should pay $25 less than her reservation price. Ann's monthly rent will thus be $375 and Betty's, $225. The result is that each is $25/month better off than if she had lived alone.

EXERCISE 11.2

As in Example 11.6, Ann and Betty can live together in a two-bedroom apartment for $600/month or separately in 2 one-bedroom apartments, each for $400/month. Ann would pay up to $250/month rather than moderate her telephone habits, and Betty would pay up to $150/month to achieve reasonable access to the telephone. But Betty would also be willing to pay up to $60/month to avoid the loss of privacy that comes with shared living space. Should the two women live together?

LEGAL REMEDIES FOR EXTERNALITIES

We have seen that efficient solutions to externalities can be found whenever the affected parties can negotiate with one another at no cost. But negotiation is not always practical. A motorist with a noisy muffler, for example, imposes costs on others, yet they cannot flag him down and offer him a compensation payment to fix his muffler. In recognition of this difficulty, most governments simply require that cars have working mufflers. Indeed, the explicit or implicit purpose of a large share—perhaps the lion's share—of laws is to solve problems caused by externalities. The goal of such laws is to help people achieve the solutions they might have reached had they been able to negotiate with one another.

When negotiation is costless, the task of adjustment generally falls on the party who can accomplish it at the lowest cost. For instance, in Example 11.6, Betty put up with Ann's annoying phone habits because doing so was less costly than asking Ann to change her habits. Many municipal noise ordinances also place the burden of adjustment on those who can accomplish it at lowest cost. Consider, for example, the restrictions on loud party music, which often take effect at a later hour on weekends than on weekdays. This pattern reflects both the fact that the gains from loud music tend to be larger on weekends and the fact that such music is more likely to disturb people on weekdays. By setting the noise curfew at different hours on different days of the week, the law places the burden on partygoers during the week and on sleepers during the weekend. Similar logic explains why noise ordinances allow motorists to honk their horns in most neighborhoods, but not in the immediate vicinity of a hospital.

As the following examples demonstrate, economic naturalists can hone their craft by focusing on laws whose purpose is to solve the problems caused by externalities.

What is the purpose of speed limits and other traffic laws?

A motorist driving a car at high speed endangers not just her own life and property but also the lives and property of others. Speed limits, no-passing zones, right-of-way rules, and a host of other traffic laws may be seen as reasoned attempts to limit the harm one party inflicts on another. Many jurisdictions even have laws requiring that motorists install snow tires on their cars by November 1. These laws promote not just safety but also the smooth flow of traffic: A single motorist who can't get up a snow-covered hill delays not only herself but also the motorists behind her.

Why do most communities have zoning laws?

Most communities restrict the kinds of activities that take place in various parts of the city. Because many residents place a high value on living in an uncongested neighborhood, some cities have enacted zoning laws specifying minimum lot sizes. In places like Manhattan, where a shortage of land encourages developers to build very large and tall buildings, zoning laws limit both a building's height and the proportion of a lot it may occupy. Such restrictions recognize that the taller a building is, and the greater the proportion of its lot that it occupies, the more it blocks sunlight from reaching surrounding properties. The desire to control external costs also helps to explain why many cities establish separate zones for business and residential activity. Even within business districts, many cities limit certain kinds of commercial activity. For example, in an effort to revitalize the Times Square neighborhood, New York City enacted a zoning law banning adult bookstores and pornographic movie theaters from the area.

Why do many governments enact laws that limit the discharge of environmental pollutants?

Limitations on the discharge of pollutants into the environment are perhaps the clearest examples of laws aimed at solving problems caused by externalities. The details of these laws reflect the cost-benefit principle. The discharge of toxic wastes into rivers, for example, tends to be most strictly regulated on those waterways whose commercial fishing or recreational uses are most highly valued. On other waterways, the burden of adjustment is likely to fall more heavily on fishermen, recreational boaters, and swimmers. Similarly, air quality regulations tend to be strictest in the most heavily populated regions of the country, where the marginal benefit of pollution reduction is the greatest.

What is the purpose of free speech laws?

The First Amendment's protection of free speech and the pattern of exceptions to that protection are another illustration of how legal remedies are used to solve the problems caused by externalities. The First Amendment acknowledges the decisive value of open communication, as well as the practical difficulty of identifying and regulating acts of speech that cause more harm than good. Yet it does allow some important exceptions. For instance, it does not allow someone to yell "fire" in a crowded theater if there is no fire, nor does it allow someone to advocate the violent overthrow of the government. In those instances, the external benefits of free speech are far too small to justify the external costs.

Why does government subsidize activities that generate positive externalities?

The laws discussed in the preceding examples are meant to regulate activities that generate negative externalities. But government also uses the law to encourage activities that generate positive externalities. The planting of trees on hillsides, for example, benefits not just the landowner but also his neighbors by limiting the danger of flooding. In recognition of this fact, many jurisdictions subsidize the planting of trees. Similarly, Congress budgets millions of dollars each year in support of basic research, an implicit acknowledgment of the positive externalities associated with the generation of new knowledge.

ECONOMIC NATURALIST 11.5

THE OPTIMAL AMOUNT OF NEGATIVE EXTERNALITIES IS NOT ZERO

Curbing pollution and other negative externalities entails both costs and benefits. As we saw in Chapter 6, the best policy is to curtail pollution until the cost of further abatement just equals the marginal benefit. In general, the marginal cost of abatement rises with the amount of pollution eliminated. (Following the low-hanging-fruit principle, polluters use the cheapest cleanup methods first and then turn to more expensive ones.) And the law of diminishing marginal utility suggests that beyond some point, the marginal benefit of pollution reduction tends to fall as more pollution is removed. As a result, the marginal cost and marginal benefit curves almost always intersect at less than the maximum amount of pollution reduction.

The intersection of the two curves marks instead the socially optimal level of pollution reduction. If pollution is curtailed by any less than that amount, society will gain more than it will lose by pushing the cleanup effort a little further. But if regulators push beyond the point at which the marginal cost and benefit curves intersect, society will incur costs that exceed the benefits. The existence of a socially optimal level of pollution reduction implies the existence of a socially optimal level of pollution, and that level will almost always be greater than zero.

As we saw in Chapter 6, because people have been conditioned to think of pollution as bad, many cringe when they hear the phrase "socially optimal level of pollution." How can any positive level of pollution be socially optimal? But to speak of a socially optimal level of pollution is not the same as saying that pollution is good. It is merely to recognize that society has an interest in cleaning up the environment, but only up to a certain point. The underlying idea is no different from the idea of an optimal level of dirt in an apartment. After all, even if you spent the whole day, every day, vacuuming your apartment, there would be *some* dirt left in it. And because you have better things to do than vacuum all day, you probably tolerate substantially more than the minimal amount of dirt. A dirty apartment is not good, nor is pollution in the air you breathe. But in both cases, the cleanup effort should be expanded only until the marginal benefit equals the marginal cost.

RECAP **EXTERNAL COSTS AND BENEFITS**

Externalities occur when the costs or benefits of an activity accrue to people other than those directly involved in the activity. The Coase theorem says that when affected parties can negotiate with one another without cost, activities will be pursued at efficient levels, even in the presence of positive or negative externalities. But when negotiation is prohibitively costly, inefficient behavior generally results. Activities that generate negative externalities are pursued to excess, while those that generate positive externalities are pursued too little. Laws and regulations are often adopted in an effort to alter inefficient behavior that results from externalities.

PROPERTY RIGHTS AND THE TRAGEDY OF THE COMMONS

People who grow up in the industrialized nations tend to take the institution of private property for granted. Our intuitive sense is that people have the right to own any property they acquire by lawful means and to do with that property much as they see fit. In reality, however, property laws are considerably more complex in terms of the rights they confer and the obligations they impose.

THE PROBLEM OF UNPRICED RESOURCES

To understand the laws that govern the use of property, we must begin by asking why societies created the institution of private property in the first place. The following examples, which show what happens to property that nobody owns, suggest an answer.

EXAMPLE 11.9

How many steers will villagers send onto the commons?

A village has five residents, each of whom has accumulated savings of $100. Each villager can use the money to buy a government bond that pays 13 percent interest per year or to buy a year-old steer, send it onto the commons to graze, and sell it after 1 year. The price the villager will get for the 2-year-old steer depends on the amount of weight it gains while grazing on the commons, which in turn depends on the number of steers sent onto the commons, as shown in Table 11.4.

The price of a 2-year-old steer declines with the number of steers grazing on the commons, because the more steers, the less grass available to each. The villagers make their investment decisions one at a time, and the results are public. If each villager decides how to invest individually, how many steers will be sent onto the commons, and what will be the village's total income?

TABLE 11.4
The Relationship between Herd Size and Steer Price

Number of steers on the commons	Price per 2-year-old steer ($)	Income per steer ($/year)
1	126	26
2	119	19
3	116	16
4	113	13
5	111	11

If a villager buys a $100 government bond, he will earn $13 of interest income at the end of 1 year. Thus he should send a steer onto the commons if and only if that steer will command a price of at least $113 as a 2-year-old. When each villager chooses in this self-interested way, we can expect four villagers to send a steer onto the commons. (Actually, the fourth villager would be indifferent between investing in a steer or buying a bond, since he would earn $13 either way. For the sake of discussion, we'll assume that in the case of a tie, people choose to be cattlemen.) The fifth villager, seeing that he would earn only $11 by sending a fifth steer onto the commons, will choose instead to buy a government bond. As a result of these decisions, the total village income will be $65/year—$13 for the one bondholder and 4($13) = $52 for the four cattlemen.

Has Adam Smith's invisible hand produced the most efficient allocation of these villagers' resources? We can tell at a glance that it has not, since their total village income is only $65—precisely the same as it would have been had the possibility of cattle raising not existed. The source of the difficulty will become evident in Example 11.10.

What is the socially optimal number of steers to send onto the commons?

Suppose the five villagers in Example 11.9 confront the same investment opportunities as before, except that this time they are free to make their decisions as a group rather than individually. How many steers will they send onto the commons, and what will be their total village income?

This time the villagers' goal is to maximize the income received by the group as a whole. When decisions are made from this perspective, the criterion is to send a steer onto the commons only if its marginal contribution to village income is at least $13, the amount that could be earned from a government bond. As the entries in the last column of Table 11.5 indicate, the first steer clearly meets this criterion, since it contributes $26 to total village income. But the second steer does not. Sending that steer onto the commons raises the village's income from cattle raising from $26 to $38, a gain of just $12. The $100 required to buy the second steer would thus have been better invested in a government bond. Worse, the collective return from sending a third steer is only $10; from a fourth, only $4; and from a fifth, only $3.

EXAMPLE 11.10

TABLE 11.5
Marginal Income and the Socially Optimal Herd Size

Number of steers on the commons	Price per 2-year-old steer ($)	Income per steer ($/year)	Total village income ($/year)	Marginal income ($/year)
				26
1	126	26	26	
				12
2	119	19	38	
				10
3	116	16	48	
				4
4	113	13	52	
				3
5	111	11	55	

In sum, when investment decisions are made with the goal of maximizing total village income, the best choice is to buy four government bonds and send only a single steer onto the commons. The resulting village income will be $78: $26 from sending the single steer and $52 from the four government bonds. That amount is $13 more than the total income that resulted when villagers made their investment decisions individually. Once again, the reward from moving from an inefficient allocation to an efficient one is that the economic pie grows larger. And when the pie grows larger, everyone can get a larger slice. For instance, if the villagers agree to pool their income and share it equally, each will get $15.60, or $2.60 more than before.

EXERCISE 11.3

How would your answers to Examples 11.9 and 11.10 differ if the interest rate were not 13 percent but 11 percent/year?

Why do the villagers in Examples 11.9 and 11.10 do better when they make their investment decisions collectively? The answer is that when individuals decide alone, they ignore the fact that sending another steer onto the commons will cause existing steers to gain less weight. Their failure to consider this effect makes the return from sending another steer seem misleadingly high to them.

The grazing land on the commons is a valuable economic resource. When no one owns it, no one has any incentive to take the opportunity cost of using it into account. And when that happens, people will tend to use it until its marginal benefit is zero. This problem, and others similar to it, are known as the **tragedy of the commons**. The essential cause of the tragedy of the commons is the fact that one person's use of commonly held property imposes an external cost on others by making the property less valuable. The tragedy of the commons also provides a vivid illustration of the equilibrium principle (see Chapter 4). Each individual villager behaves rationally by sending an additional steer onto the commons, yet the overall outcome falls far short of the attainable ideal.

tragedy of the commons the tendency for a resource that has no price to be used until its marginal benefit falls to zero

THE EFFECT OF PRIVATE OWNERSHIP

As Example 11.11 illustrates, one solution to the tragedy of the commons is to place the village grazing land under private ownership.

EXAMPLE 11.11

How much will the right to control the village commons sell for?

Suppose the five villagers face the same investment opportunities as before, except that this time they decide to auction off the right to use the commons to the highest bidder. Assuming that villagers can borrow as well as lend at an annual interest rate of 13 percent, what price will the right to use the commons fetch? How will the owner of that property right use it, and what will be the resulting village income?

To answer these questions, simply ask yourself what you would do if you had complete control over how the grazing land were used. As we saw in Example 11.10, the most profitable way to use this land is to send only a single steer to graze on it. If you do so, you will earn a total of $26/year. Since the opportunity cost of the $100 you spent on the single yearling steer is the $13 in interest you could have earned from a bond, your economic profit from sending a single steer onto the commons will be $13 per year, provided you can use the land for free. But you cannot; to finance your purchase of the property right, you must borrow money (since you used your $100 savings to buy a year-old steer).

What is the most you should pay for the right to use the commons? Since its use generates an income of $26/year, or $13 more than the opportunity cost of your investment in the steer, the most you should pay is $100 (because that amount used to purchase a bond that pays 13 percent interest would also generate income of $13/year). If the land were sold at auction, $100 is precisely the amount you would have to pay. Your annual earnings from the land would be exactly enough to pay the $13 interest on your loan and cover the opportunity cost of not having put your savings into a bond.

Note that when the right to use the land is auctioned to the highest bidder, the village achieves a more efficient allocation of its resources, because the owner has a strong incentive to take the opportunity cost of more intensive grazing fully into account. Total village income in this case will again be $78. If the annual interest on the $100 proceeds from selling the land rights is shared equally among the five villagers, each will again have an annual investment income of $15.60.

The logic of economic surplus maximization helps to explain why the most economically successful nations have all been ones with well-developed private property laws. Property that belongs to everyone belongs, in effect, to no one. Not only is its potential economic value never fully realized, it usually ends up being of no value at all.

Bear in mind, however, that in most countries the owners of private property are not free to do *precisely* as they wish with it. For example, local zoning laws may give the owner of a residential building lot the right to build a three-story house but not a six-story house. Here, too, the logic of economic surplus maximization applies, for a fully informed and rational legislature would define property rights so as to create the largest possible total economic surplus. In practice, of course, such ideal legislatures never really exist. Yet the essence of politics is the cutting of deals that make people better off. If a legislator could propose a change in the property laws that would enlarge the total economic surplus, she could also propose a scheme that would give each of her constituents a larger slice, thus enhancing her chances for reelection.

As an economic naturalist, challenge yourself to use this framework when thinking about the various restrictions you encounter in private property laws: zoning laws that constrain what you can build and what types of activities you can conduct on your land; traffic laws that constrain what you can do with your car; employment and environmental laws that constrain how you can operate your business. Your understanding of these and countless other laws will be enhanced by the insight that everyone can gain when the private property laws are defined so as to create the largest total economic surplus.

WHEN PRIVATE OWNERSHIP IS IMPRACTICAL

Do not be misled into thinking that the law provides an *ideal* resolution of all problems associated with externalities and the tragedy of the commons. Defining and enforcing efficient property rights entails costs, after all, and sometimes, as in the following examples, the costs outweigh the gains.

Why are shared milkshakes drunk too quickly?

Why do blackberries in public parks get picked too soon?

Wild blackberries grow profusely at the edge of a wooded area in a crowded city park. The blackberries will taste best if left to ripen fully, but they still taste reasonably good if picked and eaten a few days early. Will the blackberries be left to ripen fully?

Obviously, the costs of defining and enforcing the property rights to blackberries growing in a public park are larger than the potential gains, so the blackberries will remain common property. That means that whoever picks them first gets them. Even though everyone would benefit if people waited until the berries were fully ripe, everyone knows that those who wait are likely to end up with no berries at all. And that means that the berries will be eaten too soon.

ECONOMIC NATURALIST 11.6

Why are shared milkshakes consumed too quickly?

Sam and Stan are identical twins who have been given a chocolate milkshake to share. If each has a straw and each knows that the other is self-interested, will the twins consume the milkshake at an optimal rate?

Because drinking a milkshake too quickly chills the taste buds, the twins will enjoy their shake more if they drink it slowly. Yet each knows that the other will drink any part of the milkshake he doesn't finish himself. The result is that each will consume the shake at a faster rate than he would if he had half a shake all to himself.

ECONOMIC NATURALIST 11.7

Here are some further examples of the type of tragedy of the commons that is not easily solved by defining private ownership rights.

Harvesting timber on remote public land   On remote public lands, enforcing restrictions against cutting down trees may be impractical. Each tree cutter knows that a tree that is not harvested this year will be bigger, and hence more valuable, next year. But he also knows that if he doesn't cut the tree down this year, someone else will. In contrast, private companies that grow trees on their own land have no incentive to harvest timber prematurely and a strong incentive to prevent outsiders from doing so.

Harvesting whales in international waters Each individual whaler knows that harvesting an extra whale reduces the breeding population, and hence the size of the future whale population. But the whaler also knows that any whale that is not harvested today will be taken by some other whaler. The solution would be to define and enforce property rights to whales. But the oceans are vast, and the behavior of whalers is hard to monitor. And even if their behavior could be monitored, the concept of national sovereignty would make the international enforcement of property rights problematic.

Controlling multinational environmental pollution Each individual polluter may know that if he and all others pollute, the damage to the environment will be greater than the cost of not polluting. But if the environment is common property into which all are free to dump, each has a powerful incentive to pollute. If all polluters live under the jurisdiction of a single government, enforcing laws and regulations that limit the discharge of pollution may be practical. But if polluters come from many different countries, solutions are much more difficult to implement. Thus the Mediterranean Sea has long suffered serious pollution, because none of the many nations that border it has an economic incentive to consider the effects of its discharges on other countries.

As the world's population continues to grow, the absence of an effective system of international property rights will become an economic problem of increasing significance.

RECAP **PROPERTY RIGHTS AND THE TRAGEDY OF THE COMMONS**

When a valuable resource has a price of zero, people will continue to exploit it as long as its marginal benefit remains positive. The tragedy of the commons describes situations in which valuable resources are squandered because users are not charged for them. In many cases, an efficient remedy for such waste is to define and enforce rights to the use of valuable property. But this solution is difficult to implement for resources such as the oceans and the atmosphere, because no single government has the authority to enforce property rights for these resources.

POSITIONAL EXTERNALITIES

Steffi Graf received more than $1.6 million in tournament winnings in 1992; her endorsement and exhibition earnings totaled several times that amount. By any reasonable measure, the quality of her play was outstanding, yet she consistently lost to archrival Monica Seles. But in April of 1993, Seles was stabbed in the back by a deranged fan and forced to withdraw from the tour. In the ensuing months, Graf's tournament winnings accumulated at almost double her 1992 pace, despite little change in the quality of her play.

PAYOFFS THAT DEPEND ON RELATIVE PERFORMANCE

In professional tennis and a host of other competitive situations, the rewards people receive typically depend not only on how they perform in absolute terms but also on how they perform relative to their closest rivals. In these situations, competitors have an incentive to take actions that will increase their odds of winning. For example, tennis players can increase their chances of winning by hiring personal fitness trainers and sports psychologists to travel with them on the tour. Yet the simple mathematics of competition tells us that the sum of all individual payoffs from such investments will be larger than the collective payoff. In any tennis match, for example, each contestant will get a sizable payoff from money spent on fitness trainers and sports psychologists, yet each match will have exactly one winner and one loser, no matter how much players spend. The overall gain to tennis spectators is likely to be small, and the overall gain to players as a group must be zero. To the extent that each contestant's payoff depends on his or her relative performance, then, the incentive to undertake such investments will be excessive, from a collective point of view.

Consider the following example.

Why do football players take anabolic steroids?

The offensive linemen of many National Football League teams currently average more than 330 pounds. In the 1970s, by contrast, offensive linemen in the league averaged barely 280 pounds, and the all-decade linemen of the 1940s averaged only 229 pounds. One reason that today's players are so much heavier is that players' salaries have escalated sharply over the last two decades, which has intensified competition for the positions. Size and strength are the two cardinal virtues of an offensive lineman, and other things being equal, the job will go to the larger and stronger of two rivals.

Size and strength, in turn, can be enhanced by the consumption of anabolic steroids. But if all players consume these substances, the rank ordering of players by size and strength—and hence the question of who lands the jobs—will be largely unaffected. And since the consumption of anabolic steroids entails potentially serious long-term health consequences, as a group football players are clearly worse off if they consume these drugs. So why do football players take steroids?

The problem here is that contestants for starting berths on the offensive line confront a prisoner's dilemma, like the ones analyzed in Chapter 10. Consider two closely matched rivals—Smith and Jones—who are competing for a single position. If neither takes steroids, each has a 50 percent of winning the job and a starting salary of $1 million/year. If both take steroids, each again has a 50 percent chance of winning the job. But if one takes steroids and the other doesn't, the first is sure to win the job. The loser ends up selling insurance for $30,000/year. Neither likes the fact that the drugs may have adverse health consequences, but each would be willing to take that risk in return for a shot at the big salary. Given these choices, the two competitors face a payoff matrix like the one shown in Table 11.6.

ECONOMIC NATURALIST 11.8

TABLE 11.6
Payoff Matrix for Steroid Consumption

		Jones	
		Don't take steroids	Take steroids
Smith	Don't take steroids	Second best for each	Best for Jones / Worst for Smith
	Take steroids	Best for Smith / Worst for Jones	Third best for each

Clearly, the dominant strategy for both Smith and Jones is to take steroids. Yet when they so, each gets the only the third-best outcome, whereas they could have gotten the second-best outcome by not taking the drugs. Hence the attraction of rules that forbid the consumption of anabolic steroids.

POSITIONAL ARMS RACES

positional externality occurs when an increase in one person's performance reduces the expected reward of another's in situations in which reward depends on relative performance

The steroid problem is an example of a **positional externality**. Whenever the payoffs to one contestant depend at least in part on how he or she performs relative to a rival, any step that improves one side's relative position must necessarily worsen the other's. The standing-at-concerts example discussed in Chapter 10 (Economic Naturalist 10.3) is another instance of a positional externality. Just as the invisible hand of the market is weakened by the presence of standard externalities, it is also weakened by positional externalities.

"I don't know why McGillicuddy is so pleased with himself. We're all wee, darlin' men here."

Here is another example of a positional externality.

Why do many grocery stores stay open all night, even in small towns?

ECONOMIC NATURALIST 11.9

Ithaca, New York, has seven large supermarkets, five of which are open 24 hours a day. The convenience of all-night shopping could be maintained at lower cost if all but one of the stores were to close during late-night hours. Why do many remain open?

Most people do the bulk of their shopping at a single store. If other relevant factors—price, location, merchandise quality, and so on—are essentially the same, people will choose the store with the most convenient hours. Suppose the two leading stores, Tops and Wegmans, currently close at midnight and are considering whether to stay open until 1 A.M. If one does so and the other doesn't, the store that is open longer will capture the lion's share of all business, not just from midnight to 1 A.M. but during other hours as well, because most people will do most of their shopping at the store with the most attractive offering. But suppose the benefit the public receives when each store stays open an extra hour—as measured by the higher prices people will pay— is smaller than the cost to both stores of staying open the extra hour. Each store will then face a payoff matrix like the one shown in Table 11.7.

TABLE 11.7
Payoff Matrix for Extended Shopping Hours

		Wegmans	
		Close at midnight	Close at 1:00 A.M.
Tops	Close at midnight	Second best for each	Best for Wegmans / Worst for Tops
	Close at 1:00 A.M.	Best for Tops / Worst for Wegmans	Third best for each

In this situation, the dominant strategy for each store is to remain open an extra hour, even though each would be better off if both closed at midnight. And of course, the rivalry does not stop there, for if both stay open until 1 A.M., each will see an opportunity to better its rival by staying open until 2. As long as the cost of staying open another hour is small relative to the gains received, all stores will stay open 24 hours a day. But though consumers do gain when stores remain open longer, beyond some point, the benefit to consumers is small relative to the costs borne by merchants. The problem is that for any individual merchant who fails to match a rival's hours, the costs will be even larger.

In such situations, the public might be well served by an amendment to the antitrust laws that permits stores to cooperate to limit their hours, perhaps through an agreement calling for each store to serve in rotation as the only all-night grocery. Local statutes that limit business hours might serve the same purpose. Such statutes, often called *blue laws,* remain on the books in many jurisdictions.

We have seen that positional externalities often lead contestants to engage in an escalating series of mutually offsetting investments in performance enhancement. We call such spending patterns **positional arms races.**

POSITIONAL ARMS CONTROL AGREEMENTS

Because positional arms races produce inefficient outcomes, people have an incentive to curtail them. Steps taken to reduce positional arms races, such as blue laws and rules against anabolic steroids, may therefore be thought of as **positional arms control agreements.**

Once you become aware of positional arms races, you will begin to see examples of them almost everywhere. You can hone your skills as an economic naturalist by asking these questions about every competitive situation you observe: What form do the investments in performance enhancement take? What steps have contestants taken to limit these investments? Sometimes positional arms control agreements are achieved by the imposition of formal rules, or by the signing of legal contracts. Some examples of this type of agreement follow.

Campaign spending limits In the United States, presidential candidates routinely spend more than $100 million on advertising. Yet if both candidates double their spending on ads, each one's odds of winning will remain essentially the

positional arms race a series of mutually offsetting investments in performance enhancement that is stimulated by a positional externality

positional arms control agreement an agreement in which contestants attempt to limit mutually offsetting investments in performance enhancement same. Recognition of this pattern led Congress to adopt strict spending limits for presidential candidates. (That those regulations have proved difficult to enforce does not call into question the logic behind the legislation.)

Roster limits Major League Baseball permits franchises to have only 25 players on the roster during the regular season. The National Football League sets its roster limit at 49; the National Basketball Association at 12. Why these limits? In their absence, any team could increase its chance of winning by simply adding players. Inevitably, other teams would follow suit. On the plausible assumption that, beyond some point, larger rosters do not add much to the entertainment value for fans, roster limits are a sensible way to deliver sports entertainment at a more reasonable cost.

Arbitration agreements In the business world, contracting parties often sign a binding agreement that commits them to arbitration in the event of a dispute. By doing so, they sacrifice the option of pursuing their interests as fully as they might wish to later, but they also insulate themselves from costly legal battles. Other parties in the legal system may sometimes take steps to limit spending on litigation. For example, a federal judge in South Dakota recently announced—presumably to the approval of litigants—that he would read only the first 15 pages of any brief submitted to his court.

Mandatory starting dates for kindergarten A child who is a year or so older than most of her kindergarten classmates is likely to perform better, in relative terms, than if she had entered school with children her own age. And since most parents are aware that admission to prestigious universities and eligibility for top jobs upon graduation depend largely on *relative* academic performance, many are tempted to keep their children out of kindergarten a year longer than necessary. Yet there is no social advantage in holding *all* children back an extra year, since their relative performance would essentially be unaffected. In most jurisdictions, therefore, the law requires children who reach their fifth birthday before December 1 of a given year to start kindergarten the same year.

SOCIAL NORMS AS POSITIONAL ARMS CONTROL AGREEMENTS

In some cases, social norms may take the place of formal agreements to curtail positional arms races. Some familiar examples follow.

Nerd norms Some students care more—in the short run, at least—about the grades they get than how much they actually learn. When such students are graded on the curve—that is, on the basis of their performance relative to other students—a positional arms race ensues, because if all students were to double the amount of time they studied, the distribution of grades would remain essentially the same. Students who find themselves in this situation are often quick to embrace "nerd norms," which brand as social misfits those who "study too hard."

Fashion norms Social norms regarding dress and fashion often change quickly because of positional competitions. Consider, for instance, the person who wishes to be on the cutting edge of fashion. In some American social circles during the 1950s, that goal could be accomplished by having pierced ears. But as more and more people adopted the practice, it ceased to communicate avant-garde status. At the same time, those who wanted to make a conservative fashion statement gradually became freer to have their ears pierced.

For a period during the 1960s and 1970s, one could be on fashion's cutting edge by wearing two earrings in one earlobe. But by the 1990s multiple ear piercings had lost much of their social significance, the threshold of cutting-edge status having been raised to upward of a dozen piercings of each ear, or a smaller number of piercings of the nose, eyebrows, or other body parts. A similar escalation has taken place in the number, size, and placement of tattoos.

The increase in the required number of tattoos or body piercings has not changed the value of avant-garde fashion status to those who desire it. Being on the outer limits of fashion has much the same meaning now as it once did. So to the extent that there are costs associated with body piercings, tattoos, and other steps required to achieve avant-garde status, the current fashions are wasteful compared to earlier ones. In this sense, the erosion of social norms against tattoos and body piercings has produced a social loss. Of course, the costs associated with this loss are small in most cases. Yet since each body piercing entails a small risk of infection, the costs will continue to rise with the number of piercings. And once those costs reach a certain threshold, support may mobilize on behalf of social norms that discourage body mutilation.

Norms of taste Similar cycles occur with respect to behaviors considered to be in bad taste. In the 1950s, for example, prevailing norms prevented major national magazines from accepting ads that featured nude photographs. Naturally, advertisers had a powerful incentive to chip away at such norms in an effort to capture the reader's limited attention. And indeed, taboos against nude photographs have eroded in the same way as taboos against body mutilation.

Consider, for instance, the evolution of perfume ads. First came the nude silhouette; then, increasingly well-lighted and detailed nude photographs; and more recently, photographs of what appear to be group sex acts. Each innovation achieved just the desired effect: capturing the reader's instant and rapt attention. Inevitably, however, other advertisers followed suit, causing a shift in our sense of what is considered attention-grabbing. Photographs that once would have shocked readers now often draw little more than a bored glance.

Is being on fashion's cutting edge more valuable now than in the 1950s?

"We're looking for the kind of bad taste that will grab—but not appall."

Opinions differ, of course, about whether this change is an improvement. Many believe that the earlier, stricter norms were ill-advised, the legacy of a more prudish and repressive era. Yet even people who take that view are likely to believe that *some* kinds of photographic material ought not to be used in magazine advertisements. Obviously, what is acceptable will differ from person to person, and each person's threshold of discomfort will depend in part on current standards. But as advertisers continue to break new ground in their struggle to capture attention, the point may come when people begin to mobilize in favor of stricter standards of "public decency." Such a campaign would provide yet another example of a positional arms control agreement.

Norms against vanity Cosmetic and reconstructive surgery has produced dramatic benefits for many people, enabling badly disfigured accident victims to recover a normal appearance. It has also eliminated the extreme self-consciousness felt by people born with strikingly unusual features. Such surgery, however, is by no means confined to the conspicuously disfigured. Increasingly, "normal" people are seeking surgical improvements to their appearance. Some 2 million cosmetic "procedures" were done in 1991—six times the number just a decade earlier[1]—and demand has continued to grow steadily in the years since. Once a carefully guarded secret, these procedures are now offered as prizes in southern California charity raffles. And morticians have begun to complain that the noncombustible silicon implants used in breast and buttocks augmentation are clogging their crematoria.

In individual cases, cosmetic surgery may be just as beneficial as reconstructive surgery is for accident victims. Buoyed by the confidence of having a straight nose or a wrinkle-free complexion, patients sometimes go on to achieve much more than they ever thought possible. But the growing use of cosmetic surgery has also had an unintended side effect: It has altered the standards of normal appearance. A nose that once would have seemed only slightly larger than average may now seem jarringly big. The same person who once would have looked like an average 55-year-old may now look nearly 70. And someone who once would have tolerated slightly thinning hair or an average amount of cellulite may now feel compelled to undergo hair transplantation or liposuction. Because such procedures shift people's frame of reference, their payoffs to individuals are misleadingly large. From a social perspective, therefore, reliance on them is likely to be excessive.

Legal sanctions against cosmetic surgery are difficult to imagine. But some communities have embraced powerful social norms against cosmetic surgery, heaping scorn and ridicule on the consumers of face-lifts and tummy tucks. In individual cases, such norms may seem cruel. Yet without them, many more people might feel compelled to bear the risk and expense of cosmetic surgery.

■ SUMMARY ■

- Externalities are the costs and benefits of activities that accrue to people who are not directly involved in those activities. When all parties affected by externalities can negotiate with one another at no cost, the invisible hand of the market will produce an efficient allocation of resources. According to the Coase theorem, the allocation of resources is efficient in such cases because the parties affected by externalities can compensate others for taking remedial action.

- Negotiation over externalities is often impractical, however. In these cases, the self-serving actions of individuals typically will not lead to an efficient outcome. The attempt to forge solutions to the problems caused by externalities is one of the most important rationales for collective action. Sometimes collective action takes the form of laws and government regulations that alter the incentives facing those who generate, or are affected by, externalities. Such remedies work best when they place the burden of accommodation on the

[1]*The Economist*, January 11, 1992, p. 25.

parties who can accomplish it at the lowest cost. Traffic laws, zoning laws, environmental protection laws, and free speech laws are examples.

- Curbing pollution and other negative externalities entails costs as well as benefits. The optimal amount of pollution reduction is the amount for which the marginal benefit of further reduction just equals the marginal cost. In general, this formula implies that the socially optimal level of pollution, or of any other negative externality, is greater than zero.

- When grazing land and other valuable resources are owned in common, no one has an incentive to take the opportunity cost of using those resources into account. This problem is known as the tragedy of the commons. Defining and enforcing of private rights governing the use of valuable resources is often an effective solution to the tragedy of the commons. Not surprisingly, most economically successful nations have well-developed institutions of private property. Property that belongs to everyone belongs, in effect, to no one. Not only is its potential economic value never fully realized; it usually ends up having no value at all.

- The difficulty of enforcing property rights in certain situations explains a variety of inefficient outcomes, such as the excessive harvest of whales in international waters and the premature harvest of timber on remote public lands. The excessive pollution of seas that are bordered by many countries also results from a lack of enforceable property rights.

- Situations in which people's rewards depend on how well they perform in relation to their rivals give rise to positional externalities. In these situations, any step that improves one side's relative position necessarily worsens the other's. Positional externalities tend to spawn positional arms races—escalating patterns of mutually offsetting investments in performance enhancement. Collective measures to curb positional arms races are known as positional arms control agreements. These collective actions may take the form of formal regulations or rules, such as rules against anabolic steroids in sports, campaign spending limits, and binding arbitration agreements. Informal social norms can also curtail positional arms races.

■ KEY TERMS ■

Coase theorem (277)
external benefit (273)
external cost (273)
externality (273)

negative externality (274)
positional arms control agreement (289)
positional arms race (289)

positional externality (288)
positive externality (274)
tragedy of the commons (284)

■ REVIEW QUESTIONS ■

1. What incentive problem explains why the freeways in cities like Los Angeles suffer from excessive congestion?

2. How would you explain to a friend why the optimal amount of freeway congestion is not zero?

3. If Congress could declare any activity that imposes external costs on others illegal, would such legislation be advisable?

4. Why does the Great Salt Lake, which is located wholly within the state of Utah, suffer lower levels of pollution than Lake Erie, which is bordered by several states and Canada?

5. Explain why the wearing of high-heeled shoes might be viewed as the result of a positional externality.

■ PROBLEMS ■

1. Determine whether the following statements are true or false, and briefly explain why:
   a. A given total emission reduction in a polluting industry will be achieved at the lowest possible total cost when the cost of the last unit of pollution curbed is equal for each firm in the industry.
   b. In an attempt to lower their costs of production, firms sometimes succeed merely in shifting costs to outsiders.

2. Phoebe keeps a bee farm next door to an apple orchard. She chooses her optimal number of beehives by selecting the honey output level at which her private marginal benefit from beekeeping equals her private marginal cost.
   a. Assume that Phoebe's private marginal benefit and marginal cost curves from beekeeping are normally shaped. Draw a diagram of them.

    b. Phoebe's bees help to pollinate the blossoms in the apple orchard, increasing the fruit yield. Show the social marginal benefit from Phoebe's beekeeping in your diagram.

    c. Phoebe's bees are Africanized killer bees that aggressively sting anyone who steps into their flight path. Phoebe, fortunately, is naturally immune to the bees' venom. Show the social marginal cost curve from Phoebe's beekeeping in your diagram.

    d. Indicate the socially optimal quantity of beehives on your diagram. Is it higher or lower than the privately optimal quantity? Explain.

3. Suppose the supply curve of boom box rentals in Golden Gate Park is given by $P = 5 + 0.1Q$, where P is the daily rent per unit in dollars and Q is the volume of units rented in hundreds per day. The demand curve for boom boxes is $20 - 0.2Q$. If each boom box imposes \$3/day in noise costs on others, by how much will the equilibrium number of boom boxes rented exceed the socially optimal number?

4. Refer to Problem 3. How would the imposition of a tax of \$3/unit on each daily boom box rental affect efficiency in this market?

5. Suppose the law says that Jones may *not* emit smoke from his factory unless he gets permission from Smith, who lives downwind. If the relevant costs and benefits of filtering the smoke from Jones's production process are as shown in the following table, and if Jones and Smith can negotiate with one another at no cost, will Jones emit smoke?

	Jones emits smoke	Jones does not emit smoke
Surplus for Jones	\$200	\$160
Surplus for Smith	400	420

6. John and Karl can live together in a two-bedroom apartment for \$500/month, or each can rent a single-bedroom apartment for \$350/month. Aside from the rent, the two would be indifferent between living together and living separately, except for one problem: John leaves dirty dishes in the sink every night. Karl would be willing to pay up to \$175/month to avoid John's dirty dishes. John, for his part, would be willing to pay up to \$225 to be able to continue his sloppiness. Should John and Karl live together? If they do, will there be dirty dishes in the sink? Explain.

7. How, if at all, would your answer to Problem 6 differ if John would be willing to pay up to \$30/month to avoid giving up his privacy by sharing quarters with Karl?

8. Barton and Statler are neighbors in an apartment complex in downtown Manhattan. Barton is a concert pianist, and Statler is a poet working on an epic poem. Barton rehearses his concert pieces on the baby grand piano in his front room, which is directly above Statler's study. The following matrix shows the monthly payoffs to Barton and Statler when Barton's front room is and is not soundproofed. The soundproofing will be effective only if it is installed in Barton's apartment.

	Soundproofed	Not soundproofed
Gains to Barton	\$100/month	\$150/month
Gains to Statler	\$120/month	\$ 80/month

    a. If Barton has the legal right to make any amount of noise he wants and he and Statler can negotiate with one another at no cost, will Barton install and maintain soundproofing? Explain. Is his choice socially efficient?

b. If Statler has the legal right to peace and quiet and can negotiate with Barton at no cost, will Barton install and maintain soundproofing? Explain. Is his choice socially efficient?

c. Does the attainment of an efficient outcome depend on whether Barton has the legal right to make noise, or Statler the legal right to peace and quiet?

9. Refer to Problem 8. Barton decides to buy a full-sized grand piano. The new payoff matrix is as follows:

	Soundproofed	Not soundproofed
Gains to Barton	$100/month	$150/month
Gains to Statler	$120/month	$ 60/month

a. If Statler has the legal right to peace and quiet and Barton and Statler can negotiate at no cost, will Barton install and maintain soundproofing? Explain. Is this outcome socially efficient?

b. Suppose that Barton has the legal right to make as much noise as he likes and that negotiating an agreement with Barton costs $15/month. Will Barton install and maintain soundproofing? Explain. Is this outcome socially efficient?

c. Suppose Statler has the legal right to peace and quiet, and it costs $15/month for Statler and Barton to negotiate any agreement. (Compensation for noise damage can be paid without incurring negotiation cost.) Will Barton install and maintain soundproofing? Is this outcome socially efficient?

d. Why does the attainment of a socially efficient outcome now depend on whether Barton has the legal right to make noise?

10. A village has six residents, each of whom has accumulated savings of $100. Each villager can use this money either to buy a government bond that pays 15 percent interest per year or to buy a year-old llama, send it onto the commons to graze, and sell it after 1 year. The price the villager gets for the 2-year-old llama depends on the quality of the fleece it grows while grazing on the commons. That in turn depends on the animal's access to grazing, which depends on the number of llamas sent to the commons, as shown in the following table:

Number of llamas on the commons	Price per 2-year-old llama ($)
1	122
2	118
3	116
4	114
5	112
6	109

The villagers make their investment decisions one after another, and their decisions are public.

a. If each villager decides individually how to invest, how many llamas will be sent onto the commons, and what will be the resulting net village income?

b. What is the socially optimal number of llamas for this village? Why is that different from the actual number? What would net village income be if the socially optimal number of llamas were sent onto the commons?

c. The village committee votes to auction the right to graze llamas on the commons to the highest bidder. Assuming villagers can both borrow and lend at 15 percent annual interest, how much will the right sell for at auction? How will the new owner use the right, and what will be the resulting village income?

■ ANSWERS TO IN-CHAPTER EXERCISES ■

11.1 Since Fitch gains $50/day when Abercrombie operates with a filter, he could pay Abercrombie as much as $49/day and still come out ahead.

11.2 If the two were to live together, the most efficient way to resolve the telephone problem would be as before, for Betty to give up reasonable access to the phone. But on top of that cost, which is $150, Betty would also bear a $60 cost from the loss of her privacy. The total cost of their living together would thus be $210/month. Since that amount is greater than the $200 saving in rent, the two should live separately.

11.3 The income figures from the different levels of investment in cattle would remain as before, as shown in the table. What is different is the opportunity cost of investing in each steer, which is now $11/year instead of $13. The last column of the table shows that the socially optimal number of steers is now 2 instead of 1. And if individuals still favor holding cattle, all other things being equal, they will now send 5 steers onto the commons instead of 4, as shown in the middle column.

Number of steers on the commons	Price per 2-year-old steer ($)	Income per steer ($/year)	Total village income ($/year)	Marginal income ($/year)
1	126	26	26	26
2	119	19	38	12
3	116	16	48	10
4	113	13	52	4
5	111	11	55	3

THE ECONOMICS
OF INFORMATION

■

Years ago, a naive young economist spent a week in Kashmir on a houseboat on scenic Dal Lake, outside the capital city of Srinigar. Kashmir is renowned for its woodcarvings, and one afternoon a man in a gondola stopped by to show the economist some of his wooden bowls. When the economist expressed interest in one of them, the woodcarver quoted a price of 200 rupees. The economist had lived in that part of Asia long enough to realize that the price was more than the woodcarver expected to get, so he made a counteroffer of 100 rupees.

The woodcarver appeared to take offense, saying that he couldn't possibly part with the bowl for less than 175 rupees. Suspecting that the woodcarver was merely feigning anger, the young economist held firm. The woodcarver appeared to become even angrier, but quickly retreated to 150 rupees. The economist politely restated his unwillingness to pay more than 100 rupees. The woodcarver then tried 125 rupees, and again the economist replied that 100 was his final offer. Finally, they struck a deal at 100 rupees, and with cash in hand, the woodcarver left in a huff.

Pleased with his purchase, the economist showed it to the houseboat's owner later that evening. "It's a lovely bowl," he agreed, and asked how much the economist had paid for it. The economist told him, expecting praise for his negotiating prowess. The host's failed attempt at suppressing a giggle was the economist's first clue that he had paid too much. When asked how much such a bowl would normally sell for, the houseboat owner was reluctant to respond. But the economist pressed him, and the host speculated that the seller had probably hoped for 30 rupees at most.

Adam Smith's invisible hand theory presumes that buyers are fully informed about the myriad ways in which they might spend their money—what goods and services are available, what prices they sell for, how long they last, how frequently they break down, and so on. But of course no one is ever really *fully* informed about anything. And sometimes, as in the transaction with the woodcarver, people are completely ignorant of even the most basic information. Still, life goes on, and most people muddle through somehow.

Consumers employ a variety of strategies for gathering information, some of which are better than others. They read *Consumer Reports,* talk to family and friends, visit stores, kick the tires on used cars, and so on. But one of the most important aspects of choosing intelligently without having complete information is having at least some idea of the extent of one's ignorance. Someone once said that there are two kinds of consumers in the world: those who don't know what they're doing and those who don't know that they don't know what they're doing. As in the case of the wooden bowl, the people in the second category are the ones who are most likely to choose foolishly.

Basic economic principles can help you in identifying those situations in which additional information is most likely to prove helpful. In this chapter, we will explore what those principles tell us about how much information to acquire and how to make the best use of limited information.

HOW THE MIDDLEMAN ADDS VALUE

One of the most common problems consumers confront is the need to choose among different versions of a product whose many complex features they do not fully understand. As Example 12.1 illustrates, in such cases consumers can sometimes rely on the knowledge of others.

EXAMPLE 12.1

How should a consumer decide which pair of skis to buy?

You need a new pair of skis, but the technology has changed considerably since you bought your last pair, and you don't know which of the current brands and models would be best for you. Skis R Us has the largest selection, so you go there and ask for advice. The salesperson appears to be well informed; after asking about your experience level and how aggressively you ski, he recommends the Salomon X-Scream 9. You buy a pair for $600, then head back to your apartment and show them to your roommate, who says that you could have bought them on the Internet for only $400. How do you feel about your purchase? Are the different prices charged by the two suppliers related to the services they offer? Were the extra services you got by shopping at Skis R Us worth the extra $200?

Internet retailers can sell for less because their costs are so much lower than those of full-service retail stores. Those stores, after all, must hire knowledgeable salespeople, put their merchandise on display, rent space in expensive shopping malls, and so on. Internet retailers and mail-order houses, by contrast, typically employ unskilled telephone clerks, and they store their merchandise in cheap warehouses. But if you are a consumer who doesn't know which is the right product for you, the extra expense of shopping at a specialty retailer is likely to be a good investment. Spending $600 on the right skis is smarter than spending $400 on the wrong ones.

Many people believe that wholesalers, retailers, and other agents who assist manufacturers in the sale of their products play a fundamentally different economic role from the one played by those who actually make the products. In this view, the production worker is the ultimate source of economic value added. Sales agents are often disparaged as mere middlemen, parasites on the efforts of others who do the real work.

"On the one hand, eliminating the middleman would result in lower costs, increased sales, and greater consumer satisfaction; on the other hand, we're the middleman."

On a superficial level, this view might seem to be supported by the fact that many people will go to great lengths to avoid paying for the services of sales agents. Many manufacturers cater to them by offering consumers a chance to "buy direct" and sidestep the middleman's commission. But on closer examination, we can see that the economic role of sales agents is essentially the same as that of production workers. Consider Example 12.2.

How does better information affect economic surplus?

EXAMPLE 12.2

Ellis has just inherited a rare Babe Ruth baseball card issued during the great slugger's rookie year. He'd like to keep the card but has reluctantly decided to sell it to pay some overdue bills. His reservation price for the card is $300, but he is hoping to get significantly more for it. He has two ways of selling it: He can place a classified ad in the local newspaper for $5, or he can list the card on eBay, the Internet auction service. If he sells the card on eBay, the fee will be 5 percent of the winning bid.

Because Ellis lives in a small town with few potential buyers of rare baseball cards, the local buyer with the highest reservation price is willing to pay $400 at most. If Ellis lists the card on eBay, however, a much larger number of potential buyers will see it. If the two eBay shoppers who are willing to pay the most for Ellis's card have reservation prices of $900 and $800, respectively, by how much will the total economic surplus be larger if Ellis sells his card on eBay? (For the sake of simplicity, assume that the eBay commission and the classified ad fee equal the respective costs of providing those services.)

In an eBay auction, each bidder reports his or her reservation price for an item. When the auction closes, the bidder with the highest reservation price wins, and the price he or she pays is the reservation price of the second highest bidder. So in this example, the Babe Ruth baseball card will sell for $800 if Ellis lists it on eBay. Net of the $40 eBay commission, Ellis will receive a payment of $760, or $460 more than his reservation price for the card. Ellis's economic surplus will thus be $460. The winning bidder's surplus will be $900 − $800 = $100, so the total surplus from selling the card on eBay will be $560.

If Ellis instead advertises the card in the local newspaper and sells it to the local buyer whose reservation price is $400, then Ellis's surplus (net of the newspaper's $5 fee) will be only $95, and the buyer's surplus will be $0. Thus total economic surplus will be $560 − $95 = $465 larger if Ellis sells the card on eBay than if he lists it in the local newspaper.

eBay provides a service by making information available to people who can make good use of it. A real increase in economic surplus results when an item ends up in the hands of someone who values it more highly than the person who otherwise would have bought it. That increase is just as valuable as the increase in surplus that results from manufacturing cars, growing corn, or any other productive activity.

RECAP   **HOW THE MIDDLEMAN ADDS VALUE**

In a world of incomplete information, sales agents and other middlemen add genuine economic value by increasing the extent to which goods and services find their way to the consumers who value them most. When a sales agent causes a good to be purchased by a person who values it by $20,000 more than the person who would have bought it in the absence of a sales agent, that agent augments total economic surplus by $20,000, an achievement on a par with the production of a $20,000 car.

THE OPTIMAL AMOUNT OF INFORMATION

Without a doubt, having more information is better than having less. But information is generally costly to acquire. In most situations, the value of additional information will decline beyond some point. And because of the low-hanging-fruit principle, people tend to gather information from the cheapest sources first before turning to more costly ones. Typically, then, the marginal benefit of information will decline, and its marginal cost will rise, as the amount of information gathered increases.

THE COST-BENEFIT TEST

Information gathering is an activity like any other. The cost-benefit principle tells us that a rational consumer will continue to gather information as long as its marginal benefit exceeds its marginal cost. If the relevant marginal cost and marginal benefit curves are as shown in Figure 12.1, a rational consumer will acquire I^* units of information, the amount for which the marginal benefit of information equals its marginal cost.

Another way to think about Figure 12.1 is that it shows the optimal level of ignorance. When the cost of acquiring information exceeds its benefits, acquiring additional information simply does not pay. If information could be acquired free,

---

FIGURE 12.1
The Optimal Amount of Information.
For the marginal cost and benefit curves shown, the optimal amount of information is I^*. Beyond that point, information costs more to acquire than it is worth.

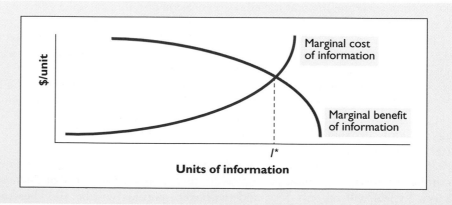

decision makers would, of course, be glad to have it. But when the cost of acquiring the information exceeds the gain in value from the decision it will facilitate, people are better off to remain ignorant.

THE FREE-RIDER PROBLEM

Does the invisible hand assure that the optimal amount of advice will be made available to consumers in the marketplace? The next example suggests one reason that it might not.

Why is finding a knowledgeable salesclerk often difficult?

People can choose for themselves whether to bear the extra cost of retail shopping. Those who value advice and convenience can pay slightly higher prices, while those who know what they want can buy for less from a mail-order house. True or false: It follows that private incentives lead to the optimal amount of retail service.

The market would provide the optimal level of retail service except for one practical problem, namely, that consumers can make use of the services offered by retail stores without paying for them. After benefiting from the advice of informed salespersons and after inspecting the merchandise, the consumer can return home and buy the same item from an Internet retailer or mail-order house. Not all consumers do so, of course. But the fact that customers can benefit from the information provided by retail stores without paying for it is an example of the **free-rider problem,** an incentive problem that results in too little of a good or service being produced. Because retail stores have difficulty recovering the cost of providing information, private incentives are likely to yield less than the socially optimal level of retail service. So the statement above is false.

Why did Rivergate Books, the last bookstore in Lambertville, New Jersey, recently go out of business?

Small independent bookstores often manage to survive competition from large chains like Borders and Barnes and Noble by offering more personalized service. Janet Holbrooke, the proprietor of Rivergate Books, followed this strategy successfully for more than a decade before closing her doors in 1999. What finally led her to quit?

According to Mrs. Holbrooke, a retired English teacher, "When Barnes and Noble came in, a few people were curious, went to look, and bought some books. But they came back and said they wanted to be able to find things more easily and have clerks that had an idea of what their grandchildren might like to read, and we held our own."[1] Customers were also drawn in by special events, such as readings and book signings by authors. But during one of these events, Mrs. Holbrooke saw that her store's days were numbered:

> I found out that Gerald Stern, who won the National Book Award for poetry, was a Lambertville man, and I asked him if he would come in and do a reading. He gave a wonderful presentation, and we had a good turnout, but we sold very few books, and then I overheard one of the women who were presenting a book for his signature say that she had bought hers through Amazon.com. Here I thought we were bringing something special to the town. But if people are going to bring in books that they got from the Internet, then we don't have a chance."[2]

ECONOMIC NATURALIST 12.1

free-rider problem an incentive problem in which too little of a good or service is produced because nonpayers cannot be excluded from using it

ECONOMIC NATURALIST 12.2

---

[1] Quoted by Iver Peterson, "A Bookseller Quits Battle With Internet," *The New York Times*, June 27, 1999, p. 21.
[2] Ibid.

"In reply to your inquiry regarding the Burke garden hoe, please visit our Worldwide Web home page at: http://www.burke1903.com."

EXERCISE 12.1

Apart from its possible contribution to free-rider problems, how is increased access to the Internet likely to affect total economic surplus?

TWO GUIDELINES FOR RATIONAL SEARCH

In practice, of course, the exact value of additional information is difficult to know, so the amount of time and effort one should invest in acquiring it is not always obvious. But as Examples 12.3 and 12.4 suggest, the cost-benefit principle provides a strong conceptual framework for thinking about this problem.

EXAMPLE 12.3

Should a person living in Paris, Texas, spend more or less time searching for an apartment than someone living in Paris, France?

Suppose that rents for one-bedroom apartments in Paris, Texas, vary between $300 and $500/month, with an average rent of $400/month. Rents for similar one-bedroom apartments in Paris, France, vary between $2,000 and $3,000/month, with an average rent of $2,500. In which city should a rational person expect to spend a longer time searching for an apartment?

In both cities, visiting additional apartments entails a cost, largely, the opportunity cost of one's time. In both cities, the more apartments someone visits, the more likely it is that he or she will find one near the lower end of the rent distribution. But because rents are higher and are spread over a broader range in Paris, France, the expected saving from further time spent searching will be greater there than in Paris, Texas. And so a rational person will expect to spend more time searching for an apartment in France.

Example 12.3 illustrates the principle that spending additional search time is more likely to be worthwhile for expensive items than for cheap ones. For example, one should spend more time searching for a good price on a diamond engagement ring than for a good price on a stone made of cubic zirconium; more time searching for a low fare to Sydney, Australia, than for a low fare to Sidney, New York; and more time searching for a car than for a bicycle. By extension, hiring an agent—someone who can assist with a search—is more likely to be a good investment in searching for something expensive than for something cheap. For example, people typically engage real estate agents to help them find a house, but they seldom hire agents to help them buy a gallon of milk.

Who should expect to search longer for a good price on a used piano?

EXAMPLE 12.4

Both Tom and Tim are shopping for a used upright piano. To examine a piano listed in the classified ads, they must travel to the home of the piano's current owner. If Tom has a car and Tim does not and both are rational, which one should expect to examine fewer pianos before making his purchase?

The benefits of examining an additional piano are the same in both cases, namely, a better chance of finding a good instrument for a low price. But because it is more costly for Tim to examine pianos, he should expect to examine fewer of them than Tom.

Example 12.4 makes the point that when searching becomes more costly, we should expect to do less of it. And as a result, the prices we expect to pay will be higher when the cost of a search is higher.

THE GAMBLE INHERENT IN SEARCH

Suppose you are in the market for a one-bedroom apartment and have found one that rents for $400 per month. Should you rent it or search further in hopes of finding a cheaper apartment? Even in a large market with many vacant apartments, there is no guarantee that searching further will turn up a cheaper or better apartment. Searching further entails a cost, which might outweigh the gain. In general, someone who engages in further search must accept certain costs in return for unknown benefits. Thus further search invariably carries an element of risk.

In thinking about whether to take any gamble, a helpful first step is to compute its **expected value**—the average amount you would win (or lose) if you played that gamble an infinite number of times. To calculate the expected value of a gamble with more than one outcome, we first multiply each outcome by its corresponding probability of occurring, and then add. For example, suppose you win $1 if a coin flip comes up heads and lose $1 if it comes up tails. Since 1/2 is the probability of heads (and also the probability of tails), the expected value of this gamble is (1/2)($1) + (1/2)(−$1) = 0. A gamble with an expected value of zero is called a **fair gamble.** If you played this gamble a large number of times, you wouldn't expect to make money, but you also wouldn't expect to lose money.

A **better-than-fair gamble** is one with a positive expected value. (For example, a coin flip in which you win $2 for heads and lose $1 for tails is a better-than-fair gamble.) A **risk-neutral** person is someone who would accept any gamble that is fair or better. A **risk-averse** person is someone who would refuse to take any fair gamble.

expected value of a gamble the sum of the possible outcomes of the gamble multiplied by their respective probabilities

fair gamble a gamble whose expected value is zero

better-than-fair gamble one whose expected value is positive

risk-neutral person someone who would accept any gamble that is fair or better

risk-averse person someone who would refuse any fair gamble

EXERCISE 12.2

Consider a gamble in which you win $4 if you flip a coin and it comes up heads and lose $2 if it comes up tails. What is the expected value of this gamble? Would a risk-neutral person accept it?

In Example 12.5 we apply these concepts to the decision of whether to search further for an apartment.

EXAMPLE 12.5

Should you search further for an apartment?

You have arrived in San Francisco for a 1-month summer visit and are searching for a one-bedroom sublet for the month. There are only two kinds of one-bedroom apartments in the neighborhood in which you wish to live, identical in every respect except that one rents for $400 and the other for $360. Of the vacant apartments in this neighborhood, 80 percent are of the first type and 20 percent are of the second type. The only way you can discover the rent for a vacant apartment is to visit it in person. The first apartment you visit is one that rents for $400. If you are risk-neutral and your opportunity cost of visiting an additional apartment is $6, should you visit another apartment or rent the one you've found?

If you visit one more apartment, you have a 20 percent chance of it being one that rents for $360 and an 80 percent chance of it being one that rents for $400. If the former, you'll save $40 in rent, but if the latter, you'll face the same rent as before. Since the cost of a visit is $6, visiting another apartment is a gamble with a 20 percent chance to win $40 − $6 = $34 and an 80 percent chance of losing $6 (which means "winning" −$6). The expected value of this gamble is thus (0.20)($34) + (0.80)(−$6) = $2. Visiting another apartment is a better-than-fair gamble, and since you are risk-neutral, you should take it.

EXERCISE 12.3

Refer to Example 12.5. Suppose you visit another apartment and discover it is one that rents for $400. If you are risk-neutral, should you visit a third apartment?

THE COMMITMENT PROBLEM WHEN SEARCH IS COSTLY

When most people search for an apartment, they want a place to live not for just a month but for a year or more. Most landlords, for their part, are also looking for long-term tenants. Similarly, few people accept a full-time job in their chosen field unless they expect to hold the job for several years. Firms, too, generally prefer employees who will stay for extended periods. Finally, when most people search for mates, they are looking for someone with whom to settle down.

Because in all these cases search is costly, examining every possible option will never make sense. Apartment hunters don't visit every vacant apartment, nor do landlords interview every possible tenant. Job seekers don't visit every employer, nor do employers interview every job seeker. And not even the most determined searcher can manage to date every eligible mate. In these and other cases, people are rational to end their searches, even though they know a more attractive option surely exists out there somewhere.

But herein lies a difficulty. What happens when, by chance, a more attractive option comes along after the search has ceased? Few people would rent an apartment if they thought the landlord would kick them out the moment another tenant came along who was willing to pay higher rent. Few landlords would be willing to rent to a tenant if they expected her to move out the moment she discovers a cheaper apartment. Employers, job seekers, and people who are looking for mates would have similar reservations about entering relationships that could be terminated once a better option happened to come along.

This potential difficulty in maintaining stable matches between partners in ongoing relationships would not arise in a world of perfect information. In such a world, everyone would end up in the best possible relationship, so no one would be tempted to renege. But when information is costly and the search must be limited, there will always be the potential for existing relationships to dissolve.

In most contexts, people solve this problem not by conducting an exhaustive search (which is usually impossible, in any event) but by committing themselves to remain in a relationship once a mutual agreement has been reached to terminate the search. Thus landlords and tenants sign a lease that binds them to one another for a specified period, usually 1 year. Employees and firms enter into employment contracts, either formal or informal, under which each promises to honor his obligations to the other, except under extreme circumstances. And in most countries a marriage contract penalizes those who abandon their spouses. Entering into such commitments limits the freedom to pursue one's own interests. Yet most people freely accept such restrictions, because they know the alternative is failure to solve the search problem.

RECAP   **THE OPTIMAL AMOUNT OF INFORMATION**

Additional information creates value, but it is also costly to acquire. A rational consumer will continue to acquire information until its marginal benefit equals its marginal cost. Beyond that point, it is rational to remain uninformed.

Markets for information do not always function perfectly. Free-rider problems often hinder retailers' efforts to provide information to consumers.

Search inevitably entails an element of risk, because costs must be incurred without any assurance that search will prove fruitful. A rational consumer can minimize this risk by concentrating search efforts on goods for which the variation in price or quality is relatively high and on those for which the cost of search is relatively low.

ASYMMETRIC INFORMATION

One of the most common information problems occurs when the participants in a potential exchange are not equally well informed about the product or service that is offered for sale. For instance, the owner of a used car may know that the car is in excellent mechanical condition, but potential buyers cannot know that merely by inspecting it or taking it for a test drive. Economists use the term **asymmetric information** to describe situations in which buyers and sellers are not equally well informed about the characteristics of products or services. In these situations, sellers are typically much better informed than buyers, but sometimes the reverse will be true.

As Example 12.6 illustrates, the problem of asymmetric information can easily prevent exchanges that would benefit both parties.

asymmetric information situations in which buyers and sellers are not equally well informed about the characteristics of goods and services for sale in the marketplace

EXAMPLE 12.6

Will Jane sell her car to Tom?

Jane's 1995 Miata has 70,000 miles on the odometer, but most of these are highway miles driven during weekend trips to see her boyfriend in Toronto. (Highway driving causes less wear and tear on a car than city driving.) Moreover, Jane has maintained the car precisely according to the manufacturer's specifications. In short, she knows her car to be in excellent condition. Because she is about to start graduate school in Boston, however, Jane wants to sell the car. 1995 Miatas sell for an average price of $8,000, but because Jane knows her car to be in excellent condition, her reservation price for it is $10,000.

Tom wants to buy a used Miata. He would be willing to pay $13,000 for one that is in excellent condition but only $9,000 for one that is not in excellent condition. Tom has no way of telling whether Jane's Miata is in excellent condition. (He could hire a mechanic to examine the car, but doing so is expensive, and many problems cannot be detected even by a mechanic.) Will Tom buy Jane's car? Is this outcome efficient?

Because Jane's car looks no different from other 1995 Miatas, Tom will not pay $10,000 for it. After all, for only $8,000, he can buy some other 1995 Miata that is in just as good condition, as far as he can tell. Tom therefore will buy someone else's Miata, and Jane's will go unsold. This outcome is not efficient. If Tom had bought Jane's Miata for, say, $11,000, his surplus would have been $2,000 and Jane's another $1,000. Instead, Tom ends up buying a Miata that is in average condition (or worse), and his surplus is only $1,000. Jane gets no economic surplus at all.

THE LEMONS MODEL

We can't be sure, of course, that the Miata Tom ends up buying will be in worse condition than Jane's—since *someone* might have a car in perfect condition that must be sold even if the owner cannot get what it is really worth. Even so, the economic incentives created by asymmetric information suggest that most used cars that are put up for sale will be of lower-than-average quality. One reason is that people who mistreat their cars, or whose cars were never very good to begin with, are more likely than others to want to sell them. Buyers know from experience that cars for sale on the used car market are more likely to be "lemons" than cars that are not for sale. This realization causes them to lower their reservation prices for a used car.

But that's not the end of the story. Once used car prices have fallen, the owners of cars that are in good condition have an even stronger incentive to hold onto them. That causes the average quality of the cars offered for sale on the used car market to decline still further. Berkeley economist George Akerlof was the first to explain the logic behind this downward spiral.[3] Economists use the term **lemons model** to describe Akerlof's explanation of how asymmetric information affects the average quality of the used goods offered for sale.

As Example 12.7 suggests, the lemons model has important practical implications for consumer choice.

lemons model George Akerlof's explanation of how asymmetric information tends to reduce the average quality of goods offered for sale

EXAMPLE 12.7

Should you buy your aunt's car?

You want to buy a used Honda Accord. Your Aunt Germaine buys a new car every 4 years, and she has a 4-year-old Accord that she is about to trade in. You believe her report that the car is in good condition, and she is willing to sell it to you for $10,000, which is the current blue book value for 4-year-old Accords. (The blue book value of a car is the average price for which cars of that age and model sell in the used car market.) Should you buy your aunt's Honda?

Akerlof's lemons model tells us that cars for sale in the used car market will be of lower average quality than cars of the same vintage that are not for sale. If you believe your aunt's claim that her car is in good condition, then being able to buy it for its blue book value is definitely a good deal for you, since the blue book price is the equilibrium price for a car that is of lower quality than your aunt's.

Examples 12.8 and 12.9 illustrate the conditions under which asymmetric information about product quality results in a market in which *only* lemons are offered for sale.

[3] George Akerlof, "The Market for Lemons," *Quarterly Journal of Economics*, **84**: 488–500, 1970.

What price will a used car fetch?

EXAMPLE 12.8

Consider a world with only two kinds of cars, good ones and lemons. An owner knows with certainty which type of car she has, but potential buyers cannot distinguish between the two types. Ten percent of all new cars produced are lemons. Good used cars are worth $10,000 to their owners, but lemons are worth only $6,000. Consider a naive consumer who believes that the used cars currently for sale have the same quality distribution as new cars (i.e., 90 percent good, 10 percent lemons). If this consumer is risk-neutral, how much would he be willing to pay for a used car?

Buying a car of unknown quality is a gamble, but a risk-neutral buyer would be willing to take the gamble provided it is fair. If the buyer can't tell the difference between a good car and a lemon, the probability that he will end up with a lemon is simply the proportion of lemons among the cars from which he chooses. The buyer believes he has a 90 percent chance of getting a good car and a 10 percent chance of getting a lemon. Given the prices he is willing to pay for the two types of car, his expected value of the car he buys will thus be $0.90(\$10,000) + 0.10(\$6,000) = \$9,600$. And since he is risk-neutral, that is his reservation price for a used car.

EXERCISE 12.4

How would your answer to the question posed in Example 12.8 differ if the proportion of new cars that are lemons had been not 10 percent but 20 percent?

Who will sell a used car for what the naive buyer is willing to pay?

EXAMPLE 12.9

Refer to Example 12.8. If you were the owner of a good used car, what would it be worth to you? Would you sell it to a naive buyer? What if you owned a lemon?

Since you know your car is good, it is worth $10,000 to you, by assumption. But since a naive buyer would be willing to pay only $9,600, neither you nor any other owner of a good car would be willing to sell to that buyer. If you had a lemon, of course, you would be happy to sell it to a naive buyer, since the $9,600 the buyer is willing to pay is $3,600 more than the lemon would be worth to you. So the only used cars for sale will be lemons. In time, buyers will revise their naively optimistic beliefs about the quality of the cars for sale on the used car market. In the end, all used cars will sell for a price of $6,000, and all will be lemons.

In practice, of course, the mere fact that a car is for sale does not guarantee that it is a lemon, because the owner of a good car will sometimes be forced to sell it, even at a price that does not reflect its condition. The logic of the lemons model explains this owner's frustration. The first thing sellers in this situation want a prospective buyer to know is the reason they are selling their cars. For example, classified ads often announce, "Just had a baby, must sell my 1999 Corvette" or "Transferred to Germany, must sell my 2000 Toyota Camry." Any time you pay the blue book price for a used car that is for sale for some reason unrelated to its condition, you are beating the market.

THE CREDIBILITY PROBLEM IN TRADING

Why can't someone with a high-quality used car simply *tell* the buyer about the car's condition? The difficulty is that buyers' and sellers' interests tend to conflict. Sellers of used cars, for example, have an economic incentive to overstate the quality of their products. Buyers, for their part, have an incentive to understate the

Why do new cars lose a significant fraction of their value as soon as they are driven from the showroom?

amount they are willing to pay for used cars and other products. Potential employees may be tempted to overstate their qualifications for a job. And people searching for mates have been known to engage in deception.

That is not to say that most people *consciously* misrepresent the truth in communicating with their potential trading partners. But people do tend to interpret ambiguous information in ways that promote their own interests. Thus, 92 percent of factory employees surveyed in one study rated themselves as more productive than the average factory worker. Psychologists call this phenomenon the "Lake Wobegon effect," after Garrison Keillor's mythical Minnesota homestead, where "all the children are above average."

Notwithstanding the natural tendency to exaggerate, the parties to a potential exchange can often gain if they can find some means to communicate their knowledge truthfully. In general, however, mere statements of relevant information will not suffice. People have long since learned to discount the used car salesman's inflated claims about the cars he is trying to unload. But as the next examples illustrate, though communication between potential adversaries may be difficult, it is not impossible.

EXAMPLE 12.10   **How can a used car seller signal high quality credibly?**

Jane knows her Miata to be in excellent condition, and Tom would be willing to pay considerably more than her reservation price if he could be confident of getting such a car. What kind of signal about the car's quality would Tom find credible?

Again, the potential conflict between Tom's and Jane's interests suggests that mere statements about the car's quality may not be persuasive. But suppose Jane offers a warranty, under which she agrees to remedy any defects the car develops over the next 6 months. Jane can afford to extend such an offer because she knows her car is unlikely to need expensive repairs. In contrast, the person who knows his car has a cracked engine block would never extend such an offer. The warranty is a credible signal that the car is in good condition. It enables Tom to buy the car with confidence, to both his and Jane's benefit.

THE COSTLY-TO-FAKE PRINCIPLE

costly-to-fake principle to communicate information credibly to a potential rival, a signal must be costly or difficult to fake

The preceding examples illustrate the **costly-to-fake principle,** which holds that if parties whose interests potentially conflict are to communicate credibly with one another, the signals they send must be costly or difficult to fake. If the seller of a defective car could offer an extensive warranty just as easily as the seller of a good car, a warranty offer would communicate nothing about the car's quality. But warranties entail costs that are significantly higher for defective cars than for good cars—hence their credibility as a signal of product quality.

To the extent that sellers have an incentive to portray a product in the most flattering light possible, their interests conflict with those of buyers, who want the most accurate assessment of product quality possible. Note that in the following example, the costly-to-fake principle applies to a producer's statement about the quality of a product.

ECONOMIC NATURALIST 12.3

Why do firms insert the phrase "As advertised on TV" when they advertise their products in magazines and newspapers?

Company *A* sponsors an expensive national television advertising campaign on behalf of its compact disc player, claiming it has the clearest sound and the best repair record of any CD player in the market. Company *B* makes similar claims in a sales brochure but does not advertise its product on television. If you had no additional information to go on, which company's claim would you find more credible? Why do you suppose Company *A* mentions its TV ads when it advertises its CD player in print media?

Accustomed as we are to discounting advertisers' inflated claims, the information given might seem to provide no real basis for a choice between the two products. On closer examination, however, we see that a company's decision to advertise its product on national television constitutes a credible signal about the product's quality. The cost of a national television campaign can run well into the millions of dollars, a sum a company would be foolish to spend on an inferior product.

For example, in 1996 Pizza Hut spent some $50 million to launch a new cheese-stuffed TripleDecker pizza. In that year, a single 30-second TV spot on the *Seinfeld* show cost advertisers $450,000, and the same spot during the Super Bowl cost $1.3 million. National TV ads can attract the potential buyers' attention and persuade a small fraction of them to try a product. But these huge investments pay off only if the resulting initial sales generate other new business—either repeat sales to people who tried the product and liked it or sales to others who heard about the product from a friend.

Because ads cannot persuade buyers that a bad product is a good one, a company that spends millions of dollars advertising a bad product is wasting its money. An expensive national advertising campaign is therefore a credible signal that the producer *thinks* its product is a good one. Of course, the ads don't guarantee that a product *is* a winner, but in an uncertain world, they provide one more piece of information. Note, however, that the relevant information lies in the expenditure on the advertising campaign, not in what the ads themselves say.

These observations may explain why some companies mention their television ads in their print ads. Advertisers understand the costly-to-fake principle and hope that consumers will understand it as well.

As the next example illustrates, the costly-to-fake principle is also well known to many employers.

Why do many companies care so much about elite educational credentials?

Microsoft is looking for a hardworking, smart person for an entry-level managerial position in a new technical products division. Two candidates, Cooper and Duncan, seem alike in every respect but one: Cooper graduated with the highest honors from MIT, while Duncan graduated with a C+ average from Somerville College. Whom should Microsoft hire?

If you want to persuade prospective employers that you are both hardworking and intelligent, there is perhaps no more credible signal than to have graduated with distinction from a highly selective educational institution. Most people would like potential employers to think of them as hardworking and intelligent. But unless you actually have both those qualities, graduating with the highest honors from a school like MIT will be extremely difficult. The fact that Duncan graduated from a much less selective institution and earned only a C+ average is not proof positive that he is not diligent and talented, but companies are forced to play the percentages. In this case the odds strongly favor Cooper.

ECONOMIC NATURALIST 12.4

CONSPICUOUS CONSUMPTION AS A SIGNAL OF ABILITY

Some individuals of high ability are not highly paid. (Remember the best elementary school teacher you ever had.) And some people, such as the multibillionaire investor Warren Buffet, earn a lot, yet spend very little. But such cases run counter to general tendencies. In competitive markets, the people with the most ability tend to receive the highest salaries. And as suggested by the cost-benefit principle, the more someone earns, the more he or she is likely to spend on high-quality goods and services. As the following example suggests, these tendencies often lead us to infer a person's ability from the amount and quality of the goods he consumes.

ECONOMIC NATURALIST 12.5

Why do many clients seem to prefer lawyers who wear expensive suits?

You have been unjustly accused of a serious crime and are looking for an attorney. Your choice is between two lawyers who appear identical in all respects except for the things they buy. One of them wears a cheap polyester suit and arrives at the courthouse in a 10-year-old rust-eaten Dodge Colt. The other wears an impeccably tailored suit and drives a new BMW 740i. If this were the *only* information available to you at the time you chose, which lawyer would you hire?

The correlation between salary and the abilities buyers value most is particularly strong in the legal profession. A lawyer whose clients usually prevail in court will be much more in demand than one whose clients generally lose, and their fees will reflect the difference. The fact that one of the lawyers consumes much more than the other does not *prove* that he is the better lawyer, but if that is the only information you have, you can ill afford to ignore it.

If the less able lawyer loses business because of the suits he wears and the car he drives, why doesn't he simply buy better suits and a more expensive car? His choice is between saving for retirement or spending more on his car and clothing. In one sense, he cannot afford to buy a more expensive car, but in another sense, he cannot afford *not* to. If his current car is discouraging potential clients from hiring him, buying a better one may simply be a prudent investment. But because *all* lawyers have an incentive to make such investments, their effects tend to be mutually offsetting.

When all is said and done, the things people consume will continue to convey relevant information about their respective ability levels. The costly-to-fake principle tells us that the BMW 740i is an effective signal precisely because the lawyer of low ability cannot afford one, no matter how little he saves for retirement. Yet from a social perspective, the resulting spending pattern is inefficient, for the same reason that other positional arms races are inefficient (see Chapter 11). Society would be better off if everyone spent less and saved more for retirement.

The problem of conspicuous consumption as an ability signal does not arise with equal force in every environment. In small towns, where people tend to know one another well, a lawyer who tries to impress people by spending beyond her means is likely to succeed only in demonstrating how foolish she is. Thus the wardrobe a professional person "needs" in towns like Dubuque, Iowa, or Athens, Ohio, costs less than half as much as the wardrobe the same person would need in Manhattan or Los Angeles.

STATISTICAL DISCRIMINATION

In a competitive market with perfect information, the buyer of a service would pay the seller's cost of providing the service. In many markets, however—the market for fire insurance is one example—the seller does not know the exact cost of serving each individual buyer.

In such cases, the missing information has an economic value. If the seller can come up with even a rough estimate of the missing information, she can improve her position. As the following examples illustrate, firms often do so by imputing characteristics to individuals on the basis of the groups to which they belong.

ECONOMIC NATURALIST 12.6

Why do males under 25 years of age pay more than other drivers for auto insurance?

Gerald is 23 years old and is an extremely careful and competent driver. He has never had an accident, or even a moving traffic violation. His twin sister Geraldine has had two accidents, one of them serious, in the last 3 years and has accumulated three speeding tickets during that same period. Why does Gerald pay $1,600/year for auto insurance, while Geraldine pays only $800?

The expected cost to an insurance company of insuring any given driver depends on the probability that the driver will be involved in an accident. No one knows what that probability is for any given driver, but insurance companies can estimate rather precisely the proportion of drivers in specific groups who will be involved in an accident in any given year. Males under 25 are much more likely than older males and females of any age to become involved in auto accidents. (Testosterone seems to have something to do with it.) Gerald pays more than his sister because even those males under 25 who have never had an accident are more likely to have one than females the same age who have had several accidents.

Of course, females who have had two accidents and accumulated several tickets in the last 3 years are more likely to have an accident than a female with a spotless driving record. The insurance company knows that and has increased Geraldine's premium accordingly. Yet it is still less than her brother's premium. That does not mean that Gerald is in fact more likely to have an accident than Geraldine. Indeed, given the twins' respective driving skills, Geraldine clearly poses the higher risk. But because insurance companies lack such detailed information, they are forced to set rates according to the information they possess.

To remain in business, an insurance company must collect enough money from premiums to cover the cost of the claims it pays out, plus whatever administrative expenses it incurs. Consider an insurance company that charges lower rates for young males with clean driving records than for females with blemished ones. Given that the former group is more likely to have accidents than the latter, the company cannot break even unless it charges females more, and males less, than the respective costs of insuring them. But if it does so, rival insurance companies will see cash on the table: They can offer females slightly lower rates and lure them away from the first company. The first company will end up with only young male policyholders and thus will suffer an economic loss at the low rates it charges. That is why, in equilibrium, young males with clean driving records pay higher insurance rates than young females with blemished records.

The insurance industry's policy of charging high rates to young male drivers is an example of **statistical discrimination**. Other examples include the common practice of paying higher salaries to people with college degrees than to people without them and the policy of favoring college applicants with high SAT scores. Statistical discrimination occurs whenever people or products are judged on the basis of the groups to which they belong.

Even though everyone *knows* that the characteristics of specific individuals can differ markedly from those of the group to which they belong, competition promotes statistical discrimination. For example, insurance companies know perfectly well that *some* young males are careful and competent drivers. But unless they can identify *which* males are the better drivers, competitive pressure forces them to act on their knowledge that as a group young males are more likely than others to generate insurance claims.

Similarly, employers know that many people with only a high school diploma are more productive than the average college graduate. But because employers usually cannot tell in advance who those people are, competitive pressure leads them to offer higher wages to college graduates, who are more productive, on average, than high school graduates. Universities, too, realize that many applicants with low SAT scores will earn higher grades than applicants with high scores. But if two applicants look equally promising except for their SAT scores, competition forces universities to favor the applicant with higher scores since, on average, that applicant will perform better than the other.

Statistical discrimination is the *result* of observable differences in group characteristics, not the cause of those differences. Young males, for example, do not generate more insurance claims because of statistical discrimination. Rather, statistical discrimination occurs because insurance companies know that young males generate more claims. Nor does statistical discrimination cause young

statistical discrimination the practice of making judgments about the quality of people, goods, or services based on the characteristics of the groups to which they belong males to pay insurance rates that are high in relation to the claims they generate. Among any group of young male drivers, some are careful and competent, and others are not. Statistical discrimination means the more able males will pay high rates relative to the volume of claims they generate, but it also means the less able male drivers will pay low rates relative to the claims they generate. On average, the group's rates will be appropriate to the claims its members generate.

Still, these observations do little to ease the frustration of the young male who knows himself to be a careful and competent driver, or the high school graduate who knows herself to be a highly productive employee. Competitive forces provide firms an incentive to identify such individuals and treat them more favorably whenever practical. When firms succeed in this effort, however, they have often discovered some other relevant information on group differences. For example, many insurance companies offer lower rates to young males who belong to the National Honor Society or make the dean's list at school. Members of those groups generate fewer claims, on average, than other young males. But even these groups include risky drivers, and the fact that companies offer discounts to their members means that that all other young males must pay higher rates.

ADVERSE SELECTION

adverse selection the pattern in which insurance tends to be purchased disproportionately by those who are most costly for companies to insure

Although insurance companies routinely practice statistical discrimination, each individual within a group pays the same rate, even though individuals within the group often differ sharply in terms of their likelihood of filing claims. Within each group, buying insurance is thus most attractive to those individuals with the highest likelihood of filing claims. As a result, high-risk individuals are more likely to buy insurance than low-risk individuals, a pattern known as **adverse selection**. Adverse selection forces insurance companies to raise their premiums, which makes buying insurance even less attractive to low-risk individuals, which raises still further the average risk level of those who remain insured. In some cases, only those individuals faced with extreme risks may continue to find insurance an attractive purchase.

RECAP   ASYMMETRIC INFORMATION

Asymmetric information describes situations in which not all parties to a potential exchange are equally well informed. In the typical case, the seller of a product will know more about its quality than the potential buyers. Such asymmetries often stand in the way of mutually beneficial exchange in the markets for high-quality goods, because buyers' inability to identify high quality makes them unwilling to pay a commensurate price.

Information asymmetries and other communication problems between potential exchange partners can often be solved through the use of signals that are costly or difficult to fake. Product warranties are such a signal, because the seller of a low-quality product would find them too costly to offer.

Buyers and sellers also respond to asymmetric information by attempting to judge the qualities of products and people on the basis of the groups to which they belong. A young male may know he is a good driver, but auto insurance companies must nonetheless charge him high rates because they know only that he is a member of a group that is frequently involved in accidents.

DISAPPEARING POLITICAL DISCOURSE

An intriguing illustration of statistical discrimination arises when a politician decides what to say about controversial public issues. Politicians have an interest in supporting the positions they genuinely believe in, but they also have an interest in winning reelection. As the next examples illustrate, the two motives often conflict, especially when a politician's statements about one subject convey information about her beliefs on other subjects.

Why do opponents of the death penalty often remain silent?

Quite apart from the question of whether execution of convicted criminals is morally legitimate, there are important practical arguments against capital punishment. For one thing, it is extremely expensive relative to the alternative of life without parole. Execution is costly because of judicial safeguards against execution of innocent persons. In each capital case prosecuted in the United States, these safeguards consume thousands of person-hours from attorneys and other officers of the court, at a cost that runs well into the millions of dollars.[4] Such efforts notwithstanding, the record is replete with examples of executed persons who are later shown to be innocent. Another argument against capital punishment is that many statistical studies find that it does not deter people from committing capital crimes. Though many political leaders in both parties find these and other arguments against capital punishment compelling, few politicians voice their opposition to capital punishment publicly. Why not?

A possible answer to this puzzle is suggested by the theory of statistical discrimination. Voters in both parties are concerned about crime and want to elect politicians who take the problem seriously. Suppose there are two kinds of politicians, some who in their heart of hearts take the crime issue seriously and others who merely pay lip service to it. Suppose also that voters classify politicians in a second way: those who publicly favor the death penalty or remain silent, and those who publicly oppose it. Some politicians will oppose the death penalty for the reasons just discussed, but others will oppose it because they are simply reluctant to punish criminals—perhaps because they believe that crime is ultimately more society's fault than the criminal's. (Politicians in the latter category are the ones voters think of as being "not serious about crime"; they are the ones most voters want to get rid of.) These two possible motives for opposing the death penalty suggest that the proportion of death penalty opponents who take the crime issue seriously, in the public's view, will be somewhat smaller than the corresponding proportion among proponents of the death penalty. For the sake of discussion, imagine that 95 percent of politicians who favor the death penalty and only 80 percent of politicians who oppose the death penalty are "serious about crime."

If you are a voter who cares about crime, how will your views about a politician be affected by hearing that he opposes the death penalty? If you knew nothing about that politician to begin with, your best guess on hearing his opposition to the death penalty would be that there is an 80 percent chance that he is serious about crime. Had he instead voiced support for the death penalty, your best guess would be that there is a 95 percent chance that he is serious about crime. And since voters are looking for politicians who are serious about crime, the mere act of speaking out against the death penalty will entail a small loss of political support even for those politicians who are extremely serious about crime.

Knowing this tendency on the part of voters, some politicians who are only marginally opposed to the death penalty may prefer to keep their views to themselves. As a result, the composition of the group that speaks out publicly against the death penalty will change slightly so that it is more heavily weighted with people reluctant to punish criminals in any way. Suppose, for example, that the proportion of death penalty oppo-

---

[4]See Philip J. Cook and Donna B. Slawson, "The Costs of Processing Murder Cases in North Carolina," The Sanford Institute of Public Policy, Duke University, Durham, N.C., 1993.

nents who are serious about crime falls from 80 to 60 percent. Now the political cost of speaking out against the death penalty rises, leading still more opponents to remain silent. Once the dust settles, very few opponents of capital punishment will risk stating their views publicly. In their desire to convince voters that they are tough on crime, some may even become proponents of the death penalty. In the end, public discourse will strongly favor capital punishment. But that is no reason to conclude that most leaders—or even most voters—genuinely favor it.

disappearing political discourse
the theory that people who support a position may remain silent, because speaking out would create a risk of being misunderstood

The economist Glen Loury was the first to call attention to the phenomenon described in the preceding example. We call it the problem of **disappearing political discourse**. Once you understand it, you will begin to notice examples not just in the political sphere but in everyday discourse as well.

ECONOMIC NATURALIST 12.8

Why do proponents of legalized drugs remain silent?

That addictive drugs like heroine, cocaine, and methamphetamines cause enormous harm is not a matter of dispute. The clear intent of laws that ban commerce in these drugs is to prevent that harm. But the laws also entail costs. By making the drugs illegal, they substantially increase their price, leading many addicts to commit crimes to pay for drugs. The high incomes of illicit drug dealers also divert many people from legitimate careers and result in turf battles that often have devastating consequences for both participants and bystanders. If these drugs were legal, drug-related crime would vanish completely. Drug use would also rise, how significantly we do not know. In short, it is at least *conceivable* that legalizing addictive drugs might be sound public policy. Why, then, do virtually no politicians publicly favor such a policy?

Many politicians may simply believe that legalizing drugs is simply a bad idea. Theoretically, legalization could lead to such a steep rise in drug consumption that the cost of the policy might far outweigh its benefits. This concern, however, is not supported by experience in countries such as England and the Netherlands, which have tried limited forms of legalization. A second explanation is that politicians who favor legalization are reluctant to speak out for fear that others will misinterpret them. Suppose that some people favor legalization based on careful analysis of the costs and benefits, while other proponents are merely crazy. If the proportion of crazies is higher among supporters than among opponents of legalization, someone who speaks out in favor of legalization may cause those who do not know her to increase their estimate of the likelihood she is crazy. This possibility deters some proponents from speaking out, which raises the proportion of crazies among the remaining public supporters of legalization—and so on in a downward spiral, until most of the remaining public supporters really are crazy.

Why did the task of reestablishing normal diplomatic relations with China fall to President Richard Nixon, the lifelong communist basher?

The disappearing political discourse problem helps to explain why the United States had difficulty reestablishing normal diplomatic relations with China, which were severed in the wake of the communist revolution. One could oppose communist expansionism and yet still favor normalized relations with China on the grounds that war is less likely when antagonists communicate openly. In the Cold War environment, however, American politicians were under enormous pressure to demonstrate their steadfast opposition to communism at every opportunity. Fearing that support for the normalization of relations with China would be misinterpreted as a sign of softness toward communism, many supporters of the policy remained silent. Not until Richard Nixon—whose anticommunist credentials no one could question—was elected President were diplomatic relations with China finally reopened.

The problem of disappearing discourse also helps explain the impoverished state of public debate on issues such as the reform of Social Security, Medicare, and other entitlement programs.

▪ SUMMARY ▪

- Virtually every market exchange takes place on the basis of less than complete information. More information is beneficial both to buyers and to sellers, but information is costly to acquire. The rational individual therefore acquires information only up to the point at which its marginal benefit equals its marginal cost. Beyond that point one is rational to remain ignorant.

- Retailers and other sales agents are important sources of information. To the extent that they enable consumers to find the right products and services, they add economic value. In that sense they are no less productive than the workers who manufacture goods or perform services directly. Unfortunately, the free-rider problem often prevents firms from offering useful product information.

- Several principles govern the rational search for information. Searching more intensively makes sense when the cost of a search is low, when quality is highly variable, or when prices vary widely. Further search is always a gamble. A risk-neutral person will search whenever the expected gains outweigh the expected costs. A rational search will always terminate before all possible options have been investigated. Thus in a search for a partner in an ongoing bilateral relationship, there is always the possibility that a better partner will turn up after the search is over. In most contexts, people deal with this problem by entering into contracts that commit them to their partners once they have mutually agreed to terminate the search.

- Many potentially beneficial transactions are prevented from taking place by asymmetric information—the fact that one party lacks information that the other has. For example, the owner of a used car knows whether it is in good condition, but potential buyers do not. Even though a buyer may be willing to pay more for a good car than the owner of such a car would require, the fact that the buyer cannot be sure he is getting a good car often discourages the sale. More generally, asymmetric information often prevents sellers from supplying the same quality level that consumers would be willing to pay for.

- Both buyers and sellers can often gain by finding ways of communicating what they know to one another. But because of the potential conflict between the interests of buyers and sellers, mere statements about the relevant information may not be credible. For a signal between potential trading partners to be credible, it must be costly to fake. For instance, the owner of a high-quality used car can credibly signal the car's quality by offering a warranty—an offer that the seller of a low-quality car could not afford to make.

- Firms and consumers often try to estimate missing information by making use of what they know about the groups to which people or things belong. For example, insurance firms estimate the risk of insuring individual young male drivers on the basis of the accident rates for young males as a group. This practice is known as statistical discrimination. Other examples include paying college graduates more than high school graduates and charging higher life insurance rates to 60-year-olds than to 20-year-olds. Statistical discrimination helps to explain the phenomenon of disappearing political discourse, which occurs when opponents of a practice such as the death penalty remain silent when the issue is discussed publicly.

▪ KEY TERMS ▪

adverse selection (312)	disappearing political discourse (314)	lemons model (306)
asymmetric information (305)	expected value of a gamble (303)	risk-averse person (303)
better-than-fair gamble (303)	fair gamble (303)	risk-neutral person (303)
costly-to-fake principle (308)	free-rider problem (301)	statistical discrimination (311)

▪ REVIEW QUESTIONS ▪

1. Can it be rational for a consumer to buy a Chevrolet without having first taken test drives in competing models built by Ford, Chrysler, Honda, Toyota, and others?

2. Explain why a gallery owner who sells a painting might actually create more economic surplus than the artist who painted it.

3. Explain why used cars offered for sale are different, on average, from used cars not offered for sale.

4. Explain why the used-car market would be likely to function more efficiently in a community in which moral norms of honesty are strong than in a community in which such norms are weak.

5. Why might leasing a new Porsche be a good investment for an aspiring Hollywood film producer, even though he can't easily afford the monthly payments?

▪ PROBLEMS ▪

---

1. State whether the following are true or false, and briefly explain why:
   a. Companies spend billions of dollars advertising their products on network TV primarily because the texts of their advertisements persuade consumers that the advertised products are of high quality.
   b. You may not get the optimal level of advice from a retail shop when you go in to buy a lamp for your bike, because of the free-rider problem.
   c. If you need a lawyer, and all your legal expenses are covered by insurance, you should *always* choose the best-dressed lawyer with the most expensive car and the most ostentatiously furnished office.
   d. The benefit of searching for a spouse is affected by the size of the community you live in.

2. Consumers know that some fraction x of all new cars produced and sold in the market are defective. The defective ones cannot be identified except by those who own them. Cars do not depreciate with use. Consumers are risk-neutral and value non-defective cars at $10,000 each. New cars sell for $5,000 and used ones for $2,500. What is the fraction x?

3. Carlos is risk-neutral and has an ancient farmhouse with great character for sale in Slaterville Springs. His reservation price for the house is $130,000. The only possible local buyer is Whitney, whose reservation price for the house is $150,000. The only other houses on the market are modern ranch houses that sell for $125,000, which is exactly equal to each potential buyer's reservation price for such a house. Suppose that if Carlos does not hire a realtor, Whitney will learn from her neighbor that Carlos's house is for sale, and will buy it for $140,000. However, if Carlos hires a realtor, he knows that the realtor will put him in touch with an enthusiast for old farmhouses who is willing to pay up to $300,000 for the house. Carlos also knows that if he and this person negotiate, they will agree on a price of $250,000. If realtors charge a commission of 5 percent of the selling price and all realtors have opportunity costs of $2,000 for negotiating a sale, will Carlos hire a realtor? If so, how will total economic surplus be affected?

4. Ann and Barbara are computer programmers in Nashville who are planning to move to Seattle. Each owns a house that has just been appraised for $100,000. But whereas Ann's house is one of hundreds of highly similar houses in a large, well-known suburban development, Barbara's is the only one that was built from her architect's design. Who will benefit more by hiring a realtor to assist in selling her house, Ann or Barbara?

5. For each pair of occupations listed, identify the one for which the kind of car a person drives is more likely to be a good indication of how good she is at her job.
   a. Elementary school teacher, real estate agent
   b. Dentist, municipal government administrator
   c. Engineer in the private sector, engineer in the military

6. Brokers who sell stocks over the Internet can serve many more customers than those who transact business by mail or over the phone. How will the expansion of Internet access affect the average incomes of stockbrokers who continue to do business in the traditional way?

7. Whose income do you predict will be more affected by the expansion of Internet access:
   a. Stockbrokers or lawyers?
   b. Doctors or pharmacists?
   c. Bookstore owners or the owners of galleries that sell original oil paintings?

8. How will growing Internet access affect the number of film actors and musicians who have active fan clubs?

9. Fred, a retired accountant, and Jim, a government manager, are 63-year-old identical twins who collect antique pottery. Each has an annual income of $100,000 (Fred's from a pension, Jim's from salary). One buys most of his pottery at local auctions,

and the other buys most of his from a local dealer. Which brother is more likely to buy at an auction, and does he pay more or less than his brother who buys from the local dealer?

10. Female heads of state (e.g., Israel's Golda Meir, India's Indira Gandhi, Britain's Margaret Thatcher) have often been described as more bellicose in foreign policy matters than the average male head of state. Using Loury's theory of disappearing discourse, suggest an explanation for this pattern.

■ ANSWERS TO IN-CHAPTER EXERCISES ■

12.1 Internet search is a cheap way to acquire information about many goods and services, so the effect of increased Internet access will be a downward shift in the supply curve of information. In equilibrium, people will acquire more information, and the goods and services they buy will more closely resemble those they would have chosen in an ideal world with perfect information. These effects will cause total economic surplus to grow. Some of these gains, however, might be offset if the Internet makes the free-rider problem more serious.

12.2 The probability of getting heads is 0.5, the same as the probability of getting tails. Thus the expected value of this gamble is $(0.5)(\$4) + (0.5)(-\$2) = \$1$. Since the gamble is better than fair, a risk-neutral person would accept it.

12.3 Since you still have a 20 percent chance of finding a cheaper apartment if you make another visit, the expected outcome of the gamble is again $2, and you should search again. The bad outcome of any previous search is a sunk cost and should not influence your decision about whether to search again.

12.4 The expected value of a new car will now be $0.8(\$10,000) + 0.2(\$6,000) = \$9,200$. Any risk-neutral consumer who believed that the quality distribution of used cars for sale was the same as the quality distribution of new cars off the assembly line would be willing to pay $9,200 for a used car.

PART

4

LABOR MARKETS AND THE PUBLIC SECTOR

The market imperfections discussed in Part 3 help explain why no country on earth leaves all important economic decisions entirely in the hands of market forces. But income disparities among individuals are perhaps an even more important source of government involvement in modern economic life. In Chapter 13 we will explore why some people earn so much more than others. We will discuss the human capital model, which emphasizes the importance of differences in personal characteristics. But our focus will be on why people with similar personal characteristics often earn sharply different incomes.

In Chapter 14 we will explore examples in which careful application of basic economic principles can help society design policies that mitigate the market imperfections discussed in Part 3. The thread uniting these examples is the problem of scarcity. In each case we will explore how intelligent application of the cost-benefit principle can help resolve the resulting trade-offs in ways that expand the economic pie.

In Chapter 15 we will tackle such questions as how big government should be, what sorts of goods and services it should provide, and how it should raise the revenue to pay for them. We will also explore why rational citizens might empower government to constrain their behavior in various ways, and how such powers should be apportioned among local, state, and federal levels.

Finally, in Chapter 16 we will investigate why poverty and income inequality have become issues of central concern to all democratically elected governments. Because government programs to redistribute income have costs as well as benefits, policymakers must compare an imperfect status quo with the practical consequences of imperfect government remedies. We will explore why policies that would expand the economic pie often cannot be adopted unless steps are simultaneously taken to assure that everyone will end up with a larger slice.

LABOR MARKETS

■

By only the slimmest of margins, Mary Lou Retton won the individual all-around gold medal in women's gymnastics at the Los Angeles Summer Olympic Games in 1984. In the years since, she has remained in the spotlight, continuing to earn millions of dollars from product endorsements and motivational speeches. In contrast, the silver medalist from 1984 has dropped completely from view. (Can you name her?) She is Ecaterina Szabo, one of the most talented Romanian gymnasts of her era, and although she came within a hairsbreadth of beating Retton, wealth and international recognition were not to be hers.

Many physicians in Szabo's homeland are likewise every bit as talented and hardworking as physicians here in the United States. But while American physicians earn an average annual income of almost $200,000, Romanian physicians earn so little that some of them supplement their incomes by cleaning the Bucharest apartments of expatriate Americans for just $10 a day.

Why do some people earn so much more than others? No other single question in economics has stimulated nearly as much interest and discussion. American citizenship, of course, is neither necessary nor sufficient for receiving high income. Many of the wealthiest people in the world come from extremely poor countries, and hundreds of thousands of Americans are homeless and malnourished.

Our aim in this chapter will be to employ simple economic principles in an attempt to explain why different people earn different salaries. We'll discuss the human capital model, which emphasizes the importance of differences in personal characteristics. But our focus will be on why people with similar personal characteristics often earn sharply different incomes. Among the factors we will consider are labor unions, winner-take-all markets, discrimination, and the effect of nonwage conditions of employment.

Why do small differences in performance sometimes translate into enormous differences in pay?

WAGE AND SALARY DETERMINATION IN COMPETITIVE LABOR MARKETS

In some respects, the sale of human labor is profoundly different from the sale of other goods and services. For example, although someone may legally relinquish all future rights to the use of her television set by selling it, the law does not permit people to sell themselves into slavery. The law does, however, permit us to "rent out" our services to employers. And in many ways the rental market for labor services functions much like the market for most other goods and services. Each specific category of labor has a demand curve and a supply curve. These curves intersect to determine both the equilibrium wage and the equilibrium quantity of employment for each category of labor.

What is more, shifts in the relevant demand and supply curves produce changes analogous to those produced by shifts in the demand and supply curves for other goods and services. For example, an increase in the demand for a specific category of labor will generally increase both the equilibrium wage and the equilibrium quantity of employment in that category. By the same token, an increase in the supply of labor to a given occupation will tend to increase the level of employment and lower the wage rate in that occupation.

As in our discussions of other markets, our strategy for investigating how the labor market works will be to go through a series of examples that shed light on different parts of the picture. In the first example, we focus on how the equilibrium principle helps us to understand how wages will differ among workers with different levels of productive ability.

EXAMPLE 13.1

How much will the potters earn?

Mackintosh Pottery Works is one of numerous identical companies that hire potters who mold clay into pots. These companies sell the pots for $1.10 each to a finishing company that glazes and fires them and then sells them in the retail marketplace. Clay, which is available free of charge in unlimited quantities, is the only input used by the potters. Rennie and Laura are currently the only two potters who work for Mackintosh, whose only cost other than potters' salaries is a 10 cent handling cost for each pot it delivers to the finisher. Rennie delivers 100 pots/week and Laura delivers 120. If the labor market for potters is perfectly competitive, how much will each be paid?

In this example, we assume that Rennie and Laura have decided to work full-time as potters, so our focus is not on how much they will work but on how much they will be paid. After taking handling costs into account, the value of the pots that Rennie delivers is $100/week, and that is the amount Mackintosh will pay him. To pay him less would risk having him bid away by a competitor. For example, if Mackintosh paid Rennie only $90/week, the company would then enjoy an economic profit of $10/week as a result of hiring him. Seeing this cash on the table, a rival firm could then offer Rennie $91 and would earn additional economic profit of $9/week by bidding him away from Mackintosh. So under the bidding pressure from rival employers, Mackintosh will have difficulty keeping Rennie if it pays him less than $100/week. And the company would suffer an economic loss if it paid him more than $100/week. Similarly, the value of the pots delivered each week by Laura is $120, and this will be her competitive equilibrium wage.

In Example 13.1, the number of pots each potter delivered each week was that potter's **marginal physical product,** or **marginal product** *(MP)* for short. More generally, a worker's marginal product is the extra output the firm gets as a result of hiring that worker. When we multiply a worker's marginal product by the net price for which each unit of the product sells, we get that worker's **value of**

marginal product of labor (MP) the additional output a firm gets by employing one additional unit of labor marginal product, or *VMP.* (In Example 13.1 the "net price" of each pot was $1.00—the difference between the $1.10 sale price and the $0.10 handling charge.) The general rule in competitive labor markets is that *a worker's pay in long-run equilibrium will be equal to his or her VMP—the net contribution he or she makes to the employer's revenue.* Employers would be delighted to pay workers less than their respective *VMPs,* to be sure. But if labor markets are truly competitive, they cannot get away with doing so for long.

In Example 13.1, each worker's *VMP* was independent of the number of other workers employed by the firm. In such cases, we cannot predict how many workers a firm will hire. Mackintosh could break even with 2 potters, with 10, or even with 1,000 or more. In many other situations, however, we can predict exactly how many workers a firm will hire. Consider Example 13.2.

value of marginal product of labor (VMP) the dollar value of the additional output a firm gets by employing one additional unit of labor

EXAMPLE 13.2

How many workers should Adirondack hire? (Part 1)

The Adirondack Woodworking Company hires workers in a competitive labor market at a wage of $350/week to make kitchen cutting boards. If the boards sell for $20 each and the company's weekly output varies with the number of workers hired as shown in Table 13.1, how many workers should Adirondack hire?

TABLE 13.1
Employment and Productivity in a Woodworking Company
(When Cutting Boards Sell for $20 Each)

Number of workers	Total number of cutting boards/week	MP (extra cutting boards/week)	VMP ($/week)
0	0		
		30	600
1	30		
		25	500
2	55		
		21	420
3	76		
		18	360
4	94		
		14	280
5	108		

In Example 13.1 our focus was on wage differences for employees whose productive abilities differed. In contrast, we assume here that all workers are equally productive and the firm faces a fixed market wage for each. The fact that the marginal product of labor declines with the number of workers hired is a consequence of the law of diminishing returns. (As discussed in Chapter 6, the law of diminishing returns says that when a firm's capital and other productive inputs are held fixed in the short run, adding workers beyond some point results in ever-smaller increases in output.) The third column of the table reports the marginal product for each additional worker, and the last column reports the value of each successive worker's marginal product—the number of cutting boards he or she adds times the selling price of $20. Adirondack should keep hiring as long as the next worker's *VMP* is at least $350/week (the market wage). The first four workers have *VMPs* larger than $350, so Adirondack should hire them. But since hiring the fifth worker would add only $280 to weekly revenue, Adirondack should not hire that worker.

Note the similarity between the perfectly competitive firm's decision about how many workers to hire and the perfectly competitive firm's output decision we considered in Chapter 6. When labor is the only variable factor of production, the two decisions are essentially the same. Because of the unique correspondence between the firm's total output and the total number of workers it hires, deciding how many workers to hire is the same as deciding how much output to supply.

As Examples 13.3 and 13.4 illustrate, the worker's attractiveness to the employer depends not only on how many cutting boards he or she produces but also on the price of cutting boards and on the wage rate.

EXAMPLE 13.3

How many workers should Adirondack hire? (Part 2)

Refer to Example 13.2. Suppose that the price of cutting boards rises from $20 to $30. If the wage rate and marginal physical products are as before, how many workers should Adirondack hire?

As shown in the last column of Table 13.2, the 14 cutting boards produced by the fifth worker now add (14)($30) = $420 to weekly revenue, and since his wage is only $350, the company should hire him.

TABLE 13.2
The Effect of a Price Increase on Employment

Number of workers	Total number of cutting boards/week	MP (extra cutting boards/week)	VMP ($/week)
0	0		
		30	900
1	30		
		25	750
2	55		
		21	630
3	76		
		18	540
4	94		
		14	420
5	108		

EXERCISE 13.1

In Example 13.3, what is the lowest cutting board price at which Adirondack should hire two workers?

EXAMPLE 13.4

How many workers should Adirondack hire? (Part 3)

Now suppose that cutting boards again sell for their original price of $20 but that the wage rate of workers is not $350/week but $370. If the company's weekly output of cutting boards again varies with the number of workers as shown in Table 13.3, how many workers should it hire?

This time note that although the fourth worker was an attractive hire at a wage of $350/week, he will not be worth hiring at a wage of $370. His *VMP* is now smaller than his wage, so the company should hire only three workers.

TABLE 13.3
The Effect of a Wage Increase on Employment

Number of workers	Total number of cutting boards/week	MP (extra cutting boards/week)	VMP ($/week)
0	0		
		30	600
1	30		
		25	500
2	55		
		21	420
3	76		
		18	360
4	94		
		14	280
5	108		

EXERCISE 13.2

In Example 13.4, how many workers would Adirondack hire if the wage rate were $275/week?

RECAP   **WAGE AND SALARY DETERMINATION IN COMPETITIVE LABOR MARKETS**

In competitive labor markets, employers face pressure to pay each worker the value of his or her marginal product. When a firm can hire as many workers as it wishes at a given market wage, it should expand employment as long as the value of marginal product of labor exceeds the market wage.

MONOPSONY: THE LONE EMPLOYER IN A LABOR MARKET

In perfectly competitive product markets, sellers have no control over product prices. Market supply and demand curves intersect, and firms take the resulting prices as given. Similarly, in perfectly competitive labor markets, firms have no control over wage rates. The wage in each market is determined by supply and demand. In Examples 13.2 to 13.4, Adirondack Woodworking was a buyer in a perfectly competitive labor market, and viewed the market wage accordingly. The supply curve of labor facing such an employer is perfectly elastic—a horizontal line at the market wage.

But now suppose that Adirondack is a **monopsony**—the only buyer of labor services in its local labor market. The labor supply curve facing the company is now the labor supply curve for the market as a whole. There is no market wage per se. Workers get paid whatever Adirondack chooses to offer. But Adirondack is not free to offer just any wage, for if its offer is extremely low, workers may decide to relocate, or they may stop working and go on welfare. Even so, Adirondack now has some discretion about the wage it pays. In general, the more

monopsony a market with only a single buyer

workers the company wishes to hire, the more it will have to pay. How much should it pay its workers?

In many ways, the problem facing the monopsonist is similar to the one facing a monopolist in the market for a product. Because the monopolist's demand curve is the same as the product demand curve for the market as a whole, the only way the monopolist can expand sales is by cutting price. Similarly, because the supply curve of labor confronting the monopsonist is the supply curve for the labor market as a whole, the only way the monopsonist can hire additional workers is by offering higher wages. But raising the wage to an additional worker generally means also having to raise the wage for the workers hired thus far. And as Example 13.5 illustrates, the monopsonist has an incentive to limit employment, much as the monopolist has an incentive to limit output.

EXAMPLE 13.5

How many workers should Adirondack hire? (Part 4)

The Adirondack Woodworking Company is the only employer in a small town in the mountains of upstate New York. It sells kitchen cutting boards for $20 each, and its weekly output again varies with the number of workers as shown in Table 13.4. If there are five workers in town whom Adirondack might hire, with reservation wages as shown in Table 13.5, and if Adirondack must pay each worker the same wage, how many should it hire? (An individual's reservation wage for a job is the smallest payment for which she or he would be willing to accept the job.)

TABLE 13.4
Output and Employment for a Monopsonist

Number of workers	Total number of cutting boards/week	MP (extra cutting boards/week)	VMP ($/week)
0	0		
		30	600
1	30		
		25	500
2	55		
		21	420
3	76		
		18	360
4	94		
		14	280
5	108		

For the monopolist in the product market, recall that the decision rule is to sell another unit if marginal revenue (the amount by which its total revenue goes up when it sells an extra unit) exceeds marginal cost. For the monopsonist in the labor market, the corresponding rule is to hire another worker if that worker's *VMP* exceeds **marginal labor cost**—the amount by which the monopsonist's total wage bill would go up if it hired the extra worker. Marginal labor cost in this example is shown in the last column of Table 13.6. (Again, we assume that the monopsonist does not know each worker's reservation wage and must therefore pay each worker the same wage.)

If Adirondack offers a wage of $200, the only worker it will attract is Alice. If the company also wants to hire a second worker (Bert), it must not only pay him $50/week more than it is currently paying Alice, but it must also raise Alice's

marginal labor cost the amount by which a monopsonist's total wage bill goes up if it hires an extra worker

TABLE 13.5
Reservation Wages for the Monopsonist's Potential Employees

Worker	Reservation wage ($/week)
Alice	200
Bert	250
Carrie	300
Donna	350
Ernie	400

TABLE 13.6
Calculating Marginal Labor Cost for the Monopsonist

Worker	Reservation wage ($/week)	Total labor cost ($/week)	Marginal labor cost ($/week)
			200
Alice	200	200	
			300
Bert	250	500	
			400
Carrie	300	900	
			500
Donna	350	1,400	
			600
Ernie	400	2,000	

pay to $250/week. Because the company's total labor cost will go from $200 to $500/week in the process, the marginal labor cost of hiring Bert is $300/week. But since Bert's *VMP* is $500/week, hiring him is clearly in Adirondack's interest. Carrie, too, is a worthwhile hire because her marginal labor cost of $400/week is less than her *VMP* of $420. But Donna's marginal labor cost of $500/week is considerably more than her $360 *VMP*. So even though Donna's reservation wage of $350 is less than her *VMP*, the cost-benefit principle tells us that Adirondack will do better by not hiring her. Thus the company will hire only three workers—Alice, Carrie, and Bert—and will pay each a wage of $300/week.

EXERCISE 13.3

In Example 13.5, how many workers should Adirondack hire if cutting boards sold not for $20 but for $30?

In Chapter 9, we saw that a monopolist in the product market produces too little output because price exceeds marginal revenue. A similar inefficiency occurs with a monopsonist in the labor market. In Example 13.5, note that Adirondack the monopsonist has the same *VMP* schedule (Table 13.4) as its perfectly competitive counterpart in Example 13.2 (Table 13.1). In both cases, the company *could* hire four workers at a wage of $350/week. Yet the monopsonist hires one less worker than its perfectly competitive counterpart in Example 13.2. With only three workers on the monopsonist's payroll, the *social* cost of adding another worker is just the fourth worker's reservation wage, namely, $350. Because the fourth worker would add 18 cutting boards to the weekly production total, for a gain in revenue of $360, society would thus gain output worth $10 more than the social cost of hiring the fourth worker. Yet the monopsonist will not hire a fourth worker, because the private cost (marginal labor cost) of doing so is $500.

The monopsonist produces too little because the private cost of an additional hire is greater than the social cost of that hire. The reason for the discrepancy is that the new hire necessitates paying existing workers more, which the monopsonist understandably views as a real cost, but which from society's perspective is merely a transfer from the monopsonist to the existing workers.

Monopsony was once far more common than it is today. One reason for the decline is that a much greater proportion of workers now live in cities, giving them a broad choice of employers within driving distance of their homes. Another reason is that geographic mobility is greater now than in the past. Thus even those who live in small communities dominated by a single employer are more likely to have the option of seeking employment elsewhere. And with the continuing rise of telecommuting, the significance of monopsony in the labor market will diminish still further. Most economists believe that today's labor markets are highly competitive and that firms must be highly aggressive if they are to recruit and retain the capable workers they need.

RECAP **MONOPSONY**

Unlike the perfectly competitive employer, who can hire as much labor as he wishes at the market wage, the monopsonist can expand employment only by offering higher wages. And unlike the perfectly competitive employer, who continues hiring only until *VMP* equals the market wage, the monopsonist continues hiring until *VMP* equals marginal labor cost, which exceeds the market wage. The profit-maximizing employment level for the monopsonist is lower than the level that would maximize total economic surplus.

EQUILIBRIUM IN THE LABOR MARKET

An employer's reservation price for a worker is the most the employer could pay without suffering a decline in profit. As discussed, this reservation price for the employer in a perfectly competitive labor market is simply *VMP*, the value of the worker's marginal product. Because of the law of diminishing returns, we know that the marginal product of labor, and hence *VMP*, declines in the short run as the quantity of labor rises. The individual employer's demand curve for labor in any particular occupation—say, computer programmers—may thus be shown, as in Figure 13.1(a), as a downward-sloping function of the wage rate. Suppose firm 1 [part (a)] and firm 2 [part (b)] are the only two firms that employ programmers in a given community. The demand for programmers in that community will then be the horizontal sum of the individual firm demands [part (c)].

What does the supply curve of labor for a specific occupation look like? Will more labor be offered at high wage rates than at low wage rates? For the economy as a whole during the past several centuries, the workweek has been declining and real wages have been rising. This pattern might seem to suggest that the supply curve of labor is downward-sloping, and for the economy as a whole it may be. Yet the supply of labor *to any particular occupation* is almost surely upward-sloping, because wage differences among occupations influence occupational choice. It is no accident, for example, that many more people are choosing jobs as computer programmers now than in 1970. Wages of programmers have risen sharply during the past several decades, which has led many people to forsake other career paths in favor of programming.

Curve *S* in Figure 13.2 represents the supply curve of computer programmers. As more tasks have become computerized in recent decades, the demand for pro-

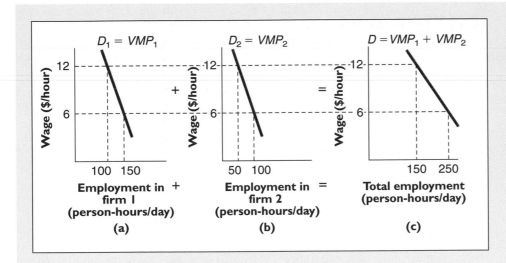

FIGURE 13.1
The Occupational Demand for Labor.
If firm 1 and firm 2 are the only firms that employ labor in a given occupation, we generate the demand curve for labor in that occupation by adding the individual demand curves horizontally.

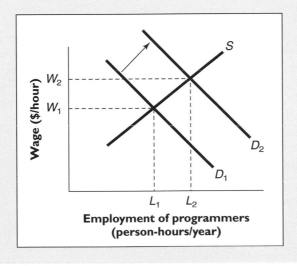

FIGURE 13.2
The Effect of an Increase in the Demand for Computer Programmers.
An increase in the demand for programmers from D_1 to D_2 results in an increase in the equilibrium level of employment (from L_1 to L_2) and an increase in the equilibrium wage (from W_1 to W_2).

grammers has grown, as shown by the shift from D_1 to D_2 in Figure 13.2. Equilibrium in the market for computer programmers occurs at the intersection of the relevant supply and demand curves. The increase in demand has led to an increase in the equilibrium level of programmers from L_1 to L_2 and a rise in the equilibrium wage from W_1 to W_2.

As discussed in Chapter 8, the market for stocks and other financial assets reaches equilibrium very quickly in the wake of shifts in the underlying supply and demand curves. Labor markets are often much slower to adjust. When the demand for workers in a given profession increases, shortages may remain for months or even years, depending on how long it takes people to acquire the skills and training needed to enter the profession.

EXPLAINING DIFFERENCES IN EARNINGS

The theory of competitive labor markets tells us that differences in pay reflect differences in the corresponding *VMP*s. Thus, in Example 13.1, Laura earned 20 percent more than Rennie because she made 20 percent more pots each week than he did. This difference in productivity may have resulted from an underlying difference in talent or training, or perhaps Laura simply worked harder than Rennie.

Yet often we see large salary differences even between people who appear equally talented and hardworking. Why, for example, do lawyers earn so much more than plumbers who are just as smart and work just as hard? And why do surgeons earn so much more than general practitioners? These wage differences might seem to violate the no-cash-on-the-table principle, which says that only differences in talent, luck, or hard work can account for long-run differences in earnings. For example, if plumbers could earn more by becoming lawyers, why don't they just switch occupations? Likewise, if general practitioners could boost their incomes by becoming surgeons, why didn't they become surgeons in the first place?

HUMAN CAPITAL THEORY

human capital theory a theory of pay determination that says a worker's wage will be proportional to his or her stock of human capital

human capital an amalgam of factors such as education, training, experience, intelligence, energy, work habits, trustworthiness, initiative, and others that affect the value of a worker's marginal product

Answers to these questions are suggested by the **human capital theory,** which holds that an individual's *VMP* is proportional to his or her stock of **human capital**—an amalgam of factors such as education, experience, training, intelligence, energy, work habits, trustworthiness, initiative, and so on. According to this theory, some occupations pay better than others because they require larger stocks of human capital. For example, a general practitioner could become a surgeon, but only by extending her formal education by several more years. An even larger additional investment in education is required for a plumber to become a lawyer.

In general, a decision to invest in human capital, like decisions to invest in other assets, requires comparing costs incurred in the present with benefits received in the future. As Example 13.6 illustrates, intelligent decisions of this sort require us to make use of the present value concept we encountered in Chapter 8.

EXAMPLE 13.6

Should Betsy get an MBA?

Betsy has a bachelor's degree and 2 years of experience as a branch manager of a small business. If she continues along her present career path, she will be promoted to positions of greater managerial responsibility, and the present value of her lifetime earnings in those positions will be $350,000. If instead she takes 2 years off and completes an MBA degree, she will be assigned to positions of significantly higher responsibility. The present value of her lifetime earnings in those positions will be $393,000. The only expenses of attending business school are two tuition payments—a $22,000 payment now and another $22,000 payment 1 year from now. Suppose that apart from monetary considerations, Betsy is indifferent between these two life courses. If the annual interest rate is 10 percent, should she go for her MBA?

The benefit of the MBA is the resulting increase in the present value of Betsy's lifetime earnings, which is $393,000 − $350,000 = $43,000. The cost of the MBA is the present value of her tuition payments, which is $22,000 + $22,000/ 1.10 = $42,000. (The opportunity cost of her lost earnings while getting the degree is reflected in the present value of her lifetime earnings with the degree.) Since the benefit of getting her MBA exceeds the cost by $1,000, Betsy should get the degree.

Someone who compared the salaries of managers with MBAs to those of managers without MBAs might be tempted to conclude that the MBAs had reaped an enormous windfall. But their advantage appears less dramatic once we include the cost of acquiring the additional human capital.

EXERCISE 13.4

Refer to Example 13.6. If Betsy had been indifferent between getting an MBA or not at an interest rate of 10 percent, which option should she choose if the interest rate is 12 percent? (*Hint:* An increase in the interest rate will change the present value of the cost of obtaining the degree by a different amount than it will change the present value of the benefit.)

Differences in demand can result in some kinds of human capital being more valuable than others. Consider again the increase in demand for computer programmers that has been occurring for the past several decades. During that same time period, the demand for the services of tax accountants has fallen as more and more taxpayers have used tax-preparation software in lieu of hiring accountants to help them with their taxes. Both occupations require demanding technical training, but the training received by computer programmers now yields a higher return in the labor market.

LABOR UNIONS

Two workers with the same amount of human capital may earn different wages if one of them belongs to a **labor union** and the other does not. A labor union is an organization through which workers attempt to bargain collectively with employers for better wages and working conditions.

labor union a group of workers who bargain collectively with employers for better wages and working conditions

Many economists believe that unions affect labor markets in much the same way that cartels affect product markets. To illustrate, consider a simple economy with two labor markets, neither of which is unionized initially. Suppose the total supply of labor to the two markets is fixed at $S_0 = 200$ workers/day and that the demand curves are as shown by VMP_1 and VMP_2 in Figure 13.3(a) and (b). The sum of the two demand curves, $VMP_1 + VMP_2$ [Figure 13.3(c)], intersects the supply curve to determine an equilibrium wage of $9/hour. At that wage, firms in market 1 hire 125 workers/day [part (a)], and firms in market 2 hire 75 [part (b)].

Now suppose workers in market 1 form a union and refuse to work for less than $12/hour. Because demand curves for labor are downward-sloping, employers of unionized workers reduce employment from 125 workers/day to 100 [Figure 13.4(a)]. The 25 displaced workers in the unionized market would, of course, be delighted to find other jobs in that market at $12/hour. But they cannot and so are forced to seek employment in the nonunionized market. The result is an excess supply of 25 workers in the nonunion market at the original wage of $9/hour. In time, wages in that market decline to $W_N = $6/hour, the level at which 100 workers can find jobs in the nonunionized market [Figure 13.4(b)].

FIGURE 13.3

An Economy with Two Nonunionized Labor Markets.

Supply and demand intersect to determine a market wage of $9/hour in part (c). At that wage, employers in market 1 hire 125 workers/day, and employers in market 2 hire 75 workers/day. The *VMP* is $9 in each market.

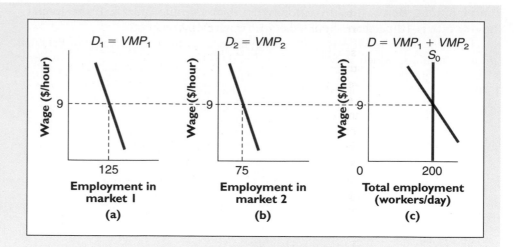

FIGURE 13.4

The Effect of a Union Wage above the Equilibrium Wage.

When the unionized wage is pegged at $W_U = \$12$/hour [part (a)], 25 workers are discharged. When these workers seek employment in the nonunionized market, the wage in that market falls to $W_N = \$6$/hour.

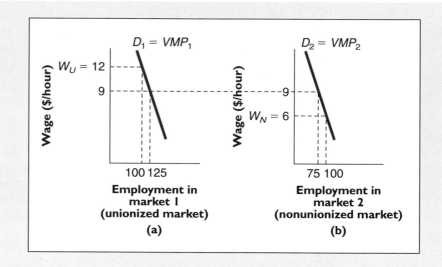

It might seem that the gains of the unionized workers are exactly offset by the losses of nonunionized workers. On closer inspection, however, we see that pegging the union wage above the equilibrium level actually reduces the value of total output. Recall from Chapter 2 that the condition for allocating a resource between two activities efficiently is for the marginal benefit of the resource to be the same in each activity. Here, the two activities are production in the unionized market and production in the nonunionized market; the marginal benefit of the resource in each market is the labor's *VMP* in that market. With the wage set initially at $9/hour in both markets, the condition for efficient allocation was met, because labor's *VMP* was $9/hour in both markets. But because the collective bargaining process drives wages in the two markets apart, the value of total output is no longer maximized. To verify this claim, note that if a worker is taken out of the nonunionized market, the reduction in the value of output there will be only $6/hour, which is less than the $12/hour gain in the value of output when that same worker is added to the unionized market.

EXERCISE 13.5

In Figure 13.4, by how much would the value of total output be increased if the wage rate were $9/hour in each market?

If unionized firms have to pay more, how do they manage to survive in the face of competition from their nonunionized counterparts?

In fact, nonunionized firms sometimes do drive unionized firms out of business, as when the American textile industry moved to the south to escape the burden of high union wages in New England. Even so, unionized and nonunionized firms often manage to compete head-to-head for extended periods. If their costs are significantly higher, how do the unionized firms manage to survive?

Wages paid to workers in a unionized firm are sometimes 50 percent or more above the wages paid to their nonunionized counterparts. But this difference actually overstates the difference between the labor costs of the two types of firms. Because the higher union wage attracts an excess supply of workers, unionized employers can adopt more stringent hiring requirements than their nonunionized counterparts. As a result, unionized workers tend to be more experienced and skilled than nonunionized workers. Studies estimate that the union wage premium for workers with the same amount of human capital is only about 10 percent.

Another factor is that unions may actually boost the productivity of workers with any given amount of human capital, perhaps by improving communication between management and workers. Similarly, the implementation of formal grievance procedures, in combination with higher pay, may boost morale among unionized workers, leading to higher productivity. Labor turnover is also significantly lower in unionized firms, which reduces hiring and training costs. Studies suggest that union productivity may be sufficiently high to compensate for the premium in union wages. So even though wages are higher in unionized firms, these firms may not have significantly higher labor costs per unit of output than their nonunionized counterparts.

Only one in six American workers currently belongs to a labor union, about half the union membership rate during the 1950s. Because the union wage premium is small and applies to only a small fraction of the labor force, union membership in the United States is probably not an important explanation for why workers with similar qualifications often earn sharply different incomes.

WINNER-TAKE-ALL MARKETS

Differences in human capital do much to explain observed differences in earnings. Yet earnings differentials have also grown sharply in many occupations within which the distribution of human capital among workers seems essentially unchanged. Consider the following example.

Why does Kathleen Battle earn millions more than singers of only slightly lesser ability?

Although the best sopranos have always earned more than others with slightly lesser talents, the earnings gap is sharply larger now than it was in the last century. Today, top singers like Kathleen Battle earn millions of dollars per year, hundreds or even thousands of times what sopranos only marginally less talented earn. Given that listeners in blind hearings often have difficulty identifying the most highly paid singers, why is this earnings differential so large?

The answer lies in a fundamental change in the way we consume most of our music. In the nineteenth century, virtually all professional musicians delivered their services in concert halls in front of live audiences. (In 1900, the state of Iowa alone had more than 1,300 concert halls!) Audiences of that day would have been delighted to listen to the world's best soprano, but no one singer could hope to perform in more than a tiny fraction of the world's concert halls. Today, in contrast, most of the music we hear comes in recorded form, which enables the best soprano to be literally everywhere at once. As soon as the master recording has been made, Kathleen Battle's performance can be burned onto compact discs at the same low cost as for a slightly less talented singer's.

Tens of millions of buyers worldwide are willing to pay a few cents extra to hear the most talented performers. Recording companies would be delighted to hire those singers at modest salaries, for by so doing they would earn an enormous economic profit. But that would unleash bidding by rival recording companies for the best singers. Such bidding assures that the top singers will earn multimillion dollar annual salaries (most of which constitute economic rents, as discussed in Chapter 8). Slightly less talented singers earn much less, because the recording industry simply does not need those singers.

winner-take-all labor market
one in which small differences in human capital translate into large differences in pay

The market for sopranos is an example of a **winner-take-all market,** one in which small differences in ability or other dimensions of human capital translate into large differences in pay. Long familiar in entertainment and professional sports, this reward pattern is becoming more common in other professions, as technology enables the most talented individuals to serve broader markets. A winner-take-all market does not mean a market with literally only one winner. Indeed, hundreds of professional musicians earn multimillion dollar annual salaries. Yet tens of thousands of others, many of them nearly as good, struggle to pay their bills.

One consequence of the spread of winner-take-all markets has been the sharp increase in the pay of top earners relative to others. Compensation of the chief executives of America's largest companies, for example, is now more than 400 times the salary of the average American production worker, up from a multiple of 42 in 1980. These executives now average roughly $4 million/year, and the highest paid among them earn considerably more.

The top earners on Wall Street have also fared well. For example, roughly 1,000 Wall Street professionals received bonuses in excess of $1 million in 1997–1998. Goldman Sachs alone made roughly $3 billion in fiscal 1997, the bulk of which was apportioned among its 190 most senior directors. In terms of their "current compensation," these directors typically earn less than $4 million annually, but many took home nearly four times that amount in bonus money. One layer down in the hierarchy, Goldman's 215 managing directors received an average of $1.5 million in 1998 bonus money.

A similar earnings explosion has taken place in publishing, where even six-figure advances for works of hardcover fiction were rare just two decades ago. For authors, the watershed event was the $5 million paid in 1985 by William Morrow for the rights to James Clavel's novel *Whirlwind*. Five years later, NAL/Viking paid Stephen King $40 million for the rights to his next four novels, and Dell/Delacourt paid Danielle Steel $60 million for her next five books.

Big winners have also become increasingly common in show business and professional sports. Both Mel Gibson and Adam Sandler now command approximately $25 million per film. In his final year of play, Chicago Bulls star Michael Jordan was paid about $30 million, and he earned a considerably larger sum for his various product endorsements.

Some social critics view the escalating salaries of top earners as a signal that labor markets are no longer effectively competitive. Yet competitive pressures in domestic and international labor markets have never been more intense than they are today. The role of growing competition in the rise of top performers' salaries is clearly evident in the salary trajectory of professional baseball players.

Why did professional baseball players' salaries remain stagnant until 1975, despite the large influx of television revenue that began in the 1950s?

Baseball as a whole grew much more lucrative in the 1950s to 1970s with the influx of national and local television revenues (another example of how new technology enables top performers to serve broader markets). Why, then, were players' salaries little higher in 1975 than in 1950?

ECONOMIC
NATURALIST
13.3

Until 1975, contract restrictions prevented players from selling their services to the highest bidder. They had to play for their current teams or not play at all. Under such restrictions, the predictions of a competitive labor market theory simply do not apply. Two important court decisions, one in 1975, the other in 1976, ushered in the modern era of free agency, in which players are essentially free to play for whichever teams they choose. As Figure 13.5 shows, player salaries began escalating sharply in the aftermath of those court decisions. The pace of salary growth escalated further with the signing of the $1 billion CBS television contract in 1988.

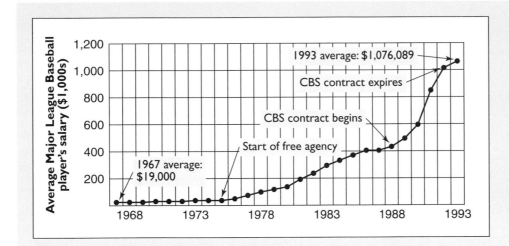

FIGURE 13.5
Salary Growth in Professional Baseball.
The value of baseball players' services rose sharply in the 1950s, when nationally televised games dramatically increased the size of the audience. But this increase in value was not reflected in salaries until 1975, when players won the right to sell their services to any team they chose. (SOURCE: Major League Baseball Players Association.)

Many critics have complained that the rapid escalation of players' salaries is a sure signal that team owners have lost their senses. This charge, too, misses the mark. The New York Yankees offered star center fielder Bernie Williams an $87 million contract in 1998 not because team owner George Steinbrenner was stupid but because Williams's presence helped fill the stands, land a more lucrative TV contract, and win the World Series. Williams was a free agent when he signed with the Yankees, and a smaller offer would have risked losing him to a rival bidder.

Why have the salaries of corporate executives been rising so rapidly?

As noted earlier, the chief executive officers of America's 200 largest companies made 42 times as much as the average production worker in 1980 but now earn more than 400 times as much. Why this dramatic increase?

Growth in productivity of the top performers and the more open bidding for their services have occurred for different reasons in different markets. In broad terms, however, the story has been much the same in the market for executive talent as in the market for professional baseball players. As a corporation's local markets have expanded into regional, then national, and finally global markets, the value of good decisions at the top of the organization has grown rapidly. But as in baseball, contributing a lot to the organization's bottom line does not guarantee a commensurate salary. There must also be open competition for the services of top performers. The almost universal practice once was to promote business executives from within the company, which often enabled firms to retain top executives for less than one-tenth of today's salaries. As recently as 1984, the business community arched its collective eyebrow when Apple Computer hired a new chief executive with a background in soft drink marketing.

But interfirm and interindustry boundaries have become increasingly permeable in the years since. As shown in Figure 13.6, for example, the number of chief executives hired from outside the company grew almost 50 percent between 1970 and 1992. This greater mobility has been accompanied by explosive growth in executive salaries.

ECONOMIC NATURALIST 13.4

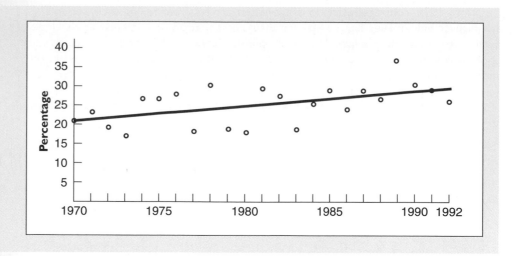

FIGURE 13.6
Percentage of CEOs with Less than 3 Years' Tenure at Time of Hire.
The number of CEOs hired from outside the company grew almost 50 percent between 1990 and 1992, a factor that helped the rapid growth of CEO pay.
(SOURCE: Robert H. Frank and Philip J. Cook, *The Winner-Take-All Society,* New York: The Free Press, 1995.)

Disney CEO Michael Eisner was paid more than $500 million in 1997 not because he duped shareholders but because he delivered an unprecedented increase in the company's value at a time when the mobility of chief executives had made them increasingly like the free agents of professional sports.

The fact that small differences in human capital often give rise to extremely large differences in pay might seem to contradict human capital theory. Note, however, that the winner-take-all reward pattern is completely consistent with the competitive labor market theory's claim that individuals are paid in accordance with the contributions they make to the employer's net revenue. The leverage of technology often amplifies small performance differentials into very large ones.

COMPENSATING WAGE DIFFERENTIALS

If people are paid the value of what they produce, why do garbage collectors earn more than lifeguards? Picking up the trash is important, to be sure, but is it more valuable than saving the life of a drowning child? Similarly, we need not question the value of a timely plumbing repair to wonder why plumbers get paid more than fourth grade teachers. Is replacing faucet washers really more valuable than educating children? As the next examples illustrate, the wage for a particular job depends not only on the value of what workers produce but also on how attractive they find its working conditions.

ECONOMIC NATURALIST 13.5

Why do garbage collectors earn more than lifeguards?

There are two summer jobs open to the 20 Wisconsin undergraduates who live in a small northeastern city: lifeguards at the local beach (10 positions) and garbage collectors for the municipal sanitation department (10 positions). All 20 summer job seekers possess the requisite skills for each job, and all view the lifeguard job as the more desirable of the two. What will happen if the city posts the same wage rate for the two jobs?

Because lifeguarding is generally regarded as pleasant work and garbage collecting is generally regarded as unpleasant, we may expect 20 applicants for the lifeguard job and none for the garbage job. If city employment directors respond in the usual way to this imbalance in supply and demand, they will keep raising the wage of garbage collectors and keep lowering the wage for lifeguards until both labor markets reach equilibrium.

Other things being equal, jobs with attractive working conditions will pay less than jobs with less attractive conditions. Wage differences associated with differences in working conditions are known as **compensating wage differentials.** Economists have identified compensating differentials for a host of different specific working conditions. Studies have found, for example, that safe jobs tend to pay less than otherwise similar jobs that entail greater risks to health and safety. Studies have also found that wages vary in accord with the attractiveness of the work schedule. For instance, working night shifts commands a wage premium, and teachers must accept lower wages because those with children value having hours that coincide with the school calendar.

As the next example illustrates, we see compensating wage differentials even for such hard-to-measure characteristics as the degree of social approval associated with different jobs.

Why do some advertising copywriters earn more than others?

Suppose you plan to pursue a career in advertising. You have two job offers, one to write ad copy for the American Cancer Society, the other to write copy for Camel Cigarette ads aimed at the youth market. Except for the subject matter of the ads, working conditions are identical in the two jobs. If the two jobs paid the same salary, which would you choose?

This question and several similar ones were recently posed to a sample of seniors about to graduate from Cornell University, who were told that the jobs in each of the six matched pairs described in Table 13.7 pay $30,000/year and have the same prospects for advancement. Suppose the same questions were put to you: Imagine, for example, that you could be an accountant for a large petrochemical company or an accountant for a large art museum, with identical salaries, offices, tasks, promotion prospects, and so on. Which would you choose? Would you choose to be a language teacher for the CIA or a language teacher for a local high school? A recruiter for Exxon or a recruiter for the Peace Corps? And so on.

compensating wage differential a difference in the wage rate—negative or positive—that reflects the attractiveness of a job's working conditions

ECONOMIC NATURALIST 13.6

Do tobacco company CEOs get paid extra for testifying that cigarette smoking does not cause cancer?

TABLE 13.7
Job Pairs Requiring Similar Ability and Experience

Ad copywriter for Camel Cigarettes	Ad copywriter for the American Cancer Society
Accountant for a large petrochemical company	Accountant for a large art museum
Language teacher for the CIA	Language teacher for a local high school
Recruiter for Exxon	Recruiter for the Peace Corps
Lawyer for the National Rifle Association	Lawyer for the Sierra Club
Chemist for Union Carbide	Chemist for Dow Chemical

After students reported which job they would choose from each pair in Table 13.7, they were asked to report the minimum pay premium they would require for switching to the job they hadn't chosen. Table 13.8 reports the percentage of students who chose jobs in the right column of Table 13.7 and the median and average pay premiums they required for switching in each case.

Conversations with these students confirmed the impression that the favored jobs were chosen at least in part because they were more likely to command the social approval of others. This does not imply, necessarily, that there is anything morally questionable about the jobs that students tended not to choose. The Dow versus Union Carbide example is especially instructive in this regard. In the early 1970s, Dow was widely seen as an "evil" company because it manufactured the napalm that was dropped on villages during the Vietnam war. But memories of this association are no longer fresh. In contrast, many people still recall vividly the disaster in which poisonous methyl cyanate gas leaked from a Union Carbide chemical plant in Bhopal, India, killing and maiming tens of thousands of sleeping villagers. Despite the fact that subsequent

TABLE 13.8
Compensating Wage Differentials for Social Approval

Job chosen	Percentage choosing	Median pay premium for switching	Average pay premium for switching
American Cancer Society	88.2	$15,000/year	$24,333/year
Art museum	79.4	$ 5,000/year	$14,185/year
High school	82.4	$ 8,000/year	$18,679/year
Peace Corps	79.4	$ 5,000/year	$13,037/year
Sierra Club	94.1	$10,000/year	$37,129/year*
Dow Chemical	79.4	$ 2,000/year	$11,796/year

*Excludes one response of $1 trillion/year.

evidence suggested the accident resulted from negligence by Union Carbide's Indian partner, the company is only now beginning to recover from the damage the incident caused to its reputation.

Faced with two otherwise equally attractive jobs, most people will choose the employer whose mission they feel best about. How else can we explain why, in the years since it gained notoriety as a napalm manufacturer, Dow has invested millions of dollars on a national advertising campaign aimed at persuading the public that Dow's employees perform services that benefit humanity?

As the next example illustrates, employers can sometimes gain advantage by offering nonwage conditions that have special appeal to the types of workers they want.

ECONOMIC NATURALIST 13.7

Why did a telecommunications equipment manufacturer recently offer "free" BMW sedans to employees with more than 1 year of service?

Arcnet, Inc., which designs and builds wireless telecommunications systems, recently started giving a "free" BMW sedan to every employee with at least 1 year of service. The cars are not really free, of course. Each one costs the company about $9,000 a year in leasing and insurance fees, and employees who get one must declare that amount as additional income each year to the Internal Revenue Service. So we're left with a puzzle: If the company had given not the car but an additional $9,000 a year in salary instead, no one should have been worse off and at least some should have been better off. After all, any worker who really wanted a BMW could have spent the extra cash to lease one. Others who happen not to want a BMW would have come out ahead by having $9,000 a year extra to spend on other things. So why give cars instead of cash?

Essentially the same question is raised by ordinary gift exchanges among family and friends. Why give someone a necktie he might never wear when you know you could trust him to spend the same money on something he really wants? Some would answer that giving cash is just too easy and is hence a less effective way of demonstrating affection than taking the time and trouble to shop for a gift. That explanation might work for small gifts, but it is surely a stretch for luxury cars.

A more promising tack was suggested by the economist Richard Thaler, who observed that the best gifts are often things we don't dare buy for ourselves. Why, for example, is a man happy when his wife gives him a $1,000 set of titanium golf clubs paid for out of their joint checking account? Perhaps he really wanted those clubs but couldn't quite justify spending so much.

The plausibility of this way of thinking about gift giving is affirmed by the advice it suggests for gift givers. For example, consider this thought experiment: Among each of the following pairs of items costing the same amounts, which item would be the more suitable gift for a close friend?

■ $20 worth of Macadamia nuts (1 pound) or $20 worth of peanuts (10 pounds)?

■ A $75 gift certificate for Lespinasse (one lunch) or a $75 gift certificate for McDonald's (15 lunches)?

■ $30 worth of wild rice (3 pounds) versus $30 worth of Uncle Ben's converted rice (50 pounds)?

For most people, the first item in each pair is almost surely the safer choice.

Arcnet and other employers in the fast lane may be giving away BMWs for essentially similar reasons. An employee might find it awkward to explain to his depression-era parents why he had bought a car costing almost twice as much as a Honda Accord. Or he may worry that buying a new BMW might make his neighbors think he was putting on airs. Or perhaps he really wants to buy the new BMW, but his wife insists on remodeling the kitchen instead. A gift car from his employer wipes away all these concerns and more.

Is the American labor market headed for a full-fledged barter system? Not likely, because the Arcnet strategy would make little sense for many employers. Burger King owners, for example, probably won't dangle used Ford Escorts the next time they find themselves short of counter help. They and other employers of unskilled labor are more likely to stick with the time-honored strategy of paying higher wages.

But in-kind compensation is almost certain to spread further among employers of the most highly skilled workers. It is these employers who have faced consistent labor shortages, and it's the people they are trying to hire and retain who have been so responsive to the new luxury offerings.

As the trend unfolds, the gifts are likely to change. The new strategy depends on the gift's ability to generate excitement. And excitement, always and everywhere, depends on context. Most readers were astonished when the young lawyer in John Grisham's 1991 novel *The Firm* was given a new German luxury sedan as a signing bonus, and the same tactic attracts media attention even today. As more and more companies adopt this tactic, however, it will inevitably lose much of its punch.

To achieve the same impact, employers will have to raise the stakes. Can anyone doubt that talented consultants and software developers will eventually snub any employer who dares offer less than a Porsche 911?

RECAP   **EXPLAINING DIFFERENCES IN EARNINGS**

Earnings differ among people in part because of differences in their human capital, an amalgam of personal characteristics that affect productivity. Two people with the same amount of human capital may earn different wages if one belongs to a labor union and the other does not. Their earnings may also differ because a given amount of human capital has greater leverage in some contexts than others. The world's most talented soprano is far more valuable, for example, if people can listen to her music not just in live performances but on compact discs as well. Earnings may also differ between equally productive individuals because of compensating wage differentials—positive or negative wage differentials attributable to differences in working conditions.

DISCRIMINATION IN THE LABOR MARKET

Women and minorities continue to receive lower wage rates, on average, than white males with similar measures of human capital. This pattern poses a profound challenge to standard theories of competitive labor markets, which hold that competitive pressures will eliminate wage differentials not based on differences in productivity. Defenders of standard theories attribute the wage gap to unmeasured differences in human capital. Critics of these theories, who reject the idea that labor markets are effectively competitive, attribute the gap to various forms of discrimination.

DISCRIMINATION BY EMPLOYERS

employer discrimination an arbitrary preference by the employer for one group of workers over another

Employer discrimination is the term used to describe wage differentials that arise from an arbitrary preference by the employer for one group of workers over another. An example occurs if two labor force groups, such as males and females, are equally productive, on average, yet some employers ("discriminators") prefer hiring males and are willing to pay higher wages to do so.

Most consumers are not willing to pay more for a product produced by males than for an identical one produced by females (if indeed they even *know* which type of worker produced the product). If product price is unaffected by the composition of the workforce that produces the product, a firm's profit will be smaller the more males it employs, because males cost more yet are no more productive. Thus the most profitable firms will be ones that employ only females.

Arbitrary wage gaps are an apparent violation of the equilibrium principle. The initial wage differential provides an opportunity for employers who hire mostly females to grow at the expense of their rivals. Because such firms make an economic profit on the sale of each unit of output, their incentive is to expand as rapidly as they possibly can. And to do that, they would naturally want to continue hiring only the cheaper females.

But as profit-seeking firms continue to pursue this strategy, the supply of females at the lower wage rate will run out. The short-run solution is to offer females a slightly higher wage. But this strategy works only if other firms do not pursue it. Once they too start offering a higher wage, females will again be in short supply. The only stable outcome will occur when the wage of females reaches parity with the wage of males. The wage for both males and females will thus settle at the common value of their *VMP*.

Any employer who wants to voice a preference for hiring males must now do so by paying males a wage in excess of their *VMP*. Employers can discriminate against females if they wish, but only if they are willing to pay premium wages to males out of their own profits. Not even the harshest critics of the competitive model seem willing to impute such behavior to the owners of capitalist enterprises.

DISCRIMINATION BY OTHERS

customer discrimination the willingness of consumers to pay more for a product produced by members of a favored group, even if the quality of the product is unaffected

If employer discrimination is not the primary explanation of the wage gap, what is? In some instances, **discrimination by customers** may provide a plausible explanation. For example, if people believe that juries and clients are less likely to take female or minority attorneys seriously, members of these groups will face a reduced incentive to attend law school, and law firms will face a reduced incentive to hire those who do.

Another possible source of persistent wage gaps is discrimination and socialization within the family. For example, families may provide less education for their female children, or they may socialize them to believe that lofty career ambitions are not appropriate.

OTHER SOURCES OF THE WAGE GAP

Family location constraints provide another possible explanation of wage differentials by sex. In two-career couples, the best job opportunities for both spouses are unlikely to be in the same local labor market. For spouses who wish to live together, one or both usually accept something less than the best available job offer. Compromises of this sort tend to be more costly the more human capital someone has.

Because women marry men who, on average, are several years older and have more education and experience than they do, the burden of those compromises tends to fall more heavily on wives. The historical pattern was that family location was dictated by the husband's best offer, and wives took the best job they could find in that particular labor market. Even within local markets, wives may be relatively more constrained in their choice of jobs by their desire to be closer to home and children's schools. Such constraints imply that part of the sex differential in wages is attributable to the fact that males can utilize their human capital more fully than females.

Related to location constraints are differences in preferences for other non-wage elements of the compensation package. Jobs that involve exposure to physical risk, for example, command higher wages, and if men are relatively more willing to accept such risks, they will earn more than females with otherwise identical stocks of human capital. (The same difference would result if employers felt constrained by social forces not to assign female employees to risky jobs.)

Elements of human capital that are difficult to measure may also help to explain earnings differentials. For example, productivity is influenced not only by the quantity of education an individual has, which is easy to measure, but also by its quality, which is much harder to measure. Part of the black-white differential in wages may thus be due to the fact that schools in black neighborhoods have not been as good, on average, as those in white neighborhoods. Differences in the courses people take in college appear to have similar implications for differences in productivity. For instance, students in math, engineering, or business—male or female—tend to earn significantly higher salaries than those who concentrate in the humanities. The fact that males are disproportionately represented in the former group gives rise to a male wage premium that is unrelated to employer discrimination.

"English lit—how about you?"

Wage differentials may also result from behavioral choices that affect productivity. As discussed earlier, for example, people earn less when they choose jobs, such as those commonly seen in the nonprofit sector, that provide a measure of moral satisfaction in exchange for smaller monetary compensation. When males choose such jobs, they earn the same low wages that women do. But women are much more likely than males to choose such jobs, and this difference further reduces the previously unexplained sex-differential in wages.

Wage rates depend not only on the total amount of experience someone has but also on the manner in which that experience accumulates. Continuous labor force participation results in significantly higher wages than intermittent labor force participation, for males and females. But because women are also more likely than men to specialize in childrearing, their labor force participation is more likely to be intermittent. Wage differentials that stem from differences in labor force participation patterns also cannot be attributed to employer discrimination.

Despite concerted efforts to explain sex and race differentials in wages, significant gaps remain. One recent survey, for example, reported that almost 40 percent of the wage gap between men and women with a high school education could not be explained by the usual human capital variables. Studies of wage differentials by race report similar findings. Debate about discrimination in the workplace will continue until the causes of these differentials are more fully understood.

COMPARABLE WORTH POLICIES: A COSTLY REMEDY?

comparable worth legislation
legislation that would set wages for a job not by market forces but by collective judgments about the social value of the job

Many social critics bemoan the fact that bond traders and personal-injury lawyers earn millions of dollars annually, while the salaries of teachers and librarians stagnate. Concern with such inequities has led some people to favor **comparable worth legislation**—statutes that would shift wage determination from private market forces to committees of government bureaucrats. The goal of those committees would be to assure that workers are paid in accord with the social value of what they produce. For example, if the committee decided that a good fourth grade teacher, or a brave soldier, is worth more to society than a good corporate tax specialist, it would set their respective salaries accordingly.

Regardless of one's views about the social concerns that motivated the comparable worth movement, there are good reasons to be skeptical about the proposed remedy. As discussed earlier, many people value employment that offers a chance to contribute to society's well-being. In perfectly competitive markets, workers in such jobs tend to earn lower wages—a compensating wage differential for morally satisfying work. Now suppose, as in Example 13.7, that a government regulation tried to prohibit compensating differentials for jobs that command social approval.

EXAMPLE 13.7

What would be the consequence of a law requiring that ad copywriters for the United Way be paid more than ad copywriters for the Philip Morris Tobacco Company?

Suppose the demand and supply curves for ad copywriters in the two settings are as shown in Figure 13.7. By how much will total economic surplus be reduced if the government says that ad copywriters for the United Way must be paid at least $60,000/year and that those who are employed by Philip Morris cannot be paid more?

In the unregulated case, ad copywriters who choose employment with the United Way will earn only $40,000/year [Figure 13.7(a)], while those who choose Philip Morris will earn $80,000/year. If comparable worth legislation then pegs the salary at $60,000/year for both employers, employment of copywriters will decline at each company: from 1,000 to 500 at United Way and from 1,000 to 750 at Philip Morris, as shown in Figure 13.8. The resulting reduction in total economic surplus is equal to the sum of the areas of the two pale blue triangles. The lost surplus at the United Way is (1/2)($40,000)(500) = $10 million/year [part (a)]. The lost surplus at Philip Morris is (1/2)($30,000)(250) = $3.75 million/year [part (b)].

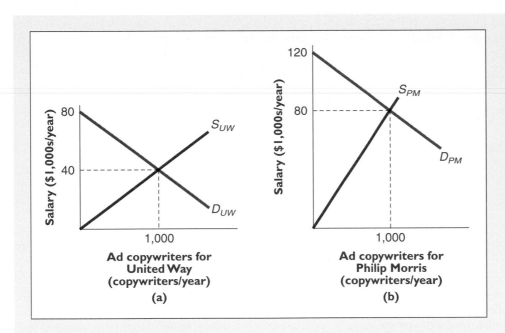

FIGURE 13.7
Equilibrium in Unregulated Markets for Ad Copywriters.
Because many ad copywriters prefer employment with the United Way to employment with Philip Morris, the equilibrium wage for copywriters will be higher at Philip Morris, part (b), than at the United Way, part (a).

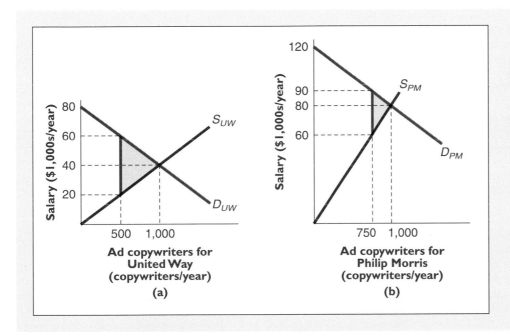

FIGURE 13.8
The Reduction in Economic Surplus Caused by Comparable Worth Legislation.
A comparable worth law that requires all ad copywriters to be paid $60,000 results in lost surplus of $10 million at United Way [area of the pale blue triangle, part (a)] and $3.75 million at Philip Morris [area of the pale blue triangle, part (b)].

Despite their manifestly benign intent, comparable worth statutes make the economic pie smaller by preventing markets from reaching equilibrium. Comparable worth legislation is thus similar in its effects to other laws that attempt to regulate prices. Any problem with an existing market equilibrium is best solved, as the efficiency principle reminds us, by altering the forces that produced that equilibrium in the first place. Any other approach inevitably results in failure to maximize total economic surplus.

> **RECAP** **DISCRIMINATION IN THE LABOR MARKET**
>
> Critics of the theory of competitive labor markets have offered a variety of theories of discrimination to explain why women and minorities continue to receive lower wages than would be predicted by standard human capital models. The theory of employer discrimination holds that the observed wage gaps are the result of prejudice against women and minorities on the part of employers. The theory of customer discrimination attributes the same wage gaps to prejudice on the part of customers. Comparable worth policies attempt to reduce wage gaps by imposing collective restraints on the amounts that different employees may be paid.

▪ SUMMARY ▪

- A worker's long-run equilibrium pay in a competitive labor market will be equal to the value of her marginal product *(VMP)*—the market value of whatever goods and services she produces for her employer. The law of diminishing returns says that when a firm's capital and other productive inputs are held fixed in the short run, adding workers beyond some point results in ever-smaller increases in output. Firms that purchase labor in competitive labor markets face a constant wage, and they will hire labor up to the point at which *VMP* equals the market wage.

- Human capital theory says that an individual's *VMP* is proportional to his stock of human capital—an amalgam of education, experience, training, intelligence, and other factors that influence productivity. According to this theory, some occupations pay better than others simply because they require larger stocks of human capital.

- Wages often differ between individuals whose stocks of human capital appear nearly the same, as when one belongs to a labor union and the other does not. Technologies that allow the most productive individuals to serve broader markets can translate even small differences in performance into enormous differences in pay. Such technologies give rise to winner-take-all markets, which have long been common in sports and entertainment and which are becoming common in other professions.

- Compensating wage differentials—wage differences associated with differences in working conditions—are another important explanation for why some earn more than oth-

ers. They help to explain why garbage collectors earn more than lifeguards and, more generally, why individuals with a given stock of human capital tend to earn more in jobs that have less attractive working conditions.

- Many firms pay members of certain groups—notably blacks and females—less than they pay white males with similar personal characteristics. If such wage gaps are the result of employer discrimination, their existence implies profit opportunities for firms that do not discriminate. Several other factors, including discrimination by customers and institutions other than firms, may explain at least part of the observed wage gaps.

- Proponents of comparable worth legislation have proposed that wages be based not on market forces but instead on government assessments of social value. Such proposals would reduce economic surplus by preventing employers and workers from making mutually advantageous exchanges.

- Competitive labor markets do a remarkable job of creating order out of chaos. Driven only by the usual mix of human motives, people sort themselves surprisingly well into the jobs that interest them most and make the most productive use of their talents and training. In the process, most workers manage to support themselves and their families without government assistance. But the labor market is not immune from the imperfections that plague product markets. Monopsonists tend to hire too few workers, just as monopolists tend to produce too little output.

▪ KEY TERMS ▪

comparable worth legislation (342)
compensating wage differential (336)
customer discrimination (340)
employer discrimination (340)
human capital (330)

human capital theory (330)
labor union (331)
marginal labor cost (326)
marginal product of labor (322)
monopsony (325)

value of marginal product (*VMP*) (323)
winner-take-all market (334)

▪ REVIEW QUESTIONS ▪

1. You are an aide to a senator who wants advice about how to vote on a proposal that would outlaw paying truck drivers more than librarians. Can you suggest a more efficient way to promote the objective of the proposal, which is to increase the salary of librarians relative to other workers?

2. Why is the supply curve of labor for any specific occupation likely to be upward-sloping, even if, for the economy as a whole, people work fewer hours when wage rates increase?

3. True or false: If the human capital possessed by two workers is nearly the same, their wage rates will be nearly the same. Explain.

4. Congress periodically holds hearings to examine the effects of smoking on health. The witnesses who testify at those hearings under the sponsorship of the Tobacco Institute (a cigarette industry organization) are generally thought to have weaker scientific reputations than the witnesses who testify under the sponsorship of the American Cancer Society. Why, then, do the former witnesses get paid much more than the latter?

5. True or false: Economic surplus would be larger if a profit-maximizing monopsonist in the labor market were required to hire one more worker than it otherwise would have chosen to. Explain.

▪ PROBLEMS ▪

1. Mountain Breeze supplies air filters to the retail market and hires workers to assemble the components. An air filter sells for $26, and Mountain Breeze can buy the components for each filter for $1. Sandra and Bobby are two workers for Mountain Breeze. Sandra can assemble 60 air filters per month, and Bobby can assemble 70. If the labor market is perfectly competitive, how much will Sandra and Bobby be paid?

2. Stone, Inc., owns a clothing factory and hires workers in a competitive labor market to cut and sew denim fabric into jeans. The fabric required to make each pair of jeans costs $5. The company's weekly output of finished jeans varies with the number of workers hired, as shown in the following table:

Number of workers	Jeans (pairs/week)
0	0
1	25
2	45
3	60
4	72
5	80
6	85

a. If the jeans sell for $35/pair, and the competitive market wage is $250/week, how many workers should Stone hire? How many pairs of jeans will the company produce each week?

b. Suppose the Clothing Workers Union now sets a weekly minimum acceptable wage of $230/week. All the workers Stone hires belong to the union. How does the minimum wage affect Stone's decision about how many workers to hire?

c. If the minimum wage set by the union had been $400/week, how would the minimum wage affect Stone's decision about how many workers to hire?

d. If Stone again faces a market wage of $250/week, but the price of jeans rises to $45/week, how many workers will the company now hire?

3. The Rainflower Cactus Nursery is the only employer in a small town in Nevada. It sells potted cacti at $5 each, and its weekly output of cacti varies with the number of workers, as shown in the following table:

Number of workers	Potted cacti/week
0	0
1	50
2	90
3	120
4	140
5	150
6	155

There are six people in town potentially available to work at Rainflower. The six people, together with their reservation wages, are shown in the following table:

Worker	Reservation wage ($/week)
Jon	75
Joe	80
Jenny	85
Jeff	90
Jessica	100
Luke	150

    a. If Rainflower must pay the same wage to all workers, how many workers will the firm hire? What wage will it pay?

    b. What is the socially optimal number of workers to hire?

    c. If Rainflower could pay each worker exactly his or her reservation wage, how many workers would the company hire?

4. Acme, Inc., supplies rocket ships to the retail market and hires workers to assemble the components. A rocket ship sells for $30,000, and Acme can buy the components for each rocket ship for $25,000. Wiley and Sam are two workers for Acme. Sam can assemble one-fifth rocket ship per month, and Wiley can assemble one-tenth. If the labor market is perfectly competitive and rocket components are Acme's only other cost, how much will Sam and Wiley be paid?

5. Carolyn owns a soda factory and hires workers in a competitive labor market to bottle the soda. Her company's weekly output of bottled soda varies with the number of workers hired, as shown in the following table:

Number of workers	Cases/week
0	0
1	200
2	360
3	480
4	560
5	600

    a. If each case sells for $10 more than the cost of the materials used in producing it and the competitive market wage is $1,000/week, how many workers should Carolyn hire? How many cases will be produced per week?

b. Suppose the Soda Bottlers Union now sets a weekly minimum acceptable wage of $1,500/week. All the workers Carolyn hires belong to the union. How does the minimum wage affect Carolyn's decision about how many workers to hire?

c. If the wage is again $1,000/week but the price of soda rises to $15/case, how many workers will Carolyn now hire?

6. Laura has a nursing degree and 2 years of experience working at George Washington University Hospital. If she continues along her present career path, the present value of her lifetime earnings will be $200,000. If she takes 2 years off and completes a midwifery degree, the present value of her lifetime earnings will be $221,000. However, she must make two tuition payments for the midwifery course, one now and one a year from now, both of $10,500. Apart from her salary, Laura is indifferent between nursing and midwifery. If the interest rate is 5 percent, should Laura go to midwifery college? Explain.

7. Stefano is thinking about getting a law degree. If he continues along his present career path, the present value of his lifetime earnings will be $500,000. If instead he takes 3 years off and gets the law degree, the present value of his lifetime earnings will be $550,000. However, he must make annual tuition payments of $20,000 at the beginning of each academic year. Apart from his salary, Stefano is indifferent between his current occupation and a career in law. If the interest rate is 20 percent, should Stefano go to law school? Explain.

8. A simple economy has two labor markets for carpenters: one for residential houses, the other for commercial buildings. The demand for residential carpenters is given by $W_R = 40 - 10L_R$, where W_R is the wage of residential carpenters in dollars per hour and L_R is the number of residential carpenters in hundreds per day. The demand for commercial carpenters is given by $W_C = 40 - 5L_C$, where W_C is the wage of commercial carpenters in dollars per hour and L_C is the number of commercial carpenters in hundreds per day. The economy has 300 carpenters, each of whom has the skills required to be either a residential or a commercial carpenter, and each of whom wants to work full-time in whichever type of carpentry pays best. What will be the equilibrium wage and employment level for each type? (*Hint:* To find the total demand curve for carpenters, first graph the two demand curves side by side and then add them horizontally.)

9. In Problem 8, suppose commercial carpenters form a union and announce that they will not work for less than $30/hour. Any union member who cannot find work in the commercial market will work in the residential market. How many carpenters work in each market, and what is the wage in the residential market?

10. Refer to Problem 9. By how much does the formation of the commercial carpenter's union reduce the total value of carpenters' services provided each hour?

■ ANSWERS TO IN-CHAPTER EXERCISES ■

13.1 Adirondack will hire a second worker only if the *VMP* with two workers is at least 300. Since $VMP = (P)(MP)$, and since the marginal product of the second worker is 25 cutting boards, the lowest P for which the company will hire two workers is found by solving $(P)(25) = 300$ for $P = 12$.

13.2 Since the *VMP* of each worker exceeds $275, Adirondack will now hire five workers.

13.3 As shown in the following table, *VMP* for each of the first four workers now exceeds marginal labor cost, so Adirondack should now hire four workers.

Number of workers	Total number of cutting boards/week	MP (extra cutting boards/week)	VMP ($/week)	Marginal labor cost
0	0			
		30	900	200
1	30			
		25	750	300
2	55			
		21	632	400
3	76			
		18	540	500
4	94			
		14	420	600
5	108			

13.4 A higher interest rate reduces the present value of both the cost of an MBA degree and the resulting higher earnings. But the cost of getting an MBA occurs during the next 2 years, while the salary increase is spread out over many years. The higher interest rate will therefore reduce the present value of the benefit of the degree by more than it will reduce the present value of its cost. Since Betsy was indifferent at an interest rate of 10 percent, she should not get the degree if the interest rate is 12 percent.

13.5 When the wage rate is $9/hour in each market, 25 fewer workers will be employed in the nonunionized market and 25 more in the unionized market. The loss in output from removing 25 workers from the nonunionized market is the sum of the VMPs of those workers, which is the pale blue area in part (b) of the following figure. This area is $187.50/hour. (*Hint:* To calculate this area, first break the figure into a rectangle and a triangle.) The gain in output from adding 25 workers to the unionized market is the pale blue area in part (a), which is $262.50/hour. The net increase in output is thus $262.50 − $187.50 = $75/hour.

(a)   (b)

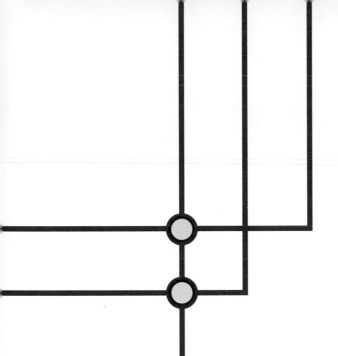

CHAPTER

14

THE ECONOMICS
OF PUBLIC POLICY

■

In 1979, in the wake of the second major oil supply interruption in a decade, officials in the Carter administration met to discuss policies for reducing U.S. dependence on foreign oil. The proposal they ultimately put forward was a gasoline tax of 50 cents per gallon. Anticipating objections that the tax would impose an unacceptable hardship on the poor, policymakers proposed to return the revenues from the tax to the citizenry by reducing the payroll tax, the tax on wages that supports the Social Security system.

Proponents of the gasoline tax argued that in addition to reducing the nation's dependence on foreign oil, the tax would reduce air pollution and ease highway congestion. But critics ridiculed the proposal, charging that if the revenues from the tax were returned to the people, the quantity of gasoline demanded would remain essentially the same. Their argument tipped the debate, and officials never managed to implement the proposal.

But whatever the ultimate merits of the administration's proposal, there was no merit at all in the argument the critics used to attack it. True, the proposed tax rebate meant that people *could* have bought just as much gasoline as before the tax. Yet the tax would have given them a powerful incentive not to do so. As we saw in Chapter 5, the cost-benefit principle leads consumers to change their behavior to escape the effects of a steep rise in the after-tax price of gasoline: by switching to cars with smaller, more fuel-efficient engines, forming carpools, and so on. Such changes free up money to spend on other goods and services, which become relatively more attractive because they are not taxed.

No society can hope to formulate and implement intelligent economic policies unless its citizens and leaders share an understanding of basic economic principles. Our aim in this chapter will be to explore how careful application of these principles can help us design policies that both expand the economic pie and make everyone's slice larger. We will begin with a discussion of government policy toward natural monopoly, and then we will explore a seemingly unrelated collection of policy issues, including the pricing of public services, health care delivery, environmental regulation, and crime control. The unifying thread running through these issues is the problem of scarcity. In each case, we will explore how the cost-benefit principle can help to resolve the resulting trade-offs.

PUBLIC POLICY TOWARD NATURAL MONOPOLY

Monopoly is problematic not only because of the loss in efficiency associated with restricted output but also because the monopolist earns an economic profit at the buyer's expense. Many people are understandably uncomfortable about having to purchase from the sole provider of any good or service. For this reason, voters in many societies have empowered government to adopt policies aimed at controlling natural monopolists.

There are several ways to achieve this aim. A government may assume ownership and control of a natural monopoly, or it may merely attempt to regulate the prices it charges. In some cases government solicits competitive bids from private firms to produce natural monopoly services. In still other cases, governments attempt to dissolve natural monopolies into smaller entities that compete with one another. But many of these policies create economic problems of their own. In each case, the practical challenge is to come up with the solution that yields the greatest surplus of benefits over costs. Natural monopoly may be inefficient and unfair, but the alternatives to natural monopoly are far from perfect.

STATE OWNERSHIP AND MANAGEMENT

Recall from Chapter 9 that a natural monopoly is inefficient because the monopolist's profit-maximizing price is greater than its marginal cost. But even if the natural monopolist *wanted* to set price equal to marginal cost, it could not do so and hope to remain in business. After all, the defining feature of a natural monopoly is economies of scale in production, which means that marginal cost will always be less than average cost. Setting price equal to marginal cost would fail to cover average production cost, which implies an economic loss.

Consider the case of a local cable television company. Once an area has been wired for cable television, the marginal cost of adding an additional subscriber is very low. For the sake of efficiency, all subscribers should pay a price equal to that marginal cost. Yet a cable company that priced in this manner would never be able to recover the fixed cost of setting up the network. This same problem applies not just to cable television companies but to all other natural monopolies. Even if such firms wanted to set price equal to marginal cost (which, of course, they do not, since they will earn more by setting marginal revenue equal to marginal cost), they cannot do so without suffering an economic loss.

One way to attack the efficiency and fairness problems is for the government to take over the industry, set price equal to marginal cost, and then absorb the resulting losses out of general tax revenues. This approach has been followed with good results in the state-owned electric utility industry in France, whose efficient pricing methods have set the standard for electricity pricing worldwide.

But state ownership and efficient management do not always go hand in hand. Granted, the state-owned natural monopoly is free to charge marginal cost, while the private natural monopoly is not. Yet private natural monopolies often face a much stronger incentive to cut costs than their government-owned counterparts. When the private monopolist figures out a way to cut $1 from the cost of production, its profit goes up by $1. But when the government manager of a state-owned monopoly cuts $1 from the cost of production, the government typically cuts the monopoly's budget by $1. Think back to your last visit to the Department of Motor Vehicles. Did it strike you as an efficiently managed organization?

Whether the efficiency that is gained by being able to set price equal to marginal cost outweighs the inefficiency that results from a weakened incentive to cut costs is an empirical question.

STATE REGULATION OF PRIVATE MONOPOLIES

In the United States, the most common method of curbing monopoly profits is for government merely to regulate the natural monopoly rather than own it. Most states, for example, take this approach with electric utilities, natural gas providers, local telephone companies, and cable television companies. The standard procedure in these cases is called **cost-plus regulation:** Government regulators gather data on the monopolist's explicit costs of production and then permit the monopolist to set prices that cover those costs, plus a markup to assure a normal return on the firm's investment.

cost-plus regulation a method of regulation under which the regulated firm is permitted to charge a price equal to its explicit costs of production plus a markup to cover the opportunity cost of resources provided by the firm's owners

While it may sound reasonable, cost-plus regulation has several pitfalls. First, it generates costly administrative proceedings in which regulators and firms quarrel over which of the firm's expenditures can properly be included in the costs it is allowed to recover. This question is difficult to answer even in theory. Consider a firm like Pacific Telesis, whose local telephone service is subject to cost-plus regulation but whose other products and services are unregulated. Many Pacific Telesis employees, from the president on down, are involved in both regulated and unregulated activities. How should their salaries be allocated between the two? The company has a strong incentive to argue for greater allocation to the regulated activities, which allows it to capture more revenue from captive customers in the local telephone market.

A second problem with cost-plus regulation is that it blunts the firm's incentive to adopt cost-saving innovations, for when it does, regulators require the firm to cut its rates. The firm gets to keep its cost savings in the current period, which is a stronger incentive to cut costs than the one facing a government-owned monopoly. But the incentive to cut costs would be stronger still if the firm could retain its cost savings indefinitely. Furthermore, in cases in which regulators set rates by allowing the monopolist to add a fixed markup to costs incurred, the regulated monopolist may actually have an incentive to *increase* costs rather than reduce them. Outrageous though the thought may be, the monopolist may earn a higher profit by installing gold-plated faucets in the company rest rooms.

Finally, cost-plus regulation does not solve the natural monopolist's basic problem, the inability to set price equal to marginal cost without losing money. Although these are all serious problems, governments seem to be in no hurry to abandon cost-plus regulation.

EXCLUSIVE CONTRACTING FOR NATURAL MONOPOLY

One of the most promising methods for dealing with natural monopoly is for the government to invite private firms to bid for the natural monopolist's market. The government specifies in detail the service it wants—cable television, fire protection, garbage collection—and firms submit bids describing how much they will charge for the service. The low bidder wins the contract.

The incentive to cut costs under such an arrangement is every bit as powerful as that facing ordinary competitive firms. Competition among bidders should also eliminate any concerns about the fairness of monopoly profits. And if the government is willing to provide a cash subsidy to the winning bidder, exclusive contracting even allows the monopolist to set price equal to marginal cost.

Contracting has been employed with good results in municipal fire protection and garbage collection. Communities that employ private companies to provide these services often spend only half as much as adjacent communities served by municipal fire and sanitation departments.

Despite these attractive features, however, exclusive contracting is not without problems, especially when the service to be provided is complex or requires a large fixed investment in capital equipment. In such cases, contract specifications may be so detailed and complicated that they become tantamount to regulating the firm directly. And in cases involving a large fixed investment—electric power generation and distribution, for example—officials face the question of how to transfer the assets if a new firm wins the contract. The winning firm naturally wants to acquire the assets as cheaply as possible, but the retiring firm is entitled to a fair price for them. What, in such cases, is a fair price?

Fire protection and garbage collection are simple enough that the costs of contracting out these functions is not prohibitive. But in other cases, such costs might easily outweigh any savings made possible by exclusive contracting.

VIGOROUS ENFORCEMENT OF ANTITRUST LAWS

The nineteenth century witnessed the accumulation of massive private fortunes, the likes of which had never been seen in the industrialized world. Public sentiment ran high against the so-called robber barons of the period—the Carnegies, Rockefellers, Mellons, and others. In 1890, Congress passed the Sherman Act, which declared illegal any conspiracy "to monopolize, or attempt to monopolize . . . any part of the trade or commerce among the several States . . ." And in 1914, Congress passed the Clayton Act, whose aim was to prevent corporations from acquiring shares in a competitor if the transaction would "substantially lessen competition or create a monopoly."

Antitrust laws have helped to prevent the formation of cartels, or coalitions of firms that collude to raise prices above competitive levels. But they have also caused some harm. For example, federal antitrust officials spent more than a decade trying to break up the IBM Corporation in the belief that it had achieved an unhealthy dominance in the computer industry. That view was proved comically wrong by IBM's subsequent failure to foresee and profit from the rise of the personal computer. By breaking up large companies and discouraging mergers between companies in the same industry, antitrust laws may help to promote competition, but they may also prevent companies from achieving economies of scale.

A final possibility is simply to ignore the problem of natural monopoly: to let the monopolist choose the quantity to produce and sell it at whatever price the market will bear. The obvious objections to this policy are the two we began with, namely, that a natural monopoly is not only inefficient but also unfair. But just as the hurdle method of price discrimination mitigates efficiency losses (see Chapter 9), it also lessens the concern about taking unfair advantage of buyers.

Consider first the source of the natural monopolist's economic profit. This firm, recall, is one with economies of scale, which means that its average production cost declines as output increases. Efficiency requires that price be set at marginal cost, but because the natural monopolist's marginal cost is lower than its average cost, it cannot charge all buyers the marginal cost without suffering an economic loss.

The depth and prevalence of discount pricing suggests that whatever economic profit a natural monopolist earns generally will not come out of the discount buyer's pocket. Although discount prices are higher than the monopolist's marginal cost of production, in most cases they are lower than the average cost. Thus the monopolist's economic profit, if any, must come from buyers who pay list price. And since those buyers have the option, in most cases, of jumping a hurdle and paying a discount price, their contribution, if not completely voluntary, is at least not strongly coerced.

So much for the source of the monopolist's economic profit. What about its disposition? Who gets it? A large chunk—some 35 percent, in many cases—goes to the federal government via the corporate income tax. The remainder is paid out to shareholders, some of whom are wealthy and some of whom are not. These shareholder profits are also taxed by state and even local governments. In the end, two-thirds or more of a monopolist's economic profit may fund services provided by governments of various levels.

Both the source of the monopolist's economic profit (the list price buyer) and the disposition of that profit (largely, to fund public services) cast doubt on the claim that monopoly profit constitutes a social injustice on any grand scale. Nevertheless, the hurdle method of differential pricing cannot completely eliminate the fairness and efficiency problems that result from monopoly pricing. In the end, then, we are left with a choice among imperfect alternatives. As the cost-benefit principle emphasizes, the best choice is the one for which the balance of benefits over costs is largest. But which choice that is will depend on the circumstances at hand.

> **RECAP** **PUBLIC POLICY TOWARD NATURAL MONOPOLY**
>
> The natural monopolist sets price above marginal cost, resulting in too little output from society's point of view (the efficiency problem). The natural monopolist may also earn an economic profit at buyers' expense (the fairness problem). Policies for dealing with the efficiency and fairness problems include state ownership and management, state regulation, exclusive contracting, and vigorous enforcement of antitrust laws. Each of these remedies entails problems of its own.

MARGINAL COST PRICING OF PUBLIC SERVICES

Suppose the government has decided to become the provider of a natural monopoly good or service. How much should it charge its customers? The theory of competitive supply, normally applied to perfectly competitive firms that can sell any quantity they choose at a constant market price (see Chapter 6), helps to answer this question. Consider Example 14.1, in which a local government supplies water to its residents.

What is the marginal cost of water in Gainesville?

EXAMPLE 14.1

The municipal water supply company in Gainesville, Florida, has three potential sources of water: an underground spring, a nearby lake, and the Atlantic Ocean. The spring can supply up to 1 million gallons/day at a cost of 0.2 cent/gallon. The lake can supply an additional 2 million gallons/day at a cost of 0.8 cent/gallon. Additional water must be distilled from the ocean at a cost of 4.0 cents/gallon. Draw the marginal cost curve for water in Gainesville.

The low-hanging-fruit principle tells us that the city will use the cheapest source of water first (the spring). Only when the quantity demanded exceeds the spring's capacity will the city turn to the next least expensive source, the lake; and only when the lake's capacity is exhausted will the city supply water from the ocean. The marginal cost curve will thus be as shown in Figure 14.1.

FIGURE 14.1
The Marginal Cost Curve for Water.
The current marginal cost of water is the cost of producing an extra gallon by means of the most expensive production source currently in use.

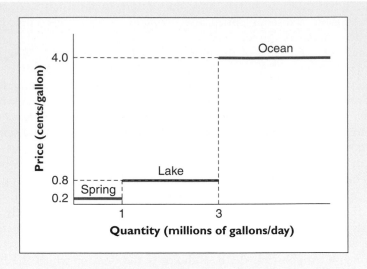

EXAMPLE 14.2   **How much should the government charge for water?**

In Example 14.1, suppose that if the price of water were 4.0 cents/gallon, citizens of Gainesville would consume 4 million gallons/day. Given the marginal cost curve shown in Figure 14.1, how much should the city charge a citizen whose water comes from the underground spring? How much should it charge someone whose water comes from the lake?

The citizens of Gainesville will enjoy the largest possible economic surplus if the price they pay for water exactly equals the marginal cost of providing it. Since the total amount of water demanded at 4.0 cents/gallon exceeds 3 million gallons/day, the city will have to supply at least some households with water distilled from the Atlantic Ocean, at a cost of 4.0 cents/gallon. At 4 million gallons/day, the marginal cost of water is thus 4.0 cents/gallon, and *that is true no matter where the water comes from*. As long as the city must get *some* of its water from the ocean, the marginal cost of water taken from the underground spring is 4.0 cents/gallon. Water taken from the lake also has a marginal cost of 4.0 cents/gallon.

This statement might seem to contradict the claim that water drawn from the spring costs only 0.2 cent/gallon, water drawn from the lake, only 0.8 cent/gallon. But there is no contradiction. To see why, ask yourself how much the city would save if a family that currently gets its water from the spring were to reduce its consumption by 1 gallon/day. The cutback would enable the city to divert that gallon of spring water to some other household that currently gets its water from the ocean, and that in turn would reduce consumption of ocean water by 1 gallon. So if a family currently served by the spring were to reduce its daily consumption by 1 gallon, the cost savings would be exactly 4.0 cents. And that, by definition, is the marginal cost of water.

To encourage the efficient use of water, the city should charge every household 4.0 cents/gallon for all the water it consumes. Charging any household less than that would encourage households to use water whose marginal benefit is less than its marginal cost. For example, suppose the city charged households who get their water from the spring only 0.2 cent/gallon. Those households would then expand their use of water until the benefit they received from the last gallon used equaled 0.2 cent. Because that gallon could have been used to serve someone who is currently using water distilled from the ocean, for whom the value of the marginal gallon is 4 cents, its use would entail a loss in economic surplus of 3.8 cents.

EXERCISE 14.1

Suppose that at a price of 0.8 cent/gallon the citizens of Gainesville would consume a total of only 2 million gallons/day. How much should the city charge for water? Should that same charge apply to people who get their water from the spring?

The general rule is that a public utility maximizes economic surplus by charging its customers the marginal cost of the goods or services it provides. Example 14.3 provides another illustration of this principle.

How should electric rates charged by a Vermont utility vary by season?

EXAMPLE 14.3

A government-owned electric utility in Vermont has two sources of power, a hydroelectric generator and a coal-burning steam generator. Electricity from the hydroelectric facility can be delivered to households at a cost of 2 cents/kilowatthour for any amount up to 4 million kilowatthours/day. Additional electricity can be produced in unlimited quantities by the steam generator, at a cost of 6 cents/kilowatthour. The company's daily demand curve for electricity during the summer months is $P = 4 - 2Q$, where P is the price in cents per kilowatthour and Q is the quantity demanded, in millions of kilowatthours per day. The demand curve for electricity in the winter months is $P = 12 - Q$. How much should this utility charge for electricity during the summer months? During the winter months? Should a family that receives its power directly from the hydroelectric generator during the winter months pay less than a family that receives its power from the steam generator?

As before, the efficient pricing rule is to set price equal to marginal cost, which depends on how much energy the utility produces each day. As shown in Figure 14.2, marginal cost *(MC)* is 2 cents/kilowatthour when production is between 0 and 4 million kilowatthours/day and 6 cents/kilowatthour when production levels exceed 4 million kilowatthours/day. To sell power efficiently, the utility should view this marginal cost curve as its supply curve and charge the market-clearing price for each season. During the winter months, demand intersects marginal cost at a price of 6 cents/kilowatthour, so that is the price the utility should charge in the winter. During the summer months, demand intersects marginal cost at a price of 2 cents/kilowatthour, so that is the optimal price during the summer months.

Note that the optimal price during the winter months is 6 cents/kilowatthour for *all* families, even those whose electricity is supplied by the hydroelectric generator. If you were the public relations spokesperson for this utility, how would

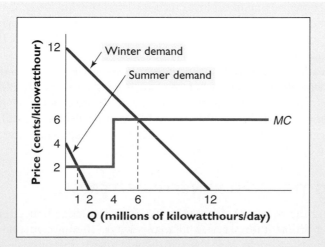

FIGURE 14.2
Seasonal Differences in Electric Rates.
The efficient price in each season is the one that equates marginal cost with seasonal demand. Given the two seasonal demand curves shown, the utility should charge 2 cents/kilowatthour in the summer months and 6 cents/kilowatthour in the winter months.

you respond to a family that complained it was being overcharged for the power it received from the hydroelectric generator in the winter? You might begin by pointing out how much the utility would save if it no longer had to supply power to this family. It could allocate the hydroelectric capacity this family used to some other family that would otherwise have been served by the steam generator, for a savings of 6 cents/kilowatthour. Whenever the utility has to supply more electricity than it can produce with the hydroelectric generator, the marginal cost of serving every user is 6 cents/kilowatthour.

EXERCISE 14.2

How would your answer to the question posed in Example 14.3 have differed if the winter demand curve had been $P = 8 - 2Q$?

RECAP MARGINAL COST PRICING OF PUBLIC SERVICES

For a good or service—private or public—to be allocated efficiently, its price must equal its marginal cost of production. This principle tells us that when a public utility supplies water or electricity from several different sources, each with different costs, all users should pay a price equal to the highest-cost source in current use.

HEALTH CARE DELIVERY

In the United States, real health care expenditures per capita have grown more rapidly than real income per capita for as long as the relevant data have been available. As a share of national income, health care costs have risen from only 4 percent in 1940 to roughly 14 percent today. Part of this increase is the result of costly new health care technologies and procedures. Diagnostic tests have grown more expensive and sophisticated, and procedures like coronary bypass surgery and organ transplantation have grown far more common. Yet a great deal of medical expenditure inflation has nothing to do with these high-tech developments. Rather, it is the result of fundamental changes in the way we pay for medical services.

The most important change has been the emergence of the so-called third-party payment system. Earlier in this century, many people insured themselves against catastrophic illness but purchased routine medical care out of their own pockets. But starting after World War II, and increasingly since the mid-1960s, people have come to depend on insurance for even routine medical services. Some of this insurance is provided privately by employers; some, by the government. In the latter category, Medicaid covers the medical expenses of the poor, and Medicare those of the elderly and disabled.

The spread of medical insurance, especially government-financed medical insurance, owes much to the belief that an inability to pay should not prevent people from receiving medical care they need. Indeed, medical insurance has surely done much to shelter people from financial hardship. The difficulty is that in its most common form, medical insurance has also spawned literally hundreds of billions of dollars of waste each year.

APPLYING THE COST-BENEFIT CRITERION

To understand the nature of this waste, we must recognize that although medical services differ from other services in many ways, they are in one fundamental respect the same—namely, that the cost-benefit test is the only sensible criterion for deciding which services ought to be performed. The fact that a medical procedure has *some* benefit does not, by itself, imply that the procedure should be performed. Rather, it should be performed only if its benefit, broadly construed, exceeds its cost.

The costs of medical procedures are relatively easy to measure, using the same methods applied to other goods and services. But the usual measure of the benefit of a good or service, a person's willingness to pay, may not be acceptable in the case of medical services. For example, most of us would not conclude that a lifesaving appendectomy that costs $2,000 is unjustified merely because the person who needs it can afford to pay only $1,000. When someone lacks the resources to pay for what most of us would consider an essential medical service, society has at least some responsibility to help. Hence the proliferation of government-sponsored medical insurance.

Many other medical expenditures are not as pressing as an emergency appendectomy, however. Following such surgery, for example, the patient requires a period of recuperation in the hospital. How long should that period last: 2 days? 5? 10? The cost-benefit principle is critically important to thinking intelligently about such questions. But as Example 14.4 illustrates, the third-party payment system has virtually eliminated cost-benefit thinking from the medical domain.

How long should David stay in the hospital?

EXAMPLE 14.4

To eliminate recurrent sore throats, David plans to have his tonsils removed. His surgeon tells him that the average hospital stay after this procedure is 2 days (some people stay only 1 day, while others stay 3, 4, or even 5 days). Hospital rooms cost $300/day. If David's demand curve for days in the hospital is as shown in Figure 14.3, how many days will he stay if he must pay for his hospital room himself? How many days will he stay if his medical insurance fully covers the cost of his hospital room?

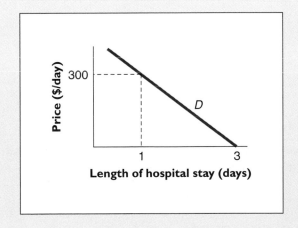

FIGURE 14.3
The Demand for Hospital Care.
The demand curve for postoperative hospital care is downward-sloping, just like any other demand curve. At higher prices, people choose shorter hospital stays, not because there is no benefit to a longer stay, but because they prefer to spend their money in other ways.

If David must pay for his hospital room himself, his best option will be to stay for just 1 day. But if the cost of his hospital room is completely covered by insurance, the marginal cost *to him* will be zero. In that case he will stay for 3 days.

Should we be concerned that people choose longer hospital stays when their expenses are fully insured? The cost-benefit principle tells us that a hospital stay should be extended another day only if the benefit of doing so would be at least as great as the cost of the resources required to extend the stay. But when hospital costs are fully covered by insurance, the decision maker sees a marginal cost of zero, when in fact the marginal cost is several hundred dollars. According to the cost-benefit criterion, then, full insurance coverage leads to wastefully long hospital stays. That is not to say that the additional days in the hospital do no good at all. Rather, their benefit is less than their cost. As Example 14.5 illustrates, a shorter hospital stay would increase total economic surplus.

EXAMPLE 14.5

How much waste does full insurance coverage cause?

Using the demand and cost information from Example 14.4, calculate how much waste results from full insurance coverage of David's hospital room.

If the marginal cost of an additional day in the hospital is $300, the supply curve of hospital room days in an open market would be horizontal at $300. If David had to pay that price, he would choose a 1-day stay, which would result in the largest possible economic surplus. If he extends his stay past 1 day, cost continues to accumulate at the rate of $300/day, but the benefit of additional care—as measured by his demand curve—falls below $300. If he stays 3 days, as he will if he has full insurance coverage, the extra 2 days cost society $600 but benefit David by only $300 (the area of the pale blue triangle under David's demand curve in Figure 14.4). The amount by which the extra cost exceeds the extra benefit will thus be $300 (the area of the dark blue triangle).

FIGURE 14.4

The Waste Resulting from Full Insurance Coverage.

The area of the pale blue triangle ($300) represents the benefit of extending the hospital stay from 1 to 3 days. Since the cost of the extra 2 days is $600, the area of the dark blue triangle ($300) represents the loss in economic surplus that results from the longer stay.

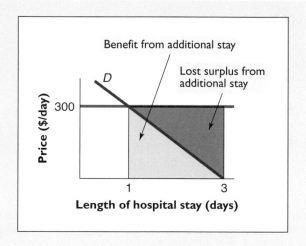

EXERCISE 14.3

Refer to Example 14.4. How much waste would be caused by an insurance policy that reimbursed hospital room expenses at the rate of $150/day?

DESIGNING A SOLUTION

In circumstances in which economic surplus has not been maximized, a transaction can always be found that will make both the patient *and* the insurance company better off. Suppose, for example, that the insurance company in Example 14.5 gives David a cash payment of $700 toward hospital expenses and lets him decide for himself how long to stay in the hospital. Confronted with a price of $300/day, David would choose to stay only a single day. The $400 cash he would have left after paying his hospital bill is $100 more than enough to compensate him for the benefit he would lose by not staying an extra 2 days. (Again, that benefit is $300, the area of the pale blue triangle in Figure 14.4.) A $700 cash payment would also leave his insurance company better off by $200 than if it had provided unlimited hospital coverage at no extra charge (since David would have stayed 3 days in that case). And since no one else is harmed by this transaction, it represents a *Pareto improvement* over unlimited coverage, meaning a change that makes some people better off without harming others (see Chapter 7).

The amount of waste caused by full insurance coverage depends on the price elasticity of demand for medical services—the more elastic the demand, the greater the waste. Proponents of full coverage believe that the demand for medical services is almost completely inelastic with respect to price and that the resulting waste is therefore negligible. Critics of full coverage argue that the demand for medical services is actually quite sensitive to price and that the resulting waste is significant.

Who is right? One way to tell is to examine whether people who lack full insurance coverage spend significantly less than those who have it. The economist W. G. Manning and several coauthors did so by performing an experiment in which they assigned subjects randomly to one of two different kinds of medical insurance policies.[1] The first group of subjects received **first-dollar insurance coverage,** meaning that 100 percent of their medical expenses were covered by insurance. The second group got "$1,000 deductible" coverage, meaning that only expenses beyond the first $1,000 a year were covered. (For example, subjects with $1,200 of medical bills would receive $1,200 from their insurance company if they belonged to the first group but only $200 if they belonged to the second.) In effect, since most people incur less than $1,000 a year in medical expenses, most subjects in the second group effectively paid full price for their medical services, while subjects in the first group paid nothing. Manning and his colleagues found that *people with $1,000 deductible policies spent between 40 and 50 percent less on health care than subjects with first-dollar coverage. More important, there were no measurable differences in health outcomes between the two groups.*

Taken at face value, the results of the Manning study suggest that a large share of the inflation in medical expenditures since World War II has been caused by growth in first-dollar medical insurance. Why not simply abandon first-dollar coverage in favor of high deductibles? People would still be protected against financial catastrophe but would have a strong incentive to avoid medical services whose benefit does not exceed their cost.

Some would say that Medicaid and Medicare should not carry high deductibles because they would impose too great a burden on poor families. But as in other instances in which concern for the poor is offered in defense of an inefficient policy, an alternative can be designed that is better for rich and poor alike. For example, all health insurance could be written to include high deductibles, and the poor could be given an annual stipend to defray the initial medical expenses not covered by insurance. At year's end, any unspent stipend would be theirs to keep. Here again, the efficiency principle reminds us that concern for the well-being of the poor is simply no reason for not adopting the most efficient policy.

first-dollar insurance coverage insurance that pays all expenses generated by the insured activity

THE HMO REVOLUTION

During the 1990s, the high cost of conventional health insurance led many people to switch to a **health maintenance organization (HMO).** An HMO is a group of physicians that provides its patients with medical services in return for a fixed annual fee. As the next example illustrates, the incentive to provide any given medical service is weaker under the standard HMO contract than under conventional health insurance.

health maintenance organization (HMO) a group of physicians that provides health services to individuals and families for a fixed annual fee

[1]W. G. Manning, J. P. Newhouse, E. B. Keeler, A. Liebowitz, and M. S. Marquis, "Health Insurance and the Demand for Medical Care," *American Economic Review* 77: 251–277, June 1987.

Why is a patient with a sore knee more likely to receive a magnetic resonance imaging (MRI) exam if he has conventional health insurance than if he belongs to a health maintenance organization?

When a patient visits his physician complaining of a sore knee, the physician has several options. After hearing the patient describe his symptoms and examining the knee manually, the physician may prescribe anti-inflammatory drugs and advise the patient to abstain from vigorous physical activity for a period, or she may advise the patient to undergo an (MRI) exam, a costly diagnostic procedure that generates images of the inner workings of the injured joint. The physician in an HMO receives no additional revenue if she orders the MRI exam, because all services are covered by the patient's fixed annual fee. Under conventional health insurance, in contrast, the physician will be reimbursed at a fixed rate, usually well above her marginal cost, for each additional service performed.

"Well, Bob, it looks like a paper cut, but just to be sure let's do lots of tests."

In many instances, the most prudent course of treatment is unambiguous, and in such cases physicians will make the same recommendation despite this striking difference in incentives. But in many other cases, it may not be obvious which decision is best. And in these cases, HMO physicians are much less likely to order expensive tests.

People who switch to HMOs pay less for their health plans than those who stick with conventional health insurance, because the HMO contract provides a strong incentive for doctors not to prescribe nonessential services. Many people fear, however, that the very same incentive may sometimes result in their not receiving valuable care. These concerns have led to proposed legislation granting patients rights of appeal when they are denied care by an HMO.

PAYING FOR HEALTH INSURANCE

It is troubling, but perhaps not surprising, that access to medical care is extremely limited in many of the world's poorest nations. After all, citizens of those nations lack enough income to buy adequate food, shelter, and many other basic goods and services. What *is* surprising, however, is that despite the movement to less expensive HMO plans, some 45 million Americans had no health coverage of any kind in 2000, almost 5 million more than in 1993. Politicians in both parties agree that something must be done to expand health coverage. But before an intelligent solution to this problem can be implemented, we must first understand why so many people are without coverage in the first place.

In the richest country on earth, experiencing the longest sustained economic boom in its history, why do the ranks of the uninsured keep swelling?

Although the incomes of most Americans are higher than ever, millions of American families continue to experience day-to-day financial distress. In 1998, for example, one of every 68 families filed for bankruptcy, more than the number of families with children graduating from college that year. Under the circumstances, it is easy to see why many families in generally good health might be tempted to press their luck. After all, health coverage for a family of four with no preexisting medical conditions costs upward of $4,000 a year, which is almost always far more than what such a family spends on medical services. The extra cash could help pay for a move into a better school district, for example, or at least keep creditors at bay.

As more people cancel their health coverage, going without insurance becomes more socially acceptable. Parents who didn't buy health insurance for their families were once viewed as irresponsible, but this stigma loses some of its sting as the number of uninsured grows. Making matters worse is the changing composition of the pool of the insured. As more healthy families forgo coverage, those left tend to be sicker and more costly to treat, forcing up premiums (an example of *adverse selection,* discussed in Chapter 12). In short, our health insurance system is in a death spiral. And as more people become uninsured, the problem will get worse, because the costs borne by those who remain insured will continue to escalate.

ECONOMIC NATURALIST 14.2

Government could eliminate the downward spiral by simply reimbursing each family up to $4,000 a year for health insurance. Government bureaucrats would not need to prescribe which doctors we see or micromanage any of the other details. They would simply process insurance receipts and send out reimbursement checks. This plan sounds expensive but would actually be less costly than the current system. The principal savings would come from delivering more cost-effective care to those who are now uninsured.

As it stands now, the untreated minor illnesses of the uninsured often develop into major illnesses, which are far more costly to treat. And when such illnesses befall the uninsured, we almost always treat them, often in costly emergency rooms. The resulting burden on hospitals leads to higher fees and increased government support—both of which now come largely out of the pockets of high-income taxpayers with health insurance.

The total budget needed to finance a $4,000 health insurance reimbursement for every American family—some $250 billion a year—would obviously require higher taxes. But for those whose employers currently provide health insurance, these taxes would be offset by an increase in salaries. After all, companies offer insurance not because they are charitable, but because they find doing so an effective way to compete for workers. Any company that did not offer higher salaries to previously insured workers would risk losing them to a company that did.

A universal reimbursement program would impose no net burden on taxpayers because of both salary adjustments and reductions in the high cost of care for the uninsured. And by providing a powerful incentive for all families to buy insurance, it would reverse the current downward spiral.

Critics of health care reform will say that if some people want to save money by going without health insurance, that's their problem or their choice. Perhaps, but it's a problem for the rest of society as well, one that if left untended will grow steadily worse.

ENVIRONMENTAL REGULATION

As we saw in Chapter 11, goods whose production generates negative externalities, such as atmospheric pollution, tend to be overproduced whenever negotiation among private parties is costly. Suppose we decide, as a society, that the best attainable outcome would be to have half as much pollution as would occur under completely unregulated conditions. In that case, how should the cleanup effort be distributed among those firms that currently discharge pollution into the environment?

The most efficient—and hence best—distribution of effort is the one for which each polluter's marginal cost of abatement is exactly the same. To see why, imagine that under current arrangements, the cost to one firm of removing a ton of pollution from the air is larger than the cost to another firm. Society could then achieve the same total reduction in pollution at lower cost by having the first firm discharge 1 ton more into the air and the second firm 1 ton less.

Unfortunately, government regulators seldom have detailed information on how the cost of reducing pollution varies from one firm to another. Many pollution laws therefore require all polluters simply to cut back their emissions by the same proportion, or to meet the same absolute emissions standards. If different polluters have different marginal costs of pollution abatement, however, those approaches will not be efficient.

TAXING POLLUTION

Fortunately, alternative policies can distribute the cleanup more efficiently, even if the government does not know firms' costs. One method is to tax pollution and allow firms to decide for themselves how much pollution to emit. The logic of this approach is illustrated in Example 14.6.

EXAMPLE 14.6

What is the least costly way to cut pollution by half?

Two firms, Sludge Oil and Northwest Lumber, have access to five production processes, each of which has a different cost and produces a different amount of pollution. The daily costs of the processes and the number of tons of smoke emitted are shown in Table 14.1. Pollution is currently unregulated, and negotiation between the firms and those who are harmed by pollution is impossible, which means that each firm uses process *A*, the least costly of the five. Each firm emits 4 tons of pollution/day, for a total of 8 tons of pollution/day.

TABLE 14.1
Costs and Emissions for Different Production Processes

Process (smoke)	A (4 tons/day)	B (3 tons/day)	C (2 tons/day)	D (1 ton/day)	E (0 tons/day)
Cost to Sludge Oil ($/day)	100	200	600	1,300	2,300
Cost to Northwest Lumber ($/day)	300	320	380	480	700

The government is considering two options for reducing total emissions by half. One is to require each firm to curtail its emissions by half. The other is to set a tax of T on each ton of smoke emitted each day. How large must T be to curtail emissions by half? What would be the total cost to society under each alternative?

If each firm is required to cut pollution by half, each must switch from process A to process C. The result will be 2 tons/day of pollution for each firm. The cost of the switch for Sludge Oil will be $600/day − $100/day = $500/day. The cost to Northwest Lumber will be $380/day − $300/day = $80/day, for a total cost of $580/day.

Consider now how each firm would react to a tax of T/ton of pollution. If a firm can cut pollution by 1 ton/day, it will save T/day in tax payments. Whenever the cost of cutting a ton of pollution is less than T, then, each firm has an incentive to switch to a cleaner process. For example, if the tax were set at $40/ton, Sludge Oil would stick with process A, because switching to process B would cost $100/day but would save only $40/day in taxes. Northwest Lumber, however, would switch to process B, because the $40 saving in taxes would be more than enough to cover the $20 cost of switching.

The problem is that a $40/day tax on each ton of pollution results in a reduction of only 1 ton/day, 3 tons short of the 4-ton target. Suppose instead that the government imposed a tax of $101/ton. Sludge Oil would then adopt process B, because the $100 daily cost of doing so would be less than the $101 saved in taxes. Northwest Lumber would adopt process D, because for every process up to and including D, the cost of switching to the next process would be less than the resulting tax saving.

Overall, then, a tax of $101/ton would result in the desired pollution reduction of 4 tons/day. The total cost of the reduction would be only $280/day ($100/day for Sludge Oil and $180/day for Northwest Lumber), or $300/day less than when each firm was required to cut its pollution by half. (The taxes paid by the firms do not constitute a cost of pollution reduction, because the money can be used to reduce whatever taxes would otherwise need to be levied on citizens.)

The advantage of the tax approach is that it concentrates pollution reduction in the hands of the firms that can accomplish it at least cost. Requiring each firm to cut emissions by the same proportion ignores the fact that some firms can reduce pollution much more cheaply than others. Note that under the tax approach, the cost of the last ton of smoke removed is the same for each firm, so the efficiency condition is satisfied.

One problem with the tax approach is that unless the government has detailed knowledge about each firm's cost of reducing pollution, it cannot know how high to set the pollution tax. A tax that is too low will result in too much pollution, while a tax that is too high will result in too little. Of course, the government could start by setting a low tax rate and gradually increase the rate until pollution is reduced to the target level. But because firms often incur substantial sunk costs when they switch from one process to another, that approach might be even more wasteful than requiring all firms to cut their emissions by the same proportion.

AUCTIONING POLLUTION PERMITS

Another alternative is to establish a target level for pollution and then auction off permits to emit that level of pollution. The virtues of this approach will become clear in Example 14.7.

EXAMPLE 14.7   How much will pollution permits sell for?

Two firms, Sludge Oil and Northwest Lumber, have access to the five different production processes described in Example 14.6. The government's goal is to cut the current level of pollution, 8 tons/day, by half. To do so, the government auctions off four permits, each one of which entitles the bearer to emit 1 ton of smoke/day. No smoke may be emitted without a permit. What price will the pollution permits fetch at auction, how many permits will each firm buy, and what will be the total cost of the resulting pollution reduction?

Process (smoke)	A (4 tons/day)	B (3 tons/day)	C (2 tons/day)	D (1 ton/day)	E (0 tons/day)
Cost to Sludge Oil ($/day)	100	200	600	1,300	2,300
Cost to Northwest Lumber ($/day)	300	320	380	480	700

If Sludge Oil has no permits, it must use process *E*, which costs $2,300/day to operate. If it had one permit it could use process *D*, which would save it $1,000/day. Thus, the most Sludge Oil would be willing to pay for a single 1-ton pollution permit is $1,000/day. With a second permit, Sludge Oil could switch to process *C* and save another $700/day; with a third permit, it could switch to process *B* and save another $400; and with a fourth permit, it could switch to process *A* and save another $100. Using similar reasoning, we can see that Northwest Lumber would pay up to $220 for one permit, up to $100 for a second, up to $60 for a third, and up to $20 for a fourth.

Suppose the government starts the auction at a price of $90. Sludge Oil will then demand four permits and Northwest Lumber will demand two, for a total demand of six permits. Since the government wishes to sell only four permits, it will keep raising the price until the two firms together demand a total of only four permits. Once the price reaches $101, Sludge Oil will demand three permits and Northwest Lumber will demand only one, for a total demand of four permits. Compared to the unregulated alternative, in which each firm used process *A*, the daily cost of the auction solution is $280: Sludge Oil spends $100 switching from process *A* to process *B*, and Northwest Lumber spends $180 switching from *A* to *D*. This total is $300 less than the cost of the original alternative, requiring each firm to reduce its emissions by half. (Again, the permit fees paid by the firms do not constitute a cost of cleanup, because the money can be used to reduce taxes that would otherwise have to be collected.)

The auction method has the same virtue as the tax method—namely, that of concentrating pollution reduction in the hands of those firms that can accomplish it at the lowest cost. But the auction method also has other attractive features that the tax approach does not. First, it does not induce firms to commit themselves to costly investments that they will have to abandon if the cleanup falls short of the target level. And second, it allows private citizens a direct voice in determining where the emission level will be set. For example, any group that believes the pollution target is too lenient could raise money to buy permits at auction. By keeping those permits locked away in a safe, the group could assure that they will not be used to emit pollution.

Several decades ago, when economists first proposed the auctioning of pollution permits, reactions of outrage were widely reported in the press. Most of those reactions amounted to the charge that the proposal would "permit rich firms to pollute to their hearts' content." Such an assertion betrays a total misunderstanding of the forces that generate pollution. Firms pollute not because they *want* to pollute, but because dirty production processes are cheaper than clean ones. Society's only real interest is in keeping the total amount of pollution from becoming excessive, not in *who* actually does the polluting. And in any event, the firms that do most of the polluting under an auction system will not be rich firms but those for whom pollution reduction is most costly.

Economists have argued patiently against these misinformed objections to the auction system, and their efforts have finally borne fruit. The sale of pollution permits is now common in several parts of the United States, and there is growing interest in the approach in other countries. Sound ideas may not always triumph over wrongheaded ones, especially in the short run, but in this instance economic education has helped society move forward.

RECAP   **ENVIRONMENTAL REGULATION**

An efficient program for reducing pollution is one for which the marginal cost of abatement is the same for all polluters. Taxing pollution has this desirable property, as does the auction of pollution permits. The auction method has the advantage that regulators can achieve a desired abatement target without having detailed knowledge of the abatement technologies available to polluters.

WORKPLACE SAFETY REGULATION

Most industrialized countries have laws that attempt to limit the extent to which workers are exposed to health and safety risks on the job. Those laws have often been described as necessary to protect workers against exploitation by employers with market power. Given the working conditions we saw in the early stages of the industrial revolution, the idea that such exploitation pervades unregulated private markets has intuitive appeal. Witness Upton Sinclair's vivid account of life in the Chicago meatpacking factories at the turn of the twentieth century:

> Some worked at the stamping machines, and it was very seldom that one could work long there at the pace that was set, and not give out and forget himself, and have a part of his hand chopped off. There were the hoisters, as they were called, whose task it was to press the lever which lifted the dead cattle off the floor. They ran along a rafter, peering down through the damp and the steam; and as old Durham's architects had not built the killing room for the convenience of the hoisters, at every few feet they would have to stoop under a beam, say four feet above the one they ran on; which got them into the habit of stooping, so that in a few years they would be walking like chimpanzees. Worst of any, however, were the fertilizer men, and those who served in the cooking rooms. These people could not be shown to the visitors—for the odor of the fertilizer-man would scare any ordinary visitor at a hundred yards, and as for the other men, who worked in tank-rooms full of

steam, and in which there were open vats near the level of the floor, their peculiar trouble was that they fell into the vats; and when they were fished out, there was never enough of them left to be worth exhibiting—sometimes they would be overlooked for days, till all but the bones of them had gone out to the world as Durham's Pure Leaf Lard.[2]

The miserable conditions of factory workers, juxtaposed with the often opulent lifestyle enjoyed by factory owners, seemed to affirm the idea that owners were exploiting workers. But given that conditions in the factories were in fact too dangerous, how much safer should they have been?

Consider the question of whether to install a specific safety device, say, a guardrail on a lathe. Many people are reluctant to employ the cost-benefit principle to answer such a question. To them, safety is an absolute priority, so the guardrail should be installed regardless of its cost. Yet most of us do not make personal decisions about our own health and safety that way. No one you know, for example, gets the brakes on his car checked every day, even though doing so would reduce the likelihood of being killed in an accident. The reason, obviously, is that daily brake inspections would be very costly and would not reduce the probability of an accident much compared to annual or semiannual inspections.

The same logic can be applied to installing a guardrail on a lathe. If the amount one is willing to pay to reduce the likelihood of an accident exceeds the cost of the guardrail, it should be installed; otherwise, it should not be. And no matter how highly we value reducing the odds of an accident, we will almost surely settle for less than perfect safety. After all, to reduce the risk of an accident to nearly zero, one would have to enclose the lathe in a thick plexiglass case and operate it with remote-controlled mechanical arms. Faced with the prohibitive cost of such an alternative, most of us would decide that the best approach is to add safety equipment whose benefit exceeds its cost, and then use caution while operating the machine.

But will unregulated employers offer the level of workplace safety suggested by the cost-benefit principle? Most nations appear to have decided that they will not. As noted, virtually every industrial country now has comprehensive legislation mandating minimum safety standards in the workplace—laws usually described as safeguards against exploitation of workers.

Yet explaining safety regulation as an antidote for exploitation raises troubling questions. One difficulty stems from the economist's argument that competition for workers prods firms to provide the socially optimal level of amenities. For example, if an amenity—say, a guardrail on a lathe—costs $50/month to install and maintain and workers value it at $100/month, then the firm must install the device or risk losing workers to a competitor that does. After all, if a competing firm were to pay workers $60/month less than they currently earn, it could cover the cost of the device with $10 to spare, while providing a compensation package that is $40/month more attractive than the first employer's.

To this argument, critics respond that in practice there is very little competition in the labor market. They argue that incomplete information, worker immobility, and other frictions create situations in which workers have little choice but to accept whatever conditions employers offer. But even if a firm were the *only* employer in the market, it would still have an incentive to install a $50 safety device that is worth $100 to the worker. Failure to do so would be to leave cash on the table.

Other defenders of regulation suggest that workers may not know about safety devices they lack. But that explanation, too, is troubling, because competing firms would have a strong incentive to call the devices to workers' attention.

Is safety regulation needed to protect workers from exploitation?

[2]Upton Sinclair, *The Jungle*, Sinclair, 1906, p. 106.

If the problem is that workers cannot move to the competing firm's location, then the firm can set up a branch near the exploited workers. Collusive agreements to restrain such competition have proved difficult to maintain, because each firm can increase its profit by cheating on the agreement.

In fact, worker mobility between firms is high, as is entry by new firms into existing markets; cartel agreements have always been notoriously unstable. Information may not be perfect, but if a new employer in town is offering a better deal, sooner or later word gets around.

Finally, if, despite these checks, some firms still manage to exploit their workers, we should expect those firms to earn a relatively high profit. But in fact we observe just the opposite. Year in and year out, firms that pay the *highest* wages are the most profitable. And so we are left with a puzzle. The fear of exploitation by employers with market power has led governments to adopt sweeping and costly safety regulations; yet the evidence suggests that exploitation cannot be a major problem. As Example 14.8 suggests, however, safety regulation might prove useful even in a perfectly competitive environment with complete information.

Will Don and Michael choose the optimal amount of safety?

EXAMPLE 14.8

Suppose Don and Michael are the only two members of a hypothetical community. They get satisfaction from three things: their income, safety on the job, and their position on the economic ladder. Suppose Don and Michael must both choose between two jobs, a safe job that pays $50/week and a risky job that pays $80/week. The value of safety to each is $40/week. Having more income than one's neighbor is worth $40/week to each; having less income than one's neighbor means a $40/week reduction in satisfaction. (Having the same income as one's neighbor means no change in satisfaction.) Will Don and Michael make the best job choices possible in this situation?

Viewed in isolation, each person's decision should be to take the safe job. Granted, it pays $30/week less than the risky job, but the extra safety it offers is worth $40/week. So aside from the issue of relative income, the value of the safe job is $90/week (its $50 salary plus $40 worth of safety), or $10/week more than the risky job.

Once we incorporate concerns about relative income, however, the logic of the decision changes in a fundamental way. Now the attractiveness of each job depends on the job chosen by the other. The four possible combinations of choices and their corresponding levels of satisfaction are shown in Table 14.2. If each man chooses a safe job, he will get $50 of income, $40 worth of satisfaction from safety, and—because each will have the same income—zero satisfaction from relative income. So if each man chooses the safe job, each will get a total of $90

TABLE 14.2
The Effect of Concern about Relative Income on Worker Choices Regarding Safety

		Michael	
		Safe job at $50/week	Risky job at $80/week
Don	Safe job at $50/week	$90 each	$50 for Don $120 for Michael
	Risky job at $80/week	$120 for Don $50 for Michael	$80 each

worth of satisfaction. If instead each man chooses the risky job, each will get $80 of income, zero satisfaction from safety, and because each has the same income as the other, zero satisfaction from relative income. If we compare the upper left cell of the table to the lower right cell, then, we can say unequivocally that Don and Michael would be happier if each took a safe job at lower income than if each chose a risky job with more income.

But consider how the choice plays out once the two men recognize their interdependency. Suppose, for example, that Michael chooses the safe job. If Don then chooses the unsafe job, he ends up with a total of $120 of satisfaction: $80 in salary plus $40 from having more income than Michael. Michael, for his part, ends up with only $50 worth of satisfaction: $50 in salary plus $40 from safety, minus $40 from having a lower income than Don. Alternatively, suppose Michael chooses the risky job. Then Don will again do better to accept the risky job, for by doing so he gets $80 worth of satisfaction rather than $50.

In short, no matter which job Michael chooses, Don will get more satisfaction by choosing the risky job. Likewise, no matter which job Don chooses, Michael will do better by choosing the risky job. Yet when each follows his dominant strategy, they end up in the lower right cell of the table, which provides only $80/week of satisfaction to each—$10 less than if each had chosen the safe job. Thus their job safety choice confronts them with a prisoner's dilemma (see Chapter 10). As in all such situations, when the players choose independently, they fail to make the most of their opportunities.

EXERCISE 14.4

How would your answer to the question posed in Example 14.8 have differed if the value of safety had been not $40/week but $20?

Example 14.8 suggests an alternative explanation for safety regulation, one that is not based on the need to protect workers from exploitation. If Don and Michael could choose collectively, they would pick the safe job and maximize their combined satisfaction. Thus each might support legislation that establishes safety standards in the workplace.

We stress that concern about relative income need not mean that people care only about having more or better goods than their neighbors. In our society, a person's relative income is important for reasons that everyone recognizes. For example, if you want to send your child to a good school, you must buy a house in a good school district. But who gets a house in a good school district? Those who have high relative income. Similarly, if you want a house with a view, and only 10 percent of homesites have views, who gets them? The people in the top 10 percent of the income distribution, of course, and only those people. Many important outcomes in life depend on where a person stands on the economic ladder. And when people care about their relative income, rational, self-interested actions will not always lead to efficient outcomes in the labor market.

That is not to say that regulation always improves matters. The labor market may not be perfect, but government regulators aren't perfect, either. Safety in the workplace is overseen by the Occupational Safety and Health Administration (OSHA), an agency that has drawn considerable criticism, much of it justified. Consider, for example, the following passage on safety requirements for ladders, taken verbatim from an early OSHA manual:

> The general slope of grain in flat steps of minimum dimension shall not be steeper than 1 in 12, except that for ladders under 10 feet in length the slope shall not be steeper than 1 in 10. The slope of grain in areas of local deviation shall not be steeper than 1 in 12 or 1 in 10 as specified above. For all ladders, cross grain not steeper than 1 in 10 are permitted in lieu of 1 in 12, provided the size is

increased to afford at least 15 percent greater strength than for ladders built to minimum dimensions. Local deviations of grain associated with otherwise permissible irregularities are permitted.[3]

This befogged passage appears in a section devoted to ladders that is 30 pages long, two columns to the page. One can easily imagine the managers of a firm deciding that their best course of action is simply to abandon any activities requiring ladders.

As an alternative to OSHA-style prescriptive safety regulation, many economists favor programs that increase employers' financial incentives to reduce workplace injuries. The **workers' compensation** system provides a mechanism through which such a change might be achieved. Workers' compensation is a government insurance system that provides benefits to workers who are injured in the workplace. As currently administered, the program does not adjust each individual employer's premiums fully to reflect the claims generated by its workers. Employers with low injury rates thus pay premiums higher than needed to cover the claims generated by their workers, while those with high injury rates pay premiums too small to cover the claims generated by their workers.

workers' compensation a government insurance system that provides benefits to workers who are injured on the job

Economists argue that revising insurance premiums to reflect the full social cost of the injuries sustained by each employer's workers would provide the optimal incentive to curtail injuries in the workplace. In effect, premiums set at this level would be an optimal tax on injuries and would be efficient for the same reason that a properly chosen tax on pollution is efficient. An injury tax set at the marginal cost of injury would encourage employers to adopt all safety measures whose benefit exceeds their cost.

As in other domains, we are far more likely to achieve optimal safety levels in the workplace if we choose among policies on practical cost-benefit grounds rather than on the basis of slogans about the merits or flaws of the free market.

Why does the government require safety seats for infants who travel in cars but not for infants who travel in airplanes?

A mother cannot legally drive her 6-month-old son to a nearby grocery store without first strapping him into a government-approved safety seat. Yet she can fly with him from Miami to Seattle with no restraining device at all. Why this difference?

In case of an accident—whether in a car or an airplane—an infant who is strapped into a safety seat is more likely to escape injury or death than one who is unrestrained. But the probability of being involved in a serious accident is hundreds of times higher when traveling by car than when traveling by air, so the benefit of having safety seats is greater for trips made by car. Using safety seats is also far more costly on plane trips than on car trips. Whereas most cars have plenty of extra room for a safety seat, parents might need to purchase an extra ticket to use one on an airplane. Most parents appear unwilling to pay $600 more per trip for a small increment in safety, either for themselves or their children.

ECONOMIC NATURALIST 14.3

RECAP   SAFETY REGULATION

Most countries regulate safety in the workplace, a practice often defended as needed to protect workers from being exploited by employers with market power. Yet safety regulation might be attractive even in perfectly competitive labor markets, because the social payoff from investment in safety often exceeds the private payoff. An injury tax set at the marginal cost of injury would encourage optimal investment in workplace safety.

---

[3]Quoted by Robert S. Smith, "Compensating Wage Differentials and Public Policy: A Review," *Industrial and Labor Relations Review,* **32:**339–352, 1977.

CRIME CONTROL

Because police and other law enforcement officials are charged with protecting our lives and personal safety, political leaders are often reluctant to discuss expenditures on law enforcement in cost-benefit terms. But because we live in a world of scarcity, we cannot escape the fact that spending more on law enforcement means spending less on other things of value. Crimes, like accidents, are costly to prevent. The socially optimal amount to spend on avoiding any specific type of crime is that amount for which the marginal benefit of reducing that crime exactly equals its marginal cost. As the next example illustrates, the cost-benefit principle helps to explain why society invests so much more heavily in preventing some crimes than in preventing others.

ECONOMIC NATURALIST 14.4

Should college professors receive Secret Service protection when they give out-of-town lectures?

Why do more Secret Service agents guard the President than the Vice President, and why do no Secret Service agents guard college professors?

When the President of the United States flies to Cleveland to give a speech, hundreds of federal agents are assigned to protect him against attack by an assassin. But when the Vice President flies to Cleveland to give a speech, many fewer agents are assigned, and when a college professor goes to Cleveland for the same purpose, no agents are assigned at all. Why this difference?

According to the cost-benefit principle, the government should keep assigning agents in each case until the cost of an additional agent equals the value of the extra protection provided. In each of the three cases, the marginal cost of assigning agents is essentially the same. As shown in Figure 14.5, marginal cost *(MC)* is likely to be upward-sloping, because of the low-hanging fruit principle, according to which the most effective agents should be assigned first.

The important difference among these three cases lies in the value of assigning additional agents. The marginal benefit of an agent assigned to the President [MB_P, (a)] is much higher than the marginal benefit of an agent assigned to the Vice President [MB_{VP}, (b)], for at least two reasons. First, opponents of the government have a stronger motive to attack the President than the Vice President, because the President's role is so much more important than the Vice President's. Thus assigning an additional agent to the President is more likely to prevent an attack. And second, the benefit of preventing an attack against the President is much higher than that of preventing an attack against the Vice President, again, because the President's role is so much more important. These observations imply that the optimal number of agents to assign to the President [N_P, part (a)] is much greater than the optimal number of agents to assign to the Vice President [N_{VP}, part (b)]. Finally, the optimal number of agents to assign to a trav-

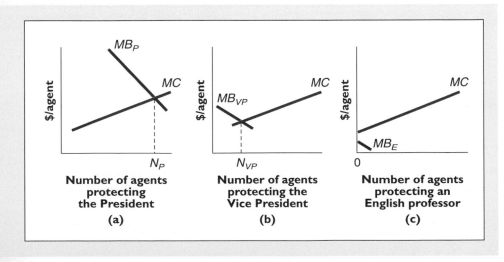

FIGURE 14.5
Differential Investment in Crime Prevention.
Because of differences in the marginal benefit of protection, more Secret Service agents are assigned to protect the President [part (a)] than to protect the Vice President [part (b)], and none are assigned to protect an ordinary citizen [part (c)].

eling professor is zero [part (c)], because the marginal benefit of such an assignment [MB_E, part (c)] is so small. After all, few people have any reason to attack a professor, and in the unlikely event of an attack, the consequences would be far less serious than if a prominent government leader were attacked.

Many critics of the cost-benefit approach complain that when applied in examples like the one just discussed, it gives short shrift to the dignity of human life. On closer inspection, however, this complaint is difficult to support. The recommendation to assign no Secret Service agents to protect a traveling college professor does not imply that the lives of ordinary citizens are not to be cherished. Rather, it simply acknowledges that even without Secret Service protection, not even a single traveling professor is likely to be assassinated in the course of the next hundred years. For the same money that we would spend to send agents on largely pointless assignments, we could install guardrails on dangerous mountain roads, purchase additional mobile emergency units, or make any number of other investments that would save thousands of lives. The logic of the scarcity principle does not cease to apply whenever the choices we must make involve human health or safety.

> **RECAP**   **CRIME CONTROL**
>
> The cost-benefit principle applies in crime policy just as in other areas of public policy. Society's efforts to curb crime should be expanded only to the point at which the marginal benefit from crime reduction equals its marginal cost.

LEGALIZED GAMBLING

Before 1964, lotteries were illegal in every state in America. Recent years, however, have witnessed the steady proliferation of legalized gambling. State lotteries now exist in 37 states and the District of Columbia, and most citizens now live within hours of the nearest legal casino.[4]

Proponents of legalization call gambling a victimless crime. They argue that since neither bettors nor casino operators can be *forced* to gamble, any gambling that occurs must be a voluntary exchange that benefits all parties. In this view, gambling is just like any other form of entertainment; to prohibit it is like prohibiting the sale of tickets to basketball games.

Why, then, did most states originally enact laws to prohibit gambling? The apparent explanation is similar to the one for bans on the sale of heroin, cocaine, and other mood-altering drugs. Although many people—perhaps most people—appear to be capable of gambling in moderation, for a small minority gambling is a highly addictive activity. When the opportunity to gamble is freely available, many of these people will gamble to excess, jeopardizing their psychological health and, more important from the state's point of view, their ability to support and care for their families.

Prior to 1970, although gambling was officially against the law, the authorities made little attempt to prosecute people who gambled discreetly. At that time, virtually all gambling occurred surreptitiously. People who really wanted to gamble could still find ways to do it, but those who wanted to avoid the temptation

---

[4]See Charles Clotfelter, Philip Cook, Julie Edell, and Marian Moore, "State Lotteries at the Turn of the Century: Report to the National Gambling Impact Study Commission," June 1, 1999, mimeograph.

could easily steer clear. As legalized gambling has proliferated, however, problem gamblers have experienced more difficulty staying out of trouble. Casinos advertise heavily, and states themselves often promote their lotteries with sophisticated multimillion dollar advertising campaigns. In New York State, for example, television commercials portrays people's fantasies about winning the lottery ("I'd buy the company and fire my boss!").

An average of 55 percent of the adults living in states that have lotteries bought at least one ticket during 1998. Most of them enjoyed the experience enough to justify the few dollars they spent. Since only about half the revenue from ticket sales is paid out in prizes, legalized gambling brings in additional revenue to pay for public services. Yet for a significant minority, the expanded gambling opportunities have not been welcome. New chapters of Gamblers Anonymous, a support group much like Alcoholics Anonymous, are forming at record rates.

Should gambling be outlawed again? Although the task of measuring the relevant costs and benefits is too complex to attempt here, one thing is clear: Any state that attempted to outlaw gambling on its own would have serious difficulty. Residents of a state that did not sponsor a lottery could still patronize lotteries in neighboring states. The lottery-free state would then lose much of its tax revenue yet fail to re-create a nongambling environment. On a state-by-state basis, each state confronts a decision to ban gambling much like the prisoner's dilemma discussed in Chapter 10.

▪ SUMMARY ▪

- Our aim in this chapter was to apply basic microeconomic principles to a variety of government policy questions. We began by looking at the various policies governments employ to mitigate concerns about fairness and efficiency losses arising from natural monopolies. Such policies include state ownership and management of natural monopolies, state regulation, private contracting, and vigorous enforcement of antitrust laws. Each of these remedies entails costs as well as benefits. In some cases, a combination of policies will produce a better outcome than simply allowing natural monopolists to do as they please. But in other cases, a hands-off policy may be the best available option.

- Basic economic principles can help to determine the optimal pricing policy when government is the direct provider of a service. We saw that the total economic surplus from the provision of a service will be largest if each user is charged the marginal cost of providing the service. In the case of public utilities, such a policy often entails charging different rates for similar services provided at different times. Economic principles can also help to show how different methods of paying for health care affect the efficiency with which medical services are delivered. In the case of health care, the gains from marginal cost pricing can often be achieved through insurance policies with large deductibles.

- An understanding of the forces that give rise to environmental pollution can help to identify those policy measures that will achieve a desired reduction in pollution at the lowest possible cost. Both the taxing of pollution and the sale of transferable pollution rights promote this goal. Each distributes the environmental cleanup effort so that the marginal cost of pollution abatement is the same for all polluters.

- A perennially controversial topic is the application of the cost-benefit principle to policies involving health and safety. Many critics feel that the use of cost-benefit analysis in this domain is not morally legitimate, because it involves putting a monetary price on human life. Yet the fundamental principle of scarcity applies to health and safety, just as it does to other issues. Spending more on health and safety necessarily means spending less on other things of value. Failure to weigh the relevant costs and benefits, then, means that society will be less likely to achieve its stated goals in law enforcement, health care, workplace safety, and pollution abatement.

- Until the 1960s most states had laws against gambling but did not vigorously enforce them. The implicit aim of those laws may have been to shield potentially vulnerable citizens from the temptation to gamble excessively, without preventing gambling entirely. In recent decades most states have repealed their gambling laws, and now actively promote the sale of tickets in state-sponsored lotteries. One result has been a steep increase in compulsive gambling, which has led to renewed calls to declare gambling illegal. But the decision to ban gambling confronts states with a prisoner's dilemma. Any state that unilaterally outlawed it would lose substantial tax revenue without reducing gambling, for many citizens would simply patronize lotteries in neighboring states.

▪ KEY TERMS ▪

cost-plus regulation (351)
first-dollar insurance coverage (359)

health maintenance organization
(HMO) (359)

workers' compensation (369)

▪ REVIEW QUESTIONS ▪

1. Since natural monopolists tend to produce less than the socially optimal level of output, does this mean that we should always try to break up natural monopolists into several smaller firms?

2. Why do economists believe that pollution taxes and effluent permits are a more efficient way to curb pollution than laws mandating across-the-board cutbacks?

3. Why is first-dollar health care coverage inefficient?

4. How would you explain to a skeptical bank manager why the socially optimal number of bank robberies is not zero?

5. Does it make sense for the Federal Aviation Administration to require more sophisticated and expensive safety equipment in large commercial passenger jets than in small private planes?

▪ PROBLEMS ▪

1. In Charlotte, North Carolina, citizens can get their electric power from two sources: a hydroelectric generator and a coal-fired steam generator. The hydroelectric generator can supply up to 100 units of power/day at a constant marginal cost of 1 cent/unit. The steam generator can supply any additional power that is needed at a constant marginal cost of 10 cents/unit. When electricity costs 10 cents/unit, residents of Charlotte demand 200 units/day.
   a. Draw the marginal cost curve of electric power production in Charlotte.
   b. How much should the city charge for electric power? Explain. Should it charge the same price for a family whose power comes from the hydroelectric generator as it does for a family whose power comes from the steam generator?

2. The municipal waterworks of Cortland draws water from two sources, an underground spring and a nearby lake. Water from the spring costs 2 cents/100 gallons to deliver, and the spring has a capacity of 1 million gallons/day. Water from the lake costs 4 cents/100 gallons to deliver and is available in unlimited quantities. The demand for water in the summer months in Cortland is $P = 20 - 0.001Q$, where P is the price of water in cents per hundred gallons and Q is quantity demanded in hundreds of gallons per day. The demand curve for water in the winter months is $P = 10 - 0.001Q$. If the waterworks wants to encourage efficient water use, how much should it charge for water in the summer months? In the winter months?

3. Refer to Problem 2. By how much would daily total economic surplus go down if, in response to complaints from summer residents, the Cortland city council passed a law requiring all water to be sold at 3 cents/100 gallons throughout the year.

4. In the event he requires an appendectomy, David's demand for hospital accommodations is as shown in the following diagram. David's current insurance policy fully covers the cost of hospital stays. The marginal cost of providing a hospital room is $150/day.

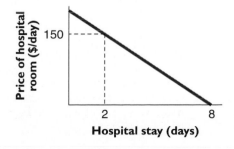

a. If David's only illness this year results in an appendectomy, how many days will he choose to stay in the hospital?

b. By how much would total economic surplus have been higher this year if David's hospital insurance covered only the cost of hospital stays that exceed $1,000 per illness?

5. Refer to Problem 4. Suppose David's employer adopts a new health care plan that pays 50 percent of all medical expenses up to $1,000 per illness, with full coverage thereafter. How will economic surplus under this plan compare with economic surplus with the policy in Problem 4b?

6. Two firms, Sludge Oil and Northwest Lumber, have access to five production processes, each one of which has a different cost and gives off a different amount of pollution. The daily costs of the processes and the corresponding number of tons of smoke emitted are as shown in the following table.

Process (smoke)	A (4 tons/day)	B (3 tons/day)	C (2 tons/day)	D (1 ton/day)	E (0 tons/day)
Cost to Sludge Oil ($/day)	50	70	120	200	500
Cost to Northwest Lumber ($/day)	100	180	500	1,000	2,000

a. If pollution is unregulated, which process will each firm use, and what will be the daily smoke emission?

b. The city council wants to curb smoke emissions by 50 percent. To accomplish this, it requires each firm to curb its emissions by 50 percent. What will be the total cost to society of this policy?

7. The city council in Problem 6 again wants to curb emissions by half. This time, it sets a tax of $T on each ton of smoke emitted per day. How large will T have to be to effect the desired reduction? What is the total cost to society of this policy?

8. Refer to Problem 7. Instead of taxing pollution, the city council decides to auction off four permits, each of which entitles the bearer to emit 1 ton of smoke/day. No smoke may be emitted without a permit. Suppose the government conducts the auction by starting at $1 and asking how many permits each firm wants to buy at that price. If the total is more than four, it then raises the price by $1, and asks again, and so on, until the total quantity of permits demanded falls to four. How much will each permit sell for in this auction? How many permits will each firm buy? What will be the total cost to society of this reduction in pollution?

9. Tom and Al are the only two members of a household. Each gets satisfaction from three things: his income, his safety at work, and his income relative to his roommate's income. Suppose Tom and Al must each choose between two jobs: a safe job that pays $100/week and a risky job that pays $130/week. The value of safety to each is $40/week. Each person evaluates relative income as follows: Having more income than his roommate provides the equivalent of $30/week worth of satisfaction, having less implies a reduction of $30/week worth of satisfaction, and earning the same income as his roommate means no change in satisfaction. Will Tom and Al choose optimally between the two jobs?

10. Refer to Problem 9. If Tom and Al could negotiate binding agreements with one another at no cost, which job would they choose? Suppose that negotiation is impractical and that the only way Tom and Al can achieve greater workplace safety is for the government to adopt safety regulations. If enforcement of the regulations costs $25/week, would Tom and Al favor their adoption?

▪ ANSWERS TO IN-CHAPTER EXERCISES ▪

14.1 At a consumption level of 2 million gallons/day, the marginal source of water is the lake, which has a marginal cost of 0.8 cent/gallon. The city should charge everyone 0.8 cent/gallon, including those who get their water from the spring.

14.2 If winter demand were $P = 8 - 2Q$, all winter power could be provided by the hydroelectric generator, and the marginal cost of producing electricity would be 2 cents/kilowatthour during both the winter and summer months.

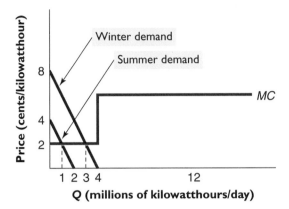

14.3 The optimal stay is still 1 day. If insurance reimburses $150/day, then the marginal charge seen by David will be the remaining $150/day, so he will stay 2 days. The cost to society of the additional day is $300, and the benefit to David of the extra day is only $225 (the area of the pale blue figure). The loss in surplus from the additional day's stay is thus $75.

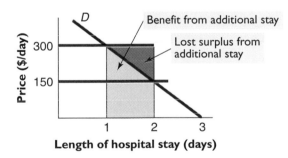

14.4 The payoff matrix would now be as follows, and the best choice, both individually and collectively, would be the risky job.

		Michael	
		Safe job at $50/week	Risky job at $80/week
Don	Safe job at $50/week	$70 each	$30 for Don $120 for Michael
	Risky job at $80/week	$120 for Don $30 for Michael	$80 each

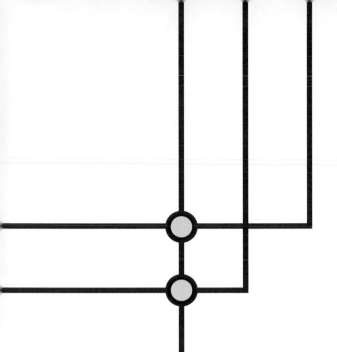

CHAPTER 15

PUBLIC GOODS AND TAXATION

∎

Government has the power to tax. Unlike a private business, which can get our money only if we voluntarily buy its product, the government can take our money even if we don't want the particular mix of goods and services provided.

Government also has a monopoly on the legitimate use of force. If people break the law, government has the power to restrain them, using force if necessary. It also has the power to deprive lawbreakers of their liberty for extended periods, and, in some places, even to execute them. Government can draft law-abiding citizens into the armed forces and send them into situations in which they must kill others and risk being killed themselves.

These are awesome powers. And although they are often used in the pursuit of noble ends, the historical record abounds with illustrations of their abuse. Voters and politicians of both parties are keenly aware of these abuses. Indeed, contemporary political rhetoric almost invariably entails criticism of bloated, out-of-control government bureaucracy. Even mainstream Democrats—ostensibly the party of activist government in the United States—have conceded the need to curb government's role. For example, as President Clinton remarked in his 1996 State of the Union Message, "the era of big government is over."

Others advocate even more radical retrenchment. For instance, Harry Browne, the 1996 Libertarian Party presidential candidate, called for abolition of the Internal Revenue Service, the agency responsible for collecting the federal income tax. This step would be tantamount to abolishing the federal government itself, for without tax revenues, there would be no way to pay for public goods and services.

Browne is right, of course, that a sure way to prevent government abuse of power is simply to have no government. But since virtually no society on earth lacks a government, we may suspect that governments, on balance, do more good than harm.

But how big, exactly, should government be? What goods and services should it provide? How should it raise the revenue to pay for them? What other powers should it have to constrain the behavior of its citizens? And how should the various powers we assign to government be apportioned among local, state, and federal levels? Our goal in this chapter will be to employ the principles of microeconomics in an attempt to answer these pragmatic questions.

GOVERNMENT PROVISION OF PUBLIC GOODS

public good a good or service that, to at least some degree, is both nonrival and nonexcludable

One of the primary tasks of government is to provide what economists call **public goods,** such as national defense and the criminal justice system.

PUBLIC GOODS VERSUS PRIVATE GOODS

nonrival good a good whose consumption by one person does not diminish its availability for others

nonexcludable good a good that is difficult, or costly, to exclude nonpayers from consuming

Public goods are those goods or services that are, in varying degrees, **nonrival** and **nonexcludable.** A nonrival good is one whose consumption by one person does not diminish its availability for others. For example, if the military prevents a hostile nation from invading your city, your enjoyment of that protection does not diminish its value to your neighbors. A good is nonexcludable if it is difficult to exclude nonpayers from consuming it. For instance, even if your neighbors don't pay their share of the cost of maintaining an army, they will still enjoy its protection.

Another example of a nonrival and nonexcludable good is an over-the-air broadcast of the *David Letterman Show.* The fact that you tune in one evening does not make the program any less available to others, and once the broadcast has been beamed out over the airwaves, it is difficult to prevent anyone from tuning in. Similarly, when the City of New York puts on a fireworks display in New York harbor to celebrate the Fourth of July, it cannot charge admission, because the harbor may be viewed from so many different locations in the city. And the fact that additional persons view the display does not in any way diminish its value to other potential viewers.

In contrast, the typical private good is diminished one-for-one by any individual's consumption of it. For instance, when you eat a cheeseburger, it is no longer available for anyone else. Moreover, people can be easily prevented from consuming cheeseburgers they don't pay for.

> **EXERCISE 15.1**
>
> Which of the following, if any, is nonrival?
> a. The website of the Bureau of Labor Statistics at 3 A.M.
> b. The World Cup Soccer championship game watched in person.
> c. The World Cup Soccer championship game watched on television.

pure public good a good or service that, to a high degree, is both nonrival and nonexcludable

Goods that are both highly nonexcludable and nonrival are often called **pure public goods.** Two reasons favor government provision of such goods. First, for-profit private companies would have obvious difficulty recovering their cost of production. Many people might be willing to pay enough to cover the cost of producing the good, but if it is nonexcludable, the company cannot easily charge for it (an example of the free-rider problem discussed in Chapter 12). And second, if the marginal cost of serving additional users is zero once the good has been produced, then charging for the good would be inefficient, even if there were some practical way to do so. This inefficiency often characterizes the provision of **collective goods**—nonrival goods for which it is possible to exclude nonpayers. Pay-per-view cable television is an example. People who don't pay don't get to watch, a restriction that excludes many viewers who would have benefited from watching. Since the marginal cost to society of their tuning in is literally zero, excluding these viewers is wasteful.

A **pure private good** is one from which nonpayers can easily be excluded and for which one person's consumption creates a one-for-one reduction in the good's availability for others. The theory of perfectly competitive supply developed in Chapter 6 applies to pure private goods, of which basic agricultural products are perhaps the best examples. A **pure commons good** is a rival good that is also nonexcludable, so-called because goods with this combination of properties almost always result in a tragedy of the commons (see Chapter 11). Fish in ocean waters are an example.

The classification scheme defined by the nonrival and nonexcludable properties is summarized in Table 15.1. The columns of the table indicate the extent to which one person's consumption of a good fails to diminish its availability for others. Goods in the right column are nonrival, and those in the left column are not. The rows of the table indicate the difficulty of excluding nonpayers from consuming the good. Goods in the top row are nonexcludable, those in the bottom row, excludable. Private goods (lower left cell) are rival and excludable. Public goods (upper right cell) are nonrival and nonexcludable. The two hybrid categories are commons goods (upper left cell), which are rival but nonexcludable, and collective goods (lower right cell), which are excludable but nonrival.

collective good a good or service that, to at least some degree, is nonrival but excludable

pure private good one for which nonpayers can easily be excluded and for which each unit consumed by one person means one less unit available for others

pure commons good one for which nonpayers cannot easily be excluded and for which each unit consumed by one person means one less unit available for others

TABLE 15.1
Private, Public, and Hybrid Goods

		Nonrival	
		Low	High
Nonexcludable	High	Commons good (fish in the ocean)	Public good (national defense)
	Low	Private good (wheat)	Collective good (pay-per-view TV)

Collective goods are sometimes provided by government, sometimes by private companies. Most pure public goods are provided by government, but even private companies can sometimes find profitable ways of producing goods that are both nonrival *and* nonexcludable. An example is broadcast radio and television, which covers its costs by selling airtime to advertisers.

The mere fact that a good is a pure public good does not necessarily mean that government ought to provide it. On the contrary, the only public goods the government should even *consider* providing are those whose benefits exceed their costs. The cost of a public good is simply the sum of all explicit and implicit costs incurred to provide it. The benefit of a public good is measured by asking how much people would be willing to pay for it. Although that sounds similar to the way we measure the benefit of a private good, an important distinction exists. The benefit of an additional unit of a private good, such as a cheeseburger, is the highest sum that any individual buyer would be willing to pay for it. In contrast, the benefit of an additional unit of a public good, such as an additional broadcast episode of *Sesame Street,* is the sum of the reservation prices of all people who will watch that episode.

Even if the amount that all beneficiaries of a public good would be willing to pay exceeds its cost, government provision of that good makes sense only if there is no other less costly way of providing it. For example, whereas city governments often pay for fireworks displays, they almost invariably hire private companies to put on these events. Finally, if the benefit of a public good does not exceed its cost, we are better off without it.

PAYING FOR PUBLIC GOODS

Not everyone benefits equally from the provision of a given public good. For example, some people find fireworks displays highly entertaining, but others simply don't care about them, and still others actively dislike them. Ideally, it might seem that the most equitable method of financing a given public good would be to tax people in proportion to their willingness to pay for the good. To illustrate this approach, suppose Jones values a public good at $100, Smith values the same good at $200, and the cost of the good is $240. Jones would then be taxed $80, and Smith would be taxed $160. The good would be provided, and each taxpayer in this example would reap a surplus equal to 25 percent of his tax payment: $20 for Jones, $40 for Smith.

In practice, however, government officials usually lack the information they would need to tax people in proportion to their willingness to pay for specific public goods. (Think about it: If an IRS agent asked you how much you would be willing to pay to have a new freeway and you knew you would be taxed in proportion to the amount you responded, what would you say?) Examples 15.1 to 15.3 illustrate some of the problems that arise in financing public goods and suggests possible solutions to these problems.

EXAMPLE 15.1   **Will Prentice and Wilson buy a water filter?**

Prentice and Wilson own adjacent summer cottages along an isolated stretch of shoreline on Cayuga Lake. Because of a recent invasion of zebra mussels, each must add chlorine to his water intake valve each week to prevent it from becoming clogged by the tiny mollusks. A manufacturer has introduced a new filtration device that eliminates the nuisance of weekly chlorination. The cost of the device, which has the capacity to serve both houses, is $1,000. Both owners feel equally strongly about having the filter. But because Wilson earns twice as much as Prentice, Wilson is willing to pay up to $800 to have the filter, whereas its value to Prentice, a retired schoolteacher, is only $400. Would either person be willing to purchase the device individually? Is it efficient for them to share its purchase?

Neither will purchase the filter individually because each has a reservation price that is below its selling price. But because the two together value the filter at $1,200, sharing its use would be socially efficient. If they were to do so, total economic surplus would be $200 higher than if they did not buy the filter.

Since sharing the filter is the efficient outcome, we might expect that Prentice and Wilson would quickly reach agreement to purchase it. Unfortunately, however, the joint purchase and sharing of facilities is often easier proposed than accomplished. One hurdle is that people must incur costs merely to get together to discuss joint purchases. With only two people involved, those costs might not be significant. But if hundreds or thousands of people were involved, communication costs could be prohibitive.

With large numbers of people, the free-rider problem also emerges (see Chapter 12). After all, everyone knows that the project will either succeed or fail independently of any one person's contribution to it. Everyone thus has an incentive to withhold contributions—or get a free ride—in the hope that others will give.

Finally, even when only a few people are involved, reaching agreement on a fair sharing of the total expense may be difficult. For example, Prentice and Wilson might be reluctant to disclose their true reservation prices to one another for the same reason that you might be reluctant to disclose your reservation price for a public good to an IRS agent.

These practical concerns may lead us to empower government to buy public goods on our behalf. But as Example 15.2 makes clear, this approach does not eliminate the need to reach political agreement on how public purchases are to be financed.

Will government buy the water filter if there is an "equal tax" rule?

EXAMPLE 15.2

Suppose Prentice and Wilson from Example 15.1 could ask the government to help broker the water filter purchase. And suppose that the government's tax policy must follow a "nondiscrimination" rule that prohibits charging any citizen more than his or her neighbor for a public good. Another rule is that public goods can be provided only if a majority of citizens approve of them. Will a government bound by these rules provide the filter that Prentice and Wilson want?

A tax that collects the same amount from every citizen is called a **head tax.** If the government must rely on a head tax, it must raise $500 from Prentice and $500 from Wilson. But since the device is worth only $400 to Prentice, he will vote against the project, thus denying it a majority. So a democratic government cannot provide the water filter if it must rely on a head tax.

head tax a tax that collects the same amount from every taxpayer

A head tax is an example of a **regressive tax,** one for which the proportion of a taxpayer's income that is paid in taxes declines as the taxpayer's income rises.

The point illustrated by Example 15.2 is not confined to the specific public good considered. It applies whenever taxpayers place significantly different valuations on public goods, as will almost always happen whenever people earn significantly different incomes. An equal tax rule under these circumstances will almost invariably rule out the provision of many worthwhile public goods.

As Example 15.3 suggests, one solution to this problem is to allow taxes to vary by income.

regressive tax a tax under which the proportion of income paid in taxes declines as income rises

EXAMPLE 15.3

proportional income tax one under which all taxpayers pay the same proportion of their incomes in taxes

Will the government buy the filter if there is a proportional tax on income?

Suppose that Prentice proposes that the government raise revenue by imposing a proportional tax on income to finance the provision of the water filter described in Example 15.1. Will Wilson, who earns twice as much as Prentice, support this proposal?

A **proportional income tax** is one under which all taxpayers pay the same percentage of their incomes in taxes. Under such a tax, Wilson would support Prentice's proposal, because if he didn't, each would fail to enjoy a public good whose benefit exceeds his share of its cost. Under the proportional tax on income, Prentice would contribute $333 toward the $1,000 purchase price of the filter and Wilson would contribute $667. The government would buy the filter, resulting in additional surpluses of $67 for Prentice and $133 for Wilson.

The following example makes the point that just as equal contributions are often a poor way to pay for public goods, they are also often a poor way to share expenses within the household.

ECONOMIC NATURALIST 15.1

Why don't most married couples contribute equally to joint purchases?

Suppose Hillary earns $2,000,000 per year while her husband Bill earns only $20,000. Given her income, Hillary as an individual would want to spend much more than Bill would on housing, travel, entertainment, education for their children, and the many other items they consume jointly. What will happen if the couple adopts a rule that each must contribute an equal amount toward the purchase of such items?

This rule would constrain the couple to live in a small house, take only inexpensive vacations, and skimp on entertainment, dining out, and their children's education. It is therefore easy to see why Hillary might find it attractive to pay considerably more than 50 percent for jointly consumed goods, because doing so would enable *both* of them to consume in the manner their combined income permits.

Public goods and jointly consumed private goods are different from individually consumed private goods in the following important way: *Different individuals are free to consume whatever quantity and quality of most private goods they choose to buy, but jointly consumed goods must be provided in the same quantity and quality for all persons.*

As in the case of private goods, people's willingness to pay for public goods is generally an increasing function of income. Wealthy individuals tend to assign greater value to public goods than low-income people, not because the wealthy have different tastes but because they have more money. A head tax would result in high-income persons getting smaller amounts of public goods than they want. By increasing the total economic surplus available for all to share, a tax system that assigns a larger share of the tax burden to people with higher incomes makes possible a better outcome for both rich and poor alike. Indeed, virtually all industrialized nations have tax systems that are at least mildly **progressive**, which means that the proportion of income that is taxed actually rises with a family's income.

progressive tax one in which the proportion of income paid in taxes rises as income rises

Progressive taxation and even proportional taxation have often been criticized as being unfair to the wealthy, who are forced to pay more than others for public goods that all consume in common. The irony in this charge, however, is that exclusive reliance on head taxes, or even proportional taxes, would curtail the provision of public goods and services that are of greatest value to high-income families. Studies have shown, for example, that the income elasticity of demand for public goods such as parks and recreation facilities, clean air and water, public safety, uncongested roads, and aesthetically pleasing public spaces is substantially greater than 1. Failure to rely on progressive taxation would result in gross underprovision of such public goods and services.

THE OPTIMAL QUANTITY OF A PUBLIC GOOD

In the examples considered thus far, the question was whether to provide a particular public good and, if so, how to pay for it. In practice, we often confront additional questions about what level and quality of a public good to provide.

Standard cost-benefit logic also applies to these questions. For example, New York City should add another rocket to its Fourth of July fireworks display if and only if the amount that citizens would collectively be willing to pay to see the rocket is at least as great as its cost.

THE DEMAND CURVE FOR A PUBLIC GOOD

To calculate the socially optimal quantity of a public good, we must first construct the demand curve for that public good. The process for doing so differs in an important way from the one we use to generate the market demand curve for a private good.

For a private good, all buyers face the same price and each chooses the quantity he or she wishes to purchase at that price. Recall that to construct the demand curve for a private good from the demand curves for individual consumers, we place the individual demand curves side by side and add them horizontally. That is, for each of a series of fixed prices, we add the resulting quantities demanded on the individual demand curves. In Figure 15.1, for example, we add the individual demand curves for a private good, D_1 and D_2 [parts (a) and (b)], horizontally to obtain the market demand curve for the good D [part (c)].

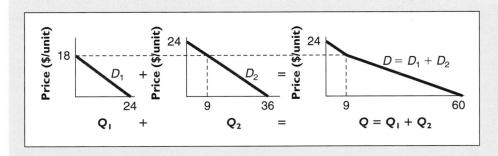

FIGURE 15.1

Generating the Market Demand Curve for a Private Good.

To construct the market demand curve for a private good [part (c)], we add the individual demand curves [parts (a) and (b)] horizontally.

For a public good, all buyers necessarily consume the same quantity, although each may differ in terms of willingness to pay for additional units of the good. Constructing the demand curve for a public good thus entails not horizontal summation of the individual demand curves but vertical summation. That is, for each of a series of quantity values, we must add the prices that individuals are willing to pay for an additional unit of the good. The curves D_1 and D_2 in Figure 15.2

(c) and (b) show individual demand curves for a public good by two different people. At each quantity, these curves tell how much the individual would be willing to pay for an additional unit of the public good. If we add D_1 and D_2 vertically, we obtain the total demand curve D for the public good [part (a)].

FIGURE 15.2

Generating the Demand Curve for a Public Good.

To construct the demand curve for a public good [part (a)], we add the individual demand curves [parts (c) and (b)] vertically.

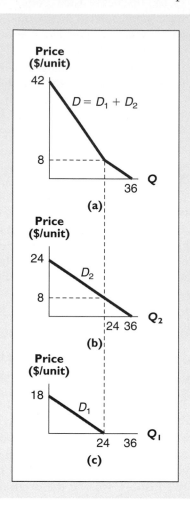

(a)

(b)

(c)

EXERCISE 15.2

Bill and Tom are the only demanders of a public good. If Bill's demand curve is $P_B = 6 - 0.5Q$ and Tom's is $P_T = 12 - Q$, construct the demand curve for this public good.

In Example 15.4, we see how the demand curve for a public good might be used in conjunction with information about costs to determine the optimal level of parkland in a city.

EXAMPLE 15.4

What is the optimal quantity of urban parkland?

The city government of a new planned community must decide how much parkland to provide. The marginal cost curve and the public demand curve for urban parkland are as shown in Figure 15.3. Why is the marginal cost curve upward-sloping and the demand curve downward-sloping? Given these curves, what is the optimal quantity of parkland?

 The marginal cost schedule for urban parkland is upward-sloping because of the low-hanging-fruit principle: The city acquires the cheapest parcels of land first, and only then turns to more expensive parcels. Likewise, the marginal will-

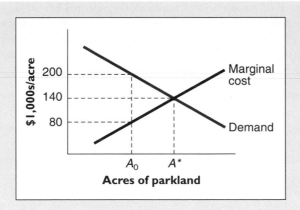

FIGURE 15.3
The Optimal Quantity of Parkland.
The optimal number of acres of urban parkland is A^*, the quantity at which the public's willingness to pay for additional parkland is equal to the marginal cost of parkland.

ingness-to-pay curve is downward-sloping because of the law of diminishing marginal utility. Just as people are generally willing to pay less for their fifth hot dog than for their first, they are also willing to pay less for the 101st acre of parkland than for the 100th acre. Given these curves, A^* is the optimal quantity of parkland. For any quantity less than A^*, the benefit of additional parkland exceeds its cost, which means that total economic surplus can be made larger by expanding the amount of parkland. For example, at A_0, the community would be willing to pay $200,000 for an additional acre of urban parkland, but its cost is only $80,000. Similarly, for any quantity of parkland in excess of A^*, the community would gain more than it would lose by selling off some parkland.

PRIVATE PROVISION OF PUBLIC GOODS

One advantage of using the government to provide public goods is that once a tax collection agency has been established to finance a single public good, it can be expanded at relatively low cost to generate revenue for additional public goods. Another advantage is that because government has the power to tax, it can summarily assign responsibility for the cost of a public good without endless haggling over who bears what share of the burden. And in the case of goods for which nonpayers cannot be excluded, the government may be the only feasible provider.

But exclusive reliance on government also entails disadvantages. Most fundamentally, the government's one-size-fits-all approach invariably requires many people to pay for public goods they don't want, while others end up having to do without public goods they want desperately. For example, many people vehemently oppose the provision of *any* sex education in the public schools, while others fervently believe that far more such instruction should be provided than is currently offered in most current public school curriculums. In addition, mandatory taxation strikes many people as coercive, even if they approve of the particular public goods being provided.

It is no surprise, then, that governments are not the exclusive providers of public goods in any society. Indeed, many public goods are routinely provided through private channels. The challenge, in each case, is to devise a scheme for raising the required revenues. Here are some methods that seem to work.

Funding by donation In 1998 Americans gave almost $175 billion to private charities, many of which provide public goods to their communities. People also volunteer their time on behalf of organizations that provide public goods. When you paint your house, mow your lawn, or plant a flower garden, you are enhancing the quality of life in your neighborhood, and in that sense you are voluntarily providing a public good to your neighbors.

Development of new means to exclude nonpayers New electronic technology makes it possible to exclude nonpayers from many goods that in the past could not be thus restricted. For instance, broadcast television stations now have the ability to scramble their signals, making them available only to those consumers who purchase descrambling devices.

Private contracting More than 8 million Americans now live in gated private communities—private homeowners' associations that wall off contiguous properties and provide various services to residents. Many of these associations provide security services, schools, and fire protection and in other ways function much like ordinary local governments. Recognizing that individual incentives may not be strong enough to assure socially optimal levels of maintenance and landscaping, these associations often bill homeowners for those services directly. Many of the rules imposed by these associations are even more restrictive than those imposed by local governments, a distinction that is defended on the grounds that people are always free to choose some other neighborhood if they don't like the rules of any particular homeowners' association. Many people would be reluctant to tolerate a municipal ordinance that prevents people from painting their houses purple, yet such restrictions are common in the bylaws of homeowners' associations.

Sale of by-products Many public goods are financed by the sale of rights or services that are generated as by-products of the public goods. For instance, as noted earlier, radio and television programming is a public good that is paid for in many cases by the sale of advertising messages. Internet services are also underwritten in part by commercial messages that appear in the headers or margins of web pages.

Given the quintessentially voluntary nature of privately provided public goods, it might seem that reliance on private provision might be preferred whenever it proved feasible. But as the following example makes clear, private provision often entails problems of its own.

ECONOMIC NATURALIST 15.2

Why do television networks favor Jerry Springer over *Masterpiece Theater?*

In a given time slot, a television network faces the alternative of broadcasting either the *Jerry Springer Show* or *Masterpiece Theater.* If it chooses *Springer,* it will win 20 percent of the viewing audience, but only 18 percent if it chooses *Masterpiece Theater.* Suppose those who would choose *Springer* would collectively be willing to pay $10 million for the right to see that program, while those who choose *Masterpiece Theater* would be willing to pay $30 million. And suppose, finally, that the time slot is to be financed by a detergent company. Which program will the network choose? Which program would be socially optimal?

A detergent maker cares primarily about the number of people who will see its advertisements and will thus choose the program that will attract the largest audience—here, the *Springer Show.* The fact that those who prefer *Masterpiece Theater* would be willing to pay a lot more to see it is of little concern to the sponsor. But to identify the optimal result from society's point of view, we must take this difference into account. Because the people who prefer *Masterpiece Theater* could pay the *Springer* viewers more than enough to compensate them for relinquishing the time slot, *Masterpiece Theater* is the efficient outcome. But unless its supporters happen to buy more soap in total than the *Springer* viewers, the latter will prevail. In short, reliance on advertising and other indirect mechanisms for financing public goods provides no assurance that the goods chosen will maximize economic surplus.

Of course, the fact that the programs that best suit advertisers' needs may not be socially optimal does not mean that government decisions would necessarily be better. One can imagine, for example, a cultural affairs ministry that would choose television programming that would be "good for us" but that few of us would want to watch.

One way to avoid the inefficiency that arises when advertisers choose programming is to employ pay-per-view methods of paying for television programming. These methods allow viewers to register not just which programs they prefer but also the strength of their preferences, as measured by how much they are willing to pay.

But although pay-per-view TV is more likely to select the programs the public most values, it is also less efficient than broadcast TV in one important respect. As noted earlier, charging each household a fee for viewing discourages some households from tuning in. And since the marginal social cost of serving an additional household is exactly zero, limiting the audience in this way is inefficient. Which of the two inefficiencies is more important—free TV's inefficiency in choosing among programs or pay TV's inefficiency in excluding potential beneficiaries—is an empirical question.

In any event, the mix between private and public provision of public goods and services differs substantially from society to society and from arena to arena within any given society. These differences depend on the nature of available technologies for delivering and paying for public goods, and also on people's preferences.

Why do detergent companies care more about audience size than about how much people would be willing to pay to see the programs they sponsor?

By how much is economic surplus reduced by a pay-per-view charge?

EXAMPLE 15.5

If *Mystery Theater* is shown on pay-per-view television at 10 P.M. on Thursdays, the demand curve for each episode is given by $P = 20 - Q$, where P is the price per household in dollars and Q is the number of households who choose to watch the program (in millions). If the regulated pay-per-view charge is $10 per household, by how much would economic surplus rise if the same episode were shown instead on "free" broadcast public TV?

With a fee of $10 per episode, 10 million households will watch (see Figure 15.4). But if the same episode were shown instead on broadcast public TV, 20 million households would watch. The additional economic surplus reaped by the extra 10 million households is the area of the blue triangle, which is $50 million. The marginal cost of permitting these additional households to watch the episode is zero, so the total gain in surplus is $50 million.

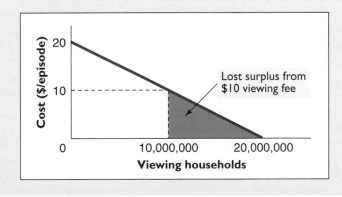

FIGURE 15.4
The Loss in Surplus from a Pay-per-View Fee.
Twice as many households would watch the program if its price were zero instead of $10. The additional economic surplus is the area of the blue triangle, or $50 million.

In general, charging a positive price for a good whose marginal cost is zero will result in a loss in surplus. As we saw in Chapter 7, the size of the loss that results when price is set above marginal cost depends on the price elasticity of demand. When demand is more elastic, the loss in surplus is greater. Exercise 15.3 provides an opportunity to see that principle at work.

EXERCISE 15.3

How would your answer to Example 15.5 have been different if the demand curve had been given instead by $P = 15 - 2Q$?

RECAP **THE OPTIMAL QUANTITY OF A PUBLIC GOOD**

Because the quantity of a public good must be the same for every consumer, the total demand curve for a public good is constructed by adding individual demand curves vertically. Optimal production of a public good occurs at the quantity for which the demand curve intersects the marginal cost curve for the public good.

Government need not always be the best way to provide public goods. Such goods can be provided by private organizations that rely on charitable contributions or the sale of by-products. Private for-profit companies can also become providers when new technologies such as pay-per-view television convert public goods into collective goods.

ADDITIONAL FUNCTIONS OF GOVERNMENT

The provision of public goods is not the only rationale for the existence of government. Government also creates and enforces the rules without which the efficient production of private goods would not be possible.

EXTERNALITIES AND PROPERTY RIGHTS

As we saw in Chapter 11, for example, externalities often stand in the way of socially optimal resource allocation in private activities. We saw, too, that optimal allocations are unlikely to result whenever property rights are poorly defined (for example, the tragedy of the commons). These observations suggest the existence of two additional important roles for government: namely, the regulation of activities that generate externalities and the definition and enforcement of property rights.

These rationales for government action explain why most governments regulate activities that generate pollution, subsidize education (on the grounds that an educated public creates positive externalities), control access to fishing waters and public timber lands, and enforce zoning laws. Most laws, in fact, represent attempts to define property rights or to control externalities. The law requiring motorists to drive on the right, for example, is an attempt to prevent the activities of one motorist from causing harm to others.

Proponents of minimalist government often object that the government unjustly curtails our freedom when it uses zoning laws to limit the size of the houses we build or imposes fines on motorists who violate highway speed limits. Yet the justification for such regulations is precisely the same as for the laws that prohibit your fist from occupying the same physical space as your neighbor's nose. You are free to swing your fists as you please, provided you cause no harm to others. But if your fist strikes your neighbor's nose, you become a violator of the law and subject to punishment. If the proponents of minimalist government approve of restricting behavior in this way, why do they disapprove of other attempts to discourage behaviors that cause harm to others?

Perhaps their fear is that because externalities are so pervasive, governments that were empowered to regulate them might quickly get out of control. This is by no means an idle fear, and we emphasize that the mere fact that an externality exists does not necessarily mean that the best outcome is for the government to regulate it. As we will see in the next section, regulation entails costs of its own. The ultimate question is therefore a practical one: Will government regulation of the externality in question do more good than harm? Slogans about being free to live without government interference provide little help in answering such questions.

LOCAL, STATE, OR FEDERAL?

Framers of the American Constitution were deeply skeptical of centralized government power. In drafting the Constitution, therefore, they explicitly tried to limit the powers of the federal government as much as possible, delegating most important powers to the states, who in turn delegated many of their powers to governments at the local level.

That the dangers of remote, centralized government ranked high among founding fathers' concerns is no surprise. After all, fresh in their memories was the autocratic treatment received by the American colonies at the hands of the monarchy in England. The founding fathers recognized that government will be more responsive the shorter the distance between officeholders and the voters who elect them.

Another obvious advantage of giving as much authority to local governments as possible is that different communities often have markedly different preferences about how much to spend on public goods, and even on what kinds of public goods to provide. When such decisions are made at the local level, people can shop for a community whose voters' preferences largely coincide with their own. Those who like high levels of public goods and services can band together and authorize high taxes to pay for them. Others who place less value on public services can choose communities in which both services and taxes are lower.

Why, given the many attractions of decisions made at the local level, did the founding fathers create federal and state governments at all? One reason is economies of scale in defense. For a country to survive politically, it must be able to deter aggression by hostile governments. A country consisting only of, say, Concord, New Hampshire, would be ill-equipped to do that. Large, well-equipped armies and navies cost a lot of money, and countries without sufficient population simply cannot afford them.

Defense, however, is not the only reason to empower governments beyond the local or state level. As discussed in Chapter 14, for example, no individual state has the authority required to significantly reduce the extent of legalized gambling in the current environment. Similarly, the problem of pollution is difficult to solve when the various sources of pollution are not subject to regulatory control by a single government. Much of the acid rain experienced in Canada, for example, is the result of sulfur dioxide emissions from industrial sources in the upper midwest of the United States. These emissions are beyond the reach of Canadian environmental regulations. In many instances, as with the discharge of greenhouse gases, not even a coalition of all the governments in North, Central, and South America would have power to take effective action. Carbon dioxide emitted anywhere on the planet disperses to uniform concentrations around the globe in a matter of months.

The choice between different levels of government, then, often confronts us with difficult trade-offs. Ceding the power of taxation to a federal government often entails painful compromises for voters in individual states. But the loss of political autonomy is an even less attractive option. Similarly, nations are understandably reluctant to cede any of their sovereign powers to a higher authority, but failure to take such steps may entail unacceptable environmental costs in the long run.

RECAP   **ADDITIONAL FUNCTIONS OF GOVERNMENT**

Government creates economic surplus not only by providing public goods but also by regulating activities that generate externalities and by defining and enforcing property rights. These rationales explain why most governments regulate pollution, subsidize education, control access to fishing waters and public timber lands, and enforce zoning laws.

Although the framers of the Constitution disliked centralized government power, they recognized that some government functions are not best performed at the local or even state level. Economies of scale argue for provision of defense at the national level. Externalities that transcend local boundaries provide an additional rationale for national or even international government.

SOURCES OF INEFFICIENCY IN THE POLITICAL PROCESS

In most countries, expenditures on public goods, tax policy, and laws regulating behavior are determined in large part by the votes of democratically elected representatives. This process is far from perfect. (Winston Churchill called democracy "the worst form of government, except for any other.") Inefficiencies often arise in the public sphere not because of incompetent or ignorant legislators but because of structural incentive problems.

PORK BARREL LEGISLATION

The following example, drawn not from the public sector but from everyday private life, illustrates one of the important incentive gaps.

Why does check-splitting make the total restaurant bill higher?

ECONOMIC NATURALIST 15.3

Sven Torvaldsen and nine friends are having dinner at la Maison de la Casa House, a four-star restaurant in Minneapolis. To simplify the task of paying for their meal, they have agreed in advance to split the cost of their meal equally, with each paying one-tenth of the total check. Having cleared the entree dishes, the waiter arrives with the dessert menu, on which Sven's two favorite items are pumpkin bread pudding ($10) and chocolate mousse ($6). Sven's reservation prices for these items are $4 and $3, respectively. Will he order dessert, and, if so, which one? Would he order dessert if he were dining by himself?

When Sven and his friends split the total check equally, Sven's payment goes up by one-tenth of the menu price of any dessert he orders. Thus the prices—to him—of the bread pudding and chocolate mousse are $1 and 60 cents, respectively. Because he gets $4 − $1 = $3 of consumer surplus from the bread pudding and only $3 − $0.60 = $2.40 from the chocolate mousse, he will order the bread pudding. If Sven were dining alone, however, his bill would increase dollar for dollar with the menu price of any dessert he ordered. And since the menu prices exceed his corresponding reservation prices, he would not order dessert at all.

The irony, of course, is that if Sven's nine friends have the same preferences regarding dessert, each will order bread pudding and each person's share of the total bill will rise not by $1 but by the full $10. Compared to the alternative of no one having dessert, each diner suffers a $6 loss in consumer surplus. Still, it made sense for each to order bread pudding, since failure to do so would have reduced each diner's bill by only $1.

EXERCISE 15.4

In the preceding example, would Sven have ordered dessert if there had been only five people splitting the check instead of 10?

Alert readers will have noticed the similarity between the problem posed in the preceding example and the one posed in Economic Naturalist 11.6, in which identical twins had a single milkshake to share with two straws. The same incentive problem leads to the inefficient outcome in both cases.

The following example illustrates how the very same incentive problem rears its head in the legislative process.

Why do legislators often support one another's pork barrel spending programs?

Pork barrel programs are government programs that benefit local areas but are of questionable value from a national perspective. Why do voters seem to support legislators who initiate such projects even when the total effect of all such projects on local tax bills far exceeds the local benefits?

Consider a voter in a congressional district that contains one one-hundredth of the country's taxpayers. Suppose that voter's representative is able to deliver a public project that generates benefits of $100 million for the district but that costs the federal government $150 million. Since the district's share of the tax bill for the project will be only $150 million/100 = $1.5 million, residents of the district are $98.5 million better off with the project than without it. And that explains why so many voters favor legislators with a successful record of "bringing home the bacon."

But why would legislator A support such a project in legislator B's home district? After all, B's project will cause A's constituents' taxes to rise—albeit by a small amount—yet they will get no direct benefit from the project. The answer is that if A does not support B's project, then B will not support A's. The practice whereby legislators support one another's pet projects is known as **logrolling**. This practice creates a bias toward excessive spending, much like the bias created when a dinner check is split equally.

ECONOMIC NATURALIST 15.4

pork barrel spending a public expenditure that is larger than the total benefit it creates but that is favored by a legislator because his or her constituents benefit from the expenditure by more than their share of the resulting extra taxes

logrolling the practice whereby legislators support one another's legislative proposals

RENT-SEEKING

A related source of inefficiency in the public sphere occurs because the gains from government projects are often concentrated in the hands of a few beneficiaries, while the costs are spread among many. This means that beneficiaries often have a powerful incentive to organize and lobby in favor of public projects. Individual taxpayers, by contrast, have little at stake in any public project and therefore have little incentive to incur the cost of mobilizing themselves in opposition.

Suppose, for example, that a price support bill for sugar will raise the price of sugar by 10 cents per pound and that the average American family currently consumes 100 pounds of sugar per year. How will this legislation affect the average family's consumption of sugar? Recall from Chapter 5 that a good, such as salt or sugar, whose share in most family budgets is small is likely to have a low price elasticity of demand. Hence each family's sugar consumption will decline only slightly as a result of the 10 cent price hike. The resulting increase in each family's annual expenditures on sugar—slightly less than $10—is scarcely a noticeable burden, and surely not enough to induce many people to complain to their representatives. The same legislation, however, will raise sugar industry revenues by nearly $1 billion annually. With a sum that large at stake, it is certain that the industry will lobby vigorously in its favor.

Why don't citizens vote those legislators who support such bills out of office? One reason is the problem of rational ignorance, discussed in Chapter 12. Most voters have no idea that a price support bill for sugar and other special-interest bills even exist, much less how individual legislators vote on them. If all voters became well-informed about such bills, the resulting increase in the quality of legislation might well be sufficient to compensate each voter for the cost of becoming informed. But because of the free-rider problem, each voter knows that the outcome of votes in Congress will not be much affected by whether he becomes well-informed.

Still other sources of inefficiency arise even in the case of projects whose benefits exceed their costs. Several years ago, for example, the federal government announced its decision to build a $25 billion high-energy physics research facility (the "superconducting supercollider"), which ignited an intense competition among more than 20 states vying to be chosen as the site for this facility. Hundreds of millions of dollars was spent on proposal preparation, consultants' fees, and various other lobbying activities. Such investments are known as **rent-seeking**, and they tend to be inefficient for the same reason that investments by contestants in other positional arms races are inefficient (see Chapter 11).

Efforts devoted to rent-seeking are socially unproductive because of the simple incentive problem illustrated in Example 15.6.

rent-seeking the socially unproductive efforts of people or firms to win a prize

EXAMPLE 15.6

Why would anyone pay $50 for a $20 bill?

Suppose a $20 bill is to be auctioned off to the highest bidder. The rules of this particular auction require an initial bid of at least 50 cents, and succeeding bids must exceed the previous high bid by at least 50 cents. When the bidding ceases, both the highest bidder and the second-highest bidder must give the amounts they bid to the auctioneer. The highest bidder then receives the $20, and the second-highest bidder gets nothing. For example, if the highest bid is $11 and the second-highest bid is $10.50, the winner earns a net payment of $20 − $11 = $9, and the runner-up loses $10.50. How high will the winning bid be, on average?

Auctions like this one have been extensively studied in the laboratory. And although subjects in these experiments have ranged from business executives to college undergraduates, the pattern of bidding is almost always the same. Following the opening bid, offers proceed quickly to $10, or half the amount being auctioned. A pause then occurs as the subjects appear to digest the fact that with the next bid the sum of the two highest bids will exceed $20, thus taking the auctioneer off the hook. At this point, the second-highest bidder, whose bid stands at $9.50, invariably offers $10.50, apparently preferring a shot at winning $9.50 to a sure loss of $9.50.

In most cases, all but the top two bidders drop out at this point, and the top two quickly escalate their bids. As the bidding approaches $20, a second pause occurs, this time as the bidders appear to recognize that even the highest bidder is likely to come out behind. The second-highest bidder, at $19.50, is understandably reluctant to offer $20.50. But consider the alternative. If he drops out, he will lose $19.50 for sure. But if he offers $20.50 and wins, he will lose only 50 cents. So as long as he thinks there is even a small chance that the other bidder will drop out, it makes sense to continue. Once the $20 threshold has been crossed, the pace of the bidding quickens again, and from then on it is a war of nerves between the two remaining bidders. It is common for the bidding to reach $50 before someone finally yields in frustration.

One might be tempted to think that any intelligent, well-informed person would know better than to become involved in an auction whose incentives so strongly favor costly escalation. But many of the subjects in these auctions have been experienced business professionals; many others have had formal training in the theory of games and strategic interaction. For example, the psychologist Max Bazerman reports that during the past 10 years he has earned more than $17,000 by auctioning $20 bills to his MBA students at Northwestern University's Kellogg Graduate School of Management, which is consistently among the top-rated MBA programs in the world. In the course of almost 200 of his auctions, the top two bids never totaled less than $39, and in one instance they totaled $407.

As Example 15.7 shows, the incentives that confront participants in the $20 bill auction are strikingly similar to those that confront companies that are vying for lucrative government contracts.

How much will cellular phone companies bid for an exclusive license?   **EXAMPLE 15.7**

The State of Wyoming has announced its intention to grant an exclusive license to provide cellular phone services within its borders. Two firms have met the deadline for applying for this license. The franchise lasts for exactly 1 year, during which time the franchisee can expect to make an economic profit of $20 million. The state legislature will choose the applicant that spends the most money lobbying legislators. If the applicants cannot collude, how much will each spend on lobbying?

If both spend the same, each will have a 50-50 chance at the $20 million prize, which means an expected profit of $10 million minus the amount spent lobbying. If the lobbyists could collude, each would agree to spend the same small, token amount on lobbying. But in the absence of a binding agreement, each will be strongly tempted to try to outspend the other. Once each firm's spending reaches $10 million, each will have an expected profit of zero (a 50-50 chance to earn $20 million, minus the $10 million spent on lobbying).

Further bidding would guarantee an expected loss. And yet, if one firm spent $10,000,001 while the other stayed at $10 million, the first firm would get the franchise for sure and earn an economic profit of $9,999,999. The other firm would have an economic loss of $10 million. Rather than face a sure loss of $10 million, it may be tempted to bid $10,000,002. But then, of course, its rival would face a similar incentive to respond to that bid. No matter where the escalation stops, it is sure to dissipate much of the gains that could have been had from the project. And perhaps, as in the $20 bill auction, the total amount dissipated will be even more than the value of the franchise itself.

From the individual perspective, it is easy to see why firms might lobby in this fashion for a chance to win government benefits. From society's perspective, however, this activity is almost purely wasteful. Lobbyists are typically intelligent, well-educated, and socially skilled. The opportunity cost of their time is high. If they were not lobbying government officials on behalf of their clients, they could be producing other goods or services of value. Governments can discourage such waste by selecting contractors not according to the amount they spend lobbying but on the basis of the price they promise to charge for their services. Society will be more successful the more its institutions encourage citizens to pursue activities that create wealth rather than activities that merely transfer existing wealth from one person or company to another.

STARVE THE GOVERNMENT?

The Nobel laureate Milton Friedman has said that no bureaucrat spends taxpayers' money as carefully as those taxpayers themselves would have. And indeed, there can be little doubt that many government expenditures are wasteful. Beyond the fact that logrolling often results in pork barrel programs that would not satisfy the cost-benefit test, we must worry that government employees may not always face strong incentives to get the most for what they spend. The Pentagon, for example, once purchased a coffeemaker for $7,600 and on another occasion paid $600 for a toilet seat. Such expenditures may have been aberrations, but there seems little doubt that private contractors often deliver comparable services at substantially lower costs than their public counterparts.

In their understandable outrage over government waste, many critics have urged major cutbacks in the volume of public goods and services. These critics reason that if we let the government spend more money, there will be more waste. This is true, of course, but only in the trivial sense that there would be more of *everything* the government does—good and bad—if public spending were higher.

One of our most extensive experiences with the consequences of major reductions in government spending comes from the Proposition 13 movement in California. This movement began with the passage of State Proposition 13 in 1978, which mandated large reductions in property taxes. As Californians have belatedly recognized, this remedy for government waste is like trying to starve a tapeworm by not eating. Fasting does harm the tapeworm, sure enough, but it harms the host even more. Residents of the Golden State, who once proudly sent their children to the nation's best schools, are now sending them to some of its worst.

The physician treats an infected patient by prescribing drugs that are toxic to the parasite but not to the host. A similar strategy should guide our attack on government waste. For example, we might consider the adoption of campaign-finance reform laws that would prevent legislators from accepting campaign contributions from the tobacco industry and other special interests whose government subsidies they support.

The question, then, isn't whether bureaucrats know best how to spend our money. Rather, it's "How much of our money do *we* want to spend on public services?" Although we must remain vigilant against government waste, we must also remember that many public services deliver good value for our money.

RECAP **SOURCES OF INEFFICIENCY IN THE POLITICAL PROCESS**

Government does much to help the economy function more efficiently, but it can also be a source of waste. For example, legislators may support pork barrel projects, which do not satisfy the cost-benefit criterion but which benefit constituents by more than their share of the extra taxes required to pay for the projects.

Rent-seeking, a second important source of inefficiency, occurs when individuals or firms use real resources in an effort to win favors from the government. Voters often fail to discipline legislators who abet rent-seeking, because the free-rider problem gives rise to rational ignorance on the part of many voters.

Concern about government waste has led many to conclude that the best government is necessarily the smallest one. The solution favored by these critics is to starve government by reducing the amount of money it can collect in taxes. Yet starving the government reduces one kind of waste only to increase another by curtailing public services whose benefit exceeds their cost.

WHAT SHOULD WE TAX?

Although the primary purpose of the tax system is to generate the revenue needed to fund public goods and other government expenditures, taxes also have many other consequences, some intended, others not. For example, taxes alter the relative costs and benefits of engaging in different activities. They also affect the distribution of real purchasing power in the economy. The best tax system is one that raises the needed revenues while at the same time having the most beneficial, or least deleterious, side effects.

On the first criterion, the federal tax system has not performed particularly well. Although the federal budget began to show a modest surplus in the late 1990s, until then it had been in continuous deficit since 1969, during which time the federal government had to borrow trillions of dollars to pay its bills.

The fact that governments and private corporations borrow money in the same capital market explains the phenomenon economists call **crowding out.** When government increases its demand in the market for borrowed funds, inter-

crowding out occurs when private firms cancel planned investment projects because of higher interest rates caused by government borrowing est rates rise, causing firms to cancel some of their planned investment projects. When the government fails to raise enough revenue from taxes to cover the amount it spends on public goods and services, it thus diverts funds from investments that would have helped the economy to grow.

What about the effect of taxes on incentives? As discussed in Chapter 7, taxes will hold production and consumption below socially optimal levels in markets in which the private costs and benefits coincide exactly with all relevant social costs and benefits. Suppose, for example, that the long-run private marginal cost of producing cars is $10,000/unit and that the demand curve for cars is as shown in Figure 15.5. The equilibrium quantity and price will be 6 million/year and $10,000, respectively. If no externalities accompany the production or consumption of cars, these will be the socially optimal levels for quantity and price. But if we now add a tax of $2,000/car, the new equilibrium price and quantity will be $12,000 and 4 million, respectively. The loss in economic surplus will be equal to the area of the blue triangle ($1 billion/year), which is the cumulative sum of the differences between what excluded buyers would have been willing to pay for extra cars and the marginal cost of producing those cars.

Economists who write for the popular press have long focused on the loss in surplus caused by taxes like the one shown in Figure 15.5. These economists argue that the economy would perform better if taxes were lower and total government expenditures were smaller.

But arguments for that claim are far from compelling. As discussed in Chapter 7, for example, even if a tax in a market like the one shown in Figure 15.5 did produce a loss in surplus for participants in that market, it might nonetheless be justified if it led to an even larger gain in surplus from the public expenditures it financed. We also saw in Chapter 7 that the deadweight loss from taxing a good (or activity) will be smaller the smaller is the elasticity of demand or supply for the good. This principle suggests that deadweight losses could be minimized by concentrating taxes on goods with highly inelastic supply or demand curves.

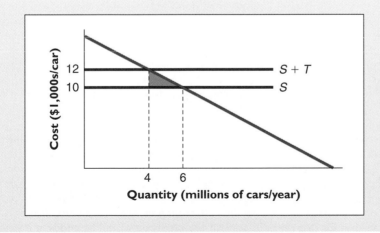

FIGURE 15.5
The Loss in Surplus from a Tax on Cars.
If the supply and demand curves for cars embody all relevant cost benefits of producing and consuming cars, then placing a tax on cars will lead to underproduction of them and a corresponding reduction in economic surplus.

Another difficulty with the argument that taxes harm the economy is more fundamental—namely, that taxes need not cause any loss in surplus at all, even in the markets in which they are directly applied. Suppose, for example, that in the market for cars considered earlier, private marginal cost is again $10,000 but that the production and use of cars now generates air pollution and congestion, negative externalities that sum to $2,000/car each year. The socially optimal quantity of cars would then be not 6 million/year but only 4 million (see Figure 15.5). Without a tax on cars, the market would reach equilibrium at a price of $10,000 and a quantity of 6 million/year. But with a tax of $2,000/car, the equilibrium quantity would shrink to 4 million/year, precisely the socially optimal number.

Here, the direct effect of the tax is not only not to reduce total economic surplus but actually to augment it by $1 billion/day. To that amount we would then add the additional daily surplus made possible by the additional $8 billion worth of public goods financed by the tax.

Could we raise enough tax revenue to run the government if we limited ourselves to taxing only those activities that generate negative externalities? No one knows for sure, but it might be possible, for the list of such activities is a long one.

For instance, when someone enters a congested freeway, he creates additional delays for the motorists already there. Existing technology would enable us to levy road-use taxes that reflect these congestion externalities. Each time fossil fuels are burned, they emit greenhouse gases into the atmosphere, which will accelerate the trend toward global warming. A tax on carbon would increase economic surplus by causing decision makers to take this external cost into account. Taxes on other forms of air and water pollution would have similarly benign effects on resource allocation. Recent experience with refundable taxes on food and beverage containers demonstrates that taxes like these can raise needed revenue while at the same time contributing to a cleaner environment.

■ SUMMARY ■

- Our aim in this chapter was to apply principles of microeconomics to the study of the government's role in modern society. One of government's principal tasks is to provide public goods, such as national defense and the criminal justice system. Such goods are, in varying degrees, nonrival and nonexcludable. The first property describes goods for which one person's consumption does not diminish the amount available for others, while the second refers to the difficulty of preventing nonpayers from consuming certain goods.

- Goods that are both highly nonexcludable and nonrival are often called pure public goods. A collective good—such as pay-per-view cable television—is nonrival but excludable. Commons goods are goods that are rival but nonexcludable.

- Because not everyone benefits equally from the provision of any given public good, charging all taxpayers equal amounts for the provision of public goods will generally not be either feasible or desirable. As in the case of private goods, people's willingness to pay for public goods generally increases with income, and most governments therefore levy higher taxes on the rich than on the poor. Tax systems with this property have been criticized on the grounds that they are unfair to the wealthy, but this criticism ignores the fact that alternative tax schemes generally lead to worse outcomes for both rich and poor alike.

- The criterion for providing the optimal quantity or quality of a public good is to keep increasing quantity or quality as long as the marginal benefit of doing so exceeds the marginal cost. One advantage of using the government to provide public goods is that once a tax collection agency has been established to finance a single public good, it can be expanded at relatively low cost to generate revenue to fi-

nance additional public goods. A second advantage is that because government has the power to tax, it can easily assign responsibility for the cost of a public good. And in the case of goods for which nonpayers simply cannot be excluded, the government may be the only feasible provider.

- One disadvantage to exclusive reliance on government for public goods provision is the element of coercion inherent in the tax system, which makes some people pay for public goods they don't want, while others do without public goods they do want. Many public goods are provided through private channels, with the necessary funding provided by donations, sale of by-products, by development of new means to exclude nonpayers, and in many cases by private contract. A loss in surplus results, however, whenever monetary charges are levied for the consumption of a nonrival good.

- In addition to providing public goods, government serves two other important roles: the regulation of activities that generate externalities and the definition and enforcement of property rights. Despite a general view that government is more responsive the shorter the distance between citizens and their elected representatives, factors such as economies of scale in the provision of public goods and externalities with broad reach often dictate the assignment of important functions to state or national governments.

- Although history has shown that democracy is the best form of government, it is far from perfect. For example, practices such as logrolling and rent-seeking, common in most democracies, often result in the adoption of laws and public projects whose costs exceed their benefits.

- To finance public goods and services, governments at all levels must tax. But a tax on any activity not only generates revenue, it also creates an incentive to reduce the activity. If the activity would have been pursued at the optimal level in the absence of a tax, taxing it will result in too little of the activity. This observation has led many critics to denounce all taxes as harmful to the economy. Yet the negative effects of taxes on incentives must be weighed against the benefits of the public goods and services financed by tax revenue. Furthermore, taxes on inelastically supplied or demanded activities may generate only small deadweight losses, while taxes on activities that create negative externalities may actually increase economic efficiency.

▪ KEY TERMS ▪

collective good (379)
crowding out (394)
head tax (381)
logrolling (391)
nonexcludable good (378)

nonrival good (378)
pork barrel spending (391)
progressive tax (382)
proportional income tax (382)
public good (378)

pure commons good (379)
pure private good (379)
pure public good (378)
regressive tax (381)
rent-seeking (392)

▪ REVIEW QUESTIONS ▪

1. a. Which of the following goods are nonrival?
   Apples
   Stephen King novels
   Street lighting on campus
   NPR radio broadcasts
   b. Which of these goods are nonexcludable?

2. Give examples of goods that are, for the most part:
   a. Rival but nonexcludable
   b. Nonrival but excludable
   c. Both nonrival and nonexcludable

3. Why might even a wealthy person prefer a proportional income tax to a head tax?

4. True or false: A tax on an activity that generates negative externalities will improve resource allocation in the private sector and also generate revenue that could be used to pay for useful public goods. Explain.

5. Consider a good that would be provided optimally by private market forces. Why is the direct loss in surplus that would result from a tax on this good an overstatement of the loss in surplus caused by the tax?

▪ PROBLEMS ▪

1. Jack and Jill are the only two residents in a neighborhood, and they would like to hire a security guard. The value of a security guard is $50/month to Jack and $150/month to Jill. Irrespective of who pays the guard, the guard will protect the entire neighborhood.
   a. What is the most a guard can charge per month and still be assured of being hired by at least one of them?
   b. Suppose the competitive wage for a security guard is $120/month. The local government proposes a plan whereby Jack and Jill each pay 50 percent of this monthly fee, and asks them to vote on this plan. Will the plan be voted in? Would economic surplus be higher if the neighborhood had a guard?

2. Refer to Problem 1. Suppose Jack earns $1,000/month and Jill earns $11,000/month.
   a. Suggest a proportional tax on income that would be accepted by majority vote and would pay for the security guard.
   b. Suppose instead that Jack proposes a tax scheme under which Jack and Jill would each receive the same net benefit from hiring the guard. How much would Jack and Jill pay now? Would Jill agree to this scheme?
   c. What is the practical problem that prevents ideas like the one in part b from working in real-life situations?

3. The following table shows all the marginal benefits for each voter in a small town whose town council is considering a new swimming pool with capacity for at least three citizens. The cost of the pool would be $18 per week and would not depend on the number of people who actually used it. The interest rate is 1 percent per week.

Voter	Marginal benefit ($/week)
A	12
B	5
C	2

a. If the pool must be financed by a weekly head tax levied on all voters, will the pool be approved by majority vote? Is this outcome socially efficient? Explain.

b. The town council instead decides to auction a franchise off to a private monopoly to build and maintain the pool. If it cannot find such a firm willing to operate the pool, then the pool project will be scrapped. If all such monopolies are constrained by law to charge a single price to users, will the franchise be sold, and if so, how much will it sell for? Is this outcome socially efficient? Explain.

4. Refer to Problem 3. Suppose now that all such monopolies can perfectly price-discriminate.

a. Will the franchise be sold, and if so, how much will it sell for? Is this outcome socially efficient? Explain.

b. The town council decides that, rather than auction off the franchise, it will give it away to the firm that spends the most money lobbying council members. If there are four identical firms in the bidding and they cannot collude, what will happen?

5. Two consumers, Smith and Jones, have the following demand curves for Podunk Public Radio broadcasts of recorded opera on Saturdays:

$$\text{Smith:} \quad P_S = 12 - Q$$
$$\text{Jones:} \quad P_J = 12 - 2Q,$$

where P_S and P_J represent marginal willingness to pay values for Smith and Jones, respectively, and Q represents the number of hours of opera broadcast each Saturday.

a. If Smith and Jones are the only public radio listeners in Podunk, construct the demand curve for opera broadcasts.

b. If the marginal cost of opera broadcasts is $15 per hour, what is the socially optimal number of hours of broadcast opera?

6. Suppose the demand curves for hour-long episodes of the *Jerry Springer Show* and *Masterpiece Theater* are as shown in the following diagram. A television network is considering whether to add one or both programs to its upcoming fall lineup. The only two time slots remaining are sponsored by Colgate, which is under contract to pay the network 10 cents for each viewer who watches the program, out of which the network would have to cover its production costs of $400,000 per episode. (Viewership can be estimated accurately with telephone surveys.) Any time slot the network does not fill with *Springer* or *Masterpiece Theater* will be filled by infomercials for a weight-loss program, for which the network incurs no production costs and for which it receives a fee of $500,000. Viewers will receive $5 million in economic surplus from watching each installment of the infomercial.

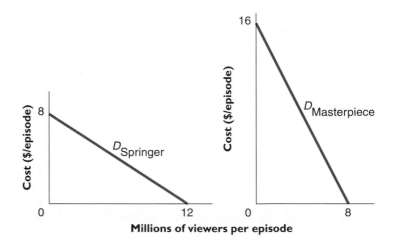

a. How will the network fill the two remaining slots in its fall lineup?

b. Is this outcome socially efficient?

7. Refer to Problem 6. By how much would total economic surplus be higher if each episode of *Masterpiece Theater* were shown on PBS free of charge than if it were shown by a profit-maximizing pay-per-view network?

8. When a TV company chooses a pay-per-view scheme to pay for programming, which of the following statements is true? Explain.

a. The outcome is socially efficient.

b. The programs selected will maximize advertising revenue.

c. The marginal cost to an additional viewer of watching the programs is lower than when advertising is used to finance programming.

d. The outcome is always more socially efficient than when advertising is used to finance programming.

e. The variety of programs provided is likely to rise.

9. When a group of people must decide whether to buy a shared public good or service, the free-rider problem frequently occurs because:

a. People have an incentive to understate how much the facility is really worth to them if they have to pay taxes to finance it.

b. Each individual's needed contribution is an insignificant amount of the total required.

c. People have an incentive to overstate how much the facility is worth to them if they don't have to pay taxes to finance it.

d. People hope that others will value the facility enough to pay for it entirely.

e. Only one of the above statements is not a reason for the existence of the free-rider problem.

10. The town of Smallsville is considering building a museum. The interest on the money Smallsville will have to borrow to build the museum will be $1,000 per year. Each citizen's marginal benefit from the museum is shown in the following table, and this marginal benefit schedule is public information.

a. Assuming each citizen voted his or her private interests, would a referendum to build the museum and raise each citizen's annual taxes by $200 pass?

b. A citizen proposes that the city let a private company build the museum and charge the citizens a lump-sum fee each year to view it as much as they like. Only citizens who paid the fee would be allowed to view the museum. If the private company were allowed to set a single fee, would any company offer to build the museum?

c. A second citizen proposes allowing the private company to charge different prices to different citizens and auctioning the right to build the museum to the highest bidding company. Again, only the citizens who pay the fee may view the museum. What is the highest bid a private company would make to supply the museum to Smallsville?

Citizen	Marginal benefit from museum ($/year)
Anita	340
Brandon	290
Carlena	240
Dallas	190
Eloise	140

■ ANSWERS TO IN-CHAPTER EXERCISES ■

15.1 a. The BLS web site at 3 in the morning has the capacity to serve far more users than it attracts, so an additional user calling up the site does not prevent some other user from doing so. Other web sites, however do not show the nonrival property, at least during certain hours, because they attract more users than their servers can accommodate.

b. The stadium at the championship game is always full, so anyone who watches the game in person prevents someone else from doing so.

c. Additional people can watch the game on television without diminishing the availability of the telecast for others.

15.2 To construct the demand curve [part (a)], we first graph Bill's demand curve [part (c)] and Tom's demand curve [part (b)] and then add the two individual demand curves vertically. The equation for the demand curve is $P = 18 - 1.5Q$.

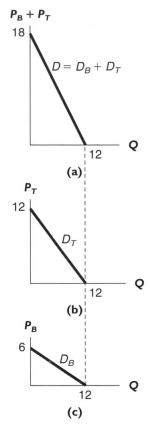

(a)

(b)

(c)

15.3 Whereas elasticity of demand was 1 at a price of $10 on the original demand curve, it is 1.5 on the new demand curve. As a result, the $10 fee now excludes 20 million viewers, and the resulting loss in surplus (again the area of the blue triangle) is now $100 million.

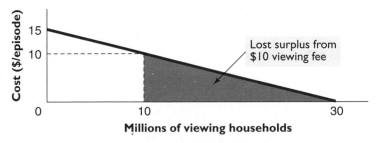

15.4 If Sven orders bread pudding, his share of the bill would now go up by $2 instead of $1. If he orders chocolate mousse, his share of the bill would go up by $1.20 instead of $0.60. So he would still order the bread pudding (surplus = $4 − $2 = $2) rather than the chocolate mousse (surplus = $3 − $1.20 = $1.80).

CHAPTER 16

INCOME REDISTRIBUTION

Patek Philippe's Calibre '89 is perhaps the most remarkably elaborate and accurate mechanical watch ever built. Among its many features is a "tourbillon," a gyroscope that turns about once each minute, whose purpose is to offset the distortionary effects of the earth's gravitational field. Yet despite its $2.7 million price tag and formidable engineering wizardry, the Calibre '89 is actually less accurate than a battery-powered quartz watch costing less than $20. The earth's gravitational field, it turns out, doesn't affect the accuracy of an electronic watch.

Accurate or not, top-of-the line mechanical wristwatches are selling briskly. A Patek Philippe watch priced at $45,000, for example, is available only on backorder, and sales of watches costing more than $2,000 are growing at almost 13 percent a year. The men who purchase these mechanical wristwatches (women almost never buy them) often own several, which confronts them with a problem: Although the watches are self-winding, they will stop if put aside for a few days. So the owner of several of these watches must often reset each one before wearing it.

One could hardly expect men of means to tolerate such a problem for long. And sure enough, there is now a ready solution. On display in Asprey & Garrard showrooms, discerning buyers will find a finely tooled calfskin-covered box with a golden clasp, whose doors open to reveal six mechanical wrists that rotate just often enough to keep the mechanical wristwatches they hold running smoothly. The price? Only $5,700.

Many people might think that if the government were to tax buyers of $50,000 wristwatches more heavily and use the proceeds to buy school lunches for poor children, the world would a better place. Yet this proposition remains a remarkably controversial one. Our aim in this chapter will be to explore whether income inequality is something society should be concerned about, and, if so, whether practical remedies exist. As we will see, government programs to redistribute income have costs as well as benefits. As always, policymakers must employ the cost-benefit principle to compare an imperfect status quo with the practical consequences of imperfect government remedies.

RECENT TRENDS IN INEQUALITY AND CONSUMER SPENDING

The period from the end of World War II until the early 1970s was one of balanced income growth in the United States. During that period, incomes grew at almost 3 percent a year for rich, middle-class, and poor Americans alike.

In the ensuing years, however, the pattern of income growth has been dramatically different. In the first row of Table 16.1, for example, notice that families in the bottom 20 percent of the income distribution saw their real incomes actually decline by more than 4 percent from 1978 to 1998. The third row of the table indicates that the real incomes of families in the middle quintile grew by less than 10 percent during the same 20-year period (a growth rate of less than one-half of 1 percent per year). But while the real incomes of middle-class and poor families were stagnant or declining, families with the highest earnings experienced much bigger gains than in the immediate postwar decades. Thus real incomes jumped more than 40 percent for families in the top quintile between 1978 and 1998, while those for families in the top 5 percent jumped by more than 68 percent.

TABLE 16.1
Mean Income Received by Families in Each Income Quintile and by the Top 5 Percent of Families, 1968–1998 (1998 dollars)

Quintile	1978	1988	1998
Bottom 20 percent	$ 13,103	$ 12,256	$ 12,526
Second 20 percent	28,415	28,541	29,482
Middle 20 percent	42,667	44,414	46,662
Fourth 20 percent	58,786	63,785	68,430
Top 20 percent	99,754	117,035	140,846
Top 5 percent	146,178	182,863	246,520

SOURCE: Census Bureau. www.census.gov/hhes/income/histinc/f03.html.

The result has been a significant shift in the overall distribution of earnings among American families. Table 16.2, for example, shows how the shares of total earnings have evolved for the different groups between 1968 and 1998. Note that the lowest three quintiles each had a significantly smaller share of the national income in 1998 than in 1968, while the share of the fourth quintile was essentially unchanged. But note in the final two rows of the table that the share of the top quintile rose more than 17 percent, and the share of the top 5 percent rose almost 33 percent.

Recent earnings growth has been even greater for those higher up the income ladder. Thus real earnings of the top 1 percent of U.S. workers have more than doubled since 1979, and those near the top of the income ladder have taken home paychecks that might have seemed unimaginable just two decades ago. For

TABLE 16.2
Share of Aggregate Income Received by Each Quintile and by the Top 5 Percent of Families, 1968–1998

Quintile	1968	1978	1988	1998
Bottom 20 percent	5.6	5.4	4.6	4.2
Second 20 percent	12.4	11.7	10.7	9.9
Middle 20 percent	17.7	17.6	16.7	15.7
Fourth 20 percent	23.7	24.2	24.0	23.0
Top 20 percent	40.6	41.1	44.0	47.3
Top 5 percent	15.6	15.1	17.2	20.7

SOURCE: Census Bureau. www.census.gov/hhes/income/histinc/f02.html.

example, though no American CEO earned as much as $1 million in 1978, Disney's CEO Michael Eisner took home more than $565 million in 1997 (including gains from exercising his stock options).

Recent decades also witnessed dramatic growth and increased concentration of personal wealth. Wealth holdings for the richest 1 percent of Americans have roughly doubled since 1980, and the combined wealth of this group now exceeds the combined wealth of Americans below the 95th percentile. The Forbes Four Hundred—the celebrated list of the 400 richest people in America—included 243 billionaires in 1998, up from 170 just a year earlier. In 1982 the list contained just 13 billionaires—five of them children of Texas oil tycoon H. L. Hunt. Together the Forbes 400 are worth more than $1 trillion, nearly one-eighth the national income of the United States, and more than the national income of China, a country of more than 1 billion people.

The recent gains in wealth have not been confined to those who were already worth hundreds of millions. For example, more than 4 million American households had a net worth of at least $1 million in 1998, 20 percent more than in 1995. Some 274,000 households had a net worth of at least $10 million in 1998, up from 190,400 households in 1995.

In sum, to say that recent changes in the distributions of income and wealth have produced a fundamental shift in the American economic landscape is hardly an exaggeration. People who had a lot of money to begin with have considerably more now, and many more people have a lot of money now than in the past.

These fortunate people have been buying more and better things, just as people with extra cash in their pockets have always done. Sales trends in the wristwatch industry are like those in virtually every other product category. For example, while total car sales in the United States went down 3 percent in 1997, Porsche sales rose 79 percent, Mercedes sales 35 percent, and BMW sales 16 percent. And while overall wine sales are down slightly from their peak in 1986, sales of ultrapremium wines have been growing more than 20 percent a year since 1980.

Houses with more than 20,000 square feet of living space are currently being constructed in record numbers. A typical house of that size has 10 or more large bedrooms, each with its own bath; an informal living room and a formal living room; a ballroom; a 500-square-foot kitchen with separate pantry; a dining room; a media room; a library; maid's quarters; and a five- or six-car garage. Many have squash courts and bowling alleys.

Suffice it to say that in purely economic terms, those near the top of the income ladder are prospering as never before. In contrast, those farther down the ladder have seen their living standards grow much more slowly, or even decline.

> **RECAP** **RECENT TRENDS IN INEQUALITY AND CONSUMER SPENDING**
>
> From 1945 until the mid-1970s, incomes grew at almost 3 percent a year for rich, middle-class, and poor families alike. In contrast, most of the income growth since the mid-1970s has been concentrated among top earners. The real earnings of low-income families have actually declined since the mid-1970s. Changes in wealth concentration have followed the same patterns. Higher income and wealth at the top of the economic pyramid has stimulated large increases in spending on luxury consumption goods.

MORAL CONCERNS RAISED BY INCOME INEQUALITY

In the United States, as in most other market economies, the vast majority of citizens receive most of their income from the sale of their own labor. An attractive feature of the free-market system, in both moral and practical terms, is that it rewards initiative, effort, and risk taking. The harder, longer, and more effectively a person works, the more she will be paid. And if she risks her capital on a venture that happens to succeed, she will reap a handsome dividend indeed.

Yet relying on the marketplace to distribute income also entails a moral drawback—namely, that those who do well often end up with vastly more money than they can spend, while those who fail often cannot afford even basic goods and services. Hundreds of thousands of American families are homeless, and still larger numbers go to bed hungry each night. Many distinguished philosophers have argued that such poverty in the midst of plenty is impossible to justify on moral grounds.

JUSTICE AS FAIRNESS

Inequality might be easier to accept if it were strictly the result of differences in effort, but it is not. Talent plays an important role in most endeavors, and although it can be nurtured and developed in those who have it, having it in the first place is essentially a matter of luck.

Yet having abundant talent is no guarantee of doing well. To become wealthy, one must have the *right* talent. Being able to hit a baseball 400 feet with consistency will earn an athlete millions annually, but being the best fourth grade teacher in the nation will earn an educator little. The baseball star earns so much more not because he works harder or has more talent, but because he is lucky enough to be good at something people are willing to pay a premium for.

John Rawls, a moral philosopher at Harvard University, has constructed a cogent ethical critique of the marginal productivity system, one based heavily on the economic theory of choice itself.[1] In thinking about what constitutes a just distribution of income, Rawls asks us to imagine ourselves meeting to choose the rules for distributing income. The meeting takes place behind a "veil of ignorance," which conceals from participants any knowledge of what talents and abilities each has. Because no individual knows whether he is smart or dull, strong or weak, fast or slow, no one knows which rules of distribution would work to his own advantage.

Rawls argues that the rules people would choose in such a state of ignorance would necessarily be fair, and if the rules are fair, the income distribution to which they give rise will also be fair.

---

[1] John Rawls, *A Theory of Justice,* Cambridge, Mass.: Harvard University Press, 1971.

What sort of rules would people choose from behind a veil of ignorance? If the national income were a fixed amount, most people would probably give everyone an equal share. That scenario is likely, Rawls argues, because most people are strongly risk-averse. Since an unequal income distribution would involve not only a chance of doing well but a chance of doing poorly, most people would prefer to eliminate the risk by choosing an equal distribution. Imagine, for example, that you and two friends have been told that an anonymous benefactor has donated $300,000 to divide among you. How would you split it? If you are like most people, you would immediately propose an equal division, or $100,000 for each of you.

Yet despite the obvious attraction of equality, it is far from absolute. Indeed, the goal of absolute equality is quickly trumped by other concerns when we make the rules for distributing wealth in modern market economies. Wealth, after all, generally doesn't come from anonymous benefactors; we must produce it. In a large economy, if each person were guaranteed an equal amount of income, few would invest in education or the development of special talents, and as Example 16.1 illustrates, the incentive to work would be sharply reduced.

Does income sharing affect labor supply?

EXAMPLE 16.1

Sue is offered a job reshelving books in the University of Montana library from noon until 1 P.M. each Friday. Her reservation wage for this task is $10/hour. If the library director offers Sue $100/hour, how much economic surplus will she enjoy as a result of accepting the job? Now suppose the library director announces that the earnings from the job will be divided equally among the 400 students who live in Sue's dormitory. Will Sue still accept?

When the $100/hour is paid directly to Sue, she accepts the job and enjoys an economic surplus of $100 − $10 = $90. If the $100 were divided equally among the 400 residents of Sue's dorm, however, each resident's share would be only 25 cents. Accepting the job would thus mean a negative surplus for Sue of $0.25 − $10 = −$9.75, so she will not accept the job.

EXERCISE 16.1

What is the largest dorm population for which Sue would accept the job on a pay-sharing basis?

In a country without rewards for hard work and risk taking, national income would be dramatically smaller than in a country with such rewards. Of course, material rewards for effort and risk taking necessarily lead to inequality. Rawls argues, however, that people would be willing to accept a certain degree of inequality as long as these rewards produced a sufficiently large increase in the total amount of output available for distribution.

But how much inequality would people accept? Much less than the amount produced by purely competitive markets, Rawls argues. The idea is that behind the veil of ignorance, each person would fear being put in a disadvantaged position, so each would choose rules that would produce a more equal distribution of income than exists under the marginal productivity system. And since such choices *define* the just distribution of income, he argues, fairness requires at least some attempt to reduce the inequality produced by the market system.

THE UTILITARIAN ARGUMENT

The branch of moral philosophy called **utilitarianism** holds that the right course of action is the one that results in the highest total level of utility. Utilitarians argue against income inequality on the grounds that the marginal utility of income is typically smaller for a wealthy person than for a poor person. In their view,

utilitarianism a moral theory in which the right course of action is the one that results in the highest total utility transferring $1,000 of income from a rich person to a poor person is justified because the extra happiness experienced when the poor person received the money would far outweigh the decline in happiness when the rich person gave it up.

Although some have objected to this argument, saying that no one knows for sure how gains and losses affect the well-being of people in different circumstances, most people accept the claim that an extra dollar generally meets more pressing demands for a poor person than for a rich person. But even utilitarians do not argue for complete equalization on these grounds. With Rawls, they recognize that a regime of complete equality would so weaken incentives that it would not, in fact, produce the greatest utility for all.

THE PSYCHOLOGICAL COSTS OF INEQUALITY

Many modern disciples of Adam Smith appear reluctant to introduce concerns about inequality into discussions of economic policy. Yet as Smith himself recognized, such concerns are a basic component of human nature. Writing more than two centuries ago, he introduced the important idea that local consumption standards influence the goods and services that people consider essential (or "necessaries," as Smith called them). In the following passage, for example, Smith described the factors that influence the amount an individual must spend on clothing in order to be able appear in public "without shame."

> By necessaries I understand not only the commodities which are indispensably necessary for the support of life, but whatever the custom of the country renders it indecent for creditable people, even of the lowest order, to be without. A linen shirt, for example, is, strictly speaking, not a necessary of life. The Greeks and Romans lived, I suppose, very comfortably though they had no linen. But in the present times, through the greater part of Europe, a creditable day-labourer would be ashamed to appear in public without a linen shirt, the want of which would be supposed to denote that disgraceful degree of poverty which, it is presumed, nobody can well fall into without extreme bad conduct. Custom, in the same manner, has rendered leather shoes a necessary of life in England. The poorest creditable person of either sex would be ashamed to appear in public without them.[2]

The absolute standard of living in the United States today is vastly higher than it was in Adam Smith's eighteenth-century Scotland. Yet Smith's observations apply with equal force to contemporary industrial societies. Consider, for instance, the journalist Dirk Johnson's recent account of the experiences of Wendy Williams, a middle school student from a low-income family in Dixon, Illinois.

> Watching classmates strut past in designer clothes, Wendy Williams sat silently on the yellow school bus, wearing a cheap belt and rummage-sale slacks. One boy stopped and yanked his thumb, demanding her seat.
>
> "Move it, trailer girl," he sneered.
>
> It has never been easy to live on the wrong side of the tracks. But in the economically robust 1990's, with sprawling new houses and three-car garages sprouting like cornstalks on the Midwestern prairie, the sting that comes with scarcity gets rubbed with an extra bit of salt. . . .
>
> To be without money, in so many ways, is to be left out.
>
> "I told this girl: 'That's a really awesome shirt. Where did you get it?'" said Wendy, explaining that she knew it was out of her price

[2]Adam Smith, *The Wealth of Nations*, New York: Everyman's Library, E. P. Dutton, 1910 (1776), book 1.

range, but that she wanted to join the small talk. "And she looked at me and laughed and said, 'Why would you want to know?'"

A lanky, soft-spoken girl with large brown eyes, Wendy pursed her lips to hide a slight overbite that got her the nickname Rabbit, a humiliation she once begged her mother and father to avoid by sending her to an orthodontist.

For struggling parents, keenly aware that adolescents agonize over the social pecking order, the styles of the moment and the face in the mirror, there is no small sense of failure in telling a child that she cannot have what her classmates take for granted.

"Do you know what it's like?" asked Wendy's mother, Veronica Williams, "to have your daughter come home and say, 'Mom, the kids say my clothes are tacky,' and then walk off with her head hanging low."[3]

An adolescent in eighteenth-century Scotland would not have been much embarrassed by having a slight overbite, because not even the wealthiest members of society wore braces on their teeth then. Rising living standards have altered the frame of reference that defines an acceptable standard of cosmetic dentistry. The toll that inequality takes on individuals like Wendy Williams is no less important because it occurs in psychological rather than explicit monetary terms.

RECAP   **MORAL CONCERNS RAISED BY INCOME INEQUALITY**

High levels of income inequality have drawn moral objections on several grounds. John Rawls has argued that the degree of inequality typical of unregulated market systems is unfair because people would favor substantially less inequality if they chose distributional rules from behind a veil of ignorance. Utilitarians favor reducing inequality because the marginal utility of income is smaller for wealthy persons than for poor persons. Others have objected to extreme inequality because it imposes significant psychological costs.

PRACTICAL CONCERNS RAISED BY POVERTY AND INCOME INEQUALITY

Even if we set moral concerns completely aside, compelling practical reasons to limit poverty and inequality would remain. One concern is that poverty imposes many costs on those who are not poor. Another is that growing income inequality raises the price of achieving many important family goals.

THE EFFECT OF POVERTY ON THE NONPOOR

The productivity of any member of a team depends on the productivity of other team members. For example, the amount by which the efforts of skilled engineers or managers contribute to national income will be many times greater in an economy with a highly skilled workforce than in one with a poorly trained workforce. Those at the top of the productivity ladder gain by working with people of the highest caliber. Yet beyond some point, poverty may inhibit those near the bottom of the income ladder from developing their skills to the fullest. For example, low-income parents often cannot afford after-school lesson programs for their

---

[3]Dirk Johnson, "When Money Is Everything, Except Hers," *The New York Times*, October 28, 1998, p. A1.

children, who are often forced to drop out of school prematurely. Low-income parents may also fail to learn about training programs for themselves or may lack transportation to get to those programs.

Even the psychological burden of being poor can result in missed opportunities. For instance, when a teacher asked Wendy Williams, the Illinois middle school student, to join an advanced class in algebra, she declined, saying "I get picked on for my clothes and living in the trailer park. I don't want to get picked on for being a nerd, too."[4] No matter what its cause, the undeveloped potential of low-income persons works not just to their own disadvantage but also to the disadvantage of those at the top.

Low-income persons are also less likely to be well nourished and less likely to obtain preventive medical care on a routine basis. Compounding these problems, the psychological stresses of living in poverty are known to foster a variety of physical illnesses. Poor people get sick more often than others, and their illnesses tend to be more serious.

These illnesses not only harm the poor but also impose costs on others. As noted in Chapter 15, some 45 million Americans currently lack health insurance. When uninsured people become seriously ill, they often receive medical care at public expense, imposing an additional tax burden on healthy people. The unpaid medical bills of the uninsured also force doctors and hospitals to increase their fees, raising the insurance premiums of those who remain insured. To the extent that illness prevents people from achieving their full potential, healthy people will miss many of the indirect benefits that spring from working with more productive colleagues.

Finally, because poverty prevents some people from capitalizing on legitimate career opportunities, it also increases the attractiveness of crime. Total U.S. spending on private security currently runs about $60 billion a year, and private security firms now employ some 1.5 million persons—more than 2 1/2 times the number in public law enforcement. When people are occupied in either committing crimes or trying to avoid them, they are diverted from producing legitimate goods and services. This pattern is profoundly wasteful from the perspective of both rich and poor.

THE EFFECT OF A WIDENING INCOME GAP ON THE MIDDLE CLASS

Since Ronald Reagan's administration, presidential aspirants have urged voters to ask themselves whether they are better off now than they were 4 years ago. At any time from 1945 to the early 1970s, the answer for most Americans would have been a resounding yes, for as noted earlier, incomes were growing at about 3 percent a year during that period for families in every income class.

Today, however, Reagan's question is more difficult to answer. Does the fact that median family income is slightly higher, in real terms, than it was in the 1970s mean that the typical middle-class family is better off now? If we measure economic well-being by the amount of goods and services such a family can buy, the answer would appear to be yes. Many respected economists have argued to that effect, invoking the Pareto criterion (see Chapter 7). According to that criterion, a change in circumstances must be counted as an improvement if it makes at least some people better off without harming others.

Yet "having more income" and "being better off" do not have exactly the same meaning. Indeed, increased spending at the top of the income distribution has caused tangible harm to families in the middle by raising the cost of achieving goals that almost every family cherishes. Few middle-income parents, for example, would be comfortable knowing that their children were attending below-average schools. But since the quality of public schools is closely linked to

[4]Johnson, ibid.

local property taxes, which in turn are closely linked to local real estate prices, people cannot send their children to a public school of even average quality if they buy a home in a school district in which house prices are well below average. The relationship between school quality and housing prices creates a problem for middle-income families, because the average new home built in the United States today, which has some 2,200 square feet of living space, is roughly 50 percent larger than the average new home built in 1970. So today's middle-income family cannot send its children to schools of average quality unless it carries a much larger mortgage than its counterparts in 1970.

Increased income inequality is the reason the average house has grown so much bigger. The process begins when higher incomes prompt top earners to build larger homes. Perhaps your parents didn't care whether your neighbors had bigger homes than yours. Yet many people *do* care about relative home size. Thus when top earners build 20,000-square-foot houses, others just below the top income level find their 10,000-square-foot houses no longer adequate. This process of comparison repeats itself all the way down the income ladder.

If an average earner doesn't envy his neighbor's larger house, couldn't he simply buy the same size house that average earners bought in 1970? He could, but then he would have to send his children to below-average schools. Rather than do that, he might prefer to buy the bigger house, even if he doesn't care about the extra space. Worse still, he might end up buying an existing 1,500-square-foot house whose price has been bid up sharply because of its location in a good school district.

Increased spending at the top also imposes other costs on those below. A soccer mom who buys a typical 3,000-pound sedan will incur risks that didn't exist in the 1970s, since she must now share the road with 6,000-pound Lincoln Navigators and 7,500-pound Ford Excursions. So in self-defense, she may want to spend more for a bulkier vehicle. And if her family does manage to buy a home in a good school district, she may need to spend more on her children's clothes or else share the embarrassment they experience at not measuring up to wealthier classmates. The clothing she and her husband buy might have to come up a notch as well. After all, others are wearing more expensive clothes now, and in job interviews they will want to make a good impression. Even the gifts they must give will be affected by the greater affluence of top earners.

The pressures that stem from increased spending at the top may help to explain why American families now carry an average of more than $5,000 in credit card debt. Those same pressures may explain why American families at the turn of the millennium were filing for personal bankruptcy at seven times the rate they did in 1980, even though the unemployment rate was at a 29-year low. The point is not that Americans should somehow turn back the clock to the 1970s. Rather, it is that the expanding income and wealth gaps appear to have caused tangible harm, even to middle-class people who earn a little more than they used to.

RECAP   **PRACTICAL CONCERNS RAISED BY POVERTY AND INCOME INEQUALITY**

Apart from moral concerns about income inequality, practical reasons would argue for limiting the gap between the rich and poor. One is that poverty imposes costs on the nonpoor. High-income persons benefit from having highly skilled people to work with, and poverty often limits the extent to which people can develop their skills. Poverty also fosters illness and crime, both of which burden the nonpoor. Even in the absence of absolute poverty, extreme income inequality raises the price of pursuing many basic goals, as when the growing gap between the rich and the middle class drives up the price of a house in a good school district.

METHODS OF INCOME REDISTRIBUTION

As we have seen, both moral and practical concerns provide grounds for reducing income inequality. But attempts to limit inequality are also fraught with practical difficulties. The challenge is to find ways to raise the incomes of those who cannot fend well enough for themselves, without at the same time undermining their incentive to work and without using scarce resources to subsidize those who are not poor.

Recall that in the absence of externalities and various other market imperfections, total economic surplus is largest when price is set at the level for which supply and demand curves intersect (see Chapter 7). Nevertheless, most governments disregard the efficiency principle by taking at least some steps to protect the poor by keeping the prices in certain markets from reaching market-clearing levels. Rent controls on apartments and price controls on home heating oil are familiar examples. In such cases, rich and poor alike would fare better if government simply gave the poor some more money. As we will see, a similar objection applies to legislation that sets minimum wages in the labor market.

MINIMUM WAGES

The United States and many other industrialized countries have sought to ease the burden of the working poor by enacting minimum wage legislation—laws that prohibit employers from paying workers less than a specified hourly wage. The federal minimum wage in the United States is currently set at \$5.15/hour, and several states have set minimum wage levels significantly higher. Massachusetts, for example, increased its minimum wage to \$6.75/hour in early 2000.

How does a minimum wage affect the market for low-wage labor? In Figure 16.1, note that when the law prevents employers from paying less than W_{min}, employers hire fewer workers (a decline from L_0 to L_1). Unemployment results. The L_1 workers who keep their jobs earn more than before, but the $L_0 - L_1$ workers who lose their jobs earn nothing. Whether workers together earn more or less than before thus depends on the elasticity of demand for labor. If elasticity of demand is less than 1, workers as a group will earn more than before. If it is more than 1, workers as a group will earn less.

At one point, economists were almost unanimous in their opposition to minimum wage laws, arguing that those laws reduce total economic surplus, much like other regulations that prevent markets from reaching equilibrium. In recent years, however, some economists have softened their opposition to minimum wage laws, citing studies that have failed to show significant reductions in employment following increases in minimum wage levels. These studies may well

FIGURE 16.1

The Effect of Minimum Wage Legislation on Employment.

If minimum wage legislation requires employers to pay more than the equilibrium wage, the result will be a decline in employment for low-wage workers.

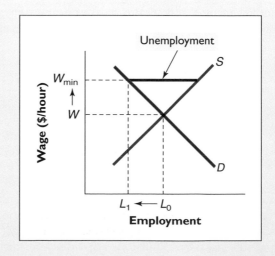

imply that as a group low-income workers are better off with minimum wage laws than without them. But as we saw in Chapter 7, any policy that prevents a market from reaching equilibrium causes a reduction in total economic surplus, which means society ought to be able to find a more effective policy for helping low-wage workers.

THE EARNED-INCOME TAX CREDIT

One such policy is the **earned-income tax credit** (EITC), which gives low-wage workers a credit on their federal income tax each year. First proposed by President Richard Nixon, the EITC was enacted into law in 1975, and in the years since it has drawn praise from both liberals and conservatives. The program is essentially a wage subsidy in the form of a credit against the amount a family owes in federal income taxes. For example, a family of four with total earned income of $18,000 in 1999 would have received an annual tax credit of about $2,500 under this program. That is, the program would have reduced the annual federal income tax payment of this family by roughly that amount. Families who earned less would have received a larger tax credit, and those who earned more would have received a smaller one. Families whose tax credit exceeded the amount of tax owed actually would have received a check from the government for the difference. (We will see more clearly how the EITC works when we discuss a closely related program in a moment.)

earned-income tax credit (EITC) a policy under which low-income workers receive credits on their federal income tax

Like the minimum wage, the EITC puts extra income into the hands of workers who are employed at low-wage levels. But unlike the minimum wage, the earned-income tax credit creates no incentive for employers to lay off low-wage workers.

Examples 16.2 to 16.4 illustrate how switching from a minimum wage to an earned-income tax credit can produce gains for both employers and workers.

By how much will a minimum wage reduce total economic surplus?

EXAMPLE 16.2

Suppose the demand for unskilled labor in the Cedar Falls labor market is given by $W = 10 - 0.001L$, where W is the wage rate in dollars per hour and L is the quantity of labor demanded in person-hours per day. If the supply curve of unskilled labor in Cedar Falls is given by $W = 0.001L$, by how much will the imposition of a minimum wage at $7/hour reduce total economic surplus? By how much do worker surplus and employer surplus change as a result of adopting the minimum wage?

In the absence of a minimum wage, the equilibrium wage for Cedar Falls would be $5/hour, and employment would be 5,000 person-hours/day (see Figure 16.2). Both employers and workers would enjoy economic surplus equal to the area of the shaded triangles, $12,500/day.

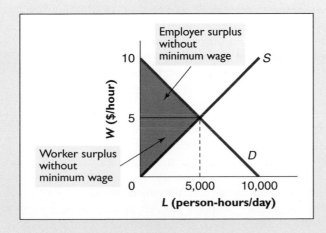

FIGURE 16.2
Worker and Employer Surplus in an Unregulated Labor Market.
For the demand and supply curves shown, worker surplus is the area of the green triangle, $12,500/day, the same as employer surplus (blue triangle).

FIGURE 16.3

The Effect of a Minimum Wage on Economic Surplus.

A minimum wage of $7/hour reduces employment in this market by 2,000 person-hours/day, for a reduction in total economic surplus of $4,000/day (area of the light blue triangle). Employer surplus falls to $4,500/day (area of cross-hatched triangle), while worker surplus rises to $16,500/day (green area).

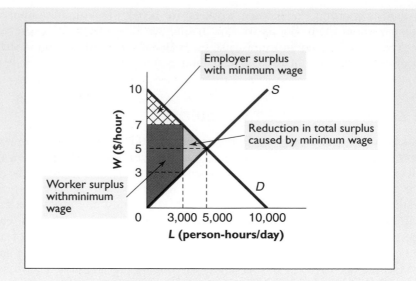

With a minimum wage set at $7/hour, employer surplus is the area of the cross-hatched triangle in Figure 16.3, $4,500/day, and worker surplus is the area of the four-sided green figure, $16,500/day. The minimum wage thus reduces employer surplus by $8,000/day and increases worker surplus by $4,000/day. The net reduction in surplus is the area of the blue triangle shown in Figure 16.3, $4,000/day.

EXERCISE 16.2

In Example 16.2, by how much would total economic surplus have been reduced by the $7 minimum wage if labor demand in Cedar Falls had been perfectly inelastic at 5,000 person-hours/day?

EXAMPLE 16.3

Refer to Example 16.2. How much would it cost the government each day to provide an earned-income tax credit under which workers as a group receive the same economic surplus as they do under the $7/hour minimum wage? (Assume for simplicity that the earned-income tax credit has no effect on labor supply.)

With an earned-income tax credit in lieu of a minimum wage, employment will be 5,000 person-hours/day at $5/hour, just as in the unregulated market. Since worker surplus in the unregulated market was $4,000/day less than under the minimum wage, the government would have to offer a tax credit worth $0.80/hour for each of the 5,000 person-hours of employment to restore worker surplus to the level obtained under the $7 minimum wage.

EXAMPLE 16.4

Can you propose an earned-income tax credit that would win unanimous support from employers and workers?

Suppose that the status quo is the unregulated labor market described in Example 16.2 and that employers and workers in that market are risk-neutral. Labor unions have sufficient political power to induce Congress to enact a minimum wage law. The President's chief economist has urged the President to persuade unions to drop their demand for a minimum wage in favor of an earned-income tax credit. Suppose neither workers nor employers would support the switch unless the expected value of each party's economic surplus under the earned-income tax credit would be at least as great as under the minimum wage. Describe an earned-income tax credit (and a tax that would raise enough money to pay for it) that would receive unanimous support from both workers and employers in the Cedar Falls labor market.

Because employer surplus is $8,000/day lower under the minimum wage than under the earned-income tax credit, employers would be willing to pay a tax up to that amount to secure the policy switch. And since worker surplus would be only $4,000/day smaller in the absence of a minimum wage, $8,000/day is more than enough to finance a tax credit that workers would support. For example, a tax of $6,000 levied on employers could be used to fund an earned-income tax credit of $1.20/hour, which would make both employers and workers better off than under the minimum wage.

The moral, as in similar examples, is that when the economic pie grows larger, everyone can have a bigger slice.

WELFARE PAYMENTS AND IN-KIND TRANSFERS

If price controls and minimum wages are inefficient, why do so many governments use them? Why don't they just transfer additional resources directly to the poor? In fact, such transfers are at the forefront of antipoverty efforts around the globe. Virtually all governments employ them, both in the form of cash transfers (such as welfare payments and EITC payments) and **in-kind transfers.**

in-kind transfer a payment made not in the form of cash but in the form of a good or service

Historically, the most important welfare program has been Aid to Families with Dependent Children (AFDC), which in most cases provides cash payments to poor single-parent households. In-kind transfers are direct transfers of goods or services to low-income individuals or families, such as food stamps, public housing, subsidized school lunches, and Medicaid.

Why did many critics charge that the AFDC program undermined family stability?

As administered in many states, a poor mother was ineligible for AFDC payments if her husband or other able-bodied adult male lived with her and her children. This provision confronted many long-term unemployed fathers with an agonizing choice. They could leave their families, making them eligible for public assistance, or they could remain, making them ineligible. Even many who deeply loved their families understandably chose to leave.

ECONOMIC NATURALIST 16.1

In most places, the extent of cash and in-kind transfers to the poor is limited, because of fear that higher transfers would weaken people's incentive to find work and support themselves. Of course, some people simply cannot work or cannot find work that pays enough to live on. In a world of perfect information, the government could make generous cash payments to those people and withhold support from those who can fend for themselves. In practice, however, the two groups are often hard to distinguish from each other.

Current welfare programs are **means-tested:** The more income one has, the smaller the benefits. The purpose of means testing is to avoid paying benefits to those who don't really need them. But because of the way welfare programs are administered, means testing often has a pernicious effect on work incentives, as Example 16.5 illustrates.

means-tested a benefit program is means-tested if its benefit level declines as the recipient earns additional income

How will earning an extra dollar affect Smith's standard of living?

EXAMPLE 16.5

Smith is an unemployed participant in four welfare programs: Food stamps, rent stamps, energy stamps, and day care stamps. Each program gives him $100 worth of stamps per month, which he is then free to spend on food, rent, energy, and day care. If Smith gets a job, his benefits in each program are reduced by 50 cents for each dollar he earns. How will his net weekly income change if he accepts a job that pays $50/week?

Smith will lose $25 in weekly benefits from each of the four welfare programs, for a total benefit reduction of $100/week. Taking the job thus leaves him $50/week worse off than before.

Low-income persons need no formal training in economics to realize that under the current welfare system, seeking gainful employment often does not pay. What is more, the system is extremely costly to administer. If the government were to eliminate all existing welfare and social service agencies, the resulting savings would be enough to raise every poor person above the poverty line. One proposal to do precisely that is the negative income tax.

THE NEGATIVE INCOME TAX

negative income tax a system under which the government would grant every citizen a cash payment each year, financed by an additional tax on earned income

breakeven income level under a negative income tax, the level of before-tax income at which a family's tax liability exactly offsets its initial tax credit

Nobel laureate Milton Friedman has proposed that current welfare programs be replaced by a single program called the **negative income tax** (**NIT**). Under the NIT, every man, woman, and child—rich or poor—receives a substantial income tax credit. The NIT is thus just like the earned-income tax credit except that it also applies to people who are not employed and hence have no earned income. A person who earns no income would receive the credit in cash. People who earn income would be taxed at some rate less than 100 percent.

Under a negative income tax, the initial credit and the tax rate would combine to determine a **breakeven income level** at which a person's tax liability exactly offsets his initial tax credit. People earning below that level would receive a net benefit payment from the government; people earning above it would make a net tax payment. Example 16.6 illustrates how the breakeven income level would be calculated.

EXAMPLE 16.6

What is the breakeven level of earned income in an NIT program?

Consider a negative income tax program with a tax credit of $6,000/year and a tax rate of 50 percent. At what income level would an individual in this program neither pay a tax nor receive a benefit? How large a net benefit would a person earning $6,000/year receive? How large a net tax payment would a person earning $18,000/year owe?

The horizontal axis of Figure 16.4 shows an individual's before-tax income, while the vertical axis measures after-tax income. With the credit payment set

FIGURE 16.4
A Hypothetical Negative Income Tax Program.
Under this negative income tax program, each person starts with a cash grant of $6,000/year, which is reduced at the rate of 50 cents for each dollar of income earned during the year. The breakeven income level is $12,000/year.

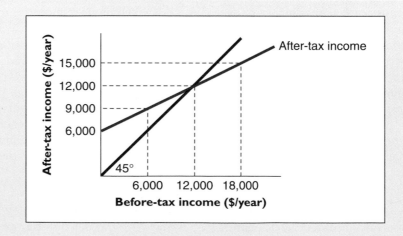

at $6,000/year, someone with a before-tax income of $0 would end up with an after-tax income of $6,000/year. From that point, his income would rise by 50 cents for each dollar earned, as shown by the red line labeled "After-tax income," until at some point it equaled his before-tax income. The 45° line shows all the points at which after-tax income equals before-tax income. In this program, the breakeven level of income is the before-tax income level at which the two lines intersect, which is $12,000/year. A person who earned $6,000/year would receive an after-tax income of $9,000, which implies that the government would send that person a check for $3,000. A person who earned $18,000/year would receive an after-tax income of $15,000, which implies that he would pay $3,000 in taxes.

EXERCISE 16.3

In Example 16.6, what would the breakeven income level have been if the tax credit had been not $6,000/year but $4,000?

The negative income tax would do much less than current programs to weaken work incentives, because unlike current programs, it would assure that someone who earned an extra dollar would keep at least a portion of it. And because the program would be administered by the existing Internal Revenue Service, administrative costs would be far lower than under the current welfare system.

Despite these advantages, however, the negative income tax is by no means a perfect solution to the income-transfer problem. Although the incentive problem would be less severe under a negative income tax than under current welfare programs, it would remain a serious difficulty. To see why, note that if the negative income tax were the *sole* means of insulating people against poverty, the payment to people with no earned income would need to be at least as large as the government's official poverty threshold.

The **poverty threshold** is the annual income level below which a family is officially classified as "poor" by the government. The threshold is based on government estimates of the cost of the so-called economy food plan, the least costly of four nutritionally adequate food plans designed by the Department of Agriculture. The department's 1955 Household Food Consumption Survey found that families of three or more people spent approximately one-third of their after-tax income on food, so the government pegs the poverty threshold at three times the cost of the economy food plan. In 1998, that threshold was $16,600 for a family of four.

For a family of four living in a city, $16,600 a year is scarcely enough to make ends meet. But suppose a group of, say, eight families were to pool their negative tax payments and move to the mountains of northern New Mexico. With a total of $132,800/year to spend, plus the fruits of their efforts at gardening and animal husbandry, such a group could live very nicely indeed.

Once a small number of experimental groups demonstrated the possibility of quitting their jobs and living well on the negative income tax, others would surely follow suit. Two practical difficulties would ensue. First, as more and more people left their jobs to live at government expense, the program would eventually become prohibitively costly. And second, the political cost of the program would almost surely force supporters to abandon it long before that point. Reports of people living lives of leisure at taxpayer expense would be sure to appear on the nightly news. People who worked hard at their jobs all day long would wonder why their tax dollars were being used to support those who were capable of holding paying jobs, yet chose not to work. If the resulting political backlash did not completely eliminate the negative income tax program, it would

poverty threshold the level of income below which the federal government classifies a family as poor force policymakers to cut back the payment so that members of rural communes could no longer afford to live comfortably. And that would mean the payment would no longer support an urban family.

PUBLIC EMPLOYMENT FOR THE POOR

An alternative method of transferring income to the poor would completely eliminate the problem with work incentives. Government-sponsored jobs could pay wages to the poor for useful work. With public service employment, the specter of people living lives of leisure at public expense simply does not arise.

But public service employment has difficulties of its own. Evidence shows that if government jobs pay the same wages as private jobs, many people will leave their private jobs in favor of government jobs, apparently because they view government jobs as being more secure. Such a migration would make public service employment extremely expensive. Other worrisome possibilities are that such jobs might involve meaningless make-work tasks and that they would prompt an expansion in government bureaucracy. By themselves, government-sponsored jobs for the poor probably are not an adequate solution to the income-transfer problem.

A COMBINATION OF METHODS

Although neither the negative income tax nor public service employment can completely solve the income-transfer problem, a combination of the two might do so. Such a program would consist of a cash grant that is far too small for anyone to live on, supplemented if necessary by a public service job at below minimum wage. Keeping the wage in public service jobs well below the minimum wage would eliminate the risk of a large-scale exodus from private jobs. And while living well on either the negative income tax or the public service wage would be impossible, the two programs together could lift people out of poverty (see Figure 16.5).

To prevent an expansion of the bureaucracy, the government could solicit bids from private management companies to oversee the public service employment program. The fear that this program would inevitably become a make-work project is allayed by evidence that unskilled workers can, with proper supervision, perform many valuable tasks that would not otherwise be performed in the private sector. They can, for example, do landscaping and maintenance in public parks, provide transportation for the elderly and handicapped, fill potholes in city streets and replace burned-out street lamps, transplant seedlings in erosion control projects, remove graffiti from public places and

Can unskilled workers perform useful public service jobs?

FIGURE 16.5

Income by Source in a Combination NIT/Jobs Program.

Together, a small negative income tax and a public job at below minimum wage would provide a family enough income to escape poverty, without weakening work incentives significantly.

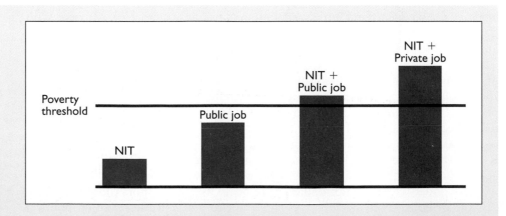

paint government buildings, recycle newspapers and containers, and staff day care centers.

This combination of a small negative income tax payment and public service employment at a subminimum wage would not be cheap. But the direct costs of existing welfare programs are also extremely large, and the indirect costs, in the form of perverse work incentives and misguided attempts to control prices, are even larger. In economic terms, dealing intelligently with the income-transfer problem may in fact prove relatively inexpensive, once society recognizes the enormous opportunity cost of failing to deal intelligently with it.

If the current approach to dealing with income transfers is highly inefficient, then there must be cash on the table that could be made available for productive uses. Yet skeptical readers may ask: If the combination of income-transfer programs just proposed would be so effective, why haven't governments around the world adopted it? Perhaps the economic logic of the proposal requires a bit of time to sink in. Such was the case with economists' proposal to auction pollution licenses, which was greeted with great hostility at first and was not adopted until decades later (see Chapter 14). In fact, many governments have shown interest in the earned-income tax credit, which was first adopted in the United States. As noted, the EITC is essentially the same as the negative income tax, except that people who are not employed are ineligible for benefits. And many cities and states have begun experiments with public service employment.

BENEFIT LEVELS: A STATE OR FEDERAL QUESTION?

An issue of current debate concerns the proper level of government for setting the welfare payments received by poor families. One side in this debate maintains that the decision is best made at the state level, because when states are free to experiment, society is more likely to discover an effective solution to the poverty problem.

Others, however, counter that allowing states to set their own welfare levels creates a budgetary prisoner's dilemma. The problem is that a state that sets its support level higher than other states will attract welfare beneficiaries, placing a greater burden on taxpayers. Compounding the problem, high-income taxpayers will be less likely to move into that state, and its current high-income taxpayers will be more likely to move out. For states that offer below-average support levels, the reverse will happen. Low-income families will be more likely to leave or not move in, and high-income families more likely to remain or move in. Thus the fear is that allowing states to set their own welfare levels will cause a race to the bottom. The end result may be a level of public assistance far too low to solve any of the important problems of poverty.

Both sides in this debate have powerful arguments. But for the time being, Congress has delegated public assistance to state governments. In 1996, it passed the **Personal Responsibility Act,** which abolished the federal government's commitment to provide cash assistance to low-income families. The new law requires the federal government to make lump-sum cash grants to the states, who are then free to spend it on AFDC benefits or other income-support programs of their own design. For each welfare recipient, the new law also sets a 5-year lifetime limit on receipt of benefits under the AFDC program.

Supporters of the Personal Responsibility Act argue that it has already reduced the nation's welfare rolls substantially and that it will encourage greater self-reliance over the long run. Skeptics fear that denial of benefits may impose severe hardships on poor children if overall economic conditions deteriorate even temporarily. This debate is unlikely to be resolved before the economy experiences its next significant downturn.

Personal Responsibility Act the 1996 federal law that transferred responsibility for welfare programs from the federal level to the state level and placed a 5-year lifetime limit on payment of AFDC benefits to any given recipient

RECAP **METHODS OF INCOME REDISTRIBUTION**

Minimum wage laws reduce total economic surplus by contracting employment. The earned-income tax credit boosts the incomes of the working poor without that drawback, but neither policy provides benefits for those who are not employed.

Other instruments in the battle against poverty include in-kind transfers such as food stamps, subsidized school lunches, Medicaid, and public housing; and cash transfers such as Aid to Families with Dependent Children. Because benefits under most of these programs are means-tested, beneficiaries often experience a net decline in income when they accept paid employment.

The negative income tax is an expanded version of the earned-income tax credit that includes those who are not employed. Combining this program with access to public service jobs would enable government to assure adequate living standards for the poor without significantly undermining work incentives.

Assigning states the responsibility of managing their own welfare programs encourages experimentation and diversity but creates an incentive for a possibly destructive competition among states to avoid attracting welfare recipients.

PAYING FOR INCOME-SUPPORT PROGRAMS: EQUITY VERSUS EFFICIENCY?

Policymakers must choose not only which policies to employ in the effort to reduce poverty and income inequality but also how to pay for them. A common proposal is to make the federal income tax more progressive. Proponents contend that such a change would not only finance additional transfers to low-income families but would also reduce the gap between the after-tax incomes of wealthy and middle-class families. Opponents of this proposal worry about the unintended side effects of increasing top tax rates.

ADVERSE EFFECTS ON INCENTIVES

Most liberals, and even many conservatives, have always considered a more progressive tax structure to be desirable on the grounds of equity. Yet many fear that steeply progressive taxes might kill the proverbial goose that lays the golden egg. Thus, as John Rawls emphasized, sufficiently high tax rates on top earners could weaken their incentive to work hard and take risks. But most empirical evidence suggests that modest increases from current tax rates would not seriously undermine the incentive to work. If tax rates at the top rose slightly, the 40 vice presidents in a large corporation who aspire to become CEO probably would not start taking Fridays off to play golf.

Another concern is that raising top marginal tax rates might compromise economic efficiency by channeling talent and effort from productive work into tax avoidance and tax evasion. Several economists saw indirect evidence for this claim when the reduction in top U.S. tax rates that was enacted in 1986 was followed by a large increase in the amount of income reported by top earners.

Without doubt, the payoff from a dollar invested in tax avoidance is higher when tax rates are high than when they are low. But although the Tax Reform Act of 1986 cut top tax rates, it also broadened the tax base significantly by eliminating a large number of deductions and exemptions. If rational tax avoiders know about a legal deduction or exemption, they will almost surely claim it whether their tax rate is 40 percent (the current top federal tax rate on income) or 60 percent. They may spend a little more effort searching out exemptions when the tax rate is higher, but their tax consultants are unlikely to advise them differently in the two cases. Thus the post-1986 increase in reported income appears more plausibly explained by the act's elimination of many existing loopholes.

Another potential efficiency loss is that higher tax rates also provide greater incentives for corporations to compensate executives with expensive perks. For instance, when top British marginal tax rates were higher than 90 percent, some companies provided top executives with chauffeur-driven Rolls Royces. For each executive, this perk might cost the company $50,000 per year, an amount most executives would hardly see fit to spend out of their own pockets. But since the after-tax value of an extra $50,000 in pay would have been less than $5,000 for these executives, a company-provided Rolls might nonetheless have seemed an attractive option.

Policymakers should weigh each of these costs carefully as they deliberate among alternative tax structures. But as we will see in the next section, a modest increase in the tax rates on top earners might also help to eliminate existing sources of economic waste.

TAX POLICY AND OCCUPATIONAL CHOICE

One way in which higher tax rates at the top could actually stimulate the economy stems from their effect on occupational choice. When an individual's reward in an occupation depends only on his or her absolute performance, the invisible hand of the market works reasonably well. That is, self-interested career choices tend to be socially efficient. But as we saw in Chapter 13, the modern economy is increasingly permeated by markets in which small differences in *relative* performance translate into large differences in reward. Given the incentives inherent in such markets, the career choices of rational individuals may not produce the largest possible economic surplus.

Increasingly, young people pursue careers in law, finance, consulting, and other professions in the hope of landing a limited number of extremely high-paying positions at the top of these professions. In the process, they forsake other careers in which pay scales at the top are less spectacular but in which additional infusions of talent appear to yield large benefits. One study estimated, for example, that while a doubling of enrollments in engineering would cause national income to grow by an additional half a percentage point each year, a doubling of enrollments in law would reduce the annual growth rate by three-tenths of a point. Other studies show that higher-quality teachers and smaller class sizes significantly increase the number of students who graduate from high school and go on to college, which would also increase the economy's growth rate. Yet average class size rose and SAT scores of entering public school teachers declined significantly between 1970 and 1990, a period during which the number of new lawyers admitted to the bar each year more than doubled.

If some labor markets attract too many contestants for a limited number of high-paying positions while other markets suffer shortages of talent, one might hope that the imbalances would fade as wages are bid up in the latter markets and driven down in the former ones. Indeed recent data show a decline in the number of law school applicants.

For two reasons, however, such adjustments are likely to fall short, even in the long run. The first is an informational problem. An intelligent decision about whether to pit one's skills against a largely unknown field of contestants for a superstar position requires a well-informed estimate of the odds of winning. Yet people's assessments of these odds tend to be notoriously inaccurate. Surveys consistently show, for example, that more than 90 percent of subjects polled think

"You will like Mr. Woofard. He has an attention-deficit disorder."

they are better than average drivers, and that more than 90 percent of workers think they are more productive than their colleagues.

Psychologists call this tendency the "Lake Wobegon Effect," after Garrison Keillor's mythical Minnesota town in which "all the children are above average." Its importance to this discussion is that it leads people to overestimate their odds of landing a superstar position. Indeed, overconfidence is likely to be especially strong in the realm of career choice, because the biggest winners are so conspicuous. Seven-figure NBA stars appear on television several times each week, but the many thousands of players who fail to make the league never attract a moment's notice. When people overestimate their chances of winning, the number of people who forsake productive occupations in traditional markets to compete in winner-take-all markets is larger than can be justified on traditional cost-benefit grounds.

The second reason for persistent overcrowding in many labor markets is a structural incentive problem we encountered in Chapter 11, the tragedy of the commons. This problem, recall, accounts for overfishing of coastal waters, overgrazing of common pastureland, and overcutting of public forests. As the next example illustrates, the same problem also accounts for why too many people crowd into certain kinds of labor markets.

Why are there too many singers and not enough teachers?

ECONOMIC NATURALIST 16.2

A small village has five residents, each of whom can earn a living in one of two ways: by singing or by teaching in a nearby town. Teachers are paid $12,000/year, but only one person receives a recording contract. The singer who is awarded this contract is paid in accordance with the quality of his or her performance, but in all cases considerably more than $12,000. The only requirement for entering the competition for a recording contract is to devote 1 year to an unpaid singing tournament. At the end of the tournament, the singer whose recording is chosen as the winner receives a payment and the losing contestants receive nothing. Thereafter, all contestants return to work as teachers.

At the beginning of the tournament, no one knows how well his or her voice compares with the voices of the other contestants, so all contestants perceive the same likelihood of winning. On average, the quality of the winning contestant's voice will be higher the more people who enter the contest (just as the fastest runner in a big high school is faster, on average, than the fastest runner in a small high school). The winning singer thus expects to receive a higher payoff when more people enter the tournament (see column 2 of Table 16.3), because a larger field of contestants generally yields a better singer. Note, however, that the expected payoff *to each contestant* decreases as the number of contestants increases, as shown in column 3 of Table 16.3. For example, with three people competing for the recording contract, each has a one-third chance of receiving a payment of $42,000, which translates into an expected payoff of $(1/3)(\$42,000) = \$14,000$. With four people competing, the expected payoff per contestant falls to $12,000. If villagers have the same tastes and are risk-neutral, how many will compete for the recording contract? What is the socially optimal number of contestants?

TABLE 16.3

The Relationship between the Number of Contestants in a Contest and the Expected Payoff

Number of contestants	Expected payment to the winner ($1,000s)	Expected payoff per contestant ($1,000s)
1	20	20
2	32	16
3	42	14
4	48	12
5	50	10

Competing for the recording contract is like buying a lottery ticket. The cost of the ticket is $12,000, the opportunity cost of not working as a teacher. The value of winning, as in many other lotteries, goes up with the number of people who enter. But whereas the prize in many lotteries rises in proportion to the number of tickets sold, the payment in this contest rises at a diminishing rate (just as the fastest runner's time improves at a diminishing rate as the size of the school increases).

By counting the number of people who are trying out for the recording contract, people can estimate their chances of winning and decide whether to enter the contest. Imagine yourself trying to choose between singing and teaching. The two occupations are equally attractive to you except for differences in the expected rate of compensation. (In other words, if both had the same expected salary, you would be indifferent between singing and teaching.) If no one else was competing for the recording contract, you would be sure to win $20,000 if you entered the contest, which is obviously better than the $12,000 you would earn as a teacher. If one other person were competing, you would get $32,000 if you won, but your chance of winning would be halved. With a 50 percent chance of winning $32,000 and a 50 percent chance of winning nothing, your expected payoff from competing in the contest would be $(1/2)\$32,000 = \$16,000$, or $4,000 more than you could earn as a teacher. Being one of two singing contestants is therefore better than a fair gamble. Armed with the cost-benefit principle, a risk-neutral person would gladly become the second contestant.

If two contestants had already announced their intention to compete for the recording contract, your entry would bring the total to three, and you would have a one-third chance of winning $42,000, or an expected payoff of $14,000. With four contestants, you would have a one-fourth chance of winning $48,000, or an expected payoff of $12,000. Finally, if all five villagers entered, you would have a one-fifth chance of winning $50,000, or an expected payoff of $10,000.

Since each villager is willing to accept a fair gamble, their decision rule will be to enter the contest as long as the expected payoff per contestant is at least equal to their $12,000 opportunity cost. In this example, a $12,000 expected payoff occurs when there are four contestants, so we would expect four people to compete for the recording contract.

With four people competing and only one working as a teacher, total village income will be $60,000/year ($48,000 for the winning singer and $12,000 for the lone teacher). That is the same as the total income the economy would have if the singer's position did not exist. Note the similarity between this result and the result in the cattle-grazing example in Chapter 11 (see Example 11.11). Indeed, the payoff structure in the singing contest is identical to the payoff structure in the tragedy of the commons. Just as the entire potential gain from the cattle industry was dissipated by excessive grazing, the entire prize in the singing contest is dissipated by the competition to obtain it.

Note too that the villagers would have generated more income if more people had become teachers and fewer had competed for the recording contract. For instance, if only two people had competed in the contest, the economy's total income would have been $68,000/year ($32,000 for the winning singer plus $36,000 for the three teachers). Two is the socially optimal number of contestants, for if a third were to enter, total income would fall to $66,000/year ($42,000 for the winning singer and $24,000 for the two teachers).

EXERCISE 16.4

In the preceding example, how many people would compete for the recording contract if the winning singer's prize increased by 20 percent?

In the singing tournament just discussed, market incentives result in a higher-quality singer than society would enjoy if labor were allocated in the socially optimal way. Thus, with four contestants (the market equilibrium number), the best singer's performance fetches $48,000 in the world recording market compared to only $32,000 with the socially optimal number, just two contestants. But the fact that total income is higher with two contestants than with four means that the market equilibrium quality of singing is too high from society's perspective. Noneconomists sometimes find such a statement jarring. ("Hey, Marge, get this: Some economist thinks the singers are too good!") But their reaction ignores the fact that the opportunity cost of higher quality in one sector of the economy is reduced output in other sectors. Society's interest would be served best by allocating additional resources to the recording sector only up to the point at which the incremental value of the resulting improvement in quality just equals the corresponding reduction in the value of other output. In the example considered, that point is reached when there are two contestants.

Once again, note the similarities between this example and the tragedy of the commons. In the cattle-grazing example, each villager decided whether to send a steer onto the commons by comparing the individual reward of doing so with the interest income forgone. Similarly, in the singing tournament example, each person decided whether to compete for the recording contract by comparing the expected reward with the teacher's salary forgone. In the commons example, the source of inefficiency was that each villager ignored the fact that sending another steer onto the commons would cause existing cattle to gain less weight. Similarly, the source of inefficiency in the singing contest is that each contestant ignores the fact that his or her entry will reduce everyone else's chances of winning. The difficulty in both the cattle and recording industries is that their payoff structures are more attractive to individuals than to society as a whole. The result is that both industries will attract too many resources.

But if misallocations arising from winner-take-all reward structures are in fact a serious problem, the solution is surely not to empower government to tell people which careers they can enter. When the rewards of competing in a market are larger for individuals than for society as a whole, the simplest solution, as Example 16.7 suggests, may be to alter the individual rewards.

How will higher taxes on top earners affect national income?

EXAMPLE 16.7

In the singing tournament described in the preceding example, how many contestants will enter the contest for a recording contract if the winning singer's income is taxed at a rate of 25 percent?

This tax is a progressive income tax, because it taxes only the winning singer's income, not the incomes of teachers. The third column in Table 16.4 shows the after-tax payment to the winning singer, and the fourth column, the expected after-tax payoff per contestant. For example, with three contestants in the contest, the winning singer will get $42,000, which means an after-tax payment of only $31,500. And since each contestant has a one-third chance to be the winner, the expected after-tax payoff is (1/3)($31,500) = $10,500 per contestant.

TABLE 16.4
A Progressive Income Tax as a Remedy for Occupational Overcrowding

Number of contestants	Expected before-tax payment to winner ($1,000s)	Expected after-tax payment to winner ($1,000s)	Expected after-tax payoff per contestant ($1,000s)
1	20	15	15
2	32	24	12
3	42	31.50	10.50
4	48	36	9
5	50	47.50	7.50

As before, an individual will enter the contest for the recording contract as long as the expected payoff is at least as large as a teacher's income, which is not taxed. That means that an individual will enter the singing contest if the after-tax expected payoff is at least $12,000. Thus the entries in the last column of Table 16.4 suggest that only two people will enter the contest—and that, recall, is the socially optimal number. Note that total income for the economy, which was $60,000 when the winning singer's income was not taxed, rises to $68,000—$36,000 for the three teachers plus $32,000 for the winning singer. (The $8,000 in income tax received by the government is included in national income because it can be used to purchase goods and services or to reduce other taxes.)

Misleading incentives like the ones in these examples confront potential contestants in a host of other high-end markets. For instance, beyond some point, an increase in the number of aspiring mergers-and-acquisitions lawyers produces much less than a proportional increase in the commissions to be had from such transactions. One law student's good fortune in landing a position in a leading Wall Street firm is largely offset by her rival's failure to land the same position. The result is an incentive gap similar to the one that encouraged too many people to compete for the recording contract: in each case, aspiring superstars tend to ignore the fact that their presence reduces other contestants' chances.

Whether misallocations of the sort just described are a serious practical problem in modern economies remains an open question. Certainly the high salaries in top law and investment banking firms appear to have lured a steadily growing number of the best and brightest into competition for those positions. And as noted, the academic qualifications of people who choose teaching as a career have been declining steadily.

To the extent that economic incentives matter at all (and economic theory tells us they do), higher taxes on top earners would discourage some people from competing for the limited number of top positions in many high-end labor markets. Moreover, those with the smallest odds of making it into the winner's circle would be the ones most likely to drop out. Thus the value of what is produced in those markets would not be reduced much by higher taxes, and any reductions would tend to be more than offset by increased output in traditional markets. Accordingly, a more progressive tax structure might help to bring about not only greater equality but also higher economic growth.

A PROGRESSIVE CONSUMPTION TAX?

Critics have also objected to progressive income taxation on the grounds that high tax rates on top earners might slow economic growth by weakening the incentive to save and invest. This is a serious concern. One way to ameliorate it is by switching from our current progressive income tax to a progressive consumption tax.

Such a tax would be straightforward to administer: Each family would pay tax not on its income but on its total spending—as measured by the simple difference between its annual income and its annual savings. And because the rich usually save and invest so much more than the poor, fairness would require that tax rates on the highest spenders be significantly higher than the current top tax rates on incomes.

For example, the current 40 percent top tax rate on income might translate into a 60 percent top rate on consumption expenditure. As shown in Table 16.5, a large standard deduction and a progressive rate structure could be employed to make sure that the tax burden of the poor and middle class remained as low as, or lower than, under the current system.

TABLE 16.5
An Illustrative Progressive Consumption Tax

Taxable consumption = Income (as currently reported to the IRS) − Annual savings − $30,000 (standard deduction for family of four)	Tax rate on each additional dollar of taxable consumption
0 – $ 39,999	20 percent
$40,000 – $ 59,999	24 percent
$60,000 – $ 79,999	28 percent
$80,000 – $ 99,999	32 percent
$100,000 – $149,999	36 percent
$150,000 – $199,999	40 percent
$200,000 – $399,999	46 percent
$400,000 – $999,999	52 percent
$1 million or more	60 percent

Under the tax shown in the table, a family of four with an annual income of $50,000 and annual savings of $5,000 would have taxable consumption of $50,000 − $5,000 − $30,000 = $15,000, and its annual tax bill would be (0.20)($15,000) = $3,000. A family of four with an annual income of $1 million and annual savings of $270,000 would have taxable consumption of $700,000, of which the first $40,000 would be taxed at 20 percent, the next $20,000 at 24 percent, and so on, for a tax bill of $306,800.

In 1943 Milton Friedman proposed a tax essentially like the one shown in Table 16.5. The federal government at that time desperately needed to raise additional revenue to finance the war effort, and Friedman argued that a progressive consumption tax was the most efficient way to do so.

To see why Friedman found this tax so attractive, note that a disproportionate share of its revenue would come from people who spend at the highest levels on consumption. Would the tax cause these people to curtail their spending? It might seem that the wealthiest individuals would simply ignore the tax, since people with billions of dollars in personal wealth could not spend it all during their lifetimes in any event. But as we saw in Chapter 5, the high prices of real estate in Manhattan induce even the city's billionaires to live in smaller houses. Would a tax that leads people to postpone building a bigger mansion cause hardship? Apparently not, and *in that fact lies a striking advantage of the progressive consumption tax*. Evidence suggests that when everyone's mansion grows a little larger, the primary effect is simply to set a new standard for how big a mansion wealthy people feel they need. Thus the current trend toward larger mansions entails an element of waste. As an individual, failure to keep pace with this trend might trigger embarrassment on social occasions, or raise troubling questions about the health of one's business. But if *everyone* postponed building a bigger mansion, such concerns would not arise.

Slowing the rate at which mansions grow larger would also generate indirect benefits for middle- and low-income families. If the biggest houses grew more slowly, so would the next biggest, and so on, all the way down. A progressive consumption tax would thus slow the rate of growth in average house size, a clear benefit to the middle-income family that already has difficulty meeting its mortgage payments.

Another beneficial effect of exempting savings from tax would be to counteract the reduction in saving that has occurred as an unintended side effect of government programs. For example, because the Social Security System replaces a significant fraction of people's earnings during retirement, they are rational to save considerably less than they would in the absence of this program. Yet Social Security is not a true savings program at all. Rather, workers pay taxes on their earnings, and the receipts are used to write checks to retirees. In the absence of Social Security, rational individuals would save much more.

Other programs such as Medicare, Medicaid, and unemployment insurance have a similar effect. Many people would save more if not for the protections these programs provide against unforeseen financial emergencies. Exempting savings from taxation can thus be justified as a way to promote saving levels closer to the ones rational consumers would have chosen under free-market conditions.

Finally, switching from a progressive income tax to a progressive consumption tax would also reduce the incentive for tax avoidance and tax evasion. Under a progressive consumption tax, a family that wants to avoid paying tax on some of its income need not participate in costly or legally questionable tax shelters. It can simply deposit that money in a savings account or mutual fund.

In sum, many of the concerns associated with the progressive income tax are reduced or eliminated by switching to a progressive consumption tax.

THE LEGISLATOR'S DILEMMA

Throughout this book, we have emphasized how the cost-benefit principle can identify ways of increasing total economic surplus. Whenever a public policy, a personal purchase, a pollution control measure, or any other action fails the cost-benefit test, an alternative can always be found that makes some people better off without harming others.

Yet government consistently implements policies that fail the cost-benefit test, especially in the realm of income redistribution. If rent controls, sugar price supports, price controls on gasoline and home heating oil, minimum wage laws, and a host of other policies reduce total economic surplus, why don't legislators replace them with more efficient measures?

A possible answer is that price and wage controls can be implemented without having to raise taxes. Thus, while policies like a negative income tax or public service employment would require funding out of general tax revenue, minimum wages and rent controls do not. Because voters fear additional tax dollars will be used to support pork barrel projects and other forms of government waste (see Chapter 15), legislators who vote for higher taxes jeopardize their political survival. Yet the mere fact that most of the costs of price and wage controls do not appear in government budgets does not make those costs any less real. Indeed, our recurring theme has been that the cost of attacking poverty with such measures is far higher than the cost of transferring income to the poor directly. The legislator's dilemma is that such inefficiencies cannot be eliminated unless the public is willing to support the necessary taxes.

REDISTRIBUTION AND COST-BENEFIT ANALYSIS

A related paradox is the question of why advocates for the poor have often been among the most vociferous opponents of cost-benefit analysis. Their objection is that because willingness to pay is based on income, cost-benefit analysis is biased in favor of high-income persons. Critics presumably have the interests of the poor in mind when they press this objection. *Yet a rational poor person would not want policy decisions to be made on any basis other than willingness to pay.*

This point is of central importance. We review the logic that supports it with the following simple example. Consider a community consisting of three voters: one rich, the other two poor. Up for decision is a proposal to switch the local public radio station from an all-music format to an all-talk format. The rich voter would be willing to pay $1,000 to see this change enacted, while the poor voters would be willing to pay $100 each to prevent it. If each voter's interests are weighted equally, the switch will not be adopted. Yet, in cost-benefit terms, failure to switch results in a net loss of $800.

Under the circumstances, little ingenuity is required to design a proposal that would command unanimous support. The programming switch could be made conditional, for example, on the rich voter paying an additional $500 in taxes, which could then be used to reduce the taxes on each poor voter by $250. This arrangement would make the rich voter $500 better off and each poor voter $150 better off than if the switch had been prevented.

Critics may respond that although such transfers would be fine in principle, the poor lack the political muscle to assure they are carried out. In an imperfect world, they argue, we get better results by resolving such issues on a one-person–one-vote basis. But this response does not withstand scrutiny. If the poor lack the political power to bargain for compensation in return for supporting a policy that harms them, what gives them the power to block that policy in the first place? Alternatively, if they have that power—and it appears they do—they necessarily have the power to bargain for compensation. After all, any policy that passes the cost-benefit test but creates net losses for the poor can be transformed into a Pareto improvement simply by making the tax system more progressive.

Critics of cost-benefit analysis are correct that measuring benefits by willingness to pay virtually assures a mix of public programs that are slanted in favor of high-income persons. But rather than abandon cost-benefit analysis, we have a better alternative. We can employ willingness-to-pay measures without apology and then use the welfare and tax system to compensate low-income families for any resulting injury. The compensation need not—indeed cannot—occur after the fact on a case-by-case basis. Rather, low-income persons could simply be granted the welfare and tax breaks required by distributive justice, *plus* additional concessions to offset their expected loss from the implementation of cost-benefit analysis using willingness to pay to measure benefits.

Rich and poor alike have an interest in making the economic pie as large as possible. Any policy that passes the cost-benefit test makes the economic pie larger. And as the efficiency principle reminds us, when the pie is larger, everyone can have a larger slice.

RECAP   **PAYING FOR INCOME-SUPPORT PROGRAMS: EQUITY VERSUS EFFICIENCY?**

Poverty is more effectively attacked by transferring additional income to the poor than by trying to regulate prices and wages. Yet many fear that the higher taxes on top earners needed to pay for such transfers will reduce effort and investment and stimulate wasteful tax avoidance. Tax avoidance can be curtailed by making the tax code simpler, and moderate increases in current top tax rates probably would not cause significant reductions in effort. The more serious concern is that higher taxes on top earners might reduce savings and investment, a danger that could be avoided by taxing consumption instead of income.

Higher tax rates on top earners have positive effects on efficiency as well as negative ones. Individuals with the highest earnings are often the winning contestants in labor markets with limited numbers of positions at the top. Such markets tend to attract too many contestants for the same reason that villagers tend to send too many cattle onto commonly owned pastureland. Higher taxes on top earners would steer marginal contestants from such markets to others in which their services would yield greater value.

Because cost-benefit analysis uses willingness to pay to measure benefits, many of its recommendations will be slanted in favor of high-income families. A democratically elected government will be unable to employ cost-benefit analysis unless it compensates low-income persons for the losses associated with that bias. Income transfers to the poor are thus a precondition for efficient economic policies.

■ SUMMARY ■

- Although incomes grew at almost 3 percent a year for all income classes during the three decades following World War II, the lion's share of income growth in the years since has been concentrated among top earners. Low-income families now have less purchasing power than in the mid-1970s.

- Apart from moral concerns about income inequality, practical reasons argue for limiting the gap between rich and poor. Poverty promotes illness and crime, both of which increase the burden on the nonpoor. Large income gaps also harm the middle class by raising the cost of pursuing basic goals.

- Policies and programs for reducing poverty include minimum wage laws, the earned-income tax credit, food stamps, subsidized school lunches, Medicaid, public housing, and Aid to Families with Dependent Children. Of

these, all but the earned-income tax credit fail to maximize total economic surplus, either by interfering with work incentives or by preventing markets from reaching equilibrium.

- The negative income tax works much like the earned-income tax credit, except that it includes those who are not employed. A combination of a small negative income tax and access to public service jobs at subminimum wages would assure adequate living standards for the poor without significantly undermining work incentives.

- Many fear that the higher taxes needed to finance such programs could curtail economic growth. This concern can be addressed by switching from the current progressive income tax to a progressive consumption tax.

▪ KEY TERMS ▪

breakeven income level (414)
earned-income tax credit (EITC) (411)
in-kind transfer (413)

means-tested (413)
negative income tax (NIT) (414)
Personal Responsibility Act (417)

poverty threshold (415)
utilitarianism (405)

▪ REVIEW QUESTIONS ▪

1. What costs does greater concentration of income among top earners impose on middle-class families?

2. Why does John Rawls believe that policies to redistribute income would command unanimous support behind a veil of ignorance?

3. Mention two self-interested reasons that a top earner might favor policies to redistribute income.

4. Why is exclusive reliance on the negative income tax unlikely to constitute a long-term solution to the poverty problem?

5. Describe the externality that makes the decision to become a contestant in a winner-take-all labor market similar to the decision to send an additional steer onto commonly owned grazing land.

▪ PROBLEMS ▪

1. Harold is one of 1,000 employees in a new start-up company. In lieu of being paid a salary, he and his coworkers were each given an equal number of shares in the company's stock. Together they own half of all stock in the company. If Harold works hard at home on company projects each evening and on weekends for the next year, the present value of the company's current and future accounting profit will grow by $1 million. How much of that gain will Harold receive? (*Hint:* As we saw in Chapter 8, a change in the present value of accounting profit will produce an equal change in the total value of the company's stock.)

2. Refer to Problem 1. If Harold's reservation price for working evenings and weekends for the next year is $10,000, what fraction of the company's stock would he have to own to induce him to put in the extra effort? On the basis of your answer, do you think the widely touted incentive effects of employee stock ownership plans may have been exaggerated?

3. Suppose the demand for unskilled labor in the Corvallis labor market is given by $W = 20 - 0.001L$, where W is the wage rate in dollars per hour and L is the quantity of labor demanded in person-hours per day. If the supply curve of unskilled labor in Corvallis is given by $W = 0.001L$, by how much will the imposition of a minimum wage at $12/hour reduce total economic surplus? Calculate the amounts by which employer surplus and worker surplus change as a result of the minimum wage.

4. Refer to Problem 3. How much would it cost the government each day to provide an earned-income tax credit under which workers as a group receive the same economic surplus as they do under the $12/hour minimum wage? (Assume for simplicity that the earned-income tax credit has no effect on labor supply.)

5. Suppose employers and workers are risk-neutral and Congress is about to enact the $12/hour minimum wage described in Problem 3. Congressional staff economists have urged legislators to consider adopting an earned-income tax credit instead. Suppose neither workers nor employers would support that proposal unless the expected value of each party's economic surplus would be at least as great as under the minimum wage. Describe an earned-income tax credit (and a tax that would raise enough money to pay for it) that would receive unanimous support from both workers and employers.

6. Suppose the equilibrium wage for unskilled workers in New Jersey is $7/hour. How will the wages and employment of unskilled workers in New Jersey change if the state legislature raises the minimum wage from $5.15/hour to $6/hour?

7. Jones, who is currently unemployed, is a participant in three means-tested welfare programs: food stamps, rent stamps, and day care stamps. Each program grants him $150/month in stamps, which can be used like cash to purchase the good or service they cover.
   a. If benefits in each program are reduced by 40 cents for each additional dollar Jones earns in the labor market, how will Jones's economic position change if he accepts a job paying $120/week?
   b. In light of your answer to part a, explain why means testing for welfare recipients has undesirable effects on work incentives.

8. What is the breakeven level of before-tax earned income in a negative income tax program with a tax credit of $5,000/year and a tax rate of 40 percent? How large a net benefit would be received by a person earning $6,000/year? How large a net tax would be paid by someone earning $15,000/year?

9. Enfield is a small economy consisting of five identical people who can earn a living in either of two ways: by acting or by growing corn. A corn farmer can earn $10,000, and the best actor in Enfield will be chosen for a film contract that pays in accordance with the performer's acting ability. The only audition requirement is to be filmed working as an unpaid actor in a theater on Broadway, which means being unable to work as a farmer. From among the filmed performances, a winner is chosen and paid. All contestants perceive the same likelihood of being chosen, and the payment to the winner increases with the number of contestants in the manner shown in the following table.

Number of contestants	Expected payment to the winner ($1,000s)	Expected payoff per contestant ($1,000s)
1	21	21
2	34	17
3	45	15
4	50	12.5
5	55	11

   a. If all villagers have the same tastes and are risk-neutral, how many will compete to become an actor? What will be the total income of the residents of Enfield?
   b. What is the socially optimal number of villagers to enter the competition? How much would village income be if only the optimal number entered?

10. Refer to Problem 9. What is the smallest lump-sum tax on the winner's earnings that would ensure that the optimal number of villagers entered the competition?

■ ANSWERS TO IN-CHAPTER EXERCISES ■

16.1 Since Sue's reservation wage is $10/hour, she must be paid at least that amount before she will accept the job. The largest dorm population for which she will accept is thus 10 residents, since her share in that case would be exactly $10/hour.

16.2 With perfectly inelastic demand, employment would remain at 5,000 person-hours/day, so the minimum wage would cause no reduction in economic surplus.

16.3 The breakeven level falls from $12,000/year to $8,000.

16.4 With a 20 percent increase in the winning singer's pay, the payoffs and expected payoffs are now as shown in the following table. Contestants will continue to enter as long as the expected payoff is at least $12,000, so five contestants will now compete for the recording contract.

Number of contestants	Expected payment to the winner ($1,000s)	Expected payoff per contestant ($1,000s)
1	24	24
2	38.4	19.2
3	50.4	16.8
4	57.6	14.4
5	60	12

A

Absolute advantage. One person has an absolute advantage over another if he or she takes fewer hours to perform a task than the other person.

Accounting profit. The difference between a firm's total revenue and its explicit costs.

Adverse selection. The pattern in which insurance tends to be purchased disproportionately by those who are most costly for companies to insure.

Allocative function of price. Changes in prices direct resources away from overcrowded markets and toward markets that are underserved.

Asymmetric information. Situations in which buyers and sellers are not equally well informed about the characteristics of goods and services for sale in the marketplace.

Attainable point. Any combination of goods that can be produced using currently available resources.

Average benefit. Total benefit of undertaking n units of an activity divided by n.

Average cost. Total cost of undertaking n units of an activity divided by n.

B

Barrier to entry. Any force that prevents firms from entering a new market.

Basic elements of a game. The players, the strategies available to each player, and the payoffs each player receives for each possible combination of strategies.

Better-than-fair gamble. A gamble whose expected value is positive.

Breakeven income level. Under a negative income tax, the level of before-tax income at which a family's tax liability exactly offsets its initial tax credit.

C

Cartel. A coalition of firms that agrees to restrict output for the purpose of earning an economic profit.

Change in demand. A shift of the entire demand curve.

Change in supply. A shift of the entire supply curve.

Change in the quantity demanded. A movement along the demand curve that occurs in response to a change in price.

Change in the quantity supplied. A movement along the supply curve that occurs in response to a change in price.

Coase theorem. If at no cost people can negotiate the purchase and sale of the right to perform activities that cause externalities, they can always arrive at efficient solutions to the problems caused by externalities.

Collective good. A good or service that, to at least some degree, is nonrival but excludable.

Commitment device. A way of changing incentives so as to make otherwise empty threats or promises credible.

Commitment problem. A situation in which people cannot achieve their goals because of an inability to make credible threats or promises.

Comparable worth legislation. Legislation that would set wages for a job not by market forces but by collective judgments about the social value of the job.

Comparative advantage. One person has a comparative advantage over another if his or her opportunity cost of performing a task is lower than the other person's opportunity cost.

Compensating wage differential. A difference in the wage rate—negative or positive—that reflects the attractiveness of a job's working conditions.

Complements. Two goods are complements in consumption if an increase in the price of one causes a leftward shift in the demand curve for the other.

Constant. A quantity that is fixed in value.

Constant returns to scale. A production process is said to have constant returns to scale if, when all inputs are changed by a given proportion, output changes by the same proportion.

Consumer surplus. The economic surplus gained by the buyers of a product as measured by the cumulative difference between their respective reservation prices and the price they actually paid.

Costly-to-fake principle. To communicate information credibly to a potential rival, a signal must be costly or difficult to fake.

Cost-plus regulation. A method of regulation under which the regulated firm is permitted to charge a price equal to its explicit costs of production plus a markup to cover the opportunity cost of resources provided by the firm's owners.

Credible promise. A promise to take an action that is in the promiser's interest to keep.

Credible threat. A threat to take an action that is in the threatener's interest to carry out.

Cross-price elasticity of demand for two goods. The percentage by which the quantity demanded of the first good changes in response to a 1 percent change in the price of the second.

Crowding out. Occurs when private firms cancel planned investment projects because of higher interest rates caused by government borrowing.

Customer discrimination. The willingness of consumers to pay more for a product produced by members of a favored group, even if the quality of the product is unaffected.

Deadweight loss. The deadweight loss caused by a policy is the reduction in economic surplus that results from adoption of that policy.

Decision tree (or game tree). A diagram that describes the possible moves in a game in sequence and lists the payoffs that correspond to each possible combination of moves.

Demand curve. A curve or schedule showing the total quantity of a good that buyers wish to buy at each price.

Dependent variable. A variable in an equation whose value is determined by the value taken by another variable in the equation.

Disappearing political discourse. The theory that people who support a position may remain silent, because speaking out would create a risk of being misunderstood.

Dominant strategy. One that yields a higher payoff no matter what the other players in a game choose.

Dominated strategy. Any other strategy available to a player who has a dominant strategy.

E

Earned-income tax credit (EITC). A policy under which low-income workers receive credits on their federal income tax.

Economic loss. An economic profit that is less than zero.

Economic profit. The difference between a firm's total revenue and the sum of its explicit and implicit costs; also called excess profit.

Economic rent. That part of the payment for a factor of production that exceeds the owner's reservation price, the price below which the owner would not supply the factor.

Economic surplus. The economic surplus from taking any action is the benefit of taking the action minus its cost.

Economics. The study of how people make choices under conditions of scarcity and of the results of those choices for society.

Efficiency, or economic efficiency. Condition that occurs when all goods and services are produced and consumed at their respective socially optimal levels.

Efficient (or Pareto-efficient). A situation is efficient if no change is possible that will help some people without harming others.

Efficient markets hypothesis. The theory that the current price of stock in a corporation reflects all relevant information about its current and future earnings prospects.

Efficient point. Any combination of goods for which currently available resources do not allow an increase in the production of one good without a reduction in the production of the other.

Efficient quantity. The efficient quantity of any good is the quantity that maximizes the economic surplus that results from producing and consuming the good.

Elastic. The demand for a good is elastic with respect to price if its price elasticity of demand is greater than 1.

Employer discrimination. An arbitrary preference by an employer for one group of workers over another.

Equation. A mathematical expression that describes the relationship between two or more variables.

Equilibrium. A stable, balanced, or unchanging situation in which all forces at work within a system are canceled by others.

Equilibrium price and equilibrium quantity. The price and quantity of a good at the intersection of the supply and demand curves for the good.

Excess demand (or shortage). The difference between the quantity supplied and the quantity demanded when the price of a good lies below the equilibrium price; buyers are dissatisfied when there is excess demand.

Excess supply (or surplus). The difference between the quantity supplied and the quantity demanded when the price of a good exceeds the equilibrium price; sellers are dissatisfied when there is excess supply.

Expected value of a gamble. The sum of the possible outcomes of the gamble multiplied by their respective probabilities.

Explicit costs. The actual payments a firm makes to its factors of production and other suppliers.

External benefit (or positive externality). A benefit of an activity received by people other than those who pursue the activity.

External cost (or negative externality). A cost of an activity that falls on people other than those who pursue the activity.

Externality. An external cost or benefit of an activity.

F

Factor of production. An input used in the production of a good or service.

Fair gamble. A gamble whose expected value is zero.

First-dollar insurance coverage. Insurance that pays all expenses generated by the insured activity.

Fixed cost. A cost that does not vary with the level of an activity

Fixed factor of production. An input whose quantity cannot be altered in the short run.

Free-rider problem. An incentive problem in which too little of a good or service is produced because nonpayers cannot be excluded from using it.

G

Game tree. *See* **Decision tree.**

H

Head tax. A tax that collects the same amount from every taxpayer.

Health maintenance organization (HMO). A group of physicians that provides health services to individuals and families for a fixed annual fee.

Human capital. An amalgam of factors such as education, training, experience, intelligence, energy, work habits, trustworthiness, initiative, and others that affect the value of a worker's marginal product.

Human capital theory. A theory of pay determination that says a worker's wage will be proportional to his or her stock of human capital.

Hurdle method of price discrimination. The practice by which a seller offers a discount to all buyers who overcome some obstacle.

I

Imperfectly competitive firm. A firm that has at least some control over the market price of its product.

Implicit costs. All the firm's opportunity costs of the resources supplied by the firm's owners.

Income elasticity of demand. The percentage by which a good's quantity demanded changes in response to a 1 percent change in income.

Increasing returns to scale. A production process is said to have increasing returns to scale if, when all inputs are changed by a given proportion, output changes by more than that proportion; also called *economies of scale*.

Independent variable. A variable in an equation whose value determines the value taken by another variable in the equation.

Inefficient point. Any combination of goods for which currently available resources enable an increase in the production of one good without a reduction in the production of the other.

Inelastic. The demand for a good is inelastic with respect to price if its price elasticity of demand is less than 1.

Inferior good. A good whose demand curve shifts leftward when the incomes of buyers increase.

In-kind transfer. A payment made not in the form of cash but in the form of a good or service.

Invisible hand theory. A theory stating that the actions of independent, self-interested buyers and sellers will often result in the most efficient allocation of resources.

L

Labor union. A group of workers who bargain collectively with employers for better wages and working conditions.

Law of diminishing returns. A property of the relationship between the amount of a good or service produced and the amount of a variable factor required to produce it; the law says that when some factors of production are fixed, increased production of the good eventually requires ever larger increases in the variable factor.

Lemons model. George Akerlof's explanation of how asymmetric information tends to reduce the average quality of goods offered for sale.

Logrolling. The practice whereby legislators support one another's legislative proposals.

Long run. A period of time of sufficient length that all the firm's factors of production are variable.

M

Macroeconomics. The study of the performance of national economies and the policies that governments use to try to improve that performance.

Marginal benefit. The marginal benefit of an activity is the increase in total benefit that results from carrying out one additional unit of the activity.

Marginal cost. The marginal cost of an activity is the increase in total cost that results from carrying out one additional unit of the activity.

Marginal labor cost. The amount by which a monopsonist's total wage bill goes up if it hires an extra worker.

Marginal product of labor. The additional output a firm gets by employing one additional unit of labor.

Marginal revenue. The change in a firm's total revenue that results from a one-unit change in output.

Marginal utility. The additional utility gained from consuming an additional unit of a good.

Market. The market for any good consists of all buyers or sellers of that good.

Market equilibrium. Occurs when all buyers and sellers are satisfied with their respective quantities at the market price.

Market power. A firm's ability to raise the price of a good without losing all its sales.

Means-tested. A benefit program is means-tested if its benefit level declines as the recipient earns additional income.

Microeconomics. The study of individual choice under scarcity and its implications for the behavior of prices and quantities in individual markets.

Monopolistically competitive firm. One of a large number of firms that produce slightly differentiated products that are reasonably close substitutes for one another.

Monopsony. A market with only a single buyer.

N

Nash equilibrium. Any combination of strategies in which each player's strategy is his or her best choice, given the other players' strategies.

Natural monopoly. A monopoly that results from economies of scale (increasing returns to scale).

Negative externality. *See* **External cost.**

Negative income tax. A system under which the government would grant every citizen a cash payment each year, financed by an additional tax on earned income.

Nominal price. Absolute price of a good in dollar terms.

Nonexcludable good. A good that is difficult, or costly, to exclude nonpayers from consuming.

Nonrival good. A good whose consumption by one person does not diminish its availability for others.

Normal good. A good whose demand curve shifts rightward when the incomes of buyers increase.

Normal profit. The opportunity cost of the resources supplied by the firm's owners; Normal profit = Accounting profit − Economic profit.

O

Oligopolist. A firm that produces a product for which only a few rival firms produce close substitutes.

Opportunity cost. The opportunity cost of an activity is the value of the next-best alternative that must be forgone to undertake the activity.

Optimal combination of goods. The affordable combination that yields the highest total utility.

P

Pareto-efficient. *See* **Efficient.**

Payoff matrix. A table that describes the payoffs in a game for each possible combination of strategies.

Perfect hurdle. One that completely segregates buyers whose reservation prices lie above some threshold from others whose reservation prices lie below it, imposing no cost on those who jump the hurdle.

Perfectly competitive market. A market in which no individual supplier has significant influence on the market price of the product.

Perfectly discriminating monopolist. A firm that charges each buyer exactly his or her reservation price.

Perfectly elastic demand. The demand for a good is perfectly elastic with respect to price if its price elasticity of demand is infinite.

Perfectly elastic supply curve. A supply curve whose elasticity with respect to price is infinite.

Perfectly inelastic demand. The demand for a good is perfectly inelastic with respect to price if its price elasticity of demand is zero.

Perfectly inelastic supply curve. A supply curve whose elasticity with respect to price is zero.

Personal Responsibility Act. The 1996 federal law that transferred responsibility for welfare programs from the federal level to the state level and placed a 5-year lifetime limit on payment of AFDC benefits to any given recipient.

Pork barrel spending. A public expenditure that is larger than the total benefit it creates but that is favored by a legislator because his or her constituents benefit from the expenditure by more than their share of the resulting extra taxes.

Positional arms control agreement. An agreement in which contestants attempt to limit mutually offsetting investments in performance enhancement.

Positional arms race. A series of mutually offsetting investments in performance enhancement that is stimulated by a positional externality.

Positional externality. Occurs when an increase in one person's performance reduces the expected reward of another's in situations in which reward depends on relative performance.

Positive externality. *See* **External benefit.**

Poverty threshold. The level of income below which the federal government classifies a family as poor.

Present value. When the annual interest rate is r, the present value (PV) of a payment M to be received T years from now is the amount that would have to be deposited today at an annual interest rate r to generate a balance of M after T years: $PV = M/(1 + r)^T$.

Price ceiling. A maximum allowable price, specified by law.

Price discrimination. The practice of charging different buyers different prices for essentially the same good or service.

Price elasticity of demand. The percentage change in the quantity demanded of a good or service that results from a 1 percent change in its price.

Price elasticity of supply. The percentage change in the quantity supplied that will occur in response to a 1 percent change in the price of a good or service.

Price floor. A law or regulation that guarantees that suppliers will receive at least a specified amount for their product.

Price setter. A firm with at least some latitude to set its own price.

Price taker. A firm that has no influence over the price at which it sells its product.

Prisoner's dilemma. A game in which each player has a dominant strategy, and when each plays it, the resulting payoffs are smaller than if each had played a dominated strategy.

Producer surplus. The economic surplus gained by the sellers of a product as measured by the cumulative difference between the price received and their respective reservation prices.

Production possibilities curve. A graph that describes the maximum amount of one good that can be produced for every possible level of production of the other good.

Profit. The total revenue a firm receives from the sale of its product minus all costs—explicit and implicit—incurred in producing it.

Profit-maximizing firm. A firm whose primary goal is to maximize the difference between its total revenues and total costs.

Progressive tax. One in which the proportion of income paid in taxes rises as income rises.

Proportional income tax. One under which all taxpayers pay the same proportion of their incomes in taxes.

Public good. A good or service that, to at least some degree, is both nonrival and nonexcludable.

Pure commons good. One for which nonpayers cannot easily be excluded and for which each unit consumed by one person means one less unit available for others.

Pure monopoly. The only supplier of a unique product with no close substitutes.

Pure private good. One for which nonpayers can easily be excluded and for which each unit consumed by one person means one less unit available for others.

Pure public good. A good or service that, to a high degree, is both nonrival and nonexcludable.

R

Rational person. Someone with well-defined goals who tries to fulfill those goals as best he or she can.

Rationing function of price. Changes in price that distribute scarce goods to those consumers who value them most highly.

Real price. Dollar price of a good relative to the average dollar price of all other goods and services.

Regressive tax. A tax under which the proportion of income paid in taxes declines as income rises.

Rent-seeking. The socially unproductive efforts of people or firms to win a prize.

Reservation price. The highest price someone is willing to pay to obtain any good or service, or the lowest payment someone would accept for giving up a good or performing a service.

Risk-averse person. Someone who would refuse any fair gamble.

Risk-neutral person. Someone who would accept any gamble that is fair or better.

S

Short run. A period of time sufficiently short that at least some of the firm's factors of production are fixed.

Shortage. *See* **Excess demand.**

Slope. In a straight line, the ratio of the vertical distance the straight line travels between any two points (*rise*) to the corresponding horizontal distance (*run*).

Statistical discrimination. The practice of making judgments about the quality of people, goods, or services based on the characteristics of the groups to which they belong.

Substitutes. Two goods are substitutes in consumption if an increase in the price of one causes a rightward shift in the demand curve for the other.

Sunk cost. A cost that is beyond recovery at the moment a decision must be made.

Supply curve. A curve or schedule showing the total quantity of a good that sellers wish to sell at each price.

Surplus. *See* **Excess supply.**

T

Time value of money. The fact that a given dollar amount today is equivalent to a larger dollar amount in the future, because the money can be invested in an interest-bearing account in the meantime.

Total economic surplus. The sum of all the individual economic surpluses gained by buyers and sellers who participate in the market.

Total expenditure = Total revenue. The dollar amount consumers spend on a product is equal to the dollar amount sellers receive.

Tragedy of the commons. The tendency for a resource that has no price to be used until its marginal benefit falls to zero.

U

Ultimatum bargaining game. One in which the first player has the power to confront the second player with a take-it-or-leave-it offer.

Unattainable point. Any combination of goods that cannot be produced using currently available resources.

Unit elastic. The demand for a good is unit elastic with respect to price if its price elasticity of demand is equal to 1.

Utilitarianism. A moral theory in which the right course of action is the one that results in the highest total utility.

V

Value of marginal product of labor. The dollar value of the additional output a firm gets by employing one additional unit of labor.

Variable. A quantity that is free to take a range of different values.

Variable cost. A cost that varies with the level of an activity.

Variable factor of production. An input whose quantity can be altered in the short run.

Vertical intercept. The value taken by the dependent variable when the independent variable equals zero.

W

Winner-take-all labor market. One in which small differences in human capital translate into large differences in pay.

Workers' compensation. A government insurance system that provides benefits to workers who are injured on the job.

A

Ability, conspicuous consumption as sign of, 309–310
Absolute advantage, 50
Abstract model, 8
Acceptance threshold, 258
Accounting profit, 198–199
    compared to economic profit, 196–197
    definition, 196
Adverse selection, 312
Advertising
    spending on, 248–250
    television costs, 308–309
Advertising copywriters, 337, 342–343
Agassi, Andre, 43–44
Aggregate income, 403
Aid to Families with Dependent Children, 413, 417
Airline industry, 43
    advertising spending, 248–250
    barriers to entry, 204
    and hurdle method, 242
    net cost of compensation policy, 181
    overbooking, 179–182
    regulated, 208–209
Akerlof, George A., 306
Allen, Paul, 113
Allocative function of price, 203–204
    with free market entry/exit, 204–205
Alternatives, next-best, 32–33
Aluminum prices, 149
Amazon.com, 301
American Cancer Society, 337, 338
Anabolic steroids, 287
Analyze This, 247, 259
Antipoverty programs, 209; *see also* Income-support programs
Antitrust laws, 234
    history of, 352–353
Apple Computer, 335
Arbitration agreements, 290
Arcnet, Inc., 338–339
Aristotle, 76
Arms races, 288–289
Asprey and Garrard, 401
Asymmetric information, 305–312
    adverse selection, 310
    conspicuous consumption, 309–310
    costly-to-fake principle, 308–309
    credibility problem, 307–308
    lemons model, 306–307
    statistical discrimination, 310–312
AT&T, 222
Attainable point, 57
Auctions of pollution permits, 364–365

Automatic teller machines, 17
Automobile industry, 17
    and gas prices, 114
    tax on cars, 184
    United Kingdom, 115
Average benefit, 39–44
Average cost, 39–44, 225
    pitfalls of using, 44
Average-marginal distinction, 39–44
    fixed versus variable cost, 42–44
    resource allocation, 41–42
Aviation Consumer Action Project, 181–182

B

Banifoot, Kösten, 39, 40
Barnes and Noble, 301
Barriers to entry, 204
Baseball, 53–54, 290
Baseball players' salaries, 334–335
Basic elements of a game, 248–249
Basketball, 156
Baskin-Robbins, 115
Battle, Kathleen, 333
Bazerman, Max, 392
Behavioral choices, 341–342
Benefit levels, state or federal issue, 417
Bennett, Danny, 247
Bennett, Tony, 247, 256, 259
Bentham, Jeremy, 106
Berkeley, Calif., 115–116
Best-managed firms, 212
Better-than-fair gamble, 303
Bhopal, India, 337
Bhutan, 49
Billionaires, 403
BMW, 17, 105–106, 115, 310, 338–339, 403
Boeing 747, 207
Borders Group, 301
Boston Red Sox, 53
Braille dots, 17
Breakeven income level, 414
Browne, Harry, 377–378
Budget constraint, 109
Budget share, 124–125
Buffett, Warren, 309
Burger King, 85, 339
Business negotiations, 242–248
    Coase theorem, 276–277
    commitment problems, 262–263
    credible threats and promises, 259–262
    strategic role of preferences, 263–266
    ultimate bargaining game, 257–259

Buyers
    asymmetric information, 305–312
    full information assumption, 298
    and hurdle method, 238–242
    optimal amount of information, 300–305
    price discrimination, 235–242
By-products, 386

C

Cable television companies, 350
Cadillac, 242
California
    Proposition 13, 393–394
    water shortage, 105–106
Camel Cigarettes, 337
Cameron, James, 129
Campaign spending limits, 289–290
Capital cost, 142
Capitalist economy, 76
Capital punishment, 313–314
Car heaters, 17
Car insurance, 310–311
Carrey, Jim, 156
Cartel agreements, 252–254
    payoff matrix, 253
    temptation to violate, 253
Cartels, 252
    and antitrust laws, 352
Carter administration, 349
Cash on the table, 86
CD players, 17
Cellular phone companies, 393
Central Intelligence Agency, 337
Central planning, 75–76
Change in demand, 88
Change in quantity demanded, 88
Change in quantity supplied, 88, 147
Change in supply, 88
Chaplin, Charlie, 64
Charitable giving, 385
Chevrolet, 242
Chief executive officer compensation, 333, 403
    reasons for increase in, 335–336
China, 75, 314
Choices
    inconsistent, 11
    and preferences, 265
    rational or irrational, 11–13
Chrysler Corporation, 251–252
Churchill, Winston, 390
Cigarette advertising, 254–255
Cigarette taxes, 125

Civil Aeronautics Administration, 208
Clapton, Eric, 7–8
Clavell, James, 334
Clayton Antitrust Act, 352
Clinton, Bill, 68, 377
Clotfelter, Charles, 372n
Coase, Ronald, 276–277
Coase theorem, 275–279
Collective goods, 379
Commitment devices, 262
Commitment problems, 262–263
    preferences as solution to, 265–266
Communist countries, 75
Comparable worth issue, 342–343
Comparable worth legislation, 342
Comparative advantage, 50
    definition, 50
    and international trade, 65–68
    noneconomic factors, 54
    principle of, 51–54
    and production possibilities curve, 55–58
    sources of, 54–55
Compensation; see also Salary, Wages
    explaining differences in, 330–339
    in-kind, 339
Competitive labor markets
    explaining earnings differences, 330–339
    general rule, 323
    wage and salary determinants, 322–325
Complements, 92
Computer game producers, 225–227
Computer programmers, 328–329
Computers
    free software, 16–17
    operating systems, 140
    RAM, 15
Conan Doyle, Arthur, 32
Conspicuous consumption, 309–310
Constant, 22
Constant returns to scale, 223–224
Consumer Reports, 298
Consumers
    information-seekers, 298
    optimal amount of information, 300–305
    reliance on others for information,
        298–300
Consumer spending, recent trends, 402–404
Consumer surplus, 170
    and hurdle method, 240–241
Consumption
    and marginal utility, 107–108
    and utility, 107
Consumption tax, 424–425
Cook, Philip J., 313n, 372n
Copernicus, N., 76
Copyright law, 204, 221
Corporate earnings forecasts, 214
Corvette, 307
Cosmetic surgery, 292
Cost-benefit analysis, 1, 4
Cost-benefit principle, 4–5, 14
    applied to price controls, 174–179
    applying, 5–13
        economic surplus, 6–7
        graphical representation, 11–13
        opportunity cost, 7–8
        pursuing uncertainties, 8–9

rationality and imperfect decision
    makers, 9–11
    reservation price, 6
    role of economic models, 8
average-marginal distinction, 39–44
cost of next-best alternative, 32–33
in crime control, 370–371
and economic naturalism, 14–18
failure to ignore sunk costs, 36–39
failure with income redistribution,
    425–427
in health care delivery, 356–358
ignoring opportunity cost, 32–36
and law of demand, 105–106
market equilibrium and efficiency,
    166–169
overview, 13
for recycling, 136–139
time value of money, 34–35
Cost-benefit test, 300–301
Costly-to-fake principle, 308–309
Cost-plus regulation, 351
Costs, 4; see also Average cost; Fixed costs;
    Implicit costs; Marginal cost; Opportunity
    cost; Start-up costs; Total cost
    relative insignificance of, 44
Cost-saving innovations, 206–207
Credibility problem, 307–308
Credible promises, 259–262
Credible threats, 259–262
Crime control, 370–371
Cross-price elasticity of demand, 127
Crowding out, 394–395
Crystal, Billy, 247
Cuba, 75
Customer discrimination, 340

D

Dahl, Roald, 31
Dartmouth College, 116
David Letterman Show, 378
Deadweight loss
    of monopoly, 234
    of taxes, 186, 187–198, 394
Death penalty issue, 313–314
Decision making
    allocating fixed income, 108–110
    imperfect, 9–11
    inconsistent, 11
    rational spending rule, 110–112
    using cost-benefit principle, 8
Decision rule
    for monopolists, 231–233
    for perfectly competitive firms, 228
Decision tree, 257
    for kidnapper game, 260–261
    for remote office game, 261
Deductibles, health insurance, 359
Dell/Delacourt, 334
Demand; see also Law of demand; Price
    elasticity of demand; Supply
    allocating fixed income, 108–110
    applying rational spending rule, 113–116
    with budget constraint, 109
    changes in, 88
    concept of utility, 106–108

effect of income, 112
effect of income decrease, 94–95
effect of income distribution, 115–116
effect of prices of substitutes, 112
elastic, 123
examples, 73–74
factors causing increase in, 96
and income differences, 115
and income increase, 93–94
inelastic, 123
maximum total utility, 110
optimal combination of goods, 110
origin of wants, 129
rational spending rule, 110–112
shaped by social forces, 129
unit elastic, 123
wants translated into, 106–113
Demand curve, 85; see also Individual
    demand curve; Market demand curve
    definition, 78
    digital, 170, 171
    for hospital care, 357
    identical, 117
    for inferior goods, 94
    for labor, 322
    and marginal revenue, 231
    and market equilibrium, 79–81
    for monopolists, 232–233
    for normal goods, 94
    of perfectly competitive firms, 140–141
    perfectly elastic, 128
    perfectly inelastic, 128
    in perfect versus imperfect competition,
        222
    for public goods, 383–385
    quantity demanded and all costs, 105
    for rental housing, 176–177
    response to regulation, 86
    rules governing, 95–97
    seasonal, 355
    shifts in, 92–95
    straight-line, 117–119, 127
    and total expenditure, 119–122
Demand for labor, 329
DeNiro, Robert, 247
Department of Agriculture, 415
Dependent variables, 22
Differential investment in crime control, 370
Digital supply/demand curves, 170, 171
Diminishing marginal utility, 107–108
Diminishing returns, 141–142
Disappearing political discourse, 313–314
Discount pricing, 238–242, 352–353
Discrimination in labor market, 339–344
    comparable worth issue, 342–343
    customer discrimination, 340
    by employers, 340
    sources of wage gaps, 340–342
Division of labor, 62–64
Dodge Colt, 310
Dominant strategy, 249, 251
Dominated strategy, 249, 251
Dow Chemical, 337, 338
Downsizing, 165
Drug legalization issue, 314
Drug-related crime, 103–104
Dylan, Bob, 7–8

E

Earned-income tax credit, 176, 411–413
Earnings, explaining differences in, 330–339; *see also* Compensation; Wages
Earnings growth, 402–403
eBay, 299–300
Economic efficiency, 87
Economic loss, 199
    effect on market exit, 202
    in regulated industries, 207–209
Economic naturalism, 14–18
Economic profit
    calculating, 197–198
    central role of, 196–201
    compared to accounting profit, 196–197
    definition, 196
    versus economic rent, 205–206
    effect of market forces, 201–202
    of natural monopolies, 352–353
    in regulated industries, 207–209
Economic rent, 205–206; *see also* Rent-seeking
Economics
    definition, 4
    main branches of, 13
Economic superpower, 65–66
Economic surplus, 6–7, 13
    calculating, 169–172
    and deadweight loss of monopoly, 234
    definition, 169
    effect of better information, 299–300
    effect of taxes collected from sellers, 185–187
    from excess supply, 168
    first-come, first-served policies, 179–183
    loss from pay-per-view fees, 387
    lost from taxes, 395
    maximization, 284–285
    opportunity for, 167
    and price ceilings, 174–178
    and price floors, 178–179
    reduced by minimum wage, 411–412
    and rent controls, 176–178
    unregulated home heating oil market, 174
Economic system
    central planning versus markets, 75–76
    invisible hand theory, 196, 203–207
    property rights, 284–286
Economies of scale, 223–224
    with fixed costs, 224–227
    total and average costs, 225
Economists, against rent control, 76, 84
Edell, Julie, 372n
Efficiency, 87
    compared to other goals, 172–173
    first-come, first-served policies, 179–183
    and market equilibrium, 166–169
    of price adjustments, 174–183
    of price ceilings, 174–178
    primary economic goal, 173
    and taxes, 183–189
Efficiency principle, 87–88
    in income-support programs, 418–427
    in price floors, 178–179
Efficient market hypothesis, 211–213
Efficient point, 58

Efficient quantity, 87
Eisner, Michael, 336
Elastic demand, 123
Elasticity of demand, 127
Electric utility rates, 355–356
Employers
    agents of discrimination, 340
    discrimination by, 340
    in-kind compensation, 339
    reservation price for workers, 328
Employment
    compensatory wage differentials, 336–339
    effect of minimum wage, 410
    effect of wage increases, 325
    labor force participation, 342
    for monopsonist, 326
    requiring similar ability/experience, 337
Environmental pollutants, 280
Environmental regulations, 362–365
Equation, 22
    constructed from table, 26–28
    constructing, 22–23
    derived from graph, 24
    graph of, 23–24
Equilibrium, 79–81
    in labor market, 328–330
    Nash equilibrium, 249–250
Equilibrium price, 79–87
    and change in technology, 91
    and complements, 92
    effect of shift in demand/supply, 96–97
    and fall in input price, 90–91
    and rise in input price, 89–90
    and seasonal price movements, 97
    and substitutes, 92–93
Equilibrium principle, 88
    effect of more than normal profit, 200–202
    and social optimum, 213–215
    and wage gaps, 340
Equilibrium quantity, 79–81, 85
    and change in technology, 91
    and complements, 92
    effect of shift in demand/supply, 96–97
    effect of taxes, 184
    with fall in input prices, 90–91
    with rise in input prices, 89–90
    and seasonal price movements, 97
    and substitutes, 92–93
Equilibrium wage, 332
Essential inputs, 146
Excess demand, 80
    and surplus-enhancing transaction, 167
Excess supply, 80
    and surplus-enhancing transaction, 168
Exchange
    and opportunity cost, 50–55
    principle of comparative advantage, 51–54
Exclusive contracting, 351–352
Expected value of a gamble, 303
Explicit costs, 196, 198–199
External benefits, 273–281
External costs, 273–281
Externalities, 273–281, 286–292
    Coase theorem, 275–279

    effect on resource allocation, 274–275
    environmental policy, 362–365
    government role, 388
    graphically portrayed, 275
    legal remedies, 279–281
Exxon Corporation, 337

F

Fabrikant, Geraldine, 247n
Factors of production, 141
    economies of scale, 223–224
    fixed or variable, 141–142
Fair gamble, 303
Fairness, 404–405
Falkland Islands war, 265
Family location decisions, 340–341
Family stability, 413
Farm price supports, 178–179
Fashion norms, 290–291
Federal government, 389
Firm, The (Grisham), 339
Firms
    best-managed, 212
    externalities from, 273–281
    imperfectly competitive, 140, 221
    present value of future costs and benefits, 210
    price setters, 221
    price takers, 140, 206
    profit-maximizing, 140
    shutdown condition, 144–145
    sources of market power, 223–227
    unionized, 333
First Amendment, 280
First-come, first-served policies, 179–183
First-dollar health insurance coverage, 359
Fiscal policy, crowding out effect, 394–395
Fixed costs, 42–44
    with economies of scale, 224–227
Fixed factors of production, 141–142
Fixed income
    allocating, 108–110
    budget constraint, 109
Florida Power and Light, 222
Food costs, 415
Football, 287
Forbes Four Hundred, 403
Ford Escort, 339
Ford Excursion, 114, 409
Fortune, 212
Free-market economy, 76
    functions of price, 203–204
    skepticism about, 165–166
Free speech laws, 280
Free-trade agreements, 68
Frequent-flyer miles, 33–34
Friedman, Milton, 393, 414, 425
Funding by donation, 385

G

Gainesville, Fla., 353–355
Gains from trade, 67, 68
Gamble inherent in search, 303
Gambling, 371–372

Game theory
  basic elements of a game, 248–249
  commitment problems, 262–263
  credible threats and promises, 259–262
  dominant strategy, 249, 251
  dominated strategy, 249, 251
  Nash equilibrium, 249–250
  payoff matrix, 248
  prisoner's dilemma, 251–256
  strategic role of preferences, 263–266
  and timing, 256–263
  ultimate bargaining, 257–258
Game tree, 257
Garbage collectors, 336
Gasoline tax, 349
Gas prices
  in United Kingdom, 115
  in United States, 114
Gated private communities, 386
Gates, Bill, 5, 205
General Motors, 242, 251–252
George, Henry, 188
Gibson, Mel, 334
Gift-giving, 338–339
Goldman Sachs, 334
Goods; see also Private goods; Public goods
  allocating fixed income between, 108–110
  inferior, 94
  normal, 94
  optimal combination of, 110
  rational spending rule, 110–112
Gould, Stephen Jay, 54n
Government
  additional functions, 388–390
  disadvantages of excessive reliance on, 385
  disregard of efficiency principle, 410
  externalities and property rights, 388
  local, state, or federal, 389
  monopoly on violence, 377
  provision of public goods
    nature of public goods, 378–380
    paying for public goods, 380–382
  sources of inefficiency
    pork-barrel legislation, 390–391
    rent-seeking, 391–393
  subsidizing positive externalities, 281
  taxing power, 377
  and taxpayer revolt, 393–394
Government franchising, 224
Government licensing, 224
Government waste, 393–394
Graf, Steffi, 286
Graph
  changes in slope and vertical intercept, 25–26
  constructed from table, 26–28
  deriving equation from, 24
  of externalities, 275
  of marginal cost, 145–146
  of marginal revenue, 230
  of price elasticity of supply, 152
  slope of a line, 24
  of straight-line equation, 23–24
  vertical intercept, 23–24
Greenspan, Alan, 186
Grisham, John, 339
Grocery stores, 288–289

H

Hanover, N. H., 115–116
Head tax, 381
Health care delivery, 356–362
  cost-benefit principle, 356–358
  designing a solution, 358–359
  HMO revolution, 359–360
  third-party payment, 356
Health care expenditures, 356
Health insurance, 358
  first-dollar coverage, 359
  and HMOs, 359–360
  paying for, 360–362
  uninsured citizens, 361
Health maintenance organizations, 359–360
Holmes, Sherlock, 32
Homeowners' associations, 386
Home size, 409
Honda Accord, 306
Honda Civic, 114
Honeybee keeper, 274
Horizontal addition, 117
Hospital care, 357
Household Food Consumption Survey, 415
Housing costs, 115–116
Housing market, 74, 81–84, 176–178
Human capital, 330
  compensating wage differentials, 336–339
  in unionized labor force, 331–333
  and wage differentials, 341
  in winner-take-all labor market, 334–336
Human capital theory, 319, 330–331
Hunt, H. L., 403
Hurdle method of price discrimination, 238–242
  efficiency, 240–241
  examples, 241–242
  perfect hurdle, 239
Hybrid goods, 379

I

IBM antitrust case, 352
Identical demand curves, 117
Illicit drugs, 103–104
Imperfect competition
  contrasted with perfect competition, 222–223
  forms of, 222
  sources of market power, 223–227
Imperfect decision makers, 9–11
Imperfectly competitive firms, 140, 221
  prisoner's dilemma confronting, 252–255
Imperfect price discrimination, 238
Implicit costs, 196, 198–199
Incentives
  adverse effects of income-support programs, 418–419
  under a consumption tax, 424–425
  and taxes on top earners, 423–424
  and tax system, 419–424
Income
  breakeven level, 414
  decrease and change in demand, 94–95
  differences and rational spending rule, 115
  increase and changes in demand, 93–94

and price elasticity of demand, 124–125
  recent trends, 402–404
Income disparities, 319, 321
  explaining differences in, 330–339
Income distribution, 403–404
  effect on demand, 115–116
  inequality problem, 404–407
Income elasticity, 127
Income inequality
  moral concerns
    justice and fairness, 404–405
    psychological costs, 406–407
    utilitarian argument, 405–406
  practical concerns
    effect of poverty on nonpoor, 407–408
    effect on middle class, 408–409
Income quintiles, 402, 403
Income redistribution
  benefit levels, 417
  failure of cost-benefit principle, 425–427
  methods
    combination of, 416–417
    earned-income tax credit, 411–413
    in-kind transfers, 413–414
    minimum wage, 410–411
    negative income tax, 414–416
    public employment, 416
    welfare payments, 413–414
Income support programs
  adverse effects on incentives, 418–419
  cost-benefit analysis, 426–427
  equity versus efficiency, 418–427
  paying for
    legislator's dilemma, 425–426
    progressive consumption tax, 424–425
    tax policy and occupational choice, 419–424
Income tax
  negative, 414–415
  progressive, 382, 423
  proportional, 382
  replaced by consumption tax, 424–425
Income transfers, 175, 176
Inconsistent choices, 11
Increasing marginal utility, 108
Increasing returns to scale, 223–224
Independent variables, 22
Individual demand curve, 116–122
  and horizontal addition, 117
Individual supply curve, 137–139
Inefficiency of political process, 390–394
Inefficient point, 58
Inelastic demand, 123
Inequality, 402–404
Infant safety seats, 369
Inferior goods, 94
Information; see also Asymmetric information
  costs of, 300
  disappearing political discourse, 313–314
  effect on economic surplus, 299–300
  known by buyers, 298
  optimal value of
    commitment problem, 304–305
    cost-benefit test, 300–301

and free-rider problem, 300–301
  gamble inherent in search, 303–304
  guidelines for rational search,
    302–303
In-kind compensation, 339
In-kind transfers, 413–414
Input prices, 148
Inputs
  effect of fall in price of, 90–91
  effect of rise in price of, 89–90
  exclusive control over, 223
  flexibility of, 154
  mobility of, 154–155
  substitute, 155
  supply bottleneck, 156
  unique and essential, 156
Insurance
  deductibles, 359
  health policies, 358
  paying for health insurance, 360–362
  waste caused by coverage, 359
  workers' compensation, 369
Insurance companies
  adverse selection, 310
  statistical discrimination, 310–312
Intel Corporation, 227
Interest, 34
  fairness issue, 35
Internal Revenue Service, 338–339
  call for abolition of, 377–378
International trade, and comparative
  advantage, 65–68
Intuit Corporation, 16
Invisible hand, 196
  in antipoverty programs, 209
  breakdown under monopoly, 233–234
  overview, 213
  in regulated markets, 207–209
  and social optimum, 213–215
  in stock market, 210–213
Invisible hand theory
  economic rent versus economic profit,
    205–206
  effect of cost-saving innovations,
    206–207
  importance of free entry/exit, 204–205
  overview, 207
  two functions of price, 203–204
Irrational choices, 11
Ithaca, New York, 195

J

James, Bill, 53
Jerry Springer Show, 386
Jevons, William Stanley, 77
Jobs requiring similar ability/experience, 337
Johnson, Dirk, 406–407, 408n
Jordan, Michael, 334
Jungle, The (Sinclair), 365–366
Jurassic Park, 94
Justice, 404–405

K

Kahneman, Daniel, 11
Kashmir, 297

Keeler, E. B., 359n
Keeler, Wee Willie, 53
Keillor, Garrison, 308, 420
Kellogg Graduate School of Management,
  392
Kidnapper game, 260–261
Kindergarten starting date, 290
King, Stephen, 334

L

Labor force participation, 342
Labor market
  competitive, 322–325
  differences in earnings
    compensatory wage differentials,
      336–339
    human capital theory, 330–331
    labor unions, 331–333
    winner-take-all markets, 333–336
  discrimination in, 339–344
    comparable worth issue, 342–344
    customer discrimination, 340
    by employers, 340
    sources of wage gaps, 340–342
  equilibrium, 328–330
  with monopsony, 325–328
  tax policy and occupational choices,
    419–424
  winner-take-all, 333–336
Labor specialization, 62–64
Labor turnover, 333
Labor unions, and differences in earnings,
  331–333
Lake Wobegone Effect, 308, 420
Law of demand, 146–147
  needs and wants, 104–106
  and price increases, 119–120
  shape of demand curve, 117–118
Law of diminishing marginal utility, 108, 281
Law of diminishing returns, 141–142, 144
  inapplicable in long run, 147
Law of supply, 146–147
Legalized drug campaign, 314
Legalized gambling, 371–372
Lemons model, 306–307
Liebowitz, A., 359n
Lifeguards, 336
Lincoln Navigator, 409
Linear demand curve, 119
Linux, 140
Local government, 389
London Philharmonic Orchestra, 135
Long run production, 141
Lopez, Armando, 165
Los Angeles Lakers, 156
Los Angeles Summer Olympics, 321
Lost World, The, 94
Lotteries, 372
Loury, Glen, 314
Low-income person
  standard of living, 408
  tied to welfare system, 414
Luxury goods, 401–402, 403

M

Macintax software, 16
Macroeconomics, 13
Magic Cards, 221–222
Managed care, 359–360
Mankiw, N. Gregory, 50
Manning, W. G., 359
Marginal, 12
Marginal benefit, 12, 13, 39
  of information, 300
Marginal benefit curve, 15–16
Marginal cost, 12, 13, 39
  with economies of scale, 224–227
  equal to price, 144
  of information, 300
Marginal cost curve
  equal to supply curve, 147
  graphing, 145–146
  for monopolists, 232–233
  in perfect competition, 145–146
  raised by wage rates, 148
Marginal cost of abatement, 281, 362
Marginal cost of production, 78
Marginal cost pricing, 353–356
Marginal labor cost, 326–327
Marginal physical product, 322
Marginal productivity, critique of, 404–405
Marginal product of labor, 322
Marginal revenue
  definition, 228
  for monopolists, 229–231
Marginal revenue curve
  algebraic form, 230
  graph of, 230
  with straight-line demand curve, 231
Marginal tax rates, in United Kingdom, 419
Marginal utility, 107–108
Market(s), 85
  barriers to entry, 204
  versus central planning, 75–76
  definition, 76
  demand and supply, 135
  effect of change in technology, 91
  effect of cost-saving innovations,
    206–207
  efficiency and other goals, 172–173
  free entry/exit, 204–205
  invisible hand in regulated, 207–209
  out of equilibrium, 86
  perfectly competitive, 139–147
  with price below equilibrium level, 167
  and prices, 76–85
  and rent control, 81–84
  and social welfare, 86–88
Market allocation of resources, 203
Market demand curve, 116–122
  and horizontal addition, 117
Market equilibrium, 79–81, 85
  compared to social optimum, 213–215
  and efficiency, 166–169
  goals other than efficiency, 172–173
  maximizing total economic surplus, 86
Market equilibrium quantity, 87
Market exit, 202
Market forces, effect on economic profit,
  201–202
Market imbalance, 203–204

Market power, sources of
  control over inputs, 223
  economies of scale, 223–224
  economies of scale and fixed costs,
    224–227
  government franchises, 224
  government licenses, 224
  patents, 224
Market supply curve, 137–139
Marquis, M. S., 359n
Marshall, Alfred, 77, 88
Marx, Karl, 64, 76
Masterpiece Theater, 386
Maximizing total economic surplus, 86
Maximum total utility, 110
McDonald's, 85
MCI Communications, 222
Mean income, 402
Means-tested welfare programs, 413
Meatpacking industry, 365–366
Medicaid, 356, 359, 413, 425
Medicare, 356, 359, 425
Mediterranean Sea, 286
Mercedes-Benz, 403
Mexico, and NAFTA, 68
Miata, 305–306
Microeconomics, 13
Microsoft Corporation, 113, 140, 204, 205,
  309
Middle class, effect of income gap, 408–409
Middleman, value added by, 298–300
Minimum wage, 410–411
  reducing economic surplus, 411–412
Mixed economies, 76
Modern Times, 64
Monopolistic competition, 222
Monopolists
  compared to monopsonists, 326–327
  earning economic profit, 350
  marginal revenue, 229–231
  perfectly discriminating, 238
  profit maximization, 228–233
  profit-maximizing decision rule, 231–233
  profit-maximizing output level, 232–233
  socially inefficient, 234
  using discount to expand market,
    235–242
Monopoly, 222; *see also* Natural
  monopolies
  antitrust laws, 352–353
  and antitrust laws, 234
  as breakdown of invisible hand,
    233–234
  deadweight loss, 234
  means of controlling, 350
Monopsonist
  employee's reservation wage, 327
  input and employment for, 326
  marginal labor cost, 326–327
  social versus private cost of hiring,
    327–328
Monopsony, 325–328
  decline of, 328
Moore, Marian, 372n
Moral sentiments, 263–264
Morisette, Alanis, 105–106
Multinational environmental pollution, 286

Municipal water supply, 353–355
Mystery Theater, 387

N

NAL/Viking, 334
Nash, John, 249
Nash equilibrium, 249–250
National Aeronautics and Space
  Administration, 39
National Basketball Association, 156, 290
National Football League, 113, 287, 290
National income, 423–424
National Rifle Association, 337, 338
Natural monopolies
  definition, 223–224
  public policy toward
    antitrust laws, 352–353
    cost-plus regulation, 351
    exclusive contracting, 351–352
    state regulation, 351
    state ownership and management,
      350–351
  source of economic profit, 352–353
Needs, and law of demand, 104–106
Negative externalities, 274
  optimal amount of, 281
  pollution permits, 364–365
  pollution tax, 362–364
Negative income tax, 414–416
Nepal, 49
Nerd norms, 290
Newhouse, J. P., 359n
Newton, Isaac, 76
New York City
  cost of taxicab medallions, 208
  food supply distribution, 73–74
  housing problems, 74
  rent control, 81–84
  zoning laws, 280
New York Times, 129, 155
Next-best alternative, 32–33
Nintendo, 225–227
Nixon, Richard M., 314, 411
No-free-lunch principle, 4
Nominal price, 114
Nonexcludable goods, 378
Nonrival goods, 378–379
Normal goods, 94
Normal profit, 197, 198–199
  earning more than, 200
Norms against vanity, 292
Norms of taste, 291–292
North American Free Trade Agreement, 68
North Korea, 75
Northwestern University, 392

O

Occupational demand for labor, 329
Occupational overcrowding, 423
Occupational Safety and Health
  Administration, 368–369
Occupations
  choices and tax policy, 419–424
  in human capital theory, 330–331
  supply curve for, 328–329

Oil prices, controls on, 174–175
Oil price shocks, 349
Oligopoly, 222
  cartel agreements, 252–254
O'Neal, Shaquille, 156
One-person economy, 55–58
Opportunity cost, 57
  and changes in productivity, 58–59
  in cost-benefit principle, 7–8
  and exchange, 50–54
  ignoring, 32–36
  increasing, 61
  of producing and selling, 77–78
  recognizing relevant alternative,
    32–33
  time value of money, 33–35
  unexploited, 88
Opportunity cost of an occupation, 135
Opportunity cost of resources, 135–136
Optimal amount of negative externalities,
  281
Optimal amount of safety, 367–368
Optimal combination of goods, 110
Optimal quantity of public good, 383–385
Optimal value of information, 300–305
Organization of Petroleum Exporting
  Countries, 254
Output
  effect of price discrimination, 236–238
  increase and marginal revenue, 229
  and marginal revenue, 228
  monopolist's decision rule, 231–233
  for monopsonist, 326
  for profit maximization, 142–144
Output-employment relationship, 141
Overbooking by airlines, 179–182

P

Pacific Telesis, 351
Parameter, 22
Pareto, Vilfredo, 166
Pareto criterion, 408
Pareto efficiency, 166
Pareto improvement, 359
Patek Philippe watches, 401
Patents, 224
Pavorotti, Luciano, 129
Payoff matrix, 248, 257
  for cartel agreements, 253
  for extended shopping hours, 289
  for relative performance, 286–288
Payoffs, depending on relative performance,
  286–288
Pay-per-view television fees, 387
Peace Corps, 337, 338
Pentium chip, 227
Perfect hurdle, 239
Perfectly competitive firms, 206
  compared to imperfect competition,
    222–223
  decision rule, 228
  demand curves, 140–141
  and law of supply, 146–147
  marginal cost, 145–146
  output to maximize profit, 142–144
  price equal to marginal cost, 144

prices, 141
  seller's supply role, 144
  short-run production, 141–142
  supply curve equal to marginal cost
    curve, 147
Perfectly competitive markets
  definition, 140
  profit maximization, 139–140
Perfectly discriminating monopolist, 238
Perfectly elastic demand curve, 128
Perfectly elastic supply curve, 153–154
Perfectly inelastic demand curve, 128
Perfectly inelastic supply curve, 153
Perot, Ross, 68
Personal Responsibility Act of 1996, 417
Peterson, Iver, 301n
Pharmaceutical industry, 224
Philip Morris, 254–255, 342–343
Picasso, Pablo, 76–77
Pizza Hut, 309
Plato, 76
Political discourse, 313–314
Political process
  and income-support programs, 425–426
  sources of inefficiency
    pork-barrel legislation, 390–391
    rent-seeking, 391–393
Pollock, Jackson, 76–77
Pollution, 87
  multinational, 286
  taxes on, 188–189, 362–364
Pollution permits, 364–365
Pontiac, 17
Poor nations, 65–66, 321
Pork-barrel legislation, 390–391
Porsche, 403
Positional arms control agreements
  examples, 289–290
  social norms, 290–292
Positional arms races, 288–289
Positional externalities
  arms control agreements, 289–290
  arms races, 288–289
  definition, 288
  payoffs on relative performance,
    286–288
Positive externalities, 274
  subsidized by government, 281
Pottery workers, 322
Poverty; *see also* Income-support programs
  practical concerns
    effect on middle class, 408–409
    effect on nonpoor, 407–408
  threshold, 415
Preferences, 129
  solution to commitment problems,
    265–266
  strategic role in negotiations, 263–266
Present value of future costs and benefits,
  210
President of the United States, 370–371
Price
  allocative function, 203–204
  in calculation of economic surplus,
    169–172
  debate over determination of, 76–77
  and demand curve, 78

and demand for substitutes, 112
  discounts, 238–242
  equal to marginal cost, 144
  above equilibrium level, 168–169
  and information, 297–298
  and invisible hand theory, 203–207
  at market equilibrium, 79–81
  and markets, 76–85
  nominal versus real, 114
  opportunity cost of resources, 135–136
  of perfectly competitive firms, 141
  predicting and explaining changes in,
    88–97
  rationing function, 203–204
  and rent controls, 81–84
  role of substitution, 113–115
  seasonal movements, 97
  with shortages or surplus, 80–81
  and shutdown decision, 144–145
  and supply curve, 77–78
Price adjustments, cost of preventing
  first-come, first-served policies, 179–183
  overview of, 183
  price ceilings, 174–178
  price floors, 178–179
Price ceilings, 85
  inefficiency of, 174–178
Price changes
  effect on total revenue, 124
  of other products, 148
Price controls
  comparable worth laws, 343
  on gasoline, 83–84
  on hamburgers, 84–85
  minimum wage, 110–112
  price ceilings, 85, 174–178
  price floors, 178–179
  rent control, 81–84, 176–178
  waste caused by, 175
Price discrimination
  definition, 235
  effect on output, 236–238
  hurdle method, 238–242
  imperfect, 238
  by monopolists, 235–242
Price elasticity of demand, 122–129
  calculating, 125–127
  definition, 122
  determinants
    budget share, 124–125
    substitution possibilities, 124
    time, 125
  effect of taxes, 187–188
  graphical interpretation, 126
  negative condition, 122–123
  along straight-line demand curve, 127
  and total expenditure, 123–124
Price elasticity of supply
  defining and calculating, 151–154
  determinants
    ability to produce substitute inputs,
      155
    flexibility of inputs, 154
    mobility of inputs, 154–155
    time, 155–156
  effect of taxes, 187–188
  effect of tax on sellers, 184

overview of, 157
  supply bottleneck, 156
  unique and essential inputs, 156
Price expectations, 148
Price floors, 178–179
Price increase, and law of demand, 119–120
Price setters, 221
Price supports, 178–179
Price takers, 140, 206
Principle of comparative advantage, 51–54
Principle of increasing opportunity cost, 61
Prisoner's dilemma
  and cartel agreements, 252–254
  and cigarette advertising, 254–255
  in everyday life, 255–256
  with imperfectly competitive firms,
    252–255
  original version, 251
Private contracting, 386
Private goods
  compared to public goods, 378–380
  individually consumed, 382
  jointly consumed, 382
  pure, 379
Private ownership, 284–285
Private property
  effect of private ownership, 284–285
  when ownership is impractical, 285–286
Private security expenditures, 408
Producer surplus, 170
  and hurdle method, 240–241
Production
  economies of scale, 223–224
  exclusive control over inputs, 223
  externalities from, 273–281
  fixed costs, 224–227
  flexibility of inputs, 154
  in long run, 141
  mobility of inputs, 154–155
  output for profit maximization, 142–144
  patent protection, 224
  pollution from, 87
  principle of increasing opportunity cost,
    61
  in short run, 141–142
  and source of market power, 223–227
  substitute inputs, 155
  supply bottleneck, 156
  time factor, 155–156
Production cost, and technology, 148
Production goals, 60–61
Production possibilities
  and comparative advantage, 55–58
  expanded by trade, 65–68
  in one-person economy, 55–58
  in two-person economy, 59–61
Production possibilities curve, 50
  attainable point, 57
  definition, 55
  efficient point, 58
  to generate supply curve, 157–159
  importance of specialization, 61–64
  inefficient point, 58
  influencing factors, 58–59
  for many-person economy, 64–65
  for one-person economy, 56–58
  for poor nations, 65–66

Production possibilities curve (*continued*)
  and scarcity principle, 57
  for two-person economy, 59–61
  unattainable point, 57
Productivity
  changes and opportunity cost, 58–59
  growth in, 135–136
  increased by specialization, 61–64
  and specialization, 49–50
  and unions, 333
Profit, 139
  quest for, 195–196
  in regulated markets, 207–209
  types of, 196–201
Profit maximization, 139–140
  and calculation of marginal revenue,
    229–231
  with cartel agreements, 252–254
  for monopolists, 228–233
  output chosen for, 142–144
  with price discrimination, 235–242
Profit-maximizing firms, 140
Profit-maximizing level of output
  for monopolists, 231–233
  perfectly competitive firms, 228
Profit-maximizing supply rule, 146
Progressive consumption tax, 424–425
Progressive income tax, 382, 423
Property, problem of unpriced resources,
  282–284
Property rights, 282–286
  government role, 388
Proportional income tax, 382
Proposition 13 revolt, Calif., 393–394
Psychological burden of poverty, 406–407,
  408
Public employment for the poor, 416
Public goods, 378–379
  compared to private goods, 378–380
  demand curve, 383–385
  optimal quantity, 383–385
  private provision of
    funding by donation, 385
    means of excluding nonpayers, 386
    private contracting, 386
    by sale of by-products, 386
Public policy
  on crime control, 370–371
  environmental regulation
    pollution permits, 364–365
    taxing pollution, 362–364
  health care delivery, 356–362
    cost-benefit principle, 356–358
    designing a solution, 358–359
    HMO revolution, 359–360
    paying for health insurance, 360–362
  on legalized gambling, 371–372
  marginal cost pricing, 353–356
  toward natural monopolies
    antitrust laws, 352–353
    cost-plus regulation, 351
    exclusive contracting, 351–352
    state ownership and management,
      350–351
    state regulation, 351
  workplace safety, 365–369

Public services, marginal cost pricing,
  353–356
Pure commons good, 379
Pure monopoly, 222
Pure private goods, 379
Pure public goods, 378–379

Q

Quantity
  market equilibrium, 87
  predicting and explaining changes in,
    88–97
  socially optimal, 87
Quantity demanded, 125–126
Quicken software, 16

R

Rationality, 9–11
Rational person, 5
  applying cost-benefit principle, 9–11
Rational spending rule
  and income differences, 115
  and income distribution, 115–116
  role of substitution, 113–115
Rationing function of prices, 203–204
Rawls, John, 404–405, 418
Raw materials, 149
Reagan, Ronald W., 408
Real price, 114
Recording contract, 420–422
Recycling
  acquisition of raw materials by, 149
  cost-benefit principle, 136–139
  and theory of supply, 149–151
Red Cross, 139
Regressive tax, 381
Regulated markets, 207–209
Regulation; *see also* Price controls; Public
  policy
    cost-plus, 351
    as government function, 388–390
    of natural monopolies, 351
    remedies for externalities, 279–281
Relative performance, 286–288
Remote office game, 261, 263–264
Rent control
  and economic surplus, 176–178
  lost rent from, 177
  results of, 74
Reservation price, 6, 13, 38, 137–139
  and perfect hurdle, 239
Reservation wage, 327
Resource allocation
  criterion, 41–42
  effect of externalities, 274–275
Resources
  market allocation of, 203
  tragedy of the commons, 284
  unpriced, 282–284
Retton, Mary Lou, 321
Rise, 24
Risk-averse person, 303
Risk-neutral person, 303
Rivergate Books, 301
RJR Tobacco Company, 254–255

Robber barons, 352
Ross, Diana, 255
Roster limits, 290
"Royal Jelly" (Dahl), 31
Run, 24

S

Salaries; *see also* Wages
  of baseball players, 334–335
  of CEOs, 333, 335–336, 403
  in competitive labor markets, 322–325
  explaining differences in, 330–339
Sale of by-products, 386
Sales, Monica, 286
Sales clerks, knowledgeable, 301
Sandler, Adam, 334
Sangam Restaurant, Boston, 39
Savings, exempt from taxes, 425
Scarcity, 1, 4, 13
  necessitating tradeoffs, 4–5
  and socially optimal amount of litter,
    149–151
Scarcity principle, 4, 14
  in production possibilities curve, 57
Schelling, Thomas, 262–263
Search
  costliness and commitment problem,
    304–305
  gamble inherent in, 303–304
Search time, 302–303
Sears Tower, 224
Seasonal demand, 355
Seasonal price movements, 97
Secret Service, 371
Sega, 225–227
Seinfeld show, 309
Self-interest, 264–265
Selfishness, 264–265
Sellers
  asymmetric information, 305–312
  and hurdle method, 238–242
  price discrimination, 235–242
Seller's supply rule, 144
Sesame Street, 379
Share prices, 210
  in efficiency market, 211–212
Sherman Antitrust Act, 352
Shopping hours, 288–289
Shortages, 80
  from price controls, 81–85
  water in California, 105–106
Short-run production, 141
Shutdown condition, 144–145
Sierra Club, 337, 338
Silver Blaze (Conan Doyle), 32
Sinclair, Upton, 365–366
Singers's audition, 420–422
Single tax, 188
Slawson, Donna B., 313n
Slope
  changes in, 25
  of line, 24
Smart-for-one-dumb-for-all principle, 87–88
Smith, Adam, 63, 76, 195–196, 203–204,
  214, 215, 219, 222, 274, 283, 298, 406
Smith, Robert S., 369n

Social efficiency, 234
Social forces, 129
Socially optimal amount of litter, 149–151
Socially optimal amount of pollution, 281
Social norms, 290–292
Social optimum, 213–215
Social Security, 425
Social welfare, 86–88
    promoted by price controls, 174–179
    promoted in private sector, 179–183
Soviet Union, 75
Space shuttle program, 39–40
Special-interest legislation, 391–393
Specialization, 49–50
    in Adam Smith, 63
    criticisms of, 64
    gains from division of labor, 62–64
    gains from expanding opportunity,
        61–62
    significance of, 61–64
Speed limits, 280
Spielberg, Steven, 94
Sport utility vehicles, 114
Sprint, 222
Standard of living, 406
Start-up costs, 224
State government, 389
State lotteries, 372
State ownership and management, 350–351
State welfare standards, 417
Statistical discrimination, 310–312
    and political discrimination, 313–314
Steel, Danielle, 334
Steinbrenner, George, 335
Stern, Gerald, 301
Stock market
    efficient market hypothesis, 211–213
    forecasts of corporate earnings, 214
    invisible hand in, 210–213
    share prices, 210
Stock portfolio, 212
Straight-line demand curve, 117–119
    and marginal revenue, 231
    and price elasticity, 127
Straight-line equation, 23–24
Substitutes, 92–93
    demand and prices of, 112
Substitution, and rational spending rule,
    113–115
Substitution possibilities, 124
Sunk costs
    compared to fixed costs, 43
    definition, 36
    failure to ignore, 36–39
Super Bowl advertising costs, 309
Suppliers, number of, 148
Supply, 136–139; see also Price elasticity of
    supply
    applying theory of, 149–151
    changes in, 88
    determinants of, 147–148
        change in price of other products,
            148
        input prices, 148
        number of suppliers, 148
        price expectations, 148
    examples, 73–74

Supply and demand
    effect of simultaneous shifts in, 96–97
    in nonunionzed labor market, 332
    and rent controls, 81–84
Supply and demand model
    changes in price and quantity, 88–97
    efficiency principle, 87–88
    and illicit drugs, 103–104
    rules governing, 95–97
Supply curve, 85
    definition, 77–78
    digital, 170, 171
    equal to marginal cost curve, 147
    generated by production possibilities
        curve, 157–159
    for labor, 322
    and market equilibrium, 79–81
    and number of suppliers, 148
    of occupations, 328–329
    in perfectly competitive markets,
        139–147
    perfectly elastic, 153–154
    perfectly inelastic, 153
    in perfect versus imperfect competition,
        222
    production in short run, 141–142
    for rental housing, 176–177
    response to regulation, 86
    rules governing, 95–97
    shifts in, 89–91
    upward-sloping, 139
Surplus, 80
Surplus-enhancing transaction
    from excess demand, 167
    from excess supply, 168
Szabo, Ecaterina, 321

T

Tables, 26–28
Taste, 129
    norms of, 291–292
Tax avoidance, 418–419
Taxes
    deadweight loss, 186, 187–198, 394
    effect on economic surplus, 185–187
    effect on equilibrium quantity, 184
    effects on incentives, 395
    and efficiency, 183–189
    elasticity and efficiency, 187–188
    external costs and efficiency, 188–189
    head tax, 381
    imposed on buyers and sellers, 183–185
    negative income tax, 414–416
    objects of, 394–396
    paying for welfare, 418–419
    progressive, 382
    proportional, 382
    for provision of public goods, 380–382
    regressive, 381
    on top earners, 423–424
Taxicab industry, 207–208
Taxpayer revolt, 393–394
Tax policy, and occupational choices,
    419–424
Tax Reform Act of 1986, 418–419

Technology
    determinant of supply, 148
    effect of changes in, 91
Teenage smoking, 125
Television advertising, 308–309
Television networks, 386–387
Television pay-per-view fees, 387
Television sets, 54–55
Textile industry, 333
Thaler, Richard, 37n, 338
Theory of supply, 149–151
Ticketmaster, 35
Tierney, John, 74n
Timber harvesting, 285–286
Time
    and price elasticity of demand, 125
    in price elasticity of supply, 155–156
Time allocation, 42
Time value of money, 33–35, 210
Timing
    acceptance threshold, 258
    of credible threats and promises,
        259–262
    decision trees, 247
    in game theory, 256–263
Titanic, 129
Tobacco company executives, 337
Total cost, 40, 225
Total economic surplus, 169, 172
Total expenditure
    and demand curve, 119–122
    and elasticity, 123–124
    as function of price, 122
Total revenue, 119, 198–199
    effect of price change, 124
Toxic waste, 276, 280
Toyota Camry, 307
Tradeoffs, 4–5
Traffic laws, 280
Tragedy of the commons, 282–286
    effect of private ownership on, 284–285
Trump, Donald, 224
TurboTax, 16
Tversky, Amos, 11
TWA, 248–250
Twain, Mark, 1
Two-person economy, 59–61

U

Ultimate bargaining game, 257–259
Unattainable point, 57
Unemployment insurance, 425
Uninsured citizens, 361
Union Carbide, 338
Unique inputs, 146
United Airlines, 248–250
United Kingdom
    gas prices, 115
    marginal tax rates, 419
United States Constitution, 389
United Way, 342–343
Unit-elastic demand, 123
University of Minnesota, 7
Unpriced resources, 282–284
Upward-sloping supply curve, 77–78, 139
Urban parkland, 384–385

Used car sales, 305–308
Utilitarianism, 405–406
Utility
    concept, 106–108
    and consumption, 107
Utility maximization, 106, 108–110
Utilomoter, 106

V

Value added, 298–300
Value of marginal product of labor, 322, 328
    exceeding marginal labor cost, 326–327
    in human capital theory, 330–331
    and unions, 331–333
Vanity, norms against, 292
Variable costs, 42–44, 224
Variable factors of production, 141–142
Variables, 22
VCRs, 54–55
Vermont, 355–356
Vertical intercept, 23–24
    changes in, 25
Vice-President of the United States, 370–371

W

Wage determination, 322–325

Wage gaps
    among women and minorities, 339–340
    based on ability and experience, 342
    from behavioral choices, 341–342
    from customer discrimination, 340
    from employer discrimination, 340
    from family location decisions, 340–341
    and human capital, 341
Wage rates, raising marginal cost curve, 148
Wages; see also Salaries
    compensating differentials, 336–339
    effect of increases in, 325
    explaining differences in, 330–339
    impact of unions on, 331–333
    and marginal labor cost, 326–327
    and minimum wage laws, 410–411
Wall Street Journal, 212
Wall Street professionals, 334
Wants
    allocating fixed income, 108–110
    applying rational spending rule,
        110–112, 113–116
    concept of utility, 106–108
    demand translated into, 106–113
    and income differences, 115
    and law of demand, 104–106
    origin of, 129
Warner Brothers, 247, 256

Wealth concentrations, 403
Wealth of Nations (Smith), 76, 195–196
Welfare payments, 413–414
Welfare reform, 417
Whales, harvesting, 286
Whirlwind (Clavell), 334
William Morrow, 334
Williams, Bernie, 335
Williams, Ted, 53–54
Williams, Wendy, 406–407
Windows operating systems, 140, 204
Winner-take-all labor market, 333–336
Women
    comparable worth issue, 342–343
    wage gaps, 339–340
Woodworking company, 323–325
Work, opportunity cost of, 135
Workers' compensation, 369
Workplace safety regulation, 365–369

Y–Z

Yosemite Concession Services Corporation,
    224
Zero-profit tendency, 202
Zoning laws, 280